COLONIAL FURNITURE
IN AMERICA

OAK CLOTHES PRESS 1675–1700

COLONIAL FURNITURE IN AMERICA

BY

LUKE VINCENT LOCKWOOD

THIRD EDITION
SUPPLEMENTARY CHAPTERS AND ONE HUNDRED AND THIRTY-SIX PLATES OF
NEW SUBJECTS HAVE BEEN ADDED TO THIS EDITION, WHICH NOW INCLUDES
OVER A THOUSAND ILLUSTRATIONS OF REPRESENTATIVE PIECES

VOLUME I
and
VOLUME II
COMPLETE

Published by arrangement with Charles Scribner's Sons

1957
CASTLE BOOKS
NEW YORK

CHARLES SCRIBNER'S SONS
MCMLI

COPYRIGHT, 1913, 1926, BY
CHARLES SCRIBNER'S SONS

Printed in the United States of America

PREFACE

THE last edition of "Colonial Furniture in America" was published in 1913. Since then, due largely to the increased interest and especially to the increased prices, many pieces have been found of sufficient importance to warrant their being included in a new edition. It seemed wise, therefore, to insert a supplemental chapter at the end of each volume to cover such material, the illustrations for which bear Roman numerals. The writer has tried, as far as was possible, to avoid showing articles which have been illustrated in other publications, and for that reason little material from that great source, the Metropolitan Museum, has been used.

Thanks are here recorded to the many collectors and dealers who have, without exception, freely furnished the writer with information to enable this edition to be brought up to date.

MEADOWREACH, RIVERSIDE, CONNECTICUT
      August, 1926.

PREFACE TO SECOND EDITION

DURING the eleven years that have elapsed since the publication of the first edition of this work, many important pieces of furniture have been brought to the attention of the writer, which substantiate the theory of development therein expressed. The writer has had the opportunity to examine several thousand pieces of American and English furniture, and from this examination it has become possible to determine in many instances the section of the country in which a piece was made. This examination has also shown the importance of mouldings in determining date and locality, and emphasis has been placed upon this feature throughout this work. So much new material has been acquired that the book has been entirely rewritten, the type reset, and the form extended to two volumes.

The writer wishes to express his thanks and appreciation to the Metropolitan Museum of Art not only for placing at his disposal for examination its various collections, especially the Bolles Collection of American Furniture, probably the most important ever assembled, but also for furnishing him with such photographs of pieces as were desired. He also wishes to express his thanks to the many collectors who have uniformly assisted him in this work, and especially to Mr. H. W. Erving for his untiring and enthusiastic aid, which has contributed much to the completeness of this book, and to Mr. Walter H. Durfee, who has furnished valuable information incorporated in the chapter on clocks.

MEADOWREACH, RIVERSIDE, CONNECTICUT,
August, 1913.

PREFACE TO FIRST EDITION

THE object of the present volume is to furnish the collector, and other persons interested in the subject of American colonial furniture, with a trustworthy handbook on the subject, having especially in mind the natural development of the various styles, and arranging them in such a way as to enable any one at a glance to determine under what general style and date a piece of furniture falls.

The sources of information from which this book has been derived are: examination of inventories and contemporary records, all available newspapers, works on the subjects of furniture, architecture, and interior wood-work by English, French, German, Italian, and American writers, general and commercial histories, books on manners and customs, ancient dictionaries, cabinet-makers' books of design, ancient and modern, and examination of specimens of furniture, both colonial and foreign.

The last of these sources is the most important, and New England is particularly rich in examples of the earliest as well as the later furniture, while the South is wofully lacking in any pieces prior to the mahogany period, although the inventories show that such pieces existed more abundantly there even than in the North.

New England possesses many fine collections, both public and private, and as these collections contain examples from both North and South, we have in many cases used them in illustrating instead of taking specimens still in the South.

In the last few years many pieces of the seventeenth-century furniture have come to light which fully carry out the idea of development

PREFACE TO FIRST EDITION

insisted on in this volume, but often it has been impossible to obtain pictures of these pieces, the owners fearing the reproducer.

As to the inventories, it must be borne in mind that they are misleading. The dates will always be late for a style, as there is no way of telling how long a piece, when mentioned in the inventories, had been in the possession of the deceased before the inventory was taken, and we believe the tendency has heretofore been to date too late rather than too early. A fairly safe guide to follow is to deduct ten years from the inventory date. Then as to valuations. The inventory valuations are, of course, very low, usually about three-fifths to one-half of the true value, and if before 1710 account must be taken of the fact that the purchasing power of money was then about five times what it is at present. Thus, if a chest is valued at £1 in an inventory of 1680, its true value at that time was from £1 13s. 4d. to £2, and the sum corresponding to this at the present time would be from £8 6s. 8d. to £10.

The method followed in dating the specimens of furniture here shown has been to suggest the time when the style represented was in common use, and no attempt has been made to place the date of any specimen exactly, for only under special circumstances could that be done.

The writer wishes to express his thanks to the various collectors and persons having family pieces for their universal kindness in allowing him to examine and photograph their furniture, and for the interest they have taken in this work.

BROOKLYN, November, 1901.

CONTENTS

I. Introduction 3

II. Chests 22

III. Chests of Drawers 52

IV. Cupboards and Sideboards 149

V. Desks and Scrutoires 210

VI. Looking-Glasses 281

Supplementary Chapter 335

LIST OF ILLUSTRATIONS

Oak Clothes Press, 1675–1700 . . . . *Frontispiece*

FIGURE		PAGE
1.	Doll House, first quarter eighteenth century	9
2.	Chippendale Commode, French taste, 1750–60	15
3.	Chippendale Settee, Chinese taste, 1750–60	16
4.	Chippendale Torchère, Gothic taste, 1750–60	17
5.	Chippendale Library Table, 1767	18
6.	Pine Ship Chest, first quarter seventeenth century	23
7.	Oak Chest, about 1650	24
8.	Oak Chest, third quarter seventeenth century	25
9.	Oak Chest, third quarter seventeenth century	26
10.	Oak Chest, third quarter seventeenth century	27
11.	Oak Chest, third quarter seventeenth century	27
12.	Oak Chest, third quarter seventeenth century	28
13.	Oak Chest, third quarter seventeenth century	28
14.	Dutch Marquetry Chest, 1616	29
15.	Oak Chest with one drawer, third quarter seventeenth century	30
16.	Oak Chest with one drawer, third quarter seventeenth century	31
17.	Oak Chest with two drawers, 1660–75	32
18.	Oak Chest with two drawers, 1675–1700	33
19.	Oak Chest with two drawers, 1675–1700	33
20.	Oak Chest, 1675–1700	34
21.	Oak Chest with one drawer, about 1675	35
22.	Oak Chest with two small drawers, 1675–1700	35
23.	Oak Chest with two small drawers, 1675–1700	36
24.	Oak Chest with two small drawers, 1675–1700	36
25.	Panelled Chest with two drawers, 1675–1700	37
26.	Panelled Chest with three drawers, about 1700	38
27.	Carved Oak Chest with one drawer, 1690–1710	39
28.	Carved Oak Chest with one drawer, 1690–1710	40
29.	Carved Oak Chest with two drawers, 1690–1710	41
30.	Carved Oak Chest with two drawers, 1690–1710	42
31.	Carved Oak Chest with drawers, 1701	43
32.	Carved Oak Chest with two drawers, 1700–10	44

LIST OF ILLUSTRATIONS

FIGURE		PAGE
33.	Carved Oak Chest with three drawers, 1690–1710	45
34.	Oak Chest with one drawer, 1690–1710	45
35.	Oak Chest with one drawer, 1675–1700	46
36.	Chest with one drawer, 1700–10	46
37.	Painted Chest with one drawer, 1700–10	47
38.	Painted Chest with one drawer, 1705	48
39.	Painted Hutch with one drawer, 1700–10	49
40.	Chest with two drawers, 1710–20	49
41.	Oak Chest of Drawers, 1675–1700	52
42.	Oak Chest of Drawers, 1675–1700	53
43.	Oak Chest of Drawers, 1675–1700	54
44.	Oak Chest of Drawers, 1675–1700	55
45.	Oak Chest of Drawers, 1675–1700	56
46.	Panelled Chest of Drawers, 1675–1700	56
47.	Panelled Chest of Drawers, 1675–1700	57
48.	Inlaid Chest of Drawers, 1690–1700	58
49.	Panelled Chest of Drawers, 1675–1700	58
50.	Walnut Chest of Drawers, 1690–1700	59
51.	Oak Panelled High Chest of Drawers, 1675–1700	63
52.	High Chest of Drawers, 1680–1700	64
53.	Marquetry High Chest of Drawers, 1680–1700	65
54.	High Chest of Drawers, 1680–1700	66
55.	Dressing-Table, 1680–1700	67
56.	Dressing-Table, 1680–1700	68
57.	High Chest of Drawers, 1690–1700	69
58.	Dressing-Table, 1690–1700	68
59.	High Chest of Drawers, 1690–1700	70
60.	High Chest of Drawers, 1690–1700	71
61.	High Chest of Drawers, 1690–1700	72
62.	Slate-Top Table, 1690–1700	73
63.	Top view of foregoing table	73
64.	Dressing-Table, 1700–10	73
65.	High Chest of Drawers, 1700–10	74
66.	High Chest of Drawers, 1700–10	75
67.	Inlaid High Chest of Drawers, 1700–10	76
68.	High Chest of Drawers, 1700–10	77
69.	High Chest of Drawers, 1710–20	78
70.	High Chest of Drawers, 1710–20	79
71.	High Chest of Drawers, 1710–20	80
72.	Dressing-Table, 1700–10	81
73.	Dressing-Table, 1700–10	82
74.	Dressing-Table, 1710–20	82

LIST OF ILLUSTRATIONS

XV

FIGURE		PAGE
75.	Dressing-Table, 1710–20	82
76.	Dressing-Table, 1710–20	82
77.	Miniature Cupboard of Drawers, about 1700	83
78.	Early Handles, 1690–1720	83
79.	Japanned High Chest of Drawers, 1700–25	84
80.	Japanned Dressing-Table, 1700–25	85
81.	High Chest of Drawers, 1710–20	86
82.	Dressing-Table, 1710–20	87
83.	Dressing-Table, 1710–20	88
84.	High Chest of Drawers, Spanish feet, 1710–20	89
85.	Dressing-Table, Spanish feet, 1710–20	89
86.	High Chest of Drawers, 1710–20	90
87.	Dressing-Table, 1710–20	91
88.	Dressing-Table, 1710–20	91
89.	Dressing-Table, 1710–20	92
90.	Japanned Scroll-Top High Chest of Drawers, 1720–30	93
91.	Scroll-Top High Chest of Drawers, about 1725	94
92.	Scroll-Top High Chest of Drawers, 1730	95
93.	Scroll-Top High Chest of Drawers and Dressing-Table, 1725–50	96
94.	Scroll-Top High Chest of Drawers, 1725–50	97
95.	Scroll-Top High Chest of Drawers, 1725–50	98
96.	Scroll-Top High Chest of Drawers, 1750–60	99
97.	Cupboard on frame, 1730–50	100
98.	Dressing-Table, 1730–50	100
99.	Scroll-Top High Chest of Drawers, 1750–60	101
100.	Block-Front High Chest of Drawers, about 1750	102
101.	Block-Front Dressing-Table, about 1750	103
102.	Scroll-Top High Chest of Drawers, 1760–75	105
103.	Scroll-Top High Chest of Drawers, 1760–75	105
104.	Scroll-Top High Chest of Drawers, 1760–75	106
105.	Scroll-Top High Chest of Drawers, 1760–75	107
106.	Scroll-Top High Chest of Drawers, 1760–75	108
107.	Scroll-Top High Chest of Drawers, 1760–75	109
108.	Dressing-Table, 1760–75	110
108a.	Advertisement in drawer of preceding figure	110
109.	Dressing-Table, 1760–75	111
110.	Dressing-Table, 1760–75	112
111.	Dressing-Table, 1760–75	112
112.	Cellarette in form of dressing-table, 1760–75	113
113.	Knee-Hole Dressing-Table, 1725–50	114
114.	Chest on Chest, about 1750	115
115.	Chest on Chest, 1750–75	116

LIST OF ILLUSTRATIONS

xvi

FIGURE		PAGE
116.	Block-Front Chest on Chest, 1750–75	118
117.	Block-Front Chest on Chest, 1750–75	119
118.	Block-Front Chest on Chest, 1750–75	120
119.	Block-Front Chest on Chest, 1750–75	121
120.	Block-Front Chest on Chest, 1750–75	122
121.	Knee-Hole Block-Front Dressing-Table, 1750–75	123
122.	Knee-Hole Block-Front Dressing-Table, 1750–75	124
123.	Knee-Hole Dressing-Table, 1750–75	125
124.	Chest on Chest, 1750–75	126
125.	Chest on Chest, 1760–75	127
126.	Chest of Drawers and Cupboard, about 1790	128
127.	Chest of Drawers, 1760–75	129
128.	Chest of Drawers, about 1775	129
129.	Chest of Drawers, Bombé-shaped, about 1760	130
130.	Block-Front Chest of Drawers, 1750–75	130
131.	Block-Front Chest of Drawers, 1750–75	131
132.	Block-Front Chest of Drawers, 1750–75	132
133.	Block-Front Chest of Drawers, 1760–75	133
134.	Block-Front Chest of Drawers, 1760–75	134
135.	Reversed Serpentine-Front Chest of Drawers, about 1780	134
136.	Reversed Serpentine-Front Chest of Drawers, 1780–90	135
137.	Serpentine-Front Chest of Drawers, about 1780–90	136
138.	Swell-Front Chest of Drawers, 1790–1800	137
139.	Swell-Front Chest of Drawers, 1790–1800	137
140.	Swell-Front Chest of Drawers, 1790–1800	138
141.	Chest of Drawers, Sheraton style, about 1800	138
142.	Chest of Drawers, Sheraton style, 1800–10	139
143.	Chest of Drawers, Empire style, 1800–10	140
144.	Chest of Drawers, Empire style, 1810–20	140
145.	Chest of Drawers, Empire style, 1810–20	141
146.	Chest of Drawers, Empire style, 1810–20	142
147.	Dressing-Table, Hepplewhite style, 1790–1800	143
148.	Dressing-Table, Sheraton style, about 1800	143
149.	Dressing-Table, Sheraton style, 1800–10	143
150.	Dressing-Table, 1800–10	144
151.	Stencilled Chest of Drawers, about 1820	144
152.	Basin-Stand, 1725–50	145
153.	Wash-Stand, 1790–1800	145
154.	Wash-Stand, 1790–1800	146
155.	Wash-Stand, 1790–1800	147
156.	Wash-Stand, 1790–1800	147
157.	Livery Cupboard, last quarter seventeenth century	150

LIST OF ILLUSTRATIONS

xvii

FIGURE		PAGE
158.	Dining-Hall, Christ Church College, Oxford. (Showing cupboard beneath windows.)	151
159.	Court Cupboard, about 1600	153
160.	Court Cupboard, third quarter seventeenth century	154
161.	Court Cupboard, third quarter seventeenth century	155
162.	Press Cupboard, third quarter seventeenth century	156
163.	Press Cupboard, 1660–80	157
164.	Press Cupboard, 1660–80	158
165.	Press Cupboard, last quarter seventeenth century	159
166.	Press Cupboard, last quarter seventeenth century	161
167.	Press Cupboard, last quarter seventeenth century	161
168.	Press Cupboard, last quarter seventeenth century	162
169.	Press Cupboard with three drawers, 1675–1700	163
170.	Press Cupboard with three drawers, 1699	164
171.	Press Cupboard with three drawers, 1690–1700	165
172.	Wainscot Cupboard, 1675–1700	166
173.	Cupboard of Drawers, 1680–1700	167
174.	Painted Kas, about 1700	169
175.	Walnut Kas, about middle of seventeenth century	170
176.	Spoon-Rack, 1675–1700	171
177.	Walnut Cupboard, 1725–50	173
178.	Cherry Cupboard, 1725–50	173
179.	Wardrobe, 1725–50	174
180.	Cupboard, 1780–90	175
181.	Wardrobe, 1810–20	176
182.	Dresser, 1725–50	177
183.	Side Cupboard, about 1725	178
184.	Cupboard, 1738	179
185.	Side Cupboard, 1725–50	180
186.	Side Cupboard with panelling, style of about 1750	181
187.	Corner Cupboard, 1725–50	183
188.	Corner Cupboard, 1725–50	182
189.	Corner Cupboard, 1725–50	183
190.	Corner Cupboard, 1750–75	184
191.	Corner Cupboard, 1750–75	184
192.	Corner Cupboard, 1750–75	185
193.	Inlaid Corner Cupboard, 1790–1800	186
194.	Corner Cupboard, 1800–10	186
195.	Carved Corner Cupboard, about 1800	187
196.	Oak Sideboard Table, 1690–1700	188
197.	Walnut Sideboard Table with marble top, 1720–40	189
198.	Carved Sideboard Table, 1725–50	190
199.	Carved Sideboard Table with marble top, 1750–60	191

LIST OF ILLUSTRATIONS

FIGURE		PAGE
200.	Chippendale Sideboard Table, about 1760	191
201.	Sideboard Table, 1760–70	192
202.	Sideboard Table, 1780–90	193
203.	Hepplewhite Sideboard, 1790–1800	194
204.	Hepplewhite Sideboard, 1790–1800	195
205.	Hepplewhite Sideboard, 1790–1800	195
206.	Hepplewhite Sideboard, 1799	196
207.	Hepplewhite Sideboard, 1790–1800	196
208.	Hepplewhite Corner Sideboard, 1790–1800	197
209.	Sheraton Sideboard, 1790–1800	198
210.	Sheraton Sideboard, 1795–1810	199
211.	Sheraton Sideboard, 1790–1800	199
212.	Sheraton Sideboard, about 1800	200
213.	Knife and Spoon Box, 1790–1800	200
214.	Sheraton Sideboard with china closet, about 1800	201
215.	Sheraton Sideboard with china closet and desk drawers, about 1800	202
216.	Mixing-Table, 1790–1800	203
217.	Sheraton Sideboard, about 1800	204
218.	Empire Sideboard, 1810–20	205
219.	Empire Sideboard, 1810–20	206
220.	Empire Sideboard, 1810–20	207
221.	Empire Sideboard inlaid with brass, 1810–20	207
222.	Empire Sideboard, about 1820	208
223.	Empire Sideboard, about 1830	208
224.	Bible-Box, 1649	211
225.	Desk-Box, 1650–75	212
226.	Desk-Box, 1650–75	212
227.	Desk-Box, 1650–75	212
228.	Two Desk-Boxes with Friesland carving, 1675–1700	213
229.	Desk-Box, 1680–1700	213
230.	Desk-Box, Hadley pattern, about 1700	213
231.	Desk-Box, 1675–1700	214
232.	Desk-Box, 1690–1700	214
233.	Desk-Box, about 1700	214
234.	Desk-Box on frame, about 1675	215
235.	Desk-Box on frame, 1680–1700	215
236.	Desk-Box on frame, about 1700	216
237.	Desk-Box on frame, about 1700	217
238.	Scrutoire, fall front, about 1700	219
239.	Ball-Foot Scrutoire, 1700	220
240.	Ball-Foot Scrutoire, about 1700–10	220
241.	Ball-Foot Scrutoire with cabinet top, 1700–10	221

LIST OF ILLUSTRATIONS

FIGURE		PAGE
242.	Ball-Foot Scrutoire, 1700–10	222
243.	Slant-Top Scrutoire on frame, 1700–25	223
244.	Slant-Top Scrutoire on frame, 1700–25	224
245.	Cabriole-Legged Scrutoire, about 1725	225
246.	Cabriole-Legged Scrutoire, 1725–40	225
247.	Cabriole-Legged Scrutoire, 1725–40	227
248.	Cabriole-Legged Scrutoire, 1740–50	226
249.	Slant-Top Scrutoire with Dutch turned legs, 1725–40	227
250.	Cabriole-Legged Scrutoire with cabinet top, 1725–40	228
251.	Cabriole-Legged Scrutoire, 1725–40	229
252.	Dressing-Table with desk drawer, 1760–75	230
253.	Knee-Hole Desk, about 1725	232
254.	Slant-Top Scrutoire, 1740–50	233
255.	Slant-Top Scrutoire with cabinet top and bird's claw and ball feet, 1725–50	234
256.	Slant-Top Scrutoire, 1740–50	235
257.	Slant-Top Scrutoire, third quarter eighteenth century	236
258.	Slant-Top Scrutoire, third quarter eighteenth century	237
259.	Slant-Top Scrutoire, third quarter eighteenth century	237
260.	Knee-Hole Writing-Table, 1750–60	238
261.	Block-Front, Slant-Top Scrutoire, third quarter eighteenth century	239
262.	Block-Front, Slant-Top Scrutoire, third quarter eighteenth century	240
263.	Block-Front, Slant-Top Scrutoire, third quarter eighteenth century	241
264.	Block-Front, Slant-Top Scrutoire, third quarter eighteenth century	241
265.	Block-Front, Slant-Top Scrutoire with cabinet top, third quarter eighteenth century	242
266.	Block-Front, Slant-Top Scrutoire with cabinet top, third quarter eighteenth century	243
267.	Block-Front, Slant-Top Scrutoire with cabinet top, third quarter eighteenth century	244
268.	Block-Front, Slant-Top Scrutoire with cabinet top, third quarter eighteenth century	245
269.	Block-Front, Slant-Top Scrutoire with cabinet top, third quarter eighteenth century	246
270.	Block-Front, Slant-Top Scrutoire with cabinet top, third quarter eighteenth century	247
271.	Block-Front, Slant-Top Scrutoire with cabinet top, third quarter eighteenth century	248
272.	Block-Front, Slant-Top Scrutoire with cabinet top, third quarter eighteenth century	248
273.	Block-Front, Slant-Top Scrutoire with cabinet top, third quarter eighteenth century	249
274.	Block-Front, Slant-Top Scrutoire with cabinet top, third quarter eighteenth century	250
275.	Block-Front, Slant-Top Scrutoire with cabinet top, third quarter eighteenth century	251
276.	Block-Front, Slant-Top Scrutoire with cabinet top, 1760–75	252
277.	Block-Front, Slant-Top Scrutoire with cabinet top, 1778	254
278.	Block-Front, Slant-Top Scrutoire with cabinet top, third quarter eighteenth century	255
279.	Bombé-Front, Slant-Top Scrutoire with cabinet top, 1750–75	257
280.	Bombé-Front, Slant-Top Scrutoire with cabinet top, 1750–75	258
281.	Bombé-Front, Slant-Top Scrutoire with cabinet top, 1750–75	259
282.	Slant-Top Scrutoire with cabinet top, 1760–75	261
283.	Slant-Top Scrutoire with cabinet top, 1760–75	261

LIST OF ILLUSTRATIONS

FIGURE		PAGE
284.	Slant-Top Scrutoire with bookcase top, 1750–70	262
285.	Slant-Top Scrutoire with bookcase top, 1750–70	263
286.	Serpentine-Front, Slant-Top Scrutoire, 1765–80	264
287.	Reversed Serpentine-Front Scrutoire, 1765–80	265
288.	Reversed Serpentine-Front Scrutoire with cabinet top, 1765–80	266
289.	Tambour Writing-Table, 1780–90	267
290.	Cylinder-Fall Desk, 1780–90	267
291.	Bookcase and Scrutoire, 1780–90	268
292.	Bookcase and Scrutoire, 1780–90	268
293.	Fire-Screen Scrutoire, 1780–90	269
294.	Writing-Table, 1789	270
295.	Knee-Hole Writing-Table, about 1790	270
296.	Inlaid Secretary, 1790–1800	271
297.	Inlaid Writing-Table, about 1800	272
298.	Inlaid Writing-Table with bookcase top, about 1800	273
299.	Inlaid Writing-Table, 1810	274
300.	Inlaid Writing-Cabinet, about 1800	274
301.	Inlaid Desk, 1800–10	275
302.	Scrutoire with bookcase top, 1800–10	276
303.	Chest of Drawers with desk drawer, 1800–10	276
304.	Empire Writing-Table, about 1820	277
305.	Empire Scrutoire, 1810–20	277
306.	Bookcase, Chippendale style, 1760–70	278
307.	Bookcase, Shearer style, 1780–90	279
308.	Bookcase, Sheraton style, 1790–1800	280
309.	Looking-Glass with stump-embroidery frame, about 1640	282
310.	Looking-Glass with marquetry frame, 1690–1700	283
311.	Looking-Glass with walnut frame, 1700–10	284
312.	Looking-Glass with walnut frame, 1700–10	284
313.	Looking-Glass with walnut frame, about 1710	285
314.	Looking-Glass with gilt frame, first quarter eighteenth century	286
315.	Looking-Glass with japanned frame, first quarter eighteenth century	286
316.	Looking-Glass with walnut frame, first quarter eighteenth century	287
317.	Two Looking-Glasses with walnut frames, first quarter eighteenth century	288
318.	Looking-Glass with gilt frame, first quarter eighteenth century	289
319.	Looking-Glass with walnut and gilt frame, first quarter eighteenth century	289
320.	Looking-Glass with japanned frame, first quarter eighteenth century	290
321.	Looking-Glass with walnut and gilt frame, first quarter eighteenth century	290
322.	Looking-Glass with walnut and gilt frame, first quarter eighteenth century	291
323.	Looking-Glass with walnut and gilt frame, first quarter eighteenth century	291
324.	Looking-Glass with walnut frame, first quarter eighteenth century	292
325.	Looking-Glass with gilt and carved frame, first quarter eighteenth century	292

LIST OF ILLUSTRATIONS

FIGURE		PAGE
326.	Looking-Glass with walnut and gilt frame, 1725–50	293
327.	Looking-Glass with walnut and gilt frame, 1725–50	293
328.	Looking-Glass with walnut and gilt frame, 1725–50	294
329.	Looking-Glass Frame with scroll pediment, 1725–50	294
330.	Looking-Glass Frame with scroll pediment, 1725–50	295
331.	Looking-Glass Frame with scroll pediment, 1750–75	295
332.	Looking-Glass Frame with scroll pediment, 1750–75	296
333.	Looking-Glass Frame with scroll pediment, 1750–75	296
334.	Looking-Glass in Chippendale style, 1750–65	297
335.	Girandole in Chippendale style, 1750–65	298
336.	Mantel Looking-Glass, Chippendale style, 1750–70	299
337.	Mantel Looking-Glass, Chippendale style, 1750–65	299
338.	Girandole in Edwards & Darley style, 1750–65	300
339.	Pier Glass and Table in Johnson style, 1750–65	301
340.	Gilt Looking-Glass in Chippendale style, 1760–70	302
341.	Gilt Looking-Glass in Chippendale style, 1760–75	302
342.	Looking-Glass with mahogany and gilt frame, 1760–75	302
343.	Two Looking-Glasses with mahogany and gilt frames, 1770–80	303
344.	Looking-Glass with mahogany and gilt frame, 1780–90	304
345.	Looking-Glass with mahogany and gilt frame, 1780–90	304
346.	Looking-Glass with mahogany inlaid and gilt frame, about 1790	305
347.	Looking-Glass with mahogany and gilt frame, 1780–90	305
348.	Looking-Glass with mahogany and gilt frame, 1790–1800	306
349.	Looking-Glass with carved and gilded frame, about 1780	306
350.	Looking-Glass with carved and gilded frame, about 1780	307
351.	Sconce, 1790–1800	307
352.	Sconce, 1790–1800	307
353.	Looking-Glass, shield-shaped, 1780–90	308
354.	Looking-Glass, filigree frame, 1785–95	308
355.	Looking-Glass, filigree frame, 1785–95	309
356.	Looking-Glass, filigree frame, 1785–95	309
357.	Looking-Glass, Sheraton style, 1785–95	310
358.	Pier-Glass, Sheraton style, 1785–95	310
359.	Looking-Glass with carved and gilt frame, 1785–95	311
360.	Looking-Glass with carved and gilt frame, 1785–95	311
361.	Looking-Glass with carved and gilt frame, 1785–95	312
362.	Looking-Glass with mahogany and gilt frame, 1785–95	312
363.	Looking-Glass with mahogany and gilt frame, 1785–95	313
364.	Looking-Glass with mahogany and gilt frame, 1785–95	313
365.	Looking-Glass with mahogany and gilt frame, 1785–95	313
366.	Looking-Glass with glass frame, 1780–90	**314**
367.	Looking-Glass with marble and gilt frame, 1780–90	314

LIST OF ILLUSTRATIONS

FIGURE		PAGE
368.	Looking-Glass with marble and gilt frame, 1780–90	315
369.	Looking-Glass with mahogany and gilt frame, about 1780	315
370.	Looking-Glass with mahogany and inlaid frame, about 1790	316
371.	Looking-Glass with medallion plaque, 1790–1800	316
372.	Mantel Looking-Glass, about 1790	317
373.	Mantel Looking-Glass, about 1790	318
374.	Mantel Looking-Glass, about 1800	318
375.	Mantel Looking-Glass, 1800–10	319
376.	Mantel Looking-Glass, 1810–20	320
377.	Pier Looking-Glass, 1798	321
378.	Pier Looking-Glass, about 1800	320
379.	Girandole, about 1800	322
380.	Girandole, about 1800	323
381.	Looking-Glass with gilded frame, 1790–1800	324
382.	Looking-Glass with gilded frame, 1790–1800	324
383.	Looking-Glass, Empire style, 1812–20	325
384.	Looking-Glass, Empire style, 1810–20	325
385.	Looking-Glass, Empire style, 1810–20	326
386.	Looking-Glass, Empire style, 1810–20	326
387.	Looking-Glass, Empire style, 1800–12	327
388.	Looking-Glass, Empire style, 1810–20	327
389.	Looking-Glass, Empire style, 1810–20	327
390.	Enamelled and Brass Looking-Glass Rosettes	328
391.	Looking-Glass with painted glass border, about 1800	328
392.	Looking-Glass with painted glass border, about 1800	329
393.	Small Looking-Glass with painting at top, 1790–1800	329
394.	Small Looking-Glass with carved and coloured frame, 1790–1800	330
395.	Dressing-Glass, 1780–90	330
396.	Dressing-Glass, about 1790	331
397.	Dressing-Glass, 1785–95	331
398.	Dressing-Glass, 1785–95	332
399.	Dressing-Glass, 1785–95	332
400.	Dressing-Glass, 1785–95	333
401.	Dressing-Glass, 1790–1800	333

SUPPLEMENTARY CHAPTER

FIGURE		PAGE
I.	Carved Oak Chest made by Nicholas Disbrowe before 1683	336
II.	Inscription of foregoing chest	336
III.	Oak Chest, third quarter seventeenth century	338
IV.	Oak Chest, third quarter seventeenth century	339

LIST OF ILLUSTRATIONS

FIGURE		PAGE
V.	Oak Chest with two drawers, third quarter seventeenth century	339
VI.	Oak Chest with two drawers, third quarter seventeenth century	340
VII.	Oak Chest with two drawers, third quarter seventeenth century	340
VIII.	Carved Oak Chest with two drawers, last quarter seventeenth century	341
IX.	Two-Drawer Oak Chest, Hadley type, first quarter eighteenth century	342
X.	Panelled Chest, about 1700	343
XI.	Painted High Chest of Drawers, about 1700	344
XII.	High Chest of Drawers, scroll legs, about 1700	345
XIII.	Cupboard on Stand, about 1700	345
XIV.	High Chest of Drawers, 1700–25	346
XV.	High Chest of Drawers, 1700–25	347
XVI.	Dressing-Table, 1700–25	348
XVII.	Dressing-Table, 1750–75	348
XVIII.	Dressing-Table, 1750–75	349
XIX.	High Chest of Drawers, 1750–75	351
XX.	Chest on Chest, 1750–75	352
XXI.	Block-Front Chest on Chest, 1760–80	353
XXII.	Block-Front Chest of Drawers, 1760–80	354
XXIII.	Block-Front Chest on Chest, 1770–80	356
XXIV.	Block-Front Chest of Drawers, 1770–80	357
XXV.	Block-Front Chest of Drawers, 1770–80	358
XXVI.	Detail capital on foregoing, 1770–80	359
XXVII.	Block-Front Chest on Chest, 1770–80	360
XXVIII.	Serpentine-Front Chest on Chest, 1770–80	361
XXIX.	Block-Front Knee-Hole Chest on Chest, 1770–80	362
XXX.	Block-Front Chest of Drawers, 1770–80	363
XXXI.	Block-Front Chest on Chest, 1770–80	364
XXXII.	Chest on Chest, 1790–1800	365
XXXIII.	Swell-Front Chest of Drawers, 1790–1800	366
XXXIV.	Swell-Front Chest of Drawers, 1790–1800	366
XXXV.	Swell-Front Chest of Drawers, 1800–10	367
XXXVI.	Swell-Front Dressing-Table, 1790–1800	368
XXXVII.	Swell-Front Wash-Stand, 1790–1800	368
XXXVIII.	Press Cupboard, 1650–75	370
XXXIX.	Clothes Cupboard, 1650–75	371
XL.	Sideboard Table, 1725–50	372
XLI.	Hepplewhite Sideboard, 1790–1800	373
XLII.	Hepplewhite Sideboard, 1790–1800	373
XLIII.	Hepplewhite Sideboard, 1790–1800	374
XLIV.	Sheraton Mixing-Table, 1800–10	374
XLV.	Sheraton Sideboard, 1800–10	375

LIST OF ILLUSTRATIONS

FIGURE		PAGE
XLVI.	Sheraton Sideboard with china-closet and drawer, about 1800	376
XLVII.	Label of Edmund Johnson on preceding sideboard	377
XLVIII.	Oak Desk-Box, 1671	378
XLIX.	Oak Desk-Box, 1670–80	378
L.	Desk-Box, Friesland Carving, about 1700	379
LI.	Standing Desk, Closed, about 1700	380
LII.	Standing Desk, Open, about 1700	381
LIII.	Small Ball-Foot Scrutoire, 1700–10	382
LIV.	Scrutoire on Frame, about 1725	382
LV.	Block-Front Scrutoire with cabinet top, 1750–75	383
LVI.	Serpentine-Front Scrutoire with cabinet top, 1770–80	384
LVII.	Block-Front Scrutoire, 1760–70	385
LVIII.	Sheraton Scrutoire with cabinet top, 1790–1800	386
LIX.	Sheraton Desk, bookcase top, 1800–10	387
LX.	Sheraton Desk, about 1810	387
LXI.	Sheraton Bookcase, 1790–1800	388
LXII.	Queen Anne Mantel Mirror, about 1725	389
LXIII.	Georgian Mantel Mirror, 1725–50	390
LXIV.	Queen Anne Pier Mirror, about 1725	391
LXV.	Georgian Pier Mirror, 1725–50	392
LXVI.	Pier Mirror, about 1750	392
LXVII.	Pier Mirror, 1750–75	392
LXVIII.	Pier Mirror, 1750–75	393
LXIX.	Two Mirrors, 1750–75	394
LXX.	Pair of Mirrors, 1780–90	395
LXXI.	Pier Mirror, 1790–1800	395
LXXII.	Gilded Mirror, 1790–1800	396
LXXIII.	Pier Mirror, 1800–10	397

COLONIAL FURNITURE
Volume I

I
INTRODUCTION

THE history of the cabinet-maker's art is the record of the unconscious struggle toward an ideal which, when finally attained, destroyed all further inspiration. This ideal persisted from one age to another, never retrograding, and each succeeding age saw it more clearly, until, at the close of the eighteenth century, it was found that its limitations had been reached. Incident to this development, many styles originated and were carried to their conclusions, and were either amalgamated with a new style or abandoned.

The ideal successfully attained was the production of furniture with a minimum of material and a delicacy of form sufficient to withstand the strain for which it was made. The medium of ornament and decoration was secondary to that of form, and when the form of any style had been perfected the decoration became more ornate, until a new style was welcomed as a return to simplicity. It therefore follows, as a general rule, that the earlier the example the greater its simplicity of line and ornamentation.

The origin and development of the various styles were dependent upon many conditions, social, commercial, and political. The earliest European furniture was crude and heavy. It consisted of only such articles as were essential to domestic life, such as chests, tables, benches, bed frames, and, occasionally, chairs. In the reign of James I, when the American colonisation began, England had not advanced far as a manufacturing country. The Dutch were still the great commercial race, carrying on a prosperous trade with Spain, Portugal, and the East Indies. Antwerp also was a great commercial centre and was exporting to England household furniture and choice dry-goods, receiving in exchange only crude raw materials, such as wool, lead, and tin, together with beer and cheese. Holland was at this time receiving from Spain and Italy the cane furniture which later came to England under Charles II.

The furniture in England of this period was rectangular in form, and such articles as stood on legs were heavily underbraced. Tables were made of oak with bulb-turned legs, often with rails carved in arabesque or lunette patterns. Occasionally a table would have a single leaf with a swinging leg, the forerunner of the gate-legged table. Many of the oak tables were arranged to be extended, one leaf lapping over the other when not extended. The dining-table of the middle class consisted of a deal board mounted on three or four standards. Chairs were either of the wainscot type, heavy and more or less carved, or of the plain turned variety with three or four legs. Oak chests and cupboards were in common use.

During the reign of Charles I there was very little change in the form of furniture, except that the French form of chair was introduced with turned legs, the back and seat of leather or embroidery making a decidedly lighter effect than the wainscot type. Chairs were not at all common, but stools and forms were used in their place. Oak was almost the universal wood, and did not lend itself to any style other than the massive. Couches or day beds were also in use among the wealthy class at this time.

In the early days of the Commonwealth little, if any, change took place in the prevailing styles of furniture, except possibly that the Puritan spirit asserted itself in a certain stiffness of form and also in the more general use of chairs. Late in the Commonwealth walnut was introduced, and with the use of this wood came a lightness not before attained. Legs were spiral or slightly turned, and cane was employed for the seats and backs of chairs. Chests became less popular, and in their place were used cupboards with drawers and chests of drawers.

With the Restoration came greater comfort and luxury, brought by Charles and his followers from France and Holland. Cane chairs of beech and walnut, with carved cresting, sides, and underbrace, took the place of the simple stiff chairs. Turnings on table legs became more refined, and the heavy oak tables were superseded by tables with two leaves. Chests of drawers took the place of chests. Marquetry was introduced, and expensive textiles and embroideries were more commonly imported to cover upholstered chairs. The Flemish scroll ʃ became the dominant form of ornamentation, and this scroll, when used as legs of chairs and tables, was the forerunner of the cabriole leg.

During the reign of William and Mary many changes took place in the style of furniture, due not only to the fact that William was distinctly Dutch and brought with him Dutch ideas and Dutch workmen, but also to the revocation of the Edict of Nantes in 1685, after which many artisans fled to England. During the first part of this reign the popularity of the Flemish furniture was at its height, but this style was gradually replaced by the Dutch style. The chests of drawers were raised from the floor on turned cup-shaped legs, and that same form of leg was extensively used on chairs and tables; marquetry and japanning became popular, and carving almost completely disappeared. Chinese objects were extensively imported and collecting became a fad. The furniture, however, did not reflect this fashion, except in fret design and japanning, until about 1740.

INTRODUCTION 5

In the American colonies the same change in style is noticeable, except that marquetry was but little used.

It would be difficult to understand the variations in style of the furniture in the American colonies up to this time without having clearly in mind the reasons for the formation of the different colonies.

In New England the first settlement was at Plymouth, made by a band of religious enthusiasts who had previously fled from England to Holland to escape religious persecution and obtain religious liberty. They lived for some years in that country, until, foreseeing that the political changes taking place in Holland might curtail their liberty, they decided to establish a colony in the New World, on the Delaware River, under the jurisdiction of the London Company. These people were poor and, because of their unsettled lives, probably had little property. This little company after crossing the Atlantic found themselves off Cape Cod, which was under the jurisdiction of the Plymouth Company. Here they landed, hoping to obtain a grant. It was a small and struggling band of men and women who faced starvation and Indian perils, and it was not until 1624 that success was assured. The grant to the land upon which they had settled was given to a joint stock company, and in 1627 the settlers bought the stock, which was not finally paid for until 1633. The colony was always small and did not exceed in number three thousand, in 1643, when emigration ceased. It could hardly be expected, therefore, that this colony would have anything but bare necessities during its early existence, and the inventories at Plymouth show this to be the fact.

The Puritan emigration was, however, quite different. The purpose of their exodus from England was to form a theocratic government in the new country moulded after the model set for them in the Old Testament. They came from the west of England, the Puritan stronghold, and were persons of means. One of the principal reasons for the exodus was the political condition of England during the early reign of Charles I, and it is more than a coincidence that between 1629 and 1640, the period when Charles tried to rule England without Parliament, that twenty-six thousand persons emigrated to New England. This exodus ceased with the beginning of the Civil War. It is undoubtedly true that these persons not only brought with them household goods and furniture, but, as they became prosperous, many of the comforts of England and Holland were imported by them in exchange for the raw products of the New World.

The influence of the Dutch in the New World was both direct and indirect. During the war for independence in Holland many thousands of artisans and skilled workers fled to England. They settled, for the most part, in the west of England among the people who founded New England. They were Protestants and lovers of liberty, and sufficiently like the persons among whom they lived to become quickly assimilated, and many of the Puritans coming to New England had this foreign blood. It is this probably that, in part at least, accounts for the similarity of design in furniture and decoration between the two countries. The Dutch settlement in America was made primarily for trading. Manhattan Island was selected, because of the Hudson River and the magnificent harbour, as the most desirable post for the fur trade. The settlements were under the direction of the Dutch West India Company, but the growth was slow, composed mostly of traders who came and went, and, of course, these people carried few household articles. It became evident that in order to secure a permanent and self-supporting community the farmer class must be encouraged to settle there, but the Dutch had obtained independence at home and were loath to leave the peace for which they had so long striven for the dangers of the New World. To overcome this feeling and to encourage emigration the West India Company in 1629 issued a charter, providing that any person bringing to New Netherlands fifty persons and settling them in homes on the Hudson River should have a grant of land to be held in a semi-feudal tenure of patroon or lord of the manor.

This charter seems to have had the desired effect of making permanent settlements, but even then the Dutch colony did not increase as rapidly as that of New England, and it was not until further inducements had been made that people of quality and education came in any numbers. This was about the year 1639, and it is probable that prior to that date only necessities had been brought over except by the patroons for their own use. Although the Dutch rule was but of short duration, its influence has been strong. Dutch customs and styles have persisted even to the present day, giving modifications of designs which are easily recognised. These colonists were rich in household goods, mostly imported in exchange for furs and raw material which were exported.

The Pennsylvania colony was founded at a later date, 1683, and was composed of emigrants, most of whom were prosperous, and from the beginning the colony had most of the luxury to which they had been accustomed at home. Many artisans were brought over, and much of the finer furniture found in this country came from that colony, much of it being made there.

The Virginia colony was largely made up of gentlemen adventurers and settlers, and always kept in close touch with the mother country, exchanging tobacco for household articles and other products.

It will thus be seen that in all probability the early furniture of this country was either brought over or imported by the settlers, but in no large quantities. Later, as more pieces were needed, they were made after the pattern with which the people were familiar, and at the time Charles II came to the throne most of the furniture used in this country was being made here. The colonial newspapers are full of advertisements of every sort of manufactured article imported from London. The list includes nails and brasses, all kinds of hardware, stuffs of all sorts, china utensils and tools, looking-glasses, and hard wood, but very little

INTRODUCTION

furniture is mentioned, and this condition continued to the Revolutionary War, although as late as 1765 the newspapers throughout the colonies were urging people to patronise and develop home industries.

Before proceeding further it will be well to consider the furniture which was in use in the colonies during the seventeenth century. Up to 1650 furniture must have been very scarce, and in the earlier inventories the only articles of furniture mentioned are tables, chairs, chests, and bedsteads. As prosperity increased furniture became very plentiful, and before the new century began the wealthier class about New York and the other seaports had all that the European markets could offer. The South seems to have been particularly well provided with court cupboards, chests, couches, and leather chairs, while in New England chests of drawers, desks, scrutoires, and Turkey-work chairs were more plentiful. The furniture in the South was largely imported, for the expression "old" is mentioned with all kinds of furniture from the very first, while in New England the low valuations lead us to believe that most of the furniture there was home-made. The high chests of drawers appear first, as might be expected, in the New York records and last in the South. In New England they seem to have been in common use as early as 1685-90. The reason for this seems to be that New England was in rather close touch with Holland, where this style originated, while the South only traded with England, where these pieces never became very popular. At Philadelphia the records show luxury from the beginning, and as a rule valuations were higher there than elsewhere. The furniture of New Amsterdam seems to have differed from that found in New England and the South in several ways. The furniture mentioned in New Amsterdam shows clearly the influence of the Continental and Eastern markets, mention being made of wicker furniture, East India cabinets, ebony chairs, and India blankets, etc., the reasons for which probably were that the Dutch still controlled the East India trade and, further, that New York was made a harbour for that large class of persons who at that time, like Captain Kidd, were engaged in piracy. Little mention is found of carved oak. There are no court or livery cupboards mentioned in the New York inventories, but nearly every family had a *kas* or *kasse*, a large linen cupboard, and this piece of furniture is found nowhere else in this country.

Nothing, perhaps, influenced the furniture of the eighteenth century so much as the introduction of mahogany, the strength of which made possible a quite new method of carving, delicate and lace-like, which reached its perfection in some of Chippendale's models. According to tradition, mahogany, although known since the time of Raleigh, was first made into furniture in England about the year 1720. If this were true, the colonies would have the honour of having discovered its great value for furniture some years before the mother country, for in the Philadelphia inventories, as early as 1708, mahogany is mentioned as made up into furniture, and there are entries at New York which seem to indicate that there was furniture there made of that wood about fifteen years earlier. The tradition of its introduction into England is, however, faulty, for it is now known that furniture was made occasionally of this wood in England during the latter half of the seventeenth century.

In the early years of the eighteenth century a radical change occurred in the form of furniture, and approximately the year 1700 marks the dividing line between ancient and modern forms. Straight lines were melted into curves; rectangular forms, whenever possible, were modified or abandoned. The turned leg was superseded by the cabriole, underbracing disappeared, and the style of carving popular in the last quarter of the seventeenth century gave way to simpler designs. More attention was paid to perfection of form than to ornament. The dominant feature of the new form was the use of the cyma curve as a substitute for straight lines wherever possible. To illustrate: Two cyma curves placed thus ∫ ⌐ formed the design of the chair backs. A cyma curve thus ∫ formed the cabriole leg. Two cyma curves placed thus ‿‿ formed the scroll top found on high-boys, secretaries, and cupboards. When placed thus ⌒⌒ they formed the familiar outline found on the skirts of high-boys, low-boys, and other pieces. Mouldings, cupboard openings, and the inner edges of mirrors were cut in the same curve.

There was less carved decoration used in this period than in that of Charles II, and it was cut on the surface instead of used to form the outline. The commonest designs were the shell, mascaron, cartouche, swags of flowers, acanthus leaves, and often classical designs. Claw feet of birds and animals grasping balls were popular, and, although these designs were sometimes found in metal work of a much earlier period, they first became popular on furniture at this time. The style came to England from Holland and to this country from both, and is known as the Dutch, Queen Anne, or early Georgian style.

Figure 1 shows the interior of a doll house, the furnishings of which are of this period. There are cabriole leg tables, double chairs and stools, a chest of drawers, a knee-hole dressing-table with dressing-glass, a slant-front secretary with cabinet top, a basin-stand, a card-table, and a fire-screen. There are three bedsteads heavily draped in the fashion of the day; there is a rug on the parlour floor. In the kitchen is a turned chair in the form usually called Carver in this country. It is a significant fact that there are no high-boys. In the American colonies at this time every house would contain several.

The Dutch style was finally superseded by the introduction of the French, rococo, Chinese, and Gothic designs a little prior to the middle of the eighteenth century. The American colonies do not seem to have adopted these designs until

Figure 1.
Doll House, first quarter eighteenth century.

somewhat later, and the French form of chest of drawers, called commodes, were never popular here.

From this time forward the history of furniture can readily be followed from the published works of architects and cabinet-makers.

One cannot but be impressed by the careful and scholarly manner in which these books were written. It is manifest that the cabinet-maker's profession at that time ranked with that of architects.

One of the first books of design of this period was "The Gentlemen's and Builders' Companion," by William Jones, published in 1739. The following are the principal published designs down to the publication by Chippendale: "The City and County Builders' and Workmen's Treasury of Designs," by Batty and Thomas Langley, published in 1740, which show French influences, and some of the tables are copied from designs by Nicholas Pineau, of Paris; "The British Architect or the Builders' Journal of Stair-cases," by Abraham Swain, published in 1745, which shows the earliest rococo designs; a book by Edwards and Darley in Chinese taste; a book by Thomas Johnson, showing designs in Gothic, Chinese, and rococo taste and making use of foxes and other animals; "A New Book of Ornament," by Mattheas Lock, published in 1752, similar to Johnson's designs, except that he does not make so much use of the figures of animals; "New Designs for Chinese Temples, Triumphal Arches, Garden Seats, Palings, etc.," by William Halfpenny, published in 1750–52; Sir William Chambers's designs showing Chinese and rustic taste; and "Gentleman's and Cabinet-makers' Director," by Thomas Chippendale, first published in 1754.

The most prominent of these designers and cabinet-makers was Thomas Chippendale, and his influence on the furniture of England and this country in 1750 to 1780 was probably greater than that of any other, so that the period can properly be called by his name. Very little of the life of Chippendale has been known until Constance Simon published her researches, entitled "English Furniture Designers of the Eighteenth Century."

It appears that Chippendale was married to Catherine Redshaw, of Saint Martin's in the Field, May 19, 1748, and that in 1749 he had a shop in Conduit Street, Long Acre, London, and removed from there, in 1753, to 60 Saint Martin's Lane, where he took over three houses adjoining his own. That his shop was large and his business prosperous would appear from a notice in the *Gentleman's Magazine* of April 5, 1755, which reads as follows:

"A fire broke out in the workshop of Mr. Chippendale, a cabinet-maker near Saint Martin's Lane, which consumed the same, wherein were the chests of 22 workmen."

Twenty-two workmen would indicate at least a small factory. In 1760 he was elected a member of the Society for the Encouragement of Arts, Manufactures and Commerce. He was in partnership for a time with James Rannil, who

INTRODUCTION

died in 1766, after which date Chippendale advertises to conduct the business on his own account. He died November 13, 1779, and his widow Elizabeth, apparently his second wife, was granted letters of administration.

The oldest son, Thomas, succeeded to the business with Thomas Haig, who had been a book-keeper in the firm, under the firm name of Chippendale & Haig, until 1796. Chippendale, Jr., died in 1822. The date of Chippendale's birth is a matter of conjecture. He must have had a well-established business at fifty, and if he lived the allotted span of seventy years he must have been born about 1709, which would have made him forty-one years old in 1750, which seems probable. It will, at any rate, be seen that as a young man he must have been familiar with the published designs above referred to, and his own designs, first published in 1754, bear out this supposition, for he refers to the fact that designers have paid but little attention to rules of architecture. He appears to have been at first a cabinet-maker, but as his business prospered it developed into that of interior decoration, and he executed not only his own but the designs of architects such as Adam Brothers. The writer has in his possession a copy of a bill rendered by Chippendale to Sir Roland Winn, Bart., for furniture, draperies, carpets, papering, and interior decoration for Nostel Abbey, covering the years 1766–70. Some of the pieces described in this bill will be illustrated in the text, and they show that by this time Chippendale had departed from the French and had adopted more of the classical style then coming into vogue.

"The Gentleman and Cabinet-maker's Director" was advertised for sale in the *Gentleman's Magazine* in 1754 in book form. The writer has been unable to find any reference to the second edition except by inference from the advertisements of the third edition. The third edition was not at first published in book form, but in folios, each containing four copper plates at 1s. each. On August 21, 1759, the following advertisement appears in the *London Chronicle:*

Saturday, October 6 will be published
No. I, being Four Folio Copper Plates, price 1 s.,

THE GENTLEMAN'S and CABINET MAKER'S DIRECTOR. To be continued Weekly and the whole completed in Fifty Numbers,

By THOMAS CHIPPENDALE,
Cabinet Maker in St. Martin's Lane.

The kind Reception this work has already met with, renders any Apology for its Republication needless, and has encouraged the Author to revise and improve several of the Plates first published and to add Fifty new ones; containing some Designs of Chimney pieces, Lanthorns, and Chandeliers, for Halls and Stair Cases. Likewise various Designs of Household Furniture, both useful and ornamental.

N. B. Scales and Dimensions are annexed, and with the last number will be given Explanation and ample Illustrations in Letter-press for the Workman. Those who purchased the first Edition may have the additional Plates separate.

On October 6, 1759, appears in the same paper the following:

This day were published,
No. I of the Third Edition being Four Folio Copper-plates,
printed on Royal Paper, Price 1 s.

THE GENTLEMAN'S and CABINET MAKER'S DIRECTOR. To be continued Weekly, and the whole completed in Fifty Numbers.

By THOMAS CHIPPENDALE,
Cabinet Maker, in St. Martin's Lane.

The kind Reception this Work has already met with, renders any Apology for its Republication needless; and has encouraged the Author to revise and improve several of the Plates first published, and to add Fifty New ones; containing some Designs of Chimney-pieces, Lanthorns, and Chandeliers, for Halls and Stair Cases. Likewise various Designs of Household Furniture, both useful and ornamental, adapted to the present Taste. The Author being determined to exert the utmost of his Abilities to make this Work more complete and worthy of the Encouragement of the Publick.

To be had of the Author; and of Robert Sayer, opposite Fetter-lane, Fleet Street; and of all the Booksellers in Great Britain and Ireland.

The various parts were thereafter advertised as published, about a week apart, until Number XXV had appeared.

On March 28, 1760, the following advertisement appears:

St. Martin's Lane, March 28, 1760.

Mr. CHIPPENDALE begs leave to acquaint those Noblemen, Gentlemen and others, who have honoured him with their Subscriptions to his DESIGNS of HOUSEHOLD FURNITURE, that he is obliged to defer the Publication thereof for a few Weeks, both on Account of his indifferent State of Health, and to allow him Time for the Executing some NEW DESIGNS, with which he intends to embellish his said Work.

The Subscribers may be assured that Number XXVI. of this Work, will be published very speedily; and Mr. Chippendale hopes to make amends for this Delay, by presenting them with near ONE HUNDRED NEW DESIGNS, instead of FIFTY, which he first proposed.

He takes this Opportunity of Thanking his worthy Subscribers for the Approbation they have shown in regard to this Publication; and the kind Reception

INTRODUCTION

it has met with determines him to spare no Pains or Cost, to render it as elegant and as useful a Work as it is in his Power to do.

Nothing further appears until June 17, 1760, when Number XXVI was advertised.

And on July 26, 1760, appears the following advertisement:

CHIPPENDALE'S DESIGNS.

T. BECKET, Bookseller, at *Tully's Head*, near *Surry-Street*, in the *Strand*:

Begs Leave to acquaint the Nobility, Gentry and others, Subscribers to Mr. CHIPPENDALE's elegant Designs of HOUSEHOLD FURNITURE, in the newest and most fashionable Taste, that the New ones are now finished; and that Number XXVI. of that Curious Work will be published on Saturday next, and continued Weekly, without Interruption until the Whole is finished.

The first twenty-five Numbers may be had together; or any Person may begin with No. 1, and continue them Weekly; and those that will be pleased to give in their Names and Place of Abode, may depend on having the Numbers regularly sent by their Most obedient humble Servant,

T. BECKET.

Strand, July 26, 1760.

On July 31, 1760, the following advertisement appeared, which was continued for subsequent numbers until September 19, 1761:

This Day was published, Price 1s.
No. XXVI. Consisting of four elegant Designs.
(To be continued Weekly).

THE GENTLEMAN's and CABINET-MAKER's DIRECTOR. Containing a great Variety of Designs of Household Furniture in the newest and most fashionable Taste. This Work will consist of 200 Copper-plates (containing upwards of 500 Designs) elegantly engraved by the best Masters, and printed on Royal Paper, and will be comprised in fifty Numbers.

In the Course of this Work will be exhibited several New Designs of Organs, Chimney-pieces both Architectal and Ornamental; with various Designs of ornamental Brass-work for Furniture, Stoves, Grates, Chandeliers, Lanthorns &c. &c.

Proper Directions will be given for executing every Design; the Mouldings are at large; and the exact Dimensions of each Design specified. The whole intended as a complete Assistant to the Nobility and Gentry in the Choice of their Furniture; as well as a Work of general Use to the Artificer, who may be greatly instructed thereby.

By T. CHIPPENDALE,
Cabinet-Maker, in St. Martin's-Lane.

Printed for the Author; and sold by T. Becket, at Tully's Head, near Surry-Street in the Strand.

∗ Any Person may begin with No. 1, and be supplied Weekly, by applying as above.

The Price of this Work, when completed will be raised to Non subscribers. No Copies will be sold under Three Guineas in Sheets.

And on March 16, 1762, the final advertisement appears, showing that the book could be obtained in different volumes, or bound in one:

This day was published
Dedicated to his Royal Highness, Prince William, the
second Volume, price 1 £ 10 s in sheets of

THE GENTLEMAN'S and CABINET MAKER'S DIRECTOR
By THOMAS CHIPPENDALE,
Cabinet Maker & Upholsterer in St. Martin's Lane.

This Volume contains 106 new Folio Copper Plates, and upwards of 260 Designs of the most curious Pieces of Household Furniture, both useful and ornamental, with some designs of Chimney Pieces, Stove-grates, Organs, Frets, Borders for Paper Hangings &c. This may be had complete, the two volumes bound in one, containing 200 Folio Copper Plates with 400 different Designs, Price 2 £ 12 s, 6 d, in Sheets. *∗* As this Work abounds with a great Variety of elegant Designs every Gentleman will have it in his Power to make his own Choice with respect to the Furniture wanted and will be enabled to point out such his Choice to the Workman, who with common Capacity may easily execute the same the Rules being plain and easy. Printed for the Author; and sold by T. Becket and P. A. de Hondt at Tully's Head in the Strand.

The third edition is much more commonly found than the first, and is almost invariably found bound in one large volume. It has been thought worth while to dwell at some length upon the publication of this work, not only because it was the most elaborate and important work on the subject produced in England, but also because it never has before been noted that the book was first issued in parts.

Chippendale's originality lay in his ability to combine inconsistent styles in a harmonious whole. His workmanship and skill as a carver were of the highest order. He was daring in his designs, and many of the pieces shown in his book would be thought impossible of execution but for the fact that they do exist. On his pieces in French taste he would carve wood where the French would use ormolu. On his Chinese pieces he would introduce entirely

INTRODUCTION

new mouldings, such as the knuckle-bone pattern, and on his Gothic pieces he would put a touch of the Chinese.

His versatility was amazing. His designs show a range from the simple lines of the Dutch school through the rococo, Gothic, and Chinese to the classic, and here and there are exquisite pieces suggesting the Louis XIV school.

It has been the fashion of late years to decry the work of Chippendale, but this is largely because few really know his work. They see only the countless articles of furniture copied by the local cabinet-makers of that day from his

Figure 2.
Chippendale Commode, French taste, 1750–60.

designs. One has but to see a veritable piece of Chippendale's best period to feel that he stands in the presence of the work of a master designer and a master cabinet-maker.

Figure 2 shows one of a pair of Chippendale commodes in Chippendale's pure French taste. It will be seen that not only is the front curved, but also the sides, and the piece is in such perfect proportion that the ornamentation, which on a less well-proportioned piece would be excessive, merely enhances its beauty.

The carving on the legs and ends has the sharpness of ormolu and illustrates the perfection to which carving can be carried. The pendent ribbons and flowers are also of wood.

Figure 3 shows one of a pair of settees in Chippendale's Chinese taste with a slight suggestion of the Gothic in the arching under the arms. Although full of Chinese motifs and feeling, an analysis will show that there is hardly a line in the piece which a Chinese workman would have used in furniture. The piece well illustrates Chippendale's ability to adapt and combine without slavishly copying.

Figure 4 shows one of a pair of torchères or guéridons in pure Gothic style. The great beauty of this piece is its architectural perfection. It rises

Figure 3.
Chippendale Settee, Chinese taste, 1750-60.

arch on arch, each apparently supporting the weight in proper proportion, so that when the stand is reached one has the feeling that it would support any strain.

These examples are taken from the famous collection of Mr. Richard A. Canfield for the purpose of illustrating the three important styles used by Chippendale. In the same collection are examples of the same master, where these various styles are mingled.

Of course the large mass of Chippendale furniture is vastly simpler than these pieces, being made for persons of moderate means, and Chippendale's book of designs was used in England, Scotland, Ireland, and America as the basis for much of the so-called Chippendale furniture.

INTRODUCTION

The next cabinet-makers of note were Ince and Mayhew, who also published designs in parts, which were afterward bound. Under date of April 12, 1760, their advertisement was published in the *Gentleman's Magazine* as follows:

To the PUBLIC.

INCE and MAYHEW return their utmost Thanks for the kind Reception their DESIGNS have met with; and assure them no Pains shall be spared to render them preferable to any like Performance, both for the Choice of the GENTLEMAN and the Use of the WORKMAN. A Determination to finish them to the utmost Exactness obliges them to be irregular, occasioned through a great Want of Time, and every Design being NEW.

No. XVII. with Four Folio Plates, is published this Day at 1 s. To be had at Webley's, Holborn; Darley's Cheapside; and of the Authors, CABINET-MAKERS and UPHOLSTERERS, Broad-Street, Carnaby Market: Where the Honour of any Commands will be observed with the most reasonable Charges.

N. B. Those who have not yet completed their Sets, are required to do so, as but a few of the first Impression is left.

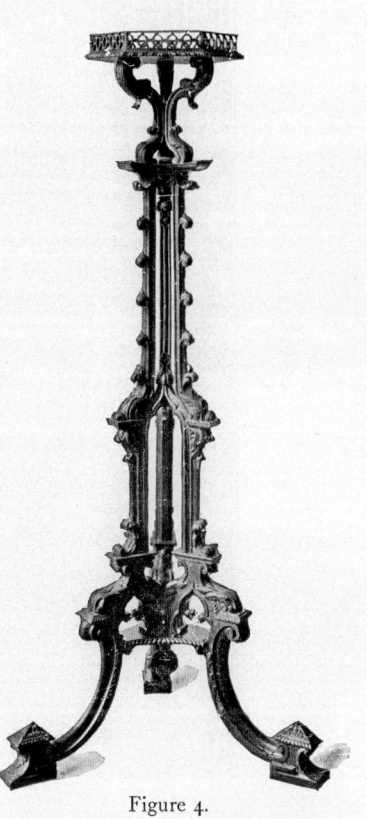

Ince and Mayhew's designs were similar to Chippendale's, but, on the whole, were not as well proportioned.

During the next ten years many other books were published, one by Decker and several by a Society of Upholsterers and Cabinet-Makers.

About 1765 the public taste began to change from the French, Gothic, and Chinese tastes to the classic, owing very largely to the research, study, and publication of classical ruins and designs by the Brothers Adam, who were the leading architects of the day.

Figure 4.
Chippendale Torchère, Gothic taste, 1750-60.

Chippendale felt the effect with others and began to execute orders from the designs made by Adam, and finally abandoned his early style for the classic, much to his detriment.

Under date of June 30, 1767, Chippendale billed to Sir Roland Winn, Bart., of Nostel Abbey, "a large Mahogany Library table of very fine wood with drawers on each side of the bottom part and drawers within on one side and partition in the other, with terms to ditto, carv'd and ornamented with Lions' heads and paws with carv'd ovals in the panels of the doors & the top cover'd with black leather & the whole completely finished in the most elegant taste. £72. 10s."

This piece is shown in Figure 5. Were it not for the bill, few persons would believe it could be made by the same person who, some ten years earlier, had made the commode shown in Figure 2, yet Chippendale, in the third edition of his "Director," shows a side-table with term legs quite suggestive of this piece.

The next cabinet-maker of this period was Shearer, who, with other cabinet-makers, published "A Cabinetmakers Book of Prices" in 1788. By this time

Figure 5.
Chippendale Library Table, 1767.

the style had completely changed, the cabriole leg had been superseded by the tapering straight leg, and there was a general lightness of construction which was entirely new, undoubtedly due to the influence of the Louis XVI style.

Shearer was the first to design a sideboard with serpentine front and inlaid drawers, now commonly called Hepplewhite.

Hepplewhite, the next of the great designers, published a book in 1789. The designs are still more delicate, almost to the point of fragility. The chair backs were usually either oval or shield-shaped, and contrasting woods were employed for ornamentation. Carving was but sparingly used.

The next and last of the great designers was Sheraton. His early style was similar to Hepplewhite's, but his chair backs were generally rectangular, and he

INTRODUCTION

often embellished pieces with a fine cameo carving. He ceased to be a cabinet-maker in 1793, and devoted the remainder of his life to writing books of design which had large sales. He died in 1806. His later designs followed the Egyptian classic style which had come into vogue in France and is known as the Empire style. He had many followers in America, notably Duncan Phyfe, of New York, a cabinet-maker who executed some exceptionally good pieces in this style.

Following Sheraton, the style became massive and heavy, with coarse carving, heavy columns, claw feet, and massive slabs of well-grained mahogany It is known as late Empire.

In America, throughout the eighteenth century, were a large number of cabinet-makers, some of whom advertised as coming from London. The number is so large, and the inventories of their estates show them to have been so prosperous, that it can only be concluded that much of the furniture was made here. On the other hand, such men as Sir William Pepperell, Faneuil, Judge Sewall, and Hancock, of Boston, Franklin, of Philadelphia, Byrd, of Virginia, and others of the wealthier class were sending to England for their furniture and household effects.

The business of furniture-making appears to have been subdivided. There were joiners, turners, chair-makers, Windsor chair-makers, carvers, and cabinet-makers, but it is doubtful whether the line of difference was sharply drawn, for some of the chair-makers are known to have made at least dressing-tables and probably other articles.

These furniture-makers seem to have kept in touch with the new English fashions. It is known that the books of the early eighteenth-century architects were freely employed here, and many of the designs from Chippendale's book were copied, including a number of his mouldings, which show familiarity with his work. For instance, the chair shown in Figure 558 bears the card of James Gillingham, cabinet and chair maker in Second Street between Walnut and Chestnut Streets, Philadelphia, and the chair is copied from Plate X in Chippendale's "Director," appearing in all editions. Further, James Rivington, of Hanover Square, New York, advertises for sale, in 1760, "Household Furniture for the year 1760 by a Society of Upholsterers, Cabinet Makers, etc. containing upwards of 180 Designs consisting of Tea Tables, Dressing, Card, Writing, Library, and Slab Tables, Chairs, Stools, Couches, Trays, Chests, Tea Kettles, Bureaus, Beds, Ornamental Bed Posts, Cornishes, Brackets, Fire Screens, Desk and Book cases, Sconces, Chimney Pieces, Girondoles, Lanthorns, etc. with Scales." This certainly indicates that the American cabinet-makers were keeping in close touch with the newest London designs. In 1762, the year that the third edition of Chippendale's book was published, an advertisement appeared in New York: "John Brinner, Cabinet and Chair Maker from London at the Sign of the Chair, opposite Flatten Barrack Hill, in the Broad-Way, New York, where every article in the Cabinet, Chair-making, Carving and Gilding Business is enacted on the most reasonable

Terms with the Utmost Neatness and Punctuality. He Carves all Sorts of Architectural, Gothic, and Chinese Chimney-pieces, Glass and Picture Frames, Slab Frames, Girondels, Chandaliers, and all Kinds of Mouldings and Frontispieces, etc., etc., Desk and Book Cases, Library Book Cases, Writing and Reading Tables, Study Tables, China Shelves and Cases, Commode and Plain Chests of Drawers, Gothic and Chinese Chairs; all sorts of plain or ornamental Chairs, Sofa Beds, Sofa Settees, Couch and Easy Chairs, Frames, all Kinds of Field Bedsteads, etc., etc. N. B. He has brought over from London six Artificers, well-skilled in the above branches."

In 1771 appears the following: "Tomorrow will be sold at public vendue at the Merchants' Coffee house at twelve O'clock by John Applegate, a very neat set of carved mahogany chairs, one carved and gilt sideboard table, and a Chinese hanging bookcase with several other things. N. B. The back of the chairs is done after the pattern of some of the queens; a sketch of which chair will be shown at the time of the sale. The chairs and other things were made by a person in the Jersies who served his time and afterward was eleven years foreman to the great and eminent cabinet maker, William Hallet, Esq., that bought the fine estate of the Duke of Shandos, called Cannon's in Middlesex; was afterwards a master for twenty years in London and hath been two years in the Jersies. He will receive any order for furniture, viz:—Plate cases or best Chinese hanging bookcases or on frames; French elbow chairs, ribbon back, Gothic or any sort of chairs, likewise carved glass frames, girrandoles, bracket branches etc."

In the late years of the century were published books of prices, apparently in imitation of the ones published yearly in London. In Philadelphia it was called "The Journeyman's Cabinet and Chair makers' Philadelphia Book of Prices," and a similar book was published by the joiners of Hartford in 1792.

The furniture found in America during the eighteenth century can be divided into four periods.

The first period was from about 1700 to 1725, when the style was a combination of the William and Mary with the Dutch style which followed it. The change in style had been so radical that the conservative colonists seem to have been loath to adopt it; consequently during this period the two styles struggled with each other for the supremacy. In an inventory as late as 1724, at Boston, turkey-work chairs are mentioned as new, and Judge Samuel Sewall, in 1719, writing to London for household goods, asked for "a dozen good black walnut chairs fine cane with a couch." However, the new style continued to persist, and in 1722 are found advertised crooked-backed chairs, clearly referring to the new form.

The next period was from 1725 to 1750. The Dutch style was now at its height. The cabinet-makers did not slavishly copy the English style, but developed along somewhat independent lines, and the high chests of drawers and their

INTRODUCTION

companion dressing-tables continued in fashion and were not replaced by the English adaptation of the French commodes.

During the Chippendale period, 1750 to 1775, furniture was made in the colonies which for workmanship compared favourably with any made in England. In Philadelphia high chests of drawers, dressing-tables, and desks were made with scroll top and elaborately carved, while in New England low chests of drawers, chest on chests, dressing-tables, and desks were being made in the block-front type. Both of these styles are original in America and are the contribution of cabinet-makers here to the art. Pie-crust tables and well-carved chairs were abundantly made here and were quite the equal of those made in England.

The last period is 1785 to 1810. America does not seem to have been greatly influenced by the transition pieces between Chippendale and the Hepplewhite and Sheraton schools. The Revolutionary War had cut off all commercial intercourse between the two countries just at the time when the transition pieces were popular in England; consequently the Chippendale style lasted longer here, and by the time the war was over the later styles had become firmly established.

The Sheraton style greatly influenced the cabinet-makers, and many dainty pieces are found here. One of the characteristics of the style in this country is that it is almost devoid of mouldings; rarely, if ever, is the cyma curve used, but the edges are often straight, relieved of bareness by inlay.

The Empire period in this country was prolific. Mahogany had become plentiful, and massive furniture was constructed with posts and columns often carved in a coarse pineapple and acanthus-leaf design.

About 1825 there was an attempt made to revive the Gothic style, and a number of pieces are found here reflecting that attempt. In England several books of design were published, notably Pugin's "Gothic Furniture" in 1826. The attempt was short-lived and was followed by a revival of the French rococo, of which many rosewood parlour suits and other furniture are still quite commonly found.

II
CHESTS

AS has often been pointed out, chests have been in use for many centuries. One of the first indications of civilisation in man is the accumulation of property, and this necessitates a place for storing what has been accumulated. Chests or coffers, therefore, are among man's oldest possessions.

In England, where we shall follow their history a little, the chests of Norman times were huge oak boxes, bound and rebound with iron, and sometimes magnificently wrought. These served as receptacles for valuables in both the churches and castles, and were furnished with strong locks the mechanism of which often occupied the entire inside of the chest's cover. For many years these chests served for seats and tables, and for trunks when the lord and lady travelled. Some ancient manuscripts show their tops furnished with chess-boards, a player sitting at either end of the chest.

Carving as an art is also very old; it is referred to in Exodus xxxv, 33, as "in carving of wood, to make any manner of cunning work." Carving was at first employed almost exclusively for the beautifying of cathedrals and churches, for even the castles of kings, up to the time of Henry III, were very bare, and showed nothing in the way of fine wood-work.

During the reign of Henry III (1216–72), however, room-panelling was introduced into England, and the archings and window-frame designs long used in the churches became the models for wood-carvings used in the castles and manor-houses for many generations. Almost every design found on the chests and cupboards preserved in the English museums are those employed in the room-panelling of the period to which the furniture belonged.

The early chests of the thirteenth, fourteenth, and fifteenth centuries had very wide stiles, sometimes as wide as twelve inches. These were frequently elaborately ornamented with carving. Stiles gradually became narrower, so that by the opening of the seventeenth century they had become about the width of the stiles used in the panelling of the period. By the time the American colonisation began the chest in England had reached the last stage of its development and was soon to be superseded by the chest of drawers.

CHESTS

What the chests were which came to the American colonies with the first settlers it is now impossible to say. There is occasional mention, in the early inventories, of wainscot chests or great oak chests, but by far the larger number are recorded simply as chests, or old chests, and their valuation is so slight as to lead us to the conclusion that they must have been of very simple design.

Ship chests or pine boxes were probably brought over by all settlers. Figure 6 shows the ship chest said to have been brought by Elder Brewster, and many

Figure 6.
Pine Ship Chest, first quarter seventeenth century.

hundreds of boxes such as this probably came from Holland and England during the years when the colonies where being settled. An entry appears at Boston, in the items of the estate of a man who died on the ship *Castle* during his voyage to Massachusetts, in 1638, of "An owld pine chest 5s"; and of two other chests without description, of still more trifling value.

The earliest carved chests found here are decorated with panels carved in arched designs identical with the patterns seen in England on mantelpieces and wall-panellings during Elizabethan and Jacobean times. Without doubt the carved chests that were brought over previous to 1650 served as the models for those made here for a long time, for the writer has identified almost every pattern used on early chests as having been used in England, and there seems to have been no originality shown in the designs employed in this country until after the middle of the seventeenth century.

There are about ten designs that appear repeatedly in the chests, cupboards, and wainscot chairs of the seventeenth century. These are used in many combinations, sometimes eight out of the ten appearing together on the large pieces and from three to five on the smaller ones. The scroll design, for instance, is often found used in single form for a border and entwined and doubled for a panel. Once familiar with these designs, a close observer will find furniture belonging to the carved-oak period in this country very easy to identify. These designs will be pointed out as they are met with in the specimens to be spoken of later.

A chest, cupboard, or chair is occasionally met with which has carved designs not traceable to England, but showing French or Dutch influence. Almost without exception such pieces will be found to be made of foreign wood, and the designs were not copied here to any extent, as were the familiar English ones.

The chests are constructed with stiles and rails, mortised and tenoned, held

Figure 7.
Oak Chest, about 1650.

in place with wooden pegs made square and driven into a round hole. The edges of the stiles and rails toward the panels are usually chamfered, and the panels, which are sometimes made of pine, are fitted into the frame. The ends are also panelled in various designs, and the back is formed of pine or oak planks nailed or framed in and occasionally panelled. The tops of American chests are usually of a single plank of pine with a slight overhang at the ends and front. Under the ends are fastened cleats which hold the top and prevent warping. When made of oak, they are in strips finished and fashioned as the pine ones. The edge of the top, except the back, is finished with a thumb-nail moulding. The hinges are composed of two iron staples interlocked, one driven into the rail and one into the top and clinched. On the inside, within the chest at one end, is usually found a small till.

Figure 7 shows a chest with the characteristic arching and pattern detail used throughout the Elizabethan and Jacobean periods. Burton Agnes Hall, built in 1601, shows this arched carving on the staircase in the great hall. This chest is constructed in the usual manner; the stiles and rails are joined with mortise and tenon (all wood-work fastened in this way is spoken of as joined), and the panels are fitted into the frame. The top rail is carved in a lunette design, and on all four stiles are carved laurelling, each surmounted by a rosette. The pilasters and arches on the panel are carved in guilloche design. This chest is the property of the Hon. and Mrs. Morgan G. Bulkeley, of Hartford, Connecticut.

The chests following the general form of Figure 7 are found in different sizes, some as large as five feet in length, and vary in size from twenty to thirty inches.

Figure 8.
Oak Chest, third quarter seventeenth century.

The arches are sometimes elaborately carved, sometimes merely indicated by slight tracery. Space between the arches is sometimes carved and sometimes inlaid in foliated designs, and any and all of the foliated border patterns are used to decorate the stiles and rails.

Figure 8 shows a very beautiful carved chest in the Bolles Collection, the property of the Metropolitan Museum of Art. The top rail is carved in a guilloche design, the outer stiles in laurelling, and the lower rail in an open chain of rectangles and circles and carved rosettes. The stile separating the panels is carved in a palm-leaf design. The design of the two outer panels is that of a stem foliated at the top, and at the centre of the stem are two flowers resembling tulips and below are drooping leaves. This pattern is one of the most popular found on American chests, and we will point out its variations as they occur. The centre panel is composed of scrolls and leaves. Carved brackets finish the inside of the lower rail.

Figure 9 shows another well-carved chest in the same collection. The top rail and four stiles are carved in a palmated scroll design and the lower rail is carved in foliated scrolls. The outer panels, it will be seen, are carved in the same design as that shown in the preceding figure, but the foliage is more realistic while the tulips are less so. The background is filled in with colour, and the lozenge-shaped centre panel is decorated in a design suggesting the flower in the outer panels, and foliations fill in the spandrels.

Figure 9.
Oak Chest, third quarter seventeenth century.

Another early pattern of chest often seen in this country is shown in Figure 10. The panels, which are four in number, are decorated in lozenge tracings in scratch carving. The top rail is in lunette design and the edges of the stiles are nicked. The tradition which attaches to this chest is that its owner, Lady Anne Millington, a daughter of Lord Millington, came to this country in pursuit of her lover, a British army officer. Failing to find him, she taught school at Greenwich, Connecticut, and married Lieutenant Gershom Lockwood. The chest is said to have been sent to her by her parents in 1660, filled with "half a bushel of guineas and many fine silk dresses." The chest now has a pine top which is not the original. It is in the possession of Professor H. B. Ferris, of New Haven, Connecticut, a lineal descendant of Gershom Lockwood and Lady Anne Millington, as is also the writer.

"A carved chest £1," at Plymouth in 1657, is one of the few references to carving found in the inventories; but as description of any kind is generally lack-

CHESTS

ing, carved chests were probably by no means as scarce as these records would make it appear.

Figure 11 shows a chest belonging to Mr. H. W. Erving, of Hartford, Connecticut. The top rail is carved in a lunette design, while the outer stiles, as well

Figure 10.
Oak Chest, third quarter seventeenth century.

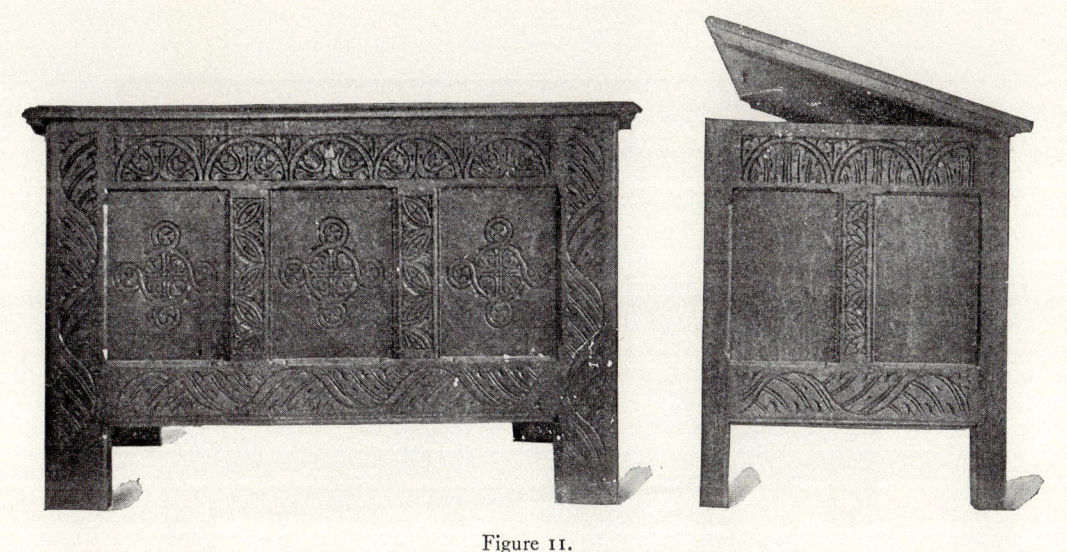

Figure 11.
Oak Chest, third quarter seventeenth century.

as the lower rail, are carved in scratch carving in waving lines with a crude suggestion of foliation. The stiles separating the panels are carved in a design of shuttle-shaped ovals, the points set at an angle. On the panels is a guilloche design of a large circle and four small ones set cruciform. The ends are carved in the same designs as the front, which is unusual in American chests.

Figure 12 shows a simple chest with no carving, except on the panels, which are carved in an excellent palmated scroll design. The chest is in the Bolles Collection, the property of the Metropolitan Museum of Art.

Figure 12.
Oak Chest, third quarter seventeenth century.

Figure 13.
Oak Chest, third quarter seventeenth century.

Figure 13 shows another oak chest in the same collection. The top rail is carved in a foliated scroll design, and each of the three panels in the same scrolls set about a rectangular centre.

CHESTS

Figure 14 shows a chest of very different order from any met with among the English settlers. This chest is undoubtedly Dutch, and was found by the writer in New York State. The panels show the arching of the English chest shown in Figure 7, but the decoration is inlay or marquetry of a crude kind. Church scenes are on the three front panels; on one end the panel is decorated with plain blocking in alternate light and dark wood, the blocks about one and one-half inches square; the other end has a church, showing side view and steeple, the windows being cut in relief. The stiles are inlaid with three stripes of dark wood, and the capitals

Figure 14.
Dutch Marquetry Chest, 1616.

are of the same dark wood. The top is panelled with heavy mouldings and decorated with two large inlaid stars. The dentilled cornice which appears beneath the moulding on the cover is about the only suggestion of English chests. It has a large spring lock, and above the lock on the inside appears the inscription "I. N. R. I.," suggesting at once that the chest was made for church use; but the lettering is so small and in so inconspicuous a place, and the chest throughout so crude in design, that we are inclined to believe that the pious inscription was placed above the lock to secure it against thieves. The small panels at the right and left of the front have inlaid the initials "L. W." and the date "1616." The W has at some time been substituted, as the panel plainly shows, but not very recently, as this, as well as the L, is badly worm-eaten. The dark wood of the marquetry is walnut, but the mouldings at the bottom and on the top are soft wood, evidently pine; the light wood is a foreign pine. The chest when found was in a most dilapidated condition, worm-eaten throughout; the parts, however, are practically all original, except the feet, which are new.

There is strong indication that in New York, where the Dutch influence was largely felt, the chests were not in general of the carved and panelled varieties in use in the English colonies. The inventories in New York, although they show a large number of chests, make very sparse mention of oak or wainscot, and we have been unable to find any chests surviving among the Dutch families that are of oak carved or panelled. A collector who has made systematic search among the Dutch towns along the Hudson River tells us that only one oak chest was found, and that of a well-known Connecticut pattern. Dutch chests were, so far as we can ascertain, largely made of pine and often painted; the finer ones were of black walnut.

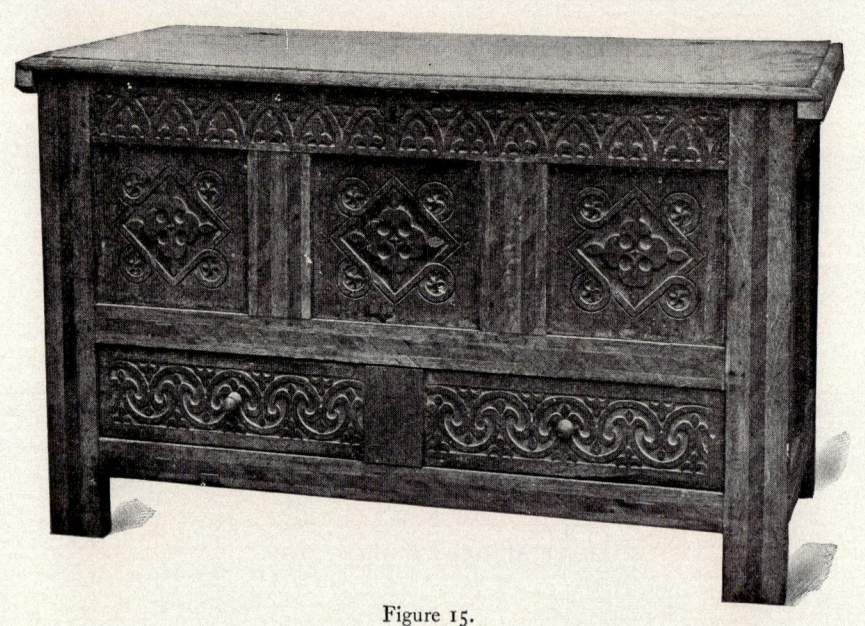

Figure 15.
Oak Chest with one drawer, third quarter seventeenth century.

The opinion prevails very generally among students of the subject that almost all the chests belonging to the first half of the seventeenth century were made without drawers. This opinion is largely based upon the fact that the chests without drawers which have come to light are carved in designs known to be early, while chests having drawers are, the majority of them, decorated with the designs of later date, or are on the panelled order, which, generally speaking, is of later origin than carving. The use of drawers, however, was certainly well known in the early part of the seventeenth century, for chests of drawers are mentioned at Plymouth as early as 1642. The first mention we have found in the inventories of a chest with a drawer is at Salem in 1653; after this time the item "chest with a drawer" or "with drawers" is frequently met with, and by far the larger number of chests which have survived are made with one or two drawers.

In England the chest seems to have passed from the chest with one drawer, or with two drawers side by side, to the pieces with the shallow chest with doors below concealing drawers, and from that it was but a short step to changing the

CHESTS

shallow chest into the drawer, making a cupboard or a chest of drawers with a top which could be used to place things upon. In America, on the other hand, the development was to add two or three drawers below the chest proper. The latter was continued with about the same depth, the result being that the piece became higher and higher. The development from the three-drawer chest to the chest of drawers made the piece lower by substituting a single drawer of perhaps a third of its depth for the chest part, thus making a four-drawer chest of drawers.

Figure 16.
Oak Chest with one drawer, third quarter seventeenth century.

The drawers on pieces dating before 1700 are almost invariably on side runners; that is, the sides of the drawers at about the centre are channelled out and a piece of wood which is fastened to the frame slides in this channelling forming the drawer runner.

Figure 15 shows a chest with one drawer in the Bolles Collection, belonging to the Metropolitan Museum of Art. The top rail is carved in an entwined lunette design with a fleur-de-lis in each opening, and the front drawer is carved in a semi-classical design. On the stiles and rails, other than the top rail, are inlaid bands of dark wood. The panels are each carved in a lozenge-shaped design with four circles.

A nicely carved chest with one drawer is shown in Figure 16 and is the property of Mr. H. W. Erving. The top rail is carved in a very good foliated scroll design. The stile separating the two panels is carved in a single foliated scroll design, and the design on the panels is formed by two foliated scrolls, one above the other. The front of the drawer is in the same design as the panels, except that the scrolls are drawn together to fit a narrower space. The outer stiles are plain.

A handsome carved chest with two drawers, which is in the same collection, is shown in Figure 17. The upper rail is carved in the familiar lunette design. The four panels are carved in a palm design and the drawer fronts in a design of

Figure 17.
Oak Chest with two drawers, 1660–75.

alternating large and small circles with carved rosettes. The stiles throughout are finished with grooving, such as was common on the chests of the period. The dimensions of the chest are as follows: Length 50 inches, width 19¼ inches, height 36½ inches.

A two-drawer chest owned by the writer is shown in Figure 18. It is of light-coloured American oak, the top, bottom, and back being of pine. About fifty chests in this design have been found in Connecticut, some with no drawers and others with one and two. The design, while not wholly new, is a combination of older designs, forming a somewhat original whole, and such chests are generally known as of the Connecticut or sunflower pattern. The outer panels are each carved in a design of a conventional flower, possibly a tulip with two leaves below on each side of the stem. The centre panel is carved in a design of three flowers suggestive of the aster with leaves. On the stiles are applied split spindles, and on the panelled drawer fronts and panels of the ends are applied turtle-back bosses. The chest is large: Length 47¾ inches, width 22 inches,

CHESTS

height 39¼ inches. This style of chest, it will be seen, is a combination of the carved and panelled chests.

Figure 18.
Oak Chest with two drawers, 1675–1700.

Figure 19.
Oak Chest with two drawers, 1675–1700.

Figure 19 shows a chest which is the property of the Connecticut Historical Society. The rails, stiles, and drawer fronts are carved in a beautiful design of tulips. The outer panels are carved in the same design as those shown in the preceding figure, while the centre panel, which has chamfered corners, shows a single aster at the centre with foliated radiates, terminating in the same flower very much smaller that appears on the end panels. The chest has top, drawers, and back, all of oak, somewhat unusual in New England made pieces, but it undoubtedly was made there, for the wood is American oak, and the person making it must have been familiar with the so-called Connecticut chest pattern.

Figure 20 shows a panelled and carved chest without drawers in the "Connecticut pattern" from the Bolles Collection, owned by the Metropolitan Mu-

Figure 20.
Oak Chest, 1675-1700.

seum of Art. The outer panels are carved in the same design as those shown in the preceding figure, while the centre panel, instead of being carved in the aster pattern, is divided into four sunken panels and a small raised one, on each of which is applied a turtle-back boss. The applied split spindles on the stiles are the same as those shown in Figure 18.

Figure 21 shows a one-drawer chest owned by the Connecticut Historical Society. Its decorated effects are obtained entirely by panelling and turned ornaments. The two outer panels are panelled in the design of double arches, but for the centre pilaster is substituted a pendant. The centre panel is in the form of a cross *potent*. On the stiles and front of drawer are applied split spindles, and on the top rail are rectangular and turtle-back bosses. The ends are nicely panelled. The chest is made of English oak throughout and was undoubtedly of English manufacture.

CHESTS

A simple chest, belonging to Mr. Dwight Blaney, of Boston, is shown in Figure 22. The panels are perfectly plain and the stiles and rails channelled.

Figure 21.
Oak Chest with one drawer, about 1675.

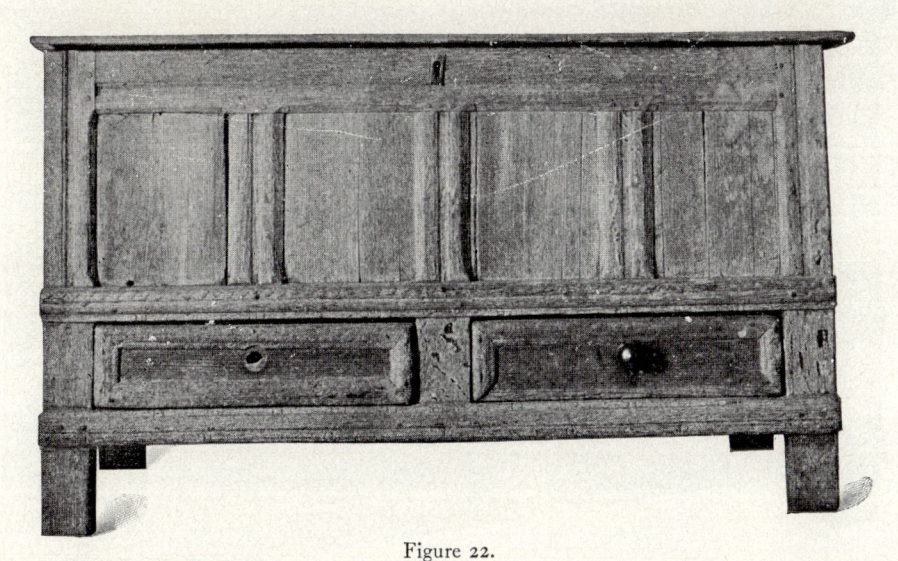

Figure 22.
Oak Chest with two small drawers, 1675-1700.

On the moulding, below the chest part, is cut a serrated design. There are two panelled drawers on side runners, placed side by side, instead of a single long drawer. This feature is occasionally found but is not at all common.

36 COLONIAL FURNITURE

Figure 23 shows a chest owned by the Pilgrim Society at Plymouth. The mouldings on the rails are slightly carved; the panels are lozenge-shaped, with

Figure 23.
Oak Chest with two small drawers, 1675–1700.

Figure 24.
Oak Chest with two small drawers, 1675–1700.

five egg-shaped, applied bosses at the centre of each. The stiles are ornamented with applied split spindles. There are two short drawers at the bottom, as in the preceding figure.

CHESTS

A fine example of a panelled chest is shown in Figure 24, the property of Miss C. M. Traver, of New York. The outer panels are divided into five panels by a raised moulding, lozenge-shaped, with cruciform extensions at each of its angles. In the centre of each of these panels is an applied boss. The centre panel is in the form of two arches; from the key-stone of each is a pendent split spindle. The intrados of the arches is notched and in the spandrels are carved wheel-shaped ornaments. Below the arches are two small rectangular panels and in the centre of each is an applied boss. The mouldings on the rails are

Figure 25.
Panelled Chest with two drawers, 1675–1700.

ornamented with a serrated design, and just above and below the drawers are two parallel lines in repetition. The back is of oak and panelled. There are two parallel drawers below the chest, as in the two preceding figures. A comparison of the mouldings and turnings on the three preceding chests rather indicates that they were made by the same person.

A two-drawer panelled chest found in the vicinity of Boston, and now belonging to Mr. H. W. Erving, is shown in Figure 25. Panelled chests, chests of drawers, and cupboards similar to this have been found in considerable numbers in the region of Boston, while they are rarely met with in other parts of New England. This fact seems to indicate that they were made near where they are found. The chest here shown has the front panelled in quite an elaborate design, the mouldings, except those on the lower drawer, being of pine and originally painted or stained red. The centre of the raised square panels on the chest section are pine and show the remains of a red stain or paint, probably in imitation of snake-wood. The upper drawer has the mouldings of oak and appears never to have been stained. The raised flat pine surfaces of the chest part and of the lower drawer were painted black. The mouldings on the rails are pine, alternately

Figure 26.
Panelled Chest with three drawers, about 1700.

black and red. The ends of the chest have two oblong panels of pine which appear to have been stained brownish red. The top is oak, but the back and the backs and bottoms of the drawers are pine. The space on the stiles above the large turned ornaments is finished with corbels.

There is a panelled chest with three drawers in the Bolles Collection (Figure 26) which stands about as high as a modern chiffonier. The chest portion occupies about one-third of the space; the drawers which fill the rest are graduated in width from narrow to wide toward the bottom. The panels are formed by mouldings simply, and each drawer is supplied with a round escutcheon and two drop handles of brass. A wide single-arch moulding runs between each drawer

CHESTS

and is mitred into a moulding which follows the stiles. Each end is formed of one large panel. This would seem to be the latest form which the chest took, and the inconvenience of having the chest portion so high must have prevented its extensive use.

The mouldings on the best panelled chests are of cedar, but, as a rule, on the American-made chests they are of pine, and painted or stained red in imitation of cedar or rosetta-wood (an East Indian wood brilliant red in colour, heavily grained in black, which was largely used by Spanish and Italian cabinet-makers

Figure 27.
Carved Oak Chest with one drawer, 1690–1710.

during the sixteenth and seventeenth centuries). The turned ornaments are seldom found made of oak, but of pine, beech, and maple, and painted black in imitation of ebony. Panelled chests were made in a great number of designs, following geometrical patterns; they are occasionally found with large ball feet, and when this is the case a heavy outstanding moulding finishes the front and ends of the chest. The foot in other cases is simply the stile prolonged from four to eight inches. The English-made panelled chests are usually made entirely of hard-wood and neither stained nor painted. The rule which seems to have been general in American panelled pieces is that where the mouldings or panels were of hard-wood, *i. e.*, oak or cedar, they were left natural; where they were of pine they were painted or stained. This rule may not always have been followed, and if a hard-wood moulding or panel shows evidence of having been coloured, it would seem safe to restore according to this evidence.

40 COLONIAL FURNITURE

A form of chest probably more often found than any other is the Hadley chest, shown in Figure 27, so called because many have come from Hadley, Massachusetts, or its vicinity.

This style of chest has a number of peculiarities. The pattern consists of a crudely carved leaf, flower, and small scroll, thus   On the surfaces of the leaves and flowers it is scratch carving. This pattern repeats itself over the entire front surface of the chest. Three repetitions of the designs

Figure 28.
Carved Oak Chest with one drawer, 1690–1710.

are on the outer stiles, and on the outer panels are two sprays of the same design, set back to back, which is suggestive of the design shown in Figure 8. The inner panel represents two palm leaves, and the lower section is left plain to receive the initials, which are E. C. The carving and design are very crude, and it will be seen that no attempt is made to have the design exactly finish the space on the rail above and below the panel, although on the drawer front and lower rail it repeats four times even. This design repeating itself is the chief characteristic of the style. No two, however, seem to be exactly alike; the design varies a little with each chest. This chest is in the Bolles Collection and is owned by the Metropolitan Museum of Art.

Figure 28 shows another one-drawer Hadley chest which is the property of Mr. H. W. Erving, of Hartford. The design on this piece differs from the design shown in the preceding figure principally in that the design on the top rail carries over onto the stiles, thus making two complete repetitions of the design on each side of the lock, whereas in the preceding figure the design on the rail is sacrificed for that on the stiles. The result is that in order to obtain three full repetitions of the designs on the stiles the legs are a trifle longer. Another difference is that the designs on the two lower rails and drawer fronts consist of one and one-half designs on each side of the centre; otherwise the pieces are similar, except that this piece does not have the carved wheel at the centre of the

Figure 29.
Carved Oak Chest with two drawers, 1690–1710.

rail below the panels. The dimensions are as follows: Length 42 inches, height 32½ inches, width 19 inches. Hadley chests are found with one, two, and three drawers and, the writer has reason to think, were always stained. The chest here shown has never been tampered with, and is stained with the three colours—red, mulberry or purplish brown, and black, as follows: The top front rail, black; centre rail, brown; bottom rail, black; two end front panels, red; centre panel, brown; drawer front, very light brown; stiles on front, black; on ends, brown. The ends are panelled but not carved; the rails are stained brown, panels black, and the short stile separating the two upper panels, red.

Figure 29 shows a two-drawer Hadley chest in the Erving Collection. It will be seen that the design is better worked out in this piece. Instead of trying to repeat the design both horizontally and vertically, the design on the rails and drawers is allowed to finish on the stiles, as it did on the top rail only in the last figure. This rather indicates that the designer was experimenting, and these chests are shown in the order in which they were probably made.

Figure 30 shows a more pretentious attempt at modifying the design, and its intricacy indicates that the designer had passed the experimental stage. The

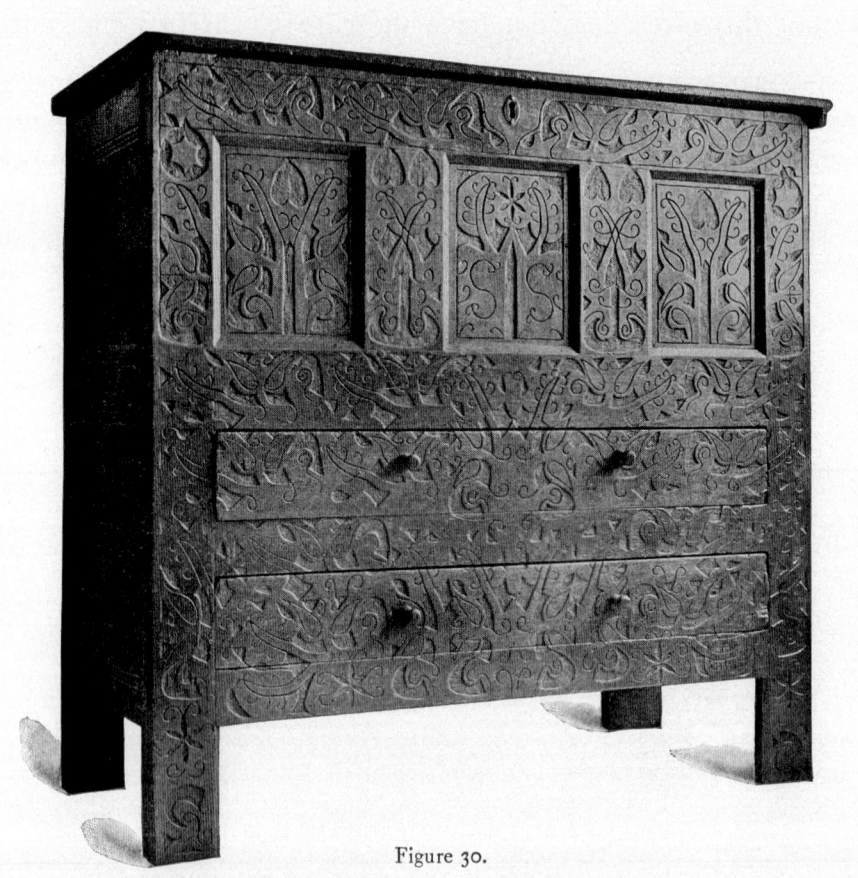

Figure 30.
Carved Oak Chest with two drawers, 1690–1710.

top rail shows a double repetition of the pattern on each side of the key-hole. On the stiles, between the panels, there is a rearrangement of the design in order that two carved hearts may be placed at the top of each. On each of the outer stiles, to correspond, is carved a star. A heart is also cut in each of the outer panels and a star is cut in the centre one. The space below the panels is divided into two distinct arrangements of the design. The first one takes in the rail and upper drawer and consists of a double repetition of the design of the top rail on both rail and drawer, extending over onto the stiles; and at the centre, continuing from the drawer over the rail, are two repetitions of the design set vertically, back to back, as in the outer panels. The two lower rails and drawer form the second arrangement of the design. It consists of a single design on each side of the centre, not extending onto the rail, and at the centre two groups of two of these designs are set vertically back to back. On the lower rail, to fill in the space, is carved a design of stars, and on the rail opposite the lower drawer is carved the design in the same size as appears on the stiles opposite the panels. The more one studies the combinations of the design in this chest the more pleasing it appears, and it contains a greater variation of the design than appears on any other Hadley chest known. The initials are S. S. in scratch carving. This chest is the property of Mr. Dwight Blaney, of Boston.

Figure 31.
Carved Oak Chest with drawers, 1701.

An interesting variation of the Hadley chest is shown in Figure 31, which is the property of Mr. William J. Hickmott, of Hartford. The top rail, instead of being carved in the flower-and-leaf design, has carved, in letters resembling the scratch carving on the leaves, the following: "Thankful Taylor February the 18 1701." At each of the upper corners is carved a geometrical design. On the stiles, between the panels as well as on the outer stiles, is carved the flower-and-leaf design in its simplest form. The three panels are in the design usually found only on the centre panel. At the base of each of the outer ones is cut two geometrical designs, and in the centre one is carved three rosettes. Below, the design consists of two of the flowers, with one of each kind of leaf, which carries over onto the stiles, and the rail at the bottom is ornamented with scrolls in scratch carving. About the panels are mouldings, which indicate that this chest is of later date than those shown above.

Still another late variation of the Hadley chest, from the same collection, is shown in Figure 32. The top rail is ornamented with two pairs of the Hadley design reversed, and the same design is repeated on the drawers and rails below. The outer panels are in the usual design, but the centre panel is decorated with two units of the design set face to face instead of back to back. The outer stiles are grooved instead of carved and the chest stands on turned feet.

Figure 32.
Carved Oak Chest with two drawers, 1700-10.

Figure 33 shows a three-drawer Hadley chest owned by the Deerfield Historical Society. The arrangement of the design is similar to that shown in Figure 28; that is, at the top the design on the rail carries onto the stiles, and then follows on the stiles a repetition of the design four times; on each rail and drawer is carved a double repetition of the design at each side of the centre; the initials are S. H., and a heart is carved above.

Figure 34 shows a further modification of the Hadley chest. The upper rail is carved in a single design on either side of the key-hole, and the panels are octagonal instead of rectangular and are reversed; that is, the two outer panels are in

Figure 33.
Carved Oak Chest with three drawers, 1690–1710.

Figure 34.
Oak Chest with one drawer, 1690–1710.

Figure 35.

Oak Chest with one drawer, 1675-1700.

Figure 36.

Chest with one drawer, 1700-10.

CHESTS

the design of the inner panel and the inner one is the same as the outer ones of the standard type. There are split spindles on the stiles, which are plain, and turtle-back bosses are on the drawer. This piece is the property of the writer.

Figure 35 shows an unusual oak chest with one drawer, the property of Mr. William F. J. Boardman, of Hartford. The top rail is ornamented with parallel vertical groovings. The panels are raised with a quarter-round edge, and there is a double set of four rectangular panels which give the appearance of eight small

Figure 37.
Painted Chest with one drawer, 1700–10.

drawers. At the centre of each of these small panels is a rosette. The surfaces of the stiles and rails are ornamented with channel mouldings, and on the drawer are four series of five rectangular bosses with rounded edges.

Figure 36 shows an example of a chest with the panels, which are of pine, painted with dark strips. Very large and ornately carved split spindles are applied, extending the entire length of the outer stiles; and double split spindles are applied to the stiles, separating the panels. This chest is in the Bolles Collection at the Metropolitan Museum of Art.

Figure 37 shows a painted chest from the Erving Collection. The painted decorations are all in their original condition and are in interesting and unusual designs. The single flower on the stiles, drawer front, and centres of the outer panels was probably intended to represent a tulip. The stiles are ornamented with applied split spindles. This chest was found near Branford, Connecticut.

Figure 38 shows an exceptionally fine painted chest in the Bolles Collection. The rails and stiles are well moulded with grooved mouldings and the surface is mottled. The outer panels are decorated with a well-executed design of what appear to be thistles, and on the centre panel is painted a circle within which are the letters E. L. and the date 1705. On the drawer front is painted a design of sprays of flowers and leaves.

Figure 38.
Painted Chest with one drawer, 1705.

Figure 39 shows a small painted chest or hutch, the property of Mr. William J. Hickmott, of Hartford. It is 21 inches long, 20½ inches high, and 12¼ inches wide. The piece is constructed like a ship chest, without stiles and rails, the sides being single planks of wood. The front of the chest part is painted to represent a spray of leaves, and on the drawer front are two similar sprays. A single-arch moulding borders the edges of the front and above the drawer.

A late form of a chest with two drawers is shown in Figure 40. The chest of drawers had already become popular, and the front of the chest part has two blind drawers to give the appearance of a four-drawer chest of drawers. The top lifts up in the same manner as the chests. These pieces, as is this one, are usually made of pine and are found sometimes with the single and sometimes

Figure 39.
Painted Hutch with one drawer, 1700-10.

Figure 40.
Chest with two drawers, 1710-20.

with the double arched moulding about the drawers and with the early drop or engraved handles. They sometimes have bracket and sometimes ball feet.

After much study of the inventories the writer is convinced that it is impossible to place the date of a chest in any exact year, for the records covering the century between 1633 and 1733 vary only slightly in the descriptions and valuations given. Practically the only way to determine the date is by the character of the decoration used.

The examples here illustrated represent the better quality of chests in use during the seventeenth century, because, as is natural, only the best of the chests would have been considered worth preserving. Their values, as given in the inventories, vary from one shilling to seventy shillings, the purchasing power of money being at that time about five times what it is to-day. At Plymouth, in 1634, "a great oak chest with lock and key 8s"; Salem, 1644, "4 chests £1"; 1673, "a wainscott chest 8s"; Plymouth, 1682, "a wainscot chest £1"; Philadelphia, 1709, "a wainscot chest £1"; in the same year, "a black walnut chest £2 5s"; Providence, 1680, "a great chest with a drawer 1s"; New York, 1697, "1 black nutt chest with two black feet £2 10s"; at Yorktown, Virginia, 1674, "2 chests £1 2s"; 1675, "3 chests 8s"; and the highest price noted, at New York, 1682, "1 chest with drawers £3 10s." Very many chests both North and South inventoried simply as chests are valued at from one to ten shillings. There is also mention in the inventories of iron-bound chests, one at Salem, in 1684, valued at five shillings. The writer knows of two such chests, both of Norwegian pine, in trunk shape with rounded tops; one is bound with wrought-iron bands about four inches wide, in the tulip pattern, and has initials and the date 1707, also in wrought-iron; the other has finely wrought bands in a Spanish design. Cedar chests are noted occasionally, valued at about thirty shillings; they were probably plain, as no description whatever is given of them.

It may be well to review briefly the facts which we have observed in connection with the examples of chests here described. First, as to the wood. Most of the English chests are entirely of oak; most of the American-made ones had the top, the back, and the bottoms of both chest and drawers made of pine. No unfailing rule can, however, be given, for the writer has seen chests, undoubtedly made abroad, which have pine used in their construction, and, on the other hand, American pieces made throughout of American oak.

The chests appear to have been mainly of three kinds—those made with all-over carving; those with carved panels, further decorated with the turned pieces; and the panelled ones. There is every reason to think that the all-over carving is the oldest, but chests of this style continued to be made long after the fashion of adding the turned ornaments became general. The carving on American-made chests is, as a rule, very shallow—what is known as peasant carving. The English carving is generally more in relief and not so crude in execution. The

CHESTS

fine relief carving, such as is seen on Continental furniture of the sixteenth and seventeenth centuries, was entirely beyond the powers of the American makers. The size of chests varied from eighteen inches in height when without drawers to forty-eight inches when with three drawers. The length varies from about thirty to sixty inches. They were almost always furnished with a small compartment, or till, at one end near the top. All the oak chests were made in the most substantial manner; the oak forming the frame and the sides of the drawers is about one and a quarter inches in thickness.

There has been much discussion by those interested in the subject as to whether most of the chests were imported or made in this country. This must be decided mainly by an examination of the woods. The English oak used is of two varieties—live-oak and swamp-oak—the former of a rich brown colour and fine grained; the swamp-oak with a long grain much like the American ash, and tending to flake with the grain as does the ash. The American white-oak is a rich golden brown with a coarser grain, which in the quarter is so highly figured as to distinguish it at once from the English live-oak. It keeps its rich golden colour with age, while the English grows darker without the golden tinge. American oak, however, when exposed to the weather, loses much of its golden colour, and it is by no means easy to distinguish it from English oak which has been subjected to the same conditions.

Chests continued to be mentioned in the inventories until the last of the eighteenth century; after 1710 they are frequently referred to as "old." They probably ceased to be made to any extent after 1730.

III
CHESTS OF DRAWERS

THE evolution of the chest of drawers from the chest with drawers was natural and practicable. The greater convenience of the drawers over the chest must have been apparent from the time the chest first had the drawer added. Then, when the piece grew higher and the two drawers were added, the top became useful to place articles upon. The inconvenience of having a chest with lifting top, from which the articles must be removed before opening, naturally suggested making the piece all drawers with no chest part.

A few chests of drawers are mentioned in the earliest New England records: One at Plymouth in 1642 valued at £1; one in 1643 valued at £2 10s.; one at Salem in 1666 valued at £2 10s.; one at New York in 1669 valued at £1 6s.; and at Philadelphia in 1685 "a chest drawers oake £1"—which are very high valuations when compared with the other articles in the same inventories. The York County, Virginia, records between the years 1633 and 1693 mention only a very small number of chests of drawers, and most of these valued at but eight to ten shillings; but the expression "cupboard of drawers" is used, perhaps, to describe the same thing, and these are valued higher. In 1674 "a cupboard of drawers £1 10s" is mentioned at Yorktown, Virginia.

Figure 41.
Oak Chest of Drawers, 1675–1700.

These chests of drawers are constructed in the same manner as the chests. The rails are mortised into the stiles. The sides and backs are panelled, and the drawer fronts are either carved or panelled or ornamented with turned applied spindles in the manner of the chests. The drawers slide on side runners; that is, the sides of the drawers, which are of heavy material, are, at about the centre, grooved out. The upper edge of the grooved surface slides on a strip of wood

CHESTS OF DRAWERS

fastened to the frame so that the drawer hangs suspended. The tops were usually rather thin and finished with a thumb-nail moulding. The handles on chests of drawers are sometimes turned wooden knobs and sometimes iron or brass drop handles, variously shaped plates of the metal being fastened to the drawer, and through these passed a heavy wire bent at right angles inside the drawers to hold the drops. How early brasses were used is difficult to say, but there is an item in a New York inventory, taken in 1692, of the estate of a store-

Figure 42.
Oak Chest of Drawers, 1675-1700.

keeper, which mentions "12 doz. wrought escutcheons, 5½ doz. filed and brasse handles." We believe them to have been in use as early as 1665, for the high chests of drawers dating as early as that had the brass drop handles. The handles and escutcheons, for the most part, were imported. The earlier papers contain among the advertisements notices of brasses and escutcheons for sale, and this continued down to the Revolutionary War. This is probably the reason that there is such a similarity in design in handles throughout the colonies and that the same designs are found on English furniture of the same period.

A beautiful two-drawer chest of drawers in the Metropolitan Museum of Art is shown in Figure 41, probably made by Nicholas Disbrowe. The stiles and rails are carved in the tulip design found on the chest shown in Figure 19. The drawers are broad, and on the surface of the upper one are carved conventional flowers set in lunettes. On the lower drawer are carved palmated scrolls set upright. The top is finished with the usual thumb-nail moulding.

Figure 42 shows a three-drawer chest of drawers in the Bolles Collection. A well-designed and executed palmated scroll design covers the surfaces of the drawers. The design is accentuated by having the background coloured. On each stile is carved a single-leaved stalk with a flower at the top. On each end is a double panel. The handles are simple wooden knobs and the top is in the usual chest form but stationary.

Figure 43 shows a chest of drawers, the property of Mr. H. W. Erving. There are four drawers, each divided into two panels. The design of the carving on the

Figure 43.
Oak Chest of Drawers, 1675–1700.

upper drawer is palmated scrolls and on the second drawer foliated scrolls, and these designs are repeated alternately on the lower drawers. On the lower rail and skirt is carved a foliated scroll design. Tall ball and ring turned feet are on the front, while the rear legs are an extension of the rear stiles. Above the top drawer and extending on the sides is a dentil moulding, alternately a wide and narrow dentil. Under the top, both on the front and sides, are a series of small corbels. On the outer stiles are pairs of split spindles applied, and two short spindles of the same design separate the panels on each drawer. A peculiar feature of this chest of drawers is the length of the legs as shown from the side view. From the front this is concealed by the lower rail and skirt.

CHESTS OF DRAWERS

Figure 44 shows a chest of drawers, the property of Mr. Dwight M. Prouty, of Boston. The drawers are panelled in two panels, the edges being straight, except those on the inside, which are redented. Split turned spindles placed in pairs horizontally finish the surfaces of the panels, a very unusual treatment, and on each stile is a very long heavy split spindle extending the full length. A single split spindle is on each drawer between the two panels. The rail between the drawers is carved in design of horizontal gouging, each pair being separated

Figure 44.
Oak Chest of Drawers, 1675–1700.

by a short reed. The skirt is serrated and a moulding finishes the overhanging top on the front. The ends are panelled in quarters.

Figure 45 shows a chest of drawers, the property of the writer. The top drawer is divided into two plain rectangular panels with heavy moulded edges. The next drawer has two octagonal panels with a rectangular panel between, and the designs repeat on the lower drawers. Between each two panels are a pair of applied split spindles, and four pairs of split spindles are applied on each stile. The rails between each drawer and at the top and bottom are moulded. The front feet are ball-turned and the rear feet are straight.

Figure 46 shows a chest of drawers which quite strongly suggests the chest shown in Figure 25. The piece is made in two parts and separates below the

Figure 45.
Oak Chest of Drawers, 1675–1700.

Figure 46.
Panelled Chest of Drawers, 1675–1700.

second drawer. The top and third drawers have narrow rectangular panels with chamfered corners, while the second and fourth drawers have heavy raised bevelled panels with the surface in rectangular indented panels. The frame is of oak and the top of Virginia walnut. The centres of all the panels are of rosewood and the mouldings are red cedar. The moulding about the bottom is also red cedar. The resulting contrast of woods is very pleasing. The backs and sides of the drawers are of American oak, which denotes its origin. The ball feet are in the type found on the desks and other pieces of the period. This chest of drawers is the property of Mr. H. W. Erving. Such a piece as this was, perhaps, described at New York in 1696 as "A chest of draws with balls at the feet £1. 16s."

Figure 47.
Panelled Chest of Drawers, 1675–1700.

Figure 47 shows another chest of drawers quite similar to the foregoing. The frame is of oak and in two parts, and the mouldings and the drawer fronts are of walnut, except the second drawer, which has a front of pine with walnut panels and mouldings. The second drawer has a raised bevelled panel on the surfaces of which are four octagonal panels. The other drawers have rectangular panels with chamfered corners. On the stiles and separating the panels of the drawer fronts are sunken panels and on the ends are two bevelled panels. At the top is a moulding quite suggestive of the late style when chests of drawers were elevated on frames, and consists of a fillet and a cyma reversa, and at the base the moulding is a cavetto, a fillet, a quarter-round, and a fillet. The feet are in the flat onion turning and the rear legs are the extension of the stiles. The handles are of the drop type with circular plates. This piece is the property of Mr. Hollis French, of Boston.

Figure 48.
Inlaid Chest of Drawers, 1690–1700.

Figure 49.
Panelled Chest of Drawers, 1675–1700.

CHESTS OF DRAWERS

Figure 48 shows an inlaid chest of drawers in the Bolles Collection. The rails and stiles and the section separating the panels on the drawers are ornamented with bands of broad inlay set diagonally and separated by a straight strip of oak. The edges of the panels are bevelled. The handles are of the drop type with round plates.

Figure 49 shows a very fine panelled chest of drawers in the Bolles Collection which quite closely resembles the lower portion of some of the press cupboards of the period. (See Figure 169.) Just below the top is a quarter-round mould-

Figure 50.
Walnut Chest of Drawers, 1690–1700.

ing cut in diagonal and vertical lines, and below is a carved serrated edge with small stars. Well-proportioned corbels, three in number, are on the stiles and at the centre of the top drawer. The panelling is very elaborate; the top and third drawers are in the design of an indented rectangle with blocks inserted at the centre of the long sides; the second drawer has three panels, the outer ones with square blocks inserted in the four corners and the centre one with four small rectangular panels. The lower drawer has also three panels. The outer ones have blocks inserted at the centre of the sides of the rectangle, while the centre one is an octagon with a small octagonal panel inside. On the stiles and separating the panels on the drawers below the top ones are applied split spindles. The piece stands on four ball feet.

Figure 50 shows the latest development of the chest of drawers which foreshadowed the upper section of the six-legged type. (See Figure 54.) In fact, except for the mouldings, it is the same. The piece is made of walnut throughout. There are two short drawers at the top, and below are three long ones, all on bottom runners. A single-arch moulding is on the frame about the drawers, and the handles are of the drop variety. The top is finished with a thumb-nail moulding, and below is the usual moulding found on the earliest form of the six-legged pieces, a fillet, a cyma reversa, and an astragal. At the bottom is a flaring moulding consisting of an astragal, a cavetto, a narrow and a broad fillet. The piece stands on ball feet at the front and the rear feet on extensions of the stiles. It is the property of Luke Burnell Lockwood.

We now come to the consideration of the high chests of drawers commonly known as high-boys, though this name is never used in the records and probably was given in derision after their appearance had become grotesque to eyes trained to other fashions.

The evolution of the high-boy from the chest of drawers was just as natural as the development of the chest of drawers from the chest. The lower drawers could only be reached by bending, and some of the chests of drawers had been made on tall legs probably for that very reason. (See Figure 43.) It must have become apparent that raising the chests of drawers from the floor on a table or frame would place all of the drawers within easy reach, and so probably the style arose. It was but a step to utilise the space in the upper part of the frame for drawers and the perfected style of the early high-boy was born. The chest of drawers having been raised to such a height, the top could not be conveniently utilised for toilet purposes. A smaller piece which matched the lower or table part of the high-boy was made and the low-boy came into existence. The style apparently at once became popular and for good reason, for its convenience and appearance left nothing to be desired.

It will be interesting in the following pages to trace how the style developed until it reached the point where its original object had been lost sight of, and pieces were built with drawers so high that they could only be reached with a step-ladder.

The development of the high-boy was peculiarly American. In England and on the Continent they never were very popular and practically went out of existence in England before 1725, being replaced by the commodes which had come into vogue from France. In America, however, very few commodes are found, and the high-boy continued to be popular and to be developed until about 1780–90 when the chests of drawers of the type of Shearer, Sheraton, and Hepplewhite superseded them.

The introduction of these chests of drawers on high legs or frames marks the time when the character of construction was changed, and from that period the use of oak was gradually discontinued and the massive style seen in the chests and early chests of drawers was no longer followed.

Just when the high chests of drawers came into fashion cannot be determined exactly. The only records which could show this are the inventories, and they cannot be depended upon for placing the date when a new style came into use, for an article may have been in use for a number of years before it was spoken of in a will or inventory. Ten years may safely be deducted from the first inventory mentioned to obtain the date when the fashion changed. Such a radical change as that from the low oaken chest of drawers to chests of drawers on high frames would seem to call for special mention in recording them, but this is seldom the case. There are, however, two new expressions used in connection with the chests of drawers which indicate that a change had taken place. The first of these is "a chest of drawers on a frame," first met with in New York in 1689, the cost price being given as £4 16s. The second expression referred to is "chest of drawers and table." As both chests of drawers and tables had very frequently been mentioned separately up to the last quarter of the seventeenth century, the very common use of the expression "chest of drawers and table" as one item denotes that they bore some relation to each other, which had not previously been the case. There can be no doubt that a "chest of drawers and table" were a high chest of drawers and dressing-table, or, in other words, a high-boy and a low-boy. In the New York records the expression "chest of drawers and table" does not occur as one item, but during the last quarter of the seventeenth century many of the chests of drawers inventoried are immediately preceded or followed by a table, and when the wood of which the chest is made is mentioned the table is invariably the same wood. The first mention of this kind is in the inventory of Dom Nicolas van Rensselaer, January 16, 1678, in which a chest of drawers of nutwood, followed by a table of the same wood, are valued at 60 guilders (about £5 in English money). Another entry in 1686 is "a wallnut table £1, 15s, a chest of drawers wallnut £3." The facts here shown and the high valuations indicate that these items refer to high chests of drawers and dressing-tables. The first mention of the chest of drawers and table is at Philadelphia in 1684: "chest of drawers and table £8." Both of these values are much above those of any chests of drawers previously mentioned, and this fact further indicates the change of style. In view of these facts we have no hesitation in naming the year 1675 as about the date when the high chests of drawers were first known in the colonies.

The frames upon which the early chests of drawers were raised were of two general varieties—those having turned legs (Figure 53) and those having bandy or cabriole legs (Figure 79). These chests of drawers on frames were quite different in construction from the early chests of drawers. In the table part, the outer turned legs dowelled into stiles which extended to the moulding separating the two parts, and the sides and fronts were framed into these stiles; the upper section had sides of planks of wood without stiles. The top, bottom, and runners for the drawers were dovetailed into these sides. This upper section was enough narrower than the lower part to take up the difference in width between the planks of wood and the stile, so that the drawers of both parts were in the same vertical line. There were six legs, four in front and two at the back. The earlier six-legged high-boys had turned legs, cup-shaped, and between each leg the skirt was cut in a simple arch above which was a single long drawer. The two mouldings separating the upper and lower sections were one on the table part and one on the upper part. That on the table part was a thumb-nail moulding, while that fastened to the upper part was a cyma curve with a broad fillet. The moulding at the top was a quarter-round, a fillet, a cyma recta. About the drawers was a single-arch or large astragal moulding. The stretchers were cut in the same design as the skirt. A little later the skirt and stretchers were cut in a double cyma curve, and in the centre an arch separated two cyma curves, and the single long drawer was replaced by two square ones with a short narrow one between. To the top moulding sometimes was added an astragal; the cut edges of the skirt were finished with a thin strip of wood slightly projecting beyond the surface.

The next type had turned legs, trumpet-shaped (Figure 65), the skirt and arrangement of the drawers remaining the same, but about the drawers on the frame were applied double-arch mouldings. The top moulding was elaborated by adding a short cove, making the top moulding a quarter-round, a fillet, a cyma recta, a fillet, and a cove, and still later was added to the moulding a large torus or cushion frieze which made the front of a cornice drawer (Figure 67). The table part would sometimes have five and six small drawers. Still later, in place of the torus moulding, was added a large cavetto which was sometimes the front of a drawer.

Such was the normal development of the six-legged high-boy. Had cabinet-makers discarded their old moulding-planes as the styles changed, one could date such a piece of furniture from the mouldings alone, but the tools were expensive and the cabinet-makers in country places continued to use their old tools long after they had become old-fashioned; consequently we find every possible variation of the pure style above described. For instance, turned legs in cup style appeared with double-arch moulding and the simple early form of the upper moulding will occasionally appear on late pieces; consequently one must date these pieces by the latest feature they contain. The handles on the earlier pieces were of the drop style, and on the later pieces—those having the double-arch mouldings about the drawers—the handles were stamped, usually called engraved plate with wire bales holding the handles. This rule is also subject to exception, depending upon whether the piece was country or city made. Occasionally these high-boys are found with a chest at the top concealed by blind drawers.

These pieces were made of walnut, maple, cherry, pine or whitewood, or with drawer fronts veneered in straight-grain or burl walnut, with a herring-bone border

CHESTS OF DRAWERS

or with a veneer of maple, either straight-grain or bird's-eye, with a herring-bone border, and rarely they were decorated with marquetry and japanning. The later pieces were sometimes painted in floral designs.

Figure 51.
Oak-Panelled High Chest of Drawers, 1675–1700.

Figure 51 shows a high chest of drawers of oak in the Bolles Collection, owned by the Metropolitan Museum of Art. It is of English make and the mouldings do not follow the usual order of the American ones above described. The upper section, it will be seen, suggests the chest of drawers (Figure 49). The moulding at the top consists of a small quarter-round, a large quarter-round, a cyma reversa, and another quarter-round. The top drawer is divided into two rectangular panels with blocks inserted at top and bottom; the second drawer is divided into four panels with blocks at the four corners of each; the third drawer is divided into two panels with blocks inserted at the centre of each side, and the fourth drawer is divided into eight rectangular panels with a

Figure 52.
High Chest of Drawers, 1680–1700.

block inserted at the centre of each group of four panels. On the frame and about the drawers is planted a single-arch moulding. The ends are panelled. The mouldings fastened to the base of the upper part consist of a quarter-round, a cyma recta, and a fillet, while those attached to the frame are a quarter-round and a thumb moulding. In the frame are two plain panelled drawers, and the skirt is cut in front in three segments of a circle and at the ends in two round arches. The piece stands on six cup-turned legs and the stretchers follow the curves of the skirt.

Figure 52 shows the earliest form of the six-legged high-boy that we have found in this country. The upper section is constructed in much the same way

CHESTS OF DRAWERS

as the early chests of drawers. The stiles and rails are mortised and tenoned and the ends are panelled. The five drawers are on side runners, and on the frame about the drawers are heavy single-arch mouldings. The moulding at the top is a quarter-round, a fillet, a cyma recta, and an astragal. The frame is quite low,

Figure 53.
Marquetry High Chest of Drawers, 1680–1700.

standing on four elaborately turned cup legs in front and two slender turned legs at the back. There are two drawers, the fronts panelled in the manner of the earlier pieces. These drawers have one runner on the side and one at the bottom. The stretchers on the front and sides are slightly curved. The back stretcher, however, is very unusual and is placed on edge and cut in a series of inverted arches. This chest of drawers when found showed traces of black and red paint on the drawer fronts and mouldings and has now been restored. It is in the Bolles Collection at the Metropolitan Museum of Art.

As the high chest of drawers developed it gradually lost its points of resemblance to the chest. The mouldings, while retaining the general form, were made narrower, the drawers did not run on side runners, and the ends were not panelled. The transition piece above described is the only one of its kind which is known to the writer, and practically the oldest form of high chests of drawers is shown in Figure 53, an exceedingly interesting specimen from the Erving Collection

Figure 54.
High Chest of Drawers, 1680–1700.

of a chest or drawers decorated with fine English marquetry, which was found at Portsmouth, New Hampshire. The carcass is of pine as are the fronts of the drawers behind the marquetry, the rest of the drawers are oak. The legs are maple, and although old did not belong to this piece. The beautifully executed designs of birds and flowers in colours extend not only around the sides but on the top. About the drawers are single-arch mouldings which, as has been said, are like those found on panelled chests, except that they are somewhat narrower. The cornice, consisting

CHESTS OF DRAWERS

of a quarter-round, a fillet, and a cyma recta, the single drawer in the table or frame part, the simple arch between the legs and the drop brasses, are all characteristic of the earliest high chests of drawers. The stretchers are new and incorrect; they should follow the curve with which the skirt is finished. The brasses on this piece, though not the original, were taken from a very early high chest of drawers. The dimensions of this piece are as follows: Total height 59 inches, upper part 31 inches, lower part 28 inches, width of upper part 38 inches, width of lower part 40 inches, depth 23 inches.

Figure 54, also from the Erving Collection, is a sycamore chest of drawers, probably of American manufacture. The stretchers on this piece are original, as

Figure 55.
Dressing-Table, 1680–1700.

are also the fine drop handles. The mouldings, cornice, arrangement of drawers, and arches between the legs are identical with the imported pieces above described. We believe these chests of drawers to be such as were referred to in the inventories already quoted, dated 1678 and 1684. The dimensions of this piece are as follows: Total height 65 inches, upper part 35½ inches, lower part 29½ inches, width of upper part 36¼ inches, lower part 39 inches, depth 21 inches.

A very early dressing-table in the Bolles Collection is shown in Figure 55. There is but a single long drawer, as in Figure 54, surrounded by a single-arch moulding, and the skirt is cut in the early arch pattern, two pendants taking the place of the two inside legs. The legs are turned in the cup shape and the handles are circular plates with drops. This is the earliest form of dressing-table known to American collectors.

Another early dressing-table in the same collection is shown in Figure 56. It is veneered with walnut with a herring-bone border on the drawer, but there are no mouldings on the frame about the drawer. The piece stands on five cup-shaped turned legs and the skirt and stretchers are cut in a simple arch. Dressing-tables with the fifth leg are rare.

Figure 57 shows a typical example of the best form of the early six-legged high-boys such as were found in New England. The drawer fronts are veneered with burl walnut with a herring-bone border about the drawers. On the frame is

Figure 56.
Dressing-Table, 1680–1700.

Figure 58.
Dressing-Table, 1690–1700.

the single-arch moulding. The mouldings at the top are in the early form, a quarter-round, a fillet, and a cyma recta. In the frame are three drawers and the skirt and stretchers are cut in the usual cyma curve pattern. The skirt at the centre is placed higher than usual, and the drawer runners are concealed by a skirt running from front to back cut in cyma curves. The legs are well turned in the cup pattern. The handles are in the early drop design with pierced round plates. This piece is in the Bolles Collection.

Figure 58 shows the dressing-table which is a companion piece to the high-boy shown in the last figure. It is in the same collection. The piece is like the frame part of the high-boy, except that it is smaller and has but four legs. Pendent drops take the place of the two inside legs of the high-boy. The underbracing is X-shaped to enable one to sit in front of it. At the crossing of the stretchers is a ball ornament. The tops of these dressing-tables were usually veneered in four rectangular sections, fitted to show the grain to best advantage, and enclosed in

Figure 57.
High Chest of Drawers, 1690–1700.

a herring-bone edge. Outside the herring-bone edge was a border with a strip two inches in width showing the straight grain running at right angles to the

Figure 59.
High Chest of Drawers, 1690–1700.

edge. The edge of the top was usually finished with a thumb-nail moulding. The veneer is missing from the top of this dressing-table.

Figure 59 shows an interesting variation of this type with five instead of six legs. The drawer fronts are painted in a flower-and-leaf design. The upper moulding is in the earliest pattern and a single-arch moulding is on the frame about the drawers.

CHESTS OF DRAWERS

The moulding on the frame is unusually heavy. There is one long drawer in the frame which, not having the usual arch moulding about it, gives the appearance of being part of the frame. The lower edge is straight, finished with an astragal on both the front and sides. The legs are turned, cup-shaped, and the stretchers are cut in double cyma curves. The handles are drops with circular plates.

Figure 60.
High Chest of Drawers, 1690–1700.

Figure 60 shows another five-legged high-boy of a little later date. The top has a thumb-nail moulding such as is found on the chests and cupboards, and below that is a moulding consisting of a cyma recta and two fillets. A single-arch moulding is on the frame about the drawers of the upper part but not about the long, narrow drawer on the frame. An astragal or single-arch moulding finishes the edges on the front and sides just above the skirt, which is cut in cyma curves,

COLONIAL FURNITURE

as are the stretchers. The legs are cup-turned; the handles are drops with circular plates. These two pieces are crudely constructed and are lower and much heavier than the usual six-legged type. They are the only ones that have come under the writer's observation, and are in the Bolles Collection, Metropolitan Museum of Art.

Figure 61.
High Chest of Drawers, 1690–1700.

Figure 61 shows a six-legged high-boy which belongs to Mr. G. W. Walker, of New York. It will be seen that the cornice mouldings are in the earliest type and the single-arch moulding is about the drawers. The surface of the drawers is of maple with a herring-bone border of walnut, giving a very pleasing contrast of woods. The skirt is cut in the arch pattern as are also the stretchers. The legs are turned cup-shaped. The handles are drops with diamond-shaped plates, which is a little later form than the circular plates.

CHESTS OF DRAWERS

A dressing-table with a slate top is shown in Figure 62 and is the property of Mr. W. F. J. Boardman, of Hartford, Connecticut. The legs are cup-shaped and the stretchers are in the usual X design. The skirt is cut in the simple arch

Figure 62.
Slate-Top Table, 1690–1700.

Figure 63.
Top view of foregoing table.

and a single-arch moulding is about the drawers on the frame. The top, which is shown in Figure 63, has a much heavier overhang than is found on the ordinary pieces. At the centre is a piece of slate stone and the border is elaborately inlaid; in each of the four corners are lions rampant, and inlaid rectangular panels are on the sides. The top in all probability was not made here, but was imported and placed on the table. These tops are thought by some to have come from Switzerland, but it is the writer's opinion that they are from Holland and were used to place hot dishes upon in much the same way as the tea-table tops with delft tiles inserted.

Mention of these tables is made in the early inventories, but only in Boston. In 1693, "In the lower room a slate table, £1, 10s"; in 1699, "In the hall a slate table £1, 10s," and in 1703, "a table with a stone in the middle £1."

These prices are high, which would rather indicate that the tops were imported.

An unusual dressing-table is shown in Figure 64. The legs are turned in the cup pattern and a single-arch moulding is about the drawers. The

Figure 64.
Dressing-Table, 1700–10.

stretchers, cut in cyma curves, are in simple waving form instead of scroll form. The handles are drops with diamond-shaped plates. The unusual feature is the drop leaf at the back and that the back is finished with the skirt cut in cyma curves similar to the front, which seems to indicate that the piece was intended to

Figure 65.
High Chest of Drawers, 1700–10.

be used where all four sides could be seen. This is the property of Mr. Dwight M. Prouty, of Boston.

Dressing-tables are also found finished alike on both sides, the back having dummy drawers. They are also occasionally found made of mahogany.

CHESTS OF DRAWERS 75

We now come to the second type of the six-legged high-boy, of which Figure 65 is a good example. It differs from the preceding style in the following particulars: The moulding at the top has a fillet and small cove added, making the mouldings a quarter-round, a fillet, a cyma recta, a fillet, and a small cove. The

Figure 66.
High Chest of Drawers, 1700-10.

mouldings about the drawers are of the double-arch type. The legs are turned in the trumpet shape, and the handles are engraved plates with two bent wires clinched on the inside of the drawer holding the bails. The drawer fronts are veneered in walnut with herring-bone border. It is the property of the writer.

A variation of the second type of high chests of drawers, the property of Mr. Hollis French, of Boston, is shown in Figure 66. The cornice consists of a

Figure 67.
Inlaid High Chest of Drawers, 1700-10.

CHESTS OF DRAWERS

quarter-round, a fillet, a cyma reversa, a wide fillet, a narrow fillet, and a cyma recta. The double-arch moulding is on the frame about the drawers. The legs are cup instead of trumpet shaped. The drawers are veneered walnut with a herring-bone border and the handles are drops with diamond-shaped plates.

Figure 68.
High Chest of Drawers, 1700–10.

An interesting inlaid high chest of drawers, the property of Mr. William W. Smith, of Hartford, is shown in Figure 67. The cornice is heavy and consists of a quarter-round, a fillet, a cyma recta, a fillet, and a cove, as in Figure 65; below this is added a wide fillet or frieze, a small torus, a large torus or cushion frieze, and a small torus. The cushion frieze conceals a drawer, a feature not uncommon in the later pieces. There are three instead of the usual two drawers

78   COLONIAL FURNITURE

at the top. Each of the drawers is divided into two panels by an inlaid border of alternately light and dark wood set diagonally. About the drawers is the single-arch moulding; the brasses are drops and the legs are cup-turned; three features uncommon in the later pieces.

Still another variation of the second type of six-legged high chests of drawers is shown in Figure 68 and is the property of Mr. Dwight M. Prouty, of Boston.

Figure 69.
High Chest of Drawers, 1710–20.

The cornice somewhat resembles that shown in the preceding figure and consists of a quarter-round, a fillet, a cyma recta, a fillet, a wide fillet or frieze, a narrow fillet, a cyma recta, a fillet, a large torus or cushion frieze, and a small torus. The cushion frieze, as is usual, conceals a drawer. The drawers are of walnut veneer with herring-bone edges, and on the frame and about the drawers is the canal moulding which is rarely found so early. The handles are drops with diamond-shaped plates and the legs are cup-turned as in the earlier type.

CHESTS OF DRAWERS

A six-legged high-boy, which is the property of the writer, is shown in Figure 69. The cornice mouldings consist of a quarter-round, a fillet, a cove, two fillets, and a cyma recta, below which is a large torus which conceals a moulding drawer.

Figure 70.
High Chest of Drawers, 1710–20.

Double-arch mouldings are about the drawers and the legs are turned in trumpet shape. There are five drawers in the frame. The piece is made throughout of whitewood.

Figure 70 shows another six-legged high-boy of whitewood, the property of Miss C. M. Traver, of New York. The cornice is composed of a quarter-round, a fillet, a cyma recta, a fillet, and a cove with the torus drawer below. There are

Figure 71.
High Chest of Drawers, 1710-20.

CHESTS OF DRAWERS

three drawers instead of two at the top and six drawers in the frame, and a double-arch moulding is about the drawers. The skirt is cut in cyma curves and segments of circles and the stretchers in double arches. The legs are turned in the cup shape. This piece illustrates the fact above noted, that a piece sometimes combines early and late characteristics, for the legs belong to the early type while the mouldings stamp it indubitably late.

A very unusual piece of this period is shown in Figure 71. The cornice is a quarter-round, a fillet, a cyma recta, a fillet, and a cove. A double-arch moulding

Figure 72.
Dressing-Table, 1700–10.

is about the drawers. The drawer fronts are veneered with walnut, the grain, beautifully matched, surrounded by a herring-bone border. There are but four instead of six legs and these are turned in cup shape. The stretchers are X shape like the dressing-tables. The skirt is cut in long cyma curves and an arch. This piece is in the Bolles Collection.

Figure 72 shows a dressing-table of the second period, in the writer's possession. The fronts of the drawers and the top are of walnut veneer with herring-bone border. The legs are turned cup shape, and double-arch mouldings are about the drawers.

82 COLONIAL FURNITURE

Another dressing-table is shown in Figure 73. The turned legs are octagon and the X-shaped stretchers are cut in Flemish scrolls. At the centre, where the stretchers cross, is a small plate-shaped piece. The skirt is cut in arches and about the drawers is a double-arch moulding. This piece is of Dutch origin.

Figure 73.
Dressing-Table, 1700–10.

Figure 74.
Dressing-Table, 1710–20.

Figure 75.
Dressing-Table, 1710–20.

Figure 76.
Dressing-Table, 1710–20.

Figure 74 shows another dressing-table with double-arch mouldings about the drawers and turned trumpet-shaped legs. A fifth ball foot supports the point where the X-shaped stretchers cross. The top is not original. Trumpet-turned legs appear but rarely on dressing-tables of this style, and then they are usually

CHESTS OF DRAWERS

of pine and rather cheaply made. The last two tables are in the Bolles Collection, owned by the Metropolitan Museum of Art.

Figure 75 shows a dressing-table, the property of Mr. H. W. Erving. It is made of whitewood and has the double-arch mouldings about the drawers, and trumpet-turned legs. The handles are drops with diamond-shaped plates.

Figure 76 shows an unusual dressing-table with four well-turned legs in a vase-and-ring pattern, with turned stretchers between the legs, in the manner of the tables of this period. About the drawers are double-arch mouldings, and the skirt is cut in the usual curves. The handles are drops with diamond-shaped plates. This table is in the Bolles Collection.

Figure 77 shows a miniature cupboard of drawers standing on a frame with six cup-shaped turned legs. It is but 26¾ inches high and 7¾ inches wide. Inside the cupboard part are ten small drawers surrounded by single-arch mouldings, and in the lower section are three small drawers without mouldings. This piece is the property of the Metropolitan Museum of Art.

Figure 77.
Miniature Cupboard of Drawers, about 1700.

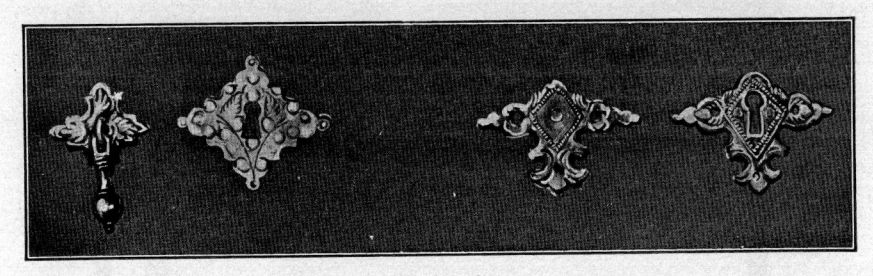

Figure 78.
Early Handles, 1690–1720.

The types of handles which were used on the chests of drawers with turned legs are shown in Figure 78. The first, known as drop handles, had the drops both solid and hollow, the latter having the appearance of being cut in two. The plates and escutcheons are in many shapes, some being round with the edges pierced, others shield shape. These drop brasses we will call handles of the first period. The second style has a bail handle fastened with bent wires, and the plates are generally the shape of those shown, but not always stamped. The

84 COLONIAL FURNITURE

drop handle is the older and is sometimes found on chests in both iron and brass. These brasses with bail handles held by bent wire we will call handles of the second period.

Figure 79.
Japanned High Chest of Drawers, 1700–25.

The transition from the turned-legged high-boys to the bandy or cabriole legged ones was simple and followed the general fashion which became popular in the early eighteenth century. Their general construction was similar to the later six-legged type. They are occasionally found with a double-arch moulding about the drawers and veneered walnut fronts, and the writer has seen one with a single-arch moulding and drop brass handles, but that was a crudely made piece of pine. There is also found the canal moulding, which consists of two small parallel astragals placed upon the frames about the drawers (Figure 68), and also a single astragal or bead moulding is found about the drawers on some of the later pieces (Figure 79). As a rule, however, the drawers were overlapped; that is, there was a thumb-nail moulded edge which projected slightly over the edges of the frame. The cornice mouldings of the earlier bandy-legged high-boys were

Figure 80.

Japanned Dressing-Table, 1700–25.

similar to those found on the later six-legged pieces—a quarter-round, a fillet, a cyma recta, a fillet, and a cove with and without an astragal. But this soon was superseded by the almost universal moulding found on the earlier flat and scroll-top pieces, consisting of a quarter-round, a fillet, a cove, an astragal, a fillet, and a small cove, and this form of moulding continued to be used until the high-boy went out of fashion. The mouldings separating the two sections also changed, and after the style was well established the thumb-nail moulding on the frame part disappeared as did also the moulding which was fastened to the upper part. In their places was substituted a single moulding fastened to the top of the table part into which the top set. The woods used were walnut and walnut veneer, pine, maple, cherry, and, later, mahogany.

Figure 79 shows a japanned high-boy in the Bolles Collection. The cornice is composed of a quarter-round, a fillet, a cyma recta, a fillet, a small cove, a fillet and a large cove, an astragal, a fillet and small cove, and the two mouldings which separate the parts are fastened, one on the frame and one on the upper section, in the early manner. On the edge of the frame about the drawers are small bead mouldings, and the skirt is cut in cyma curves separated by straight lines, which is the usual form of skirts throughout that period. The japanning

Figure 81.
High Chest of Drawers, 1710–20.

is of unusually good quality and well preserved. Each drawer is in a different design of raised figures, houses, animals, and flowers in gilt, and on the lower drawer is an architectural attempt in the form of two columns on each side of a shell, and cupids above.

The art of japanning became very popular in England about the year 1685; in fact, it was almost a craze, and the learning of the art was taken up by gentlemen and ladies. It was supposed to make the wood indestructible. Macquoid, in "A History of English Furniture," quotes from a work, entitled "A Treatise on Japanning and Varnishing," published in 1688 by John Stalker, of the Golden

CHESTS OF DRAWERS 87

Ball, and George Parker, of Oxford, in which the writer says, in speaking of the art: "No damp air, no mouldering worm or corroding time can possibly deface it, and which is more wonderful, though its ingredients, the gums, are in their own nature inflammable; yet this most vigorously resists the fire, and is itself found to be not combustible."

No wonder japanning was popular if it could accomplish all this, but, unfortunately, corroding time does deface it, and very little is found to-day that is not in rather bad condition. It was composed of a kind of varnish, and the decoration was sometimes in colours, but more generally was built up with plaster and gilded, as in this piece.

Japanning continued to be popular until about 1720, and mention is made in the newspapers of the practising of the art in Boston in 1712 and even earlier. This early form of japanning must not be confused with that which came about 1790 to 1800. The decoration on the latter was composed entirely of drawings in gilt, but without any raised work.

Figure 82.
Dressing-Table, 1710–20.

Figure 80 shows the dressing-table in the same collection which was the companion piece to the preceding figure. It follows the high-boy in every line, the decorations on the surface of the drawers alone differing. The top is japanned but badly worn. A thumb-nail moulding with curved corners finishes the edges.

Figure 81 shows a maple piece which is literally a chest of drawers on a frame, for the table part has no drawers. The cornice consists of a quarter-round, a fillet, a cyma recta, an astragal, a fillet, and a cove, and the moulding separating the two parts is on the frame. The arrangement of the drawers, which overlap, is unusual in that there are two drawers at the bottom. The handles are in the early form, wires supporting the bails.

Figure 82 shows a dressing-table in the Bolles Collection, with bandy legs terminating in club feet, with heavy shoes below. That the piece is early is evident from the double-arch moulding about the drawers on the frame. The cutting of the skirt in ogee curves and the edge which finishes them, also the handle plates which are engraved, are early features.

88   COLONIAL FURNITURE

Figure 83 shows a beautiful dressing-table with a walnut veneer front and top, after the manner of the turned variety. About the drawers on the frame is a canal moulding which consists of a strip of wood about half an inch wide with a bead moulding on the edge. This form of moulding differs from that shown in Figure 79, which it closely resembles, in that on the latter the bead is only about the drawers, making it appear between the drawers to be a

Figure 83.
Dressing-Table, 1710–20.

canal moulding, but on the stiles it has but a single bead on the inner edge next to the drawer. The skirt is cut and finished in the form of the turned type of dressing-tables.

Figure 84 shows an early walnut high-boy. The cornice consists of a fillet, a cove, and an astragal. There are three small drawers at the top, two next, and then three long ones, and in the table part there are four drawers of equal size. The drawers are overlapped, with a thumb-nail edge. The peculiar feature of this piece is the Spanish feet with which the bandy legs are finished. Only four or five of these high-boys have come under the writer's observation, and they can all be traced to New Jersey, where they were probably made. Bandy legs on such pieces are always cut rectangular instead of round, and there is always the moulding about the legs just above the Spanish foot. The handles are engraved with wires supporting the bails. This piece is the property of the writer.

Figure 85 shows a dressing-table in the same style as the preceding, which is also in the writer's possession. It is made of walnut and has five drawers with overlapping edges. The skirt is cut very high at the centre to permit of its being

Figure 84.
High Chest of Drawers, Spanish feet, 1710–20.

Figure 85.
Dressing-Table, Spanish feet, 1710–20.

90　　COLONIAL FURNITURE

used by a person seated. The legs are cut in a more pronounced cyma curve than usual and the Spanish feet are well formed; the handles are engraved and have posts supporting the bails. The dressing-tables of this type are more commonly found than the high-boys and several have been found in New England. This piece came from New Jersey and has the lines of a piece made there.

Figure 86.
High Chest of Drawers, 1710–20.

The common form of a flat-top, bandy-legged high-boy is shown in Figure 86. The cornice is composed of a quarter-round, a fillet, a cove, an astragal, a fillet, and a cove, which was the form of cornice most used from 1730 to 1770. The moulding separating the two sections is a quarter-round, a fillet, and a cove. The skirt is cut in two sections of an arch separated by a straight line and the pendent drops are original. The knees of the bandy legs are finished with a scroll. In the upper section is a large drawer with a carved rosette, and on either side

CHESTS OF DRAWERS

are two short drawers, and below are long drawers graduated in width. In the frame are four drawers, the centre one having carved on the surface a design known as the rising-sun pattern. The handles are in the medium-size willow pattern. The steps, such as are shown on the top of this piece, were often used to display china and glass. A Boston inventory of 1713 mentions earthenware on top of a chest of drawers. This piece is the property of the writer.

Figure 87 shows a dressing-table of about the same period as the preceding high-boy and, like that high-boy, is made of cherry. The arrangement of the drawers and the cutting of the skirt is in the early form. The legs are unusually

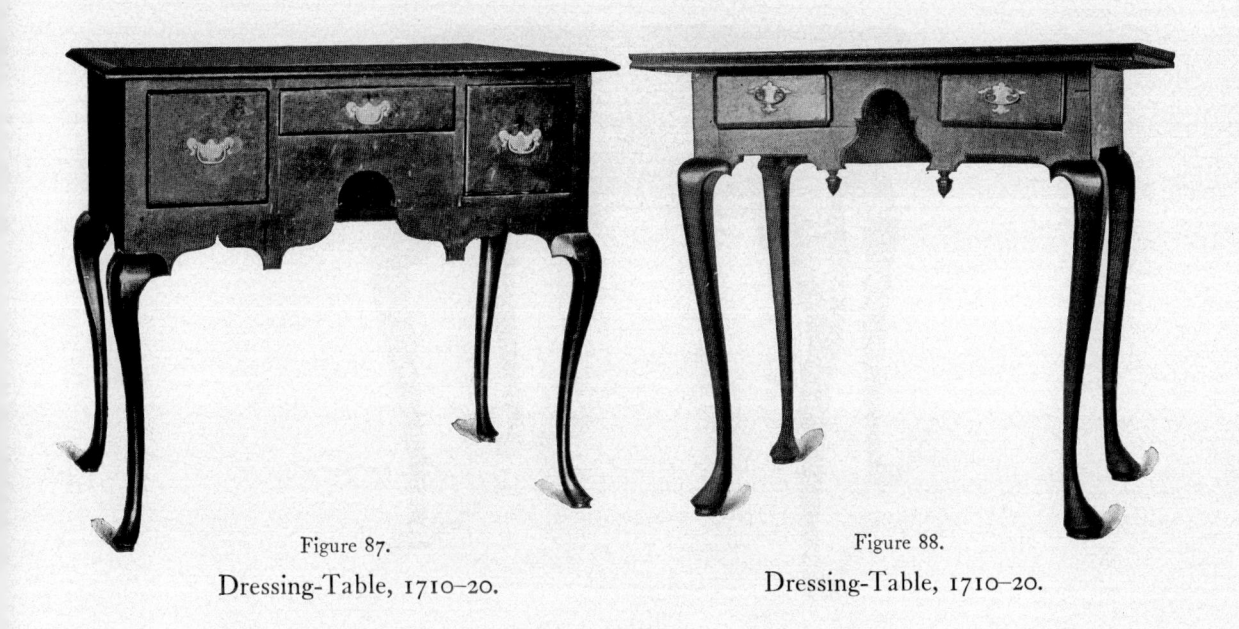

Figure 87.
Dressing-Table, 1710–20.

Figure 88.
Dressing-Table, 1710–20.

slight and the sweep of the curve is much greater than usual. The handles are in the early willow pattern. This piece belongs to the writer.

Figure 88 shows another dressing-table of the bandy-legged variety. It has but two drawers, the skirt at the centre cutting too high to admit of a centre drawer. The skirt is cut under the drawer in two cyma curves separated by a straight line and at the centre two cyma curves and an arch. The legs are bandy, terminating in club feet, and a projection at the back of the legs gives the suggestion of a hoof. The handles are the early engraved type with wires supporting the bails. This piece is the property of Mr. Dwight Blaney, of Boston.

A small dressing-table with one drawer is shown in Figure 89. About the drawer on the frame is a bead moulding and the skirt is plain. The legs are bandy, and in the upper part are carved C scrolls, an early feature more popular in England than America.

Between the years 1710 and 1730 the flat-top variety of high-boy was superseded by the scroll-top, which differs from those heretofore described in that the top, instead of having a flat cornice, has one composed of two large cyma curves separated at the centre, giving somewhat the appearance of the broken pediment. The top was generally hooded; that is, the curve of the top carried through to the back. Such pieces are also called bonnet-top (Figure 92). Because of this top the pieces are taller, and the centre of the upper drawer was usually above the base of the cornice, and sometimes the drawers were curved under the

Figure 89.
Dressing-Table, 1710–20.

cornice conforming to it. The cornice moulding and construction of the earlier scroll-top high-boys were the same as the later flat-top variety.

The flat-top pieces did not disappear after 1730, but because of their simpler construction continued to be made for many years, but they had ceased by that time to be fashionable.

There is a flat-top high chest of drawers belonging to Mr. George M. Curtis, of Meriden, Connecticut, which has burned on the front "made by Joshua Read of Norwich in the year 1752."

There is a house at Wethersfield, Connecticut, which belonged to Dr. Ezekiel Porter, which was furnished about the year 1730. The sleeping-rooms, five in number, were each supplied with a high chest of drawers and a dressing-table, and each chest of drawers had a scroll top. We find advertised, in 1757, "A mahogany case of drawers with an O. G. top," and in 1756 one with an "ogier top."

CHESTS OF DRAWERS 93

Figure 90 shows a japanned high chest of drawers from the Bolles Collection that combines a number of characteristics of both the early and late styles. The scroll top has practically the same mouldings as those on the flat top of the japanned high chest of drawers shown in Figure 79, a quarter-round, a fillet, a cyma recta, a fillet, a large cove, an astragal, a fillet, and a little cove. A

Figure 90.
Japanned Scroll-Top High Chest of Drawers, 1720-30.

moulding is fastened to the base of the upper part and also to the top of the frame, as in the other japanned piece, and the skirt is cut in the same design. About the drawers on the frame is a double-arch moulding and the handles are engraved with bails held by wires. There are seven drawers in the frame. The japanning is in poor condition. This is the earliest scroll-top high chest of drawers that has come under the writer's observation.

Figure 91.
Scroll-Top High Chest of Drawers, about 1725.

CHESTS OF DRAWERS 95

Figure 91 shows another early scroll-top high chest of drawers, the property of Mr. Hollis French, of Boston. The cornice consists of a quarter-round, a fillet, a cove, an astragal, a fillet, and a small cove, and the top is finished with three spiral finials. About the drawers and on the frame is the canal moulding. On the square drawers at the top and bottom is a sunken rounded blocking. The

Figure 92.
Scroll-Top High Chest of Drawers, 1730.

front is walnut veneer with the herring-bone border, and the handles are engraved, having wires to support the bails.

Figure 92 shows the regular type of a scroll-top high chest of drawers which is one of those purchased by Dr. Ezekiel Porter in 1730, above referred to. The cornice is composed of the following mouldings: A quarter-round, a fillet, a cyma recta, a fillet, a large cove, an astragal, a fillet, and a small cove. At the ends and the centre of the top are the original turned finials. At the front of the top and lower drawer are carved the rising-sun pattern. All of the drawers overlap and the skirt is cut in cyma curves separated by straight lines. The handles are in the willow pattern.

Figure 93 shows a high chest of drawers and its companion dressing-table of walnut, the property of Mr. G. W. Walker, of New York. The cornice is in the next later pattern than that shown in the preceding figure, consisting of a quarter-round, a fillet, a large cove, an astragal, a fillet, and a small cove. The turned flame finials are original and unusually fine. The outer drawers at the top are curved with the cornice, and the centre one is carved in the rising-sun pattern, as is also the centre drawer at the bottom. The skirt is cut in two quarter-rounds separated by a straight line, the same as shown in Figure 86. The drop pendants on the dressing-table are original. The handles are in the willow pattern.

Figure 93.
Scroll-Top High Chest of Drawers and Dressing-Table, 1725–50.

Figure 94 shows a scroll-top high chest of drawers in the Bolles Collection. It is made of walnut veneer, and a border of checkered inlay is on the drawers and a simple band of inlay outlines the top and bottom. On either side of the top drawer is inlaid in light and dark woods a cruciform ornament. The piece is very

Figure 94.
Scroll-Top High Chest of Drawers, 1725–50.

beautifully made. The cornice consists of the usual quarter-round, a fillet, a large cove, an astragal, a fillet, and a small cove, and each stile is finished with a fluted pilaster which carries through the cornice and forms the base for the acroterium.

Figure 95.
Scroll-Top High Chest of Drawers, 1725–50.

The finials are urn-shaped with spiral flames. The centre drawers at the top and bottom are both carved in a well-executed shell pattern such as appears on the mirrors of the period. The skirt is cut in the same design as that shown in Figure 93.

Figure 95 shows another scroll-top chest of drawers in the same collection which in general appearance is similar. The cornice and pilasters and the cutting of the skirt are the same as in Figure 94. The piece, however, is not

CHESTS OF DRAWERS

veneered or inlaid. The drawers, instead of overlapping, are flush, with a bead moulding finishing the frame about them, and the top and lower centre drawers are carved in the rising-sun pattern. The finials are urns with long spiral flames.

Figure 96.
Scroll-Top High Chest of Drawers, 1750–60.

Figure 96 shows a scroll-top high chest of drawers, the property of Mr. H. W. Erving. The cornice mouldings are unusual, consisting of a cyma reversa, a dentil moulding, a cove, an astragal, a fillet, and a small cove. On the inner ends of the scroll and on the centre acroterium are carved rosettes. The corners have square recessed edges and quarter-spiral columns are inserted. The drawers at the centre of the top and bottom are carved in a fan pattern. The legs terminate in bird's claw and ball feet and acanthus leaves are carved on the knees. The skirt is cut in the design of quarter circles separated by straight lines.

Figure 97 shows an interesting cupboard on frame which was part of the purchase of Dr. Ezekiel Porter about 1730, above referred to. The cornice has the same mouldings as those shown in Figure 93, and a narrow moulding extends horizontally across the piece about three inches below the cornice, giving the suggestion of a pediment. A small drawer is in the cornice. The skirt is cut in two long cyma curves and the rising-sun pattern is carved on the centre drawer.

A low-boy in the same collection, all of which belonged to the late Miss Bidwell, of Wethersfield, Connecticut, is shown in Figure 98. There are four drawers, the centre lower one ornamented in a shell pattern, and the skirt is cut in two long cyma curves with two small cyma curves in the centre. The skirts of the last two pieces are so cut that no pendent drops are required, and thus the last suggestion of the six-legged high-boy disappeared.

Figure 97.
Cupboard on Frame, 1730-50.

A crudely made but rather interesting scroll-top high chest of drawers is shown in Figure 99. The cornice is composed of a quarter-round, a fillet, a cyma recta, a fillet, a large cove, an astragal, a fillet, and a small cove. Large, coarsely carved rosettes finish the inner ends of the scrolls. On the stiles and front are carved scrolls and other designs. On the lower drawer is carved a shell pattern with a double edge; the legs are bandy, terminating in bird's claw and ball feet, and the knees are slightly carved.

An interesting block-front high chest of drawers, the property of Mr. G. G. Ernst, South Norwalk, Connecticut, is shown in Figure 100. A very heavy and unusual cornice finishes the top, composed of a fillet, cyma recta, fillet, cove, wide

Figure 98.
Dressing-Table, 1730-50.

CHESTS OF DRAWERS

fillet or frieze, cove, cyma reversa, fillet, large cove, astragal, fillet, and small cove. The large cove conceals a drawer. The blocking carries through the cornice and the cornice is broken at the centre by a carved shell. On the stiles of the upper

Figure 99.
Scroll-Top High Chest of Drawers,
1750–60.

part are fluted pilasters and the stiles of the lower part are also fluted. A double-arch moulding finishes the frame about the drawers. The upper section has two raised blockings and the frame part has three with six small drawers. The skirt is curved in the same design as found on the early bandy-legged type. (See Figure

Figure 100.
Block-Front High Chest of Drawers, about 1760.

CHESTS OF DRAWERS

86.) At the centre is a carved shell. The legs terminate in bird's claw and ball feet. Block-front high chests of drawers are very rare, and this example is the earliest block-front piece of any description that has come under the writer's observation. This piece dates about 1760.

Figure 101 shows a block-front dressing-table which is the property of Mr. A. W. Wellington, of Boston. The top is cut in the shape of the block-front chests of drawers. There are six small drawers with overlapping edges, and on

Figure 101.
Block-Front Dressing-Table, about 1760.

the skirt, which is also blocked, are three handles to carry out the appearance of drawers. The skirt is cut in the same pattern as in the preceding figure. The bandy legs terminate in club feet with wide shoes.

Block-front pieces became popular during the third quarter of the eighteenth century and appear to have been of American origin, or if not at least they were more developed here than elsewhere. The drawer fronts were cut from a large piece of wood of sufficient thickness to take the convex and concave surfaces. The blocking was seldom applied. They are most commonly found in desks or chests on chests, and the vast majority have come from New England. Many of the simpler varieties have come from New Hampshire, and the best examples come from Rhode Island. This subject will be more fully discussed a little later in this chapter.

Between 1760 and 1770 the form of the high chest of drawers became much more ornate, Chippendale motifs being worked into the simpler forms of the earlier types. This development was also American, and the late high chests of drawers have no counterpart in any other country. The best of these pieces came from Philadelphia, and the type is so pronounced that they are commonly called "Philadelphia high-boys and low-boys." They are found in two types, one where the front carries into the scroll cornice and the other where the cornice is separated from the front by a moulding, making a pediment.

Figure 102 shows a very good example of the first style. The chief characteristics are the shell carving on the lower centre drawer, which was usually repeated on the upper drawer under the cornice. The shell is carved into the surface, while the scroll foliations, as a rule, are applied, or partly applied and partly carved. There are usually three small drawers at the top, two below that, and then three long drawers. Another characteristic is the beautifully carved rosettes finishing the inner edge of the scrolls. The legs are shorter and the enclosed part is higher than in the New England pieces. These pieces are very tall and represent the last development of the high chest of drawers. The cornice of this piece is also characteristic of the first type and is composed of a fillet, a cyma recta, a fillet, a large cove, and a quarter-round. The corners have square recessed edges and quarter-fluted columns are inserted. The uppermost and lower drawers are carved in shell pattern with foliated streamers. It is a little unusual to have the carved drawer at the top above the three short drawers. It is usually the middle drawer of the three top ones, as in the next figure. The finials are urns with flames. The skirt is cut in scrolls with a shell at the centre, and a carved shell is on the knees. The bandy legs terminate in bird's claw and ball feet. This piece is the property of Mr. Richard A. Canfield.

Figure 103 shows another high chest of drawers of the first type which is in the Pendleton Collection, owned by the Rhode Island School of Design. The cornice is composed of the same mouldings as appear in the preceding figures but the top is not hooded. Well-carved rosettes finish the inner ends of the scrolls and the finials are the usual urn and flame found on these pieces. The corners have square recessed edges and quarter-fluted columns are inserted. The shell drawer at the top is inserted between two small drawers in the manner most commonly found. The mouldings separating the two carcasses are a fillet, cyma reversa, fillet, torus, fillet, and cove. Occasionally a cove, fillet, and quarter-round are substituted for the cyma reversa, as in the next figure. At the centre of the skirt is carved a shell and on the knees are carved acanthus leaves. The legs terminate in bird's claw and ball feet.

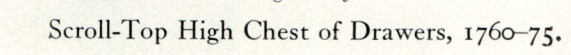

Figure 103.
Scroll-Top High Chest of Drawers, 1760–75.

Figure 102.
Scroll-Top High Chest of Drawers, 1760–75.

106   COLONIAL FURNITURE

Figure 104 shows a slight variation of this type. The cornice is composed of the usual fillet, cyma recta, fillet, cove, and quarter-round. The rosettes are

Figure 104.
Scroll-Top High Chest of Drawers, 1760–75.

beautifully executed five-petal flowers. The end finials are urns with flames, while at the centre is a foliated and rococo cartouche, showing very strongly the Chippendale influence, and probably suggested by the cartouche which is over the

CHESTS OF DRAWERS

pulpit at Saint Peter's Church, Philadelphia. The shell-carved drawer at the top is replaced by beautifully carved foliated scrolls applied. The corners have square recessed edges and quarter-fluted columns are inserted. The lower drawer in the frame is carved in the characteristic shell design with streamers, and the knees are carved in acanthus-leaf design extending well down the legs. The legs

Figure 105.
Scroll-Top High Chest of Drawers, 1760–75.

terminate in bird's claw and ball feet. This piece is made of fine-grain mahogany. The handles are of the large willow type. It is the property of Mr. George S. Palmer, of New London.

Figure 105 shows another high chest of drawers quite similar to the preceding one, which is the property of Mr. William W. Smith, of Hartford. The cornice mouldings and the flame finials are in the characteristic form, and at the centre is an ornament composed of a rococo cartouche. In place of the shell drawer at the top is applied a carved shell with streamers, filling the space above the three small drawers. The corners are finished with the usual quarter-fluted columns. The edge of the skirt is carved in a foliated scroll design and at the centre is a shell. Acanthus leaves are carved on the legs, which terminate in bird's claw and ball feet.

Figure 106 shows the second type of these high chests of drawers. It will be seen that it has a pediment top and the mouldings are a trifle lighter. They consist of a narrow fillet, a cyma recta, an astragal, a fillet, a large fillet, a short fillet, a quarter-round, a fillet, a dentil moulding, a fillet, a cove, and two astragals and fillets bordering a broad applied fret. These mouldings to the fret are repeated in the scroll top. It will be seen that the top also differs from the other and is not hooded. Rosettes finish the scrolls, and at the centre of the top is a cartouche similar but less elaborate than that shown in the preceding figure. A lattice finishes between the scrolls, another characteristic of the type. Upon the upper centre drawer is carved a shell without streamers. A shell in the same design is repeated in the lower outer drawers at the bottom, and at the centre of the skirt is carved a large shell. The corners of the stiles of the upper part have square recessed edges and quarter-fluted columns are inserted. The knees are carved in a shell and pendent flower design and the legs terminate in bird's claw and ball feet. The handles are of the open-work pattern. This piece is in the Pendleton Collection, owned by the Rhode Island School of Design, Providence, Rhode Island.

Figure 106.
Scroll-Top High Chest of Drawers, 1760–75.

Figure 107 shows another high chest of drawers in the second type which is the property of Mr. George S. Palmer. The mouldings of the pediment are less in number than those in the preceding piece and consist of a fillet, a cyma recta,

Figure 107.
Scroll-Top High Chest of Drawers, 1760–75.

a small fillet, a large fillet, a small fillet, a dentil moulding, a short cove, a fret, an astragal, and a fillet. The fret does not extend on the sides. The rosettes are beautifully carved with foliated streamers extending above the top, and the lattice under the scrolls is foliated. At the centre is a carved bust and on each end is a draped urn in pure Chippendale style. The edges of the stiles are recessed, and a Corinthian capital and quarter-round, with surface carved in

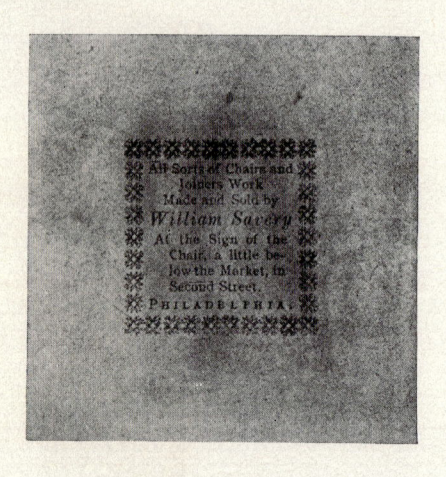

Figure 108.
Dressing-Table, 1760–75.

Figure 108a.
Advertisement in drawer of preceding figure.

foliated scrolls, are inserted. The fret design is carved at the top of the frame. The lower drawer is beautifully carved in a design of foliated scrolls, in the centre of which are two swans, and the edges of the skirt are carved in rococo foliations very suggestive of Chippendale designs. On the knees are carved foliated scrolls and the legs terminate in bird's claw and ball feet. The handles are missing, but they were probably of the large willow type.

It is a surprise to many that beautiful pieces, such as these which are described and the dressing-tables following, could have been made in this country. They were certainly the work of cabinet-makers of the first rank, and not only are such pieces found, but chests on chests, desks, and tables with pie-crust edges of the same quality are to be found, all traceable to Philadelphia. Who the cabinet-maker was, or whether there was more than one, is not known, but a dressing-table of this type has been found (Figure 108) in which is pasted an advertisement of the maker (Figure 108a), which reads as follows: "William Savery, at the Sign of the Chair, near the market on Second Street." He, at least, was one of these cabinet-makers.

CHESTS OF DRAWERS

This last-mentioned dressing-table is the property of Van Cortlandt Museum, New York. The corners of the top are cut in the usual curves. The ends are recessed, with quarter-fluted columns inserted, and on the knees and centre of the skirt are carved shells. The centre drawer has the usual shell, but the streamers are more feathery than usual.

Figure 109 shows a dressing-table, a companion piece to Figure 102. On the lower drawer are the characteristic shell streamers and the skirt is cut in scrolls. At the centre is a carved shell. The same design is repeated on the knees. The

Figure 109.
Dressing-Table, 1760–75.

edge of the top is moulded in a cove, a fillet, and a quarter-round. The edges are recessed and quarter-round fluted columns inserted. This piece is the property of Mr. Richard A. Canfield.

Figure 110 shows another dressing-table, the property of the writer. The top is moulded in the usual manner, described in the preceding figure, and below the top is a moulding consisting of a cyma recta and quarter-round; the outer edges of the stiles are chamfered and fluted. The skirt is elaborately cut and a shell is carved at the centre. There is the usual shell and streamer drawer, and on the knees is carved an acanthus-leaf design extending well down the legs, which terminate in bird's claw and ball feet. This piece is made of Virginia walnut.

Figure 110.
Dressing-Table, 1760–75.

Figure 111.
Dressing-Table, 1760–75.

CHESTS OF DRAWERS

Figure 111 shows one of the most elaborately carved dressing-tables that has been found which belongs to the Pendleton Collection. The top is moulded in the usual way, and below is a fillet, a cove, and two astragals separated by an applied carved fret of scrolls and shells extending across the front and sides. The outer corners of the stiles have square recessed edges, and quarter-round columns with surfaces carved in sprays of leaves are inserted. The edge of the skirt is carved with foliated scrolls and at the centre is a group of flowers. The knees are carved in an acanthus-leaf design. The handles are in the open-work pattern.

Figure 112.
Cellarette in Form of Dressing-Table, 1760–75.

A very unusual piece in the form of a dressing-table is shown in Figure 112, the property of Mr. George B. Foster, of Hartford. It will be seen that the drawers are blind but have overlapping edges to aid the deception, and the upper section is a chest with a lid. It was apparently intended to hold bottles and to be used in a dining-room as a cellarette. The panel, which corresponds to the drawer which is usually carved in the shell and streamer design, is carved in a series of Gothic arches with Chippendale foliated scrolls above. The knees are carved in acanthus-leaf designs and the skirt is plain with irregular cutting. On either end are handles.

Not all of the dressing-tables prior to this time were of the low-boy variety. In England, where the high-boy early went out of fashion, the knee-hole dressing-table, such as is shown in the upper centre bedroom of the doll house (Figure 1), was substituted for the low-boy, and a few of these tables have been found here.

Figure 113 shows such a dressing-table with its dressing-glass, which is in the home of Professor Barrett Wendell, at Portsmouth, New Hampshire. The wood is walnut and the interior is of American pine which denotes its origin. There is one long drawer and on either side of the recessed portion are three small drawers, and a shallow drawer is above the cupboard. The feet are of the straight bracket type. The dressing-glass is in the second type of cut-work mirrors.

These dressing-tables are also made with a desk drawer, and occasionally they are found with a baize top, in which case they were intended to be used as writing-tables. Knee-hole dressing-tables were never popular in America, and but few are found until the time of their revival in the block-front type (Figure 121) in the third quarter of the eighteenth century.

Figure 113.
Knee-Hole Dressing-Table, 1725-50.

Chests on chests differ from the high chests of drawers above described in that the lower part is a chest of three or four drawers upon which is placed another chest of drawers. They, of course, have more room, but because they are close to the floor are less graceful than the high chests of drawers. They became popular about 1750, and the various cabinet-makers and designers, from Chippendale to Sheraton, give designs for them, but not for high chests of drawers, which would indicate that they were of later date. In 1768, at New York, a mahogany fluted double chest of drawers was advertised and in 1769 chests on chests were offered. The cornices on these pieces are made up of the same mouldings as are found on contemporaneous high chests of drawers, and flat tops, scroll tops, and broken or interrupted pediment tops are found.

Figure 114 shows an example of the early chest on chest. The cornice is the usual one found on the high chests of drawers after 1730—a quarter-round, a fillet, a cove and an astragal, a fillet and a small cove. The small upper drawers

CHESTS OF DRAWERS 115

are curved under the cornice and on the upper centre drawer is carved a rosette. The lower section has three long drawers and the piece stands on ball and claw bracket feet. The wood is cherry and the drawers overlap.

Figure 114.
Chest on Chest, about 1750.

Figure 115 shows a chest on chest, the property of Mrs. Anna Babbitt, of Wickford, Rhode Island. The corner mouldings, the finials, and the astragal, fillet, and small cove mouldings of the cornice finishing the circles at the centre of the top are all peculiarities of the Rhode Island pieces. The corners have square recessed edges and quarter-round fluted columns are inserted. The feet are of the ogee bracket type.

116 COLONIAL FURNITURE

High chests of drawers with these same characteristics are occasionally found. Pieces of furniture having what is known as blocked fronts were very popular in this country during the third quarter of the eighteenth century. They are usually found on chests on chests, desks, chests of drawers, knee-hole dressing-

Figure 115.

Chest on Chest, 1750–75.

tables, and occasionally on cabriole-leg dressing-tables, and rarely on high chests of drawers, probably because the style did not become popular until after the high chests of drawers had disappeared. It seems to be the fact that while in the South the high chests of drawers were being extended and enriched (Figure 102), in the North the development of such pieces had stopped, and in their place were substituted either the chests on chests or the later low chest of drawers, and the best of these had block fronts. The origin of the style is not known, but it is

CHESTS OF DRAWERS

probably American. We find practically nothing in England or on the Continent which suggests it, except that one or two pieces have been found in England, but these could have come from America with some Tory family at the time of the Revolution. They are found all through New England. Those found in the north are plain, without a carved shell at the top of the blocking, while in the southern part, especially in Rhode Island and Connecticut, they are frequently found with carved shells. There is one unusually fine type which is found in Rhode Island, and it is possible that block-front pieces of this type were made by John Goddard, of Newport, because in a letter by Goddard to Moses Brown, dated "ye 30th of ye 6th mo 1763" (Moses Brown papers, Vol. I, document 81), he writes with reference to an order from Jabez Bowen, "if he inclines to wate for me I would know whither he means to have them differint from what is common—as there is a Sort which is called a Cheston Chest of Drawers & Sweld front which are costly as well as ornimental." This must have been a block-front piece, as that was the only form at that time to which the adjective swelled could have referred. The mouldings on these so-called Rhode Island pieces are unusual and consist of a fillet, a cyma reversa, a fillet, a cove, an astragal, a fillet, and a small cove, while those found on the other pieces consist of a quarter-round, a fillet, a large cove, an astragal, a fillet, and a small cove.

Block-front pieces are usually made of mahogany or maple and are found with the straight bracket, ogee bracket, or bird's claw and ball feet. The fronts of the drawers are cut from a block of wood sufficiently thick to make the convex and concave surfaces. The surfaces are almost universally broken into two convex surfaces on the outside and a concave one of the same size at the centre. This blocking was usually carried through the bottom moulding and often onto the feet. Occasionally the drawers overlapped, but, as a general rule, they were flush with a bead moulding on the frame about them. There are two distinct types of blocking, one where the edges and the surface of the blocks are almost straight (Figure 119), and the other where the blocking is a continuous curve (Figure 131). There are also two ways of making the drawer fronts. The usual way is where the depressed centre section is back of the plane of the drawer front, thus: The other is where the depressed section is on the same plane with the drawer front, and the effect of the depression is obtained by making the raised portion with two raised sections, thus:

Figure 116 shows a block-front chest on chest in the Bolles Collection. The cornice mouldings are the quarter-round, the fillet, the cove, an astragal, a fillet, and small cove. The cornice is scrolled and the centre ends are finished with rosettes, and three flame finials finish the top. The drawers overlap and the arrangement of drawers in the upper part is the same as that found in the high chests of

118   COLONIAL FURNITURE

drawers. For this reason we place this piece among the early examples of the style. On the stiles are fluted pilasters with Corinthian capitals; on the centre

Figure 116.
Block-Front Chest on Chest, 1750–75.

drawer at the top is carved the rising-sun pattern, and the four long drawers below are slightly blocked by cutting out the centre section. The blocking in the lower section, however, is exceedingly good. On the surface of the upper drawer are carved two convex shells and one concave shell, and the two drawers below are blocked in such a way that the shells on the upper drawer seem to finish the top of a continuous blocking. This is the usual method, and the shell carving indicates that the piece belongs to the southern New England type of block-front

Figure 117.
Block-Front Chest on Chest, 1750–75.

pieces, but the cornice mouldings are not of the Rhode Island type. The chest stands on bird's claw and ball bracket feet and the skirt is cut in a design suggestive of the Vitruvian scroll.

Figure 117 shows a little later chest on chest which is the property of Smith & Beck, of Philadelphia. The cornice is composed of the same mouldings as those on the preceding figure, but at the centre the scrolls are finished with a return moulding instead of a rosette, and three flame finials finish the top. The upper drawers are curved under the cornice and the centre drawer is carved in the rising-sun pattern. Fluted pilasters finish the stiles on the upper part and the drawers are flush with bead mouldings on the frame about them. The lower section has four drawers handsomely blocked, and the blocking extends onto the straight bracket feet. The piece has large willow brasses. This is the type found in northern New England.

A rather unusual block-front chest on chest is shown in Figure 118 which is the property of Mr. H. W. Erving. The cornice consists of a quarter-round, a fillet, a cyma recta, two fillets, a cove, and a quarter-round. Rosettes finish the inner ends of the scrolls. On the centre upper drawer is carved a rising-sun pattern. The edges of the stiles are recessed and quarter-round fluted columns are inserted. About the drawers is a canal moulding which is unusual on such a late piece, as are also the five drawers in the lower part, there generally being but three or four. The piece stands on ogee bracket feet.

Figure 119 shows a block-front chest on chest, the property of Mr. Nathaniel Herreshoff, of Bristol, Rhode Island. The cornice mouldings differ a little from the regular Rhode Island type and consist of a quarter-round, a fillet, a cyma recta, a fillet, a cove, an astragal, a fillet, and a small cove.

Figure 118.
Block-Front Chest on Chest, 1750-75.

This same moulding appears on the scrutoire (Figure 270), as do also the boxes at either end of the scrolls. The carved shells, the finials, the astragal, fillet, and cove, carrying about the circular opening at the top, the bracket feet with the extra scroll carved on the inside, are points found only on the Rhode Island type.

A splendid block-front chest on chest in the Bulkeley Collection is shown in Figure 120. It will be seen at once that it belongs to the southern New England type. The cornice is the same as is found on the Rhode Island pieces and is com-

Figure 119.
Block-Front Chest on Chest, 1750–75.

Figure 120.

Block-Front Chest on Chest, 1750–75.

CHESTS OF DRAWERS

posed of a fillet, a cyma reversa, a fillet, a cove, an astragal, a fillet, and a small cove. Rosettes finish the inner ends of the scrolls and spiral finials are on the top. A carved shell design finishes the surface of the centre acroterium. The blocking on the upper part extends to the lower part through the mouldings at the base and onto the ogee bracket feet, giving the piece a tall slender appearance. The blockings are surmounted with shell carvings, but it will be noted that they are quite different from the usual type in that they are composed of reedings without being separated by concave sections. (See preceding figure.) In the

Figure 121.
Knee-Hole Block-Front Dressing-Table, 1750–75.

upper section the outer blocks are narrower than the centre concave one, and in the lower section the convex blocks are enlarged and the concave one correspondingly decreased. In the corners are inserted spirally twisted columns. The mouldings separating the two carcasses and at the base are unusual and consist of a cove, a fillet, a quarter-round, a fillet, a cove, and a fillet.

When the block-front type of chests of drawers came into use, the popularity of the high-boy and low-boy was on the decline, and consequently a different form of dressing-table had to be adopted, which brought about a revival of the earlier knee-hole type shown in Figure 113.

Figure 121 shows a block-front knee-hole dressing-table of this later period from the Pendleton Collection. On the upper drawer are carved shells in the usual way; on each side of the recessed section are three drawers with convex blocking; in the recess is a panel door hiding shelves. The mouldings below the top are a cove and a bead. The feet are ogee bracket of the peculiar shape found in Rhode Island, and the blocking which extends on them is finished with a scroll. The moulding above the scroll feet is composed of a cyma reversa and a fillet, which is a familiar Chippendale moulding. This form of foot with the scroll finish and the moulding is characteristic of the block-front pieces which were made in Rhode Island. Such pieces as this are sometimes called knee-hole desks.

Figure 122.
Knee-Hole Block-Front Dressing-Table, 1750–75.

There is one at Kingston, Rhode Island, that has a desk in the upper drawer, but that seems to be unique.

Figure 122 shows another knee-hole dressing-table which is in the Bolles Collection, owned by the Metropolitan Museum of Art. It is the same as that shown in the preceding figure, except in two respects. The moulding under the top has a fillet and cove added and the recessed drawer is concave with a shell similar to the one on the drawers immediately above it. In design and execution these forms of block-front pieces are the best that are known.

Figure 123 shows a knee-hole dressing-table, the property of Mr. Thomas G. Hazard, of Narragansett Pier, Rhode Island. Although not blocked, it

CHESTS OF DRAWERS

clearly belongs to the type shown in the preceding figures, and the door in the recessed part conceals drawers with depressed blocking. Although the bracket feet on this piece have not the extra scroll, yet the mouldings under the top and the base mouldings are identical with the blocked pieces, and it was probably made by the same cabinet-maker.

Figure 124 shows a chest on chest the lower section of which is reverse serpentine, the curve commencing on the upper drawer in much the same way as

Figure 123.
Knee-Hole Dressing-Table, 1750–75.

does blocking in the block-front pieces. This form is found quite frequently in desks (Figure 287); the drawers are flush and on the frame is a bead moulding. The corners are recessed and quarter-round columns are inserted. On the square drawer at the top is carved a design of foliated scrolls. The handles are brass rosettes which belong to a much later period than the piece, and as these drawers show that there never had been any other handles it was probably not supplied with handles until some time after it was made. The piece belonged to the late Miss Esther Bidwell, of Wethersfield, Connecticut.

A number of pieces of furniture have been found with handles of a later period, and also without any handles. Practically all handles were imported, and it is possible that the stock of brasses had given out in the town where the cabinet-maker lived.

COLONIAL FURNITURE

Figure 125 shows a chest on chest of the Philadelphia type, very similar to the high chests of drawers shown in Figures 106 and 107. The cornice is identically the same as that in Figure 106, as is also the lattice-work under the scrolls. Well-carved foliated rosettes finish the scrolls, and the arrangement of drawers at the top is the same as that in Figure 107. The finials are Chippendale urns with flowers. The edges are recessed with fluted quarter columns inserted and

Figure 124.
Chest on Chest, 1750–75.

the piece stands on ogee bracket feet. The handles are bails held by posts with circular plates and the escutcheons are in a Chippendale pattern.

Almost an exact duplicate of this piece is owned by Mr. George M. Curtis, of Meriden, Connecticut, and several others, very similar, have come from Philadelphia. This piece is in the possession of the writer.

Figure 126 shows another piece with a cupboard above and drawers below. It is of French walnut and inlaid with medallions of coloured wood. Similar pieces

Figure 125.
Chest on Chest, 1760–75.

are called clothes presses by Chippendale. This piece stands on French bracket feet and the simple cornice indicates that it belongs to the Sheraton period.

As we have said above, high chests of drawers remained popular in America for many years after they had gone out of fashion in England, for the English had adopted the low chest of drawers from the French. In this country, after the form shown in Figure 50 had disappeared, there were practically none found here until after the middle of the eighteenth century, and then they were scarce until about 1780, when they practically superseded the high variety. In this country they have generally been called bureaus, probably because in some of the later varieties one of the drawers contains a desk (Figure 303).

Figure 126.
Chest of Drawers and Cupboard, about 1790.

An unusually handsome low chest of drawers in Chippendale style is shown in Figure 127. The front is cut in the serpentine shape; that is, it is composed of two cyma curves so placed that there are two concave curves separated by a convex one. To avoid an acute angle at the corners, the edges are chamfered and ornamented with a fret carving. The top follows the curve of the front, and is finished with a characteristic Chippendale moulding, a fillet, a cove, and a quarter-round. The piece stands on four well-proportioned bird's claw and ball feet and the surfaces are cut in acanthus and C-scroll designs. The top drawer is divided into many compartments and small drawers, some of them ingeniously hidden by sliding partitions, and at the right end is a quarter-round drawer which swings out. A wooden slide covers the top drawer and acts as a dressing-shelf. The handles are silvered. This piece can be traced to Pennsylvania and is of the same class of workmanship as some of the high chests of drawers above described coming from Philadelphia. It is the property of the writer.

Another later chest of drawers in the same collection is shown in Figure 128. Its construction is the same as that last described and the carved frets on the ends are in the identical design. The top drawer is also divided in the same way, including the quarter-round drawer, all of which makes it quite probable that it was the work of the same cabinet-maker at a slightly later date. The moulding

Figure 127.
Chest of Drawers, 1760–75.

Figure 128.
Chest of Drawers, about 1775.

Figure 129.
Chest of Drawers, Bombé-shaped, about 1760.

Figure 130.
Block-Front Chest of Drawers, 1750–75.

CHESTS OF DRAWERS

edge is composed of a fillet and a torus. The piece stands on ogee bracket feet, which carry out the curves and lines of the front and ends.

Figure 129 shows a form of low chest of drawers known as *bombé* or kettle shape. The front is serpentine and the sides swell at the bottom, the edges of the lower drawers taking the same curve. This form was used by Chippendale on some of his best pieces and is found in this country also on desks. The piece stands on four plain bird's claw and ball feet. It is in the Pendleton Collection, owned by the Rhode Island School of Design.

Figure 131.
Block-Front Chest of Drawers, 1750–75.

Figure 130 shows a low chest of drawers with block front, the blocking extending to the top, which is cut in block form. The drawers are flush with a bead on the frame about them and the feet are in straight bracket type. This piece represents the type of low chest of drawers which was developed in New England at the time the type shown in the three preceding figures was developed in the South. The form of the piece shows that it belongs to the northern New England type of block front. This piece is the property of Mr. Dwight M. Prouty.

Figure 131 shows a block-front low chest of drawers from the Pendleton Collection. The blocking is in the second form, the blocks being swelled instead of square or nearly so. (Compare this with Figure 130.) The mouldings on the edge of the top are the fillet, cove, and torus. The feet are of the bird's claw and ball bracket type well fashioned. The drawers are flush with a bead on the frame about them.

Figure 132 shows another of the block-front low chests of drawers in the same collection. The form of blocking is the same. The four drawers are graded in

Figure 132.
Block-Front Chest of Drawers, 1750–75.

height. The piece stands on ogee bracket feet with a scroll finish, which is characteristic of the Rhode Island type. The moulding at the bottom, however, is not in the usual form, being a cove, a fillet, a quarter-round, and a fillet instead of a cyma reversa and two fillets. The drawers are flush with a bead on the frame about them.

By far the largest number of blocked front chests of drawers are without the shell carved at the top of the drawers. Such as are found are of two varieties—those having bird's claw and ball bracket feet and those having the ogee bracket

CHESTS OF DRAWERS

feet. Figure 133 shows one of the former type, the property of Mr. H. W. Erving. The shell, it will be seen, is the same as appears on the chest on chest shown in Figure 120. The mouldings under the top consist of a fillet, a cove, and a bead. The corners have square recessed edges filled in with quarter-fluted columns. The drawers, four in number, are flush with a bead moulding on the frame about them. The base mouldings are unusual, consisting of a quarter-round, a fillet, a cove, and a fillet.

Figure 133.
Block-Front Chest of Drawers, 1760–75.

Figure 134 shows the second type of these chests of drawers which it will be interesting to compare with the preceding one. It is of the pure Rhode Island type, the shell differing materially from that shown in the preceding figure, and there are three drawers instead of four, a characteristic of the type. The edge of the top is cut in a fillet and a cyma recta, and the mouldings below are a fillet, a cove, an astragal, a fillet, and a small cove. The base mouldings are a cyma reversa and a wide fillet as is usual. The legs are ogee brackets with scrolls carved on the inner sides. This chest of drawers is the property of Dr. Frank I. Hammond, of Providence.

Figure 134.
Block-Front Chest of Drawers, 1760–75.

Figure 135.
Reversed Serpentine-Front Chest of Drawers, about 1780.

CHESTS OF DRAWERS

Figure 135 shows a reverse serpentine low chest of drawers; that is, the outer curves are convex and the centre one concave; the drawers are flush and the piece stands on bird's claw and ball feet. At the centre of the skirt is carved a small shell.

Figure 136 shows another reverse serpentine low chest of drawers of a little later date. The edges of the stiles are recessed and quarter-round columns are

Figure 136.
Reversed Serpentine-Front Chest of Drawers, 1780–90.

inserted. The feet are of the ogee bracket type and the handles are bails supported by posts and oval plates.

After about 1780 the low chests of drawers became almost universally used, and the cabinet designers of the period—Shearer, Hepplewhite, and Sheraton—give many examples. They were commonly inlaid, and the majority found in this country have swelled rather than serpentine fronts.

A fine example of a serpentine-front chest of drawers is shown in Figure 137 and is the property of Mr. John H. Buck, of Hartford. On each drawer is inlaid a delicate rope border. The corners are chamfered and have inlaid panels. The feet are of the straight bracket type and the handles are oval, of the Hepplewhite school.

136 COLONIAL FURNITURE

Figure 138 shows a swell-front low chest of drawers. Each drawer is inlaid about an inch and a half from the edge with a narrow band of walnut, and the edge of the top and the frame at the bottom have a border about three-quarters of an inch wide of inlay. The corners are recessed and filled in with fluted quarter columns. The oval brasses, with bails fastened to the outer edge of post, are in the usual form for the period. This piece is the property of Miss E. R. Burnell, of Hartford.

Figure 137.
Serpentine-Front Chest of Drawers, about 1780–90.

Figure 139 shows a swell-front low chest of drawers in the Bolles Collection. The frame is of mahogany veneer. There are two long panels and a short panel of satin-wood veneer on each drawer and a small panel of the same is inserted on the skirt. The feet are of the long French bracket type. The handles are oval and on each is embossed an urn. The edges of the drawers are finished with a bead.

Figure 140 shows another swell-front low chest of drawers with square and oval panels of satin-wood outlined with a border of walnut, rosewood, and ebony. An oval panel also finishes the skirt. The piece stands on French bracket feet. One of the characteristics of this style is the fact that there are no mouldings either on the edge of the top or skirt. This piece was the property of the late Mrs. Alexander Forman, of Brooklyn.

Figure 138.
Swell-Front Chest of Drawers, 1790–1800.

Figure 139.
Swell-Front Chest of Drawers, 1790–1800.

Figure 140.

Swell-Front Chest of Drawers, 1790–1800.

Figure 141.

Chest of Drawers, Sheraton style, about 1800.

CHESTS OF DRAWERS 139

Figure 141 shows a chest of drawers in Sheraton style. There are two narrow upper drawers, and below is a very deep drawer giving the appearance of being a desk drawer (Figure 303), and below that are three long drawers. The edges of the drawers are beaded. At either end is a reeded column which extends to form the feet and the top is shaped to cover the columns. The handles are oval.

Figure 142 shows a late form of Sheraton serpentine-front chest of drawers of which a number have been found in the vicinity of New York. The drawer

Figure 142.
Chest of Drawers, Sheraton style, 1800–10.

fronts are in serpentine form but the stiles are straight with reeded surface. The wood is cherry with a holly inlay about the edges of the drawers, and in the centre of the top drawer is an oval inlay of mahogany, and a border of mahogany is on the top rail below the top. The skirt is cut in ogee curves and the feet are turned. This piece is the property of the writer.

The Sheraton style gradually developed into the Empire style, of which many examples are found in this country, especially in low chests of drawers. They were heavy and massive, with reeded columns, claw feet, and coarse but effective carving. Few, if any, mouldings were used, which is one reason they have not the beauty of the earlier pieces. These pieces are erroneously called colonial.

Figure 143.
Chest of Drawers, Empire style, 1800–10.

Figure 144.
Chest of Drawers, Empire style, 1810–20.

CHESTS OF DRAWERS

Figure 143 shows an Empire chest of drawers belonging to the writer. The upper part is straight with two drawers, and below are three swell drawers, and the base is again straight. The overhang is supported by two reeded columns and the piece stands on claw feet.

Figure 144 shows a very typical chest of drawers of the period. There are three short drawers at the top and below are four drawers slightly recessed. On

Figure 145.
Chest of Drawers, Empire style, 1810–20.

the stiles are heavy columns carved in a coarse pineapple pattern and the feet are carved animals' claws.

Figure 145 shows another chest of drawers in Empire style. The top is backed and supported at the ends by short columns carved in the pineapple pattern. There are three small drawers at the top and four long ones below, a little recessed, and at the corners are columns carved in an acanthus leaf and pineapple pattern. The piece stands on carved animals' claw feet.

Figure 146 shows another chest of drawers of the same period. On the top are two small drawers and below are four long ones. About the drawers is an inlaid border of holly. The corners are finished with columns with pineapple carving and spiral twisting.

When the high-boy had gone out of fashion and the low chests of drawers had taken its place, there was not so great demand for dressing-tables because

Figure 146.
Chest of Drawers, Empire style, 1810–20.

the tops of the chests of drawers could be used for toilet articles. In sections of the country, however, where a certain degree of luxury was maintained, dainty little dressing-tables were in use.

Figure 147 shows one of a pair of dressing-tables in the Hepplewhite style, the property of Mrs. James R. May, of Portsmouth. The piece resembles a miniature sideboard except that it is not so high. The front swells, and there is one long drawer at the top, one square drawer on each side, and a short drawer at the centre. The drawer fronts have inlaid panels of satin-wood and rosette handles. The centre is arched to enable a person to sit at the table. Such pieces

CHESTS OF DRAWERS 143

as this were intended to have upon them small dressing-glasses similar to the one shown in the succeeding figure.

A number of these dressing-tables have been found with several drawers extending down the sides, leaving a centre section open.

Another dressing-table of a little later date is shown in Figure 148. It is made like a card-table but without the folding leaf. The front is swelled. There is one drawer in front, and on either side at the back is a lid which conceals a small receptacle occupying the sections on either side of the drawer. On the top of this piece is the original dressing-glass in the lower part of which is a shallow drawer. This dressing-table is the property of Mrs. Joseph E. Davis, of York Harbor, Maine.

Figure 147.
Dressing-Table, Hepplewhite style, 1790–1800.

Figure 148.
Dressing-Table, Sheraton style, about 1800.

Figure 149.
Dressing-Table, Sheraton style, 1800–10.

Figure 149 shows a dressing-table in Sheraton style. This, also, is in the form similar to a card-table. The front is reverse serpentine in form, and the

144 COLONIAL FURNITURE

sides are sections of a circle. On top of the piece is a raised section with two small drawers on which is placed the dressing-glass, which in this case was probably on a standard. The legs are turned and reeded. This dressing-table is the property of Mrs. James R. May, of Portsmouth.

Figure 150.
Dressing-Table, 1800–10.

Figure 151.
Stencilled Chest of Drawers, about 1820.

Figure 150 shows a dressing-table of a later period in the Erving Collection. A mirror is fastened to the top with scroll brackets; reeded columns extending to the top support the piece, and below the drawer is a shelf.

About this time it became fashionable to stencil furniture, and Figure 151 shows a characteristic chest of drawers in this style. On the top is fastened, with carved scroll supports, a rectangular mirror, the frame of which is stencilled. On the top are three small drawers and under the top is a cushion frieze concealing a drawer on the surface of which is stencilled a pattern of fruit and flowers and two rosettes. Below this are three drawers recessed and at the ends are columns stencilled in an acanthus-leaf pattern. The piece stands on turned feet.

CHESTS OF DRAWERS

Figure 152 shows a basin stand in the Pendleton Collection, owned by the Rhode Island School of Design. These stands were popular in England during the Dutch and Chippendale periods but were never common here. This piece, as is usual, stands on three legs. At the bottom is the place for the ewer. Above

Figure 152.
Basin-Stand, 1725–50.

Figure 153.
Wash-Stand, 1790–1800.

are two small drawers and a soap-dish, and the rim at the top is intended for the basin. A basin-stand very similar to this is shown in miniature in the doll house (Figure 1).

Figure 153 shows a wash-stand or night table of a later period which is in the Blaney Collection. There are two drawers with veneered panels and below is a shelf with a nicely scalloped edge. Reeded columns extending from the top form the legs and support the piece.

A well-proportioned corner wash-stand of the Hepplewhite period is shown in Figure 154 and was the property of the late William G. Boardman, of Hartford. The front is swelled. At the corners of the doors are inlaid fans and a line of inlay is on the bottom.

Figures 155 and 156 show two examples of corner wash-stands of the period. Figure 155 has the long, tapering outstanding legs of the Hepplewhite period and Figure 156 is in the Sheraton style.

As bureaus are so commonly associated with mahogany, it will perhaps be well to say something of the history of the use of that wood for furniture in general. The tradition of its introduction into England by Sir Walter Raleigh,

Figure 154.
Wash-Stand, 1790–1800.

in 1595, is quite generally accepted, and at the same time it is as generally believed that it was not used there to any extent until about 1720. It is not likely that the century which divides its discovery from its popular use was absolutely ignorant of it, and some pieces are now known to have been made of mahogany in England previous to 1700. As far as this country is concerned, there is no indication whatever that it was known or used much previous to 1700; none of the furniture, such as chairs, tables, or chests of drawers, which was made at this time, was made of mahogany, and there is no mention in the inventories or contemporary documents of any kind, that the writer has been able to find, of mahogany previous to

CHESTS OF DRAWERS

1700. At Philadelphia, in 1694, the inventory of a cabinet-maker named John Fellows contained the following list of material in a shop: "pyne loggs, walnutt loggs, pyne boards, walnutt planks, walnutt scantling, oak boards and cedar boards, one case of drawers, partlie made, stuff for a side table partlie made, stuff partlie wrought for a hall table, a parcel of brass work for drawers, four sutes of locks for chests of drawers, three dressing box locks"; but in 1720 Joseph Waite, also of Philadelphia, had in his shop "a chest of mahogany drawers unfinished."

Figure 155.
Wash-Stand, 1790–1800.

Figure 156.
Wash-Stand, 1790–1800.

Previous to this there is mention of a "broaken mahogany skreen" in the inventory of John Jones, in 1708, at Philadelphia, valued at two shillings. If we conclude, then, that the use of mahogany for furniture in this country was contemporaneous with the opening of the eighteenth century, we shall certainly place it early enough, and we are equally safe in concluding that it was not in general use earlier than 1720–30. The Boston *Evening Post* throughout the year 1741 advertises mahogany boards in large quantities, and after this time the newspapers and inventories frequently mention mahogany tables, chairs, and desks.

It may be well, while on this subject, to speak here of the difference between the old mahogany and the new. There are in the market to-day in commonest use two kinds of mahogany. One, from Mexico, is quite a soft wood, and light in colour, which does not darken with age, and consequently must be stained. It weighs but about two and a half pounds to a square foot, an inch in thickness, while West Indian mahogany weighs about six pounds. The other kind of mahogany is from Honduras, and is even softer than the Mexican, with a much coarser grain. It is therefore often possible to tell by the weight of a piece of furniture whether it is old or new, and this is particularly true in respect to chairs.

The best mahogany to-day, as well as in former days, comes from the West Indies, and is sometimes called Spanish mahogany. There is also a very beautiful grained mahogany now in the market coming from Africa.

IV
CUPBOARDS AND SIDEBOARDS

AT the time when the American colonies were settled, cupboards had been in common use for generations. As the name implies, they were originally "bordes" on which to set drinking-cups. The earliest of these cupboards now known are constructed with shelves arranged like steps, and having often a "tremor" or canopy of wood; they are Gothic in style, and are spoken of sometimes as ambries or almeries, the names long used in the churches for a niche or cupboard near the altar, built to contain the utensils requisite for conducting worship.

The frequent mention of cupboards of all kinds throughout our probate records shows them to have been in very common use in all the colonies, and the spelling of the word is various enough to suit all tastes: cubboard, cubberd, cubbord, cubbert, cupbard, and cubart are some of the spellings employed. Court, wainscot, livery, standing, hanging, press, joined, plain, great, and painted are the descriptions most often met with. Court and livery, the words most often used in connection with the cupboards of New England and the South, seem to have lost their original meanings sometime before their use in this country. It is fair to suppose that they must have had some definite descriptive meanings when first applied, and these seem to have been derived from the French words *court* and *livrer*, *court* meaning low or short, and pointing to the conclusion that this must have been a low piece of furniture much like a modern serving-table. *Livrer* has been variously translated to mean service and delivery, perhaps referring to a custom in vogue during the fifteenth and sixteenth centuries of delivering to the household the rations required during the day and night. An old English dictionary defines livery as "something given out in stated quantities at stated times." For a note on the word cupboard in the "Promptuarium Parvulorum Clericorum," published by Wynkyn de Worde in 1510, and republished by the Camden Society in 1865, reads as follows: "The livery cupboard often mentioned in accounts and ordinances of the household was open and furnished with shelves whereon the ration called a livery allowed to each member of the household was placed." The English inventory records throughout the sixteenth century, published by the Surtees and Camden societies, make frequent mention of court and livery cupboards, but their values, even in the estates of persons of consequence, are so exceedingly low as to indicate that they must have been very simple in style and workmanship, hardly more than shelves supported by a frame.

We have found no examples of American livery cupboards, although mention is made of them in the inventories. It is probable, therefore, that they were so simple that they were not preserved, or that the name was used indiscriminately by the persons making the inventories with court and press cupboards.

Figure 157.
Livery Cupboard, last quarter seventeenth century.

Figure 157 shows a small livery cupboard from the Bulkeley Collection. The stiles and rails are carved in a foliated design similar to the design found on some of the chests. The lower part of the door is in the shape of a double arch, a pendant being substituted for the pilaster in the centre. The pilaster and arches are carved in an imbricated design and in the spandrels are carved foliations. The inner edges of the intrados are scalloped. The upper section of the door is open to admit of the free circulation of air and the space is filled in with balusters, and split balusters and turtle-back bosses ornament the surface. Inside are shelves. The design of this piece shows that it is late.

The picture of the dining-hall at Christ Church College, Oxford (Figure 158), shows a court cupboard beneath the window, which must have been far finer than

Figure 158.
Dining-Hall, Christ Church College, Oxford.
(Showing cupboard beneath windows.)

the bulk of those of the time to which it belongs (sixteenth century). The upper shelf will be seen to be supported by well-carved dragons, the lower by pilasters carved after the manner of Elizabethan pieces, and the centre shelf is ornamented with deeply carved godrooning. This cupboard doubtless represents very fairly the style in which cupboards were built during the fifteenth and sixteenth centuries. Toward the close of the sixteenth century the English records show the court and livery cupboards to have increased in value, and this undoubtedly means that these pieces had been elaborated in some way, probably by the addition of enclosures in the form of cupboards and drawers and also by the addition of ornaments in the form of carving and inlay. This we know to be true, for a number of cupboards dating early in the seventeenth century are preserved in the collections of English museums which have enclosures and drawers and are carved and inlaid.

A very few specimens of cupboards with only the upper portion enclosed remain in this country, and the theory that the court cupboard has evolved from open shelves to the fully enclosed cupboards, of which comparatively large numbers remain, is well supported. The upper portion, as we have seen, was first enclosed, the lower remaining an open shelf; then a drawer was added below the middle shelf, and, finally, the lower portion was entirely enclosed, first with cupboards and then with drawers. Properly speaking, then, the terms court and livery do not apply to the cupboards which are to be found in this country, which are, technically speaking, press cupboards, that is, enclosed with doors; but there is every reason to think that these press cupboards were referred to as court and livery, for there is express mention of court cupboards with drawers and livery cupboards with drawers, which are not qualifications of real court or livery cupboards.

As far as this country is concerned, court and livery are used quite interchangeably, if one may judge from values given, for the prices of both are equally small or large, as the case may be: a court cupboard at Salem in 1647, 14s.; a livery cupboard at the same place in 1656, 18s.; a livery cupboard and cloth in 1674, £1 5s.; a court cupboard and cloth at Boston in 1700, £1; a court cupboard with a drawer at Boston in 1658, 16s.; a livery cupboard with drawers, 1666, 10s.

The cloth was mentioned quite as often with court as with livery, and suggests that their make-up must have been much the same. There is no mention of either court or livery cupboards in the early New York records, and the *kasses* or cupboards in use among the Dutch will be spoken of separately.

The Southern records contain quite frequent mention of both court and livery cupboards, but, as far as the writer has been able to determine, these pieces have utterly disappeared, and it may be assumed that they were in character and material the same class of furniture as those remaining in New England, as the source of supply for North and South was the same.

CUPBOARDS AND SIDEBOARDS 153

The wood is usually oak, with pine freely used for the cupboard tops, bottoms, and backs, and for the bottoms of the drawers when drawers are used. In the panelled cupboards the mouldings are occasionally found of cedar, but are more often of pine, beech, or maple, painted, and the turned ornaments, drops, nail-heads, turtle-backs, and triglyphs are of the same woods, also painted. The predominance of American oak in the construction of these cupboards denotes,

Figure 159.
Court Cupboard, about 1600.

of course, their manufacture here, and as they are such bulky, difficult pieces to transport, it would seem likely that comparatively few of them were brought over. The tops are finished with a thumb-nail moulding similar to that found on the chests.

Figure 159 shows a very beautiful court cupboard, the property of the Metropolitan Museum of Art. The lower section is open and in the upper section is a cupboard with splayed sides. The ends are supported by large, bulbous, turned columns similar to those found on the feet of tables of the Elizabethan period.

(See Figure 674.) The surfaces of the upper pair are carved in an arabesque design and the upper surfaces of the lower pair are godrooned, while the lower section is carved in an acanthus-leaf design. Beautifully carved corbels are placed beneath each of the two boards. On the drawer is a well-executed arabesque design. The top rail is ornamented with a spray of flowers and leaves, and on each of the panels is inlaid a floral spray. The mouldings about the panels are carved in a guilloche design. On the lower rail is inlaid a checker-board design. This is one of the

Figure 160.
Court Cupboard, third quarter seventeenth century.

most beautiful court cupboards that has come under the writer's observation and is, of course, English, dating about 1600.

Figure 160 shows an American example of a court cupboard in the Bolles Collection, and its plainness is in striking contrast to the English piece shown in the foregoing figure. There is no carving on the piece, the ornamentation being obtained entirely by split spindles and bosses applied. The cupboard has splayed sides, and each panel is in an arched design from the centre of which is a pendent split spindle. The drawer front is a large torus moulding. Cupboards open below are very rarely found in this country. The arching and construction of this piece indicated that it was made in the third quarter of the seventeenth century.

CUPBOARDS AND SIDEBOARDS 155

The best American court cupboard that has come under the writer's observation is shown in Figure 161 and is in the Bolles Collection, the property of the Metropolitan Museum of Art. At the top is a moulding cut to resemble blocks with a serrated lower edge, and three large corbels, between which are pairs of rectangular bosses with chamfered edges. The sides are finished as the front. The recessed portion is straight and contains two cupboards; the doors of each are

Figure 161.
Court Cupboard, third quarter seventeenth century.

panelled in lozenge shape with a nail-head boss in the centre, and between the doors is a panel in arch form with split-spindle bosses. At each end is a cruciform panel with two small panels below. The lower moulding is cut in pairs of small vertical lines, a serrated line in scratch carving and the block design which appears above. Below the cupboard shelf is the same moulding that appears at the top. There are two drawers with a pair of split-spindle bosses at either side and in the centre. The skirt is cut in ogee curves and the straight legs have been slightly cut off.

Figure 162 shows a press cupboard constructed in the way most commonly employed. The cupboard in the upper portion is splayed at the corners and the overhanging cornice is supported by heavy turned posts. The torus moulded drawer is well carved in the familiar foliated design, as is also the top rail. The lower section is entirely enclosed with doors panelled in the simplest manner and the stiles and rails are perfectly plain. The panels on the upper cupboard are practically in the same design as those shown in the foregoing figure, and it is of about the same date.

Figure 162.
Press Cupboard, third quarter seventeenth century.

Figure 163 shows a beautiful press cupboard in the Bulkeley Collection. It is constructed in the usual way, *i. e.*, the upper cupboard having splayed sides, the torus moulded drawer, and a lower cupboard. The top rail is well carved in a foliated scroll design; at the corners and centre are applied ornaments known as nail-heads, taking the place of corbels. Under the top is a series of small corbels closely resembling a dentil cornice. The door panel of the upper cupboard is carved in a design of one large and four small circles with a rosette in each with foliation between. The side panels are double and in the designs of rosettes and foliation, while at the back is a band of foliated scrolls. On the moulded drawer is again the foliated scroll. On each outer stile are carved six rosettes and on the centre stile a guilloche design. On the lower rail is a lunette design. The panels of the door are carved in a waving circular design with foliations.

CUPBOARDS AND SIDEBOARDS

Such examples of carving as that last shown make it appear rather remarkable that the New England inventories do not mention carving in connection with cupboards and only very occasionally in the description of chests; it would seem that the original cost of such work as these cupboards show would necessarily be high; but on looking through a long list of cupboard values taken at Plymouth, Salem, Boston, Philadelphia, and Yorktown, the values vary, as a rule, from

Figure 163.
Press Cupboard, 1660–80.

5s. to £1 5s., and valuations above these figures are very rare. An entry of a "court cubbert" at Boston, 1681, places the value at £4, and at Yorktown a court cupboard with drawers, in 1657, is valued at £5; at Salem, in 1733, we find "one best cupboard £3," and the "next best, £2"; but the currency inflation suffered at this time in Massachusetts may bring the actual value of the last-named down to the average. The inside arrangement of these cupboards does not vary much. The upper cupboard is usually open—that is, without shelves—but sometimes has a shelf in the centre; and when the cornice at the top is not a drawer it often has a shelf concealed which is reached through the cupboard. The lower cupboard has from one to three long shelves. These cupboards, as well as the joined oak furniture in general, are fastened together mortise and tenon fashion with wooden pegs throughout; no nails whatever were used in them.

Figure 164.
Press Cupboard, 1660–80.

A press cupboard somewhat similar to the one just described is shown in Figure 164 and was the property of the late Walter Hosmer. The construction is practically the same, except that the drawer is straight instead of having a torus moulding, and it stands on ball feet. The upper rail is carved in a foliated scroll design separated by well-carved corbels, and a dentil cornice finishes the top. The door of the upper cupboard is in a very good design of entwined foliated scrolls, and on all the stiles is laurelling with rosettes. The side panels are double, as in the preceding piece, carved with rosettes. The drawer and lower panels are carved in a double foliated scroll design, and corbels finish the top of the stiles and centre of the drawer. On the stiles on either side of the door is nicked carving.

CUPBOARDS AND SIDEBOARDS 159

The wide outstanding moulding and the ball feet will be observed. The turned columns are of oak instead of pine, painted, which is the manner common on American cupboards, and a semi-classic effect is given by the crude Ionic capitals with which they are finished. The cupboard is of American white-oak and

Figure 165.
Press Cupboard, last quarter seventeenth century.

of unusual size, being 5 feet 1½ inches high; the lower section being 3 feet in height, 4 feet wide, and 21 inches deep; the upper part, 2 feet 1½ inches high and 18¾ inches deep.

Figure 165 shows a very good example of a panelled press cupboard dating in the last quarter of the seventeenth century. It is constructed in the same way as has been described with regard to the preceding pieces. The raised panels on the doors suggest the panels on the chest (Figure 25). The drawer fronts and the centre of each panel are inlaid in checker-board design. This inlay is quite often found in the better cupboards abroad, but it is not very common in this country. The top rail and the tops of the stiles of the lower part are finished with corbels and the surfaces are embellished with split spindles and bosses. This cupboard was found neglected in a stable some years ago and carefully restored; but the feet, which are new, should have been of the ball variety illustrated in Figure 164, for, almost without exception, chests and cupboards having the wide outstanding moulding at the bottom have these ball feet, while the straight feet are merely the continuation of the stiles and uninterrupted by any moulding in most cases.

The feet of chests and cupboards being often missing, it may be of service to collectors to know that if the place where the feet were applied originally can be examined, the presence of an auger-hole with rounded end denotes the use of a very old style of instrument, for the modern auger leaves a straight surface where it finishes a hole. The ball feet were furnished with dowel-pins which fitted into the holes.

The cupboard from Mr. Erving's Collection, shown in Figure 166, has come to be quite generally known among collectors as the Connecticut cupboard, for a number of them have been found in Connecticut and the writer has been unable to trace any that have been found elsewhere.

This cupboard differs from those previously shown, in that the upper cupboard instead of being splayed is recessed, making a shallow cupboard the entire width of the piece. In place of corbels on the top rail are carved tulip designs. The two outer panels on the upper cupboard are doors, the centre being stationary. The surfaces of these panels are ornamented with bosses and split spindles, and at the centre between the two posts is a pendant. The drawer is panelled and has applied turtle-back ornaments on the surface. The lower panels, it will be seen, are in the same design as that found on the Connecticut chests (Figure 18). The stiles are ornamented with strap work and split spindles. Cupboards are occasionally met with in which both upper and lower sections are recessed, the lower cupboard finished in the same manner as the upper, and also having the turned posts at the corners. A drawer sometimes is added at the bottom. A cupboard of this description is in the Waters Collection at Salem, Massachusetts.

Figure 167 shows a press cupboard, the property of Mr. George Dudley Seymour, of New Haven, which is constructed in the same way as that shown in the preceding figure. On the rail under the top are three groups of three applied rectangular bosses with chamfered sides. Under the upper and lower boards are the same kind of applied blocks, set diagonally, as appear on the preceding

Figure 167.
Press Cupboard, last quarter seventeenth century.

Figure 166.
Press Cupboard, last quarter seventeenth century.

cupboard. The upper cupboard has three panels, the outer ones blocked in the corners and the centre one blocked in the corners and centre of the sides. A turtle-back boss is applied at the centre of each panel in both sections. The doors in the lower part are also constructed in the same manner as in the preceding figure but are without carving.

Figure 168.
Press Cupboard, last quarter seventeenth century.

Figure 168 shows a press cupboard, the property of Mr. Maxwell C. Greene, of Providence, which, although English, has been in this country from colonial times. The top edge is carved in a chevron design. Under the top are four corbels and the space between is ornamented with carved foliated scrolls. The upper cupboard is recessed and the top is supported by two columns turned in the vase-and-ring pattern. The two doors are panelled with blocks inserted in the corners

CUPBOARDS AND SIDEBOARDS 163

and a split spindle and two rosettes are applied on each. At the centre is carved a fleur-de-lis with a crown above. On the drawer front are two panels carved in the foliated scroll design. The two lower doors are panelled with blocks inserted on the four sides and on the panels are split spindles and rosettes. One large and two small split spindles finish each stile.

Figure 169.
Press Cupboard with three drawers, 1675–1700.

A very fine cupboard with drawers, known as the "Putnam cupboard," which was presented to the Essex Institute, Salem, by Miss Harriet Putnam Fowler, of Danvers, Massachusetts, a descendant of John Putnam, who settled in Salem about the year 1634, is shown in Figure 169. It differs from all the preceding in having the lower section entirely of drawers, a development which we may regard as the extreme to which these cupboards came, although a court cupboard with three drawers is mentioned in a Boston inventory as early as 1677. The panelling on the drawers is especially fine, all the mouldings being of cedar. The first and second drawers are identically like the third and fourth drawers of Figure 49, and the bottom drawer is divided into three panels, the outer ones

Figure 170.
Press Cupboard with three drawers, 1699.

having the four sides indented and the centre one having blocks inserted at the centre of the sides and through the centre. The arch shape of the recessed panels of the cupboard portion would make it appear that this cupboard may be an early example of its kind. It probably dates in the last quarter of the seventeenth century. The piece is made in two parts, the cupboard proper and the drawer section separate.

CUPBOARDS AND SIDEBOARDS 165

Figure 170 shows an interesting cupboard with drawers in the Bolles Collection, owned by the Metropolitan Museum of Art. It is of American oak, and the maker apparently had in mind such a piece as is shown in the preceding figure. The three drawers are panelled in a simpler adaptation of the top drawer of Figure 169. The cupboard portion is also very similar, with the two arches on each side and split spindles. The supporting bulbous posts of each are turned in the same design. The chief differences are the designs of the panels on the cupboard door and the fact that the stiles on this piece are extended to form the feet, while in

Figure 171.
Press Cupboard with three drawers, 1690–1700.

the preceding cupboard the feet are onion-shaped and a moulding finishes the lower rail. This cupboard is dated 1699.

Figure 171 shows a late, rather crude cupboard with drawers in the Bolles Collection. The workman had rather pretentious ideas which he was incapable of executing. The general proportions of the piece are good, but the carving is shallow and lacks the freedom of line found on the Bulkeley cupboard (Figure 163) which it quite closely resembles. The top rail is finished with a dentil cornice and three nail-head bosses take the place of the corbels. The spaces between are crudely carved in foliated scrolls. The panels of the cupboard and the two lower drawers are painted in circles in red and white with nebuly or waving parallel lines within and surrounding the circles, giving a rather startling effect. The frame of the cupboard door and the stiles of the lower portion of the piece are carved in a foliated design. The upper drawer is slightly rounded, carved in a design of double foliated scrolls and circles. Within each of the outer circles is carved a four-leaf flower, which is represented in paint on the panels of the cupboard, and within the centre circle is an eight-looped decoration. The skirt is serrated. Quite a number of chests and cupboards have been found in New England painted in a

Figure 172.
Wainscot Cupboard, 1675–1700.

similar fashion, but it is extremely difficult to determine what design it is intended to represent. The paint on this piece has been restored, but the writer saw the piece in the rough before restoration, and there is no doubt that it is restored correctly but probably too brilliantly.

Figure 172 shows a wainscot or joint cupboard in the collection of Mr. H. W. Erving, which is made throughout of oak, no pine whatever appearing in its construction, a fact quite noteworthy, as the wood is American oak, and most American pieces show pine, while the majority of English pieces are much more sparing in the use of it. The cupboard is divided at the centre, and a long drawer runs across the bottom, the mouldings on this drawer being worked on, not applied as

CUPBOARDS AND SIDEBOARDS 167

is usual. The stiles may have originally had turned ornaments, but the piece shows no evidence of having been painted. Its date is about 1675–1700.

Cupboards of this variety, with panelling in various geometrical designs, are very often constructed with the receding portions of the panel in pine, and painted black, and with the mouldings painted red.

Figure 173 shows a piece very rarely found in this country which belonged to the late Walter Hosmer, of Wethersfield, Connecticut, which may, perhaps, be

Figure 173.
Cupboard of Drawers, 1680–1700.

such a piece as was referred to in several Yorktown (Virginia) inventories before 1700—"a cupboard of drawers." It is 53 inches high, 43 inches wide, and 30 inches deep, and is made in two sections, as were the high chests of drawers and the cupboard last shown. The upper section consists of two drawers, one about 4½ inches wide, extending entirely across the front just beneath the moulding, and a larger drawer 10½ inches wide. The lower section is in appearance a cupboard, the doors enclosing three long drawers. The wood is English oak, and the face of the centre panels and the entire front of the narrow drawer, as well as the face of the applied ornaments of the upper section, are veneered with snake-wood, an extremely hard wood growing in Brazil. The mouldings are cedar, and there is no paint on the piece, except on the turned ornaments, which are painted black. The knob handles are of bone and the drop handles on the enclosed drawers are of iron. This piece was found in Connecticut, but is undoubtedly of English origin.

Cupboard cloths and cushions are mentioned frequently in all the records, and often inventoried separately as articles of considerable value, sometimes higher than the cupboard itself. We know that the cupboard tops were used for the display of china, pewter, and glass, for this is often included in the appraised value of the cupboard; therefore the cupboard cloths or carpets are easily accounted for, as covers made of various materials (linen, tapestry, and needle-work are some of the kinds mentioned) would very naturally have been in use. But what a cupboard cushion could be does not at first appear, as there seems to have been no cupboard that could possibly have been used as a seat, and cushions meant cushions in those days as now, and are almost invariably mentioned with joined chairs and settles. The only solution for the riddle of the cushion on the cupboard seems to be that the cushion was probably a very thin one, placed over or under the cloth as a protection to the china and glass against striking a hard surface with force enough to break or injure it.

The cupboards discussed so far in this chapter represent the kind of furniture with which the homes of the seventeenth century in this country were furnished, and to the average American of the present day are absolutely unknown.

The consensus of opinion among students of the subject is that the design for the wainscot cupboards came from Germany, and Herr von Falke, in his lectures on "Art in the House," shows a few designs for German Renaissance sideboards, mostly from the designs of Hans Vriedeman de Vries (painter, designer, and architect, born at Leeuwarden, in Friesland, 1527; died at Antwerp some time after 1604), which may easily have been the models for the heavily panelled cupboards so common here. The taste for the brilliant colours with which the cupboards were sometimes stained and painted probably also came from the Germans, for Dr. von Falke remarks that the magnificent inlay in coloured woods, metals, and precious stones achieved by the great artists of Italy and Spain created a desire for these same colour effects without the same expense and skill, thus giving rise to the use of paint or stain among the German cabinet-makers of the seventeenth century. Practically all the American cupboards show traces of having their mouldings and turned ornaments painted, and the carved pieces, many of them, show the presence of a black stain or paint used as a background to set off the carving more effectively. A cupboard is occasionally found where judicious scraping will show the original ornament to have been principally a design in paint, simulating carving or panelling.

It has been previously remarked that the words court and livery do not appear in the inventory records at New York, and, likewise, the words oak and wainscot are almost entirely lacking. The word *kas*, sometimes spelled *kasse*,

CUPBOARDS AND SIDEBOARDS

appears very often, and this was the Dutch name for cupboard. The records speak of plain cupboards, great cupboards, walnut cupboards, great presses, Holland cupboards, cedar cupboards, and Dutch painted cupboards, and a search among the treasures of Dutch families in the vicinity of New York has not revealed a single oak piece or a cupboard in any way resembling the court and livery cupboards of New England.

Figure 174.
Painted Kas, about 1700.

A Dutch painted cupboard, now preserved at the Van Cortlandt Mansion, Van Cortlandt Park, New York, is shown in Figure 174. The quaint designs in fruit and flowers are in shades of grey and seem never to have been tampered with. There is a long drawer across the bottom on side runners, and the cupboard doors conceal wide shelves. Kasses of this kind are made in three parts; the heavy cornice lifts off and the frame and drawer are separated from the cupboard proper. The cornice consists of a short cyma recta, a fillet, and a large cyma reversa. These kasses always stand on ball feet in the front, while the rear legs are simply an extension of the stiles. Many kasses are found in the neighbourhood of New York and in the Dutch settlements along the Hudson and in New Jersey. They are made of pine, cherry, maple, and walnut, and the doors are often panelled. A shallow drawer is sometimes found under the middle shelf.

A Dutch painted cupboard valued at £1 is mentioned in the New York inventories in 1702.

Figure 175 shows a kas in the possession of Mrs. Henry R. Beekman, of New York. The wood is walnut throughout, and the carving, which is well executed, is applied in the method common in such pieces. The cornice is heavier than in

Figure 175.
Walnut Kas, about middle of seventeenth century.

the preceding figure and consists of a quarter-round, a fillet, a cyma recta, a fillet, a cove, a fillet, a cyma reversa, a fillet, and a cove. The dimensions are 7 feet 3 inches in height, 6 feet 2½ inches in width. The cornice overhanging measures 8 inches and the ball feet are 9 inches in diameter. The wide drawer at the bottom is on side runners, and the inside shelves, three in number, are each

CUPBOARDS AND SIDEBOARDS 171

finished with a 3-inch drawer, also on side runners. This kas probably represents the finest of the cupboards in use among the Dutch, and the tradition in the Beekman family is that it came to New York with the first Beekman in Governor Stuyvesant's ship in the year 1647. The piece is of Holland origin and could date as early as the tradition states.

The records of New York speak of great black walnut kasses, referring to such cupboards as this.

So far as the writer can ascertain, these kasses were the only style of large cupboard used by the Dutch in this country, and their character is certainly quite different from that of similar pieces in the New England colonies.

An interesting little piece of Dutch carving found at Coxsackie, New York, which now belongs to the writer, is shown in Figure 176. The wood is beech, and the design is what is known as Friesland carving and is not common in this country. The three narrow shelves are each pierced with five oval openings designed to hold spoons. The wood of the shelves around these openings is much worn by long years of use. These spoon-racks are mentioned in some of the early Dutch records, called by their Dutch name, *lepel-borties*. The Dutch, with their housewifely tastes, loved to have their walls adorned with bright pewter and china, and devised shelves of various kinds for the holding of these valued articles. "A painted wooden rack to sett china ware in" is mentioned at New York in 1696.

Figure 176.
Spoon-Rack, 1675–1700.

Something should perhaps be said of the length of time that early cupboards remained in fashion—much longer, no doubt, in the villages than in the towns, where a change of fashion was followed more closely. At Boston the records begin to speak of chests of drawers on frames about 1680, and we may date the decline of cupboards from this time, though in some parts of New England they continued to be made for some twenty years or more. A will dated at New York in 1708 specifies that the wife of the testator shall be allowed to take "a new cubbard that is now amaking by Mr. Shaveltie"; and Mrs. Vanderbilt's "Social History of Flatbush" mentions a Dutch cupboard which sold for £4 in 1790. At Philadelphia, which was not settled until 1682, the records make very little mention of cupboards. From 1683 until 1720 only six are found, all valued very low, and described as old or old-fashioned. On the other hand, chests of drawers and tables are freely mentioned, showing that the cupboards were superseded by the high chests of drawers which came into use in the last quarter of the seventeenth century.

In New England and other portions of America not under direct Dutch influence were found cupboards which were used for much the same purpose as were kasses, and these continue to be occasionally found throughout the eighteenth century.

Probably the most important piece of American oak which has been found is the clothes press, illustrated as a frontispiece, which belongs to Mr. William F. J. Boardman, of Hartford, in whose family it has always been. The upper and lower panel sections conceal a closet with wooden pegs. The dimensions of the piece are as follows: Length 4 feet 10 inches, height 5 feet 6½ inches, depth 19 inches. The piece is of beautifully grained oak, except for the large panels, which are of pine, painted black. The nail-head applied ornaments are so placed as to appear to secure the panels to the surface, and the large panels are of unusual shape, redented at the corners and centres of the sides. The hinges are of wrought-iron in the form of a cock's head. Below the cupboard are two drawers placed side by side. This is the only fine example of a press cupboard found in this country known to the writer, and they are not common anywhere.

Figure 177 shows a panelled cupboard of walnut, the property of Mr. Charles R. Morson, of Brooklyn. The cornice consists of a quarter-round, a fillet, a cyma recta, a fillet, a cove, an astragal, and a fillet. The doors each have six bevelled panels and there are three panels on each end. The corners have square recessed edges with fluted quarter columns inserted. Below the cupboard are five drawers with overlapping edges, and the handles are of the early willow pattern. The piece stands on ogee bracket feet.

Another cupboard is shown in Figure 178. It is made of cherry in two carcasses, both sections having shelves concealed by doors. The cornice is unusual, consisting of a small fillet, a small cyma recta, a dentil moulding, a cyma recta, a dentil moulding, a cove, a quirk, an astragal, a fillet, a small cove, a dentil moulding, a fillet, and a small quarter-round. A dentil moulding finishes the under side of the moulding separating the two carcasses. There is one long narrow panel on each side of the doors, both top and bottom, and the doors are also panelled. The panels are all applied on the frame. The feet are of the ogee bracket type. The original H hinges and escutcheons appear on the piece. This cupboard is the property of the writer.

Figure 179 shows a wardrobe belonging to Mrs. Russell, of Woodstock, Connecticut. It is built exactly like the cabinet top of a scrutoire, and it belongs to the period of scroll-type high chests of drawers. Its dimensions are 6 feet 1 inch

Figure 178.
Cherry Cupboard, 1725–50.

Figure 177.
Walnut Cupboard, 1725–50.

high, 3 feet 1½ inches wide, and 15½ inches deep. The cornice is composed of the usual mouldings of the period, a quarter-round, a fillet, a cove, an astragal, a fillet, and a small cove. The doors have long bevelled panels. The piece stands

Figure 179.
Wardrobe, 1725–50.

on ogee bracket feet. This is the only wardrobe of this period which has come under the writer's observation, and down to the Empire period they are very scarce, probably because the houses had ample closet room.

Figure 180 shows a cupboard, the property of the Tiffany Studios. The cornice, which is in the form of a broken pediment, is composed of a fillet, a cyma recta, a fillet, a quarter-round, a dentil moulding, a cove, and an astragal. On the cyma recta is carved an acanthus-leaf design. Across the front is a fillet, a cyma recta, a fillet, a dentil moulding, and a cove. The latter is decorated with

CUPBOARDS AND SIDEBOARDS 175

arches and pendent drops. This form of ornament was quite frequently used during the Sheraton period (Figures 291 and 292), and is found in some houses

Figure 180.
Cupboard, 1780–90.

in this country dating about 1800. At each side are columns fluted about three-quarters of the way down, and then fluted and reeded. The capitals are of the Corinthian order. The corners of the lower carcass are carved to represent blocks of stone, a not uncommon design of the period. In this carcass are two short and two long drawers, and the piece stands on straight bracket feet. The handles are of the open-work type.

Figure 181 shows a wardrobe of the Empire period, the property of Mrs. George Hyde Clark, of Cooperstown, New York. At either end is a plain column

Figure 181.
Wardrobe, 1810-20.

with a carved acanthus-leaf capital, and the front feet are carved to represent animals' claw feet. Many massive clothes presses, some much larger than these, are found in the Empire period and were possibly made to match a suite of bedroom furniture.

Figure 182 shows a dresser, the property of Miss C. M. Traver, of New York. The upper section is composed of three open shelves backed and surmounted by

CUPBOARDS AND SIDEBOARDS 177

a cornice composed of a quarter-round, a fillet, a cyma recta, a fillet, and a small cyma reversa. In the lower section are three drawers at the centre and

Figure 182.
Dresser, 1725-50.

a cupboard with panelled doors is at each end. The piece is made of pine throughout and was intended to be used to display china or pewter. It is of New York Dutch origin.

Figure 183 shows a side cupboard, the property of the writer. This piece differs from those shown in the succeeding figures in that it is a piece of furniture and not set into the wall. The cornice is a fillet, a cyma recta, a fillet, and a cyma reversa. What appears to be panelling is wood cut to resemble it. The opening

Figure 183.
Side Cupboard, about 1725.

of the upper section is composed of ogee or cyma curves, and a rosette is carved in the square panel on each side of the door. The sides are of American oak and extend to the floor, forming two legs upon which it rests.

A fine example of an early Georgian cupboard is shown in Figure 184. It was presented to the old Philadelphia Library Building by John Penn in 1738. The interrupted pediment is full-hooded; the mouldings are ornamented with carving in the acanthus-leaf and egg-and-dart designs, and the latter design frames

CUPBOARDS AND SIDEBOARDS

the door; the two fluted pilasters are well proportioned and appear to support the heavy pediment. At the centre is an urn with drapery.

About the years 1725–30 houses with panelled walls and with cupboards built in to match the panelling were quite generally the style throughout the colonies.

Figure 184.
Cupboard, 1738.

The majority of these cupboards were fastened into side walls and were not, therefore, movable; but some, especially in the South, were fine pieces of workmanship with scroll tops and detached. The dining-room often had a corner cupboard or buffet, while the house throughout was supplied liberally with cupboards skilfully placed in various ways in the panelling of the walls. Corner cupboards appear in the inventories earlier than buffets, and are evidently not the same thing, as their values are much lower; two at Boston, one in 1720 and the other in 1725, are valued, respectively, at 7s. and 5s., two at Philadelphia as late as 1750 are valued at 10s. and 12s., while buffets are almost invariably valued at more than a pound, and often at two or three pounds and higher. Thus at Yorktown, Virginia, are mentioned in 1745, "1 beaufet £1 10s," 1753, "1 unfinished beaufet £5 10s," and one in 1763 valued at £7 10s. The buffets were usually corner pieces, but sometimes recessed into the side walls. They were furnished with a door or doors, the upper portion of which was usually of glass and the lower panelled to

Figure 185.
Side Cupboard, 1725–50.

match the room. The shelves of the upper cupboard are cut in graceful curves, and the top at the back is often finished with a shell.

Figure 185 shows a side cupboard built into the Robinson house, at Saunderstown, Rhode Island. Inside are two fluted pilasters supporting the shell arch on each of which is carved a rosette. At the centre of the shell is also carved a large rosette. The interior of the cupboard is painted a greenish blue and seems to be in its original condition. The edges of the shell are gilt and

CUPBOARDS AND SIDEBOARDS 181

the top of the arch and rosette are red. In the spandrels of the cupboard outside are cupids painted in gilt.

Figure 186 shows a side cupboard and a portion of the panelling of a room which is the property of Mr. George S. Palmer, of New London. The upper door is of glass and the lower one is panelled. The top of the cupboard is carved in the

Figure 186.
Side Cupboard with panelling, style of about 1750.

scallop shell pattern. The method of doing this was to place a number of planks, one on the other, to the desired height and then carve out the shell. The cupboard, as is usual, is of pine and has never been painted. It is said to have come from a house built in 1785. The style of panelling, however, is earlier than that date, and one would expect to find such panelling about 1750.

A corner cupboard with panelled doors top and bottom is shown in Figure 187. The cupboard part sets back from the outside several inches, and fluted pilasters support the top, which is carved in the scallop shell pattern, the edges of which and the pilasters do not show in this picture. The outer case of the cupboard is panelled, and large fluted pilasters run from the floor to the cornice. The cornice is in the familiar form already shown, a fillet, a large cyma recta, a fillet, and a small cyma reversa. This cupboard is the property of the writer.

Figure 188.
Corner Cupboard, 1725–50.

Figure 188 shows a corner cupboard similar to the foregoing, except that it has two glass doors covering the upper cupboard. The edge of the scallop shell shows very distinctly. The sides and front of the outer case are well panelled. This cupboard is the property of Mr. Albert H. Pitkin, of Hartford.

The corner cupboard shown in Figure 189 differs in some respects from those already described. The cupboard is flush with the outside edge of the case, instead of being recessed, as in the preceding cupboards, and is covered by a single large glass door. The closed cupboard below is very short and there is no panelling except on the doors. The inside is very beautiful; engaged fluted shafts standing on very high bases support the shell top, which is boldly carved, but its edges are left flat, probably because the frame of the door covers the edge when closed. At

Figure 189.
Corner Cupboard, 1725-50.

Figure 187.
Corner Cupboard, 1725-50.

the centre of the shell is carved an urn with foliations. This cupboard is the property of Mr. George M. Curtis, of Meriden, Connecticut.

Cupboards like those shown in the preceding figures were commonly called "Beaufatts," "beaufets," or "beaufats," and a village in the vicinity of Northampton, Massachusetts, has acquired the name "Beaufat" from the fact that one of these cupboards, which was considered quite remarkable, was built into a house there.

Figure 190.
Corner Cupboard, 1750–75.

Figure 191.
Corner Cupboard, 1750–75.

Figure 190 shows a corner cupboard, in Chippendale style, which is the property of the Metropolitan Museum of Art. The cornice, which is scrolled, consists of a fillet, a cyma recta, a fillet, a dentil moulding, a cyma recta, a fillet, an astragal, and a fillet. The sides are chamfered in the usual manner, and the cornice projects, giving the appearance of a pilaster. Across the top and at the sides are carved fret designs. The glass door is broken up into an oval and C scrolls in a very charming manner. Across the top of the base is a fret design suggestive of

CUPBOARDS AND SIDEBOARDS

the Gothic, and the chamfered edges are fluted. The moulding about the panel of the cupboard is carved in an acanthus-leaf design.

Figure 191 shows a corner cupboard which is the property of Mr. G. W. Walker. The scroll of the cornice is composed of a quarter-round, a fillet, and a

Figure 192.
Corner Cupboard, 1750–75.

cove, below which is a narrow reel and bead moulding which carries partly down the sides. The ends are chamfered. A simple panel moulding follows the lines of the door. There are two flush drawers in the lower part and below is a cupboard with two panelled doors. The feet are of the ogee bracket type.

Figure 192 shows a cupboard with a flat top, the property of Mr. Hollis French, of Boston. The sides are chamfered and there is a fluted pilaster, top and bottom, on each side. The glass in the doors is plain, except that the upper series is domed. The panelled door below is perfectly plain.

A well-made mahogany inlaid corner cupboard is shown in Figure 193 and is the property of Mr. Robert H. Schutz, of Hartford. The moulding at the top

Figure 193.
Inlaid Corner Cupboard, 1790–1800.

Figure 194.
Corner Cupboard, 1800–10.

is very simple, consisting of a fillet and a cyma reversa. The top is scrolled and the inside ends are finished with rosettes inlaid in a star pattern. At the centre, above the doors, is an inlaid fleur-de-lis in a medallion, and about the doors is a delicate waving line of inlay. On the chamfered sides is inlaid a guilloche. There are three drawers in the lower part and two cupboard doors. In the centre of the latter are inlaid medallions.

CUPBOARDS AND SIDEBOARDS 187

Figure 194 shows another corner cupboard, the property of Mr. H. W. Erving, of Hartford. The cornice consists of a fillet, a cyma recta, a fillet, and a cove. A carved rosette finishes the inner ends of the scrolls. On either side of the upper and lower sections are spiral turned columns with capitals suggestive of the Ionic order, and the same capital finishes the front of the centre acroterium

Figure 195.
Carved Corner Cupboard, about 1800.

Figure 195 shows a corner cupboard of pine very elaborately carved in Sheraton designs. The cornice is very similar to the mirrors of the period with pendent balls. Below this is a frieze of half-rosettes and rosettes, and below that is a raised lozenge-shaped border bordered by astragals. The stiles and chamfered ends are fluted, broken at the centre by rosettes, and across the base is a border composed of lozenges separated by two vertical pellets. The skirt is ornamented with three rosettes. The front is convex and the glass is made on the curve. There are two doors at top and bottom, the centre glass and panel being stationary. At the centre is a drawer. The three panels in the lower part are ornamented with a border of reeding set at right angles to the stiles and rails. This piece is the property of the writer.

SIDEBOARDS

Sideboards, as we know them, are comparatively recent inventions belonging to the latter half of the eighteenth century. The court and livery cupboards were extensively used in the dining-rooms, or "parlours," as they were generally called, their drawers and compartments making a convenient storing-place for

Figure 196.
Oak Sideboard Table, 1690–1700.

linen and china, and their flat tops were commonly utilised for exhibiting the china, silver, and pewter. When the oak cupboards were no longer in favour, the corner cupboards or buffets replaced them and served the same purposes. During this time, however, when cupboards were in general use, there is occasionally mention of side tables and sideboard tables. At New York, in 1689, mention is made of "a sideboard table 15s"; in the same year "1 side table with a drawer" cost 18s.; and in 1677 "four sideboard cloths" are mentioned; and there is record at Boston, in 1707, of "a sideboard table 6s."

No oak sideboard tables of American manufacture have been found, but there is no reason to doubt that such as there were followed the fashion of the oak pieces with which they were contemporary.

Figure 196 shows an English-made sideboard table in the writer's possession which has all the characteristics of the oak period, the drawers being similar to

CUPBOARDS AND SIDEBOARDS 189

those on the oak chests of drawers (Figure 49). There are three drawers, all on side runners, and the fronts of the drawers are panelled in geometrical shapes. On the stiles are applied split spindles, and between each two panels of a drawer are a pair of split spindles in the same design but smaller. The edge of the top is finished with a thumb-nail moulding, and under the edge is a moulding composed of a fillet, a cyma recta, a fillet, and a small cyma recta. Above the legs is a fillet and cyma reversa moulding. The ends are panelled with bevelled edges; the two front legs are turned and the rear ones are an extension of the stiles.

About 1740 marble tables began to be mentioned as part of the dining-room furniture: Boston, 1741, "in ye parlour 1 marble slab and table"; in 1748, "in

Figure 197.
Walnut Sideboard Table with marble top, 1720–40.

the parlour 1 marble table with mahogany frame"; in 1759, "in the dining room 1 marble table"; in 1767, "1 marble sideboard and frame"; and the Boston *Evening Post* for July, 1751, advertises "a variety of fashionable furniture including stone tables." Chippendale's designs, published in 1754, show no sideboards with drawers or cupboards, but sideboard tables having marble tops and elaborately carved mahogany frames. The fashion of making the sideboard tops of marble was certainly a practical one, far better adapted for serving purposes than the polished wood tops so sensitive to heat and moisture. As the English fashions were so closely followed here, the entries quoted above we believe to have reference to such marble-topped serving-tables as Chippendale made use of.

Figure 197 shows a marble-top sideboard table, the property of Mrs. Babbitt, of Wickford, Rhode Island. The legs are straight instead of bandy, with Dutch feet, which is a form found in Rhode Island. The upper ends of the legs are not square where they become the stiles but remain rounded, and the marble top is cut to cover them. A number of marble tables of this type are known, and occasionally tables are found with imitation marble tops.

Figure 198 shows a sideboard table made of walnut. The frame is plain, but the flaring skirt is cut in scrolls and carved in leaf designs. At the centre is a well-carved shell and at each end is a rosette. The knees are carved in an acanthus-leaf pattern, and about half-way down the legs is carved a series of acan-

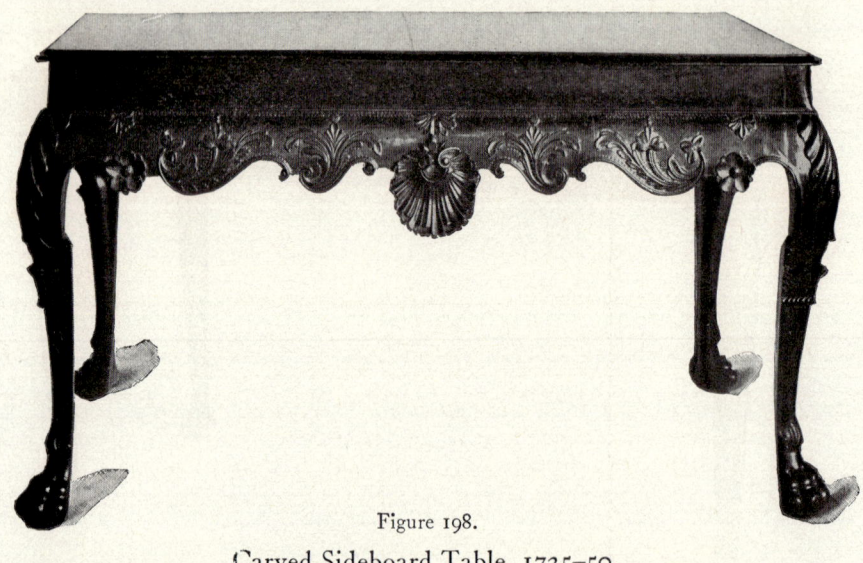

Figure 198.
Carved Sideboard Table, 1725–50.

thus leaves supported by a rope moulding. Just above the feet is again carved an acanthus leaf, and the feet are of the animal's claw and ball type.

An elaborately carved sideboard table with a marble top, the property of Mr. George S. Palmer, of New London, is shown in Figure 199. The frame is cut in a torus moulding and carved in a series of frets separated by foliated cartouches. Below is a small guilloche design and a reel and bead moulding. The skirt flares and is carved in a godrooned design with carved foliations at the centre. On the knees are carved acanthus leaves extending well down the legs, and the legs terminate in bird's claw and ball feet.

For the purpose of comparison, the Chippendale sideboard table (Figure 200) is shown. It is the property of Mr. Richard A. Canfield. The design is taken from Plate LXI of Chippendale's "Director," third edition, which bears the date of 1760. The only marked difference between the pieces is that this one has four

Figure 199.
Carved Sideboard Table with marble top, 1750–60.

Figure 200.
Chippendale Sideboard Table, about 1760.

legs in front, while the one shown by Chippendale has the corners splayed and the outer legs are set facing the sides. Above each leg is a lion's head, and between, on the frame, are carved Vitruvian scrolls. At the centre of the frame is a panel upon which swags of flowers are carved in relief. The legs are typically Chippendale. At the upper end is a scroll with acanthus leaves carved on what would be the knee, and acanthus leaves are likewise carved at the base extending upward. The legs terminate in plain square blocks. Between each of the pairs of front legs is a swag of beautifully carved leaves and flowers.

Figure 201.
Sideboard Table, 1760–70.

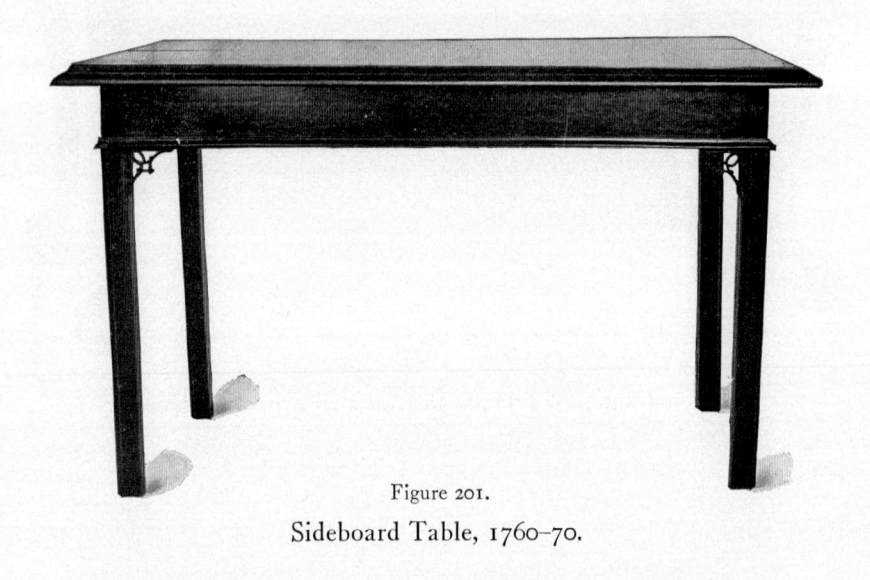

Figure 201 shows a sideboard table, the property of Professor Barrett Wendell. It stands high from the ground on straight legs whose surfaces are cut in double ogee mouldings. The lower edge is finished with a moulding and the corners with brackets.

Figure 202 shows a sideboard table of a little later date. It has a long swell on the front and at the back is a serpentine shelf. In the centre of the skirt and the back are carved, in cameo carving, urns and festoons, and at the ends, on the back, and above the legs are carved rosettes. A thumb-nail moulding finishes the edges. The piece stands on Marlborough legs which are fluted. This piece is the property of the Tiffany Studios.

The first style of sideboard which is commonly found in this country is the slender-legged inlaid mahogany one commonly credited to Chippendale. It is, however, not in any sense Chippendale either in design or workmanship. The statement is repeatedly met with, and usually supported by traditions as to date of importation or purchase, that sideboards of this kind date before 1750. This,

CUPBOARDS AND SIDEBOARDS

of course, is impossible, as there is no trace of any furniture made with a straight, tapering leg, and decorated with inlay, as these sideboards invariably were, as early as 1750. The fact is that this fashion originated with an English designer named Thomas Shearer, a member of the London Society of Cabinet-makers, whose book of prices was published in 1788. The designs therein shown for serpentine inlaid sideboards are signed by Shearer. In Hepplewhite's own book of designs, published a little later, he adopts this same fashion in his sideboards, and as his reputation seems to have much outlasted Shearer's, they generally bear his name.

Figure 202.
Sideboard Table, 1780–90.

The book of prices gives this interesting list of woods which were principally employed by these makers for marquetry and inlay: "satin wood, either solid or veneered, manilla, safisco, havannah, king, tulip, rose, purple, snake, alexandria, panella, yew and maple," the principal wood being, of course, always mahogany. Great numbers of sideboards made after these designs are still to be seen in this country, which were undoubtedly made here, judging from the fact that the veneering is on pine, and the insides of the drawers and back are of the same wood. The outlines of the fronts and sides are varied in many ways, as is also the arrangement of drawers and cupboards. The inlay also is sometimes but an outline of holly and satin-wood around the top, drawer fronts, and legs, and sometimes quite elaborate marquetry designs in many-coloured woods are used. The handles are almost invariably the brass ones with oval plates.

A Shearer or Hepplewhite sideboard of very graceful design, belonging to Mrs. L. A. Lockwood, is shown in Figure 203. The front is serpentine in shape, an extra curve being added below its two centre drawers; the drawer fronts and top are veneered in very finely grained mahogany on whitewood. This is usually the case, a sideboard of this kind being seldom met with where the drawer fronts are solid. The fan inlay in the corners of drawers and cupboard doors, as well as the wreath design on the legs, is characteristic. At least one drawer is usually arranged in sections to hold bottles.

Figure 204, the effect of which is very much marred by the cheap modern handles, is also a fine example of Hepplewhite sideboard, belonging to Mr. Ethridge,

Figure 203.
Hepplewhite Sideboard, 1790–1800.

of Salem, Massachusetts. Each drawer has a panel in light mahogany bordered with fine lines of inlay in white holly and ebony; the edge of the drawer outside of the panel is in dark mahogany. The small oval panels set into the stiles above the legs are in satin-wood. The narrow drawers each side of the centre cupboards are in this piece the bottle drawers. The knife or spoon boxes shown on the top of this sideboard were very generally made to accompany them, and are usually fine pieces of cabinet work beautifully inlaid; the inside is arranged with a wooden section set on a slant pierced in proper shapes for the holding of knives and spoons, and often each little hole is surrounded with a fine band of inlay. The handles and escutcheons are sometimes silver.

Figure 205 shows a sideboard with but four legs, although it is six feet two inches long. The ends are curved and the centre is straight and recessed. There is an inlay border about the drawers and doors. At the two ends are cupboards

Figure 204.
Hepplewhite Sideboard, 1790–1800.

Figure 205.
Hepplewhite Sideboard, 1790–1800.

Figure 206.
Hepplewhite Sideboard, 1799.

Figure 207.
Hepplewhite Sideboard, 1790–1800.

CUPBOARDS AND SIDEBOARDS 197

and at the centre is a drawer with a cupboard below. This piece is the property of Mr. Frederic T. Bontecou, of Orange, New Jersey.

Figure 206 shows a sideboard with six legs, the property of the Misses Andrews. It was purchased in 1799. The corners are curved and the straight centre projects. A narrow border of inlay is about the drawers, and at the ends are bottle drawers, and two long drawers are at the centre. The oval handles have stamped upon them a basket with a pineapple.

Figure 208.
Hepplewhite Corner Sideboard, 1790–1800.

Figure 207 shows a very beautiful sideboard with eight legs; the outer ends are concave, then a short, straight section, and the centre is serpentine. On the left end is a drawer and on the right a cupboard. In the short, straight section are bottle drawers, and a recessed cupboard is below the centre drawer. The piece is quite elaborately inlaid. In addition to the oval lines on the drawers and doors, on the stiles are inlaid shells and oval panels of satin-wood, and on the legs are pendent flowers. This piece is the property of Mr. R. T. Smith, of Hartford.

Figure 208 shows a corner sideboard in the Bulkeley Collection. The front is curved, and the piece stands on four legs in front and a single leg at the back, in the corner. About the drawers and doors are bands of inlay.

Sideboards of which those above shown are types remained in favour for a considerable period. They probably were known and used here at about the same date as in England, and if we deduct ten years from the date of the published design, on a reasonable supposition that they may have been already executed before the designs were published, 1778 would be as early a date as we should obtain for the introduction of this style. That they were made as late as 1804 is certain, for the writer has seen a bill for a sideboard very similar to Figure 206 dated in that year.

These sideboards average about six feet in length and twenty-four inches in width, though they were made in many shapes and sizes, sometimes in miniature,

Figure 209.
Sheraton Sideboard, 1790–1800.

and occasionally one is seen which is made to fit the corner of a room, the top being triangular.

In 1791 Thomas Sheraton, of London, published a book containing a number of designs for sideboards. He professes great dislike for Hepplewhite's work, but nevertheless his designs show the influence of that maker. He made great use of the slender fluted leg in place of the square tapering one, and used inlay both in wood and metal. Some of his extravagant pieces are elaborately painted and trimmed with brass.

The majority of sideboards in this country which are modelled after his designs are comparatively plain, most of them having no inlay.

Figure 209 shows a Sheraton sideboard which very closely resembles the Hepplewhite ones above described. The front is curved, and on the front of the

CUPBOARDS AND SIDEBOARDS

drawers are bevelled panels of satin-wood. Oval panels of the same wood are on the bottle drawers. At either end and at the centre are cupboards. The handles are lions' heads holding rings. The legs, six in number, are turned and reeded in

Figure 210.
Sheraton Sideboard, 1795–1810.

Figure 211.
Sheraton Sideboard, 1790–1800.

the manner popular in Sheraton's work. The piece is the property of Mr. Samuel Pray, of Boston.

Figure 210 shows a Sheraton sideboard, the property of Mr. Dwight Blaney, of Boston. There are three drawers across the top, below which are bottle drawers at either end of the cupboard. The drawer fronts are of bird's-eye maple with mahogany border, and the cupboard doors are inlaid with strips of the woods alternating, and on either side of the doors is a fine network. The turned legs, which are reeded, extend to the top, which is cut to cover them.

Figure 211 shows a large sideboard, the property of Mr. Marsden J. Perry, of Providence. At either end are large cupboards extending close to the floor. The centre section is raised higher from the floor and the drawers have a swelled

Figure 212.
Sheraton Sideboard, about 1800.

front, while the cupboard below is recessed. A bottle drawer is at either end of the centre. An oval band of inlay is about the drawers and door, and about the stiles are inlay panels and fleur-de-lis. The piece stands on stub feet. The top is a large slab of marble.

Figure 213.
Knife and Spoon Box, 1790–1800.

A sideboard which belongs to Mr. Meggat is shown in Figure 212. The knife-boxes are attached to the top and furnished with sliding scroll covers. Two small drawers pull out from the ends of these, as shown in the illustration. Many sideboards similar to this in general style are found which have, instead of the attached knife-boxes, the end sections raised about four inches above the centre, probably designed to hold knife-boxes in urn shape, one of which is shown in Figure 213.

CUPBOARDS AND SIDEBOARDS

The top of these urn-shaped boxes is not on a hinge, but is supported by a rod of wood running through the centre, which, when the top is raised sufficiently, releases a spring, thus holding the top in that position. This box belongs to Mr. Meggat. The fashion of making the knife-boxes in urn shape is not original with

Figure 214.
Sheraton Sideboard with china closet, about 1800

Sheraton, as it had been extensively used by other English cabinet-makers before this time. They are very fine specimens of cabinet work, the fitting of the graduated sections requiring a skilful workman.

Figure 214 shows a Sheraton sideboard with a china closet above, the property of Mr. Francis H. Bigelow, of Cambridge, Massachusetts. The cornice is

Figure 215.
Sheraton Sideboard with china closet and desk drawers, about 1800.

CUPBOARDS AND SIDEBOARDS

composed of a fillet, a cyma recta, a broad and narrow fillet, a cove, an astragal, and a fillet, and on the top are five urns. The glass in the doors is shaped in curves. In the cupboard part are two long cupboards, and at the centre is a desk drawer and a cupboard hidden by a tambour slide. The feet are of the stub type with pendent flowers inlaid. On the stiles are inlaid parallel lines and an inlay edge is on the doors and drawers. On the cupboard drawers are also inlaid panels. The handles are brass rosettes.

Figure 215 shows another Sheraton sideboard with china closet, the property of Mr. R. H. Maynard, of Boston. The cornice consists of a fillet, a cyma

Figure 216.
Mixing-Table, 1790–1800.

recta, a fillet, an astragal, and a fillet, below which is a band of inlay. On the top are seven urns and at the centre is an inlaid urn. The doors are unusual. Each has an upper painted panel, those on the outside representing ladies gardening and the inner one representing flowers and flower pots. On each of the inner doors below the painted panel is an oval mirror with black-and-gilt border. In the cupboard is a desk drawer and on either side is a drawer and a cupboard. The lower section, which in the preceding figure is a cupboard covered with a tambour slide, is open to allow for the knees of the person sitting at the desk. The piece stands on turned feet.

Figure 216 shows a mixing-table, the property of Mr. George S. Palmer, of New London. The table is a marble slab, and a tambour cover closes over it.

On either side are bottle drawers. The piece is inlaid with panels of satin-wood, and the same wood is inlaid on the legs, which are of the slender tapering type.

A sideboard very much like one of the designs in Sheraton's book, except that it is much simplified, is shown in Figure 217. The drawers are decorated with a narrow inlay strip, and the handles are the rosette and ring which in many styles and sizes were much used by Sheraton on furniture of all kinds.

The distinguishing characteristic of Sheraton sideboards in this country is the slender reeded leg. The sideboards here shown represent fairly well the general character of American Sheraton, though, of course, endless variations in shape, size, and arrangement are to be found. The wood is generally mahogany.

Figure 217.
Sheraton Sideboard, about 1800.

With the decline in favour of early Sheraton designs, about the year 1800, the character of construction for furniture in general was radically changed. The graceful effects obtained by the use of the slender, square, and reeded legs were entirely lost by the substitution of the massive round or rope-carved pillars, extending nearly to the floor, and finished with the bear or lion's claw foot. This massive design was adopted from the French Empire style, but the American makers omitted the elaborate trimmings in brass and ormolu and depended for effect upon the grain of the wood and the heavy carving. In the vocabulary of the dealer of to-day the term colonial is applied to this plain and massive style—a misapplied name, for the fashion was not known until some time after the American colonies had become States. The sideboards in Empire style are almost always furnished with three drawers beneath the top, the fronts of which are sometimes made on a curve; the handles are rosette and ring, lion head and ring, and the brass or glass rosette. The doors of the cupboards which filled the lower

CUPBOARDS AND SIDEBOARDS

portion are nearly always panelled, often in oval or Gothic form, as is also the board which finishes the back of the top. Veneering is used extensively to obtain elaborate grain effects, and the mahogany used is very fine. Trimmings in brass are occasionally employed, but the majority make use of panelling and carving for decorative purposes.

Figure 218 shows an Empire sideboard of conventional design having the rope-carved column extending to the floor, forming the feet. The back-board

Figure 218.
Empire Sideboard, 1810–20.

makes use of a style of broken arch which was quite often used with the Empire designs, although it is a survival of a much earlier style.

Figure 219 illustrates very well the circular pillars and bear-claw feet which are most characteristic of American Empire furniture in general. Sideboards constructed after the fashion of this one are commonly without the raised drawers at the end and are often furnished with a serving-board which pulls out from beneath the top at the ends. The centre cupboard portion is sometimes omitted, leaving the section between the two inside columns open to accommodate a cellaret.

206   COLONIAL FURNITURE

Figure 220 shows a sideboard in late Empire style, which is a type of many which were made in the South, especially in Virginia and Maryland. The rear board is raised sufficiently to accommodate a large mirror, and at either side are carved grapes and leaves. The raised panels on the fronts of the end cupboards will be seen to terminate in claw feet, which rest on a little platform extending across the front. The feet proper are plain balls, which often replace the claw in the last surviving forms of Empire sideboards. Both the last two sideboards belong to Mr. Meggat.

Figure 219.
Empire Sideboard, 1810–20.

Figure 221 shows a sideboard with the knife-boxes at either end which is the property of the Pennsylvania Museum at Philadelphia. At the back is a panel on which is carved a lion and foliated scrolls, and below, a guilloche pattern. The ornamentation on the rest of the piece is of beautifully inlaid brass. The doors of the cupboards at the ends are heavily panelled, finished with columns at either end. The knife-boxes are made similar to the cupboards with the panelled fronts and columns. They stand on ball feet as does the cupboard.

Figure 222 shows a late sideboard. The front is straight, except at the centre, which is swelled. There are three cupboards below and three drawers above. At the corners are columns with carved acanthus-leaf capitals, and the piece stands on melon feet with coarse acanthus-leaf carving.

Figure 220.
Empire Sideboard, 1810–20.

Figure 221.
Empire Sideboard inlaid with brass, 1810–20.

Figure 222.
Empire Sideboard, about 1820.

Figure 223.
Empire Sideboard, about 1830.

CUPBOARDS AND SIDEBOARDS

About 1820-30 great numbers of sideboards after the fashion of Figure 223 were made in New England, the drawers and cupboard being ornamented with veneered panels of bird's-eye maple; the front of the wide drawer at the top was sometimes arranged with a spring and quadrant and the inside finished with drawers and pigeon-holes for use as a desk.

Empire furniture, which preserved a semblance of the original French designs from which it was taken, continued to be made as late as 1850, when monstrosities following somewhat its outline, but utterly without merit or beauty, paved the way for the machine-made furniture.

V
DESKS AND SCRUTOIRES

DESKS, in one form or another, have been known from the eighth century. In his "Natural History," Bacon makes the following remark: "Some trees are best for planchers, as deal; some for tables, cupboards and desks, as walnut"; showing that at the beginning of the seventeenth century desks were apparently in common use in England.

The word desk, in the early inventories in England and this country, had a different meaning from that now given to it. It meant a box which held the writing materials, the lid of which was sometimes used as a smooth surface upon which to write. These early desks were inventoried at very low figures, anywhere from 1s. to £1. The highest prices we have found are: At Salem, in 1647, "His deske £1"; one at 30s. at New York, in 1691; a walnut desk at Philadelphia, in 1705, 30s.; and at the same place, in 1706, "a walnut tree deske inlaid £6," which is so far above the highest valuations elsewhere found that if it were not for the early date, and the fact that a distinction was made all through these years between desks and scrutoires, we should believe it to have been a scrutoire and not a desk-box.

Most of the desk-boxes were undoubtedly perfectly plain deal, maple, oak, or walnut boxes, and it is safe to assume that they have been lost because not considered worthy of care. Consequently, nearly all that are now to be found are carved more or less, and some so beautifully that it is difficult to reconcile the low inventory valuation with the pieces.

These boxes or desks were apparently used for two purposes: one as a place in which to keep books, more especially the Bible, and the other for valuable papers and writing materials.

In the early days, when the Bible was a treasure possessed by but few, it was kept under lock and key in a box of this kind, often beautifully carved, to be taken out and read at a gathering of the neighbours. By some these boxes are called "Bible-boxes" to this day. Thus at Philadelphia, in 1726, we find "Escritore, small table, deske Holy Bible £5 10s," the desk very likely being on the table and the Bible either in or on the desk. Again, in the same place, the same year, "a book desk 26s."

DESKS AND SCRUTOIRES

Some of these boxes were carved on the front, sides, and top; sometimes the top was flat and sometimes slanted. We are inclined to believe that the boxes with carved or steeply slanted tops were, as a rule, Bible-boxes, the slanting top being of a convenient slope to hold the book while it was being read, while the flat-top or slightly slanted ones, uncarved on top, were for desks.

The boxes vary in size from seventeen to thirty inches in length, and the inside, especially in those intended for desks, often contained the small till or compartment so frequently found in the chests, which was doubtless intended to hold the writing materials, and sometimes they contained pigeon-holes and sometimes a shelf running the long way of the box. This style of box is sometimes spoken of in the inventories as a "paper-box," as recorded at New York in 1691, "a small black walnutt paper box," and in 1702, "In the writing closett 1 old desk for papers."

The first mention in the inventories of anything to do with writing is at Plymouth in 1633, which is the earliest year for which inventories are given in this country: "A writing table of glass 4d." This word here probably means tablet, and it was, we believe,

Figure 224.
Bible-Box, 1649.

a plate of glass, perhaps framed, which was laid on the lap or table to obtain a perfectly smooth surface, in much the same way as is sometimes done to-day; and in Philadelphia, in 1687, appears "A writing slab & frame 8d," clearly indicating such a piece.

Probably the first mention of a desk in this country is that at Plymouth, in 1644, "1 little desk 1s," which modest price would lead us to suppose it was but a pine box. Again, at Boston, in 1676, "2 cedar desks 1£"; and in New York, in 1689, "one desk 16s"; and in 1691, "one desk or box 30s."

These pieces are not constructed like the chests with stiles and rails, but the sides are composed of slabs of wood, occasionally dovetailed at the corners, but generally simply nailed together. The bottom is also nailed and the top is usually of pine and made like chest tops with the thumb-nail moulding and with the staple hinges.

Figure 224 is a good example of a Bible-box in the possession of the Connecticut Historical Society. It is made of English oak throughout and is, therefore, probably of English make. It bears the inscription "M. S. 1649" on its front panel. The carving is of a very early pattern, and the circles on the sides and top suggest a design popular in Holland early in the century, while that on the front suggests an English design first appearing in James I's reign.

Figure 225 shows a desk-box, the property of Mr. H. W. Erving, of Hartford. The lid is slanted and fastens to a straight strip forming a part of the top. On the ends are carved flowers and leaves suggestive of the outer panels of the Connecticut chest (Figure 18), and a rosette, and the front design is two groups of two branches of flowers and leaves springing from a single stem. Between the two groups are rosettes.

A well-made small desk-box is shown in Figure 226. The front and sides are decorated with foliated scrolls, and at the centre of the front is an entwined cruci-

Figure 225.
Desk-Box, 1650–75.

Figure 226.
Desk-Box, 1650–75.

Figure 227.
Desk-Box, 1650–75.

form scroll. The edges are notched as is usual. This box is the property of Mr. William J. Hickmott, of Hartford.

Figure 227 shows a box from the Bolles Collection. The front and sides are carved in a guilloche pattern in series of three circles with rosettes in the centre and foliations about them. There is a border of scratch carving above and below. The pattern quite closely resembles that found on the drawer fronts of the chest (Figure 17).

Two interesting boxes in the Bolles Collection are shown in Figure 228. They are carved in the design known as Friesland, which consists of geometrical

Figure 234.
Desk-Box on frame, about 1675.

Figure 235.
Desk-Box on frame, 1680–1700.

of the same bosses; on the stiles are split spindles. The legs are turned as are also the stretchers.

Figure 236 shows another desk-box on frame in the Erving Collection. The pattern is the one most commonly found; on the desk part are two panels with the upper corners chamfered and on the panels are painted sprays of leaves. The drawer is divided into two panels. The legs and stretchers are knob-turned.

Figure 236.
Desk-Box on frame, about 1700.

Figure 237 shows a still different variety of a desk-box on frame in which the nature of its origin is more apparent. It consists of two sections. The upper one contains a box with a drawer; the lower section contains a drawer on a frame. The upper section sets into the lower one and is held in place by a heavy moulding in the same way as were the chests of drawers on frames. The surfaces are ornamented with painted foliations and a fleur-de-lis above and a foliated scroll below. The legs are turned and terminate in ball feet and the stretchers are scalloped. This piece is in the Bolles Collection and is a rare form.

But few of these desk-boxes on frames have survived, and they were probably rarer than any other form of oak furniture. There has been considerable conjec-

DESKS AND SCRUTOIRES

ture as to what these pieces were intended for. It has been thought by some that they were small chests. This, however, we think erroneous. It was undoubtedly the fashion to place the boxes on low tables, and it was but a step to make the table and box in one piece. That this was probably so is evidenced by the desk shown in Figures 238 and 239, which is really a desk-box set on a frame.

Throughout the inventories, whenever the words "on frame" are used they refer to a piece raised from the floor as distinguished from those resting on feet or

Figure 237.
Desk-Box on frame, about 1700.

directly on the floor. This, as is shown in the chapter on "Chests of Drawers," was the way the change from low chests of drawers to those commonly called highboys was first designated in the inventories, and as it was during this very time that this distinction was first noted with respect to chests of drawers, we conclude that the same distinction was intended wherever this expression is used. Furthermore, in none of the inventories does any expression appear but this which could possibly refer to such pieces, nor are any other pieces extant to which the expression desk and frame could apply.

From about the year 1660, or possibly a little earlier, a new style of furniture for writing purposes seems to have come into use called "scrutore," or "scriptoire," as some of the inventories call them. It may be assumed that the influence of Charles I and Charles II, with their French ideas and fancies, had something to do with the change.

One is instantly impressed, on reading the early inventories, with the fact that up to the end of the first quarter of the eighteenth century scrutoires are inventoried at much higher figures than desks, it being very seldom that they are placed at a lower valuation than £1, while the average is easily from £6 to £7. A good illustration of the above appears in a Boston inventory of 1709: "a desk 3s," "1 scriptore £6." Among the various inventories we find the following: At Boston, 1669, "scritoire and desk £10"; in 1683, "a scriptore £2," "a small scriptore 10s"; in 1704, "a black walnut scrutoire"; in 1717, "a scriptore £8"; and in 1723 one for £12; at Salem, in 1684, "a large scriptoire £5"; at New York, in 1691, "a scrutore without a lock 20s"; and in 1704, "2 schrutoors £13," the last a spelling which none but a Dutchman could have executed; at Philadelphia, in 1687, "1 screwtor £1"; in 1705, "a scrutor & large Bible £2 5s"; and in 1720, "1 black pine screwtor £4."

There are three types of early scrutoires found in this country, those having a falling front on which to write, and those having a slant top and ball feet, and those having a slant top resting on turned legs.

Figure 238 shows an example of the first type in the Bolles Collection. It is made in two carcasses; the lower one contains three drawers with the early single-arch moulding on the frame about them. About the bottom is a heavy moulding, and the piece stands on ball feet. The upper carcass consists of a solid front concealing drawers and pigeon-holes. The cornice is heavy and consists of a quarter-round, a fillet, a cyma recta, a wide fillet, a quarter-round, a torus or cushion frieze which contains a shallow drawer, an astragal, a fillet, and a cove. The wood is walnut veneered and the handles are of the early drop variety. This piece has many of the characteristics of the six-legged variety of high chests of drawers which belongs to the same period.

Very few scrutoires of this type have been found in this country, but they were fairly common in Holland and England. In an inventory of a store-keeper in New York in 1692 appears "4 Pr. Scrutore Chains with two dozen bolts." These chains must have been used to hold the front which lets down to write upon; and as all slant-top desks are supported with two frames which pull out to hold the front, such chains were probably intended for the style of scrutoire above shown.

The next type of scrutoire, and the one most commonly found of the early varieties, is shown in Figure 239. The characteristics of this type are the arrangement of the interior, with the pigeon-holes and drawers at each end advanced;

Figure 238.
Scrutoire, fall front, about 1700.

Figure 240.
Ball-Foot Scrutoire, about 1700–10.

Figure 239.
Ball-Foot Scrutoire, 1700.

DESKS AND SCRUTOIRES

the slide opening into the well which lies above the two drawers; the four drawers, two long ones and two side by side; the mouldings about the bottom, and the ball feet. The scrutoire here shown has all these characteristics. The moulding about the drawers is of the single-arch type and the handles are in the early drop form. These scrutoires are found made of maple, walnut, and of whitewood, and sometimes with veneered panels of bird's-eye maple or walnut on the face of the slant top and drawers.

Figure 240 shows another scrutoire of the same type which is in the Bolles Collection. The outer wall of the well above referred to can be seen just above the two drawers. This piece has all of the characteristics above mentioned and differs from the preceding only in that it has the double-arch instead of the single-arch moulding about the drawers, and also a variation in the ball feet, those shown in this piece being in the usual form with the flaring shoe below the ball. The surfaces of the drawers and lid are beautifully veneered with burl walnut with a herring-bone border in the manner found on some of the high chests of drawers.

Figure 241 shows the earliest form of scrutoire with a top. The lower part has all the characteristics above mentioned as belonging to this type. The upper

Figure 241.
Ball-Foot Scrutoire with cabinet top, 1700–10.

section is composed of two doors with rounded tops. In each is inserted a bevelled panel, the upper outline composed of a half-round and a cyma reversa on each side, a characteristic design of the period and identically like the mirror shown in Figure 315. The cornice is composed of two arches on the front and one at each side, and the mouldings are all cut on the circle and are as follows: a quarter-round, a fillet, a cyma recta, a fillet, and a cove, which is the same moulding as that shown on the high-boy (Figure 65). About the drawers and the doors are double-arch mouldings. The brasses are engraved and the bails are held with wires. Behind the doors are pigeon-holes, each tier having a different style of fret across the top. There are two slides below the doors to hold candle-sticks. These scrutoires are also found with flat tops and with the panels in the upper section planted instead of sunken. There is one of this description in the Philadelphia Library, which is said to have belonged to William Penn. This piece was found in Maine and is the property of the writer.

A crude scrutoire of the same period is shown in Figure 242 and is in the Bolles Collection. A number of such pieces have been found in New England and

Figure 242.
Ball-Foot Scrutoire, 1700–10.

they closely resemble the chest shown in Figure 40. It will be seen that there are but three drawers, although with the use of handles and escutcheons the impression is conveyed of four drawers. The slant top is hinged at the back instead of the front and within is practically a desk-box. One is supposed to write on the slant lid. Single-arch mouldings are about the drawers and the handles are of the early drop variety. The piece stands on four large ball feet.

The third type of early scrutoire is shown in Figure 243. This type stands on four turned and underbraced legs and is found in two styles, those where the frame is separate from the desk part, as in this case, and those in which the desk

DESKS AND SCRUTOIRES

and frame are of one piece. The frame part of this scrutoire is like the turned tables of the period, with a single long drawer. The desk part sets into the moulding of the frame and is in the usual slant-front type, the lid being supported by pulls. The inside is plain with three pigeon-holes and three drawers. This piece is in the Bolles Collection.

Figure 244 shows the second style of these scrutoires, where the desk and frame are in one piece. It will be seen that the form of construction is quite different.

Figure 243.
Slant-Top Scrutoire on frame, 1700–25.

The legs are extended to form the frame of the desk part, and this necessitates the cutting out of a quarter section of the front legs where the ends extend into the desk, and the sides are mortised and tenoned into the stiles. There is one overlap drawer below the desk. This piece is made of walnut and the handles are the original. Within are pigeon-holes and drawers cut in double ogee curves. This piece is the property of the writer. Such pieces as these would seem to be referred to in a Salem inventory of 1684, "One scritoire and frame £1. 10s."

It was a natural development when the cabriole-legged tables came into favour that this type of desk should be made in that way. The earliest one that has come under the writer's observation is the child's desk shown in Figure 245. This piece is but three feet high, made of walnut, with the early black and white check inlay on each of the three drawers and on the lid. In the centre of the lid is inlaid a star in the early form, which is the same as that found on the high chest of drawers shown in Figure 94. The frame part has no drawers and stands on four cabriole legs terminating in angular Dutch feet with groovings. The handles are in the willow pattern. This piece is the property of Miss Jane E. Lockwood.

Figure 244.
Slant-Top Scrutoire on frame, 1700–25.

One of the plainer varieties of this style is shown in Figure 246. It has but a single drawer, and the hip pieces, which should form a continuous curve from the leg to the lower edge of the scrutoire, are missing, marring the otherwise somewhat graceful effect, and the lower lines, being perfectly straight, make the piece seem even more severe. The scrutoire does not seem to have any slides to support the flap lid when let down, but has a slide, such as is used in other pieces for a candle-stand, directly in the centre above the drawer, which may have been intended to hold the top on a downward slant, as we can see no reason for a candle-slide in such a place. The inside is perfectly plain, in keeping with the exterior, and the brass hinges are, of course, new, having been placed on the outside when those on the inside were broken. The brasses are not original.

Figure 245.
Cabriole-Legged Scrutoire, about 1725.

Figure 246.
Cabriole-Legged Scrutoire, 1725–40.

225

Figure 247 shows a cabriole-legged scrutoire, the lower part of which is a lowboy upon which is placed a slant-top desk with one long drawer. The inside is plain, with drawers and pigeon-holes. The legs terminate in the usual Dutch feet. This piece is the property of the writer.

One of the most beautiful scrutoires of this type is shown in Figure 248. It has three drawers in the low-boy part, with the rising sun carved in the centre drawer, and the lower line is practically the same as appeared in the cupboard

Figure 248.
Cabriole-Legged Scrutoire, 1740–50.

high-boy shown in Figure 97, but because of the elaborate interior we would date it somewhat later—between 1740 and 1750. The legs are in good proportion, with well-defined shoes at the bottom, and there is a little column finishing each corner. In the lower part of the scrutoire proper are two small square drawers for pens, etc., which on drawing out hold the slant top for writing purposes. The interior contains eighteen drawers set into a frame made of a series of graceful curves, while the upper centre drawer has the carving to correspond with the lower part.

This piece is in almost faultless proportions, and has a grace and charm which it would be difficult to improve. It belonged to the late Mr. Walter Hosmer.

Figure 249 shows a variation of this type which was found in Flatbush, Long Island, and clearly indicates that it was made by a Dutch cabinet-maker.

Figure 249.
Slant-Top Scrutoire with Dutch turned legs, 1725-40.

Figure 247.
Cabriole-Legged Scrutoire, 1725-40.

Figure 250.
Cabriole-Legged Scrutoire with cabinet top, 1725-40.

DESKS AND SCRUTOIRES

There is no drawer in the table part and the skirt is cut in a serrated edge. The legs are turned, ending in flat balls, and resemble inverted tenpins. The desk section has one drawer below the lid, and the interior is arranged exactly like that in the ball-foot scrutoires (Figure 239), with the slide opening into the top drawer instead of into a well. The fronts of the little drawers on the inside are cut in double ogee curves. This piece is the property of the writer.

An unusual scrutoire of this type with a cabinet top is shown in Figure 250, the property of Mr. H. W. Erving. The table section has three drawers side by side and the centre one is carved in the rising-sun pattern. The legs are cabriole, terminating in large Dutch feet. The desk part is made in one piece with a cabinet top, which is an unusual form of construction. The natural way would seem to have been to make the piece in three parts, consisting of the base, the desk, and the cabinet top. Below the lid are two drawers. There are two doors in the cabinet part with fret designs planted on the panel. The cornice is in scroll form with foliated rosettes, and the space beneath the scrolls is filled in with a fret of C scrolls. At each end and at the centre are turned pointed finials, the centre one resting on a circular fluted acroterium. The cornice is composed of the following mouldings: a fillet, a cyma recta, a narrow fillet, a wide fillet, a narrow fillet, a cove, an astragal, and a fillet. This piece is of cherry and is supposed to have been made at Windsor, Connecticut.

Figure 251.
Cabriole-Legged Scrutoire, 1725-40.

Scrutoires of this type with cabinet tops are very rare in this country, and this one is probably the best example that has been found.

Another unusual scrutoire of the same type is shown in Figure 251, the property of Miss C. M. Traver, of New York. The table part is low with short cabriole legs and Dutch feet. In this part are two square drawers with a full-sun pattern carved on the surfaces, and a narrow drawer. In the desk part are three long drawers and three small ones side by side, the centre one having carved upon it the same full-sun pattern. The interior is plain, with a long drawer and four small ones below and no pigeon-holes. Above the desk part is imposed another section, consisting of two drawers, upon which is carved the rising-sun pattern placed vertically, and above are two drawers side by side. This piece is so tall that it must have been intended to be used by a person standing, and was probably made for some special purpose. The wood is maple.

Figure 252.
Dressing-Table with desk drawer, 1760–75.

Still another form of the so-called low-boy scrutoire is shown in Figure 252. When closed it appears to be a regular dressing-table of the Philadelphia type (Figure 110), but the front of the top drawer falls, disclosing a desk. The top is finished with a cove, a fillet, and a quarter-round, and below is a deep cornice composed of a fillet and a large cove. The corners have square recessed edges and quarter-reeded columns are inserted. On the base of the frame and extending onto the knees are carved flowers and leaves and on the knees are carved two flowers with a long spray of acanthus leaves extending well down the legs. The feet are of the bird's claw and ball type. The skirt is beautifully cut and carved in C scrolls with leaves, with a shell at the centre. On the centre lower drawer is carved a shell and streamer so familiar on the Philadelphia pieces. This piece, so far as the writer knows, is unique, and is in the Pendleton Collection, owned by the Rhode Island School of Design.

After the first twenty years of the eighteenth century the marked distinction before noted in the prices given for desks and scrutoires disappears, and thereafter the inventories almost indiscriminately use the terms to denote the same kind of piece at the same price. Thus, at Salem, in 1734, we find "1 desk £5, 10s."; the high valuation showing that the old distinction was no longer made. And, later still, the word scrutoire seems to disappear entirely, and writing pieces of every sort are called desks.

It was also about this time that the word bureau first came into use. The word is of French origin. Some assert that it comes from a word denoting a writing piece of any kind, while others claim that the name was derived from the word *burrel*, or *bureau*, a coarse russet cloth of mediæval times with which such pieces were covered. This latter derivation is probably the correct one, the first being a secondary meaning, for in Cotgrave's French and English dictionary, published in 1611, the following appears: "Bureau, a thick and course cloth of a browne russett or dark mingles colour; also the table thats within a Court of audit or of audience (belike, because tis usually covered with a carpet of that cloth)."

The word is used by Swift in its modern spelling with its early meaning in the following much-quoted stanza:

> "For not a desk with silver nails
> Nor bureau of expense
> Nor standish well Japann'd avails
> To writing of good sense."

This word is compounded in two ways in the inventories, bureau-desk and bureau-table or -chamber-table. Dr. Lyon, in his splendid work on Colonial Furniture, thinks the former referred to a scrutoire, while the latter referred to a low chest of drawers, or bureau in the modern sense, and cites such entries as: at Boston, in 1721, "a burow desk £3 10s"; in 1725, "1 buroe £5"; in 1739, "1 buro table"; and in 1749, "In the front chamber 1 buro table with drawers £15"—all of these valuations, of course, being in inflated currency.

This distinction hardly seems to us probable, because a low chest of drawers could have been properly described by calling it by that name, as had been the custom in the inventories of the oak period, and as was still occasionally done in this; and, furthermore, the word table could hardly be applied to such a piece.

It is undoubtedly true that when the expression first appeared it referred to some new style in furniture, and we believe, from a study of old dictionaries, as well as the inventories and the pieces still extant belonging to those times, that the word was always used in connection with writing in some way.

The word bureau appears to have had two meanings, either a piece on which to write or a chest of drawers of some sort. In the expression "bureau-desk" the word seems to have been used in its second meaning, otherwise it would not be a qualifying word and would be redundant. The furniture best answering this description would be the slant-top desks with the chest of drawers below, which was a new style. The other expression, "bureau-table" or "bureau-chamber-table," would seem to use the word in its first sense. The expressions "table" and "chamber-table," as used in the inventories we have

Figure 253.

Knee-Hole Desk, about 1725.

seen, refer to what are commonly called low-boys; so if the word bureau was there used to denote a piece to write upon, we should have a low-boy plus a desk, such pieces as are shown in Figures 246 and 247; and as such pieces came into existence at about the time this expression first appears in the inventories, we believe them to have been there described.

The word bureau does not seem to have been used to any extent in its modern meaning until the last quarter of the eighteenth century, and we believe it was then so called because of the desk appearing in the upper drawer of such pieces; the desk drawer later was dropped, but the name remained.

Chippendale shows designs for ladies' secretaries, which he calls bureaus; and he, Hepplewhite, and Sheraton call chests of drawers commodes, so it is hardly

DESKS AND SCRUTOIRES

likely that the word bureau could at that time have been very commonly used to denote a simple chest of drawers. The word secretaire is the same word as secretary, a corruption of escritoire.

It will therefore be seen that after about the first twenty years of the eighteenth century there were four words used interchangeably to denote a piece of furniture for writing purposes, viz., desk, scrutoire, escritoire, and bureau.

Another early form of desk and dressing-table is shown in Figure 253. It is in knee-hole form; that is, the centre portion is recessed to allow a person to sit at the desk. The front of the top drawer falls on a quadrant and forms a surface upon which to write, and within are pigeon-holes and drawers. On each side of the centre are three drawers, and just above the recessed portion is a shallow drawer. A cupboard is built in the recessed portion. This piece stands on straight bracket feet. The fronts of the drawers are made of walnut veneer with herringbone edges in early fashion, and the handles are in the early open-work willow pattern, the same as appears in Figure 244. This type of desk is also found with a baize top upon which to write. This piece is very similar to the dressing-table shown in Figure 113, which was the model for the knee-hole dressing-tables such as are shown in Figures 121 and 122, but which are of a considerably later date. This desk is the property of Messrs. Cooper and Griffith, of New York.

Figure 254.
Slant-Top Scrutoire, 1740–50.

As time went on more space was wanted in the drawer portion of the scrutoire than could be obtained from the low-boy type; consequently such pieces as that shown in Figure 254 came into fashion. The table part consists of a narrow frame on short, bandy legs terminating in Dutch feet. In the desk section are four drawers. It is 37½ inches high, 27½ inches wide, and 16 inches deep, and its diminutive proportions make it graceful. The use of this low frame with bandy legs seems to have been popular principally in Connecticut.

An interesting slant-top scrutoire with cabinet top, the property of Mr. George Dudley Seymour, of New Haven, is shown in Figure 255. It is made in

234 COLONIAL FURNITURE

three parts; first the frame with short cabriole leg terminating in bird's claw and ball feet, then the desk part with four drawers below, and above this is the cabinet. The top is scrolled and the mouldings consist of the usual quarter-round, fillet, cove, astragal, fillet, and small cove. Below the scroll top is a

Figure 255.
Slant-Top Scrutoire with cabinet top and bird's claw and ball feet, 1725–50.

bevelled panel, the upper surface following the outline of the top, and at the centre is carved the sun pattern. On either side of the doors is a fluted pilaster, and in each door is a bevelled panel with a domed top. Elaborate H hinges are on the doors. The interior of the desk part has four pigeon-holes on each side of the centre and two drawers, on each of which is carved the rising-sun pattern. This scrutoire is made of cherry.

DESKS AND SCRUTOIRES 235

Figure 256 shows a scrutoire with a rather good interior consisting of eight pigeon-holes with gracefully cut partitions. The drawers are all curved, four below the pigeon-holes and one at each end below, while at the centre is a long open space to hold a ledger. At the centre are also two narrow vertical drawers for paper, and two drawers, the upper one cut with a shell. Below the desk

Figure 256.
Slant-Top Scrutoire, 1740–50.

part are four drawers with overlapping edges, and the feet are of the Dutch bandy-legged type with a heavy shoe. This desk is the property of Mr. Francis H. Bigelow, of Cambridge.

Figure 257 shows a scrutoire in which the drawers in the desk part are cut in ogee curves and the decoration is obtained by carving and burning the design into the wood. It was found in central Pennsylvania. The door at the centre conceals a series of little drawers, and under the frame of these drawers is a spring which, upon being pressed, releases the whole centre and discloses a secret drawer back of the two carved columns. The lid is supported by two square drawers instead of two pulls.

In many of the scrutoires the maker exercised great ingenuity in contriving a series of secret drawers and receptacles in which deeds, wills, and other valuable papers could be kept. These secret places were sometimes arranged back of the centre compartment. The whole centre would draw out on being released by pressure of a hidden spring, which was sometimes concealed above a little drawer at the top which must first be removed; sometimes the spring would be concealed at the bottom or on the side, always ingeniously hidden from the uninitiated. This centre, being drawn out, discloses either a series of small shallow drawers, a shelf, or two narrow upright drawers on either side of the centre. This is the commonest place to find secret compartments, but if they are not in the places mentioned a narrow shelf may be found between the top drawer and the bottom of the scrutoire part, to which an entrance can be obtained by means of a sliding panel in the bottom of the scrutoire part, often securely fastened by a spring hidden in various ways. Again, there is occasionally a hollow place at the back of the slides which holds the lid.

Figure 257.
Slant-Top Scrutoire, third quarter eighteenth century.

Figure 258 shows a scrutoire with an unusually good interior. There are two tiers of three carved drawers on each side of the centre. On the upper tier are carved rosettes and on the lower ones shells. Above are three pigeon-holes on each side and above that are three drawers. On each side of the door is a fluted pilaster which is the front of a paper drawer. The door front contains a panel with the edges cut in ogee and simple curves on which a vase with prune blossoms and leaves is beautifully carved. There are four plain drawers below, and the piece stands on bird's-claw and ball bracket feet in front, with the knees carved in an acanthus-leaf and scroll design. The rear legs are in the ogee bracket type. This scrutoire is the property of Mr. C. R. Morson, of Brooklyn.

Figure 259 shows a scrutoire belonging to Mr. H. W. Erving. A rope moulding and a shell is carved on the lid, and on the centre of the lower drawer is carved a

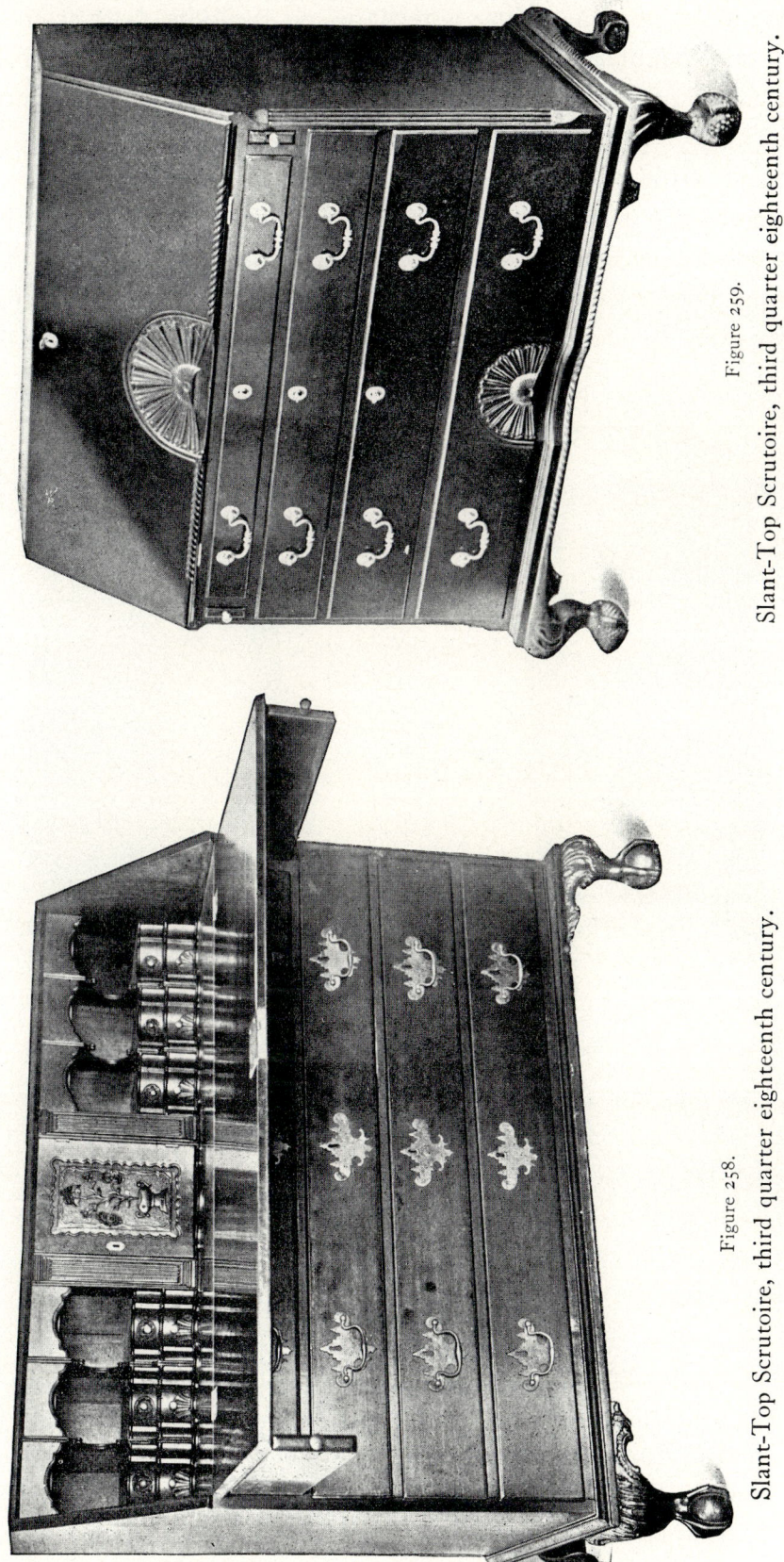

Figure 258.
Slant-Top Scrutoire, third quarter eighteenth century.

Figure 259.
Slant-Top Scrutoire, third quarter eighteenth century.

similar shell, and a rope moulding is repeated on the skirt, both front and sides. The corners are chamfered and fluted, the feet are bird's claw and ball bracket feet with carved knees, and the balls are ornamented with small indentations.

A form of writing-desk which strongly resembles the modern office desk is shown in Figure 260. This form was used in France as early as the Louis XIV period. It did not become at all common in England until Chippendale's time. Chippendale shows several designs of this form in his "Director," and a late one executed by him is shown in Figure 5. In this country the model was not

Figure 260.
Knee-Hole Writing-Table, 1750–60.

popular. The one here shown is English and the cabinet work is of exceptional quality. It will be seen that the bases are *bombé*-shaped, the sides of the drawers being cut on the curve of the frame. The top is covered with a tooled leather. The mouldings on the edges of the top are carved in a dainty acanthus-leaf design and the stiles are all carved in acanthus scrolls. The feet are of the ogee bracket type, the handles are in Chippendale style, and on the ends are mounts of cast brass in imitation of French ormolu work. The proportions, simplicity, and refinement of this writing-table make it one of the best examples known. It is the property of Mr. Richard A. Canfield.

In no piece of furniture probably did the block-front type reach such perfection as in the scrutoire.

In studying the block-front type the reader will do well to compare the desks here shown with the block-front chests of drawers (Chapter III), where will be found a discussion of the style.

DESKS AND SCRUTOIRES

Figure 261 shows a typical block-front scrutoire. The blocking is raised and depressed beyond the plane of the drawer. This is the common method. This piece stands on four bird's claw and ball feet, and the blocking extends through the moulding onto the brackets of the legs. The brasses are original and are of the type usually found on these pieces. This piece is the property of Mr. Albert H. Pitkin, of Hartford.

Figure 261.
Block-Front, Slant-Top Scrutoire, third quarter eighteenth century.

Figure 262 shows another block-front scrutoire with the same style of blocking as is shown in the preceding figure, and there is the same moulding on the frame about the drawers. The feet, however, are unusual, being animals' claw and ball bracket feet with carved knees. The mouldings at the base of most of the block-front pieces, other than the Rhode Island type, generally consist of a cove, a fillet, and a quarter-round, with a wide fillet below, as in this piece. The interior of this desk is good; the blocking idea is carried out by the hollowed fronts of the outer drawers and the single door, above each of which is carved the rising-sun pattern. The handles, of course, originally were similar to those shown in the preceding figure. This scrutoire was the property of the late William G. Boardman, of Hartford.

Figure 263 shows a block-front scrutoire of a little different type. It will be seen that the depressed section is in the same plane as the outer edges, instead of being depressed, and this gives the appearance of a double block. The usual mouldings, a cove, a fillet, a quarter-round, and a fillet, finish the bottom, and the piece stands on ogee bracket feet. The blocking does not extend through the moulding but is finished on the lower drawer. The interior is finished with curved

Figure 262.
Block-Front, Slant-Top Scrutoire, third quarter eighteenth century.

drawers and above the pigeon-holes is cut a fret design. This piece is the property of Mr. Dwight M. Prouty, of Boston.

One of the finest block-front scrutoires known is that shown in Figure 264, the property of Mr. George S. Palmer, of New London. The blocking is of the usual form and extends through the brackets of the feet. On each edge is a reeded and fluted pilaster, and the bird's claw and ball feet are well fashioned, the knees being carved. The most interesting feature, however, is the interior, arranged in amphitheatre fashion. At the base are three drawers curved both horizontally and vertically. Above those are four drawers on each side of the centre curved in the same manner, and above these on each side are four pigeon-holes surmounted by four drawers on which are carved the rising-sun pattern. On either side of the centre are three narrow vertical drawers and at the centre are three drawers with depressed blocking. The cabinet-maker was so full of his design that he

Figure 263.
Block-Front, Slant-Top Scrutoire, third quarter eighteenth century.

Figure 264.
Block-Front, Slant-Top Scrutoire, third quarter eighteenth century.

overlooked the fact that some portions of the interior projected too much to allow for the lid, consequently the lid on the inside at the two ends has been gouged out.

Figure 265.
Block-Front, Slant-Top Scrutoire with cabinet top, third quarter eighteenth century.

Figure 265 shows a block-front scrutoire with cabinet top, from the Bolles Collection. The top is scrolled and hooded, and the mouldings of the cornice consist of a quarter-round, a wide fillet, a cove, an astragal, a fillet, and a small

DESKS AND SCRUTOIRES 243

cove. There are pilasters on the doors which fit the capitals on the cornice. Behind the rounded section of the doors are carved recessed shells. The interior is composed of drawers and pigeon-holes with depressed blocking. The piece stands on short cabriole legs terminating in Dutch feet. The mouldings at the

Figure 266.

Block-Front, Slant-Top Scrutoire with cabinet top, third quarter eighteenth century.

bottom are the same found in those of the so-called Newport type, a cyma recta and a wide fillet. The blocking on the drawers is narrower than is usual and the drawers overlap.

Figure 266 shows the typical block-front, cabinet-top scrutoire found in northern New England. The cabinet top is tall and is scrolled but not hooded. The mouldings are the same as those shown in the preceding figure, except that

244 COLONIAL FURNITURE

the upper fillet is narrow. The pilasters are on the doors connecting with the capitals on the cornice, and there are recessed shells above the pigeon-holes and

Figure 267.
Block-Front, Slant-Top Scrutoire with cabinet top, third quarter eighteenth century.

a fan carving at the centre of the top. The drawers on the interior are blocked and at the centre is a panelled door. Fluted pilasters finish the stiles on either side of the drawers, and the piece stands on straight bracket feet which have

DESKS AND SCRUTOIRES

been slightly cut off. This piece is the property of Mr. Francis H. Bigelow, of Cambridge.

An interesting block-front scrutoire from the Bolles Collection is shown in Figure 267. The cabinet section is very tall and the scroll top is hooded. The mouldings consist of a quarter-round, a fillet, a large cove, an astragal, a fillet, and a small cove. The acroteriums are surmounted by two full-length figures of mahogany. At the centre of the top is a carved shell. Behind the curve of the doors are two carved recessed shells and on the doors are fluted pilasters which connect with the capitals on the frame. There are two candle-slides below the cabinet. The drawers in the interior of the desk are curved and blocked, and a small panel like those on the doors is at the centre. The blocking is in the usual form with a bead on the frame about the drawers, and the piece stands on bird's claw and ball bracket feet. The mouldings at the bottom are the usual cove, fillet, quarter-round, and fillet. At the centre of the skirt is carved a shell. This piece represents the best of the northern New England type.

Figure 268 shows a block-front, cabinet-top scrutoire, the property of Mr. H. W. Erving. The top is scrolled and hooded. The mouldings are a quarter-round, a fillet, a cove, an astragal, a fillet, and a small cove. The sides of the upper section have square recessed edges with fluted quarter-columns inserted. In the lower section are four flush drawers without any beading on the edge of the frame. The piece stands on bird's claw and ball feet in front and ogee bracket feet at the back. An unusual feature is the inlay on the rosettes, on the centre acroterium, on the lid, and about the drawers.

Figure 268.
Block-Front, Slant-Top Scrutoire with cabinet top, third quarter eighteenth century.

A southern New England block-front, cabinet-top scrutoire is shown in Figure 269. The top is scrolled and hooded, and the mouldings are a quarter-round, a fillet, a cove, an astragal, a fillet, and a cove. The doors are panelled and at the top of each is carved a raised shell. The usual candle-stick slides are below the cabinet. The lid is blocked, and at the top are shells, the outer ones raised and the centre one depressed. There are four drawers in the lower part with overlapping edges, which is rather unusual, as the drawers are usually flush with the beading on the frame. The legs are of the ogee bracket type and the base mouldings are the cove and a wide fillet. This piece may be an early example of the Rhode Island type, as it has some of its characteristics. It is the property of Mr. Richard A. Canfield.

We now come to a consideration of the Rhode Island pieces, so called because they can all be traced to Rhode Island and appear to have been made by the same man. It is thought that they were made in Newport by John Goddard, a cabinet-maker of that place. There are several cabinet-top scrutoires of this type known, and they are probably as fine pieces of cabinet work as are found in the country and differ only in minor details. These scrutoires are found in two forms, those where a rosette finishes the inner ends of the scrolls and those where the inner ends are finished with a returned moulding. Probably the earliest of these pieces is the one owned by Brown & Ives, of Providence, and is shown in Figure 270. The cabinet section is tall and stately. The top is scrolled and hooded and the inner ends of the scroll are finished with carved rosettes. The mouldings are a quarter-round, a fillet, a cyma recta, a fillet, a cove, an astragal, and a fillet.

Figure 269.
Block-Front, Slant-Top Scrutoire with cabinet top, third quarter eighteenth century.

This form of moulding is found only on this scrutoire and the chest on chest (Figure 119). The astragal and fillet carry around the circular openings at the centre. This is common to all the Rhode Island pieces. Above the doors are three raised panels with rounded edges. On all the other pieces there are but two. At the corners are boxes on which are placed the acroterium with urns and flames. This feature only appears in this piece and on the chest on chest (Figure 119). The

DESKS AND SCRUTOIRES 247

corners have square recessed edges and quarter-round fluted and reeded columns are inserted. There are three doors, two of which are hinged together, and the

Figure 270.
Block-Front, Slant-Top Scrutoire with cabinet top,
third quarter eighteenth century.

doors lock in the hinge, the inner door fastening to the outer one with a metal tongue. The beauty of this construction is that the blocking can thus be carried from the bottom to the top of the piece. The outer doors are raised with a shell carved at the top and the centre one is depressed with the sunken carved shell.

248   COLONIAL FURNITURE

The lid is also blocked with two raised shells and one depressed shell. There are four drawers and all overlap. This feature also appears only in the chest on chest (Figure 119). The upper drawer is carved with the raised and depressed shells, a feature unique in this piece. The blocking is of the usual type, carry-

Figure 271.
Block-Front, Slant-Top Scrutoire with cabinet top, third quarter eighteenth century.

Figure 272.
Block-Front, Slant-Top Scrutoire with cabinet top, third quarter eighteenth century.

ing down to the ogee bracket feet, on the inside of which is carved a scroll, a feature found only in the Rhode Island type. The base mouldings are composed of a cove, a fillet, and a quarter-round, which differ from the regular type which are a cyma reversa and a fillet. At the ends of both the upper and lower sections are handles. The urn-and-flame pattern used on all of the Rhode Island pieces is of a distinctive character and aids in identifying them.

DESKS AND SCRUTOIRES

Figure 271 shows another of these Rhode Island block-front scrutoires, the property of Mrs. A. S. Chesebrough, of Bristol. The cornice is composed of a fillet, a cyma reversa, a fillet, cove, astragal, fillet, and small cove, and these mouldings appear on all of the pieces known except the two above mentioned. The astragal, fillet, and cove carry about the centre openings in the usual manner. Above the doors are two raised panels with rounded edges. The three doors with the carved shells in the centre are the same as in the preceding figure, as is also the lid of the desk. The corners have square recessed edges with quarter-round fluted columns inserted. There are but three drawers in the lower part without any shell carving, set flush with a bead moulding on the frame about them, which is the usual construction for Rhode Island pieces. Above the drawers is a sliding shelf, a feature unique with this piece. The base mouldings are a cyma reversa and a wide fillet, mouldings found on all of these pieces except the two above mentioned. The feet are the same as those shown in the preceding figure.

Another example of these scrutoires is shown in Figure 272 and is the property of Mr. Marsden J. Perry, of Providence. With the exception of the slide above the drawers, this piece is identical with the preceding one, except that there are eleven radiates in the upper shell and twelve radiates in the lower shell, while in the preceding piece there are fourteen and fifteen radiates respectively.

Figure 273.
Block-Front, Slant-Top Scrutoire with cabinet top, third quarter eighteenth century.

The second type of these scrutoires are those in which the mouldings on the inner ends of the scroll are finished with a returned moulding instead of a rosette.

Figure 273 is an example of this kind, the property of Mr. B. E. Helme, of Kingston. This piece is the simplest of the scrutoires and was probably an early

250   COLONIAL FURNITURE

example of the type. The mouldings are the usual ones on these pieces, a fillet, cyma reversa, fillet, cove, astragal, fillet, and small cove. The two panels at the top are not finished with the raised sections, although it is possible these were applied and have fallen off. There is the usual three-door construction and shells,

Figure 274.
Block-Front, Slant-Top Scrutoire with cabinet top,
third quarter eighteenth century.

but the edges are plain and are not finished with the usual square recessed edge with quarter-column inserted. The interior is as fine as in any of the pieces. The legs have been cut off as has also the centre urn and flame. This second type of Rhode Island scrutoire differs from the first type in that it is generally enclosed directly back of the centre acroterium and also in that it has a slide on the inside of the desk opening into the top drawer.

DESKS AND SCRUTOIRES

Another of these scrutoires is shown in Figure 274, from the Pendleton Collection, owned by the Rhode Island School of Design. The top is scrolled and hooded

Figure 275.
Block-Front, Slant-Top Scrutoire with cabinet top,
third quarter eighteenth century.

and the inner ends of the scroll are finished with a returned moulding instead of a rosette. The mouldings are the same as those appearing in the last figure, and

252   COLONIAL FURNITURE

there are two raised panels with rounded edges above the doors in the usual manner. The urns and flames are also in the usual form. This piece is shown open. On the left are two doors and on the right is one. The key which locks the doors will be seen on the inside of the two doors. The interior is finished with pigeon-

Figure 276.
Block-Front, Slant-Top Scrutoire with cabinet
top, 1760–75.

holes with movable slides set in grooves. The front of these slides is cut in a long ogee curve and a half-round. The interior of the desk part has three doors at each end with depressed blocking and carved shells, and the door at the centre is in the same form. Three pigeon-holes are on each side of the centre and above each is a depressed half-round. The drawers below the pigeon-holes are in raised blocks. The interior of the piece is practically the same as that shown in the preceding figure, the only important variation being that the hood top is not backed at the

DESKS AND SCRUTOIRES

centre and the centre acroterium is not as large and is not reeded. There are three flush drawers below with bead moulding on the frame about them, and the base mouldings and the feet are in the usual form.

Another of these scrutoires is shown in Figure 275 and is the property of Mr. Richard A. Canfield. A number of refinements show that this was probably the last made of those shown. The top is scrolled and hooded and the inner ends of the scroll are finished with a returned moulding instead of rosette. The opening at the centre of the top is backed. The mouldings are the same as those on the preceding figure, as are also the two raised panels with rounded edges above the doors. The finials are also in the same design. The doors are three in number, arranged in the usual way above described, and the shells have thirteen radiates at the top and sixteen on the lid. The corners have square recessed edges in which are inserted quarter-round reeded and fluted columns. There are three flush drawers in the lower part with a bead moulding on the frame. The base moulding is in the usual style found on these pieces, a cyma reversa and a wide fillet. The piece stands on the usual bracket feet, but the carved scroll on the inner edge comes to a point.

An interesting variation of the Rhode Island type is shown in Figure 276, the property of Mr. George M. Gunn, of Milford, Connecticut. The cabinetmaker apparently had either seen or heard of a Rhode Island piece and was copying it from memory. The cornice is composed of a quarter-round, a fillet, a cyma reversa, a dentil moulding, a cove, an astragal, a fillet, and a small cove, but the astragal, fillet, and cove do not extend about the circular openings at the top as they do in the Rhode Island pieces. The cabinet is concealed by but two instead of three doors, consequently it was necessary to cut through the centre shell and depressed blocking. The shells are not made like those on the Rhode Island pieces, but are exactly like those on the chest on chest (Figure 120), as is also the carved support for the centre acroterium. There are four drawers set flush with a bead moulding on the frame about them, and the piece stands on bird's claw and ball feet with shells carved on the knees and at the centre of the skirt. The base mouldings are a cyma recta and a fillet instead of the cyma reversa and fillet found on the Rhode Island pieces.

A different type of block-front, cabinet-top scrutoire is shown in Figure 277. In those above shown the top is simply scrolled, but in this one there is a pediment top with a hood and scroll. The mouldings are more elaborate than is usual, consisting of a quarter-round, a cyma recta, a fillet, and a small cyma reversa, a dentil moulding, a cove, an astragal, and a fillet. The cymatium has the quarter-round, the cyma recta, a fillet, and a cove with a dentil moulding, and the section carrying across the front has the same mouldings, commencing with the cyma reversa. On either side of the doors are fluted pilasters the capitals of which extend through to the top of the mouldings. The two doors are panelled with ogee curved edges. The lower part has four drawers with a bead moulding on the frame about them, and the blocking is in the type where the depressed sections are in the plane of the drawer, giving the appearance of the double blocking as

Figure 277.
Block-Front, Slant-Top Scrutoire with cabinet top, 1778.

in Figure 263. The base mouldings are the cove, a fillet, a quarter-round, and a wide fillet, and the piece stands on four bird's claw and ball feet. This piece was made in New Hampshire in 1778 and is the property of the writer.

Figure 278 shows another block-front, cabinet-top scrutoire in which the pediment effect was obtained by a fret extending across the ends and front. The top

DESKS AND SCRUTOIRES

is scrolled and hooded. The scrolls terminate in a carved rosette. The mouldings consist of a quarter-round, a fillet, a cove, an astragal, a fillet, and a small cove, the fret frieze, a fillet, a cyma reversa, and a broad fillet. The finials are unusually beautiful with carved urns and flames which are cut through and wave in a realistic manner. On either side of the two doors are fluted pilasters. The panels

Figure 278.
Block-Front, Slant-Top Scrutoire with cabinet top, third quarter eighteenth century.

of the doors are cut in ogee curves. There are four drawers below in the usual blocking, and the base mouldings are a cove, a fillet, a quarter-round, and a fillet. The piece stands on bird's claw and ball feet. This piece is in the Pendleton Collection, owned by the Rhode Island School of Design.

Another form of cabinet-top scrutoire is the *bombé* type, of which three beautiful examples are shown in the following figures.

The simplest one is shown in Figure 279 and is in the Pendleton Collection, owned by the Rhode Island School of Design. The top is in the form of an interrupted or broken-arch pediment. The mouldings are a fillet, cyma reversa, wide fillet or corona, a soffit, narrow fillet, quarter-round, fillet, dentil moulding, fillet, cyma reversa, and a frieze. The moulding returns at the centre of the top to the back of the piece and a wide cove is added. On the capitals of the fluted pilasters on either side of the doors are the fillet, cyma reversa, wide fillet, and cyma reversa, which is repeated below, except that an astragal takes the place of the lower cyma reversa. It will thus be seen that the dominant theme of the mouldings is the use of the cyma reversa, which gives the piece a certain reserve and adds greatly to its beauty. An unusual feature of the pediment is that the cymatium does not extend over the top of the horizontal mouldings. The panels of the doors are bevelled and cut in a series of cyma curves in a manner found on many of the mirrors. The lower section is beautifully made. It is not only *bombé*, but the fronts of the drawers are also in serpentine form and the sides of the drawers follow the curves on the frame. This necessitated cutting the sides of all of the drawers on a curve. The base mouldings are the same as those appearing on many block-front pieces, a cove, a fillet, a quarter-round, and a fillet. The piece stands on bird's claw and ball feet. This scrutoire was found at Portsmouth, New Hampshire, and the drawers are of American pine, which would rather indicate its origin. The urn at the centre of the top is not original.

Figure 280 shows another *bombé*-shaped, cabinet-top scrutoire somewhat more ornate than that shown in the preceding figure. The top has an interrupted or broken-arch pediment and does not carry through, making the enclosed hood, as does the one shown in the preceding figure. The mouldings consist of a fillet, cyma recta, fillet, small cyma reversa ornamented with a leaf carving, wide fillet or corona, soffit, narrow fillet, quarter-round ornamented with egg-and-dart pattern, fillet, dentil moulding, fillet, small cyma reversa ornamented with leaf carving. It will be seen that the mouldings are the same as those shown in the preceding figure except that on this one are added at the top the extra fillet and cyma recta. The mouldings below the frieze are the same as those in the preceding figure, the cyma reversa being, however, ornamented with a leaf carving. The capitals of the pilaster are a long cyma recta carved in an acanthus-leaf design. The panels of the doors are bevelled and cut in series of cyma curves, as in the preceding figure, and the mouldings about the edges of the panels are carved in a leaf design. The lower part is not only *bombé*-shaped, but the fronts of the drawers are blocked, making an unusual combination. The sides of the drawers, however, do not follow the curve of the sides, as in the preceding figure, but the width of the frame takes up the swell, leaving the sides of the drawers straight. The base mouldings are the usual cove, fillet, quarter-round, and fillet,

Figure 279.
Bombé-Front, Slant-Top Scrutoire with cabinet top, 1750-75.

Figure 280.
Bombé-Front, Slant-Top Scrutoire with cabinet top, 1750–75

Figure 281.
Bombé-Front, Slant-Top Scrutoire with cabinet top, 1750–75.

and the piece stands on ogee bracket feet with carved surfaces. On the edges of the lower part is carved a leaf design. This piece is the property of Mr. George S. Palmer, of New London.

Figure 281 shows another *bombé*-front, cabinet-top scrutoire, in the Bulkeley Collection, which is more ornate than any of the foregoing. It has the same interrupted pediment top, and the mouldings are a fillet, a cyma recta, a fillet, a cyma reversa ornamented with leaf carving, a wide fillet or corona, soffit, a narrow fillet, a quarter-round ornamented with the egg-and-dart pattern, a dentil moulding, a fillet, a cyma reversa ornamented with a carved leaf pattern. It will be seen that this cornice is identical with that shown in the preceding figure. Below the frieze is a fillet, a cyma reversa carved, a wide fillet, a reel and bead moulding. Above the reeded pilaster on either side of the door is a well-carved Corinthian capital. In each door is a mirror with upper edges cut in the cyma curves with a carved moulding. A carved moulding finishes the base of the cabinet top. The lower section consists of a plain *bombé* carcass, the drawers having straight sides instead of following the curves of the frame, and in that respect is the same as that shown in the preceding figure. The base moulding consists of a fillet, a large ovolo or quarter-round carved with a flower-and-leaf design with a large shell at the centre, and the piece stands on animal's claw and ball feet.

All of these pieces, with the exception of the *bombé* feature, are very similar to early Chippendale designs, and may have been made by the same cabinet-maker, who undoubtedly was familiar with Chippendale's book.

Figure 282 shows a cabinet-top scrutoire from the Pendleton Collection, belonging to the Rhode Island School of Design, which represents the Philadelphia type and has many of the characteristics of the Philadelphia high chests of drawers (Figure 105). The top is scrolled and hooded, the inner ends of the scrolls being finished with well-carved rosettes. The mouldings are of the usual type in these pieces, a fillet, a cyma recta, a fillet, a cove, and a small quarter-round. Above the doors is applied a shell carving with foliations and flowers similar to that shown in the figure above mentioned. Urns and flames finish the ends and centre. The two doors have semicircular tops and the mouldings about the panels are carved in leaf design. The lower carcass is plain with four drawers, and the base mouldings are the usual cove, fillet, quarter-round, and fillet. The piece stands on four bird's claw and ball feet.

Figure 283 shows an interesting cabinet-top scrutoire, in the collection of Mr. George S. Palmer, which closely resembles some of the Chippendale designs. The top is finished with a scroll pediment, the inner ends of the scrolls being finished with rosettes having outstanding foliations. The mouldings are a fillet, a cyma

DESKS AND SCRUTOIRES

recta, a fillet, a wide fillet or corona, soffit, a fillet, a quarter-round, a fillet, a dentil moulding, a fillet, a cove, and an astragal. Below this is a Chinese fret frieze and then an astragal and a fillet. About the two panel doors is a Chinese fret of the same design, and below the doors, separated by an astragal, is another Chinese

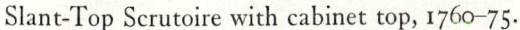

Figure 282.
Slant-Top Scrutoire with cabinet top, 1760–75.

Figure 283.
Slant-Top Scrutoire with cabinet top, 1760–75.

fret in the same design. In the lower carcass is the slant-top desk, and below that is one drawer below which are two doors concealing sliding shelves. On the doors are planted carved scrolls and leaves in a characteristic Chippendale pattern. The base moulding is the usual Chippendale one, a cyma reversa and a fillet, and the piece stands on carved ogee bracket feet. Were it not for the fact that the interior of this piece is finished with American pine, we should pronounce it English of the Chippendale school.

262 COLONIAL FURNITURE

Before leaving the subject of cabinet-top scrutoires, it has been thought well to show two examples of English scrutoires of the same period by way of comparison

Figure 284.
Slant-Top Scrutoire with bookcase top, 1750–70.

Figure 284 is a beautiful example from the Pendleton Collection. It has a scrolled pediment, the inner ends of the scrolls being finished with beautifully carved acanthus-leaf rosettes finer than any we have found in this country. The

DESKS AND SCRUTOIRES

mouldings are a quarter-round, a fillet, a cove, a pearl bead moulding, a wide fillet or corona, soffit, a small fillet, a quarter-round, a fillet, a dentil moulding, a fillet, a quarter-round, and a fillet. The frieze is plain and below it is a cove, a fillet, and a cyma reversa carved in a leaf design. Around the outer edges of the glass doors is applied a beautifully carved design of foliated scrolls and flowers. On the upper

Figure 285.
Slant-Top Scrutoire with bookcase top, 1750–70.

edge of the frame of the lower carcass is a cyma reversa carved in a leaf design, and below the top drawer is a small torus or astragal carved in a similar design. The base moulding is a cyma reversa carved in a flowing foliated design and a fillet. The piece stands on well-carved ogee bracket feet. The handles are silvered.

Figure 285 shows another English cabinet-top scrutoire which is the property of Mr. Marsden J. Perry, of Providence. The top is finished with a scroll pediment with acanthus-leaf foliations extending over the entire scrolls. Beneath the scrolls is a lattice design. The mouldings are a fillet, a cyma recta, a small fillet, a large fillet or corona, soffit, a small fillet, a quarter-round, a fillet, a dentil moulding, a fillet, and a small cove. The frieze is ornamented with a beautiful fret below which is an astragal. Each door has eight panes of glass and the frame about them is carved in a leaf design. Below the upper drawer in the lower carcass

Figure 286.
Serpentine-Front, Slant-Top Scrutoire, 1765-80.

is a small torus or astragal carved in a leaf design. The base is particularly beautiful. There is a small plain torus moulding, and the skirt is enriched with a finely carved rococo scroll design. The piece stands on scroll feet with an acanthus leaf projecting from the outer surfaces.

A form of scrutoire quite common in New England is shown in Figure 286. The front of the drawers is in the serpentine curve raised at the centre and depressed at the two ends. The base mouldings are a cyma reversa and a fillet, and the piece stands on bird's claw and ball feet. These pieces are found made of mahogany, cherry, and maple, and occasionally have cabinet tops. The table of the desk part is usually a little higher than in any other forms of scrutoire. This piece is in the Bolles Collection.

DESKS AND SCRUTOIRES

Figure 287 shows another form in which these pieces are found. The drawer front is in a reverse serpentine curve; that is, with the centre depressed and the two ends swelled. The base moulding is the cove, fillet, quarter-round, and wide fillet, and the piece stands on bird's claw and ball feet. It is the property of Mr. William Meggat, of Wethersfield, Connecticut.

Figure 288 shows a reverse serpentine-front, slant-top scrutoire with cabinet top which is in the Bolles Collection. The pediment top is very unusual in that

Figure 287.
Reversed Serpentine-Front Scrutoire, 1765–80.

the mouldings of the scroll do not extend into the horizontal mouldings, but both sets of mouldings are complete and distinct. The mouldings of the scroll are the usual quarter-round, fillet, cove, astragal, fillet, and cove, and on the inner ends of the scrolls are rosettes. The horizontal mouldings consist of a fillet, a cyma reversa, a dentil moulding, a fillet, and a cove. On each side are fluted pilasters, and the doors have sunken panels with the edges about them cut in cyma curves. Below the doors are candle-stick slides. The interior arrangement is quite like that found in Figure 274, except that it has three long plain drawers at the base. The end and centre drawers are concave blocked with shell carving, and the drawers under the pigeon-holes are in raised blocking. The base moulding is a cyma reversa and a fillet, and at the centre of the skirt is carved a half-rosette. The feet are ogee brackets.

Figure 289 shows a scrutoire of the Sheraton period. The desk part is covered with a tambour lid, which rolls back like a modern office desk and is made of alternate strips of rosewood and satin-wood. When open the bed of the table pulls out and there is a rest that can be raised to any desired angle. The drawers and pigeon-holes are of satin-wood. The front is of satin-wood with mahogany inlay, and on the stiles at either end is a medallion of an urn with flowers. The

Figure 288.
Reversed Serpentine-Front Scrutoire with cabinet top, 1765–80.

legs are tapering, made of mahogany with inlay of satin-wood. This piece is American made and was found in Philadelphia. It is the property of the writer. Such pieces were called tambour writing-tables.

Figure 290 shows two views of a beautiful little scrutoire which is the property of Mr. John J. Gilbert, of Baltimore. It is made of mahogany and satin-

Figure 289.
Tambour Writing-Table, 1780–90.

Figure 290.
Cylinder-Fall Desk, 1780–90.

wood beautifully enriched with marquetry. On the top is inlaid a rosette with streamers, and a rosette is inlaid on each end. The desk front is solid and in oval form, and at the centre is the figure of a kneeling woman and festoons of flowers and leaves with bow knots. The two drawer fronts are inlaid with similar festoons

Figure 291.
Bookcase and Scrutoire, 1780–90.

Figure 292.
Bookcase and Scrutoire, 1780–90.

as are also the ends. The legs are in the form known as Marlborough legs and have an inlay of pendent flowers. The table section of the desk pulls out and furnishes a large surface to write upon. The interior is finished with pigeon-holes and drawers with festoons, and at the centre is a door on which is inlaid an urn surrounded by a wreath. On either side of the doors are the two narrow paper-drawers on which are inlaid pendent flowers. This style of scrutoire was called by Shearer, who designed many of them, "cylinder-fall."

DESKS AND SCRUTOIRES

Figure 291 shows a scrutoire with bookcase top in the Sheraton style which belongs to Mr. John J. Gilbert, of Baltimore. The pediment top is scrolled, the inner ends being finished with simple rosettes, and below is an elaborate lattice-work composed of C scrolls. The mouldings consist of a fillet, a cyma recta, a fillet, a quarter-round, and a cove in the upper section, and below is added a moulding somewhat resembling the meander pattern. The cove across the sides and front is cut with Gothic openings in a manner which was often used by Sheraton. The glass doors are also cut in Gothic form. What appears to be the two upper drawers is the front of a desk which lets down on a quadrant in the usual manner, and below are three drawers. The piece stands on straight bracket feet.

Another Sheraton scrutoire with bookcase top, the property of Mr. Francis H. Bigelow, is shown in Figure 292. The pediment top and lattice-work is very similar to that shown in the preceding figure, but the cove moulding is cut into arches with points terminating in acorns. Below this is an inlaid frieze. The glass in the doors is cut in geometrical shapes. The desk portion is concealed behind what appear to be two drawers in the same manner as in the preceding piece. Inside are pigeon-holes and drawers, with a door at the centre and paper-drawers at the sides. Below are three drawers. The piece stands on slightly ogee bracket feet.

Figure 293.
Fire-Screen Scrutoire, 1780–90.

Another style of scrutoire found occasionally in this country, but more often in England, is a fire-screen scrutoire, an example of which appears in Figure 293, which is at the Van Cortlandt Manor, at Croton, New York. The front drops, disclosing a set of shallow pigeon-holes. Such pieces were made by Shearer and Hepplewhite in the last quarter of the eighteenth century, and this piece is almost identical with one of the illustrations among Shearer's designs, and is undoubtedly of English make.

We now come to a very different type of desk from those hitherto described. Figure 294 is a desk used by General Washington when President of the United States in 1789, and is now in the Governor's Room in the City Hall, New York. The wood is mahogany and the fluted legs and rosette trimmings are of the Sheraton style. The brass handles are found on both sides and ends, and there are seven drawers on each side, while the brasses at either end and the moulding

Figure 294.
Writing-Table, 1789.

Figure 295.
Knee-Hole Writing-Table, about 1790.

DESKS AND SCRUTOIRES

about imaginary drawers convey the impression that the ends are also furnished with drawers. At each end of the top are shelves for papers.

Figure 295 shows a knee-hole writing-table, the property of the writer. The top folds upon itself and when open is supported by pulls. There is a long drawer at the top and on each side of the recessed portion are four drawers. In the

Figure 296.
Inlaid Secretary, 1790–1800.

recessed portion is a cupboard with shelves. The base mouldings are a cove and a fillet and the piece stands on ogee bracket feet. The wood is mahogany with a border of the same wood and a narrow band of ebony about the drawers. The handles are the original. This desk is very similar to the one shown in Figure 253, and the veneered front of mahogany is made in imitation of the veneered walnut front on such a piece. The handles, however, show that it belongs to the Sheraton period. It was found in Philadelphia.

Figure 296 shows a pretty little secretary, the property of Mrs. Thomas G. Hazard, of Narragansett Pier, Rhode Island. It is made in mahogany and satin-wood. At the top is a cupboard concealed behind two doors which are inlaid in broad bands, alternately mahogany and satin-wood, set in fan shape. The front of the lower part folds over on hinges and discloses a desk shelf, and below is a drawer made of satin-wood with a mahogany border. The legs are turned and reeded in the typical Sheraton fashion.

Figure 297 shows a form of desk quite popular about 1800. The upper section contains pigeon-holes covered with tambour slides with alternating strips of mahogany and satin-wood. The writing-table, when open, is supported by pulls. In the lower section are three long drawers with satin-wood panels. A bead moulding is on the edge of the drawers instead of on the frame about them, the method

Figure 297.
Inlaid Writing-Table, about 1800.

of the earlier period. The legs are tapering, with a square block near the feet, on the surface of which are turned rosettes. This piece is the property of Mr. Francis H. Bigelow, of Cambridge.

Figure 298 shows another desk of the same general description as that shown in the preceding figure. It is in three carcasses. The cornice moulding consists of a fillet, a cove, an astragal, and a fillet, and above are three acroteriums with urns. The upper carcass has shelves for books and each of the two doors has three lights with rounded tops. Above the doors is inlaid a modification of the meander pattern. The middle section has pigeon-holes and drawers concealed behind three solid doors, and below are three small drawers. The lower section

Figure 298.
Inlaid Writing-Table with bookcase top, about 1800.

contains the writing-table which opens out and is supported by pulls. Below are three drawers of satin-wood with mahogany. A bead moulding finishes the edges of the drawers. The piece stands on simple turned legs. Such pieces as these are found principally in New England and closely resemble the sideboards shown in Figures 214 and 215. This desk is in the Bolles Collection.

Figure 299 shows a Sheraton writing-table inlaid with satin-wood, ebony, and box. The writing-board is hinged and folds back on

Figure 299.

Inlaid Writing-Table, 1810.

itself in the usual manner. At the top are three drawers below which are two recessed sections containing pigeon-holes and drawers covered with tambour slides, and at the centre is a solid door with a medallion inlaid. This piece was purchased in 1810 and is now owned by Miss Mary Bulkley, of Hartford.

An interesting little scrutoire belonging to Mr. George S. Palmer is shown in Figure 300. The upper section is a box or cabinet, the front of which falls, making a surface upon which to write and disclosing six drawers and a centre pigeon-hole. The lower part is a table with one drawer of mahogany and satin-wood. The piece has tapering fluted legs.

Figure 300.
Inlaid Writing-Cabinet, about 1800.

DESKS AND SCRUTOIRES 275

A desk in Sheraton style is shown in Figure 301 and is the property of Mr. Marsden J. Perry, of Providence. It is composed of two pedestals with a desk drawer between. In the upper section of each pedestal is a glass door

Figure 301.
Inlaid Desk, 1800–10.

with an oval centre medallion on which is painted a dancing girl. A looking-glass border is about the medallion, and at the spandrels are painted grapes and leaves. The centre section of each pedestal has cupboards concealed behind doors, inlaid in two medallions of satin-wood and a satin-wood border; the rest of the surface is of mahogany. The lower section of each pedestal is supported by four turned legs, and between these legs are four drawers graduated in width, the smallest being at the bottom, which is finished with a wide cove moulding. Each pedestal stands on short turned feet. At the top are round finials. Between the pedestals is a drawer with four oval medallions inlaid in satin-wood. The front of the drawer falls, disclosing a desk, which contains pigeon-holes, cupboards, and drawers inlaid in a similar manner to the outside. This desk is of American origin, and the theme is taken from Sheraton's design called "The Sisters' Cylinder Bookcase," the difference being that in his design provision is made for two persons to sit facing each other; a cylinder covers the writing-table, the upper section of the pedestals are bookcases with globe terminals, and the feet are more elaborately turned.

Figure 302.
Scrutoire with bookcase top, 1800–10.

Figure 303.
Chest of Drawers with desk drawer, 1800–10

Figure 302 shows a still later form of scrutoire with bookcase top. The cornice mouldings are a quarter-round, a fillet, a dentil moulding, a fillet, a cove, an astragal, and a fillet, and the top is in the same form as that shown in Figure 298 except that the finials are of brass. The glass of the doors is cut in geometrical shapes. The front of the upper drawer in the lower section falls on a quadrant and discloses a desk with pigeon-holes and drawers. Below are three drawers all of which are finished with a bead moulding. The piece stands on straight bracket feet.

DESKS AND SCRUTOIRES

A chest of drawers, the top drawer of which contains a desk, is shown in Figure 303. Below the desk drawer are three drawers all of which have the oval brasses. This piece stands on French bracket feet and belongs to F. T. Bontecou.

Chests of drawers are commonly called bureaus in this country, and they probably derive the name from the fact that many were made with the writing-drawer.

Figure 304.
Empire Writing-Table, about 1820.

Figure 305.
Empire Scrutoire, 1810–20.

Figure 304 shows a late form of scrutoire. The upper section is a small bookcase with four panes of glass with rounded tops. The top is scrolled. The writing-table folds over in the usual way. The upper drawer overlaps and is supported with twisted columns and the piece stands on turned legs.

Figure 305 shows an inlaid scrutoire of the Empire period. It will be seen that it is built on the same principle as the early ball-foot scrutoire shown in Figure 238. There is a drawer above the desk part. The writing-table is formed by the front which falls forward and is held by chains. This piece is elaborately inlaid in floral designs. The corners are chamfered and are filled in with the head and feet of a woman in brass, and there is a raised brass beading about the drawers. Another inlay of brass is about a quarter-inch from the edge.

Many pieces of this general form are found in this country. They are usually of mahogany and often have brass mounts.

Very few bookcases prior to 1790 have been found in this country. The cabinet tops of scrutoires were often used for holding books, and those with glass doors were always intended for books, and it is probable that such pieces would hold practically all of the books that the ordinary family would have, consequently

Figure 306.
Bookcase, Chippendale style, 1760–70.

there was no great need for large separate bookcases. There is, however, a very good example of an early bookcase in the Warner house in Portsmouth.

In England bookcases are common. They are usually made with a projecting central section with two wings, as is the one in the Warner house.

A very handsome mahogany bookcase in the Chippendale style is shown in Figure 306 and is the property of the Honourable Morgan G. Bulkeley, of Hartford. It is made in three sections. The central section projects and has an interrupted pediment top. The mouldings consist of a fillet, a cyma recta carved in an acanthus-leaf design, a narrow fillet, a corona, a fillet, a quarter-round, a

DESKS AND SCRUTOIRES 279

fillet, a cove, a dentil moulding, a fillet, and a quarter-round. On the front, below the cornice on both sections, is carved a very beautiful fret design. At the centre of the top is a carved eagle. The doors are cut in geometrical designs, and below them are nine small drawers with the surface ornamented with fluting. At the ends of the lower section are cupboards and at the centre are ten

Figure 307.
Bookcase, Shearer style, 1780–90.

drawers. The skirt flares and is carved in a scroll-and-leaf design with a shell at the centre of each section. The feet are ogee feet with acanthus-leaf carving on the legs.

Figure 307 shows a library bookcase, the property of Professor Henry T. Fowler, of Providence. The piece is made in three sections, the outer ones slightly recessed. The three doors contain looking-glass, the panes cut in Gothic form. The outer doors conceal bookcases and the centre ones, bookcases and a desk, which is disclosed by the falling of the desk front. In the lower section are cupboards and sliding shelves. In the centre of each of the lower doors is inlaid a fan medallion. The piece stands on straight bracket feet. The bookcase

Figure 308.
Bookcase, Sheraton style, 1790–1800.

is very similar to a design by Shearer shown in Plate 1 of the "Cabinet Makers' Book of Prices." It was formerly the property of General Knox and is said to have come from the Tuileries.

Figure 308 shows a small bookcase of a little later date which belongs to the writer. The mouldings consist of a fillet, a small cyma reversa, a quarter-round, a fillet, a cove, an astragal, a fillet, and a small cove, and just above the doors is an astragal and a fillet. The doors are cut in geometrical design and in the lower section are three long drawers. Just above the drawers is a slide, which pulls out, upon which to place books. The front of this slide is supported by legs which, when the slide is closed, form part of the stiles.

VI
LOOKING-GLASSES

THE use of mirrors dates from prehistoric times. They were of polished metal, small, and generally intended to be used in the hand. It was not until the early sixteenth century that glass was used for mirrors, and at that time Venetian workmen received state protection for the manufacture of looking-glasses, and for more than a century Venice supplied practically the whole world. The word looking-glass in the place of mirror occurs throughout the American inventories. In England the first looking-glass plates for mirrors were made in the year 1673 at Lambeth, and from that time were in general use. The records throughout the colonies for the first few years mention looking-glasses valued at from two to five shillings. As these must have been Venetian ones previous to 1673, and consequently expensive, the inference is that at that low estimate of value they must have been mere hand-glasses. After 1680, however, the records show them to have been of considerable value, very much above most of the furniture. Other records are: at Salem, in 1684, "a large looking glass and brasses" valued at £2, 5s.; at New York, in 1689, "a large looking glass 36s.," and in 1696 one at £5; at Boston, in 1698, "a large looking glass," £2, 15s.; at Philadelphia, in 1686, "a square looking glass with diamonds," and in 1687, "an olive wood diamond cut looking glass"; at New York, in 1696, "a looking glass with a gilded frame and one with an ebony frame," and in 1697, "one large looking glass with a walnut tree frame."

The descriptions above enumerated cover practically all the hints that the records give of the character of looking-glasses previous to 1700. Fortunately, however, a number of these looking-glasses have survived and will be illustrated in the following pages. The glasses, of course, were all imported in colonial times, and, as might be expected, the advertisements frequently contain notices of their importation, giving the sizes and sometimes the prices. For instance, the following advertisement appears in the Newport *Mercury*, May 13, 1765: "To be sold by Peckham & Gould at their shop in Thames Street, an assortment of looking-glasses, viz: mahogany, sconce, gilt edge and shell, thirty inches by seventeen, plain ditto twenty five inches by thirteen, twenty three by twelve and down to seven by five." Mention is also made of the importation of the looking-glasses in their frames as early as 1686, and a number of looking-glasses found here still bear the London maker's name. The Boston *News Letter* for August 10, 1719, advertises "looking glasses of divers sorts and sizes lately imported from London to be sold at the glass shop Queens Street."

It has been thought by many that practically all of the glass and frames were imported. This hardly seems probable, not only because glasses are mentioned as separately imported, but because there were good cabinet-makers, japanners, and gilders here who were undoubtedly able to construct such a simple thing as a looking-glass frame. Stephen Dwight, of New York, had his place of business between the Ferry Stairs and Burling Slip, and in 1755 advertised to carve picture and looking-glass frames. The truth probably is that many of the better frames were imported and the large number of plainer ones were made by local men who copied the imported designs, limited only by their skill and the price at which the looking-glass was to be sold. The earlier plates were so expensive that probably many persons could not afford an expensive frame, and doubtless some of them were simply enclosed in a plain frame for the protection of the glass.

Figure 309.
Looking-Glass with stump-embroidery frame, about 1640.

It also seems to have been the fashion to have old looking-glasses remodelled, and many advertisements to this effect are found in the newspapers. In 1730 James Foddy advertised "to alter and amend old looking glasses."

The following characteristic advertisement appears at New York, in 1775, of "Minshiells looking glass store, removed from Smith Street to Hanover Square (opposite Mr. Goelet's, The Sign of the Golden Key)." He advertised, "an elegant assortment of looking glasses in oval and square ornamental frames, ditto mahogany; the greatest variety of girondoles ever imported to this city; brackets for busts or lustres, ornaments for chimney pieces, as tablets, friezes, etc. Birds and baskets of flowers for the top of book cases or glass frames, gilt

LOOKING-GLASSES

bordering for rooms by the yard. Engravings by Strange, Woollet, Vivans and other eminent masters. A pleasing variety of mezzotintoes well chosen and beautifully colored. Also an elegant assortment of frames without glass. Any lady or gentleman that have glass in old fashioned frames may have them cut in ovals or put in any pattern that pleases them best. The above frames may be finished white or green and white, purple, or any other color that suits the furniture of the room, or gilt in oil or burnished gold, equal to the best imported."

An early form of looking-glass frame is shown in Figure 309. The edges are cut in curves and the entire surface is ornamented with very fine stump embroidery. On the sides are represented Charles I and his queen and at the two upper corners are castles. At the centre of the top is an angel playing on a musical instrument, and the remaining spaces are filled in with birds, animals, trees, and flowers. The frame is fastened into an oak box. This frame was sold at the sale of the property of the Right Honourable the Viscountess Wolseley and is the property of the Rosenbach Company, Philadelphia.

The earliest frames mentioned in the American inventories were of ebony. A little later walnut and olive wood were freely mentioned.

Figure 310.
Looking-Glass with marquetry frame, 1690–1700.

There are two kinds of early looking-glasses, those having the square or slightly rectangular glass, and those having long frames with two glasses, one above the other. The latter type is called a pier-glass.

In Virginia, in 1678, is mentioned "1 olive wood glass, 1 large walnut tree glass £4 14s"; at Philadelphia, in 1687, "an olive wood diamond cut looking glass."

A number of these olive-wood looking-glasses are to be found in this country, and an excellent example is shown in Figure 310. This piece was found at Portsmouth, New Hampshire, where it had been from colonial times, and it is still in the original condition except for the glass. It is in the characteristic shape of the seventeenth-century looking-glasses, nearly square with an extension top in the form of a half circle at the centre and on either side a fillet and a quarter circle. The mouldings of the frame are also characteristic of the period, consisting of a small ovolo, a broad one, a bead, and a narrow ovolo next to the glass. On the small ovolo the veneer of olive wood is composed of cross-sections. The frame, of course, must have been imported. It is ornamented with exceedingly fine

Figure 311.
Looking-Glass with walnut frame,
1700–10.

Figure 312.
Looking-Glass with walnut frame,
1700–10.

marquetry in shades of brown toned into each other. The design on the frame is of foliated scrolls and flowers, and on the top are foliated scrolls and two birds with beaks together and a crown above. The frame is a little larger than usual, measuring 33 inches by 28 inches exclusive of the top. It is in the writer's possession.

Only a few of these frames have been found in this country. There is a small one at the Whipple house, Ipswich, the top of which is missing, and there are two or three others in private collections. This form of looking-glass was popular in the last quarter of the seventeenth century, and a number of silver frames substantially in this form are known, hall-marked from 1685 to 1701.

LOOKING-GLASSES

Another form of early looking-glass, which was made of walnut, is shown in Figure 311. The mouldings are the same as those in the preceding figure, and the top, except for the fretwork, is also the same. The fret design is in scrolls and fleur-de-lis. The veneer on the small ovolo is applied in the same way as in the preceding figure. This form of early looking-glass is more commonly found than the marquetry ones, although all seventeenth-century looking-glasses are scarce. This piece is in the Blaney Collection.

Figure 313.
Looking-Glass with walnut frame, about 1710.

Figure 312 shows a small looking-glass of the same type which is in the possession of Mr. Francis H. Bigelow, of Cambridge. The mouldings of the frame are the same as those shown in the preceding figure, but the top has a single circle deeply cut in a double-fret design consisting of foliated scrolls with a fleur-de-lis at the centre.

Still another of these early walnut looking-glasses in the same collection is shown in Figure 313. The mouldings of the frame are the same as in the preceding figure, except that the one nearest the glass is a cyma instead of an ovolo, and this shows it to be of a little later date than the others. The fret design at the top is quite ornate and consists of foliated scrolls and fleur-de-lis with a crown above.

286 COLONIAL FURNITURE

The second type of early looking-glasses was a pier-glass of which an early example is shown in Figure 314. The edges of the cresting are cut in Flemish scrolls with acanthus-leaf foliations, and at the centre is a plain oval cartouche with an egg-and-dart moulding about it. Just above the frame, on either side, is a long acanthus-leaf scroll extending nearly to the cartouche. The entire back-

Figure 314.
Looking-Glass with gilt frame, first quarter eighteenth century.

Figure 315.
Looking-Glass with japanned frame, first quarter eighteenth century.

ground of the cresting is covered with diagonally crossed lines. The urn and flame at the top is an improper restoration, otherwise the piece is in the original condition. The upper section of the frame is cut in cyma curves, and on either side, extending to the straight part of the frame, are carved acanthus leaves. On the frame is carved a design of a shell, with acanthus-leaf streamers separated by an arched band from which is a pendent flower. The glass was originally in two sections and bevelled. The designs above described are the familiar ones of the Marot school to which this particular frame belongs. For the purpose of obtain-

LOOKING-GLASSES

ing different colours the entire surface is covered with gold and silver leaf and Dutch metal. This looking-glass was found in America, where it had been from colonial times. It is the property of the writer.

Such elaborately carved frames were, of course, rare in this country, but the shape was quite common. There are many frames found here with the upper sections curved, and often a cresting of wood cut in the general outline of these carved scrolls was added.

Figure 315 shows such a frame. The top is half-round and on either side is a cyma reversa, otherwise the frame, which is moulded, has straight edges. It will be seen that the panels of the doors of the scrutoire shown in Figure 241 are in the same outline. The frame is japanned and the mouldings consist of a beading on the outer edge and an ovolo. The design cut on the upper glass consists of leaves and flowers, and the edges following the curve of the frame are bevelled and the lower edge is scalloped and bevelled. It is probable that pier-glasses mentioned in the early advertisements refer to such looking-glasses as this, and it is also probable that the references in Philadelphia to "diamond cut looking glasses" refer to the ornament cut on the upper glass, as in this piece. This style of looking-glass is found also with a cut-work cresting, which in the earlier ones slipped in back of the mouldings but in later ones was part of the frame, the moulding being planted on the cresting.

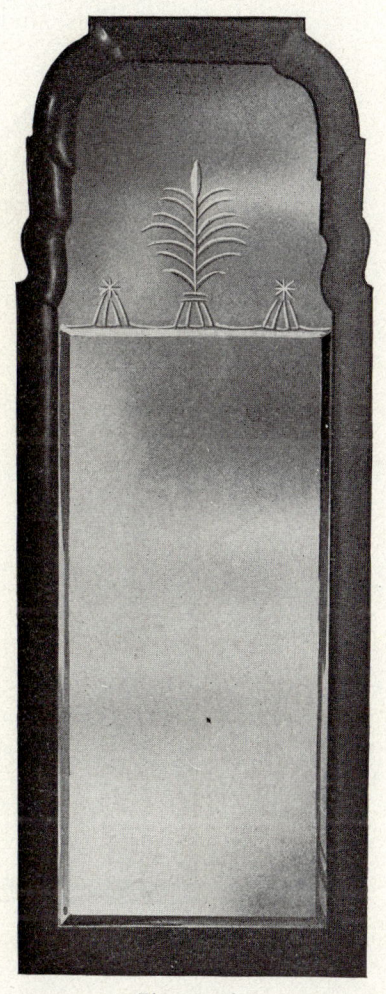

Figure 316.
Looking-Glass with walnut frame, first quarter eighteenth century.

Another looking-glass of the type under discussion is shown in Figure 316. The frame is walnut and the mouldings are a bead on the outer edge and an ovolo. The upper plate is cut in a leaf design with a star on either side. This frame probably had a cut cresting. The curves in the upper section are very similar to those shown in Figure 314. Both of the last-mentioned looking-glasses are in the possession of the writer.

Two looking-glasses of the same general type but of a slightly later date are shown in Figure 317 and are in the Bolles Collection, the property of the Metropolitan Museum of Art. The cresting on each of these looking-glasses is made separate from the frame. The upper section of each frame is in curves and the cresting on the first one has two scrolls and a central rounded projection. The other one is so crudely cut that it is difficult to determine what it was intended to represent.

Figure 318 shows another early pier-glass with sconces attached. At the centre of the top is carved a shell the edges of which are finished with out-turning acanthus leaves. This shell is supported by two large Flemish scrolls. At the

Figure 317.

Two Looking-Glasses with walnut frames, first quarter eighteenth century.

base are two large S scrolls between which is a woman's head with a shell-shaped head-dress. This design was one of the most popular of the Marot school. At the base of the upper scroll and near the base of the frame are spiral-twisted volutes. The frame is gilded throughout. It is in the Pendleton Collection, owned by the Rhode Island School of Design.

During the reign of Queen Anne looking-glass frames more closely followed architectural lines.

Figure 319 shows a looking-glass of the period, the property of Mr. John J. Gilbert, of Baltimore. The cresting is of walnut and gilt. At either side of the centre are cyma scrolls, the inner ends finished with rosettes with pendent

LOOKING-GLASSES

leaves. The mouldings of these scrolls are a fillet and a cyma recta enriched with carving in acanthus-leaf design. At the centre is a cartouche bordered with acanthus-leaf designs and spiral volutes in the centre of which is a grotesque mascaron. Below the scroll top are scrolls with acanthus leaves and rosettes. The upper section of the frame is cut in curves and the looking-glass is bordered

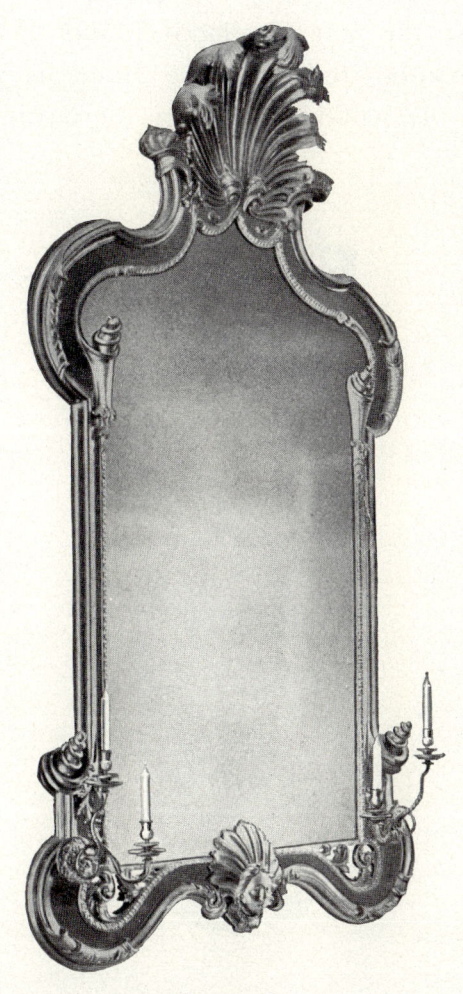

Figure 318.
Looking-Glass with gilt frame, first quarter eighteenth century.

Figure 319.
Looking-Glass with walnut and gilt frame, first quarter eighteenth century.

by a band of glass. At the base are foliated scrolls and at the centre is applied a shell with acanthus-leaf streamers. All of the carved portions are gilded. It was such a looking-glass as this that was the model for many of the so-called cut-work looking-glasses which were popular both here and in England.

Figure 320 shows a japanned looking-glass, the property of Mr. Francis H. Bigelow, of Cambridge. The cresting, which is simply cut, suggests the preceding looking-glass frame. It has the scrolls on either side and a raised centre with scalloped edges. On the surface of the cresting are a house, birds, and flowers in raised japanning. The upper section of the frame is curved and the frame has a flat strip bordered on either side by a small half-round. On this flat surface is raised japanning.

Figure 321 shows a pier-glass which is at the Van Cortlandt Manor House, Croton-on-Hudson. The frame is very tall. It will be seen that the outline of

Figure 320.
Looking-Glass with japanned frame, first quarter eighteenth century.

Figure 321.
Looking-Glass with walnut and gilt frame, first quarter eighteenth century.

the cresting is suggestive of that shown in Figure 319 and the edges of the scrolls are slightly carved and gilded. The centre ornament is missing. The upper section of the frame is cut in curves, and down the sides are carved and gilded flowers, fruits, and leaves. There are two glasses, the upper one overlapping the lower one in the usual manner of this period.

Figure 322 shows another looking-glass in this same general style which is in the writer's possession. The general outline of the cresting is the same, with the scrolls at either side and the centre raised, and at the centre is a circle cut out and filled in with a carved and gilded conventional shell. The upper section of the frame is curved in the usual manner and there is an inner moulding carved in an acanthus-leaf design and gilded. The frame is made of walnut. This style of looking-glass is the one most commonly found of all the early forms.

Figure 322.
Looking-Glass with walnut and gilt frame, first quarter eighteenth century.

Figure 323.
Looking-Glass with walnut and gilt frame, first quarter eighteenth century.

A variation of the preceding form is shown in Figure 323. The cresting is cut with the scrolls and raised centre, and at the centre is applied a carved and gilded shell and streamers. The edges of the frame at the top are curved and there is a carved and gilded border on the inside. This looking-glass is the property of Mr. G. W. Walker, of New York.

A very simple form of the type of looking-glass now under discussion is shown in Figure 324 and is the property of Mr. C. R. Morson, of Brooklyn. The cresting is cut in the form of two shallow scrolls with a suggestion of foliations on either side of the centre. There is a simple curving of the frame at the upper end.

COLONIAL FURNITURE

The second type of looking-glass that was popular during this period was one in which the frame was rectangular except for a slight curve in the corners of the top. A very fine example of such a looking-glass is shown in Figure 325 and is the property of the Tiffany Studios in New York. On either side of the top are series of scrolls, the edges carved in an acanthus-leaf design. At the centre

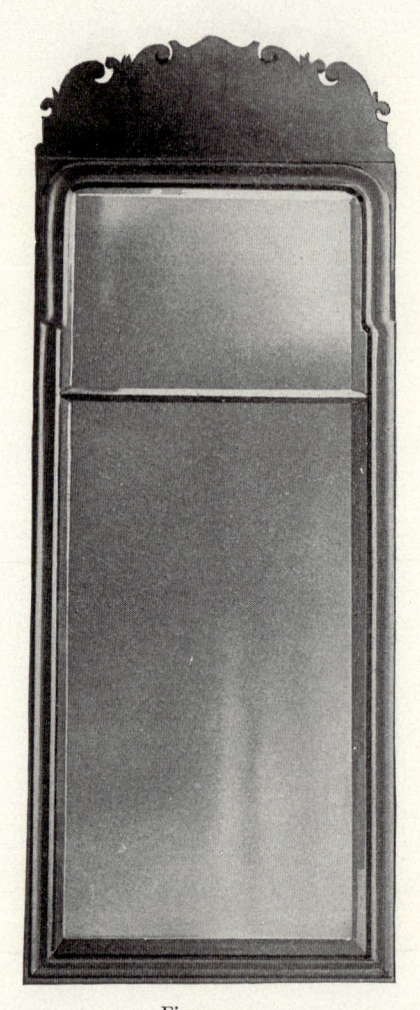

Figure 324.
Looking-Glass with walnut frame, first quarter eighteenth century.

Figure 325.
Looking-Glass with gilt and carved frame, first quarter eighteenth century.

is a three-branch cartouche, the edges of which are finished in a manner suggesting acanthus leaves, and on the surface is a rosette and leaves. On either side of the centre are two birds standing on small pedestals and at the centre three rosettes and leaves. On the sides are acanthus-leaf scrolls and on the surfaces are carved leaves and flowers, and there is a pendent flower ornament on either side. At the base are carved acanthus-leaf scrolls and at the centre a shell with streamers. The edge of the frame is carved in acanthus-leaf design and the whole piece is gilded. This looking-glass represents the best work of the period and, as before stated, such ornate mirrors were probably very scarce in this country. The form, however, was very common.

LOOKING-GLASSES

Figure 326 shows a looking-glass in the Bolles Collection which is of this type and is in a design quite commonly found here. It will be seen that it has practically the same design as that shown in the preceding figure except that instead of being carved the outline is merely indicated in the cutting. At the centre of the cresting is applied a carved and gilded scroll design with leaves and

Figure 327.
Looking-Glass with walnut and gilt frame,
1725–50.

Figure 326.
Looking-Glass with walnut and gilt frame,
1725–50.

flowers and at the bottom is a conventionalised shell with acanthus streamers. The edge of the looking-glass is straight except for the small curves at the two upper ends, which are the same as those shown in the last figure, and the moulding on the frame nearest the glass is carved in scroll and flower design and gilded.

Figure 327 shows another looking-glass of this same type, the principal difference being in the fact that the centre of the cresting is pierced and a carved and gilded crown is inserted. This general form of looking-glass continued to be used throughout the eighteenth century and the later examples will be shown below.

A different type of looking-glass with the so-called cut-work frame is shown in Figure 328. There are a number of examples found of this style, most of them being rather small. The distinguishing feature is that the cresting is very much higher than is usual, and the cutting is not in an architectural form but seems to be composed of scrolls. At the centre of the cresting is applied a carved and gilded urn and flame with acanthus-leaf streamers, and at the base is a carved and gilded scroll design with streamers. These pieces invariably have an applied carved and gilded ornament which is in the form of scrolls, urns, or cartouches. The sides of these frames are straight and apparently never had cut-work projecting edges. This form of looking-glass also remained popular and was adopted by the later styles, examples of which will be shown below.

Another form of looking-glass frame which was introduced prior to 1750 and which continued popular throughout the eighteenth century was that having a pediment top with architectural outlines.

An early example of such a looking-glass is shown in Figure 329 and is the property of Mrs. John R. Matthews, of Croton, New York. The piece has a scroll pediment, the inner edges of the scroll finished in rosettes similar to the high chests of drawers and the cabinet-top scrutoires of the period, and at the centre is an urn. Below this top is planted a moulding with projecting square corners at the top and scrolled at the bottom, a design which was popular for the mouldings about windows and doors of the houses of the period. On the outer edges are carved pendent fruit and leaves. The glass is in two sections, the upper one curved as in the earlier pieces.

Figure 328.
Looking-Glass with walnut and gilt frame, 1725–50.

Figure 329.
Looking-Glass Frame with scroll pediment, 1725–50.

Figure 330 shows another example of a looking-glass with a scroll pediment. The inner edges of the scrolls terminate in rosettes with pendent leaves, and the mouldings consist of a fillet and cyma recta ornamented with acanthus-leaf carving, a fillet, a cove, a corona, a fillet, a quarter-round ornamented with

LOOKING-GLASSES

egg-and-dart moulding, a fillet and a small cove, all gilded. At the centre is a cartouche with carved outstanding acanthus-leaf scrolls and on the surface of the cartouche are carved pendent flowers. Below the pediment on either side are two carved and gilded ornaments representing rosettes with long pendent leaves, and at the centre is carved a conventionalised shell with streamers of leaves, flowers, and fruit, gilded. Below this is the moulding which appears in the former figure, with the raised square corners and scroll base, on the surface of which is carved the same design as appears in Figure 314. On the sides are carved pendent leaves, flowers, and fruit. The inner edge of the looking-glass is rectangular and the moulding is carved in acanthus-leaf design. This looking-glass is the property of the Metropolitan Museum of Art.

Figure 330.
Looking-Glass Frame with scroll pediment, 1725–50.

Figure 331.
Looking-Glass Frame with scroll pediment, 1750–75.

Another looking-glass with a scroll pediment, the property of the writer, is shown in Figure 331. On either side is the scroll, the inner edges finished with carved rosettes with pendent flowers. The mouldings consist of a fillet and a cyma recta carved in a crude acanthus-leaf design, a fillet, a cove, a corona, a fillet, and a cyma reversa carved in acanthus-leaf design. The mouldings do not carry across the front, but are broken at the centre to admit a carved scroll and foliated design. At the centre is carved a pheasant with wings overt, standing on a rococo scroll base. The frame is bordered with the mouldings

Figure 332.
Looking-Glass Frame with scroll pediment, 1750–75.

Figure 333.
Looking-Glass Frame with scroll pediment, 1750–75.

described in the preceding figure, and on the outer edges are carved and gilded pendent flowers and fruit. The edges of the mouldings are carved in acanthus-leaf design. This piece shows the Chippendale influence and is somewhat later than the preceding piece.

Figure 332 shows another scroll-pediment looking-glass, the property of Mr. H. W. Erving, of Hartford. The surfaces of the scrolls are elaborately carved, and at the inner ends are rosettes with beautifully carved acanthus-leaf pendants. The mouldings consist of a fillet, a cyma recta with acanthus-leaf carving, a fillet,

LOOKING-GLASSES

and a quarter-round finished with an egg-and-dart moulding on the scroll, and on the moulding extending across the front is a fillet and a cyma recta carved in an acanthus-leaf design. At the centre is a pheasant with wings extended and head raised standing on a diminutive tree. Below the pediment top is a conventionalised shell with a pendent flower and acanthus-leaf scrolls. The mouldings on the outer edge are the usual kind with the projecting square corners at the top and a scroll below, and in each square at the top is applied a carved and gilded rosette. On each side are carved pendent leaves. At the centre of the base are two acanthus leaves bound together by a flower design. The upper corners on the looking-glass frame are curved in the manner shown in Figure 325.

Another scroll-pediment looking-glass is shown in Figure 333, the property of Mr. Dwight M. Prouty, of Boston. The scrolls at the top are unusually straight up and down and the mouldings are the same as those in the last figure. The inner edges of the scrolls are finished with the usual rosettes with pendent leaves. At the centre is a bird with an eagle's head and a pheasant's tail standing on a ball. The mouldings about the edge are of the same type above described and on either side are carved pendent leaves. At the centre of the squares at the top are carved and gilded stars. This frame has a number of points in common with the preceding one, and especially should be noted the curve of the sides and lower edges which are identical and are different from those shown in the earlier examples.

Figure 334.
Looking-Glass in Chippendale style, 1750–65.

About 1750 the style of the more elaborate looking-glasses completely changed. Instead of the massive architectural or solid effects of the cresting were substituted light, open, flowing lines in what is known as the Chippendale style. About this time many designers appeared who published designs for looking-glass frames, among them H. Copeland, who published in 1746; Locke, who published in 1752;

Johnson, and Chippendale. All of these designers were steeped in the designs of the Louis XV school with rococo ornamentation, or, as in the case of Edwards & Darley, in the Chinese taste. Of all these cabinet-makers the designs of Thomas Chippendale were the most refined, and a splendid example of one of his designs for a looking-glass is shown in Figure 334 and is the property of Mr. Richard A. Canfield. At the top are branches of leaves, fruits, and flowers, supported by a foliated scroll design, upon which is carved the dripping-water effect so popular in this period. This in turn is supported by large foliated C scrolls within which is an oval-shaped looking-glass, and on either side are urns with leaves and flowers. These urns and flowers are supported by the main outlines of the frame, which consist of an elongated double scroll outstanding from which are carved flowers and leaves. The main looking-glass is surrounded by foliated scrolls, and between this frame and the outer frame are inserted sections of looking-glass which tend to give the piece a delicate effect. At the centre of the base are two C scrolls separated by rococo and leaf ornamentation.

Figure 335.
Girandole in Chippendale style, 1750–65.

An interesting girandole is shown in Figure 335, the property of Mr. H. W. Erving, of Hartford. The upper end of the frame, which is small, is in a rococo design with foliated scrolls and flowers, as are also the sides. Across the base is a scroll design with flowers and at either corner is a sconce holding one candle. This frame has been in this country from colonial times, and represents the better class of looking-glasses of the Chippendale period that were found in this country. It will be seen, however, that the details of the scrolls are not so finely worked out as in the preceding looking-glass which is of English origin.

During this period long mantel looking-glasses were popular in England, but only a few examples have been found in this country.

Figure 336 shows a mantel looking-glass in the Pendleton Collection, owned by the Rhode Island School of Design. At the top are C scrolls with acanthus-leaf borders and dripping-water effects, and within the centre is a scroll design.

LOOKING-GLASSES

On the sides are smaller scrolls filled in with leaves and flowers and on the sides at the bases are represented castles. About the upper edge of the looking-glass

Figure 336.
Mantel Looking-Glass, Chippendale style, 1750–70.

Figure 337.
Mantel Looking-Glass, Chippendale style, 1750–65.

frame are a series of C scrolls. There are columns at the ends and two columns divide the looking-glass into three parts. Across the base are similar C scrolls with dripping-water effects.

A very beautiful mantel looking-glass in the same collection is shown in Figure 337. At the centre is a cartouche composed of C scrolls and conventionalised acanthus leaves at the top. Within is a painting. Extending from the central cartouche is a very beautiful series of scrolls filled in with flowers and leaves, and at the upper corners and above the scrolls at the base are acroteriums. About the frame is carved a very beautiful design in rococo and at the centre of the top over this surface are carved sprays of flowers. No such looking-glass as this has been found in this country, but it is shown to give the reader an idea of the beauty of some of the English looking-glasses of the period, which must have been seen by the American cabinet-makers who had come from England.

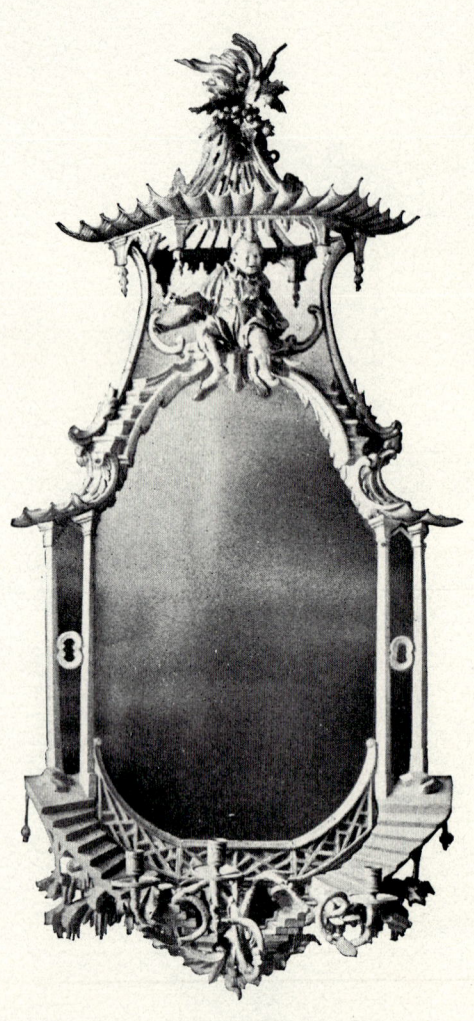

Figure 338 shows a looking-glass which is in the style most used by Edwards & Darley. The entire looking-glass is in Chinese taste. The top consists of an open-work pagoda within which sits a Chinaman with a dagger in his hand. On either side are represented steps leading up to him. Below, on each side, are two columns and series of steps leading to the base, and around the lower section of the glass is a fretwork rail. At the centre of the bottom is a sconce with three branches.

Figure 338.
Girandole in Edwards & Darley style, 1750–65.

Next to Chippendale, probably the greatest designer of looking-glass frames was Johnson, and a pier-glass and table in his style is shown in Figure 339, the property of Mr. Marsden J. Perry. The general outline of the frame, with its foliated scrolls and flowers, is similar to Chippendale's designs. At the top is a stag standing on a foliated acroterium, which is supported by two large C scrolls within the arc of which are garlands of flowers. Between the C scrolls is a panel of glass over which are hung garlands of flowers, and below these is the figure of a woman. There is a glass border between the lines of scrolls on either side of the looking-glass as is usual. At about the centre of the sides on either side is a crane and at the top on either side is a dog. At the centre of the base is a small hut. The frame is supported

LOOKING-GLASSES

by C-scroll feet. The pier-table is a companion piece. The legs are composed of scrolls with glass between, and a stretcher extends between the legs crowned at the

Figure 339.
Pier Glass and Table in Johnson style, 1750–65.

centre by a summer-house with a pagoda top. On either side is a monkey climbing toward the summer-house. The motifs of human figures and animals are the chief characteristics of Johnson's style and were rarely employed by Chippendale.

A simple looking-glass in Chippendale style is shown in Figure 340. The surface and the cresting are carved in rococo designs and scrolls, and similar designs are represented at the base. The upper section of the frame is curved in the manner of the earlier period, and the execution is simple and not elaborately worked out as in the English pieces. This looking-glass is somewhat suggestive of the looking-glass shown in Figure 335.

Another simple looking-glass of the period is shown in Figure 341. At the top on a solid background are carved scrolls, leaves, and flowers, and at the centre is an urn within which are flowers. On the lower section are foliated C scrolls with a rosette at the centre. The upper section of the glass is curved. This looking-glass is the property of the writer.

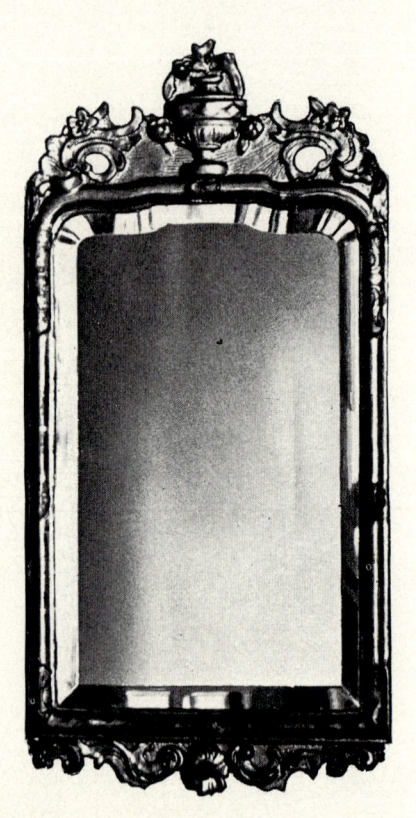

Figure 340.
Gilt Looking-Glass in Chippendale style, 1760–70.

Figure 341.
Gilt Looking-Glass in Chippendale style, 1760–75.

Such elaborate looking-glasses as the English ones above shown were only used in the houses of the wealthier classes. The type of looking-glass that was probably used by the people of moderate means throughout this period was that of which Figure 342 is a fairly good example. It will be seen that the cresting is in the cut-work pattern enriched by C scrolls with rococo effects on either side, and at the centre is a pheasant with wings overt. On the sides are the pendent leaves, flowers, and fruits which are so commonly found, and at the centre of the base is scratched a design of a rosette with streamers which is gilded. The inner edges of

Figure 342.
Looking-Glass with mahogany and gilt frame, 1760–75.

LOOKING-GLASSES

the frame are cut in cyma and simple curves, and the gilded edge is carved in an acanthus-leaf design. This looking-glass is the property of the writer.

We now come to the later example of the cut-work looking-glasses of which Figure 325 was a prototype. It will be seen that the upper edges of the looking-glasses in Figure 343 are curved in the same manner as in that figure. The cut-

Figure 343.

Two Looking-Glasses with mahogany and gilt frames, 1770–80.

work scroll tops are enriched with applied gilded and curved scrolls. On the first one is a small pediment top the inner surface of which is finished with rosettes and pendent leaves, and at the centre is a pheasant with wings overt. On the other one are acanthus scrolls on either side with a similar bird at the centre. Both looking-glasses have on either side the carved pendent leaves and flowers, gilded. These looking-glasses are in the Bolles Collection, owned by the Metropolitan Museum of Art.

Figure 344 shows another example of this same type of looking-glass, the property of the writer. On either side of the top are scrolls, the inner ends finished with rosettes and pendent flowers, and at the centre is a pheasant with wings overt. Below the pheasant is an applied oval with a pearl edge beading and on the sides are the usual pendent leaves and fruits.

Another form of this same style of looking-glass is shown in Figure 345 and is the property of the Tiffany Studios of New York. The cresting is of the usual cut-work type, but on the surfaces are scratched leaf designs instead

Figure 344.
Looking-Glass with mahogany and gilt frame, 1780–90.

Figure 345.
Looking-Glass with mahogany and gilt frame, 1780–90.

of plain surfaces as in those heretofore shown. At the centre is cut a circle and within the circle is a pheasant with wings overt. At the base is applied a carved shell.

A still later example of this same style of looking-glass is shown in Figure 346 and is in the Bolles Collection. The glass in this case is rectangular without the curved upper corners. In the centre of the cresting is a circular opening within which is inserted a pheasant with wings overt, and below are inlaid swags of flowers caught in three places with rosettes.

Figure 347 shows another cut-work looking-glass which is the property of Mr. H. W. Erving. The scrolls at the top are cut in a waving edge, and at the

LOOKING-GLASSES

centre is an urn with carved wood flowers and leaves supported on wire stems. At the centre of the cresting is a leaf design which is repeated at the base. On the sides are pendent leaves, flowers, and fruit. The inner edge of the frame is cut in a similar cyma scroll design as is shown on Figure 342. On the back of this looking-glass is pasted the advertisement of the maker, which reads as follows: "Thomas Aldersey, looking glass maker in London."

Figure 346.
Looking-Glass with mahogany inlaid and gilt frame, about 1790.

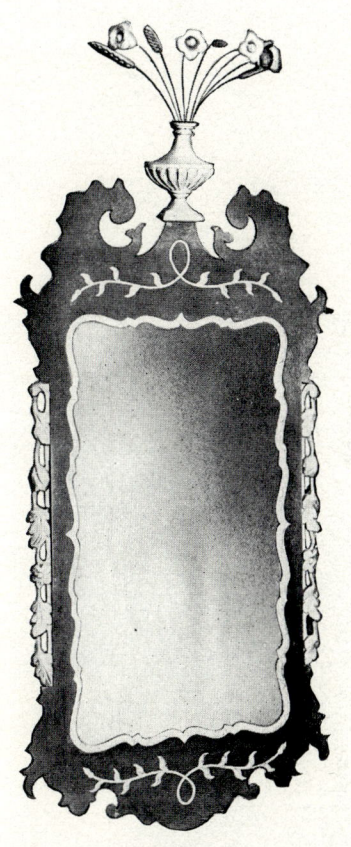

Figure 347.
Looking-Glass with mahogany and gilt frame, 1780–90.

A late form of a pediment-top looking-glass is shown in Figure 348. At either side of the centre of the top is a scroll, the inner edge finished with a simple rosette, and at the centre is an urn in which are flowers and leaves made of composition fastened on wires. The surfaces of the frame are veneered mahogany, and below the urn at the top is an inlaid medallion. On the sides are pendent leaves and flowers made of composition and hung on wires. About the frame, which is square, is a border of inlay.

Another form of small looking-glass is shown in Figure 349. At the centre of the top are leaves and flowers on an arch which is supported by two capitals, between which are swags of flowers and leaves extending from the top of the columns down over the sides. At the bottom are likewise swags of leaves caught up at the ends and the centre, and at the centre are also ribbon effects. This looking-glass is the property of Mrs. Brown, of Salem.

Figure 350 shows another looking-glass of the same general type. At the centre is an urn within which are flowers and leaves and from which depend scrolls with acanthus leaves which twist and terminate in flames. The outer and inner edges of the frame are carved and at the base are swags of leaves caught up at the ends and centre. This looking-glass is the property of the writer.

After about 1760 advertisements are

Figure 348.
Looking-Glass with mahogany and gilt frame, 1790–1800.

Figure 349.
Looking-Glass with carved and gilded frame, about 1780.

frequently found of sconces, but very few have been found in this country. It is probable that they were so fragile that they have become broken.

Figure 351 shows a sconce at the top of which is a bow knot, and below is an eagle with flowers and grasses. The eagle stands on a base from the bottom

LOOKING-GLASSES

of which spring scrolls which hold the two candle-sticks, and below are ribbons terminating in two tassels. Brass chains extend from the top and from the eagle's mouth down to the candles and the rosettes, and from the rosettes are two chains terminating in bells.

Figure 352 shows another sconce at the top of which is carved a bow knot, and below is an eagle with a chain and ball suspended from its mouth. Below are

Figure 350.
Looking-Glass with carved and gilded frame, about 1780.

Figure 351.
Sconce, 1790–1800.

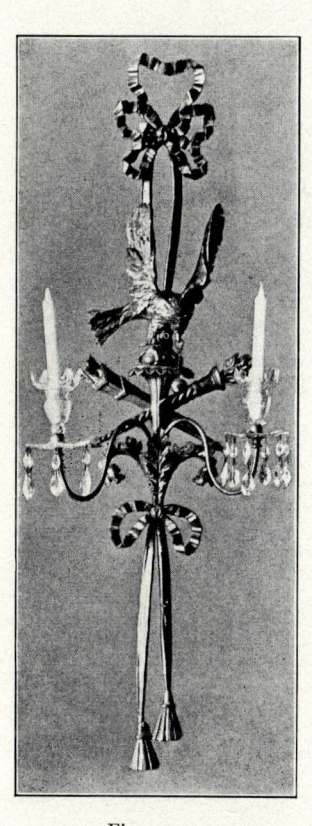

Figure 352.
Sconce, 1790–1800.

a torch and a quiver with arrows crossed. There are two candle-sticks with pendent cut-glass drops, and the base is finished with a bow knot and ribbon ending in a tassel. These sconces are the property of Mr. Marsden J. Perry, of Providence.

A few sconces similar to the one last shown have been found in this country in the South.

Figure 353 shows a shield-shaped looking-glass, the property of Mrs. E. B. Watkinson, of Hartford. The shape is exactly that of the back of Hepplewhite chairs, and the looking-glass belongs to that period. At the top is an urn from which extend grasses and from the ends of the urn are scrolls. A pearl bead moulding finishes the inner edge of the frame and at the base are pendent leaves. On the back of the looking-glass is printed the advertisement of the maker, which reads as follows: "Looking glasses and all sorts of frames with carving and gilding done by George Cooper, real manufacturer, 82 Lombard Street, London." This looking-glass is one of a pair.

The Boston *Gazette*, in 1780, advertised pairs of looking-glasses, and the New York *Gazette and Mercury*, in the same year, contains the advertisement of Duncan Barckley & Co., 16 Hanover Square, "large pier and looking glasses, oval sconces and girondoles."

We now come to a form of looking-glass very common in the later years of the eighteenth century and now known as filigree looking-glasses. The ornamentation on these looking-glasses is of a composition gilded and fastened on wires instead of being cut from the solid wood which was the fashion of an earlier date. Figure 354 shows such a looking-glass, the property of Mr. Albert H. Pitkin, of Hartford. At the centre of the top is an urn with flowers and leaves, and below are scrolls of leaves and flowers extending from the top and down on the sides. At the centre of the base is a half-rosette and there are swags of leaves and flowers.

Figure 353.
Looking-Glass, shield-shaped, 1780–90.

Figure 354.
Looking-Glass, filigree frame, 1785–95.

A similar looking-glass is shown in Figure 355, the property of Mr. Robert T. Smith, of Hartford. The usual urn with flowers is at the top, and below are scrolls and pendent leaves and flowers extending down the sides. At the base are the same pendent leaves and flowers and a central fluted ornament.

LOOKING-GLASSES

Still another looking-glass of the same sort is shown in Figure 356. There is an urn with fluted sides at the centre with flowers. The urn stands on acanthus-leaf scrolls, and pendent flowers extend from the sides of the urn and are caught by rosettes some little distance above the sides on the frame, and from these

Figure 355.
Looking-Glass, filigree frame, 1785–95.

Figure 356.
Looking-Glass, filigree frame, 1785–95.

rosettes are pendent leaves and flowers. The leaves seem to be intended to represent holly. At the base are the same leaves and flowers and a central ornament with pendent leaves.

A very fine example of this style is shown in Figure 357 and is the property of Mr. Marsden J. Perry. At the centre of the top is an oval panel with a pearl edge moulding upon which in relief is carved an urn with festoons, and above are flowers. On either side of the oval medallion are scrolls and grasses, and at the corners are two smaller medallions representing heads. The outer edges of the frame are carved in a pendent flower design, and at the base are a scroll and

310 COLONIAL FURNITURE

flowers and at the centre an oval rosette with a pearl bead edge containing a rosette.

Figure 358 shows a pier-glass, the property of the writer. It will be seen that the design is of the same order as those now under discussion, but the flowers and leaves are all cut from the solid wood instead of being made of composition

Figure 357.
Looking-Glass, Sheraton style, 1785–95.

Figure 358.
Pier-Glass, Sheraton style, 1785–95.

with wires. There is an urn at the centre with a leaf, and from this urn are festoons of flowers and leaves. On either side of the looking-glass frame are acanthus-leaf scrolls which terminate in a flower with fruit, and a similar festoon is on the sides above the base. On the surface of the frame is carved a leaf design. Below the frame are two feet composed of acanthus-leaf scrolls, and at the centre is a small swag of acanthus leaves caught at the centre.

It seems to have been the fashion in the late years of the eighteenth century to make looking-glasses showing harvesting scenes, and several are found in this country. Such a looking-glass is shown in Figure 359 and is the property of the Tiffany Studios. The top is composed of three spiral cornucopias, one upright and two lying on their sides and bound together by a wreath. In the mouth of each of the cornucopias are various kinds of flowers. The frame is rectangular. In each corner is carved a rosette, and between the rosettes is carved a leaf

Figure 359.
Looking-Glass with carved and gilt frame, 1785–95.

Figure 360.
Looking-Glass with carved and gilt frame, 1785–95.

pattern and on the edge nearest the frame is a reel and bead moulding. At the base are scrolls of leaves and flowers.

Figure 360 shows another of these looking-glasses which is the property of Mr. Marsden J. Perry, of Providence. At the centre is a figure probably intended to represent Ceres, and above her head is a bow knot and flowers and leaves. On either side of the figure are cornucopias filled with fruits and flowers which extend partially down the sides. Below the looking-glass frame are two doves standing on a quiver with arrows. The edges of the

312   COLONIAL FURNITURE

frame are carved in a guilloche pattern and the inner edge is finished with a pearl bead moulding.

Another of these looking-glasses is shown in Figure 361 and is the property of Mr. Erving. At the centre is a basket filled with fruits and a sheaf of wheat. On either side are farming implements—a rake, a pitch-fork, a flail, and a scythe—and around each are swags of leaves and flowers which extend down over the sides. At the base are ribbons and drapery. On

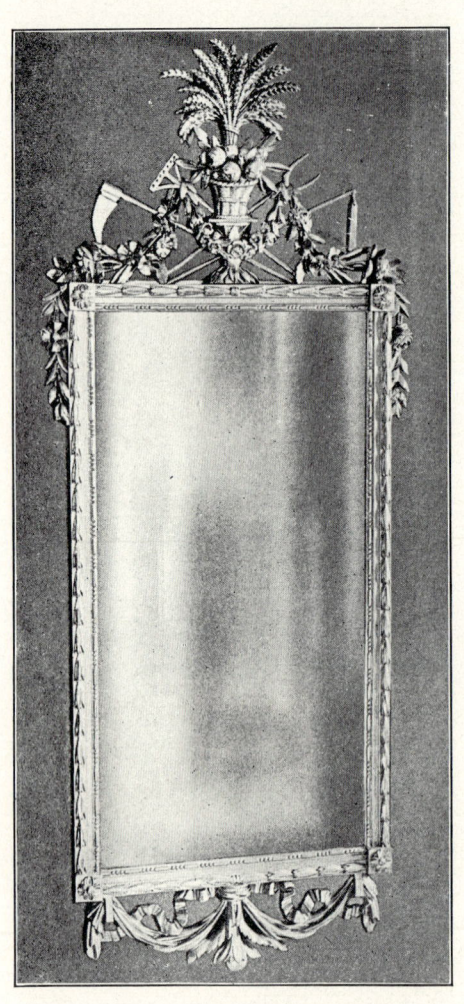

Figure 361.
Looking-Glass with carved and gilt frame,
1785–95.

Figure 362.
Looking-Glass with mahogany and gilt frame,
1785–95.

the edges of the frame are carved pendent leaves with rosettes at the corner, and the inner surface is finished with the reel and bead moulding.

Another form of small looking-glass popular at this time is shown in Figure 362. It will be seen that it is practically a revival of the earlier cut-work looking-glass shown in Figure 328. The cresting is tall and is edged with scrolls, oak leaves, and acorns. At the centre is a basket with scrolls, and acorns and leaves within. The lower edge is finished in a scroll design. All of the carving is gilded.

LOOKING-GLASSES

The inner edge of the frame is finished with a pearl bead moulding. This looking-glass is the property of the writer.

A more elaborate looking-glass of the same general character is shown in Figure 363, the property of Mr. H. W. Erving. On the top is applied an arch upon which is a bow knot with pendent leaves and fruit. Below this are scrolls

Figure 363.
Looking-Glass with mahogany and gilt frame, 1785–95.

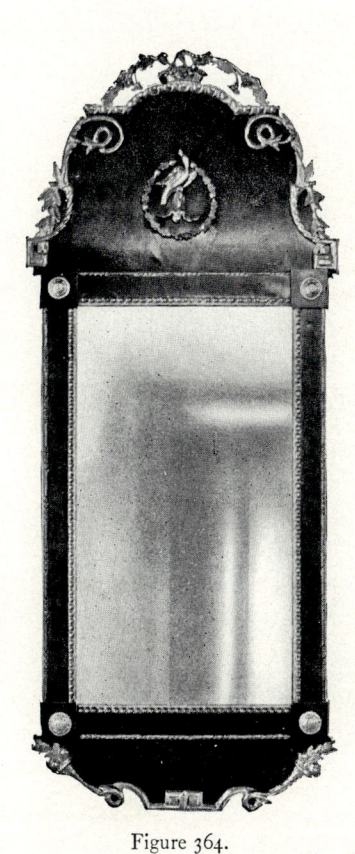

Figure 364.
Looking-Glass with mahogany and gilt frame, 1785–95.

Figure 365.
Looking-Glass with mahogany and gilt frame, 1785–95.

which support at the centre a basket containing leaves and fruits. At the base are C scrolls and a vase containing fruit and leaves.

Figure 364 shows another looking-glass of the same character, the property of Mr. George M. Curtis, of Meriden. An egg-and-dart moulding outlines the arch-shaped top, above which is a basket from which are streamers of leaves and flowers, and scrolls extend down the sides of the cresting. At the centre is applied a pheasant surrounded by a wreath. On the outer edges of the frame is a reel and bead moulding and on the inner edge a pearl bead moulding is carved. At the corners are blocks within which are inserted rosettes. At the base are scrolls terminating in cornucopias with fruit and leaves.

314 COLONIAL FURNITURE

A very elaborate looking-glass of this type is shown in Figure 365 and is the property of Mr. Norman F. Allen, of Hartford. At the top is the same arched moulding, above which are scrolls of flowers and leaves and at the centre a vase. The arch is supported by scrolls, and across the base of the cresting is a fret railing and at the centre is an urn with leaves and flowers. The corners of the frame are

Figure 366.
Looking-Glass with glass frame, 1780–90.

Figure 367.
Looking-Glass with marble and gilt frame, 1780–90.

blocked and have rosettes planted on them, and on the outer edge of the frame is a reel and bead moulding and on the inner side a pearl edge moulding. At the base are feet with leaves carved on them and a festoon of leaves and flowers.

An interesting looking-glass which is suggestive of this type is shown in Figure 366 and is the property of Mr. Frederick E. Haight, of Brooklyn. The cresting is of glass with bevelled edges, on the surface of which are cut sprays of flowers and leaves. Squares of glass are placed at the corners, and the outer edges of the frame are of glass as is also the curved base. This looking-glass came from the West Indies in the last quarter of the eighteenth century.

A form of looking-glass a number of which have been found, all coming from the seaport towns, is shown in Figure 367 and is the property of Mr. George S.

LOOKING-GLASSES

Palmer, of New London. The frame is made entirely of coloured marble. On the sides are engaged columns at the tops of which are carved and gilded finials, and at the base are feet. At the centre of the top is an arch supported on columns on top of which is an urn with flowers and scrolls of wire thinly coated with plaster. Beneath the arch is an oval framing a small picture. Such pieces

Figure 368.
Looking-Glass with marble and gilt frame, 1780-90.

Figure 369.
Looking-Glass with mahogany and gilt frame, about 1780.

as these have commonly been called "bilboa" looking-glasses and are supposed to have been imported from Portugal by persons engaged in foreign trade.

Another "bilboa" looking-glass is shown in Figure 368 and is in the Bolles Collection, owned by the Metropolitan Museum of Art. On the sides are engaged columns above which are urn finials, and at the base are carved feet. At the top are scrolls of leaves and flowers supporting an oval frame within which is a painting. On the outer edges are reel and bead mouldings, gilded, and on the inner edges a pearl bead moulding.

A form of looking-glass of which several have been found in the vicinity of Hartford is shown in Figure 369 and is the property of the writer. At the centre of the top is a pitcher with flowers and at the corners are urns. The central portion is filled by an applied ornament of scrolls. Beneath the top and around the looking-glass frame is a border suggesting the meander pattern of light wood, and the outer edges of the frame are of light wood, the balance being of mahogany, making a pleasing contrast. In the corners are blocks upon which are placed rosettes. There is a pearl edge moulding about the glass, and at the base are feet and in the centre are carved and gilded leaves.

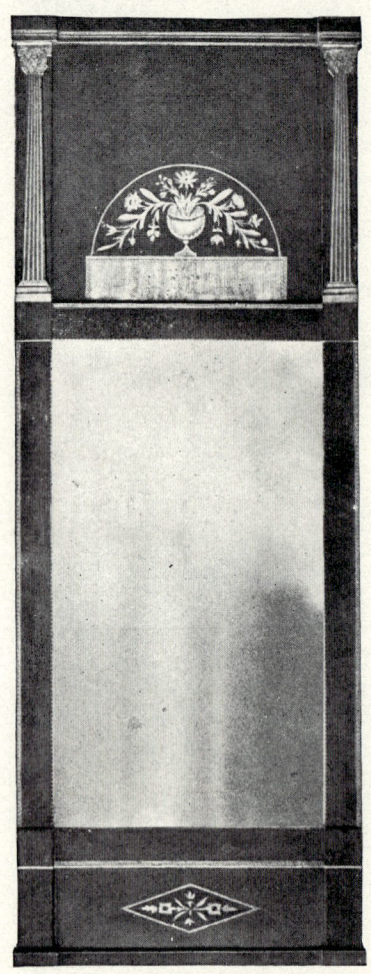

Still another form of looking-glass is that shown in Figure 370, the property of Mr. John J. Gilbert, of Baltimore. The frame is rectangular and the ornamentation is entirely obtained by inlay. On the outer edges of the upper part are inlaid columns with acanthus-leaf capitals above which is inlaid the meander pattern. At the centre of the top is inlaid a cup with flowers and leaves standing on a large base of light wood bordered with a modification of the meander pattern. At the base is an inlaid, lozenge-shaped medallion within which are leaves and flowers. A narrow band of inlay follows both the outer edge of the frame and the glass.

Figure 370.
Looking-Glass with mahogany and inlaid frame, about 1790.

Figure 371.
Looking-Glass with medallion plaque, 1790–1800.

Another looking-glass of the same general character is shown in Figure 371 and is the property of Mr. H. W. Erving, of Hartford. At the centre of the top is a medallion in which is inserted a cameo plaque representing the marriage of Cupid and Psyche. This was copied from a medallion plaque by Wedgwood of the same subject.

Figure 372 shows a mantel looking-glass from the Nichols house, Salem, Massachusetts. The cornice is in a Sheraton design with pendent balls attached

LOOKING-GLASSES

to its under surface. This form of ornamentation was not used to any extent before Sheraton's time. Below this cornice is a lattice-work applied on the sur-

Figure 372.
Mantel Looking-Glass, about 1790.

face and at the centre a festooned drapery. Below this is a panel painted on glass; at the ends, representing crossed horns, and in the centre two branches of leaves crossed. There are four reeded columns with a slight acanthus-leaf carving at the top of each. This looking-glass is supposed to have been bought at the time the

Figure 373.
Mantel Looking-Glass, about 1790.

Figure 374.
Mantel Looking-Glass, about 1800.

LOOKING-GLASSES

house was built in 1783. If so it is the earliest example of Sheraton work that the writer has seen. It would seem more probable that the mirror had been purchased some few years after the house had been built, for it is in the style which was popular about 1790.

Figure 373 shows another mantel looking-glass belonging to about the same period, from the Pendleton Collection. The cornice consists of a wide quarter-round ornamented with leaves and flowers, a short fillet from the bottom of which are pendent acorns, a wide cove, a fillet, and an ovolo with the egg-and-

Figure 375.
Mantel Looking-Glass, 1800–10.

dart moulding. There are four columns with entwined flowers and leaves about them, with Ionic capitals at the top. Rosettes appear above and below the columns.

Figure 374 shows another mantel looking-glass in the same collection. Below the top moulding are pendent acorns, and on the frieze below are applied ornaments in the anthemion pattern and at the centre is drapery. There are but two columns, each reeded and entwined with a leaf and surmounted by composite capitals.

Figure 375 shows another mantel looking-glass of a still later date. The same pendent acorns appear at the top and the caps of the columns carry up through the upper cornice. On the frieze are carved acanthus leaves and about the frame and on the columns are ring-turned half circles. This looking-glass is the property of Mr. Albert H. Pitkin, of Hartford.

Figure 376 shows another mantel looking-glass which is in the Erving Collection. Above the top of the glass and on either side are half columns set into a

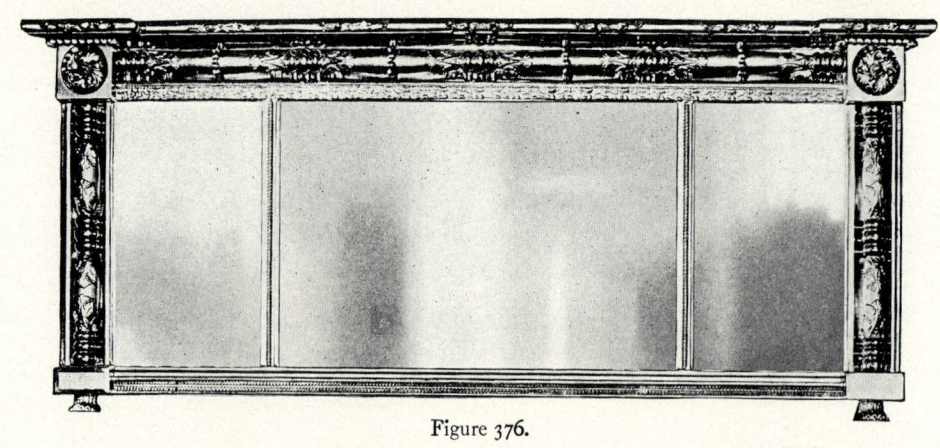

Figure 376.
Mantel Looking-Glass, 1810–20.

half-round hollow which is of burnished gold. At the two upper corners are square blocks which are hollowed out, and within are inserted rosettes and under the end columns are brass claw feet of the Empire period. The glass is divided into three sections. On the back of this mirror is the following advertisement: "Philadelphia Gilt Looking Glass Manufactury. Mahogany, toilet, dressing and pier looking glasses, etc., etc. Joseph Hillier informs his friends and the public, that he has opened a store number 76 Market Street, Baltimore, for the convenience of his Western and Southern customers, wholesale and retail, at the Philadelphia price, N. B., old glass new silvered and framed, prints, needlework, etc., framed and glazed. Cornishes and brackets made, etc. Printed by J. Robinson, 94 Market Street, Belvidere, Baltimore."

This Joseph Hillier appears in the Baltimore Directory in 1819.

Figure 377 shows a very handsome pier looking-glass, the property of Mr. Dwight Blaney, of Boston. The cornice is composed of a series of reedings bound together with straps, and on the cove moulding below are vertical leaves. On the frieze is an ornament composed of a series of scrolls suggestive of the Vitruvian scroll, and at the centre of each is a rosette. Above the columns are lions' heads. The columns are long and slender, with fluted surface, and the capitals are of the

Figure 378.
Pier Looking-Glass, about 1800.

composite order. Above the looking-glass are three panels of painted glass each representing a female figure. The centre panel represents a woman looking at a tomb around which are willow trees. On the tomb is the name "Werter." This central panel is signed "J. Phillips, 1798." Below these painted panels, on either

Figure 377.
Pier Looking-Glass, 1798.

side between the columns, are long, narrow glasses and a large central glass, and below are two small rectangular glasses and a long, narrow one.

Figure 378 shows another looking-glass of this period, the property of Mrs. Annie B. Swan, of Providence. At the two corners are pointed Gothic finials and at the centre an eagle. Pendent balls are attached to the cornice and chains with balls are swung between the two finials. In the upper section is a landscape on glass representing a building with trees about it and a river with some ships.

There are long, slender columns on either side finished with capitals of the composite order.

During this period circular girandoles with concave or convex glass were very popular. They were made in all sizes, and some were perfectly plain with a

Figure 379.
Girandole, about 1800.

moulded edge and others were highly ornamented with leaves, grapes, or flowers, with eagles or other birds in composition and gilded.

Figure 379 shows a girandole, one of a pair owned by Mrs. Charles Clarence Torr, of Philadelphia. The surface of the frame is hollow and within are set a series of balls. At the top is a dragon, with tail in the air, standing upon rocks with dripping-water effects, on either side of which are acanthus-leaf scrolls. At the sides are acanthus rosettes with dripping-water effect, and at the base are dragons' heads and acanthus leaves with two branches, each intended to hold two candles.

LOOKING-GLASSES

This rock-and-water effect, which was in imitation of the Chippendale school, was revived in the early nineteenth century, but the latter work was very much coarser than that of the Chippendale school.

Figure 380 shows another circular girandole having four lights with glass pendants. At the centre of the top are two dolphins, with tails crossed, lying on

Figure 380.
Girandole, about 1800.

rocks, and on either side are acanthus-leaf scrolls. Below are acanthus-leaf scrolls with a pendent flower. The moulding about the looking-glass is a half-round, and at the top, bottom, and two sides are cabochons with scrolls and flowers. The glass is convex. This girandole is one of a pair, the property of Mr. R. H. Maynard, of Boston.

A very beautiful oval looking-glass, but not a girandole, is shown in Figure 381, the property of the Tiffany Studios, of New York. It is composed of two cornucopias fastened together at the base by a ribbon and pendent leaves with grapes. From the mouths of the cornucopias extend heads of wheat over the top, making the upper side of the looking-glass. At the centre of the top is a large eagle.

324 COLONIAL FURNITURE

Figure 382 shows a very good early Empire looking-glass in the Bolles Collection. The mouldings are a quarter-round and a fillet on which is a pearl bead moulding, a cove, a fillet, and a small cyma reversa carved in leaf pattern. At the two ends of the top are well-shaped urns with flames and at the centre a large urn with a pineapple at the top, and festoons of leaves

Figure 381.
Looking-Glass with gilded frame, 1790–1800.

and flowers connect the urns. On the centre acroterium is a basket with fruits and flowers. The glass is divided into two sections, the upper one containing a painting representing Liberty. On either side of the frame is carved an acanthus leaf, and on either side of the looking-glass are fluted columns and on the capitals are carved acanthus leaves. At the base of the columns are carved rosettes.

Figure 382.
Looking-Glass with gilded frame, 1790–1800.

At the time of the War of 1812 it became the fashion to make looking-glasses with a painting representing scenes from the war. Figure 383 shows such a looking-glass on which is depicted the *Macedonian* fight. The looking-glass is in the usual Empire style with pendent balls, and on either side the moulding is hollowed and a narrow spiral-turned column is inserted. This looking-glass is in the Bolles Collection.

LOOKING-GLASSES

Figure 384 shows another looking-glass of about the same period. The same pendent balls are under the cornice, and on the upper section in relief is an angel flying and festoons of leaves and flowers. The columns are clustered and extend the whole length of the sides, and the centre one is hollowed, within which is inserted a pearl bead moulding. This looking-glass is in the Bolles Collection.

Figure 383.
Looking-Glass, Empire style, 1812–20.

Figure 384.
Looking-Glass, Empire style, 1810–20.

Figure 385 shows another looking-glass in the same collection. At the top are pendent acorns, and on either side in relief are classical figures and at the centre is a shell. On either side of the looking-glass are spiral-turned columns with vase-shaped capitals ornamented with acanthus leaves.

Figure 386 shows another Empire looking-glass which is the property of Mr. R. T. Smith, of Hartford. The upper edge of the cornice is carved in a leaf pattern and there are pendent ball drops, and above each column is a profile head of a man which appears to be intended to represent Cæsar. There is a star in the centre portion with a rose on each side. There are two looking-glass plates and on either side are turned columns swelled at the middle.

Figure 387 shows a small looking-glass, the property of Mr. John R. Buck, of Hartford, which quite closely resembles the mantel looking-glass shown in Figure

Figure 385.
Looking-Glass, Empire style, 1810–20.

Figure 386.
Looking-Glass, Empire style, 1810–20.

372. At the top are pendent balls and below is a painted glass on which is a rosette within which is a quiver with arrows. On the sides are columns with Ionic capitals.

Figure 388 shows still another looking-glass of this period. There are pendent acorn drops and above each column and at the centre is a rosette. The columns are turned in the heavy, rather ungraceful fashion of the later Empire period.

LOOKING-GLASSES

A slightly different form of looking-glass of this period is shown in Figure 389. It is made of mahogany without any gilt. Above each column is inlaid a lyre. The columns are partially spiral-turned and partially carved in the acanthus-leaf pattern so popular in the Empire period. On the right-hand side of the looking-glass is a miniature looking-glass belonging to a miniature chest of drawers of the period. It has the acorn pendent drops and turned columns on either side. Both of these pieces are the property of the writer.

It was the custom throughout the eighteenth century to support the looking-glasses on small rosettes, thus making them tilt forward. The rosettes were of various kinds, usually of brass, and frequently are mentioned with the looking-glass in the inventories.

Eight examples of these rosettes are shown in Figure 390. The first six are enamelled, bound in brass, and date about Revolutionary times. The seventh is of brass with an urn in openwork, and the last is a brass bust of George III which probably dates prior to the Revolution. In the Empire period

Figure 387.
Looking-Glass, Empire style, 1800–12.

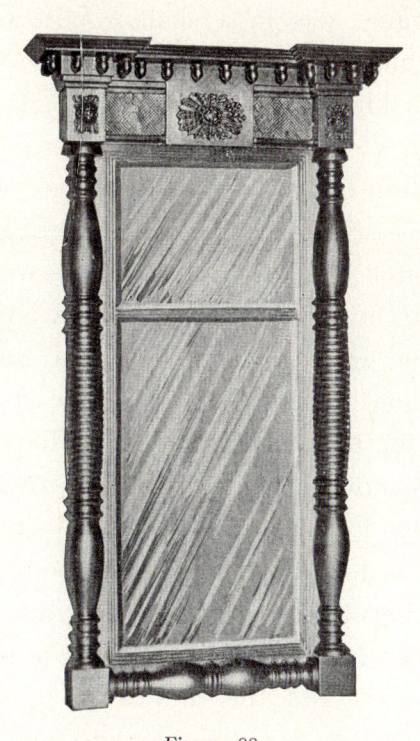

Figure 388.
Looking-Glass, Empire style, 1810–20.

Figure 389.
Looking-Glass, Empire style, 1810–20.

many rosettes were made both in this small size for looking-glasses and in the large size for window-curtains. These were usually of thin brass and in the form of conventional rosettes.

Figure 390.
Enamelled and Brass Looking-Glass Rosettes.

In the vicinity of many of the seaport towns, especially about Salem, has been found a form of looking-glass which was very small and usually set in a box, of which Figure 391 is a good example. These looking-glasses are very crudely made, the mouldings simply being glued together and covered with a very thin metal resembling what is known as Dutch metal. Between these mouldings are strips of painted glass and at the centre of the top is painted a basket of flowers. The entire frame sets in a shallow box, as is shown, and had a wooden slide cover. These looking-glasses have acquired the name of courting-glasses for which no good reason can be assigned. It has been puzzling to trace their origin, but after an examination of a large number the writer is convinced that they are of Chinese origin and were brought to this country from China by sea-captains. Some of the reasons for this conclusion are: That the frame is not made in the method employed by Europeans. The wood is the same as is found on frames of a number of paintings on glass which are indisputably of Chinese origin, and all that the writer has seen which were in their original condition have between the plate of glass and the thin wooden back strips of Chinese paper. The painting on the glass is done in the same manner and in the same peculiar colours as are those that were made in China. The

Figure 391.
Looking-Glass with painted glass border, about 1800.

LOOKING-GLASSES

frame also indicates its Eastern origin, not being in a form used in Europe at the time. This looking-glass is in the writer's possession.

Figure 392 shows another looking-glass, similarly constructed, from the Bolles Collection. The edge consists of a fillet and a quarter-round moulding very

Figure 392.

Looking-Glass with painted glass border, about 1800.

Figure 393.

Small Looking-Glass with painting at top, 1790–1800.

similar to that found on the early cut-work looking-glass frames. Within this outer frame is a border of strips of paintings on glass between two mouldings, and at the centre of the top is painted a basket of flowers.

Figure 393 shows another style of small looking-glass of the same period. Quite a number of looking-glasses like this one and the one shown in the next figure are found in this country, and they appear to be of European make and were probably inexpensive looking-glasses which were brought over by the sea-captains. At the top of this looking-glass frame are C scrolls within which is a painting of a lady.

Figure 394 shows another of these looking-glasses at the top of which are carved in wood, and coloured, flowers, leaves, and fruit, and at the base are C scrolls and flowers. These frames quite closely resemble in form those shown in

Figure 394.
Small Looking-Glass with carved and coloured frame, 1790–1800.

Figure 395.
Dressing-Glass, 1780–90.

Figures 328, 363, and following figures. Both of these two last-described looking-glasses are in the Bolles Collection, owned by the Metropolitan Museum of Art.

It was the fashion throughout the eighteenth century to place upon dressing-tables or low chests of drawers dressing-glasses attached to two uprights which enabled them to swing back and forth. The earliest example we have found in this country is shown on the knee-hole dressing-table shown in Figure 113, which is practically the same as that in the middle room on the top floor of the doll house shown in Figure 1.

Figure 395 shows a dressing-glass the top and bottom of the frame of which is in cut-work, and the stand has a small slant-top desk containing three drawers

LOOKING-GLASSES

with a drawer below. At the centre of the top and bottom, around the glass, on the uprights and desk front are inlay. A dressing-glass very similar to this, except without inlay, is shown in a woodcut in an advertisement of Weyman & Carne, of Queen Street, Charleston, in the copy of the South Carolina *Gazette* dated October 31, 1765. This piece, because of the character of inlay, appears to be of a little later date.

Figure 396.
Dressing-Glass, about 1790.

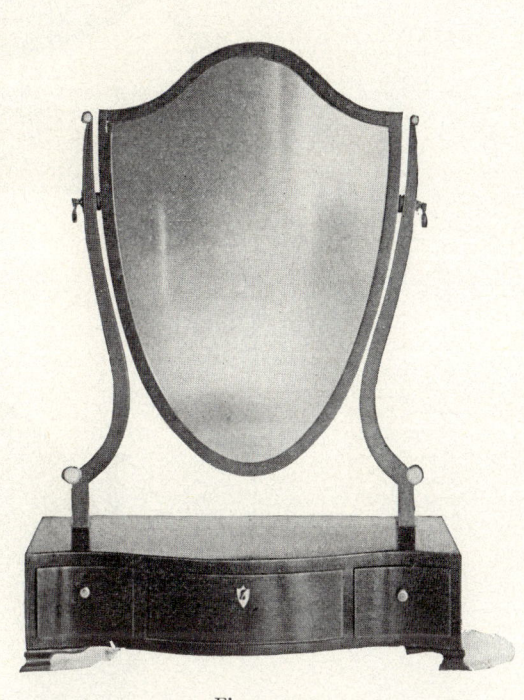

Figure 397.
Dressing-Glass, 1785-95.

A japanned dressing-glass is shown in Figure 396. This piece is of Chinese origin, and quite a number were imported to this country just prior to 1800. In the base are two long drawers below a small shelf and then two more drawers.

During the Hepplewhite and Sheraton period these dressing-glasses became very plentiful in this country, and by far the greater part of those found here belong to that period.

Figure 397 shows a typical dressing-glass of the Hepplewhite period. The frame is of mahogany and is shield-shaped. The lower section has a serpentine front with three drawers and stands on small bracket feet. This dressing-glass is the property of the Tiffany Studios of New York.

Figure 398 shows another glass of the same period in the same collection. The frame of the glass is oval, placed horizontally, and the base contains three

Figure 398.
Dressing-Glass, 1785–95.

Figure 399.
Dressing-Glass, 1785–95.

drawers, the outer ones with a convex curve and the inner one with a long, concave curve. The piece stands on short stump feet.

LOOKING-GLASSES 333

Another dressing-glass in the same collection is shown in Figure 399. The frame is oval, placed vertically. The base is serpentine and the fronts of the

Figure 400.
Dressing-Glass, 1785–95.

Figure 401.
Dressing-Glass, 1790–1800.

drawers are decorated with parallel fluting. The piece stands on small ogee bracket feet.

Still another shape of the dressing-glass of this period in the same collection is shown in Figure 400. It is shield-shaped, coming to a point at the centre of the top instead of having a serpentine curve at the top. In the base are two drawers with concave fronts and the piece stands on small ogee bracket feet.

Figure 401 shows another of these dressing-glasses which is in a little later style and of which many are found in this country. The frame of the glass is rectangular and the base has two drawers with swelled fronts. The handles are of the oval variety and the piece stands on small ogee bracket feet.

SUPPLEMENTARY CHAPTER

IT is the purpose of this chapter to illustrate and describe some subject-matter not covered by the previous chapters, which has been discovered since the publication of the Second Edition, in 1913.

CHESTS

NICHOLAS DISBROWE

Figure I shows a two-drawer chest, the property of the writer, upon the back of the lower drawer of which is written, in seventeenth-century handwriting, "Mary Allyn's Chistt, cutte and joyned by Nich. Disbrowe" (Figure II). Nicholas Disbrowe was born at Walden, Essex, England, in 1612–13, and was the son of a joiner. He appears in the records as the owner of property in Hartford in 1639. He lived at the north end of Burr Street, now North Main Street, near the tunnel. In 1660 he obtained permission to build a shop sixteen feet square on the highway. He served in the Pequot war, and was granted fifteen acres of land for his services. He was chimney viewer for the years 1647, 1655, 1663, and 1669, and held other offices. He died at Hartford in 1683, leaving a large estate for those days, amounting to £260 10s. 1d. Mary Allyn was the daughter of Col. John Allyn, secretary of the Colony, and was born at Hartford in 1657, and died in 1724. In 1686 she married William Whiting. The distinguishing features of Disbrowe's designs are well shown on the chest in question. On the upper rail the design consists of two pairs of tulips and leaves. On the stiles and rails are undulating carved bands with conventionalised tulip designs to fit the spaces. The initial A is worked into the design once on each stile, once on each side of the centre panel, three times on the upper drawer, and once on the lower drawer, the cross-bar of the A in each case being a small tulip. At the centre of the outer panels is a diamond-shaped design with tulips and leaves, radiating; in the centre of one is carved an M, and in the other an A.

The centre panel has two tulips and leaves, back to back. There is no way of distinguishing the early work of this cabinet-maker, but it is apparent from this chest that his later work was characterised by the use of conventional tulips and

Figure I.
Carved Oak Chest made by Nicholas Disbrowe before 1683.

Figure II.
Inscription of foregoing chest.

leaves, and a number of pieces thus treated have been found in the vicinity of Hartford and were probably his work, such as Figures 41, 166, 225, III, IV, V, and VI. This design, though original in its adaptation, was based upon designs already known in England. In the text is shown a drawing of an Elizabethan

CHESTS

panel from Owen Jones's "Grammar of Ornament," Plate LXXXIII (A), and also a drawing from a chest shown in Miss Jekyll's "Old West Surrey" (B). These are both similar to the outer panels in this chest and the centre panel in Figures IV, V, and VI.

Figure III, the property of the Museum at Deerfield, Massachusetts, shows a chest probably made by Disbrowe, the designs on the panels of which are identically like those shown on the preceding chest. The single drawer is heavily moulded, as are also the stiles and rails. This chest has characteristics of an earlier period than the foregoing.

A   B

Figure IV shows a chest without drawers, the property of the Rhode Island School of Design, the panels of which are in the characteristic Disbrowe design, the outer panels with tulips radiating from an octagon with carved sides, the centre panel with tulip and leaves surrounding the initials H S. The stiles and rails are ornamented with a double row of grooved mouldings.

A comparison of the chest shown in Figure V with the one described in Figure I shows so many points in common that it would be difficult to believe that they were not made by the same hand, and this is borne out by the fact that the stippled background of these two chests was apparently made by the same instrument. The rails and stiles are carried in undulating curves with a tulip in each corner, and on each drawer is a design of tulips and leaves. There is, however, much less variety and originality in this chest. The interesting feature is that the outer panels are carved in identical designs found on the so-called Connecticut chests shown in Figure VII, while the inner panel suggests the outer panels of the Disbrowe chests last shown, except that the tulips and leaves radiate from a rosette instead of a diamond or octagon shape design. This chest is the property of the Connecticut Historical Society.

Figure VI shows a two-drawer chest with the Disbrowe designs. The centre panel has the same radiating tulip and leaves shown in the preceding figures, and the outer panels have a large tulip on a stalk with smaller tulip and leaves

Figure III.
Oak Chest, third quarter seventeenth century.

below. This latter design is the one so familiar on the so-called Connecticut chests, Figure VII, of which many are known. This chest also has the same applied spindles and bosses, and is constructed in the same way as the Connecticut chests; in fact, it differs only in the design of the centre panel. It is the property of Mrs. John I. Blair.

The latest development of this style of chest is the so-called Connecticut chest shown in Figure VII, the property of the writer. The outer panels are carved in the same tulip design that appears on the chest in the preceding figure. The design on the inner panel consists of tulips on either side of a stem and three rosettes. That these were intended as rosettes and not asters or sunflowers, as usually stated, is apparent when one notes that in the centre panel of Figure III is the same rosette used in the proper way. On the stiles are applied split spindles and on the panelled drawer fronts and panels of the ends are applied turtle-back bosses. Such chests as these would be much cheaper to make than the all-over carved ones, and therefore one would expect, as is the fact, to find them more plentiful. A large number are known and some at least were probably made

Figure IV.
Oak Chest, third quarter seventeenth century.

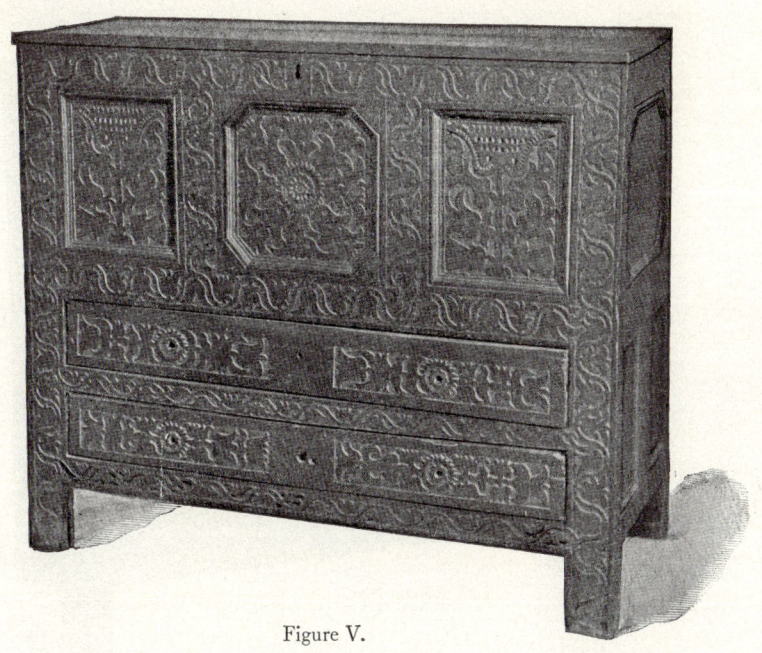

Figure V.
Oak Chest with two drawers, third quarter seventeenth century.

by Disbrowe, although a rather crude one is dated 1704, long after his death. They have been called for many years Connecticut chests, and there is little doubt now that they were made at Hartford or in its vicinity.

Few, if any, designs used in this country in the seventeenth century were original. They were either suggested by or copied from other articles, or perhaps

Figure VI.
Oak Chest with two drawers, third quarter seventeenth century.

Figure VII.
Oak Chest with two drawers, third quarter seventeenth century.

from a design suggested in a woodcut, a head or tail piece in some book accessible, or from a book of designs, of which there were many. There was plenty

CHESTS

of material available to the man with imagination, and the very strange thing is that there was so little variety. With the exception of Disbrowe, the Hadley carver and paintings on some pine pieces, no originality was shown.

HADLEY TYPE

Figure VIII shows an interesting chest with two drawers, belonging to Rev. George P. Eastman, of Orange, New Jersey. The initials E A are those of Eliza-

Figure VIII.
Carved Oak Chest with two drawers, last quarter seventeenth century.

beth Allis, who was born at Hatfield, Massachusetts, in 1679. Her father was Captain John Allis, a carpenter of that place and a prominent man. At first sight it would appear that this chest was made by the same hand as the Disbrowe one shown in Figure I, but an examination of the two chests shows they could not have been made by the same person. The wood of the front of this chest is sycamore, except for the panels and sides, which are oak. The carving is not as deep and the form of the tulip is different and much more like that used on the Hadley chests later described. It is apparent, however, that the maker of this chest had seen the Mary Allyn chest, for they are too nearly alike to warrant any other hypothesis. A study of the genealogy of the Allis and

Disbrowe families reveals some interesting facts. William Allis married in 1678 a niece of Disbrowe, and Elizabeth was the first child born to his son John after this marriage. The people of Hatfield and Hadley were in close contact with Hartford. Many of them had come from Hartford as founders of these towns, which were originally one town on the east and west side of the Connecticut River, and during the Indian wars the people of Hartford rendered assistance

Figure IX.
Two-Drawer Oak Chest, Hadley type, first quarter eighteenth century.

continuously to these stricken towns. It would seem probable, therefore, that John Allis knew Disbrowe and had seen the Mary Allyn chest, and that when his daughter Elizabeth was born he made this chest for her. These towns were very small, and a carpenter would have been both joiner and cabinetmaker, much as Joshua Hemstead was at New London, whose diary has been published. This chest required much greater skill to design and make than did the so-called Hadley chests hereafter referred to, where the design consisted simply of a repetition of the single motif of a tulip and leaf crudely carved. John Allis died in 1689 and his widow married Samuel Belden, a carpenter, who entered into a partnership with John's son Ichabod, who had married Belden's daughter by a former marriage, under the firm name of Belden & Allis, and this firm prospered and lasted for many years, building the Hadley church in 1702. The Hadley chests

CHESTS

were made during the term of the partnership, and it is the writer's belief that they were made by this firm, and had for their model the leaf and tulip design on the upper rail of the Elizabeth Allis chest, which is a crude copy of the design on the top rail of the Disbrowe chest, Figure I. This assumption is in keeping

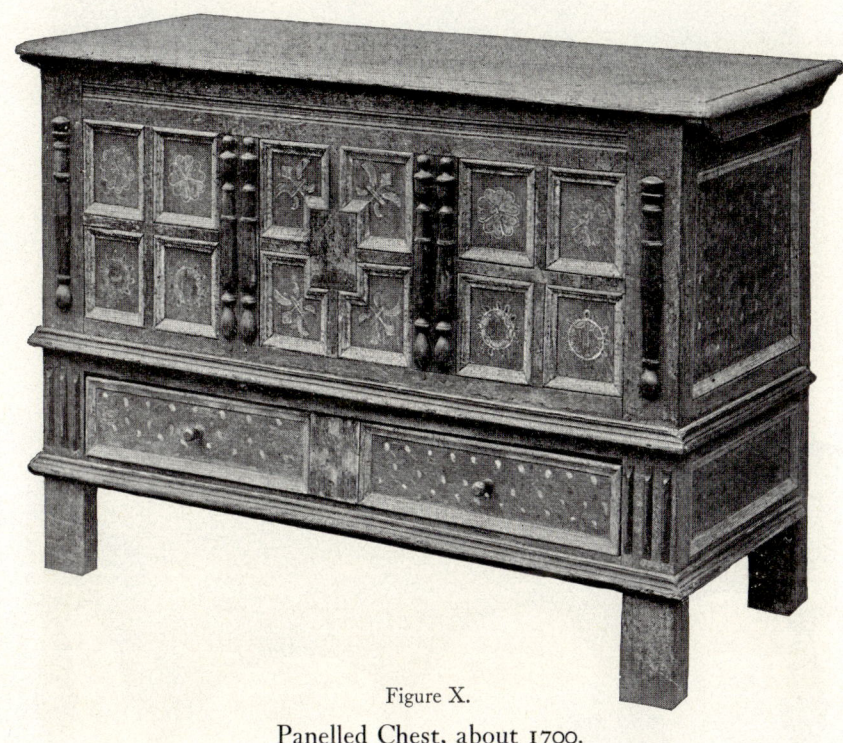

Figure X.
Panelled Chest, about 1700.

with a tradition long existing in Hadley, that these chests were made by a local carpenter.

Figure IX shows a Hadley chest, the property of the writer, which differs in some particulars from any shown in the chapter on chests. The repeat design on the top rail usually carries through the stiles. In this chest the complete design stops at the stiles and this necessitates the crowding of the design. At the centre of the top rail is the usual place for the escutcheon, and on each of the rails below and drawer fronts, the space at the centre, caused by the crowding of the repeat design, is filled by geometric designs, each different, thus giving the chest a slightly greater variety than usual. The brass rings are of course modern, the holes for the original wooden knobs having been filled.

A full discussion of the designs on the Hadley chests will be found in the chapter on chests, Figures 27 to 34 both inclusive.

Figure X shows a chest by courtesy of Mr. Charles Woolsey Lyon. The three panels are each divided into four small panels, in the centre of each of the

Figure XI.
Painted High Chest of Drawers, about 1700.

outer ones a rosette and in the centre one a fleur-de-lis. The panel of the drawers and the sides are ornamented with small dots of paint.

CHESTS OF DRAWERS

Figure XI shows a painted six-legged high-boy of great interest. The upper carcass has one drawer less than usual. The cornice consists of a quarter-

Figure XIII.
Cupboard on Stand, about 1700.

Figure XII.
High Chest of Drawers, scroll legs, about 1700.

Figure XIV.
High Chest of Drawers, 1700-25.

Figure XV.
High Chest of Drawers, 1700–25.

Figure XVI.
Dressing-Table, 1700–25.

Figure XVII.
Dressing-Table, 1750–75.

round, a fillet, a cyma, a fillet, and a quarter-round, and the moulding at the bottom of the upper section is the same as the cornice except reversed. The design of the painting is quite charming. The little drawers have rosettes and flowers, the first long drawer a vase with streamers of leaves and flowers, the lower drawer in the upper section thistles, roses, and fleur-de-lis with three crowns. This design has been found on several painted pieces. It is also found on head-pieces of books published in the first quarter of the seventeenth century, and probably commemorates the Stuart accession to the English throne.

Figure XVIII.
Dressing-Table, 1750–75.

On each end is a large tulip and a small repeat of the design on the lower part. This piece is the property of Mr. John Davidson, of New London.

A rare form of high-boy is shown in Figure XII. The arrangement of drawers, the single arch moulding and the general appearance is similar to that shown in Figure 60, but the legs are composed of scrolls, a style which came into England about 1690. These scrolls, however, on the foreign pieces are usually in the Flemish scroll and have a flat upper surface, which is generally veneered, while the scrolls on this piece are in the S form, with moulded upper surface. This piece is made of cherry, and was found in Connecticut. It is the only American scroll foot high-boy that has come under the writer's observation.

A pine cupboard on a five-legged frame is shown in Figure XIII. The lower part is much the same as that on the five-legged high-boys, but the legs are more slender. The cupboard is plain except for the mouldings about the panels of the doors, and the cornice is the usual early one consisting of a quarter-round, a fillet, and a cyma. It is the property of Mr. Willet Seaman, of New York.

Figure XIV is a very early bandy-leg high-boy, the property of Mr. Charles Woolsey Lyon. The cornice, the cushion frieze, the double-arch moulding about the drawers, the double mouldings at bottom of upper carcass, and the arrangement of drawers are the same as on the six-legged high-boy shown in Figure 68. The bandy legs are unusually well shaped, as are also the drop ornaments. The handles are stamped second-period type. The piece dates in the first quarter of the eighteenth century.

Figure XV shows a high-boy somewhat similar to the japanned one, Figure 79, except that the surface of the front is walnut veneer and inlay. The sides and legs are maple. The cornice consists of a broad fillet, a quarter-round, small fillet, cove, large fillet, cove, an astragal and a fillet. The large cove conceals a drawer. About the drawers are small bead mouldings. The veneer on the drawers is beautifully matched and is framed in a band of inlay alternating light and dark, outside of which is a broad herring-bone border. The handles are stamped. This piece is the property of the writer.

A charming little low-boy is shown in Figure XVI, also the property of the writer. The wood is maple, and the top has an inlaid star and is edged with a dark and two light bands of inlay, as are the drawer frames and ends. In the centre drawer is an inlaid shell.

A Maryland low-boy, the property of Mrs. Miles White, is shown in Figure XVII. The drawers are flush, with beaded edges, and the centre drawer has a concave shell carved upon it in an unusual design. The skirt is cut differently from those farther north and the club feet are more rounded; a shell with pendant flowers is carved on each of the front knees.

Another and very small Maryland low-boy owned by Mrs. White is shown in Figure XVIII. On the centre drawer is carved an interesting half-rosette, the knees are scratch carved, and the legs terminate in the thin pointed feet so often found in Pennsylvania and New Jersey.

Figure XIX shows a high-boy, the property of Mr. Charles R. Morson. The cornice consists of a fillet, a cyma, a fillet, a cove, an astragal, a fillet and a small cove. The latter three members carry about the central openings. This is the typical Goddard cornice, as are also the finials and the cyma moulding separating the two carcasses. At the centre of the skirt is a concave shell. The

Figure XIX.
High Chest of Drawers, 1750–75.

Figure XX.
Chest on Chest, 1750–75.

Figure XXI.
Block-Front Chest on Chest, 1760–80.

bandy legs terminate in front in ball and claw feet, and in the rear with Dutch feet. There is a slight carving on the knees of the front legs. The handles are original.

Another Goddard piece, a chest on chest, is shown in Figure XX, also the property of Mr. Charles R. Morson. The cornice and other mouldings are identical. This piece is quite similar to Figure 115, except the quarter-round fluted columns are larger and those in the lower carcass are stopped.

Figure XXII.
Block-Front Chest of Drawers, 1760–80.

John Goddard, one of the best American cabinet-makers, was born in Newport in 1724, and was the son of David and Mary Goddard. He was made a Freeman April 3, 1745. On August 6, 1746, he married, at Newport, Hannah Townsend, daughter of Job and Rebecca. He is supposed to have learned his trade of Job. He had fifteen children, among them Thomas, born April 2, 1765, who became a noted cabinet-maker. John died at Newport in July, 1785. In the Providence *Gazette and Country Journal,* June 15, 1782, appears the following advertisement:

Goddard and Engs Cabinet Makers from Newport, at their shop on the wharff of Mr. Moses Brown, a little below Messeurs Tillinghast & Holroyds

near the Baptist Meeting House. Have ready furnished for sale several articles of mahogany household furniture, such as chairs, tables. Any kind of cabinet makers work made at said shop on the shortest notice and in a neat workman like manner.
Providence, June 14, 1782

This Goddard may have been one of John Goddard's sons.

In the Newport *Mercury*, August 28, 1786, appears the following advertisement:

The Creditors to the Estate of JOHN GODDARD, Cabinet-Maker, late of Newport, deceased, represented Insolvent, are requested to bring in their Claims to the Subscribers, within Six Months, the Time allowed for that Purpose. And all those indebted to said Estate, are desired to make immediate Payment to Townsend Goddard, Executor of said Estate.

EDMUND TOWNSEND,
Commissioners.
WILLIAM ENGS, jun.

Newport, August 12, 1786.

Townsend Goddard was a son of John. Edmund Townsend may have been one of the brothers of John's wife, and William Engs jun. probably the man who advertised at Providence in 1782, or may have been his son.

A beautiful example of a Goddard type of chest on chest, with blocking on both carcasses, is shown in Figure XXI. The cornice and other mouldings are in the usual form, as are also the carved shells and the scrolls on the bracket feet. The finials are not the conventional type (see those on Figure XXII), and the set of shell carvings on the lower drawer of the upper carcass are unique. The handles are in very handsome openwork pattern, and the boxing above the cornice and the rosettes are similar to those on Figure 270.

Figure XXII shows an unusual block-front chest of drawers. Although without the shell carved on the top drawer, the mouldings and feet are true Goddard type. There is a slide at the top, and six drawers of irregular width, the one next to the bottom being the narrowest, a quite unique arrangement. The handles are beautiful examples of the openwork pattern.

There is a chest on chest, the property of Mr. George D. Pratt, in the drawer of which is a label stating that it was made by John Townsend, Newport, 1767. The cornice consists of a quarter-round, a fillet, a cove, an astragal, a fillet and a small cove.

Figure XXIII.
Block-Front Chest on Chest, 1770–80.

CHESTS OF DRAWERS

Figure XXIII shows, through the courtesy of Mr. W. Farr, a chest on chest, the lower part blocked, the cornices and other mouldings the same as on the John Townsend piece above referred to. A card in this chest reads "John Townsend, Middletown, Conn." As his pieces closely resemble the Goddard pieces from Newport, it is fair to assume that he worked first in Newport, and either

Figure XXIV.
Block-Front Chest of Drawers, 1770–80.

worked with Goddard or was familiar with his work, and that he subsequently moved to Middletown.

John Townsend was the son of Christopher and Patience, and was born February 17, 1732–33. He married Philadelphia Feke, at Newport, September 6, 1764, and a daughter was born there February 10, 1769, so he must have moved to Middletown after that date. The records at Middletown, Connecticut, have been searched but no mention is found of John Townsend, but his wife died at Newport March 15, 1802, so he probably moved back to Newport.

There have been a number of block-front pieces all traced to the Connecticut Valley which closely resemble these pieces, and they may have been made by John Townsend while working at Middletown. The cornices of the Goddard pieces consist of a fillet, a cyma, a fillet, a cove, an astragal, a fillet and a small cove, while the cornices on the Townsend pieces consist of a quarter-round, a fillet, a cove, an astragal, a fillet and a small cove. Townsend did not use a cyma in any of his mouldings, but substituted a cove, a fillet, and a quarter-round therefor.

Figure XXIV shows a chest of drawers, a companion piece to the foregoing, which has the same mouldings and handles. About each of the four drawers is a bead moulding.

Figure XXV.
Block-Front Chest of Drawers, 1770–80.

A most interesting block-front chest of drawers is shown in Figure XXV, the property of Mrs. John I. Blair. It represents one of those cherry pieces which came from the Connecticut Valley, which the writer believes was made by John Townsend. At any rate, it would appear to have been made by the maker of Figure 116, for the ball and claw feet and the scrolled skirt, which are peculiar, are common to both. The quarter-columns are fluted and terminate in a very interesting capital of acanthus leaves, Figure XXVI.

The writer has seen, since the publication of the last edition, a serpentine front chest of drawers exactly like Figure 136, with the label of Daniel Clay, Greenfield, Massachusetts, November 4, 1794.

CHESTS OF DRAWERS

A very fine chest on chest, the property of Mr. G. A. Cluett, is shown in Figure XXVII. The cornice is like those on the Townsend pieces except for an extra fillet at the top. The rosettes with streamers and the pierced finials are unusually well carved, the shell drawer is in the design found on Chippendale pieces, and the pilasters are surmounted by well-carved composite capitals.

Figure XXVIII shows a chest on chest of the general type under discussion, with the same cornice. The lower carcass, however, is in serpentine instead of block front.

Figure XXIX and XXX shows a chest on chest and a companion knee-hole dressing-table, the property of the writer. The lower portion of the chest on chest has a knee-hole recess, a very unusual treatment. The cornice consists of a quarter-round, a fillet, a cove, a fillet, a cove, an astragal, a fillet and a small cove. This is the same cornice used by John Townsend above referred to, but as this form of cornice is quite commonly found throughout New England, there is no way of identifying these pieces as his work. The columns are fluted, with Ionic capitals. The finials, the cornice, except the large cove, the fan in the square drawer at the top and on the door in the recessed part below, and the columns, are all in original gilt. This feature is unusual on American pieces, and adds greatly to the appearance. There is a chest on chest the exact duplicate of this, with the same gilding, at the Warner house, Portsmouth. The skirt at the top of the recess opening on both pieces here shown is the front of a shallow drawer. The handles are all original. The pieces bear every earmark of having been made by the same person who made Figure 117.

Figure XXVI.
Detail capital on foregoing,
1770–80.

Another knee-hole block-front chest on chest, the property of Mr. G. A. Cluett, is shown in Figure XXXI. The cornice, other mouldings, and the feet are in the same design as those shown in the preceding figure. The pilasters instead of being fluted are covered with raised carving in undulating forms. The lower part has four drawers on each side of the recessed portion instead of a single drawer across the top and three singles on each side. This enabled the

Figure XXVII.
Block-Front Chest on Chest, 1770–80

CHESTS OF DRAWERS

designer to make the cupboard higher, but somewhat at the expense of the symmetry. There are fluted pilasters on either side of the recessed door.

Figure XXXII shows one of the most ornate double chests found in this country. It is believed to have been made or designed, with other elaborate pieces, for Elias Hasket Derby, the wealthy Salem ship-owner, by the architect

Figure XXX.
Block-Front Chest of Drawers, 1770-80.

Samuel McIntire, who designed his mansion. It has a peculiar mixture of styles—the upper carcass strongly under the Adam influence, while the lower carcass is almost pure Chippendale. The piece is well proportioned and beautifully executed, and reflects the great wealth of the seaboard towns at the beginning of the nineteenth century. It is the property of Mr. Francis P. Garvan.

Figure XXXIII shows a swell-front chest of drawers, the property of the writer. The wood is mahogany and the panels satin-wood, each bordered by a small inlay of alternating light and dark squares. On the edge of the top, on each drawer squaring the oval panels, and as a finish on the skirt, are bands of

Figure XXXI.
Block-Front Chest on Chest, 1770–80.

Figure XXXII.
Chest on Chest, 1790–1800.

Figure XXXIII.
Swell-Front Chest of Drawers, 1790–1800.

Figure XXXIV.
Swell-Front Chest of Drawers, 1790–1800.

inlay of mahogany, satin-wood, and ebony. The piece stands on French bracket feet.

A similar chest of drawers, owned by Mr. G. A. Cluett, is shown in Figure XXXIV. There is a light and dark inlay about the oval panels of satin-wood,

Figure XXXV.
Swell-Front Chest of Drawers, 1800–10.

and the edge of the top and the skirt have inlay of parallel lines, dark between two light woods.

Still another inlaid chest of drawers is shown in Figure XXXV, the property of Mr. Cluett. The inlay is in mahogany, but holly lines are on the edge of the top, and on the skirt the dark strip is broken with dots of holly inlay. There are two drawers at the top instead of one long one, and the legs are turned, showing that the piece is of a slightly later date.

A very beautiful and dainty dressing-table, also the property of Mr. Cluett, is shown in Figure XXXVI. It is made of mahogany with satin-wood panels. It stands on reeded Sheraton legs. A tambour slide covers a little swell-front cupboard on the top.

A corner wash-stand owned by Mr. Cluett is shown in Figure XXXVII.

Figure XXXVI.
Swell-Front Dressing-Table, 1790–1800.

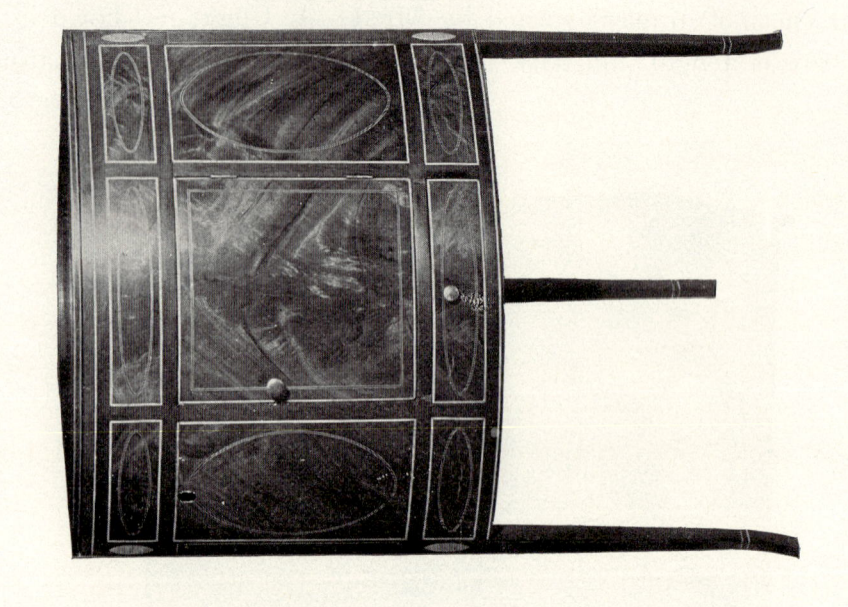

Figure XXXVII.
Swell-Front Wash-Stand, 1790–1800.

368

CUPBOARDS AND SIDEBOARDS 369

CUPBOARDS AND SIDEBOARDS

Figure XXXVIII shows a press cupboard owned by Dr. Wallace Nutting, and now in the Wadsworth Athenæum, Hartford, which apparently was made by the same cabinet-maker who made the cupboard shown in Figure 161. The moulding at the top is cut to resemble blocks with a serrated lower edge, then a flat surface and another serrated edge. There are three large corbels on the front, cut to appear as three each. The recessed portion has the same blocks and serrated edges both top and bottom, except that there are two vertical gouges at the point of each serration. The outer panels are rectangular with sides indented and a boss is in the centre of each. The centre panel consists of a raised diamond-shaped panel with a boss in the centre and two small rectangular panels below. The blocks and serrated edges appear as a cornice to the lower part, and above the two lower drawers are serrated mouldings with pairs of vertical gouges and the base moulding is enriched with similar gouges. There are two plain panels below on each side, and on each of the upper ends is a cross-shaped panel with two small rectangular panels below. The writer has seen two other cupboards of this same arrangement with serrated decoration differing from this one only in minor details.

There are a number of oak pieces known with the serrated edge, and it is thought that they were made in Plymouth. (See Figures 22, 23, 24, and 49.) The maker seems to have had great ability in panel work and composition, and was one of the great seventeenth-century American cabinet-makers. There is not sufficient evidence to establish who the maker was, but it has been suggested that it was John Alden.

An early clothes-cupboard is shown in Figure XXXIX. Across all of the panels from corner to corner are raised mouldings, and at the centre are raised rectangular panels. The hinges are early H form. The wood is Southern pine, which identifies its origin. The cornice is in early form, a wide fillet, a cyma, and a bead. The piece originally stood on ball feet. It is interesting to compare this cupboard with the frontispiece in this volume. The latter is from New England and the former from the South. It is the property of Mr. Francis P. Garvan.

A walnut sideboard table, the property of the Brooklyn Museum, is shown in Figure XL. The front is straight and the sides are curved, and the marble top follows the lines of the frame. At each front corner over the legs is a rounded section, and this feature, together with the pointed feet, mark the piece as having been made south of New York.

A very interesting sideboard, the property of Mr. Clifford S. Drake, is shown in Figure XLI. The front is curved on a long oval. The edge of the top is

Figure XXXVIII.
Press Cupboard, 1650–75.

Figure XXXIX.
Clothes Cupboard, 1650–75.

carved in a series of three parallel vertical channels with a rosette between, a design found frequently in McIntire's work. Over each leg is carved a rosette with pendant flowers, and there is a slight bead inlay on the edge of each leg and on the edge of the centre opening. The feet are in spade form. This sideboard came from Salem, Massachusetts, and could have been designed by McIntire, or at least by some one under his influence.

A very good sideboard, the property of Mr. G. A. Cluett, is shown in Figure

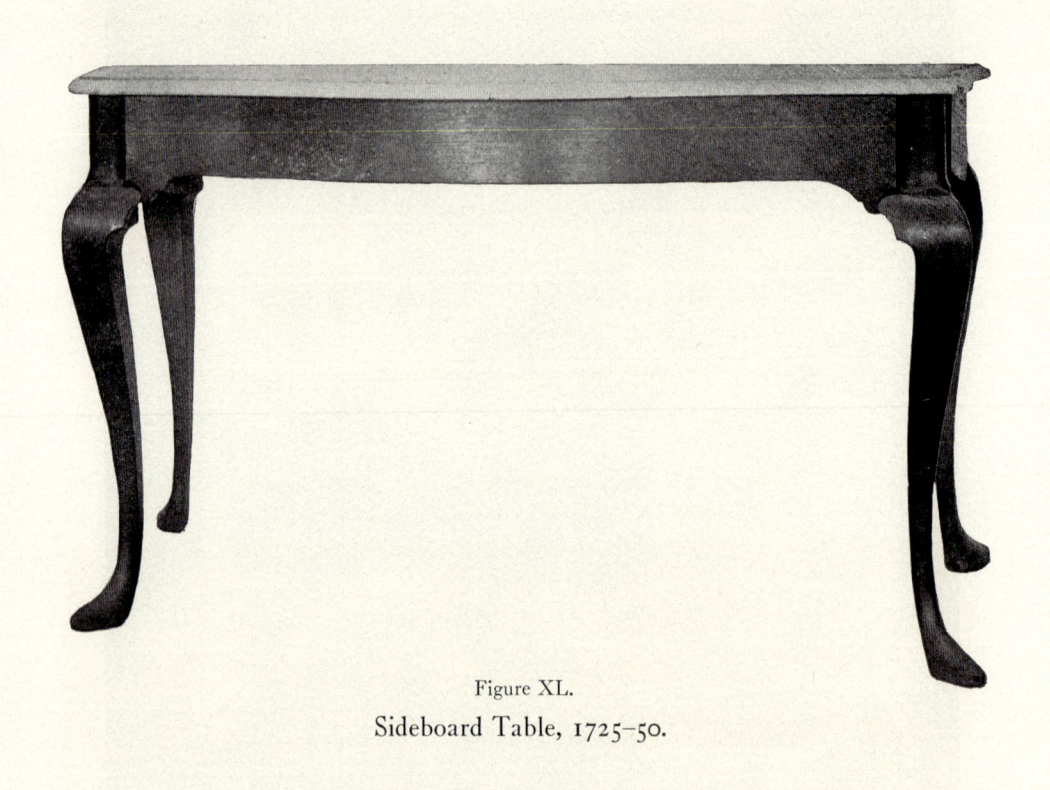

Figure XL.
Sideboard Table, 1725-50.

XLII. The front is in a long serpentine curve, with the centre portion below recessed, coved at either end and swelled in the centre. The drawers and doors are panelled in mahogany veneer, with a band of holly and ovals of light and dark beaded inlay. Across the bottom is a herring-bone design in dark and light inlay.

Another sideboard owned by Mr. Cluett is shown in Figure XLIII. The front is curved between the outer and inner legs, and the centre portion is in serpentine shape. The surfaces all have holly inlay, with inlaid rosettes on the extension of the legs. The piece stands on spade feet.

An interesting Sheraton sideboard, also the property of Mr. Cluett, is shown in Figure XLV. Both the upper and lower sections are shaped in swelled sec-

Figure XLI.
Hepplewhite Sideboard, 1790–1800.

Figure XLII.
Hepplewhite Sideboard, 1790–1800.

Figure XLIII.
Hepplewhite Sideboard, 1790–1800.

Figure XLIV.
Sheraton Mixing-Table, 1800–10.

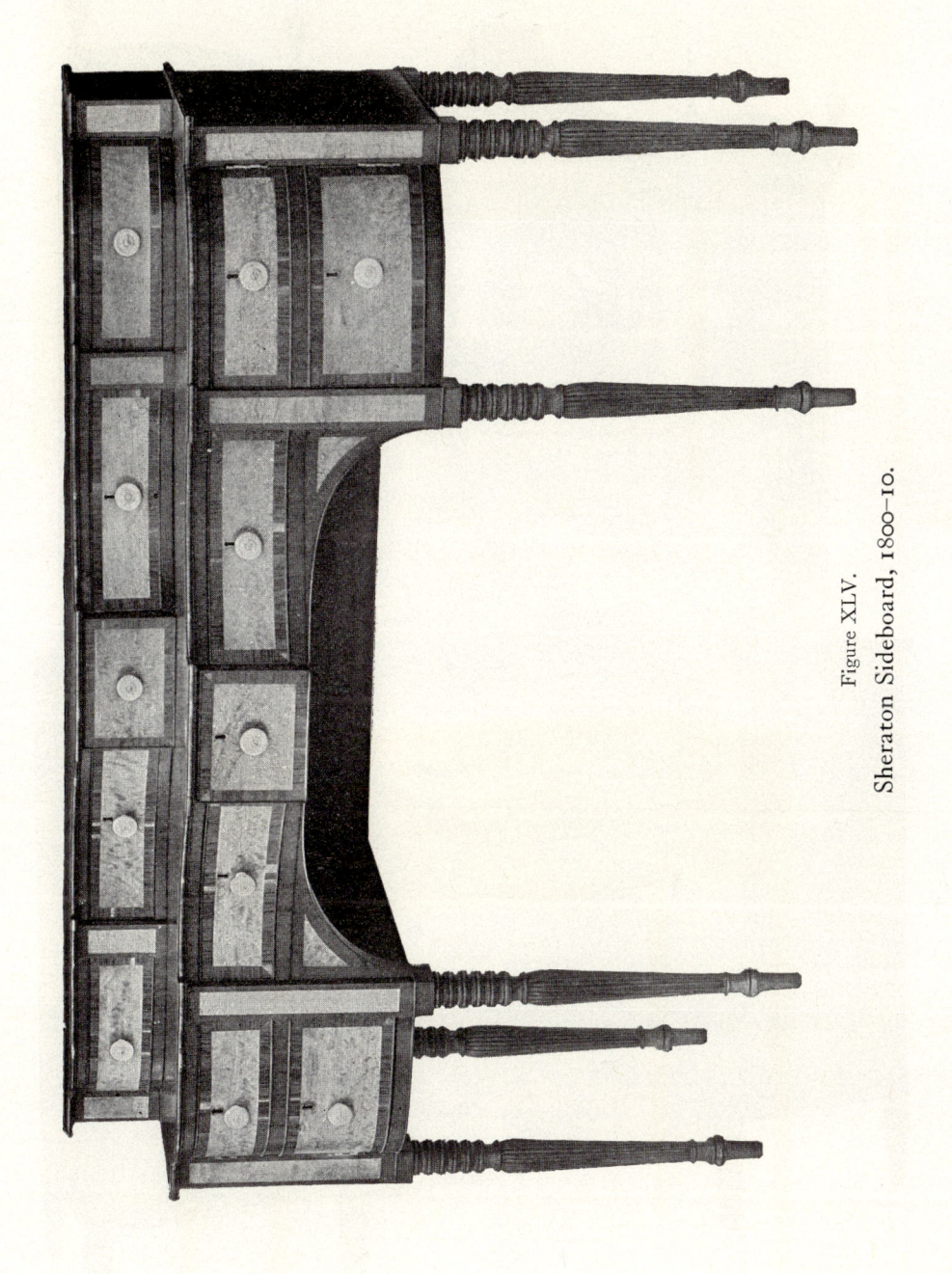

Figure XLV.
Sheraton Sideboard, 1800–10.

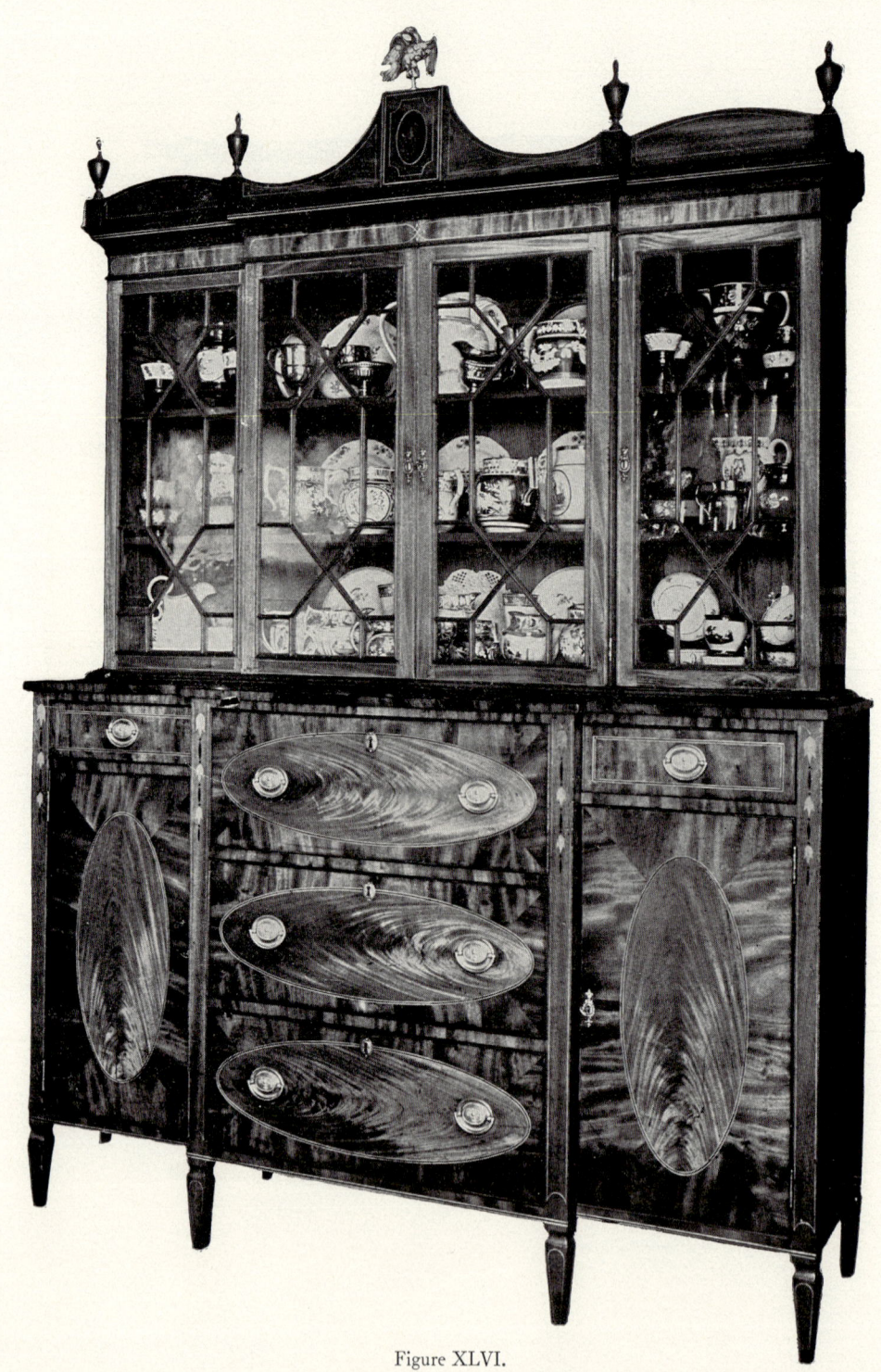

Figure XLVI.
Sheraton Sideboard with china closet and drawer, about 1800.

CUPBOARDS AND SIDEBOARDS

tions on the ends, and the depressed surfaces inside separated by a square drawer. Each division is separated by a panel of satin-wood, and the drawers are satin-wood with mahogany border. The legs are turned and reeded.

Figure XLIV shows a mixing-table with slides on the ends, the property of Mr. Cluett. The front is serpentine. The legs are turned and reeded and carry through to the top and are finished with a rosette.

Figure XLVI shows a Sheraton sideboard with china-closet, the property of Mrs. Walter P. Wright. The cornice is the same as that on Figure 214, a fillet,

Figure XLVII.
Label of Edmund Johnson on preceding sideboard.

a cyma, a broad and narrow fillet, a large cove, an astragal, and a fillet. On the top are four urns and a brass eagle at the centre. The wood is beautifully grained. Three ovals are on the three centre drawers below, set horizontally, and one on each cupboard door set vertically. The oval handles are stamped with an eagle. On each leg are inlaid pendant flowers. The feet are of the stub type with an inlaid line. The upper drawer falls forward on a quadrant disclosing a desk. These pieces have for many years been called Salem desks, but this is the only one the writer has seen which has the original label (Figure XLVII) of Edmund Johnson, Federal Street, Salem. He probably also made the sideboard shown in Figure 214, for the similarity is very striking.

DESKS AND SCRUTOIRES

A very unusual desk-box, the property of the writer, is shown in Figure XLVIII. It is a half octagon in shape. Each of the surfaces has carved upon it lunettes with a crude acanthus-leaf design. On the back is cut D ^{E} M 20 of 12 mo 1671. The piece is entirely of American oak except the bottom, which is of pine. The original iron escutcheon appears on the front. It was found in Greenfield, Massachusetts.

Figure XLVIII.
Oak Desk-Box, 1671.

Figure XLIX.
Oak Desk-Box, 1670–80.

Figure XLIX shows a desk-box, also the property of the writer, upon the front of which is carved the familiar tulip and leaf design used by Disbrowe. (See subdivision on chests above.) The front, sides, and back are of American oak, and the top and bottom of pine.

A desk-box, the property of the Brooklyn Museum, carved in the so-called Friesland design, is shown in Figure L. It is the most elaborately carved box in this design which has come under the writer's observation. The entire

DESKS AND SCRUTOIRES 379

top is carved in designs of wheels and rosettes, as are also the sides. The front has a rosette and a star either side of a heart-shaped design at the centre. Inside are pigeonholes. The piece is made of pine throughout and the hinges are original, in the butterfly pattern.

An early standing desk, the property of Mr. Philip L. Spalding, is shown both closed and open in Figures LI and LII. It is made throughout of pine. It is so designed that when closed a person standing at it can use it as a desk, and when opened the slant top raises and the front falls disclosing pigeonholes and two long drawers. It stands on a frame with six turned legs, turned stretchers and three small drawers. The early form of moulding, similar to

Figure L.
Desk-Box, Friesland carving, about 1700.

that of the clothes-cupboard, Figure XXXIX, separates the two carcasses. There are single-arch mouldings on the outer edges of the front, and the butterfly hinges are original. It was probably used in a counting-house, as there are paintings extant which show clerks standing at similar desks.

A little cherry desk, the property of the writer, is shown in Figure LIII. It is made like the ball-foot desks of the period, with a well above the drawer reached through a slide on the inside, and with pigeonholes and drawers arranged in the usual form of such pieces, with outer drawer and pigeonhole on each side advanced. (See Figure 239.) The drawer overlaps with a quarter-round moulding, the handles are second-period stamped, and the ball feet are unusually delicate. It is 20⅛ inches high and 21½ inches wide. There is an exact duplicate of this piece at the Warner house, Portsmouth, New Hampshire.

380   COLONIAL FURNITURE

It was intended to be used on a table, much as the desk-boxes of the earlier period were used.

Figure LIV shows a desk on a frame, the property of the writer. It is made of cherry throughout. The interior is finished in pigeonholes and drawers.

Figure LI.
Standing Desk, closed, about 1700.

The legs and bracings are well turned, and the skirt is cut in cyma curves with a quarter-round at the centre. The handles are original.

An uncommon form of block-front scrutoire, the property of Mr. G. A. Cluett, is shown in Figure LV. The cornice is in the usual form found outside of Rhode Island, but the top is finished with a straight dentil moulding across

DESKS AND SCRUTOIRES

the front and sides, which adds much to its appearance. The doors are bevel-panelled, straight-sided, except at top, which is cut in cyma curves. The pilas-

Figure LII.
Standing Desk, open, about 1700.

ters are fluted. The blocking extends on the lid, and the piece stands on four very well-carved animal's feet.

Figure LVI shows a maple serpentine-front scrutoire, the property of Mr. Cluett. The cornice is in the usual form, with a narrow moulding across the front and sides. The doors have sunken panels, the edges about them cut in

Figure LIV.
Scrutoire on Frame, about 1725.

Figure LIII.
Small Ball-Foot Scrutoire, 1700–10.

Figure LV.
Block-Front Scrutoire with cabinet top, 1750–75.

Figure LVI.
Serpentine-Front Scrutoire with cabinet top, 1770–80.

cyma curves. Below the lid is a long slide. The piece stands on four ball-and-claw feet. This type of piece seems to have originated in the vicinity of Salem, Massachusetts, and is frequently called a Salem desk.

Figure LVII shows a block-front scrutoire, the property of Mr. Israel Sack. It is well proportioned, with bold blocking which extends on the lid. The

Figure LVII.
Block-Front Scrutoire, 1760–70.

mouldings at the base are a cove, a fillet, and a quarter-round, the form found in northern New England. It stands on four well-proportioned ball-and-claw feet, and a shell is carved at the centre of the skirt.

Figure LVIII shows a secretary with cupboard top, the property of Mr. G. A. Cluett. The tall, slender top rather indicates Southern origin. There is no carving on the piece, but that effect is obtained by inlaid rosettes. The doors have a border of inlay with fan corners, an oval and rosette in the centre of each. The lid is finished in the same manner, and the quarter-columns carry an inlay to resemble fluting.

Figure LVIII.
Sheraton Scrutoire with cabinet top, 1790–1800.

Figure LX.
Sheraton Desk, about 1810.

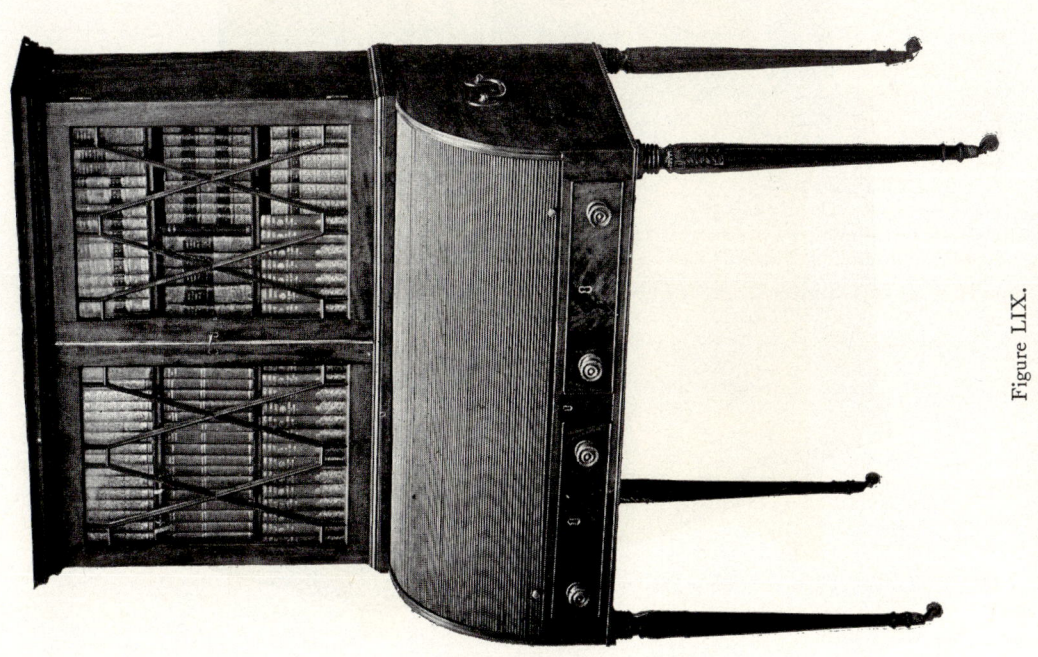

Figure LIX.
Sheraton Desk, bookcase top, 1800–10.

387

Figure LXI.
Sheraton Bookcase, 1790–1800.

LOOKING-GLASSES

Figure LIX shows a tambour desk with bookcase top, also the property of Mr. Cluett. The legs are reeded and capped with acanthus-leaf carving.

Figure LX shows a bird's-eye maple and mahogany desk with tambour slides concealing pigeonholes and drawers. There are four long drawers below. The top opens out and is supported by slides to write upon. The upper section is inlaid about the door and edges with a narrow line, and on the two outer surfaces are inlaid columns.

Figure LXI shows a bookcase, the property of the Brooklyn Museum. The piece is Baltimore made, and the upper section has the characteristic height of the pieces of that section, greatly enhancing its dignity. At the top is a broken

Figure LXII.
Queen Anne Mantel Mirror, about 1725

arch pediment and a bracket. The cornice is embellished with a dentilled moulding and a frieze composed of a series of parallel vertical channels so interrupted as to form a festoon. The lower portion has cupboards behind four doors panelled with raised moulding in the usual Sheraton fashion.

LOOKING-GLASSES

MANTEL MIRRORS

Figure LXII shows a walnut-veneer mantel mirror, the property of the writer. It is finished with a cyma moulding, and the inside strip next the glass has a border carved in an acanthus-leaf design and gilded. At each end the frame is extended to hold the brass candle-sockets and cut in a series of cyma curves. There are three sections of glass, each bevelled.

Figure LXIII shows a walnut and gilt mantel mirror, also the property of the writer. It is similar to the pier mirrors of the same period (Figure LXV) with carved and gilded scroll and leaf edge, pendant flowers and leaves, and inside acanthus-leaf edge next the glass. The glass is in one piece and bevelled.

The mantel mirrors above shown represent those popular in the Queen Anne period and the early Georgian period respectively, and they are rare. In the chapter on mirrors will be found mantel mirrors of the Chippendale, Sheraton, and Empire periods.

PIER MIRRORS

This form of mirror was intended to be used in narrow places, over tables.

Figure LXIV shows a walnut-veneer pier mirror of the Queen Anne type, the property of the writer. It belongs to the same class as the mantel mirror,

Figure LXIII.
Georgian Mantel Mirror, 1725–50.

Figure LXII. The edge is a cyma moulding, the upper section outlined in shallow curves, with the carved and gilded inner edge usual to this period. The side-brackets are cut out in a more graceful manner than usual, and being a pier glass the frame is straight on the bottom. In the opening of the top is a carved and gilded shell, the streamers being carved into the solid cresting and gilded.

Figure LXV shows a pier mirror of the same period as the mantel mirror, Figure LXIII. It is over seven feet tall. The outer edge is carved in the usual scroll and leaf design, gilded, and the form of the frame is architectural of the Georgian period. The swags of leaves, fruit, and flowers are well executed, as are also the scroll top, the rosettes with streamers, and the pheasant. The mirror came from the Smith house, Sharon, Connecticut, and is the property of the writer.

Figure LXIV.
Queen Anne Pier Mirror, about 1725.

Figure LXVII.
Pier Mirror, 1750–75.

Figure LXVI.
Pier Mirror, about 1750.

Figure LXV.
Georgian Pier Mirror, 1725–50.

392

Figure LXVIII.
Pier Mirror, 1750–75.

394 COLONIAL FURNITURE

Figure LXVI shows a slightly smaller pier mirror. It differs from any of the others shown in that the raised carved and gilded moulding has projecting square corners, both top and bottom, whereas the general method is to scroll the lower edge. The rosettes, pheasant, and pendant carvings are exceptionally well done. The height is 5 feet 2 inches, the width 22½ inches.

Another pier mirror of a little later date, the property of Mr. Charles Woolsey Lyon, is shown in Figure LXVII. The carved and gilded edge on the

Figure LXIX.
Two Mirrors, 1750–75.

sides is in an egg-and-dart design, and at the bottom and top in rococo. A very charming carved and gilded rococo finish is about the glass. At the centre of the top is carved a vase and flowers, leaves and fruit. The swags are unusually full and well carved. Height is 6 feet; width, 24 inches.

A slightly smaller pier mirror of the same period, the property of Mr. G. A. Cluett, is shown in Figure LXVIII. The carved and gilded framing and edge

Figure LXXI.
Pier Mirror, 1790–1800.

Figure LXX.
Pair of Mirrors, 1780–90.

are in the same pattern as the earlier mirrors, and the cresting and base show the Chippendale rococo motifs. At the centre of the top are beautifully carved Prince of Wales feathers with ribbons, and a heart.

Two nice cutwork mirrors, also the property of Mr. Cluett, are shown in Figure LXIX. The first one is elaborately cut, and the surfaces of the wood are carved to resemble foliage. The cresting is the Prince of Wales feathers. The second has a gilded edge and rococo designs, the upper edge elaborately cut, surmounted by a flying pheasant.

Figure LXXII.
Gilded Mirror, 1790–1800.

Figure LXX shows a pair of mirrors of the Bilboa type, the property of Mr. Cluett. They are quite similar to the one shown in Figure 369. On the top is an urn with heads of wheat, and on each side on pedestals are small urns with wheat. Beneath the top and all around the outer edge of the frame is a meander pattern of light wood, and the Grecian-key design appears at top and foot of each side and under the central pendant. At the centre of the top is an oval bead in which is a marble column, on top of which are two doves. The design is different on the two mirrors. At the four corners are rosettes of marble and arabesque designs. This pair is the finest of the type which has come under the writer's observation.

Figure LXXIII.
Pier Mirror, 1800–10.

A very good Empire mirror is shown in Figure LXXI. The eagle is standing on a pedestal of acanthus leaves, and on either side is an urn with flowers. The long slender columns have a modified form of Ionic capital. On the base of the pedestal is a cartouche within which is a basket of flowers. The panel above the mirror has a very charming Adam design of an urn with festoons of flowers caught up by rosettes.

Figure LXXII is shown because of its variation from Figure 381. As in that figure, the design is composed of two cornucopias fastened by a band from the top. Heads of wheat extend, making the top of the mirror. The heads of wheat are raised in the centre to form a cresting instead of an eagle, which appears in the other mirror.

Figure LXXIII differs from most Empire mirrors in that across the top are bold scrolls. The pedestal under the eagle and the section above the mirror-glass have painted landscapes. The mirrors just described are the property of Mr. G. A. Cluett.

COLONIAL FURNITURE
Volume II

WHEEL CHAIR ABOUT 1700

COLONIAL FURNITURE IN AMERICA

BY

LUKE VINCENT LOCKWOOD

THIRD EDITION

SUPPLEMENTARY CHAPTERS AND ONE HUNDRED AND THIRTY-SIX PLATES OF
NEW SUBJECTS HAVE BEEN ADDED TO THIS EDITION, WHICH NOW INCLUDES
OVER A THOUSAND ILLUSTRATIONS OF REPRESENTATIVE PIECES

VOLUME II

NEW YORK
CHARLES SCRIBNER'S SONS
MCMLI

Copyright, 1913, 1926, by
CHARLES SCRIBNER'S SONS

Printed in the United States of America

CONTENTS

CHAPTER		PAGE
VII.	CHAIRS	3
VIII.	SETTEES, COUCHES, AND SOFAS	127
IX.	TABLES	167
X.	BEDSTEADS	243
XI.	CLOCKS	270
	SUPPLEMENTARY CHAPTER	298
	INDEX	345

LIST OF ILLUSTRATIONS

Wheel Chair about 1700 . . . . *Frontispiece*

FIGURE		PAGE
402.	Dining-Hall, Christ Church, Oxford	4
403.	Joined Stool or Short Form, about 1650	5
404.	Turned Three-Legged Stool, early seventeenth century	6
405.	Dutch Stool, about 1650	6
406.	Turned Three-Legged or Boffet Chair, sixteenth century	7
407.	Turned Three-Legged or Boffet Chair, early sixteenth century . . .	8
408.	Turned Chair, late sixteenth and early seventeenth century	9
409.	Turned Chair, Carver style, first quarter seventeenth century . . .	9
410.	Turned Chair, Carver style, about 1650	10
411.	Turned Chair, Carver style, 1650–1700	10
412.	Turned Side Chair, Carver style, 1650–1700	11
413.	Turned Chair, Carver style, 1650–1700	11
414.	Spinning-Chair, Carver style, 1650–1700	11
415.	Turned Chair, Brewster style, first quarter seventeenth century . .	12
416.	Turned Chair, first quarter seventeenth century	12
417.	Turned Chair, first quarter seventeenth century	13
418.	Turned Chair, first quarter seventeenth century	14
419.	Turned Slat-Back Chair, 1625–50	14
420.	Turned Slat-Back Chair, 1650–1700	15
421.	Turned Slat-Back Chair, 1675–1700	15
422.	Turned Slat-Back Rocking-Chair, 1650–1700	16
423.	Turned Slat-Back Chair, 1675–1700	16
424.	Turned Slat-Back Chairs, 1700–25	17
425.	Turned Slat-Back Rocking-Chairs, 1725–50	18
426.	Turned Slat-Back Chair, 1725–50	18
427.	Turned Slat-Back Chair, 1725–50	18
428.	Turned Slat-Back Chair, 1725–50	19
429.	Turned Slat-Back Chair, Pennsylvania type, 1725–50	19
430.	Turned Slat-Back Chair with cabriole legs, Pennsylvania type, 1725–50	20
431.	Carved Oak Wainscot Chair, about 1600	21
432.	Carved Oak Wainscot Chair, first quarter seventeenth century . . .	22
433.	Oak Wainscot Chair, first quarter seventeenth century	22

vii

LIST OF ILLUSTRATIONS

FIGURE		PAGE
434.	Child's Wainscot Chair, first quarter seventeenth century	22
435.	Carved Oak Wainscot Chair, about 1650	23
436.	Carved Oak Wainscot Chair, about 1650	23
437.	Carved Oak Wainscot Chair, 1650–75	24
438.	Carved Oak Wainscot Chair, about 1650	24
439.	Oak Wainscot Chair-Table, about 1650	25
440.	Turned Wainscot Chair-Table, about 1700	26
441.	Turned Wainscot Chair-Table, 1725–50	26
442.	Leather Chair, about 1650	27
443.	Leather Chairs, about 1640	28
444.	Leather Chair, about 1650	29
445.	Turkey-Work Chair, about 1650	29
446.	Knob-Turned Chair, 1650–60	30
447.	Spiral-Turned Arm-Chair, 1650–60	31
448.	Cane Chair, 1660–80	32
449.	Cane Chair, Flemish legs, last quarter seventeenth century	34
450.	Cane Chair, Flemish legs, last quarter seventeenth century	34
451.	Cane Chair, Flemish legs, last quarter seventeenth century	35
452.	Cane Chair, Flemish legs, last quarter seventeenth century	35
453.	Cane Chair, scroll feet, last quarter seventeenth century	36
454.	Cane Chair, scroll feet, last quarter seventeenth century	36
455.	Cane Chair, last quarter seventeenth century	37
456.	Cane Chair, scroll legs, last quarter seventeenth century	37
457.	Cane Chair, Flemish legs, last quarter seventeenth century	38
458.	Cane Chair, turned legs, first quarter eighteenth century	38
459.	Upholstered Chair, turned legs, about 1700	39
460.	Upholstered Chair, turned legs, about 1700	39
461.	Banister-Back Chair, first quarter eighteenth century	40
462.	Banister-Back Chair, first quarter eighteenth century	40
463.	Banister-Back Chair, first quarter eighteenth century	41
464.	Banister-Back Chair, first quarter eighteenth century	41
465.	Banister-Back Chair, first quarter eighteenth century	42
466.	Banister-Back Chair, first quarter eighteenth century	42
467.	Banister-Back Chair, first quarter eighteenth century	43
468.	Banister-Back Chair, 1730–40	44
469.	Banister-Back Chair, 1740–50	44
470.	Cane Chair, Flemish feet, 1680–1700	45
471.	Cane Chair, Spanish feet, 1680–1700	45
472.	Cane Chair, scroll feet, 1680–1700	46
473.	Cane Chair, Spanish feet, 1680–1700	46
474.	Cane Chair, turned legs, about 1700	46

LIST OF ILLUSTRATIONS

FIGURE		PAGE
475.	Cane Chair, Spanish feet, 1680–1700	47
476.	Spanish Leather Chair, latter half of seventeenth century	48
477.	Cane Chair, Spanish feet, about 1700	49
478.	Cane Chair, scroll legs, about 1700	49
479.	Cane Chair, Spanish feet, 1690–1700	50
480.	Upholstered Chair, turned legs, about 1700	50
481.	Leather Chair, Spanish feet, 1700–10	51
482.	Cane Chair, Spanish feet, 1700–10	51
483.	Banister-Back Chair, 1710–20	52
484.	Leather Chair with Spanish feet, 1700–10	52
485.	Leather Chair, turned legs, 1700–10	53
486.	Cane Chair with cabriole legs, 1710–20	53
487.	Cane Chair with cabriole legs, 1710–20	53
488.	Cane Chair, cabriole legs, 1710–20	54
489.	Chair showing Dutch influence, 1710–15	54
490.	Chairs showing Dutch influence, 1710–20	55
491.	Chair showing Dutch influence, 1710–20	56
492.	Chair showing Dutch influence, 1710–20	56
493.	Chair showing Dutch influence, 1710–20	57
494.	Chairs in Dutch style, 1710–30	57
495.	Chairs in Dutch style, about 1725	58
496.	Chair in Dutch style, about 1725	58
497.	Chair in Dutch style, about 1725	58
498.	Chair in Dutch style, about 1725	59
499.	Chairs in Dutch style, about 1725	60
500.	Chair in Dutch style, about 1725	61
501.	Chair in Dutch style, 1725–50	61
502.	Seat in Dutch style, about 1725	62
503.	Library Chair, Dutch style, about 1725	63
504.	Upholstered Chair, Dutch style, 1725–50	63
505.	Chairs in Dutch style, 1725–50	63
506.	Chairs in Dutch style, common throughout the eighteenth century	64
507.	Turned Easy-Chair, 1700–10	65
508.	Easy-Chair, about 1725	65
509.	Easy-Chair, 1725–50	66
510.	Easy-Chair, 1725–50	66
511.	Easy-Chair, 1725–50	67
512.	Easy-Chair, 1725–50	67
513.	Easy-Chair, third quarter eighteenth century	68
514.	Easy-Chair, last quarter eighteenth century	68
515.	Easy-Chair, Empire period, first quarter nineteenth century	69

LIST OF ILLUSTRATIONS

FIGURE		PAGE
516.	Cane-Back Wheel Chair, about 1700	70
517.	Roundabout Chair, 1720–30	70
518.	Roundabout Chair, 1720–30	71
519.	Roundabout Chair with extension top, second quarter eighteenth century	71
520.	Roundabout Chair, second quarter eighteenth century	71
521.	Roundabout Chair, third quarter eighteenth century	72
522.	Roundabout Chair, third quarter eighteenth century	72
523.	Roundabout Chair, third quarter eighteenth century	73
524.	Roundabout Chair with extension top, third quarter eighteenth century	73
525.	Roundabout Chair, third quarter eighteenth century	73
526.	Windsor Chair, third quarter eighteenth century	74
527.	Windsor Chair, third quarter eighteenth century	75
528.	Windsor Chairs, third quarter eighteenth century	76
529.	Windsor Chair, third quarter eighteenth century	77
530.	Fan-Back Windsor Chairs, last quarter eighteenth century	76
531.	Windsor Slipper-Chair, Dutch feet, last quarter eighteenth century	78
532.	Windsor Chairs, last quarter eighteenth century	78
533.	Windsor Chair, last quarter eighteenth century	78
534.	Windsor Writing-Chair, last quarter eighteenth century	79
535.	Windsor Chair, about 1800	80
536.	Windsor Chair, first quarter nineteenth century	80
537.	Types of Chair Backs	82
538.	Chair in Chippendale style, Spanish feet, third quarter eighteenth century	84
539.	Chair in Chippendale style, Dutch feet, third quarter eighteenth century	85
540.	Chair in Chippendale style, third quarter eighteenth century	85
541.	Chair in Chippendale style, third quarter eighteenth century	85
542.	Chair in Chippendale style, third quarter eighteenth century	85
543.	Chair in Chippendale style, third quarter eighteenth century	86
544.	Chair in Chippendale style, third quarter eighteenth century	86
545.	Chair in Chippendale style, third quarter eighteenth century	87
546.	Chair in Chippendale style, third quarter eighteenth century	87
547.	Chair in Chippendale style, about 1760	88
548.	Chair in Chippendale style, third quarter eighteenth century	88
549.	Chair in Chippendale style, third quarter eighteenth century	89
550.	Chair in Chippendale style, 1770–80	89
551.	Chair in Chippendale style, third quarter eighteenth century	90
552.	Chair in Chippendale style, third quarter eighteenth century	90
553.	Chair in Chippendale style, third quarter eighteenth century	90
554.	Chair in Chippendale style, third quarter eighteenth century	90
555.	Chair in Chippendale style, 1750–60	91
556.	Chair in Chippendale style, French taste, 1750–60	92

LIST OF ILLUSTRATIONS

xi

FIGURE		PAGE
557.	Chair in Chippendale style, ribbon back, 1750–60	93
558.	Chair in Chippendale style, Gothic taste, third quarter eighteenth century	94
559.	Advertisement on back of foregoing chair	94
560.	Chair in Chippendale style, Gothic taste, third quarter eighteenth century	95
561.	Chair in Chippendale style, Gothic taste, third quarter eighteenth century	95
562.	Chair in Chippendale style, Gothic taste, third quarter eighteenth century	96
563.	Chair in Chippendale style, Gothic taste, 1760–70	96
564.	Chair in Chippendale style, Gothic taste, 1760–70	96
565.	Chair in Chippendale style, Gothic taste, 1760–70	97
566.	Chair in Gothic taste, 1760–70	98
567.	Chair in Manwaring style, Gothic taste, 1760–70	98
568.	Chair in Chippendale style, Gothic taste, 1760–70	99
569.	Chair in Chippendale style, Gothic taste, 1770–80	99
570.	Chair in Chippendale style, 1760–70	99
571.	Chinese Chair, about 1800	100
572.	Chair in Chippendale style, Chinese taste, third quarter eighteenth century	101
573.	Chair in Chippendale style, Chinese taste, third quarter eighteenth century	102
574.	Chair in Chippendale style, Chinese taste, about 1760	103
575.	Chair in Chippendale style, third quarter eighteenth century	104
576.	Chair in Chippendale style, imitating bamboo, 1760–70	105
577.	Ladder-Back Chair in Chippendale style, third quarter eighteenth century	105
578.	Ladder-Back Chairs, 1770–80	107
579.	Ladder-Back Chair, 1760–70	107
580.	Chair in Chippendale style, classic taste, 1768	107
581.	Upholstered Chair in Chippendale style, 1750–60	108
582.	Upholstered Chair in Chippendale style, 1750–60	109
583.	Upholstered Chair in Chippendale style, 1760–70	110
584.	Upholstered Chair in Chippendale style, 1770–80	110
585.	Chair in transition style, about 1790	111
586.	Chairs in transition style, 1780–90	111
587.	Chair in Hepplewhite style, 1785–95	112
588.	Chair in Hepplewhite style, 1785–95	113
589.	Chair in Hepplewhite style, 1785–95	113
590.	Chair in Hepplewhite style, 1785–95	113
591.	Chair in Hepplewhite style, 1785–95	114
592.	Chair in Hepplewhite style, 1785–95	114
593.	Chair in Hepplewhite style, about 1790	115
594.	Chair in Hepplewhite style, 1785–95	115
595.	Chair in Hepplewhite style, 1785–95	116
596.	Chairs in Sheraton style, 1785–90	117
597.	Chairs in Sheraton style, 1785–90	117

LIST OF ILLUSTRATIONS

FIGURE		PAGE
598.	Chair in Sheraton style, 1785–95	118
599.	Chair in Sheraton style, 1790–1800	118
600.	Chair in Sheraton style, 1785–95	118
601.	Chair in Sheraton style, 1785–95	119
602.	Chair in Sheraton style, 1785–95	120
603.	Chair in Sheraton style, 1785–95	120
604.	Red Lacquer Chair in Sheraton style, about 1800	121
605.	Painted Chair in Sheraton style, about 1800	120
606.	Painted Chair in Sheraton style, about 1800	120
607.	Upholstered Chair in Sheraton style, 1790–1800	121
608.	Upholstered Chair in Sheraton style, 1790–1800	122
609.	Upholstered Chair in Sheraton style, 1790–1800	122
610.	Painted Chairs in Sheraton style, about 1800	123
611.	Chair in Sheraton style, 1800–10	123
612.	Carved Chair in Sheraton style, 1800–10	124
613.	Chair in Phyfe style, 1810–20	124
614.	Chair in late Sheraton style, 1810–20	125
615.	Painted Chair, 1810–25	125
616.	Empire Chair, 1825–30	125
617.	Empire Chairs, about 1840	125
618.	Carved Oak Settle, last half seventeenth century	128
619.	Pine Settle, first half eighteenth century	128
620.	Cane Settle with three chair backs, about 1675	129
621.	Wagon Chair, first half eighteenth century	130
622.	Turned Slat-Back Settle with three chair backs, 1725–50	130
623.	Settee with double chair back in Dutch style, first quarter eighteenth century	131
624.	Settee with double chair back in Dutch style, about 1725	132
625.	Settee with three chair backs, Dutch style, 1725–50	133
626.	Settee with two chair backs, Chippendale style, 1750–60	133
627.	Settee with two chair backs in Chinese taste, 1750–60	134
628.	Settee with two chair backs, Chippendale style, third quarter eighteenth century	135
629.	Settee with two chair backs, Chippendale style, third quarter eighteenth century	136
630.	Settee with four chair backs, Chippendale style, 1770–80	137
631.	Settee in Chippendale style with two chair backs, 1760–80	137
632.	Settee with three ladder-back chair backs, about 1770	138
633.	Settee with two chair backs, transition style, 1775–85	139
634.	Settee with three chair backs, Hepplewhite style, 1785–95	139
635.	Settee with two chair backs, Sheraton style, about 1800	140
636.	Settee with three chair backs, Sheraton style, 1800–20	140
637.	Cane Couch, Flemish style, 1670–80	142
638	Cane Couch with Spanish feet, 1680–90	142

LIST OF ILLUSTRATIONS

xiii

FIGURE		PAGE
639.	Turned Couch, Pennsylvania type, about 1700	143
640.	Turned Couch, Pennsylvania type, about 1700	144
641.	Turned Couch, New England style, about 1700	145
642.	Turned Couch, Dutch style, 1700–15	145
643.	Turned Couch, Dutch style, about 1720	146
644.	Cabriole-Legged Couch, Dutch style, 1725–50	147
645.	Cabriole-Legged Couch, Chippendale style, about 1750	147
646.	Ball-and-Claw-Foot Couch, Chippendale style, 1750–60	148
647.	Couch, Chippendale style, 1760–70	148
648.	"Duchesse," Chippendale style, about 1760	149
649.	Couch, Chippendale period, 1770–80	150
650.	Chaise-Longue, 1790–1800	150
651.	Window-Seat, Chippendale style, third quarter eighteenth century	151
652.	Window-Seat, Chippendale style, third quarter eighteenth century	151
653.	Turned Sofa upholstered in Turkey work, about 1660	153
654.	Sofa, about 1700	154
655.	Sofa, Chippendale style, 1760–80	155
656.	Sofa, Chippendale style, third quarter eighteenth century	156
657.	Sofa, Chippendale style, third quarter eighteenth century	156
658.	Upholstered Sofa, 1770–80	157
659.	Sofa, Sheraton style, about 1785	158
660.	Sofa, Sheraton style, 1790–1800	158
661.	Sofa, Sheraton style, 1790–1800	159
662.	Sheraton Sofa, about 1800	160
663.	Sofa, Phyfe style, 1800–10	160
664.	Cane Sofa, Phyfe style, 1800–10	161
665.	Cane Sofa, Phyfe style, 1800–10	162
666.	Sofa in Phyfe style, 1800–10	163
667.	Sofa in late Sheraton style, 1800–10	163
668.	Empire Sofa, 1810–20	164
669.	Empire Sofa, 1810–20	164
670.	Empire Sofa, 1810–20	165
671.	Sofa, Empire style, 1810–20	165
672.	Table Board and Frame, about 1650	167
673.	Wainscot Table, about 1650	168
674.	Carved Oak Dining-Table, first quarter seventeenth century	169
675.	Oak Drawing-Table, early seventeenth century	171
676.	Walnut Turned Table, about 1700	171
677.	Gate-Legged Table, first half seventeenth century	172
678.	Gate-Legged Table, about 1650	172
679.	Gate-Legged Table, third quarter seventeenth century	173

LIST OF ILLUSTRATIONS

FIGURE		PAGE
680.	Double Gate-Legged Table, last quarter seventeenth century	173
681.	Double Gate-Legged Table, last quarter seventeenth century	174
682.	Gate-Legged Table, last quarter seventeenth century	174
683.	Gate-Legged Table, late seventeenth century	175
684.	Gate-Legged Table with Spanish feet, 1690–1700	176
685.	Gate-Legged Table with Spanish feet, 1690–1700	177
686.	Gate-Legged Table, late seventeenth century	177
687.	Folding-Table, third quarter seventeenth century	178
688.	Folding-Table, late seventeenth century	179
689.	Folding-Table, last quarter seventeenth century	179
690.	Folding-Table, last quarter seventeenth century	180
691.	Folding-Table, last quarter seventeenth century	181
692.	Turned Table with leaves, last quarter seventeenth century	181
693.	"Butterfly" Table, about 1700	182
694.	"Butterfly" Table, about 1700	182
695.	Turned Table, about 1675	183
696.	Turned Table with panel drawer, last quarter seventeenth century	184
697.	Turned Table, last quarter seventeenth century	185
698.	Turned Table, last quarter seventeenth century	185
699.	Spiral Turned Table, about 1650	186
700.	Turned Table, second half seventeenth century	187
701.	Turned Table, last quarter seventeenth century	187
702.	Turned Table, last quarter seventeenth century	188
703.	Turned Table, about 1700	189
704.	Turned Table, about 1700	189
705.	Turned Table, last quarter seventeenth century	190
706.	Top of foregoing table	191
707.	Three-Legged Table, about 1700	192
708.	Turned Table, about 1700	192
709.	Two Turned Tables, 1700–10	193
710.	Candle-Stand, about 1700	193
711.	Tripod Candle-Stand, first quarter eighteenth century	193
712.	Tea-Table with tile top, 1690–1700	194
713.	Slate-Top Table, last quarter seventeenth century	195
714.	X-Braced Table, about 1700	195
715.	Card-Table, 1690–1700	196
716.	Hutch-Table, about 1700	197
717.	Turned Table, first quarter eighteenth century	198
718.	Dining-Table with eight legs, second quarter eighteenth century	199
719.	Dining-Table with six legs, second quarter eighteenth century	200
720.	Drop-Leaf Table, second quarter eighteenth century	200

LIST OF ILLUSTRATIONS

XV

FIGURE		PAGE
721.	Drop-Leaf Table, second quarter eighteenth century	201
722.	Drop-Leaf Table, second quarter eighteenth century	201
723.	Twelve-Sided Table, drop leaves, second quarter eighteenth century	202
724.	Drop-Leaf Table, second quarter eighteenth century	202
725.	Rectangular Table, about 1750	203
726.	Drop-Leaf Table, third quarter eighteenth century	204
727.	Three-Legged Drop-Leaf Table, third quarter eighteenth century	204
728.	Oak Table Frame with bandy legs, first quarter eighteenth century	205
729.	Tea-Table, about 1725	205
730.	Tea-Table, about 1725	206
731.	Tea-Table, about 1725	206
732.	Tea-Table, second quarter eighteenth century	207
733.	Tea-Table, third quarter eighteenth century	207
734.	Tea-Table, second quarter eighteenth century	208
735.	Tea-Table, second quarter eighteenth century	208
736.	Tea-Table, third quarter eighteenth century	208
737.	Tea-Table, third quarter eighteenth century	209
738.	Tea-Table, domed stretchers, third quarter eighteenth century	209
739.	Tea-Table, domed stretchers, about 1760	210
740.	Pembroke Table, Chippendale style, 1760–70	211
741.	Pembroke Table, Chippendale style, 1770–80	211
742.	Bedside-Table, second quarter eighteenth century	212
743.	Tripod-Table with tray top, second quarter eighteenth century	212
744.	Tripod-Table with pie-crust top, 1750–75	213
745.	Tripod-Table with pie-crust top, 1750–75	213
746.	Tripod-Table, pie-crust top, 1750–75	214
747.	Tripod-Table, pie-crust top, 1750–75	215
748.	Tripod-Table, ogee edge, 1750–75	215
749.	Tripod-Table, Chippendale style, 1750–60	216
750.	Tripod-Table with gallery top, 1750–75	217
751.	Tripod-Table with human legs, 1750–75	217
752.	Tripod-Table with dish top, 1750–75	218
753.	Dumb-Waiter Table, 1750–75	219
754.	Small Tripod-Table with tray top, second quarter eighteenth century	219
755.	Small Tripod-Table with godrooned edge, second quarter eighteenth century	219
756.	Small Tripod-Table, last half eighteenth century	220
757.	Tripod-Table with octagonal gallery top, 1725–50	220
758.	Candle-Stand, 1725–50	220
759.	Card-Table, 1725–50	221
760.	Card-Table, 1725–50	221
761.	Card-Table, 1750–75	222

LIST OF ILLUSTRATIONS

FIGURE		PAGE
762.	Card-Table, 1725–50	223
763.	Card-Table, 1750–75	223
764.	Pier-Table, marble top, 1750–75	224
765.	Pole Screen, third quarter eighteenth century	225
766.	Pole Screen, second quarter eighteenth century	225
767.	Dining-Table, about 1775	226
768.	Dining-Table, last quarter eighteenth century	226
769.	Dining-Table, 1800–10	227
770.	Dining-Table, 1800–20	228
771.	Dining-Table, about 1810	228
772.	Dining-Table, about 1820	229
773.	Part of Dining-Table, about 1820	229
774.	Card-Table, 1775–1800	230
775.	Card-Table, 1790–1800	231
776.	Card-Table, 1790–1800	231
777.	Card-Table, 1790–1800	232
778.	Card-Table, Phyfe style, about 1810	233
779.	Card-Table, 1810–20	234
780.	Card-Table, about 1820	234
781.	Pembroke Table, last quarter eighteenth century	235
782.	Pembroke Table, 1780–90	235
783.	Pembroke Table, 1780–90	236
784.	Table, Phyfe style, 1800–10	236
785.	Table, Phyfe style, 1800–10	237
786.	Tripod-Table, about 1780–90	238
787.	Tripod-Table, 1790–1800	238
788.	Tripod-Table, about 1800	239
789.	Dumb-Waiter Table, 1785–90	239
790.	Pole Screen, about 1790	240
791.	Pole Screen, about 1790	240
792.	Toilet-Case, 1800–10	241
793.	Music-Rack, 1810–20	241
794.	Sewing-Table, 1800–10	241
795.	Sewing-Table, 1800–10	241
796.	Sewing-Table, 1810–20	242
797.	Sofa-Table, 1810–20	242
798.	Oak Bedstead, late sixteenth century	245
799.	Oak Cradle, sixteenth century	249
800.	Wicker Cradle, early seventeenth century	250
801.	Miniature Bed-Room, showing draperies, first quarter eighteenth century	251
802.	Walnut Bedstead, about 1725	252

LIST OF ILLUSTRATIONS

xvii

FIGURE		PAGE
803.	Bedstead, about 1725	252
804.	Bedstead draped in crewel-work, 1745	253
805.	Mahogany Bedstead, about 1725	254
806.	Cabriole-Legged Bedstead, 1725–50	255
807.	Cabriole-Legged Bedstead, 1725–50	256
808.	Cabriole-Legged Bedstead, about 1750	257
809.	Bedstead in Chippendale style, about 1760	258
810.	Bedstead in Chippendale style, 1750–60	259
811.	Draped Bedstead, late eighteenth century	260
812.	Bedstead, Sheraton style, about 1790	261
813.	Bedstead in late Sheraton style, about 1800	262
814.	Mahogany Bedstead in Sheraton style, 1790–1800	263
815.	Field Bedstead, 1790–1800	264
816.	Empire Bedposts, 1800–20	265
817.	Empire Bedstead, about 1810	266
818.	Low-Post Bedstead, 1820–30	267
819.	Low-Post Bedstead, 1800–20	267
820.	French Bedstead, about 1830	268
821.	French Bedstead, about 1830	268
822.	Portable or Table Clock, 1710–20	271
823.	Portable or Table Clock, 1750–60	271
824.	Portable or Table Clock, last quarter eighteenth century	272
825.	Chamber or Lantern Clock, last half seventeenth century	273
826.	Chamber or Lantern Clock, last half seventeenth century	273
827.	Chamber or Lantern Clock, last half seventeenth century	274
828.	Chamber or Lantern Clock, last quarter seventeenth century	275
829.	Dutch Chamber Clock, late seventeenth or early eighteenth century	276
830.	Tall Clock, last quarter seventeenth century	277
831.	Dial and side view of works of foregoing clock	278
832.	Tall Clock, 1690–1700	279
833.	Tall Clock, 1700–10	280
834.	Dial to foregoing clock	280
835.	Tall Clock, marquetry case, about 1700	281
836.	Tall Clock, about 1700	281
837.	Dial of tall clock showing arched top, 1725–30	282
838.	Tall Clock with japanned case, 1700–25	282
839.	Tall Clock made by Claggett, about 1725	283
840.	Tall Clock made by Claggett, 1725–35	283
841.	Dial to Claggett clock, 1730–40	284
842.	Tall Clock with japanned case made by Claggett, 1730–40	285
843.	Dial to following clock	284

LIST OF ILLUSTRATIONS

xviii

FIGURE		PAGE
844.	Wall or Mural Clock, about 1740	286
845.	Tall Clock, about 1740	286
846.	Musical Clock, Chippendale case, 1760–70	287
847.	Dial of clock shown in following figure	287
848.	Tall Clock, japanned case, about 1770	288
849.	Tall Clock, inlaid case, last quarter eighteenth century	289
850.	Burnap Clock, 1799	288
851.	Tall Clock, about 1801	289
852.	Miniature Tall Clock, about 1800	290
853.	Miniature Tall Clock, about 1800	290
854.	Tall Clock with painted face, about 1800	291
855.	Advertisement in following clock	291
856.	Willard Thirty-Day Clock, about 1800	292
857.	Willard or Banjo Clock, about 1800	292
858.	Willard Clock, about 1800	292
859.	Curtis Clock, 1800–20	293
860.	Curtis Clock, 1800–20	294
861.	Lyre-Shaped Clock, 1815–25	294
862.	Lyre-Shaped Clock, 1815–25	294
863.	Willard Bracket Clock, 1800–20	295
864.	Mantel Clock, 1800–20	295
865.	French Clock, 1800–20	295
866.	Mantel Clock, 1812	296
867.	Mantel Clock, 1820–30	296

SUPPLEMENTARY CHAPTER

FIGURE		PAGE
LXXIV.	Turned Chair, about 1650	299
LXXV.	Turned Slat-Back Chair, about 1700	299
LXXVI.	Turned Slat-Back Chair, 1725–50	299
LXXVII.	Carved-Oak Wainscot Chair, about 1650	300
LXXVIII.	Cane Chair, about 1700	301
LXXIX.	Leather Arm-Chair, Spanish feet, 1700–10	301
LXXX.	Turned Easy-Chair, 1700–10	302
LXXXI.	Arm-Chair, Dutch style, 1710–30	303
LXXXII.	Chair, Dutch style, 1725–50	304
LXXXIII.	Chippendale Arm-Chair, Gothic taste, 1760–70	305
LXXXIV.	Chippendale Arm-Chair, 1760–70	305
LXXXV.	Pair of Chippendale Side-Chairs, 1760–70	306
LXXXVI.	Chippendale Side-Chair, 1760–70	306
LXXXVII.	Hepplewhite Arm-Chair, 1780–90	307

LIST OF ILLUSTRATIONS

xix

FIGURE		PAGE
LXXXVIII.	Sheraton Inlaid Chair, 1790–1800	308
LXXXIX.	Sheraton Chair, 1790–1800	309
XC.	Sheraton Chair in Phyfe style, 1810–15	309
XCI.	Three "Fancy Chairs," 1810–20	310
XCII.	Settee with Three Chair-Backs, Hepplewhite style, 1785–95	312
XCIII.	Settee with Two Chair-Backs, Hepplewhite style, 1785–95	312
XCIV.	Settee, Painted, Sheraton style, 1810–20	313
XCV.	Pair Window-Seats, 1775–85	314
XCVI.	Window-Seat, 1785–95	314
XCVII.	Window-Seat, Painted, 1810–20	315
XCVIII.	Sofa, Chippendale style, 1760–80	316
XCIX.	Sofa, Hepplewhite style, 1785–95	316
C.	Sofa, Hepplewhite style, 1790–1800	317
CI.	Sofa, Sheraton style, 1790–1800	317
CII.	Sofa, Phyfe style, 1800–10	318
CIII.	Sofa, Sheraton style, about 1800	318
CIV.	Sofa, Phyfe style, 1800–10	319
CV.	Sofa, Phyfe style, 1800–10	320
CVI.	Couch, Sheraton style, about 1810	321
CVII.	Sofa, Empire style, 1810–20	322
CVIII.	Oak Wainscot Table, 1650–75	323
CIX.	Gate-Leg Table, about 1700	325
CX.	Folding-Table, 1675–1700	325
CXI.	Turned Table, 1675–1700	326
CXII.	Turned Table, 1675–1700	326
CXIII.	Tea-Table, about 1700	327
CXIV.	Tripod-Table, 1760–70	327
CXV.	Dining-Table, Chippendale style, 1760–70	328
CXVI.	Pair of Card-Tables, 1790–1800	329
CXVII.	Card-Table, 1790–1800	330
CXVIII.	Side-Table, about 1790	330
CXIX.	Painted Card-Table, 1800–10	331
CXX.	Oval Stand, 1790–1800	331
CXXI.	Sofa-Table, Phyfe style, 1800–10	332
CXXII.	Phyfe Table, 1800–10	332
CXXIII.	Bedstead, 1725–50	333
CXXIV.	Bedstead with Cabriole Legs, 1725–50	334
CXXV.	Bedposts, 1760–70	334
CXXVI.	Phyfe style Bedstead, 1800–10	335
CXXVII.	Tall Clock by Claggett, about 1745	337
CXXVIII.	Miniature Tall Clock by Tho Claget, about 1745	337

LIST OF ILLUSTRATIONS

FIGURE		PAGE
CXXIX.	Tall Clock by Hosmer, about 1790	338
CXXX.	Tall Clock by Whiting, 1790–1800	338
CXXXI.	Three A. Willard Bracket Clocks, 1800–10	339
CXXXII.	Three Banjo Clocks, 1800–10	340
CXXXIII.	Banjo Clock, A. Willard, 1800–10	341
CXXXIV.	Curtis Clock, 1800–20	341
CXXXV.	Two Willard Eddystone Lighthouse Clocks, 1810–20	342
CXXXVI.	Two Willard Eddystone Lighthouse Clocks, 1810–20	343

COLONIAL FURNITURE
IN AMERICA

VII
CHAIRS

IN no article of furniture is the development of style so easily traced as in chairs, for, although they have no mouldings, handles, or other such earmarks of the period as chests of drawers, each style is distinct, and its variations through gradual changes to a later form are so marked that step by step the evolution can be traced in no uncertain manner. In order, therefore, to emphasise this development it has been thought well in this chapter to show each style in its period and carry it through its various stages until it disappears or is absorbed in a succeeding style. The result of this method will be to interfere with the chronological arrangement, but it is believed that this loss will be more than compensated for by keeping before the reader the trend of development. For, after all, a knowledge of the style brings with it a knowledge of the dates.

If chairs had all been made in a single fashion the task would have been easier, but every country village had its own chair-makers, and often they were so out of touch with the prevailing fashions that their creations formed independent variations of a style which was carried only in the memory, and this is probably the reason that we find the continuance of a style in pieces which date long after the style had become old-fashioned. The date of a chair in a pure style is not a very difficult task to determine, but when a style covers a long period one is often puzzled to know whether to place the piece early or late in that period. No unfailing rule can be given, for the form, decoration, and other elements enter into the problem, but the general proposition can be laid down, other things being equal, that the heavier the frame and the underbracing of a chair in a given style the earlier the piece.

We find chairs mentioned sparsely in the earliest inventories of New England and the South, for they were not yet in common use in England, and the idea of the chair being a seat of honour was still general. "The Gate of Language Unlocked" (sixth edition, printed at London in 1643) has the following: "The chair belongeth to the teacher, the lower seats (fourms & benches) to the learner." Forms were for many years used almost exclusively in the place of chairs, and we constantly find mention of "short form" and "long form and table" in the

Figure 402.
Dining-Hall, Christ Church, Oxford.

inventories. These forms were popular in England, and were similar to those still found in the dining-halls of some of the English colleges and schools, benches heavily supported, as shown in Figure 402, which is the dining-hall at Christ Church College, Oxford.

The short form was a short bench, sometimes called in the inventories joined stool, for the ends of the tables, and the long forms were used on the long sides, those shown in Figure 402 being all long forms. Thus we find at New York, in 1680, "a long table and 2 long formes," one apparently for each side of the table; at Providence, in 1712, occurs the following entry of furniture in the parlour: "a great table, 3 formes, a great chair and 2 cushions," a form for each side and one end, and the chair for the head of the house, with one cushion for the seat of the chair and the other for a footstool.

Figure 403 shows a short form, the property of Mr. H. W. Erving, which is made of American oak. It is strongly built, with legs slightly raked, and the heavy stiles and bracing are mortised and tenoned and fastened with draw-bore pins in the method usually employed in oak pieces. American short forms are scarce, and the writer has never seen an American long form, although the English ones are fairly common.

Figure 403.
Joined Stool or Short Form, about 1650.

In nearly all of the early inventories we find stools and joined stools commonly mentioned; thus, at Plymouth, in 1641, "2 joined stools," and in the same inventory, "4 joyned stools and 2 joined chairs," which recalls a definition in Watts's "Logick," written early in the eighteenth century: "if a chair be defined a seat, for a single person, with a back belonging to it, then a stool is a seat for a single person, without a back." We also find the expression joint or "joynt" stools, which old dictionaries define as folding three-legged stools. Thus at New York, in 1677, we find "the table in the parlor and the five joynt stools"; at Yorktown, in 1658, "3 joint stools"; at Philadelphia, in 1694, "3 old 3 legged stools." A description of such stools is given by Cowper in "The Task":

"Joint stools were then created; on three legs
  Upborne they stood; three legs upholding firm
A massy slab."

Figure 404 shows an example of such a three-legged stool as was above described. The turning is in a simple early style, the only break in the surface of each leg being three beads. The stretcher between each pair of legs is joined to the seat with a spindle, and the stool has generally a very substantial yet light appearance. It is in the Bolles Collection in the Metropolitan Museum of Art.

Stools continued to be used all through the seventeenth century, and although abundantly mentioned in the inventories, they are to-day extremely rare and few are to be found in this country.

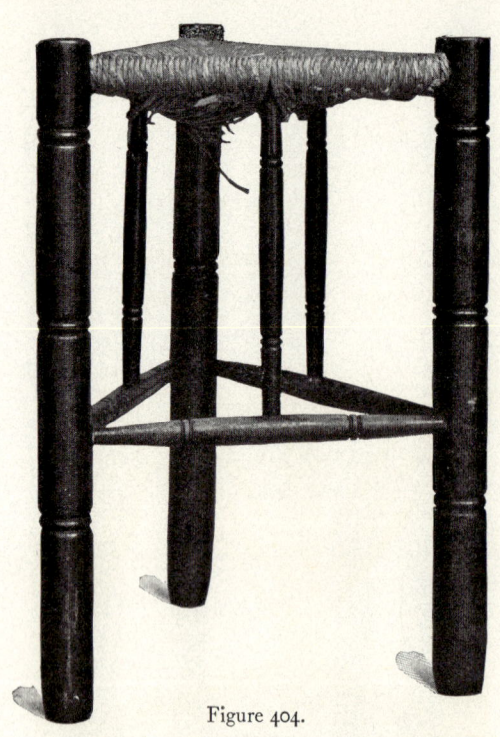

Figure 404.
Turned Three-Legged Stool, early seventeenth century.

Figure 405 shows another stool such as are found among the Dutch settlers. The rail is painted and the skirt is cut in two arches with engrailed edges. In the spandrels are carved rosettes. The legs are turned in the vase fashion and the seat finished in the thumb-nail moulding. This stool is in the Bolles Collection.

Figure 405.
Dutch Stool, about 1650.

In the American colonies down to 1650 there were two distinct styles of chairs in use, both of which had been long in use in England. They were the turned chairs and the wainscot chairs. The turned chairs are subdivided into two kinds, the spindle back and the slat back.

TURNED SPINDLE-BACK CHAIR

The turned chairs were of simple construction. The rails were let into holes bored to receive them, mortised and tenoned, and were often held in place with draw-bore pins holding all the joints tight, thus giving the chair a solidity and strength which has resisted the ravages of time to such an extent that many specimens of the seventeenth-century chairs of this type are extant which are apparently as strong and sound in their joints as if made to-day.

These chairs were made sometimes of oak or maple, but usually, at least so far as concerns this country, of ash with hickory spindles.

The earliest turned chairs are the three-legged variety. They, of course, far antedate the settlement of America and probably were never made here, but several, notably the so-called Harvard College chair, came to this country in the early days and there is some mention of them in the inventories. They were made with two legs in front and one at the back; the back projecting the width of the front was supported from the front post by arms and by a projection of the rear leg. These chairs were called buffet or boffet chairs. In a Salem inventory of 1673 is mentioned "Three bufet chairs 12s." In

Figure 406.
Turned Three-Legged or Boffet Chair, sixteenth century.

the "Promptuarum Parvalorum" of Galfridius, published in the sixteenth century, is the following definition: "Bofet, thre fotyd stole."

It is thought that this sort of chair is Byzantine and was introduced into Europe by the Normans and by them to England. There are not enough examples, however, surviving to enable one to draw positive conclusions.

Figure 406 shows a typical three-legged chair with two legs in front and one at the back. The rear leg extends up to and is fastened to the centre of the turned rail on the back. The back is further supported by three turned spindles extending from the rear leg to the under side of the rail and by two heavy spindles on each side extending from the ends of the rail to the front posts. There is a wooden seat, and a turned spindle strengthens the stretchers between each pair of legs.

8 COLONIAL FURNITURE

Figure 407 shows an ornate chair in this style. The three legs are very large, as are all the turnings. The rear leg only extends a short distance above the seat, instead of carrying through to the top rail, and supports a rectangular back composed of two heavy turned rails with nine bead-turned spindles. This rectangular back is strengthened by two turned supports on each side extending from the front posts, one fastening to the top rail and one to the lower rail, and the back is still further supported by three turned supports on each side running from the rear leg below the seat to the lower back rail. The legs are underbraced and between

Figure 407.
Turned Three-Legged or Boffet Chair, early sixteenth century.

each two legs are two spindles extending from the brace to the seat. The surfaces are ornamented with little circles in scratch carving and a large number of small projecting balls dowelled on. It would be very difficult to give a proper date to this piece, but it is probably of the late fifteenth or early sixteenth century. This and the preceding chair are in the Bolles Collection, owned by the Metropolitan Museum of Art.

Figure 408 is a very early specimen of a four-legged turned chair belonging to the Connecticut Historical Society. It is suggestive both of the preceding and succeeding styles. A peculiar feature is the apparently weak construction of the back. The back legs extend but slightly above the seat and across them is a rail supported by braces which extend to and fasten into the extension of the front legs. From this rail arises the back which in turn is strengthened by another brace which fastens into the extension of the front legs. The underbracing is similar to that shown in the preceding figure. The back is similar to the so-called Carver type which is shown in the succeeding figure.

Figure 409 shows the type of turned chair most commonly found in this country and which seems to have remained popular throughout the seventeenth

Figure 408.
Turned Chair, late sixteenth and early seventeenth centuries.

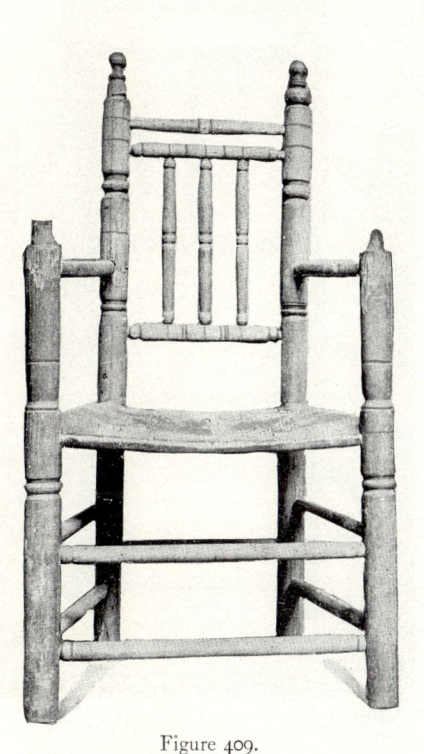

Figure 409.
Turned Chair, Carver style, first quarter seventeenth century.

century, for many specimens are found both of early and late variety. This style of chair is commonly known in this country as the Carver chair because of this specimen which is at Pilgrim Hall, Plymouth, and is said to have belonged to Governor Carver and to have been brought over by him in the *Mayflower*. They are found in large and small size and occasionally without arms. The earlier ones have heavy turned posts, the turning being very simple, while the later ones have smaller turned posts and the turning is in vase or other form. The chief characteristic of the type is the three rails and the three spindles in the back. These chairs are probably of Holland origin. They appear in the early Dutch paintings and in the interior views of the humbler homes, and were probably introduced into England from the Low Countries in the reign of Elizabeth.

A Carver chair in an unusually good state of preservation is shown in Figure 410 and is the property of Mr. George Dudley Seymour, of New Haven. The finials of the back and front legs are large balls and the line of the stiles is slightly broken with bulb turning. The construction in other respects is the same as that shown in the preceding figure.

Figure 410.
Turned Chair, Carver style, about 1650.

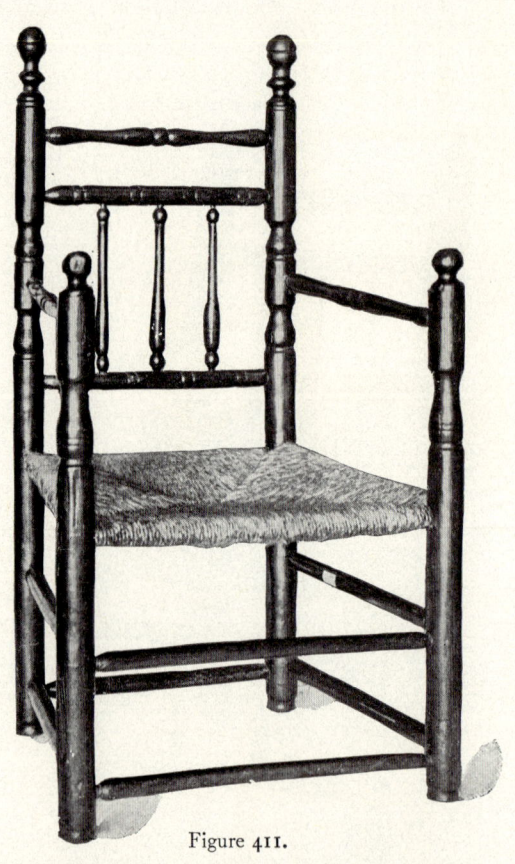

Figure 411.
Turned Chair, Carver style, 1650–1700.

A later form of the Carver chair in the possession of the writer is shown in Figure 411. The turnings are smaller and are vase-shaped and the spindles and rails are lighter. Many of these chairs are found with legs cut down and the knobs on the front post cut off, but this piece is in its original condition except that the feet are probably worn off about a quarter to one-half inch.

Figure 412 shows a side chair of the turned type under discussion. It will be seen that the turning of the knobs at the back and the three spindles are the same as those shown in the preceding figure. There is, however, but a single instead of a double rail at the top. Side chairs of this type are not at all common in this country. This chair is in the Bolles Collection at the Metropolitan Museum of Art.

CHAIRS

Figure 413 shows another chair of Carver type which is in the Blaney Collection. The turning at the top is more elaborate and the vase-shaped turnings are more pronounced than in the preceding pieces. The three spindles in the back are also more elaborately turned, all of which point to the fact that this chair is of somewhat later date than those shown in the preceding figures.

Figure 414 shows another chair of the Carver type, which is known as a spinning-chair. It stands high from the floor, as high as a child's high chair, but it is full size and is a side instead of an arm chair. The back is in the conventional form of the Carver chairs, but the spindles are much more elaborately turned and are in the form shown on the chair in the succeeding figure. The finials are also more intricately turned. The chair is in the possession of the writer.

Figure 412.
Turned Side Chair, Carver style, 1650–1700.

Figure 414.
Spinning-Chair, Carver style, 1650–1700.

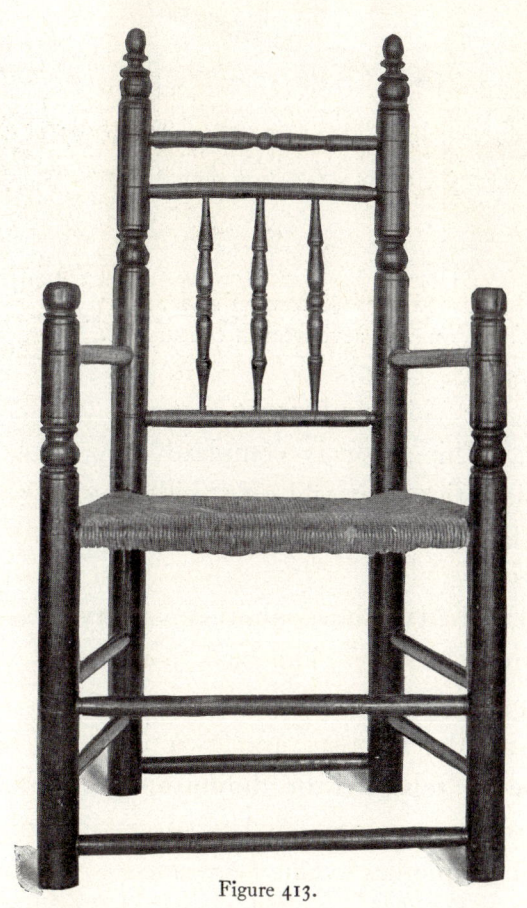

Figure 413.
Turned Chair, Carver style, 1650–1700.

We now come to the next type of turned chair (Figure 415), which is commonly called in this country the Elder Brewster chair, because this specimen, which is at Pilgrim Hall, Plymouth, is supposed to have been brought over by Elder Brewster in the *Mayflower*. It is the most beautiful of the turned types. The back is composed of a double tier of four spindles, each much more delicately turned than those of the Carver type. A series of four of the same spindles finishes the space under each arm, and originally a double tier of four spindles each fin-

Figure 415.
Turned Chair, Brewster style, first quarter seventeenth century.

ished the side and front beneath the chair. This chair is complete only on one side, the front and other side having lost the lower tier.

Figure 416 shows another variety of the turned chair. The back consists of an upper section and two rails fastened into the back posts and two uprights fastened into these rails. This same theme is repeated in diminishing size as the square becomes smaller. The spaces between are filled with small turnings. The lower portion of the back has five spindles. On each side of the back project wings and long turnings supported at the post by two short ones, giving the suggestion of an easy-chair of a later period.

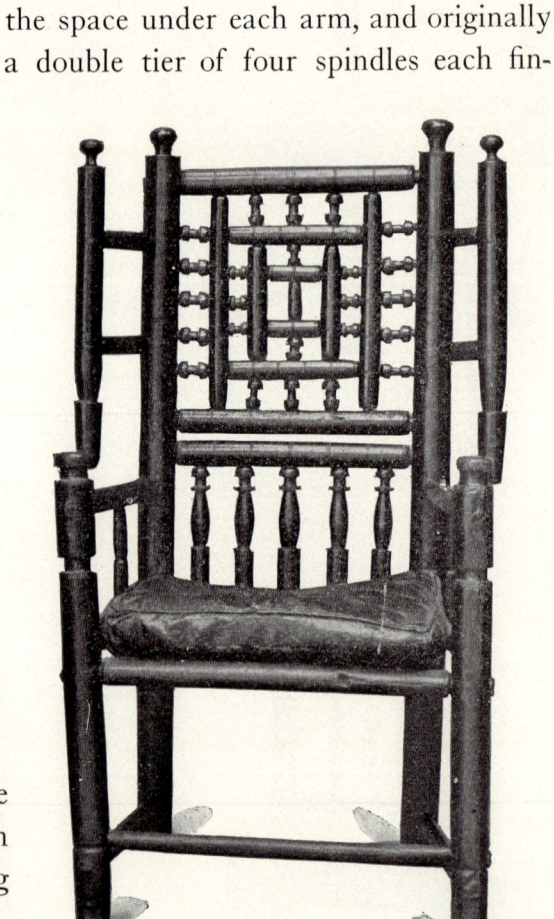

Figure 416.
Turned Chair, first quarter seventeenth century.

CHAIRS

Figure 417 shows still another variation of a turned chair. Four ornately turned parallel rails finish the top of the back, and the back itself is composed of a series of rectangles, four in number, one inside the other, filling in the entire space. The space between the arms and in front under the seat has sausage-turned spindles, and short projecting wings are at each side of the top.

These last two types, which are from the Bolles Collection, are of English origin and are extremely uncommon.

The spindle-turned chair seems to have been a hybrid, for it completely disappears about the end of the seventeenth century, except that it was, perhaps, the prototype of the turned and cane chairs of the last quarter of the seventeenth century.

SLAT-BACK TURNED CHAIRS

The second type of turned chair has a much longer history and is found late in the eighteenth century; in fact, it probably suggested the so-called ladder backs to the cabinet-makers of the Chippendale school. One reason for its popularity over the spindle type was because a series of slats in the back are more comfortable than the spindles. We will trace the development of the slat-back turned chairs consecutively, although it will result in a disarrangement of the chronological order.

Figure 417.
Turned Chair, first quarter seventeenth century.

Figure 418 shows an early example of the slat-back chair. It will be seen that there are three slats across the back instead of turned rails. These are mortised and tenoned into the back posts and the space between is filled with spindles of similar turnings to those found in the Elder Brewster chair (Figure 415). On each slat is also an insert of small spindles. The arms have a flat surface instead of being turned and the bracing is very elaborately turned. This chair is in the Bolles Collection, owned by the Metropolitan Museum of Art.

Figure 419 shows another early slat-back chair from the Bolles Collection. The slats are cut in the early form with quarter-round curves at either end. The turnings are about the size and form of the early Carver-type chairs.

Another slat-back chair is shown in Figure 420 and is the property of Mr. H. W. Erving, of Hartford. There are four slats across the back and the piece is more ornately turned, which would indicate that it is of a later date. There is a flat arm and below that is a turned support.

Figure 421 shows still another variety of the slat-back turned chairs in the Blaney Collection, the unusual feature being that the back is narrower at the top

Figure 418.
Turned Chair, first quarter seventeenth century.

Figure 419.
Turned Slat-Back Chair, 1625–50.

than at the bottom, like a ladder, and the turned supports of the arms are raked. The upper turning in the front under the seat is in what is known as the sausage form.

The earliest rocking-chair that the writer has found is shown in Figure 422. It will be seen that the turnings are almost identical with those shown in Figure 419, and, as in that chair, there are three slats. The rear legs at the back are widened out and a groove is cut in them to hold the rocker, showing that this chair must have originally been made for a rocking-chair and not cut down as have been many of the stationary chairs. It seems strange that so few early rocking-chairs should be known, because the principle of the rocker was well known and

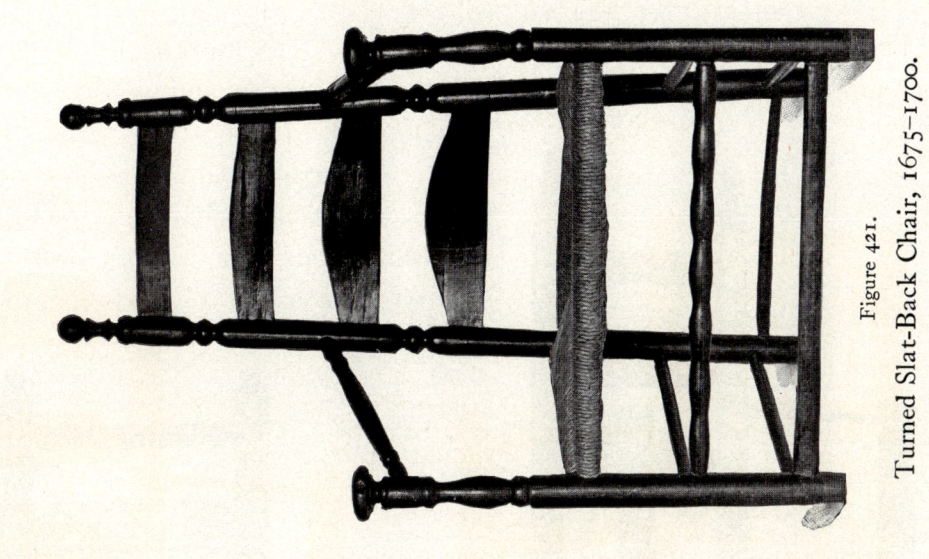

Figure 421.
Turned Slat-Back Chair, 1675–1700.

Figure 420.
Turned Slat-Back Chair, 1650–1700.

used on the cradles of the earlier period, but rocking-chairs are scarce prior to the type which is shown in Figure 425. This chair is the property of Mr. G. H. Buek and is in the "Home Sweet Home" cottage, East Hampton, Long Island.

Figure 423 shows a slat-back chair in the writer's possession. It has a turned upper rail and two slat backs. All of the turnings, including the arms and the top rail, are in the knob pattern which is rather unusual.

Slat-back chairs are found with two, three, four, five, and six slats. The slat varies considerably between those found in New England and those found in or about Philadelphia. The reason for the difference is traceable to the section of England from which the colonists came. New England was settled by persons mostly from the east of England, many of whose ancestors had come from Holland, while Philadelphia was largely settled by people from Surrey, and the same difference in type of slat-back chairs is noticeable there as here.

Figure 422.
Turned Slat-Back Rocking Chair, 1650–1700.

Figure 423.
Turned Slat-Back Chair, 1675–1700.

Figure 424 shows three slat-back chairs of the type commonly found in New England. There was hardly a household that did not own one or more, and many of them have survived to this day, cut down, with short rockers attached. The one on the left is a four-back and the centre one, a child's chair, is a two-back and at the right is a three-back. The mushroom knobs as a finish to the arms are characteristic.

Figure 425 shows two examples of slat-back rocking-chairs in the possession of the writer. These are the earliest type of rocking-chairs which are known in

Figure 424.
Turned Slat-Back Chairs, 1700–25.

this country next after the early turned style shown in Figure 422. The distinguishing feature of these pieces is the short arm, the support for which, instead of being an extension of the front legs, is a spindle which extends through the seat rail into the upper side stretcher. The first one has slats cut in waving lines and the other one has a simple slat cut in long ovals.

Figure 426 shows a New England slat-back with five slats which is in the Bolles Collection. It will be noted that the arms have changed from the turned type to the type found on the better quality of chairs of the day. The slats have oval tops and straight edges below. At the top is a turned ball and on the stiles between each slat is a turning, and the same turning appears on the front legs.

Figure 427 shows a very good example of a five-slat-back chair without arms, the property of Mrs. A. S. Chesebrough, of Bristol, Rhode Island. The stiles are turned between each slat and also on the legs between the stretchers. The chair is very similar to that shown in the preceding figure.

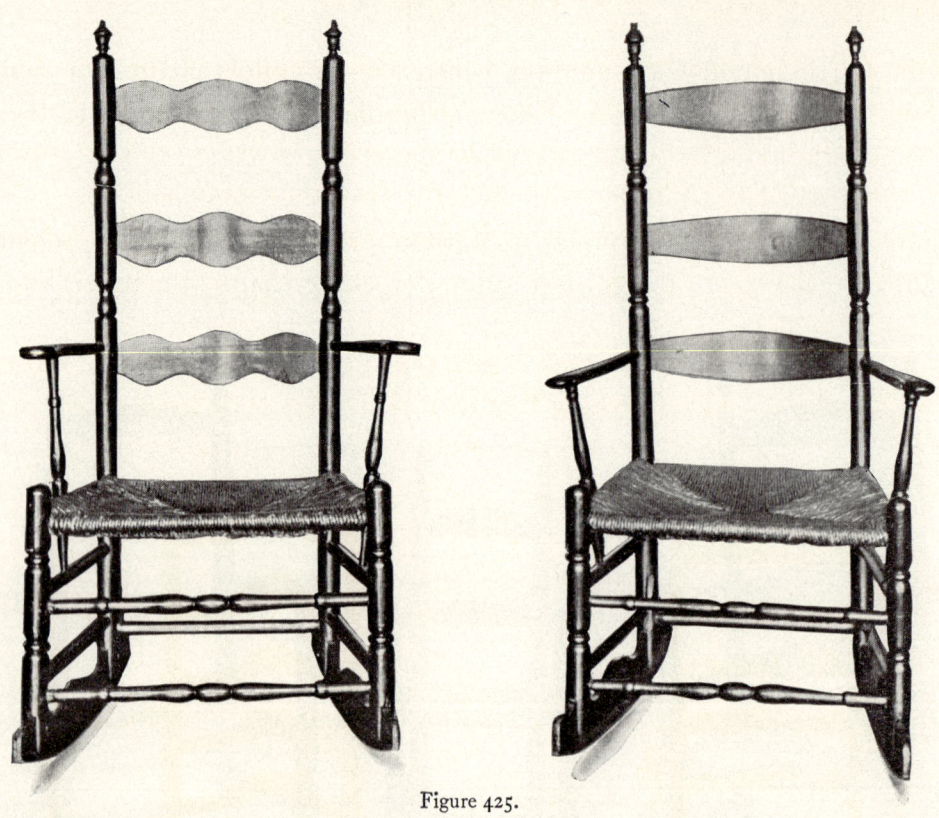

Figure 425.
Turned Slat-Back Rocking-Chairs, 1725-50.

Figure 426.
Turned Slat-Back Chair, 1725-50.

Figure 427.
Turned Slat-Back Chair, 1725-50.

18

Figure 428 shows another slat-back chair, with five slats, of the New England type. The slats are cut in cyma curves. There is no turning on the back posts except the finials. The front legs extend to the arms, however, and are turned in the vase, ring, and bulb pattern, as are also the two front stretchers.

Slat-back chairs are found both with and without arms, but the former are more common.

We will now consider the Pennsylvania type of this chair which is well exemplified in Figure 429. The distinguishing features of this type from those found in

Figure 428.
Turned Slat-Back Chair, 1725–50.

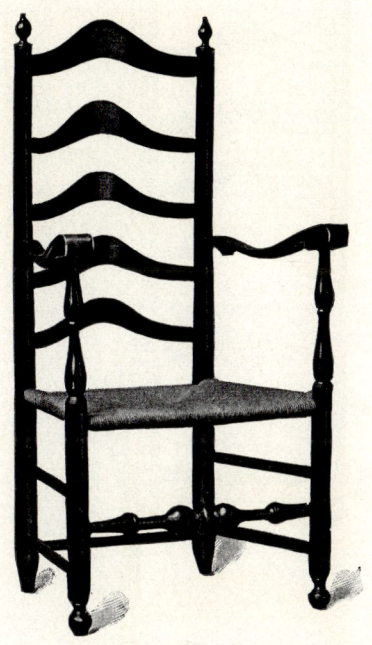

Figure 429.
Turned Slat-Back Chair, Pennsylvania type, 1725–50.

New England are that the back is simply turned without a break, while in the New England type a bulb is usually turned between each two slats, and the slat of this type always has the high curve at the centre and is more concave. The arms are always cut in on the under side, as appears in this piece, and the front legs always terminate in the same peculiar-shaped ball, the rear legs merely tapering. In New England the five-slat-back chair is not common, while in the Pennsylvania type it is the most common. This chair is the property of Mr. Frank C. Gillingham, of Germantown.

A very interesting variation of the Pennsylvania type of slat-back in the possession of the writer is shown in Figure 430. The back is very similar to that shown in the preceding figure except that it has six instead of five slats. A skirt hides the front of the rush seat and is cut in the double ogee curves found so commonly on the high-boys and chairs of the early eighteenth century. The legs are cabriole and terminate in angular Dutch feet, a form of foot commonly found south of New York. The old style of double bracing shows on the side, while the front has but the single turned brace. This is the only specimen of a slat-back chair with cabriole legs which has come under the writer's observation, and it is an interesting transition piece between the early and late styles.

These chairs are referred to in the inventories as follows: At Plymouth, 1643, "2 flag bottomed chairs & 1 frame for a chair"; Salem, 1673, "3 turned chairs"; Boston, 1698, "5 straw bottomed chairs"; 1699, "1 great turned chair"; New York, 1685, "9 Mat bottomed chairs"; 1680, "a high Matted chair & an elbow matted chair"; 1692, "12 chairs latticed with reeds"; Philadelphia, 1709, "2 turned chairs, one armed"; and at Yorktown, Virginia, 1667, "5 old bulrush chairs."

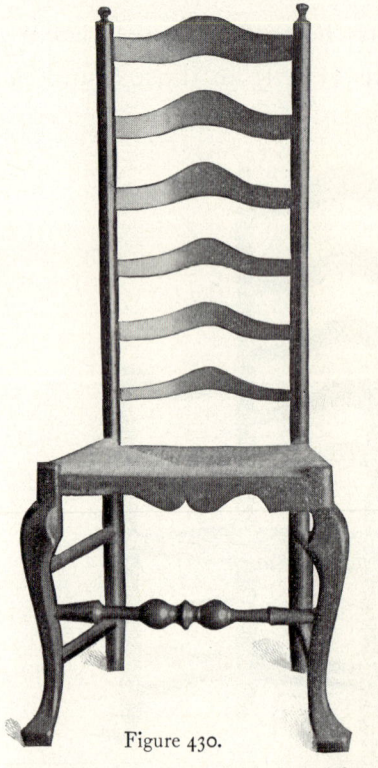

Figure 430.
Turned Slat-Back Chair with cabriole legs, Pennsylvania type, 1725-50.

WAINSCOT CHAIRS

The second style of chair found prior to 1650 is the oak chair known as the wainscot chair. The word "wainscot" is derived from the Dutch "wagenschot," literally a wagon partition, referring to the best oak timber, well grained and without knots, such as was used in the best coaches of the period. These chairs were much more massively built than the turned chairs, the construction being the same as was found on the oak chests and cupboards of the period. The backs were framed and panelled, and all joints were mortised and tenoned, fastened with draw-bore pins, and the legs were heavily underbraced. The seats were of oak slabs and were made more comfortable with cushions, which were frequently mentioned in the inventories in connection with the chairs, as in Salem, in 1644, "2 cheares & two cushans"; also the following entries refer to these chairs: Plymouth, 1634, "a joyned chair"; 1682, "a chair and cushion"; at New York, 1691, "7 chairs and four old cushions"; at Philadelphia, 1694, "4 framed oak chairs and cushions"; 1695, "large oak arm chair and cushion"; at Providence, 1712, "a great chair and 2 cushions"; 1727, "2 cushons for grate chear"; 1730, "a greate cheiar and quoshen"; at Yorktown, Virginia, 1658, "2 wainscoate chairs"; 1659, "3 wainscoate chairs." They are also frequently referred to as wooden chairs.

CHAIRS

There is mention of the wainscot chairs in the English inventories in the sixteenth and seventeenth centuries, and they were probably more generally used there than here, comparatively few being mentioned in the New England inventories, although a fairly large number are mentioned in those of the South. They are valued at from two to three times as much as the turned chairs, which

Figure 431.
Carved Oak Wainscot Chair, about 1600.

undoubtedly accounts for this fact. The chairs, when carved, show the same designs as the chests and cupboards of the period.

A massive wainscot chair which is at the Essex Institute, Salem, is shown in Figure 431. The cresting is composed of two S scrolls with foliation between, and three turned finials finish the top. The upper rail of the panel is carved in an arabesque design, and the stiles are in a foliated scroll design and the lower rail is in a double-foliated scroll. The panel is in a design of leaves, flowers, and scrolls, and it will be interesting to compare this panel with the centre panel in the chest shown in Figure 8, for it is the same theme worked out a little differently. On either side of the stiles are applied carvings and scroll designs. It is rather unusual for the top rail to set inside the stiles; the construction usually is the other way, the stiles setting into the rails.

Figure 432 shows a chair which tradition says was brought to America in 1660 but belongs to an earlier date. It will be noted that the front feet are not turned but are cut on the square in a turned de-

Figure 432.
Carved Oak Wainscot Chair, first quarter seventeenth century.

Figure 433.
Oak Wainscot Chair, first quarter seventeenth century.

Figure 434.
Child's Wainscot Chair, first quarter seventeenth century.

sign. The upper panel is in the familiar double-scroll design, and on the lower rail of the panel is carved a lunette design. The cresting extends over the stiles and is carved in two arched designs in different planes. An applied ornament of wood undoubtedly originally finished the space under the projections of the top rail, as in Figure 437.

Figure 433 is supposed to have been made at Cheapside, London, in 1614, and to have been used by Governor Winslow in

CHAIRS

his council chamber in 1633. The top rail is crested in a scroll design and a grooving on the rails is the only ornament. The skirt is cut on an angle to give the appearance of flaring and is serrated in a design found on many chests and tables of the period, and an applied ornament of wood probably finished the sides under the projecting top rail.

An interesting child's chair from the Bolles Collection is shown in Figure 434. The back is low and the top rail is cut in three arches, and four spindles connect these with the rail. The same theme is

Figure 436.
Carved Oak Wainscot Chair, about 1650.

Figure 435.
Carved Oak Wainscot Chair, about 1650.

repeated in the front below the seat. The stiles extend high above the rail on either side in the manner that was popular in the Italian and Flemish schools.

A wainscot chair of American oak in the Bolles Collection is shown in Figure 435. The panel is arched, with a narrow carved palmated design surrounding it. In each spandrel is a carved circle and a small circle is carved in the centre above the arch. The cresting, the lower edge of the back, and the skirt are all cut in the serrated design shown in Figure 432. This chair has been restored with oak of a different grain in order to clearly show the old parts.

Figure 436 shows another wainscot chair with rather crude carving. The panel is in the familiar double-foliated scroll found on other oak pieces. The top rail sets within the stile and there is a cresting of two scrolls. The surfaces of the stiles are carved in alternate circles and lozenges, and on the rail under the seat is carved a lunette design. This chair is the property of Mrs. C. S. Merriam, of Meriden, Connecticut.

A rather ornate wainscot chair from the Bulkeley Collection is shown in Figure 437. Across the top is a large double scroll. The panel is in a lozenge

Figure 437.
Carved Oak Wainscot Chair, 1650–75.

Figure 438.
Carved Oak Wainscot Chair, about 1650.

design with four semicircular projections. Above the panel is carved an entwined lunette design, and the sides of the stile under the top rail are finished with the applied pieces which are missing on the specimens shown in Figures 432 and 433. A very good reeded design finishes the seat rail and is repeated below the top rail. The front legs are rather slender for a wainscot piece, and the turning is of a later period than that on any of the other wainscot pieces shown.

Figure 438 shows a wainscot chair in the Bolles Collection which was found at Scituate, Massachusetts. It appears to be made of American oak. The carving, however, is of much better quality than is usually found in this country. The cresting is composed of two grotesque fishes with tails, terminating each in a leaf and a rosette. Below the cresting is a rectangular panel carved in a well-executed guilloche design, and on the rail below the panel is carved a foliated and flower design. The main panel is recessed by an applied arch in the spandrels of which are carved flowers and leaves, and the panel itself has a charming design of flowers and leaves after the manner of some of the chest panels. The arms are in scroll forms and slightly carved. The graceful front legs and supports of the arms are carved in godrooning and fluting. The legs have been partly cut off, judging from the height of the seat, and were probably finished like the legs of the stool shown in Figure 405. The seat rail is ornamented with reeding.

Another form of wainscot chair is the chair-table. It has all the characteristics of the wainscot chair except that the back is pivoted and swings forward, resting on the arms, forming a table. They were apparently quite common in this country, and the plainer types are still to be found. We find mentioned in a Salem inventory of 1673 "a chair table 7s 6d"; and again, in 1690, and at Yorktown, Virginia, 1666, "1 table chair"; and in 1675, "one new chair table 8s." This chair is practically the same as the famous Theodore Hook chair, although it is not carved.

Figure 439 shows the finest specimen of a chair-table that has been found in this country. It is in the Bolles Collection. It

Figure 439.
Oak Wainscot Chair-Table, about 1650.

will be seen that the frame very closely resembles the chairs of the period, except that the rear legs are turned like the front ones instead of being plain. The under sides of the stretchers are serrated and under the seat is a drawer on side runners. The back makes a long rectangular table and the cleats and mouldings on the under side are much better finished than is usual.

Figure 440 shows another unusual chair-table in the same collection. The construction is the same but there is no drawer under the seat; instead the skirt is cut in the well-known double cyma curve. The top when down forms a large square table.

Figure 440.
Turned Wainscot Chair-Table, about 1700.

Figure 441.
Turned Wainscot Chair-Table, 1725–50.

CHAIRS

Figure 441 shows a later variety, which is the more common form, with a round top, the chair-seat having a drawer on bottom runners.

LEATHER CHAIRS

The third style, which may be called a modification of the wainscot, is the leather chair, which dates a little later and by some is called Cromwellian, although it appears in the inventories in this country a little earlier than that time. It was really of Italian design, coming to England through Holland during the commonwealth, and very likely reached the Pilgrims, who had come from Holland, earlier than it did England, for we find these chairs first mentioned at Plymouth as early as 1643: "3 leather chairs, 3 small leather chairs £1 10s." We continue to find them mentioned freely until the close of the seventeenth century, as in the inventory of the famous Captain Kidd, at New York, 1692, "two dozen single nailed leather chairs, £1 16s"; and in New York, 1703, "8 leather cheares very old," undoubtedly referring to chairs similar to that shown in Figure 442. The earlier ones had a straight frame without turning with a band of leather stretched across the back and a leather seat, each fastened with large, heavy nails. The later ones had turned frames and were lighter.

Figure 442.
Leather Chair, about 1650.

Figure 442 shows an interesting specimen of a leather chair belonging to Trinity College, Hartford, Connecticut. The leather in the back is carved while that in the seat is plain. The waving line of the stretcher is suggestive of the carved stretchers of the cane period. This chair originally stood somewhat higher from the floor, but the legs are worn away.

Figure 443 shows two arm-chairs in this early leather style belonging to the Bolles Collection. These chairs stand high from the floor in the usual manner, the feet not having worn off. The front stretcher on each is a plain slab of wood, and on the one to the right the surface is ornamented with a design which has disappeared from the other.

28   COLONIAL FURNITURE

Wainscot and leather chairs in general stood much higher from the floor than either the turned ones or those appearing later; in fact, the seats are often as high as twenty or twenty-two inches. They were apparently intended to be used with footstools, as were the benches, for we find the following description in "The Gate of Language Unlocked," before referred to:

"When the table is spread with the table cloth, dishes are set upon it and trenchers 'whether they be round or square' and also a salt sellar.

"Out of the bread basket, loaves (shives) of bread are set on the table, or pieces 'morsels'; and then messes of meat.

Figure 443.
Leather Chairs, about 1640.

"The ghests that are bidden are brought (led) in by the feast-maker into the dining room (parlour) and when they have washed over a bason out of a ewer and have wiped with a towell; they sit down upon benches or stools set in order with cushions having foot stools set under them."

These leather chairs must not be confounded with the Spanish leather chairs, which are of later date and totally different style: Boston, 1653, "8 red leather backe chairs and 2 low leather backe stools"; Salem, 1647, "3 red leather chairs"; Boston, 1700, "6 russia leather chairs"; Philadelphia, 1683, "14 russia leather chairs"; 1686, "6 calfe leather chairs"; New York, 1691, "3 doz. russia leather chairs"; and Yorktown, 1668, "6 turkey leather chairs." These are references, perhaps, to the style of chair shown in Figures 442 and 444.

The York County (Virginia) records after 1660 show that a large number of these chairs were in use, one hundred and three of them being mentioned between the years 1657 and 1670; as many as twenty-eight in one inventory in 1667 are spoken of as old. Their values vary from one to ten shillings each.

A little later form of a leather chair is shown in Figure 444. The front legs and stretcher are knob-turned. The chair is smaller and lower than the earlier form. It belongs to the writer.

Figure 444.
Leather Chair, about 1650.

Figure 445.
Turkey-Work Chair, about 1650.

Figure 445 shows a chair quite similar to the foregoing which was originally covered with Turkey work. It differs from the preceding type of leather chairs in that the back is considerably higher and there are two knob turnings on each side below the upholstery. The front legs are knob-turned as is also the front stretcher. This chair is the property of the writer.

In the inventories are mentioned both Turkey carpets and Turkey work. Carpets were the imported rugs, and their usefulness seems to have been appreciated by the Dutch who brought them from the East. The Turkey work was made in imitation of the rugs. It was made on coarse canvas or sacking, on which the pattern was drawn, exactly as the hooked rugs were made except that worsted was used in place of cloth cut in strips. We find Turkey-work chairs mentioned in English inventories as early as 1589, the English having received permission, in 1579, from Amurath III to trade with Turkey. In New York we find, in 1677, "12 old Turkey chairs £1 4s"; Boston, 1669, "12 turkey work chairs £1 7s 4d"; at Yorktown, Virginia, 1674, "6 Turkey worked chairs £2 2s"; at Salem, 1684, "9 turkey work chairs without backs £2 4s"; "4 turkey work chairs with backs £1 12s"; at Philadelphia, 1687, "12 small turkie carpett chairs 2 of them broken £6"; and "6 turkie work chairs 1 of them broken £1 16s."

Turkey work and leather were very evidently not the only coverings used for these square-framed chairs, as the following inventory entries will show: Salem, 1698, "6 old serge chairs"; New York, 1680, "6 old red cloth chairs"; 1698, "6 chairs with red plush and 6 with green plush"; Philadelphia, 1687, "6 camlett silk fringe low chairs"; 1668, at Yorktown, "6 wrought chairs"; and, as upholstery was not in use for the turned or wainscot chairs, these entries must refer to the square-framed chairs just described.

Figure 446.
Knob-Turned Chair, 1650–60.

Very few of these Turkey-work or leather chairs have survived, although through a period of some thirty years they are frequently mentioned in the inventories both in the North and South, and it is not at all uncommon to find a large number, from one to three dozen, in a single inventory. The probable reason is that when the leather or Turkey work was worn out the frames were of little use and were broken up or thrown away.

After 1650 chairs became lighter in appearance, the leather chair just described affording the type.

Figure 446 indicates how this effect was secured. The front legs and stretcher resemble quite closely the chair shown in the preceding figure, but the entire frame of the piece is knob-turned. The back is composed of two turned rails and five turned spindles. This chair is in the Bolles Collection.

A very beautiful chair of this period is shown in Figure 447. The form and construction are the same as shown in the preceding figure, but the turning

CHAIRS

is all spiral-twisted, giving a rhythm of form which is extremely pleasing. It will be seen that even the rails of the seat are turned in the same manner, and a wooden seat is sunken into the rail. This chair is also in the Bolles Collection.

Figure 447.
Spiral-Turned Arm-Chair, 1650–60.

The most notable change in this period was the introduction of cane chairs from Holland. Their graceful and beautifully carved frames were in striking contrast to the turned and wainscot pieces then generally in use.

This style of furniture came into general use in England in the reign of

Charles II (1660), and continued until the Dutch style became dominant in the reign of Anne in 1702.

The fact that furniture should be exported from the Low Countries was not strange, for Antwerp seems to have been a great centre for that trade from about 1560 down, and Anderson, in his "History of Commerce," says that in that city were Germans, Danes, Italians, English, and Portuguese, and the commerce included exchanges with all the civilised countries of Europe. Antwerp was exporting household furniture to Genoa, England, and Spain as early as 1560, and, in fact, was one of the most important places in the commercial world.

So far as this country is concerned, these chairs appear in the inventories not earlier than the last quarter of the seventeenth century. We find at Yorktown, 1687, "2 old cained chairs 16s," and in New York, in 1691, "13 cane chairs broken and out of order," which would indicate at least that at that date the style was not new. At Philadelphia, 1686, "8 cane chairs"; 1687, "8 cane chairs"; Boston, 1732, "1 doz. cane chairs"; Salem, 1734, "6 cane chairs."

The style remained in fashion until after 1719, for in that year in the Boston *News Letter* is mention of "fine cane chairs just imported from London."

Figure 448.
Cane Chair, 1660–80.

The chief characteristics of the cane chair in its purity are that the cresting and front stretcher are carved, and usually there are rare exceptions, in the same design. The seat is high from the floor and the backs are tall and stately. The original caning is always composed of very narrow double strands running vertically and horizontally and a single wider strand running diagonally. The holes for the cane are in a straight line on the upper surface, but are bored diagonally, so that on the reverse side they alternate in two parallel lines. The back legs and stiles of the back, which are in one piece, are raked to an angle where the seat joins the back. The wood is beech or walnut, and occasionally, in English specimens, oak. In the later pieces the cane in the back is sometimes replaced by carved strips, but no American example of the type has come under the writer's observation.

CHAIRS

It is probable that many of these chairs found in America were imported, for chairs in the same design are found in England, but it is also probable that many of the simpler sort were made here.

There are three well-defined types of the cane chair:

First.—Those in which the turned stiles of the back terminate in finials with a carved cresting between, as in Figure 448.

Second.—Those in which the carved cresting extends over the stiles of the back which set into them, as in Figure 470.

In these two classes there is inserted between the stiles a frame of cane.

Third.—Those in which the stiles of the back are not turned, but moulded, and appear to carry in a continuous line over the top, as in Figure 475.

Each of these types persisted beyond the time when it was in fashion, and the third can be traced into the Dutch period. In order to show clearly the development of each of these types, we will take them up separately and carry them through to the time each either disappeared or was absorbed in a later style.

FIRST TYPE OF CANE CHAIRS

The first type is a continuation and refinement of the earlier turned chairs, the earliest form being similar to Figure 447 except for a panel of cane in the back and seat. This simple form was quickly superseded by the new form of chair with high seats and backs with carved crestings and front stretchers. The spiral turning was probably retained for some time, and the carving at first was on the wood and not cut to form the outline. The construction of this type was good. The cresting was mortised and tenoned into the uprights, thus giving the requisite strength for the stretching of the cane. Figure 448 is a good example of this new form. It will be seen that the spiral turning of the earlier period is still retained in the stiles and bracing. The cresting and front stretcher are carved in a design of acanthus leaves and cupids upholding a crown, a theme popular after the Restoration. The frame of the cane back is also carved in acanthus scrolls and rosettes. The legs are alternately spiral-turned and carved with roses and leaves. This chair belongs to the Tiffany Studios.

Figure 449 shows an example of a little later date. It will be seen that the Flemish scroll predominates. The sides of the frame for the cane are each carved in two Flemish scrolls, slit, and forming two volutes at one end; a conventional fleur-de-lis separates the Flemish scrolls. A similar design is carved on the front stretcher and the legs are in the form of the simple Flemish scroll. The cresting is composed of foliated C scrolls. This chair is the property of the writer.

Figure 450 shows a side chair in which the cresting, front brace, and sides of the frame for cane are carved in Flemish scrolls separated in each instance by a thistle or bunch of thistles. The legs are in the form of the Flemish scroll, with an additional foliated scroll just above the lower volute, and the legs terminate in turned feet. This form of leg is called the elaborated Flemish scroll. The finials are carved to represent grotesque heads. On the back of this chair is branded the name "J. Newell," probably that of the maker. The chair is sup-

Figure 449.
Cane Chair, Flemish legs, last quarter seventeenth century.

Figure 450.
Cane Chair, Flemish legs, last quarter seventeenth century.

posed to have belonged to Judge Samuel Sewall, of witchcraft fame, and is now in the possession of the writer.

Figure 451 is a side chair quite similar in design to that shown in Figure 450. The cresting, front stretcher, and sides of the frame for cane are each carved in two simple Flemish scroll designs separated by conventional fleur-de-lis. The legs are in the form of Flemish scrolls with an additional foliated scroll at the centre between the two volutes. The legs terminate in turned feet. This form of leg is another variation of the elaborated Flemish scroll and differs from the one shown

CHAIRS

in the preceding figure only in the placing of the foliated scroll. The seat and back of this chair were originally cane. It is the property of Mr. H. W. Erving.

Figure 452 shows a side chair in which the carved frame of the cane is a slightly different variation of the Flemish scroll, one section of the scroll being

Figure 451.
Cane Chair, Flemish legs, last quarter seventeenth century.

Figure 452.
Cane Chair, Flemish legs, last quarter seventeenth century.

split into two separate volutes. The front brace is carved in the design of two C scrolls, instead of Flemish scrolls, separated by conventional fleur-de-lis. The legs are in the form of the elaborated Flemish scroll already described and shown in Figure 450.

Figure 453 is very similar to that shown in Figure 451. The cresting, the carved frame for the cane, and the front stretcher are identical. The legs on this chair, however, are turned down to the lower brace, and from that point there is a foot in the form of a unilateral S scroll with in-turning volutes. This chair belonged to Richard Lord, whose will was probated in Hartford in 1712, and the chair is now at the Connecticut Historical Society's rooms.

Figure 454 shows a side chair with the same style of foot as appears in the preceding figure. The carving, however, is on the surface instead of forming the

Figure 453.
Cane Chair, scroll feet, last quarter seventeenth century.

Figure 454.
Cane Chair, scroll feet, last quarter seventeenth century.

outline in the manner shown in Figure 448. On the cresting is carved an eagle and foliated scrolls. On the frame for the cane back are also carved foliated scrolls and rosettes and the design on the front stretcher is the same. On the finials are carved grotesque heads similar to those in Figure 450.

Figure 455 shows an example of a chair in which the simple C-scroll design predominates. All the turned portions are in the spiral-twist pattern. The cresting is composed of two scrolls with cupids upholding a basket of flowers. The frame for the cane is in the form of two long S scrolls, and two of the same scrolls finish the bottom of the back and form the front stretcher. The legs, which are

CHAIRS

partly missing, are animals' claws with fur, crudely carved. This chair is the property of Mr. Dwight M. Prouty, of Boston.

Figure 456 shows an example of this type in which there are no Flemish scrolls. The turning is spiral and the cresting is carved in the design of two S scrolls with

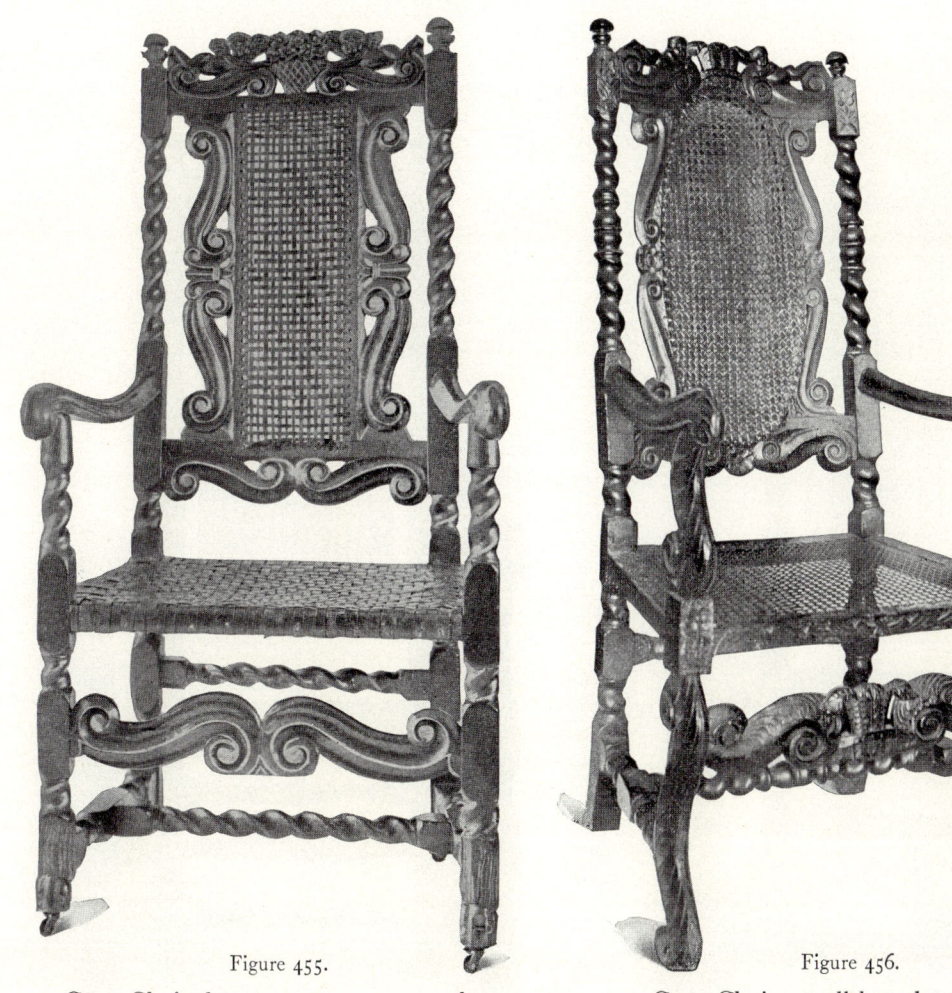

Figure 455.
Cane Chair, last quarter seventeenth century.

Figure 456.
Cane Chair, scroll legs, last quarter seventeenth century.

two cupids supporting three feathers. The cane panel in the back is oval and is in a frame carved in the design of two S scrolls separated by a rosette. The supports for the arms are S scrolls and the carved stretcher represents two S scrolls separated by three feathers. The legs are in the form of unilateral S scrolls. The surfaces of the scrolls supporting the arms, the legs, and the front stretcher are carved in acanthus-leaf designs. The edges of the seat rail are also carved. This chair is, of course, English.

Figure 457 shows a side chair of later date. The cresting is carved in the design of C scrolls, and at the centre was an inlaid star the inlay of which is missing. The finials are in the form of acorns. The front stretcher is carved in a scroll design suggesting the Flemish scroll. The legs are in the form of a Flemish scroll with an additional out-turning scroll above. The two last-mentioned chairs belong to the writer.

Figure 458 illustrates a late form of the chair shown in Figure 451. The only carving is on the cresting and is in the familiar design of the Flemish scroll. The

Figure 457.
Cane Chair, Flemish legs, last quarter seventeenth century.

Figure 458.
Cane Chair, turned legs, first quarter eighteenth century.

frame for the cane is perfectly plain and a turned-front stretcher takes the place of the carved one. The legs are turned in a simple design. This chair belongs to Mr. H. W. Erving.

Figure 459, the property of the writer, illustrates a further differing type from those under discussion. The only carving is on the cresting and front brace. The design differs from that shown in the preceding figure in that it is composed

CHAIRS

of two C scrolls instead of Flemish scrolls, separated by the conventional fleur-de-lis. The design is similar to that shown on the front brace of Figure 452. The back and seat were intended for upholstering, as the frame is heavy and unpierced.

Figure 460 shows a later variation of this type. The carved cresting has disappeared as well as the cane, and yet it clearly suggests the preceding design.

Figure 459.
Upholstered Chair, turned legs, about 1700.

Figure 460.
Upholstered Chair, turned legs, about 1700.

Figure 461 is in the style known as banister-back, which is one of the late variations of the type under discussion. Split balusters take the place of cane or upholstery and the seat is made of rush. The carved cresting is in the design of two C scrolls separated by conventional fleur-de-lis, and the legs terminate in the Spanish scroll foot. Such chairs undoubtedly were made by local cabinet-makers in imitation of the cane models, but without proper material. This is the only form of the first type which has Spanish feet.

Figure 462 shows an arm-chair of this type. The cresting is unusually well carved, in the same design as in the last figure. The front legs, which extend to hold the arms, are turned in the vase, ring, and bulb pattern and terminate in

Figure 461.
Banister-Back Chair, first quarter eighteenth century.

Figure 462.
Banister-Back Chair, first quarter eighteenth century.

Spanish feet. The stretchers, including the back one, are also well turned. This chair is in the Bolles Collection.

Figure 463 shows an arm-chair in the same style as the preceding. The cresting of C scrolls separated by a fleur-de-lis is the same, and the front stretcher is in the same design, which is rather unusual, as banister-back chairs usually have the turned stretcher. The legs terminate in the ball feet which appear on six-legged high-boys and desks of the period. Another unusual feature is that it has five instead of four split balusters, one of them missing. This chair is also in the Bolles Collection.

CHAIRS

Figure 464 shows another variation of the style. The cresting is almost invariably in the form shown in the two preceding figures, but it will be seen that this is an exception to the rule, for in this chair there are two foliated

Figure 463.
Banister-Back Chair, first quarter eighteenth century.

Figure 464.
Banister-Back Chair, first quarter eighteenth century.

scrolls, really portions of the Flemish scroll, the two sections joining at the centre to make a C scroll with foliations below. The legs terminate in unusually good Spanish feet, and the side stretchers are vase-and-ring-turned the same as the front one. This chair is the property of Mr. G. W. Walker, of New York.

Another chair of this same general type, the property of Mr. Dwight M. Prouty, of Boston, is shown in Figure 465. The carved cresting is repeated reversed at the base of the back, otherwise the chair is very similar to that shown in Figure 461.

Another and later variation of the banister-back chair is shown in Figure 466. Not only the cresting is carved but also the lower rail holding the balusters. It is a little unusual to find two turned-front braces. The balusters are usually in the same designs as the stiles of the back, as in this example.

Figure 465.
Banister-Back Chair, first quarter eighteenth century.

Figure 466.
Banister-Back Chair, first quarter eighteenth century.

A very unusual form of the banister-back chair from the Bolles Collection is shown in Figure 467. The cresting consists of a pierced circle with a C scroll on either side, and below are two circular openings. The finials of the stiles are acorns, and three small acorns are attached to the cresting. There are but three split banisters, and the lower rail of the back is cut in curves. The front legs, at the point where the front stretcher joins them, are bulb-shaped, and the legs terminate in what were probably a form of Spanish feet but which are now considerably worn off. The legs of this chair quite closely resemble those on Figure 471.

CHAIRS

A little later variety of banister-back chairs in which is but a slight suggestion of the type under discussion is shown in Figure 468. The cresting is cut in a curve as though the maker had a carved piece in mind. The balusters do not follow the general rule but are straight-grooved strips instead

Figure 467.
Banister-Back Chair, first quarter eighteenth century.

of being turned and split. The chair belongs to Mrs. L. A. Lockwood, of Riverside, Connecticut.

Figure 469 shows one of the latest developments of the banister chair back. No suggestion of carving is anywhere to be seen and the balusters are plain grooved slats. This chair belongs to Mr. Albert H. Pitkin, of Hartford.

We have now traced the development of the first type of cane chairs to the point where they disappeared, and we have shown practically every style of leg in which it is found except the unilateral Flemish scroll, of which the writer has been unable to find an example in this country although he has seen a few in England.

We now take up the second type of cane chairs in the same manner.

Figure 468.
Banister-Back Chair, 1730–40.

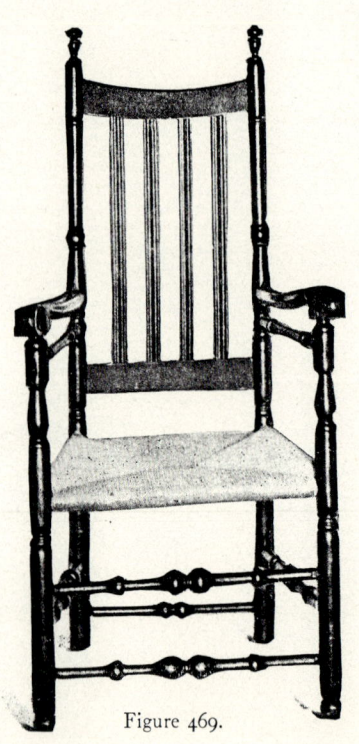

Figure 469.
Banister-Back Chair, 1740–50.

SECOND TYPE OF CANE CHAIRS

As has been stated above, the second type of cane chair consists of those in which the carved cresting extends over the stiles of the back. These are later than the first type, not having appeared much before 1685. The writer has never seen a specimen which had the simple Flemish scroll foot and only very rarely one which used that scroll in the design. They are occasionally found, however, with the elaborated scroll foot and the scroll foot shown on the chair illustrated in Figure 457. It is most generally found with a simple scroll or Spanish scroll foot. The form of construction is faulty, as the back is very much weakened by having the cresting dowelled into the stiles instead of being mortised and tenoned into it.

Figure 470 shows a side chair in this style belonging to Mr. Dwight M. Prouty, which is a fairly early specimen of the kind, for the legs are in the

CHAIRS

design of the elaborated Flemish scroll and the Flemish scroll is carved on the lower rail of the back. The cresting which extends over the stiles is composed of a large unilateral scroll with volutes at the two ends and C scrolls, while the front stretcher is an arch studded with balls.

Figure 470.
Cane Chair, Flemish feet, 1680–1700.

Figure 471.
Cane Chair, Spanish feet, 1680–1700.

Figure 471 is a good example of an arm-chair in this style. The cresting is high, carved with a scroll design, and the upper part of the frame for the cane is cut in curves and so pierced as to give the effect of a separate piece. The carved front stretcher is in a similar design to the cresting. The legs are bulbous-turned, terminating in Spanish feet. The cane in the back is original.

Figure 472 shows an arm-chair of about the same period. The cresting and front stretcher are carved in the design of foliated C scrolls supporting a crown. The legs are turned and terminate in a simple inward scroll foot.

Figure 472.
Cane Chair, scroll feet, 1680–1700.

Figure 473.
Cane Chair, Spanish feet, 1680–1700.

Figure 474.
Cane Chair, turned legs, about 1700.

CHAIRS

Figure 473 is an example of a side chair of the type under discussion. The cane extends into the cresting with a Gothic effect and the front stretcher is suggestive of that shown in Figure 471. The legs are turned, terminating in well-formed Spanish feet.

Figure 474 is of a later date, but the cresting and front stretcher are in the same design as that shown in Figure 471. The upper frame of the cane is pierced so as to appear to be separate from the cresting and is in the same Gothic form as that shown in the preceding figure. The four preceding chairs are in the possession of the writer.

This type of chair did not remain long in favour, but was superseded by the third type.

THIRD TYPE OF CANE CHAIRS

The third type of cane chairs are those in which the stiles of the back are not turned, but moulded, and appear to carry in a continuous line over the top. In this type the stiles of the back are often the frame for the cane.

A very fine example of this type is shown in Figure 475. It will be seen that the entire space between the stiles of the back is filled with cane without any suggestion of a splat. The cresting is cut in a design which is a mixture of Moorish and European styles known as the Mudejar style. The legs and supports of the

Figure 475.
Cane Chair, Spanish feet,
1680–1700.

arms originally had reeded, bulbous turnings, but a number of applied parts have been lost. The legs terminate in Spanish feet. The curving of the front stretchers follows the outline of the cresting. The chair is made of walnut and is probably of European origin. It belonged at one time to the Wyllys family, of Hartford, and is now in the collection of the Connecticut Historical Society.

Figure 476 shows an example of a Spanish chair of this period. The seat and back are covered with Spanish carved leather embellished with large brass nails. The legs are turned and terminate in Spanish feet, and the front stretcher is carved in a design of entwining scrolls. This chair is at the Pennsylvania Museum, Philadelphia.

Figure 476.
Spanish Leather Chair, latter half of
seventeenth century.

CHAIRS

Figure 477 is a simple example of the style without carving, the stiles of the back being moulded instead of turned and the moulding extending over the top. Although the piece has a separate splat, it is classified as belonging to this third type, because the stiles are moulded instead of turned, as in Figure 475. The legs are turned and terminate in Spanish feet.

Figure 477.
Cane Chair, Spanish feet, about 1700.

Figure 478.
Cane Chair, scroll legs, about 1700.

Figure 478 shows another interesting variation of the style. The cresting is formed of a series of steps without any curves. The supports to the arms are S scrolls and the legs are quite suggestive of the unilateral S-scroll feet shown in Figure 456, and are clearly the forerunners of the cabriole leg then about to come into fashion. The skirt is cut in two arched curves. The last two mentioned chairs belong to the writer.

Figure 479 shows a later variation of this style in the writer's possession. The sweep of the back is in a deep, continuous curve instead of being broken at the seat. A bird's head is carved at each end of the cresting and at the centre are two birds' heads with beaks together. The legs are cup-shaped and terminate in Spanish feet. The X underbracing is particularly graceful. The legs, bracing, and cutting of the skirt strongly suggest that on the chamber-table or low-boy illustrated in Figure 72, to which period this chair belonged.

Figure 479.
Cane Chair, Spanish feet, 1690–1700.

Figure 480.
Upholstered Chair, turned legs, about 1700.

Figure 480 is an example of an upholstered chair belonging to this period. The frames of the back and seat are entirely covered, but the outline clearly indicates the period. The skirt is cut in the cyma curve designs which were so popular in the Dutch period. The legs and bracings are turned. This chair is the property of the writer.

Figure 481 shows a side chair the outline of which is almost the same as that shown in Figure 477. The back and seat, however, are upholstered instead of caned. This chair is in the Bolles Collection and belongs to the Metropolitan Museum of Art.

CHAIRS

Figure 482 shows a side chair very similar to that shown in the preceding figure, except that it has a cane back and, originally, a cane seat, the legs terminating in simple Spanish feet. The chair is owned by the Connecticut Historical Society.

Figure 483 is an unusual chair belonging to the Connecticut Historical Society. It will be seen that it is a banister-back chair but belongs to the third type of cane

Figure 481.
Leather Chair, Spanish feet, 1700–10.

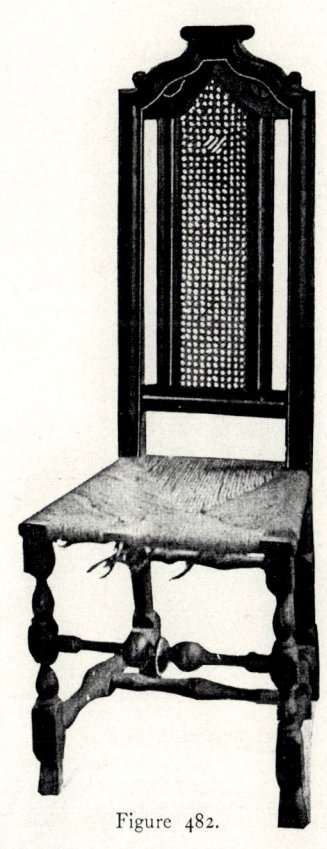

Figure 482.
Cane Chair, Spanish feet, 1700–10.

chairs because the stiles are moulded. Very few banister-backs are found in this design, most of them belonging to the first type, as shown in Figure 461. The legs are turned and terminate in Spanish feet.

Figures 484 and 485 show two variations of the same style with upholstery instead of cane. They are practically alike, except that one has Spanish feet and the other turned feet. Figure 484 belongs to Mr. William Meggat and Figure 485 to the writer.

We now come to another variation of this style which shows markedly the influence of the Dutch style then coming into vogue.

Figures 486 and 487 have backs of cane similar to Figure 482, but the legs are cabriole in form terminating in the Dutch or club foot. The former has the earlier form of leg showing a suggestion of turning above the cabriole leg. It belonged to the late Mrs. Frank H. Bosworth and Figure 487 belongs to the writer.

Figure 488 shows a still later variation of this chair, and is especially interesting in that it so successfully combines the cane with the succeeding Dutch

Figure 483.
Banister-Back Chair, 1710–20.

Figure 484.
Leather Chair with Spanish feet, 1700–10.

style. The back has the Dutch wooden splat. The legs are cabriole terminating in Dutch feet. The earlier style, however, is indicated by the cane which fills in the space between the splats and the stiles, and the seat is also cane. The carved cresting is also suggestive of the earlier style and is composed of scrolls and a shell ornament. This chair must be about contemporaneous with the introduction of the Dutch style so beautifully are the two mingled. It is in the Bulkeley Collection.

Figure 485.
Leather Chair, turned legs,
1700–10.

Figure 486.
Cane Chair with cabriole legs,
1710–20.

Figure 487.
Cane Chair with cabriole legs,
1710–20.

Figure 489 shows another transition piece. The outline of the back is similar to that shown in Figure 477, but it has the Dutch splat instead of cane. The legs are turned and terminate in Spanish feet. This chair is the property of Miss Augusta Manning, of Hartford.

Figure 490 shows an arm and a side chair in which the backs are in the pure Dutch style (Figure 494), but the legs are in the earlier turned form ter-

Figure 488.
Cane Chair, cabriole legs, 1710–20.

Figure 489.
Chair showing Dutch influence, 1710–15.

minating in Spanish feet. This type of chair was very common throughout New England, and, judging from the number found, must have been made in sets. These pieces are in the Bolles Collection.

Figure 491 shows another chair of this type from the Blaney Collection. The back is not so well worked out, but the interesting feature to note is that the turned legs terminate in short, bandy legs with Dutch feet instead of Spanish feet.

CHAIRS

Another interesting variation is shown in Figure 492 which is in the Bolles Collection in the Metropolitan Museum of Art. The only suggestion of an earlier style is the carved cresting, otherwise the chair very closely resembles the chairs in the Dutch style. It will be noted that there are two Flemish scrolls with a C scroll between, a very unusual decoration in so late a piece. The legs are turned for a short distance below the seat and then are cabriole with Dutch feet and underbrace.

It will be seen from the foregoing illustrations that this third type of cane chair was finally carried into the Dutch style.

Figure 490.
Chairs showing Dutch influence, 1710–20.

Figure 493 shows a chair very similar to that in the preceding figure but of a later date. The back is in the Dutch style, and the only suggestion of the carved cresting shown on the preceding piece is the slight carving at the centre of the top. In other respects the chairs are almost identical, having the same mouldings at the base of the splat and the same turning on the legs and stretchers. This chair is in the possession of the writer.

DUTCH TYPE OF CHAIRS

The new style, which we have seen foreshadowed in the preceding illustrations, was, from the structural point of view, a distinct advance in the evolution toward lightness. It seems strange that, a few years after the very elaborate carved cane chairs were in vogue, the wheels of fashion should have turned to such simplicity.

The chief characteristics of the style were the use of the cyma curve in the place of straight lines wherever possible and the introduction for the first time of the splat, which has become the distinguishing feature of the English and colonial

Figure 491.
Chair showing Dutch influence, 1710–20.

Figure 492.
Chair showing Dutch influence, 1710–20.

chairs of the Georgian period. The style originated in Holland, but was developed in England and the colonies more than at the place of its birth. It will be hard to overestimate the importance of this new style. It came into fashion about 1700, and it influenced the chairs for the entire century. The backs were composed of two cyma curves so placed that the stiles form a continuous curve with the top. The back is raked in a cyma curve. (See side view of chair, Figure 494.) The front legs are composed of this curve, as is often the seat; the splat is of wood so cut as to leave a uniform space between its edge and the stiles. (See Figure 496.)

The splat, at first plain, became more and more ornate, until in Chippendale's time it became the principal part ornamented.

An example of an early form is shown in Figure 494. This type is found quite commonly in New England and is usually made of maple or walnut. The

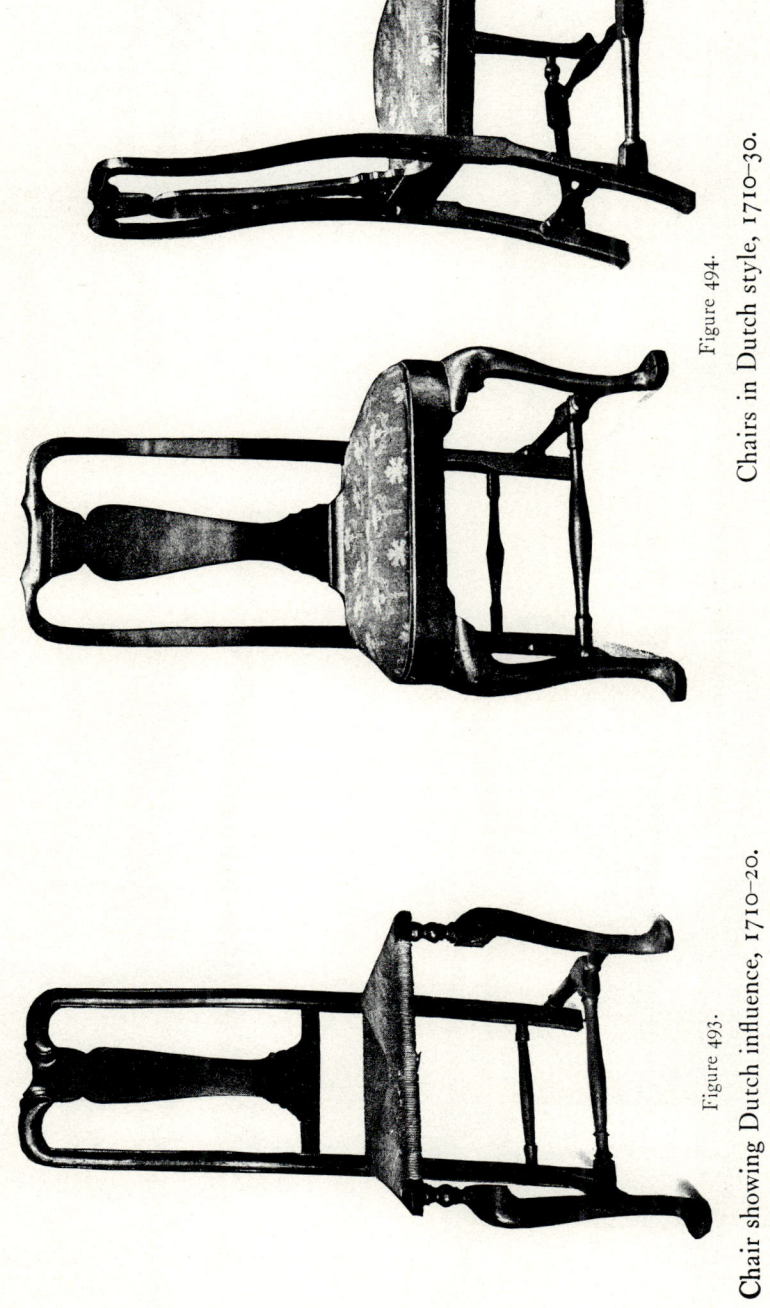

Figure 494.
Chairs in Dutch style, 1710–30.

Figure 493.
Chair showing Dutch influence, 1710–20.

Figure 495.
Chairs in Dutch style, about 1725.

Figure 496.
Chair in Dutch style, about 1725.

Figure 497.
Chair in Dutch style, about 1725.

CHAIRS

legs are underbraced with turned stretchers, a survival of an earlier period, and the legs terminate in club or Dutch feet. One of the characteristics of these chairs is the chamfered edges of the rear legs between the stretchers. These chairs belong to the Misses Andrews.

Figure 495 shows the next form of this style of chair. The general appearance is the same as that shown in the preceding figure except that the underbracing has been done away with. The seats are in the same curves with the rounded front and the bandy legs terminate in Dutch feet. These chairs belonged to Dr. Ezekiel Porter and date about 1725.

Figure 496 shows an arm-chair in this style in which the cyma curves are quite exaggerated, and the piece well illustrates the fact that the splat obtained its shape by making a uniform space between the solid centre and the stiles. The underbracing is curved and not turned except between the rear legs. The seat is composed of straight lines instead of curves which indicate a little later date. The bandy legs terminate in pointed Dutch feet. It is a form found more commonly in the South.

Figure 497 shows a chair in the Dutch style. The lines of the back, instead of

Figure 498.
Chair in Dutch style, about 1725.

being in a cyma curve, have a rounded section at the top and then continue down straight. The seat is curved in the usual manner of the earlier chairs, and the legs are cabriole terminating in Dutch feet. On either side of the knees are carved scrolls. The underbracing consists of two curved pieces of wood extending from the front to the rear legs, with another circular piece adjoining them at the centre, as in the preceding figure, which is a rather unusual feature on American chairs. The wood is walnut. This chair is one of a set and is the property of Mr. Thomas G. Hazard, Jr., of Narragansett Pier.

A well-proportioned arm-chair of the period is shown in Figure 498. The splat is solid but it is not cut in the conventional fiddle shape. The seat is curved and at the centre of the front rail is carved a shell. A shell with pendent flowers is carved on each knee and the legs terminate in bird's claw and ball feet. The arms, as is usual in chairs of this period, are very graceful. The chair is the property of the Tiffany Studios.

The surface of the stiles of these chairs is often rounded instead of flat.

The claw and ball foot has been known for many years in metal work and was found on pieces in the early seventeenth century. It also is occasionally found on the cane pieces, but in such pieces it is generally an animal's instead of a bird's claw on the ball. It does not seem to have been at all common in furniture until after 1710. It began to appear in the inventories about 1737. At that date at Boston "6 crow foot chairs" are mentioned, and in 1750 "7 chairs

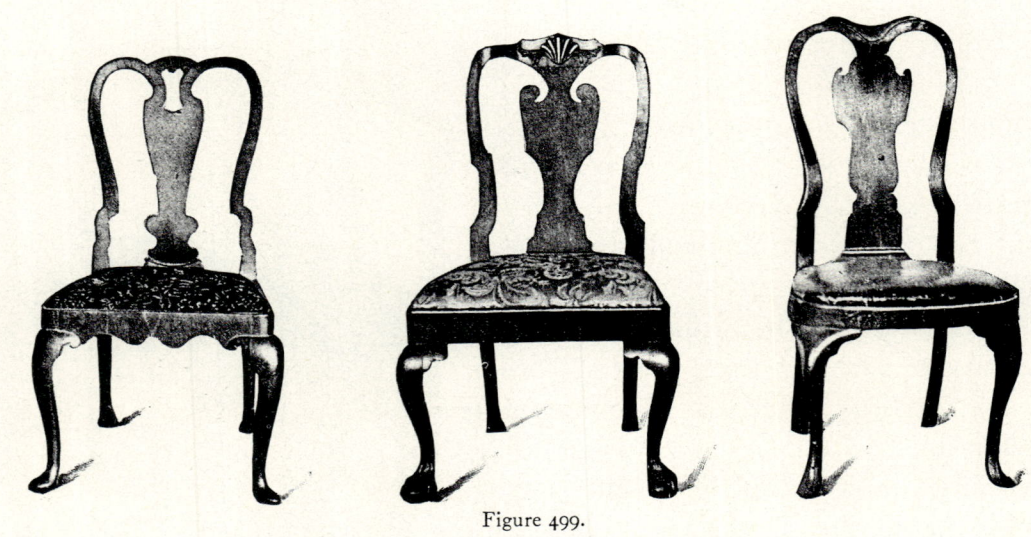

Figure 499.
Chairs in Dutch style, about 1725.

with eagle feet and shells on the knees"; and at Yorktown, Virginia, in 1745, claw-foot furniture of various kinds is mentioned; ten years at least can be safely deducted from that date to determine when the style appeared.

The style originated with the Dutch and it is generally believed to have been an adaptation of the Chinese design of the dragon's claw grasping a pearl. The claw and ball feet were of two kinds, those representing an animal's claw on a ball and those representing a bird's claw. The former is more common in England than in America.

Figure 499 shows three chairs with different splats, all of them in the shapes known about 1730.

The one on the left is of walnut veneer and has a pierced splat. The one at the centre is of mahogany and has a carved shell in the crest and bird's claw and ball feet. The one on the right is of Virginia walnut and the feet are of the pointed Dutch type.

CHAIRS

One of the best designs of the period is shown in Figure 500. The back is high and graceful and at the top is a carved shell with scrolls at either side. The splat is well proportioned and slightly pierced. On the knees are carved shells and the feet are of the angular Dutch type with grooving, which is probably a survival of the Spanish foot and is the type most found in New Jersey and the South. This chair is the property of the writer.

Chairs such as these are often called Hogarth chairs, due to the fact that

Figure 500.
Chair in Dutch style, about 1725.

Figure 501.
Chair in Dutch style, 1725–50.

in his "Analysis of Beauty" Hogarth maintains that the line of beauty is the cyma curve, and one of his illustrations is a chair of this type composed of cyma curves.

A very elaborate arm-chair of the period is shown in Figure 501 and is the property of the Metropolitan Museum of Art. On the cresting are five medallions. Within each are carved flowers. Below this is a large pendant of foliation and flowers. The splat is pierced, and on the edges are carved acanthus leaves and rosettes, and the same design is on the stiles under the arms. On the support of the arm are also carved acanthus leaves. The knees are carved with the same leaf and the legs terminate in animal's claw feet.

62 COLONIAL FURNITURE

Figure 502 shows a seat of the Georgian period, the property of Mr. John J. Gilbert, of Baltimore. Many suites of chairs were made during this period in which were several seats of this sort. They were finished alike on all sides, and the legs were in the fashion of the chairs. The legs on this piece are cabriole, terminating in bird's claw and ball feet, with a ring carved a little above the foot. On the knees are carved acanthus leaves and a scroll extending outward up onto the frame.

Figure 503 shows a style of chair known as a library chair belonging to the Dutch period. The back is built on a curve and is solid. The top is in circular form; the sides above the arms are in a concave form, and below, the arms are cut in cyma curves. The seat of the chair is round. The front legs are cabriole, terminating in Dutch feet with a high-pointed shoe. On the knees are carved shells with pendent flowers. The rear legs are straight with turned bracing and are considerably closer together than are the front legs. The result is that the stretchers between the front and the rear legs are turned in a curve until they reach the width of the rear legs, and are then straight, and are further strengthened by a turned spindle connecting the two outer stretchers at about the centre. This chair is the property of the Tiffany Studios.

Figure 502.
Seat in Dutch style, about 1725.

Figure 504 shows an upholstered chair of the period, in the possession of the writer. The back is straight, and the only wood showing is found on the legs, the front ones being cabriole, with bird's claw and ball feet, having a slight scroll carving on the inside under each knee.

We will now consider the simpler type of this form of chair.

Figure 505 shows a style of Dutch chair in the form most commonly found about New York. The top and splat are in the characteristic style, but the stiles and legs are turned and terminate in Dutch feet. The swelling of the turning on the legs was probably intended to give a slight bandy effect. Another feature of these pieces is that the splat is set on a lower rail instead of into the seat rail. This method of construction was quite common in this type of chairs abroad,

Figure 503.
Library Chair, Dutch style, about 1725.

Figure 504.
Upholstered Chair, Dutch style, 1725–50.

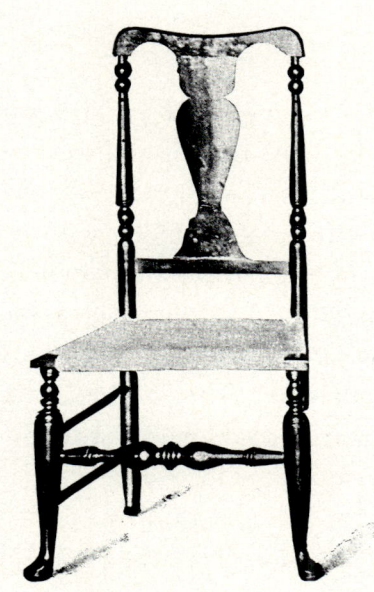

Figure 505.
Chairs in Dutch style, 1725–50.

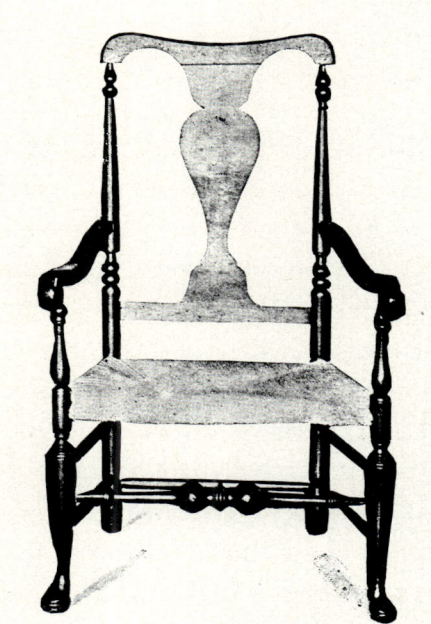

63

especially on the Continent, but is usually found in America only on these simpler pieces. These chairs are the property of the writer.

Figure 506 shows two of these simpler chairs which are more commonly

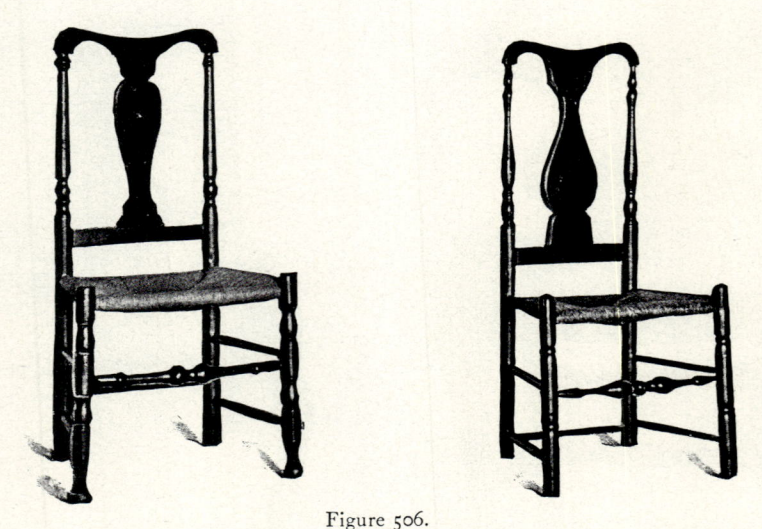

Figure 506.
Chairs in Dutch style, common throughout the eighteenth century.

found in New England. They are made of maple with rush seats, and turned throughout, except for the top rail and the splat.

EASY-CHAIRS

Not all of the chairs of the early eighteenth century were as straight and austere as those above shown. The records make frequent mention of easy-chairs. This form of chair had a high back and wings extending into the arms, low seat, and was heavily cushioned and upholstered. In the inventories they were valued much higher than other chairs, probably because of the fabric with which they were covered, which at this period was always imported. Most of these easy-chairs are of the period now under discussion. It is, therefore, thought well to insert the illustrations of all of the types here, so that they may be studied together, rather than scatter them through the chapter in their chronological order. They appear in the inventories among the chamber furniture; in New York, 1708, "An easy chair lined with red, £2. 10s."; in Boston, 1712, "an easy chair £1"; in 1713, another for £4; at Philadelphia, in 1720, "an easie chair £7. 10s."

The earliest form of easy-chair belonged to the cane period. It was upholstered and the legs and underbracing were carved in the manner of the cane chairs. None of these pieces have been found in this country, and it is probable that the transition piece shown in Figure 507 is the earliest form here. There were

CHAIRS

two forms of the earlier type of this chair, one in which the front of the arms are finished in scrolls, as in this piece, and the other in which the front of the arms are straight. (See Figure 508.) In these types the arms extend only to the wings, never through to the back, the latter being the distinctive feature of the Hepplewhite form. (See Figure 514.)

Figure 507, it will be seen, has the earliest form of arms with the scroll finish. The legs are turned and the piece not only has the side, back, and centre stretchers, but also one across the front, which indicates an early

Figure 507.
Turned Easy-Chair, 1700–10.

date, for the front turned stretcher is a survival of the carved stretcher of the former period. This piece is the property of Mr. Hollis French, of Boston.

Figure 508.
Easy-Chair, about 1725.

Figure 508 shows an easy-chair with the second type of arm. The seat is much wider, probably due to the change of fashion of dress. The legs are cabriole, terminating in Dutch feet, and side, back, and centre stretchers strengthen the piece. The rear legs between the stretchers are chamfered in the early manner. This chair is the property of the writer.

Figure 509 shows another chair with the second type of arm. It has a rounding seat with a cushion, and bandy legs terminating in Dutch feet; on each

66 COLONIAL FURNITURE

knee is carved a shell with a pendent flower, and the piece is underbraced in the manner shown in the preceding figure. This chair is the property of Mr. H. W. Erving, of Hartford.

Figure 510 shows an easy-chair, the property of the writer, which has the earlier form of arms; the legs are cabriole, terminating in grooved Dutch feet.

Figure 509.
Easy-Chair, 1725-50.

Figure 510.
Easy-Chair, 1725-50.

Although this form of arm is early, yet rarely are the legs on these pieces strengthened by stretchers.

Figure 511 shows another easy-chair of this same type in the rough. The seat should be finished with a cushion. The legs are cabriole, terminating in bird's claw and ball feet, and the knees are plain.

Figure 512 shows an easy-chair with the early form of arms. The legs are cabriole, terminating in bird's claw and ball feet, and on the knees are well-carved shells with pendent flowers. This piece is the property of Mr. John H. Buck, of Hartford.

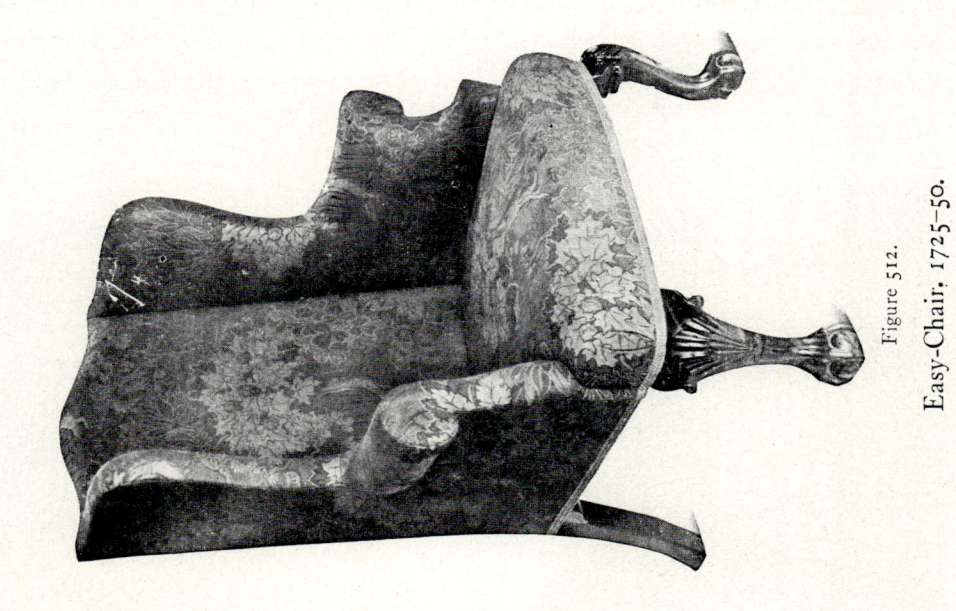

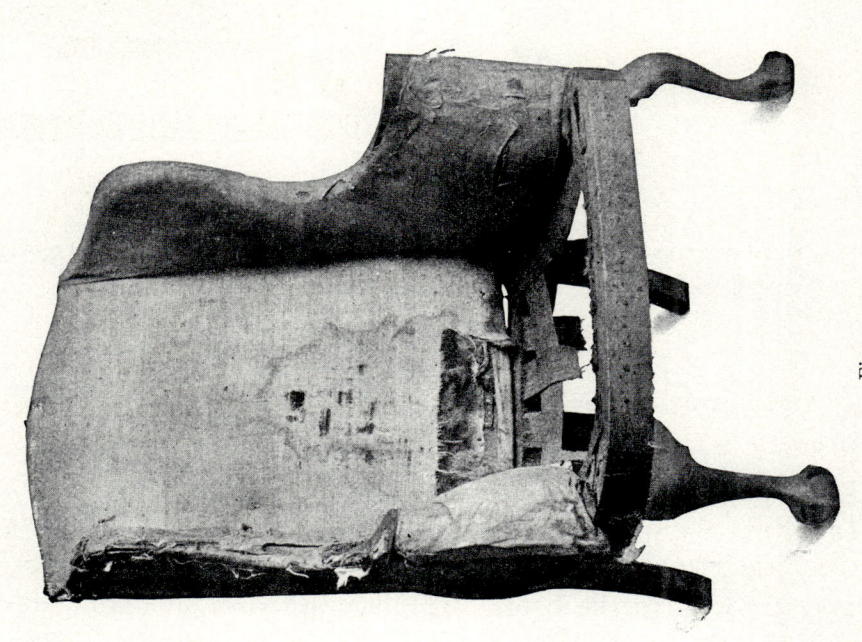

Figure 511.
Easy-Chair, 1725–50.

Figure 512.
Easy-Chair, 1725–50.

68   COLONIAL FURNITURE

Figure 513 shows a rather late variety of an easy-chair with the early form of arms, and it represents the perfection of the style. A characteristic of this type is that the seat is built on a curve with a separate cushion, and the legs are set nearer together and not on the corners as in those above shown. The legs are cabriole, terminating in bird's claw and ball feet, and on the knees are carved

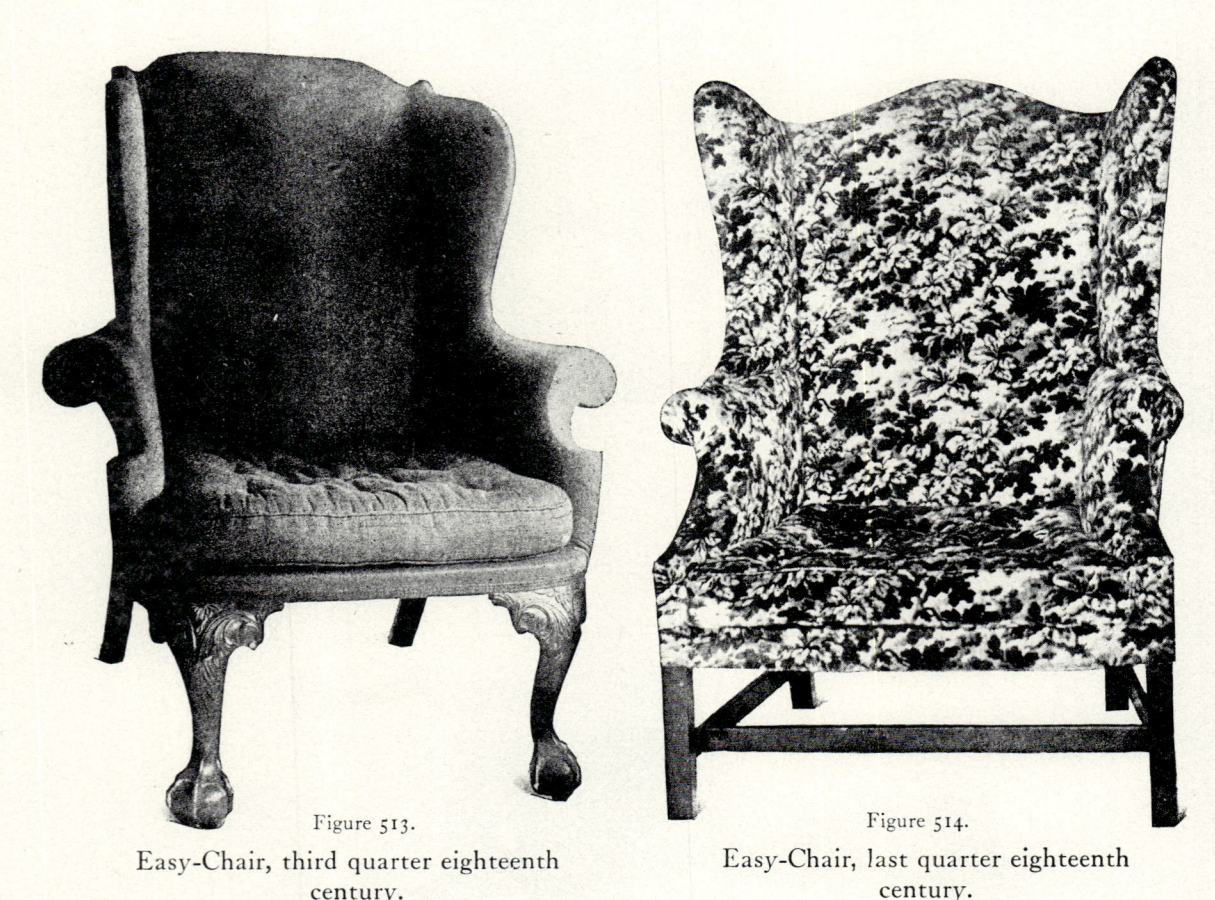

Figure 513.
Easy-Chair, third quarter eighteenth century.

Figure 514.
Easy-Chair, last quarter eighteenth century.

acanthus leaves and flowers extending well down the legs. This chair is the property of the writer.

Figure 514 shows an easy-chair in Hepplewhite style. The distinguishing features are the large wings, which are higher than the back, and rest on the arms which carry through to the back. The legs are straight and underbraced, after the manner of the chairs of the later period. The seat, although straight, has a cushion. This chair is the property of the writer.

In Figure 515 we find a very unusual easy-chair in the late Empire style. The arms are scrolls and carved with rosettes and acanthus leaves, similar to the sofas

CHAIRS

of the period, and carry through to the back, while the wings rest on the outer edge. On the rail above the legs are carved rosettes, and the legs terminate in claw feet with heavy carved acanthus leaves on the knees. This is the only easy-chair of so late a period that has come under the writer's observation. It is the property of Mr. C. R. Morson, of Brooklyn.

Figure 515.
Easy-Chair, Empire period, first quarter nineteenth century.

ROUNDABOUT CHAIRS

A style of chair very popular in the first half of the eighteenth century is the roundabout chair. Its popularity was probably due to its comfort, obtained from the curved back. It is constructed with one leg in front, and the other three legs carry through the seat to support the arms and back which are built on a curve. They are found in three styles, the transition, the Dutch, and the Chippendale.

Figure 516 shows a form of chair known as a wheel chair, owing to the fact that the underbracing has the appearance of spokes of a wheel. It is probably the forerunner of the roundabout chair. The back is circular in form and is supported by the extension of the four back legs. The outer ends terminate in finials. The back is in three sections, each mortised and tenoned into the upper section of the legs and each oval-shaped opening, which was originally caned both front and back as was also the seat. There are two legs in front and a round moulded stretcher connects all of the six legs, which are turned and terminate in plain feet. Wheel chairs are very uncommon. They are probably of Eastern origin, for the one in the frontispiece, which is the property of the writer, has bamboo pegs and the cane is very fine, after the Eastern fashion. The writer has seen several in England which have the carved cresting between the legs in the manner of the caned chairs. This

Figure 516.
Cane-Back Wheel Chair, about 1700.

chair is the property of Mr. William W. Smith, of Hartford.

Figure 517 shows a roundabout chair in the transition style. The legs and the stretchers on the front are nicely turned, while at the back the stretchers are plain. The front leg terminates in a Spanish foot and the others are plain turned. Chairs of this early

Figure 517.
Roundabout Chair, 1720–30.

style are also found with two splats, either plain or slightly pierced. The seat is sometimes finished with rush and sometimes with a slip seat. This chair is the property of the Misses Andrews.

Figure 518 shows another roundabout chair in the transition style built in the usual manner. The simple Dutch splats in the back fasten to a lower rail instead of extending to the seat rail. The legs have double underbracing, as in the preceding figure, and the front leg terminates in a short Dutch foot similar to those

CHAIRS

appearing on the chair in Figure 491. This chair is the property of Mrs. Charles P. Cooley, of Hartford.

Figure 519 shows a roundabout chair with extension top, in the early Dutch style, quite closely resembling the chair shown in Figure 495. The legs are cabriole, terminating in Dutch feet, and the arms are rounded on the edge instead of having the usual flat surface. This chair is the property of Mr. Albert H. Pitkin, of Hartford.

Figure 520 shows a very good roundabout chair, the property of Mr. Francis H. Bigelow, of Cambridge. It is in the graceful Dutch style. The legs, supports for the arms, the seat, and the splat are all in cyma curves. The arms end in a scroll and the legs terminate in Dutch grooved feet.

A well-proportioned roundabout chair is shown in Figure 521, the property of Mr. Nathaniel Herreshoff, of Bristol. The supports to the arms are curved, as in the preceding figure, and the slat is cut in a double C-scroll design. At the front

Figure 519.
Roundabout Chair with extension top, second quarter eighteenth century.

Figure 518.
Roundabout Chair, 1720–30.

Figure 520.
Roundabout Chair, second quarter eighteenth century.

of the arms is a slight hollowing. The rail on either side of the front leg is cut in cyma curves, and the piece stands on four cabriole legs terminating in bird's claw and ball feet. Several chairs identical with this have been found in Rhode Island.

Figure 522 shows another chair quite similar to that shown in the preceding figure. The legs and supports for the arms and the splat are composed of cyma

Figure 521.
Roundabout Chair, third quarter eighteenth century.

Figure 522.
Roundabout Chair, third quarter eighteenth century.

curves, but the seat rail is straight. A deep skirt extends below the seat rail. The arms are in the usual flat form and the legs terminate in bird's claw and ball feet, and on the front knee is carved a shell. This chair is the property of Mr. H. W. Erving.

Figure 523 shows another roundabout chair, the property of Mr. H. W. Erving. The front leg is cabriole, terminating in a Dutch foot; the other legs are straight, terminating in the same feet. The legs are underbraced with a turned X bracing. The splat is pierced in a scroll design the same as that shown on the Chippendale chair (Figure 543). The seat rail is curved.

Figure 524 shows a very handsome roundabout chair with extension top. There are four cabriole legs, terminating in bird's claw and ball feet, and on the

CHAIRS

knee of the front leg is carved a shell. The legs are underbraced with turned X bracing. The supports for the arms are turned and the splats are cut in a Chip-

Figure 523.
Roundabout Chair, third quarter eighteenth century.

Figure 524.
Roundabout Chair with extension top, third quarter eighteenth century.

pendale design. The extension of the back is also in the Chippendale style. This chair was the property of the late Mr. Walter Hosmer.

Figure 525 shows an interesting armchair which at first glance seems to be a roundabout, but it has two legs in front. The back and arms are, of course, in the roundabout form and cover three sides instead of two. The splat is cut in a Chippendale design. This chair is the property of Mr. Dwight M. Prouty, of Boston.

WINDSOR CHAIRS

Probably no variety of chair was so popular in this country during the last half of the eighteenth century as the Windsor chair. The origin of the chair is

Figure 525.
Roundabout Chair, third quarter eighteenth century.

not known. Tradition says it received its name by having been found by one of the Georges in a peasant's hut near Windsor. It was very popular in England all through the eighteenth century and appears to have been made in this country first in Philadelphia. There can be little doubt that the standard was set by that city, for advertisements are found in the Boston papers stating that a local chair-maker has Windsor chairs for sale "as good as those made in Phila-

Figure 526.

Windsor Chair, third quarter eighteenth century.

delphia," and at New York, in 1763, are advertised "Philadelphia made Windsor chairs." That the trade was a large one is evidenced by the fact that the early directories and advertisements show that the work was specialised, and the expression "Windsor Chairmaker" is common.

Fortunately we are able to determine which were the earlier types of the chair, because advertisements often give illustrations. In the earliest form the arms extended round the back, as in roundabout chairs, and there was an extension top either made of a bent piece of wood with either end fastened into the arms and supported by spindles, or with a curved piece of wood so supported. (See Figures 526 and 527.)

In the next form of construction the arms and back are formed of a piece of bent wood supported by spindles. (See Figure 532.)

CHAIRS

The third form is the late form with the rectangular lines following the outlines of the Sheraton school (Figure 535).

By far the largest number of Windsor chairs found are in the earliest type, not only because that form was the strongest and easiest to make, but also because that style continued to be made in large numbers well into the nineteenth century. These chairs are usually found painted, and the popular colour seems to have been green, because many of the advertisements mention "Green Windsor chairs." The great popularity of these chairs was undoubtedly due to the fact

Figure 527.
Windsor Chair, third quarter eighteenth century.

that they were cheap and light and much more comfortable than the ordinary chairs with which they were contemporaneous. They were, in fact, the everyday chair of the period.

The English variety differed in some particulars from the colonial. In the first place, many of them had a splat as well as spindles, a feature never seen on American Windsors, and the turning on the legs was not so elaborate on the English as on those found here.

Figure 526 shows an English Windsor chair. It has a comb top and a pierced splat in each section. The arms extend from the back in the usual way and the legs are cabriole, terminating in Dutch feet and underbraced.

Figure 527 is an early form of Windsor chair which is the property of Mr. Albert H. Pitkin, of Hartford. The legs are turned in vase turning and raked. The legs on Windsor chairs usually pass through the seat and fasten with a fox-

76 COLONIAL FURNITURE

tailed wedge. The bulb-turned underbracing connecting the back and front legs and the stretcher through the centre give further rigidity. The spindles directly

Figure 528.
Windsor Chairs, third quarter eighteenth century.

under the arms are turned, while the others are plain, slightly swelling. The long spindles which support the back extend through the back and fasten into the seat.

Figure 530.
Fan-Back Windsor Chairs, last quarter eighteenth century.

All of these features are common to all Windsor chairs. The ends of the arms on this piece are carved to represent an open hand; they are also found carved to represent a closed hand. These carved types are rare.

CHAIRS

77

Three good types of Windsor chairs are shown in Figure 528. The first one, on the left, is in the early type with a very high back. The legs and supports for the arms are turned in the usual way. The centre chair has what is known as the comb back because of its resemblance to the old-fashioned back

Figure 529.
Windsor Chair, third quarter eighteenth century.

comb. It consists of a curved bow-shaped piece usually, as in this case, with scroll ends and supported by spindles passing through the back into the seat. The third chair is in the same type of comb back but a little more elaborate. The centre of the back is a little raised, like the roundabout chairs, and the arms are carved in a scroll. These chairs are in the Bolles Collection.

Figure 529 shows another comb-back Windsor chair in the Bolles Collection. The turning of the legs and stretchers is finer than in the preceding figures, as are also the supports for the arms. The comb top is taller and bow-shaped and finished with well-carved scrolls.

Figure 531.
Windsor Slipper-Chair, Dutch feet, last quarter eighteenth century.

Figure 533.
Windsor Chair, last quarter eighteenth century.

Figure 532.
Windsor Chairs, last quarter eighteenth century.

Figure 530 shows a pair of what are called fan-back Windsors. It will be seen that they are really the side chair of the comb-back type and, as is the case with the side chairs of the Windsor type, are less strong than the arm-chairs. These chairs are the property of the Honourable John R. Buck, of Hartford.

Figure 531 shows an interesting slipper-chair of the fan-back type, the property of the writer. The seat is but fourteen inches high, while the back is of the regular height. The turnings are unusually large and the front legs terminate in Dutch feet, a most unusual feature for American Windsors.

Figure 532 shows the next type of Windsor chairs, in which the arms, instead of passing through the back in a horizontal line, are bent to form a high back quite similar in appearance to the extension back in Figure 527. This form of the chair is very graceful. It is quite common, but is structurally much weaker than the other type, as the chair invariably breaks at the point where the arms so sharply bend to form the top. The side chair, it will be seen, has the same general appearance, but the curved strip is fastened into the seat. The back of the arm-chair is supported by two spindles fastened into the top and extending to a projection of the seat.

Figure 534.
Windsor Writing-Chair, last quarter eighteenth century.

Another chair of the same type with a comb-back extension top is shown in Figure 533 and is in the Bolles Collection. The comb top is supported by five spindles which pass through the top and fasten into the seat. The back is supported by two spindles, as in the last figure.

The rarest form of the Windsor chair is that known as the writing-chair, of which a very beautiful example is shown in Figure 534. The back is of the same type as that shown in the preceding figure and has a large comb top supported by seven spindles. The right arm is enlarged into a table and is supported by spindles set into the extension of the seat. Under the seat is a drawer on side runners, and a similar drawer is under the table. In front, under the table, is a candle slide which, when closed, locks the drawer. This piece is in the writer's possession and at one time belonged to the first Congregational minister of Chesterfield, Massachusetts, and was not new in 1790. Such a piece may have been referred

Figure 535.
Windsor Chair, about 1800.

Figure 536.
Windsor Chair, first quarter nineteenth century.

to in a Boston inventory of 1760, "A writing chair, 3s. 8d." One can hardly realise what a comfortable and convenient piece this is, both for reading and writing.

A later type of Windsor chair is shown in Figure 535. All the lines are rectangular except the comb top, which is in the usual bow shape, and the turnings are very simple. The rockers on the chair are original.

Figure 536 shows the latest type of Windsor chair. The back and spindle slats are painted, as is also the comb top, which is supported by five spindles which extend only to the main back instead of to the seat. This piece is in the Bolles Collection.

CHAIRS

THE PERIOD OF THE CABINET-MAKERS, 1750–1840

The period now under consideration is marked by an extravagance of taste and fluctuation of fashions never before attained, which were primarily due to the sudden increase in wealth in the colonies and in England. The furniture was drawn exclusively from English models down to the introduction of the Empire style, and in their eagerness for something new the people, following the English fashions, rushed from the plain, stately pieces of the Queen Anne period to the rococo French designs of Chippendale; then, tiring of that, back to the classic for a brief time under Adam; then, in a revolt against the heavy pieces of Chippendale, to the over-light and perishable pieces of Hepplewhite and Shearer; then on to the gaudily painted pieces of Sheraton, who, under the stress of public taste, at last succumbed to the Empire style and sank into a mere copiest of the French school. Such is, in brief, the history of the chairs of this period.

This fickleness was, of course, felt more in the cities than in the country, where we often find two, or even three, of these styles existing side by side equally popular. In the cities, however, we find that the published books of design were offered for sale in the same year as they were in London, which shows the close touch kept with the London fashions.

Chippendale's designs remained popular longer than any of the others, for the reason that at the time the style changed in England the Revolutionary War was at its height and all intercourse between the two countries had practically ceased; consequently our cabinet-makers, not having the new models to work from, continued to work in the Chippendale style. By the time intercourse was resumed the Hepplewhite and Shearer styles were firmly established, and consequently we find few pieces here in the transition style, but there was a sudden change from the old to the new style. From the following coincidence we are able to determine fairly closely when the change took place.

In Wethersfield, Connecticut, were two men in good circumstances. One married in 1791 and the other in 1799, and each furnished his house in the prevailing fashion. The furniture of the one married in 1791 is Chippendale in character entirely, while that of 1799 had not a single example of that kind but was entirely Sheraton. This would seem to indicate that the Chippendale style gave way to the Sheraton somewhere between these two dates, although, of course, we find at much earlier dates Sheraton pieces, as in the Nichols house, at Salem, built and said to have been furnished in 1783 almost entirely in Sheraton style, with but little of the Chippendale; and the furniture used by General Washington, when President in 1789, and now preserved in the City Hall, New York, is pure Sheraton in style.

It is of the greatest service in placing the date of a chair to be able to tell with a degree of accuracy under the style of which cabinet-maker it falls, and we

82 COLONIAL FURNITURE

are of the opinion that the safest guide to follow is the general outline of the backs. There are, of course, a few instances where a piece will combine two styles, or perhaps be such that no single rule will enable one to determine; but these are the rare exceptions, and the following will be found to be the almost universally true characteristics of the various styles.

Figure 537 shows the backs of the four different styles.

A shows the Dutch back. It will be noted that the top curves down to the upright pieces forming the back, so that they appear to be one piece. This will universally be found true in the Dutch chairs, either in this form or in its modification shown in Figure 505.

B is Chippendale in its simplest form. It will be seen that it differs from the Dutch in that the top rail is bow shape and the ends of the top curve up instead

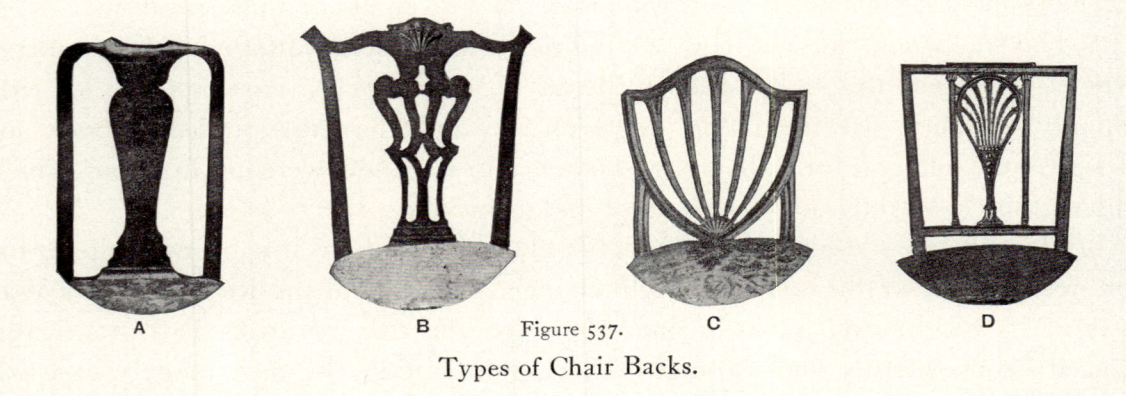

Figure 537.
Types of Chair Backs.

of down, and the centre is a rising curve. This form has infinite variations, and occasionally the ends drop, but never to form an unbroken line with the sides, and there is usually a centre rise.

C is Hepplewhite. These chairs are very easily distinguished, as the back is always either heart, shield, or oval in shape, and there are but few variations.

D is Sheraton, the general characteristic of the backs being that they are rectangular in shape, the upper edge often being raised in the centre and sometimes curved instead of straight. They never have a simple splat to form the back, which never joins the seat, but is supported by a cross-rail.

By bearing these figures in mind and allowing for the variations, one can readily tell at a glance under which of these influences a given piece falls.

When Chippendale's influence first began to be felt it is difficult to determine, for his name is not mentioned, so far as we have been able to find, until the time his published designs appeared in 1753; but judging from the spirit in which the "Director" was written, and the extremely well-made copper plates with which it was illustrated, and the price at which it sold, he must have before that time established his reputation. He died in 1779, and consequently may have been born as early as 1709, so that he could have been working for himself as early as 1735. On the whole, however, we think the conservative date of 1750 is the safest to give as the time when his influence had become somewhat general.

Chippendale excelled as a chair-maker in the designs he created for chair backs. As has previously been said, the development of the splat was distinctly English, and in Chippendale's masterful hands this became the principal beauty of the chairs. These designs were new and are his chief contribution to the cabinet-maker's art. His chairs were in Dutch, Gothic, French, and Chinese style, and more than one style was often combined in the same chair. In upholstered chairs he frankly copied the French, calling them French chairs, and some of his designs were exact copies of some already published fifteen years earlier in France.

Not by any means were all the Chippendale chairs of the ornate type so commonly associated with his name. Such chairs were expensive, and many of his designs, even in England, were very simple, but in both countries are to be found magnificent examples of his best work. The chief fault in most of Chippendale's chairs is that the arms and seat rails are not sufficiently good for the back. The rails seem to have been his chief foible. In the Dutch period the rails were usually curved so that the lack of ornamentation was not noticeable, beauty of line compensating for their plainness. On the Chippendale chairs, however, the rail was generally straight and, except in the finest specimens, did not sufficiently harmonise with the other portions of the chair, which were often carved. This seems rather strange, because French chairs of the period with which he appears to have been familiar excelled in this particular.

It must be borne in mind that Chippendale was not the only designer of chairs during the third quarter of the eighteenth century. There were also Ince and Mayhew, Robert Manwaring, and others of less importance; consequently it is not strictly accurate to call all chairs having the bow-shaped back by Chippendale's name, but they should rather be called of his period. It is highly improbable that the few designs of chair backs shown by these cabinet-makers were the only ones used by them. These designs were undoubtedly the newest, but judging from the large number of chairs extant which are not in any published book of designs it seems probable that the cabinet-makers did not confine themselves to these new designs.

The chairs in Chippendale designs whose splats are in the general outline of the fiddle are probably earlier and represent the effort of the local cabinet-makers to keep pace with the times.

Before taking up the principal designs of the period we will illustrate a few chairs showing the transition from the earlier pieces.

Figure 538 shows a chair with a Chippendale bow-shaped cresting and a pierced splat in a design shown by Manwaring. The legs, however, are turned and braced and terminate in Spanish feet. The splat does not extend to the seat, but is set into a rail after the fashion seen on some of the earlier chairs. This combination of the early transition and the Chippendale is not at all uncommon in America. This chair is in the Bolles Collection.

Figure 538.
Chair in Chippendale style, Spanish feet, third quarter eighteenth century.

Figure 539 shows another transition chair with bow-shaped cresting, splat setting into a lower rail, and turned legs and stretchers. The legs terminate in short Dutch feet. This chair is very low and is in the form known as a slipper chair. It is the property of Mr. Dwight Blaney, of Boston.

Figure 540 shows a chair with a bow-shaped cresting and a solid splat, which is the simplest form of the chair of the period. The legs are cabriole, terminating in angular Dutch feet of the New Jersey type.

Figure 541 shows a form of chair quite commonly found. The back is high, the cresting well shaped, and a carved shell is at the centre. The splat is slightly pierced and the legs are cabriole, terminating in bird's claw and ball feet, and on each knee and centre of skirt is carved a shell. This chair is the property of Mr. William Meggat, of Wethersfield, Connecticut.

Figure 539.
Chair in Chippendale style, Dutch feet, third quarter eighteenth century.

Figure 540.
Chair in Chippendale style, third quarter eighteenth century.

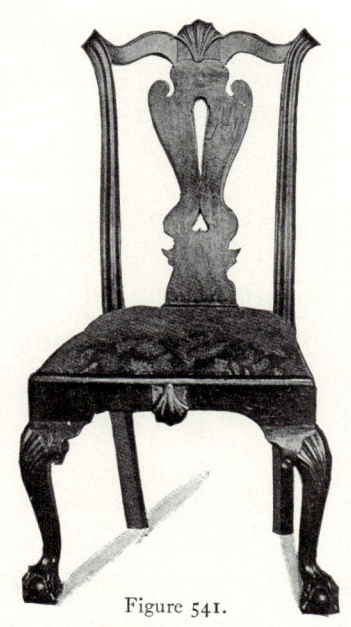

Figure 541.
Chair in Chippendale style, third quarter eighteenth century.

Figure 542.
Chair in Chippendale style, third quarter eighteenth century.

Figure 542 is quite similar to the foregoing, except that the splat is pierced in scroll designs. A shell is carved at the centre of the cresting and on each knee, and the cabriole legs terminate in bird's claw and ball feet. This chair is the property of the Honourable John R. Buck, of Hartford.

Figure 543.
Chair in Chippendale style, third quarter eighteenth century.

Figure 544.
Chair in Chippendale style, third quarter eighteenth century.

Another of the earlier designs is shown in Figure 543, the property of Mr. F. O. Pierce, of Brooklyn. The splat is composed of a rather long concave curve, below which is a large curve extending back into the top rail. The same theme is found in the late chairs of the Dutch period and in many variations in the Chippendale period. The legs are cabriole, terminating in Dutch feet, and the skirt is cut in cyma curves after the manner of the earlier period.

Figure 544 shows a chair, the property of Dr. Frank I. Hammond, of Providence, in which the splat is in the same general outline as that shown in the preceding figure, except that it is slightly better and has an additional entwined design at the centre. At the centre of the cresting are carved acanthus leaves and scrolls, and a rope moulding finishes the bottom of the skirt. The legs are cabriole, terminating in bird's claw and ball feet, and on the knees are carved acanthus leaves.

CHAIRS

Figure 545 shows another chair of the same design in which the design is worked out in its purity. Of course such a chair as this was the model from which the other simpler ones were made. On the cresting are carved acanthus leaves, and there is an acanthus-leaf carving on the edges of the scrolls in the splat.

Figure 545.
Chair in Chippendale style, third quarter eighteenth century.

Figure 546.
Chair in Chippendale style, third quarter eighteenth century.

The arms are in the shape used in the Dutch period and on the knobs and supports is leaf carving. The legs are cabriole, terminating in Dutch feet, and the entire front of each leg is carved in acanthus-leaf and rococo designs. A chair with carving on the legs usually stands on bird's claw and ball feet or French scroll feet. This chair is the property of Miss Augusta Manning, of Hartford.

Figure 546 shows still another chair with the same design of splat but of considerably later date. The only carving is at the top of the cresting and at the centre. The legs are straight and underbraced in the manner of the late pieces. This chair was new in 1791 and was part of a wedding outfit at Wethersfield, Connecticut, and was the property of the late Miss Esther Bidwell. Of course, at the large centres this style had long since disappeared, but this chair was probably made by a local cabinet-maker who still clung to the old style.

88 COLONIAL FURNITURE

Figure 547 shows a cnair in the possession of Mr. Richard A. Canfield, the splat of which strongly suggests the style now under discussion, but the plain scrolls have been broken into irregular curves. The cresting is well carved in acanthus-leaf and scroll designs which extend partly down the stile. The stiles for the balance of the distance are fluted and reeded. The edges and surface of the splat are carved in scrolls and acanthus-leaf designs. The rail of the seat is carved in a fret design. The legs are straight and are fluted and reeded and the underbracing has chamfered edges.

Figure 547.
Chair in Chippendale style, about 1760.

Figure 548.
Chair in Chippendale style, third quarter eighteenth century.

Another of the earlier designs is shown in Figure 548. The splat consists of a concave curve and a long cyma curve, and a scroll extends back into the top, but it is not a continuous curve as in the preceding designs. At the centre is carved a ribbon and tassel. The carving is of the highest order. The cresting is carved in an acanthus-leaf scroll, as are also the edges, and at each end is carved a shell. The edges of the splat are also carved with acanthus-leaf scrolls. The stiles are fluted, and at the centre of the seat rail is carved a shell with streamers and at the corners a carved shell extends on each knee. The edge of the skirt is carved in the

CHAIRS

rope design. The legs are cabriole, terminating in bird's claw and ball feet, and on the knees are acanthus-leaf scrolls. This chair represents one of the best types found in this country. There are several known which differ only sufficiently to show that they were not of a set, but probably made by the same cabinet-maker. This chair is the property of the writer.

Figure 549 shows a chair in the Blaney Collection in which the splat is in the identical outline of that shown in the preceding figure, except that there are no ribbon and tassel at the centre. The splat, however, is simply cut out and not enriched with carving. This and the preceding chair illustrate how a fully worked out model would be copied

Figure 549.
Chair in Chippendale style, third quarter eighteenth century.

by local cabinet-makers, in which the outline will be faithfully given but all detail omitted. At the centre of the cresting is carved a shell. The arms are scrolled and the supports for the arms are hollowed. The piece stands on cabriole legs, terminating in bird's claw and ball feet, and on the knees are carved shells.

Figure 550.
Chair in Chippendale style, 1770–80.

Figure 550 shows a chair with a still different form of splat. The outline of the splat is fiddle-shaped, composed of a concave and a long cyma curve. At the top is carved drapery, three tassels, and below the wood is so cut as to form intertwining ribbons. The legs are cabriole, terminating in bird's claw and ball feet, and the knees are beautifully carved in a leaf design. The stiles are fluted and reeded. The cresting is carved in a leaf

90 COLONIAL FURNITURE

Figure 551.
Chair in Chippendale style, third quarter eighteenth century.

Figure 552.
Chair in Chippendale style, third quarter eighteenth century.

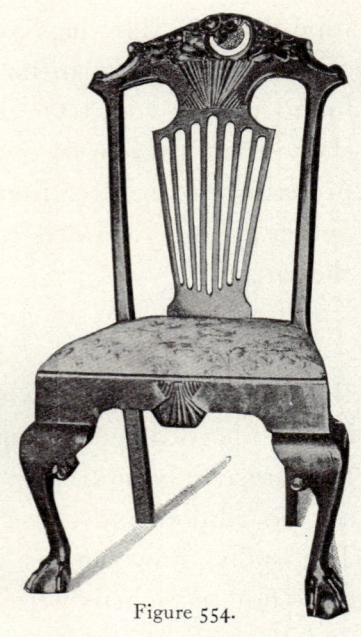

Figure 554.
Chair in Chippendale style, third quarter eighteenth century.

design. This design is quite often found in England and in this country, especially in Philadelphia and the South, and although it does not appear in any of the published designs it is one of the best of the period. The seat rail, however, is its only fault. The straight plain surface is out of keeping with the flowing lines of the drapery. It is the property of the Metropolitan Museum of Art.

Figure 551 shows a chair in the writer's possession in which the splat is cut in another early design. The scroll of the splat appears to commence at the outer ends of the cresting and to carry through to about the centre of the splat in a Flemish scroll which splits, forming a C scroll at the upper end. The illusion is further carried out by having a shell carved at the centre of the cresting, apparently joining the two curves. Below the scrolls are simple concave scrolls. This design is found on some of the late chairs of the Dutch period and was carried through into the Chippendale period. The legs are cabriole, terminating in Dutch feet standing on shoes. The chair is

Figure 553.
Chair in Chippendale style, third quarter eighteenth century.

underbraced in the same manner as appears on the chair in Dutch style (Figure 494).

Another form of splat consisting of a long concave curve is shown in Figure 552. The legs are cabriole, terminating in bird's claw and ball feet, and the piece is underbraced in the earlier style. This chair is the property of Mr. William Meggat.

Figure 555.
Chair in Chippendale style, 1750–60.

Another chair having a splat with a long cyma curve is shown in Figure 553. The top rail is almost straight, with scroll ends, and the legs are cabriole, terminating in bird's claw and ball feet.

A form of chair of which several have been found in Philadelphia is shown in Figure 554. The cresting is carved with flowers quite like the design found on rosewood pieces of a much later date. The splat is composed of a series of parallel slats and above is carved a large shell ornament. The legs are cabriole, terminating in bird's claw and ball feet, and at the centre of the rail is carved a shell. The chair is made of Virginia walnut. It is the property of the writer.

Figure 556.
Chair in Chippendale style, French taste, 1750–60.

Figure 555 shows an interesting chair in the Bulkeley Collection which came from Philadelphia. The design is one found in the first edition of Chippendale's "Director," but is not found in the third edition. The cresting is carved in scrolls after the French fashion, and the splat, although rather simple, is well carved and finished. The legs are cabriole, terminating in the French scroll foot with carved acanthus leaves. On the scroll and on the knees are carved scrolls and leaves.

CHAIRS

Another chair found in Philadelphia is shown in Figure 556 and is the property of Mr. H. W. Erving. The design is that of Plate XV in the third edition of Chippendale's book, except that in the plate the splat is composed of ribbons. The cresting is beautifully carved in rococo pattern, and the splat is composed of a short and long concave curve. Rococo and leaves are the dominant ornamentation and so graceful and light that the splat seems fragile. As a matter of fact,

Figure 557.
Chair in Chippendale style, ribbon back, 1750–60.

however, the splat is very strong and heavy, the light effect being obtained by cutting away the edges of the back. The stiles are in two cyma curves and are pierced in two places in what would be considered the weak spots of chair construction, but made extra heavy in this case to meet the strain. The rails above the seat are elaborately carved in a rococo design. The legs are cabriole, with French scroll feet, and the legs and skirt are carved in a rococo design, forming a graceful whole. The proportions of this chair, its construction and ornamentation, its lightness, grace, and apparent disregard of the rules of construction, all point to the conclusion that it was made by a master who thoroughly understood his

94 COLONIAL FURNITURE

Figure 558.
Chair in Chippendale style, Gothic taste, third quarter eighteenth century.

subject. It is the best chair that has been found in this country, and was probably made by Chippendale and imported.

It is a far cry from the simple Dutch splat to the one shown in this chair.

Figure 557 shows a chair, the property of Lord Saint Oswald, of Nostel Priory, which was made by Chippendale and is similar to one of the chairs shown in Plate XV of Chippendale's book. It is in the design known as a ribbon back. A double chair which opened into a day bed is in the same set. This chair is not so graceful as that shown in the last figure. The stiles and cresting are quite plain and the legs are of the usual bird's claw and ball type. The splat, however, is very fine. In outline it somewhat resembles that shown in the last figure, and within the scrolls are carved a bow knot and streamers of ribbons turning around the scrolls to the bottom of the splat, and at the centre is a large tassel supported by a cord.

It is rather interesting to note that Chippendale, in speaking of the ribbon-back chairs, says: "Several sets have been made which have given entire satisfaction. If any of the small ornaments should be thought superfluous, they may be left out without spoiling the design. If the seats are covered with red morocco this will have a fine effect."

Figure 558 shows a chair, the property of Dr. Frank I. Hammond, of Providence, in which the design of the splat is in Gothic style. On either side of the centre of the cresting is a small spiral scroll and at the ends of the crestings are carved acanthus leaves. The edges of the splat are finished in a beaded

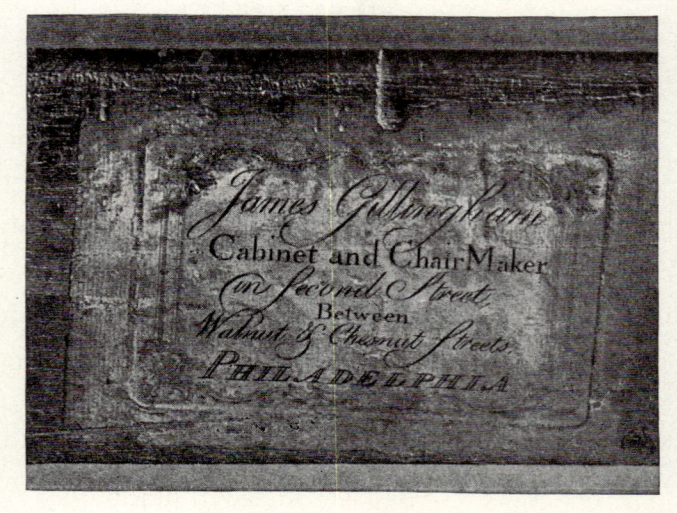

Figure 559.
Advertisement on back of foregoing chair.

scroll, as are also the skirt and the sides of the knees. The piece stands on well-proportioned cabriole legs terminating in bird's claw and ball feet. The chair has a reserve of design which makes it very pleasing. The most interesting feature of this chair, however, is the fact that the design is that shown in Plate X of Chippendale's third edition. It also appeared in his first edition. On the back of the seat is pasted the advertisement of the maker, which is shown in Figure 559. The border of the card is engraved in Chippendale scrolls, and the

Figure 560.
Chair in Chippendale style, Gothic taste, third quarter eighteenth century.

Figure 561.
Chair in Chippendale style, Gothic taste, third quarter eighteenth century.

card reads: "James Gillingham, cabinet and chair maker in Second Street, between Walnut and Chestnut Streets, Philadelphia." It is perfectly apparent, therefore, that the maker of this chair was familiar with Chippendale's book, and this may account for the fact that so many beautiful examples in the Chippendale style were found in Philadelphia.

Figure 560 shows an arm-chair in which there is a suggestion of the Gothic style caused by the interweaving of ribbon-like pieces. The cresting is carved in rococo and leaf design, and pendent flowers finish the surfaces where the two loops of the ribbon touch. The stiles are fluted, as are also the arm supports and the straight legs. On the outer edge of the legs is carved a reel and bead moulding. This chair is the property of the Tiffany Studios.

Figure 562.
Chair in Chippendale style, Gothic taste, third quarter eighteenth century.

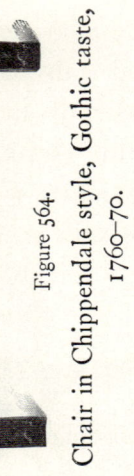

Figure 563.
Chair in Chippendale style, Gothic taste, 1760–70.

Figure 564.
Chair in Chippendale style, Gothic taste, 1760–70.

CHAIRS

Figure 561 shows a chair very similar to one shown in Plate X of Chippendale's book. The splat has a suggestion of the Gothic, and the chair, though plain, is well proportioned and finished. The legs are straight and not underbraced, and at the corners are fret brackets. This chair is the property of Miss Augusta Manning, of Hartford.

Figure 562 shows a chair having the splat composed of three concave curves in the Gothic fashion. This design seems to have been one of the most popular, and is to-day, for there are many reproductions. The legs are cabriole with bird's claw and ball feet. This chair is the property of the Tiffany Studios.

Figure 563 shows a chair, the property of the Tiffany Studios, which has a very interesting form of Gothic back. The outer edges of the splat are composed of three C scrolls. Within these scrolls are Gothic arches in a series of three, two, and one, the top arches cutting into the cresting and being pierced on either side and between in quatrefoil piercings. The upper surface of the cresting is cut in Gothic designs and there is a slight carving at either end.

Figure 565.
Chair in Chippendale style, Gothic taste, 1760–70.

The fronts of the stiles and of the legs are cut in Gothic designs, and at the base of the splat are two quatrefoil piercings with a trefoil between.

A very elaborate Chippendale Gothic chair is shown in Figure 564. The splat is composed of archings above which is a species of quatrefoil piercings extending into the top rail. On the stile, rails, and legs are Gothic designs in flat carving. This chair is the property of the Metropolitan Museum of Art.

Figure 565 shows another chair in the Gothic taste, the property of Mr. Richard A. Canfield. This chair has no splat, but the entire back is filled in with Gothic interlacing arches and on the cresting between are pierced Gothic designs. The entwined arches are carved so as partially to extend over the stiles. The underbracing is pierced in quatrefoil and lozenge form. The legs are straight and are carved in strap design. The design of this chair is quite similar to some of those shown in Chippendale's book.

A totally different kind of a Gothic chair is shown in Figure 566. The back represents columns and Gothic arches, and the effect is carried to the legs which are in the form of cluster columns. The arms are plain and quarter-round. This chair is the property of Mr. John J. Gilbert, of Baltimore.

Figure 566.
Chair in Gothic taste, 1760–70.

Figure 567.
Chair in Manwaring style, Gothic taste, 1760–70.

Figure 567 shows an interesting chair in the Gothic taste, the property of Mr. Richard A. Canfield. The Gothic effect is obtained by series of C scrolls so placed as to make a cruciform figure through the centre. These scrolls are strengthened by diagonal bands which cross at the centre and are finished with a rosette. Beneath the arms are cut ornaments in cruciform. The legs are straight and on the surface are carved rosettes and scrolls. This chair is very similar to some of Manwaring's designs and is supposed to have been made by him.

Figure 568 shows another form of Chippendale Gothic splat, the outline of which is composed of a concave, a convex, and a long concave curve. The splat is pierced to resemble a Gothic window and the surfaces are carved with a slight acanthus-leaf pattern which is also on the top rail. The legs are straight and plain with fret brackets at the corners. This chair is the property of the writer.

CHAIRS

Another attractive Chippendale Gothic chair with splat in the same curve, but differently treated, is shown in Figure 569. The ends of the top turn down instead of up; the legs are plain and straight and underbraced. This chair is the property of Mr. George T. Kendal, of Grand Rapids, Michigan.

Another form of splat consisting of three concave curves is shown in Figure 570. This form of splat, as has been seen, is almost always found in the Gothic design, and this chair appears to be an exception to the rule, for inside the outer scrolls are oval and round openings ornamented with carving. The surfaces of the stiles, rails, arm supports, and legs are carved in a simple design which increases very much the beauty of the piece.

Figure 569.
Chair in Chippendale style, Gothic taste, 1770–80.

Just as, a half-century before, the Dutch, then the controllers of the Eastern trade, had borrowed the ball and claw foot from the Chinese, so now Chippendale borrowed extensively from other Chinese designs for English use. The cabinet-makers of his day seem to have doubted the

Figure 568.
Chair in Chippendale style, Gothic taste, 1760–70.

Figure 570.
Chair in Chippendale style, 1760–70.

practicality of many of Chippendale's designs, especially those in the Gothic and Chinese styles, for in his preface Chippendale, referring to these designs as "fit for eating parlours," says: "Upon the whole I have given no design but what may be executed with advantage by the hands of a skilful workman, though some of the profession have been diligent enough to represent them (especially those after the Gothick and Chinese manner) as so many specious drawings, impossible to be worked off by any mechanick whatsoever. I will not scruple to attribute this to malice, ignorance and inability; and I am confident I can convince all noblemen, gentlemen, or others, who will honour me with their commands, that every design in the book can be improved, both as to beauty and enrichment in the execution of it, by their most obedient servant Thomas Chippendale." Quite a number of chairs in the Gothic and Chinese styles found their way to this country, especially about the seaports of New England, and they also seem to have been made here, for John Briner, a cabinet-maker at New York in 1762, advertises to make "Gothic and Chinese Chairs."

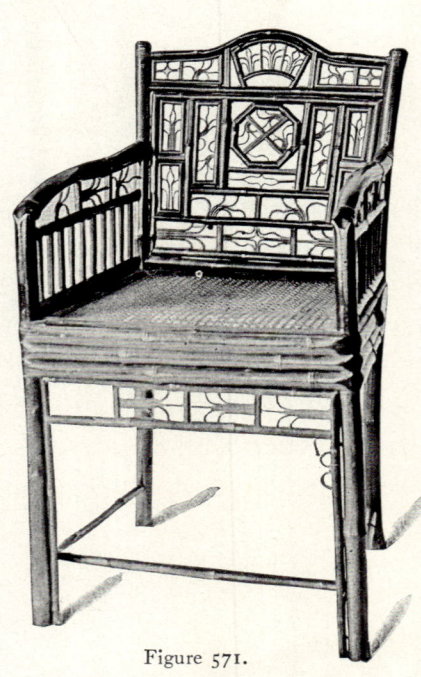

Figure 571.
Chinese Chair, about 1800.

Figure 571 shows an example of a Chinese bamboo and rattan chair which was brought from China about one hundred years ago. It was apparently such chairs as this that were copied by the cabinet-makers of the middle of the eighteenth century.

A very beautiful arm-chair in Chippendale style, showing the Chinese taste, is shown in Figure 572 and is at the Ladd house, Portsmouth, New Hampshire, where it has been from colonial times. The back of this chair is extremely elaborate and is different from any of the designs contained in Chippendale's book. The combination of C scrolls and the slight Gothic effect in the lattice design is strong indication, however, that the chair was made by Chippendale. The cresting rather suggests the third figure in Plate XXVII of Chippendale's book. The design is so ornate that it defies description. The general scheme, however, is a pagoda top, on the cresting below a series of three pagoda tops hanging pendent between C scrolls, and below the centre one another pagoda top in a half circle. The central section is supported by two columns with a suggestion of a capital, within which are well-known Chinese scroll designs. On either side of this centre are four openings within which are lattices in quatrefoil form. To enhance the

Figure 572.
Chair in Chippendale style, Chinese taste, third quarter eighteenth century.

102   COLONIAL FURNITURE

Chinese effect the seat is caned. The space under the arms is filled with a Chinese fret design. The legs are straight and C-scroll brackets are at the corners formed by the joining of the legs to the rails. On the flat surfaces of the rails, stiles, and legs are clusters of reedings. This chair is one of a set with a settee (Figure 627) which are undoubtedly of English origin, and they illustrate the fact that furniture of the highest quality was being imported to the colonies from England.

Figure 573.
Chair in Chippendale style, Chinese taste,
third quarter eighteenth century.

Figure 573 shows a Chinese Chippendale chair in which the entire back is composed of a fret design. At the centre of the top rail is the same suggestion of a pagoda as is found in the preceding figure, and on the legs are fret designs. The arms are curved much like those of the Dutch period. This chair is the property of Mr. Marsden J. Perry, of Providence.

Figure 574 shows a very interesting Chippendale chair combining French, English, and Chinese motifs. The pattern is known as the rope and bell and is one of the most beautiful of the period. The cresting is suggestive of a pagoda and is edged with rococo, from which hang little bells on ropes which give the name to the design. The splat is broken into irregular curves and piercings to carry out the Eastern flavour, and a bell on a long rope is carved on the surface.

Figure 574.
Chair in Chippendale style, Chinese taste, about 1760.

The surfaces of the stiles, rails, and legs are carved in a wonderful Chinese fret design interspersed with ropes and bells and leaves. This chair is the property of Mr. Richard A. Canfield.

In many respects the pieces which carry the Chinese motif into English form are more interesting than those which too closely copy the Chinese.

Figure 575 shows still a different design of splat, the scroll being in the Flemish form instead of the simple. On the surface of the scroll is carved an acanthus-

Figure 575.
Chair in Chippendale style, third quarter eighteenth century.

leaf design, with carved drapery connecting each side, above which is a tassel suspended by a cord which extends to the top. The cresting is well carved in an acanthus-leaf design and at the centre is a slight suggestion of the Chinese. The stiles are fluted and the arms appear to make a continuous whole with the supports in the form common in the Dutch period. The legs are cabriole and terminate in bird's claw and ball feet, with an acanthus-leaf carving on the knee, and on the skirt is a rope carving. This chair is the property of the Tiffany Studios.

It was also the fashion in this period for furniture to be made in imitation of bamboo, and a splendid example of an arm-chair made in that manner is shown in Figure 576. The back is composed of intertwined loops and the same design is repeated under the arms, and the wood throughout is carved to resemble bamboo. The chair in reality is made of beech and the loops are cut and carved from solid pieces of wood. This chair is one of a set of four in the writer's possession.

The next form of Chippendale chair is that which is known as the ladder-back. It was the latest form of the earlier slat-back chair, which probably suggested it. It consists of three or four curved rails instead of splats forming the back. This form was popular both here and in England, and many forms are

Figure 576.
Chair in Chippendale style, imitating bamboo, 1760–70.

Figure 577.
Ladder-Back Chair in Chippendale style, third quarter eighteenth century.

found, although the most common back is that shown in Figure 577 which is the property of the Metropolitan Museum of Art. It will be seen that the slats are bow-shaped and are so cut that they seem to entwine at the centre. The arms are gracefully carved at the ends in acanthus-leaf pattern and the supports of the arms are in Chippendale scrolls and pierced. The seat is slightly hollowed. The unusual feature about this chair is the cabriole legs which terminate in French scroll feet, and it is the only ladder-back chair with cabriole legs which has come under the writer's observation. These chairs are rather late, and consequently they usually have a straight leg with underbracing which superseded the cabriole type. The knees are carved in scroll design and the chair has the characteristic back of the Chippendale chair, although Chippendale shows no ladder-back designs.

Figure 578 shows three varieties of ladder-back chairs of the simpler type. The first is perfectly plain with plain slats and straight legs. The next one has pierced slats and plain, straight legs. The right-hand one is carved in the same design as that shown in the preceding figure. The legs are straight with double ogee fluting and the front rail serpentine.

Figure 579 shows a very handsome ladder-back chair. The top rail is carved and each slat has Gothic piercings, and the outer edges are cut in the pearl pattern, as are also the stiles and supports for the arms. This chair is hollowed and the front serpentine. The legs are straight and on their surfaces and on the stretchers is carved a guilloche pattern with rosettes between. This chair is the property of Mr. Richard A. Canfield.

It will be remembered that Chippendale lived and worked until 1779, that he ceased to be a designer of note after the Adam Brothers became popular, and that he continued to manufacture and do a general business as an interior decorator, executing designs made by others.

Figure 580 is a particularly interesting chair because it was made by Chippendale for Sir Roland Winn, Bart., the bill for which is still extant. The entry is dated January 27, 1768, and reads as follows: "To 6 Mahogany chairs with arms for the library, the carving exceedingly rich in the antique taste; the seats covered with green haircloth, £36." This chair is one of a set owned by Lord Saint Oswald, of Nostel Priory. It has not the grace and flow of Chippendale's earlier work, and the wood seems thick, but the detail and construction are of the highest order. The splat is lyre-shaped with well-carved acanthus leaves and rosettes, and the base is carved with acanthus leaves and pendent flowers in much the same manner as in Chippendale's earlier work. The seat rail is carved in a beautiful guilloche pattern with rosettes, all carved in the minute cameo style of the Sheraton school and without any of the freedom of his earlier work. Cameo-carved rosettes are on the square blocks of the legs, and the legs are turned with acanthus carving and reeding and the feet are of the melon type. By "antique taste," Chippendale, of course, referred to the classic, which was then much in vogue. It is hard to realise that the same designer could have made this chair and the one shown in Figure 556, the entire theme and execution are so different, and yet these two chairs only date about fifteen years apart.

Upholstered chairs were popular throughout the Dutch and Chippendale period, but they were expensive owing to the cost of the fabric with which they were covered, and some of them designed by Chippendale were works of art. Such a chair is shown in Figure 581 and is the property of Mr. Marsden J. Perry, of Providence.

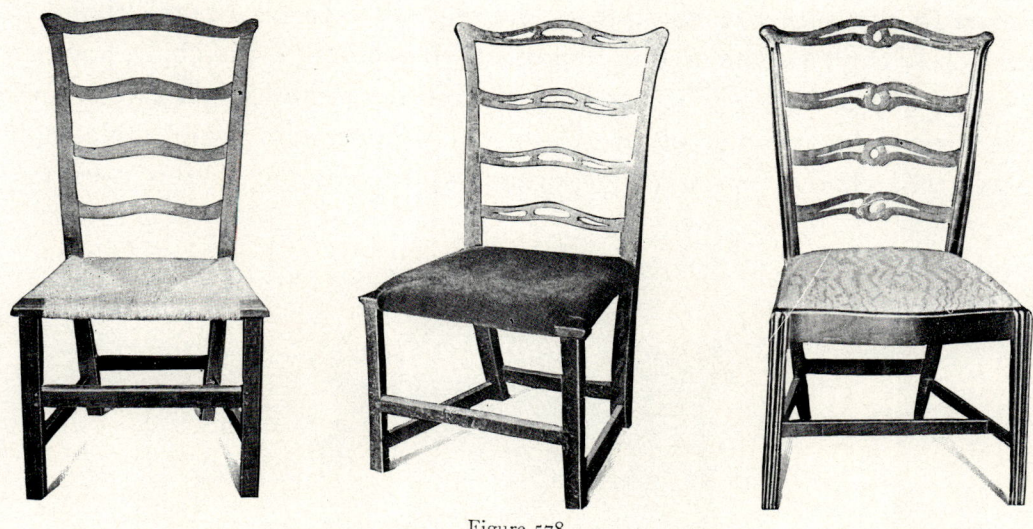

Figure 578.
Ladder-Back Chairs, 1770–80.

Figure 579.
Ladder-Back Chair, 1760–70.

Figure 580.
Chair in Chippendale style, classic taste, 1768.

COLONIAL FURNITURE

Chippendale called these chairs French chairs, and it can readily be seen that it is almost in the pure French style of the regency. In his French chairs Chippendale closely copied some of the designs of Meissonier. This chair, however, is of mahogany and not gilt. The design is a mixture of the French rococo and the Chinese, with a few touches of the Gothic in Chippendale's inimitable manner. No upholstered chair of such a high order has been found in this country and

Figure 581.
Upholstered Chair in Chippendale style, 1750–60.

they were exceedingly rare also in England. The chair is shown, however, to enable the reader to compare it with the beautiful specimens of Chippendale chairs, such as Figures 556 and 572, which did find their way to this country in colonial times, and also to show the extent to which simple models could be enriched.

The upholstered chairs that are most frequently found in England and here are of the types following.

Figure 582 shows an earlier upholstered chair of the Chippendale period, as indicated by its high back, curved seat, and bird's claw and ball feet and shell carving on the knees. It is the property of Mr. Dwight Blaney, of Boston.

Another form of upholstered chair is shown in Figure 583 and is what would be called in French a *bergère*. The legs are cabriole, terminating in French scroll feet, with a cabochon, scrolls, and leaves carved on each knee. The back legs are also cabriole and raked, and terminate in Dutch feet with a slight leaf carving. This chair is the property of the writer.

Figure 582.
Upholstered Chair in Chippendale style, 1750–60.

Figure 584 shows the simplest form of Chippendale upholstered chair most commonly found in this country. They are often made in sets with side chairs to match. The arms are upholstered and the supports are raked on a curve. The legs and stretchers are perfectly plain. This chair is the property of the writer.

The Hepplewhite, Shearer, and Sheraton styles did not immediately follow the Chippendale and Adam styles, but there was a period of transition in which the two were harmonised. As before stated, this transition, however, took place during the years of our Revolutionary War, with the necessary result that these pieces did not come here; but the cabinet-makers in this country jumped from the Chippendale into the Hepplewhite and Shearer styles without the

Figure 583.
Upholstered Chair in Chippendale style, 1760–70.

Figure 584.
Upholstered Chair in Chippendale style, 1770–80.

CHAIRS

intervening transition pieces. This probably accounts largely for the great number of plain, straight-leg Chippendale chairs found here.

A few transition pieces are however found, one of which is in Figure 585. The top rail is in the shield shape of the Hepplewhite school, but the stiles are extended through the seat to form the rear legs, and the splat is shaped as it was in the Chippendale period. A number of chairs like this have been found in and about Hartford, Connecticut, and in a table of prices published by the joiners of Hartford, in 1792, we find advertised "A chair with urn'd banisters" which could be made for £1 9s. This probably referred to this design of chair.

Figure 585.
Chair in transition style, about 1790.

Figure 586 shows an arm and side chair in transition style which belong to Mrs. N. E. Church, of Belmar, New Jersey. The stiles curve into the top, which is depressed at the centre, and the surfaces are well moulded. The splat

Figure 586.
Chairs in transition style, 1780–90.

is pierced in the anthemion design inverted. At the top is a festoon of leaves. The front rail is both hollowed and serpentine and the legs are tapering, with spade feet.

The regulation shield-backed Hepplewhite chair is shown in Figure 587. This form of construction is faulty because the centre of the back is not fastened to the seat rail. It is finished with four reeded and carved flat spindles setting into a half-rosette. The legs are reeded and terminate in spade feet. This chair is the property of Mr. H. W. Erving.

Figure 588 shows another form of the shield back the centre of which is filled in with three supporting stems with flowers. The legs are tapering and plain.

Figure 587.
Chair in Hepplewhite style, 1785-95.

Still another shield-back Hepplewhite chair is shown in Figure 589. At the centre of the back is an urn with streamers and the usual half-rosette is at the base.

A very beautiful shield-shaped Hepplewhite chair is shown in Figure 590. The centre design is drapery caught up at three places and a fleur-de-lis is at the top. The legs taper and terminate in spade feet. The seat is upholstered over the edge and finished with brass-headed nails.

Figure 591 shows another shield-shaped Hepplewhite chair. The design is drapery caught at two ends and passing over an inlaid medallion. Below are

Figure 588.
Chair in Hepplewhite style,
1785-95.

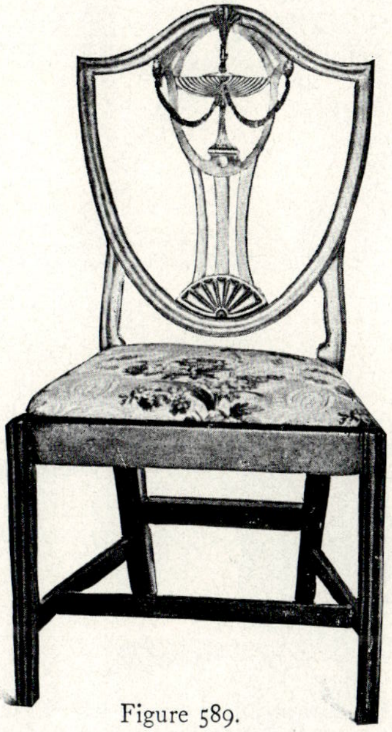

Figure 589.
Chair in Hepplewhite style,
1785-95.

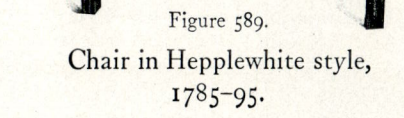

Figure 590.
Chair in Hepplewhite style,
1785-95.

carved foliated scrolls and acanthus leaves. The arms and supports are in graceful scrolls. This chair is the property of the writer.

Figure 592 shows a very beautiful shield-shaped Hepplewhite chair in the Pendleton Collection. The back consists of three conventionalised lilies from the

Figure 591.
Chair in Hepplewhite style, 1785–95.

Figure 592.
Chair in Hepplewhite style, 1785–95.

spathes of which are streamers of grass and heads of wheat. The legs are tapering, reeded and fluted, terminating in spade feet.

Figure 593 shows a chair in Hepplewhite style, the property of Mr. Richard A. Canfield. The back is shield-shaped and the cresting is carved at the centre with flowers. There are three central supports, the centre one being pierced and carved in a guilloche pattern within the centre circle of which is a carved rosette. On the outer ones is a slight leaf carving with pearl drops. The legs are square, in the Marlborough form.

Figure 594 shows a Hepplewhite chair with an oval back which gives even a more delicate effect than the shield shape. There are four curved strips forming the splat, and festoons of carved flowers are attached to the under surface of the frame of the back. The arms and supports are curved and the straight legs have moulded surfaces. This chair belongs to the Tiffany Studios.

Figure 595 shows a Hepplewhite chair with a heart-shaped back. The drapery, leaves, and flowers are well carved and the design is one of the best

Figure 593.
Chair in Hepplewhite style, about 1790.

Figure 594.
Chair in Hepplewhite style, 1785-95.

found. The legs are tapering and reeded, with spade feet. This chair was the property of the late Reverend Samuel J. Andrews, D.D.

The influence of Thomas Sheraton, the last of the great furniture designers, was very great in this country. His designs were often literally copied, and practically all of the furniture here of the period showed his motifs. The chief characteristics of his style in chairs were the rectangular lines, sometimes with a rectangular panel at the centre of the top rail upon which was cameo carving.

Figure 596 shows a pair of arm-chairs which are exactly like Plate XXXIII in Sheraton's "The Cabinet-Maker and Upholsterer's Drawing-Book." A set like these and those shown in the following figure were imported from London by the Nichols family, of Salem, Massachusetts. The backs of these chairs are composed of three arcades. On the surface of the two inner pilasters are carved pendent flowers. The front legs are rounded.

Figure 597 shows a pair of side chairs also belonging to the Nichols family. Between the frame of the back is a lattice design and at the centre of the back is a rectangular panel in which is carved a basket of flowers. The legs are straight and plain.

Figure 595.
Chair in Hepplewhite style, 1785–95.

Figure 598 shows a chair in Sheraton style the top rail of which is perfectly straight, and the stiles are raked toward the centre. Within the frame is carved drapery caught at the centre and at the two ends, falling down the inside of the stiles, and in the centre is a bow knot and drapery with a cord and two tassels. This is one of a set of six chairs in the writer's possession.

Figure 599 shows another form of Sheraton chair which is substantially like Plate XXXVI, No. 1, in Sheraton's book. In effect the back is rectangular with another rectangular frame imposed and extending above the main frame.

Figure 596.
Chairs in Sheraton style, 1785–90.

Figure 597.
Chairs in Sheraton style, 1785–90.

Figure 598. Chair in Sheraton style, 1785-95.

Figure 599. Chair in Sheraton style, 1790-1800.

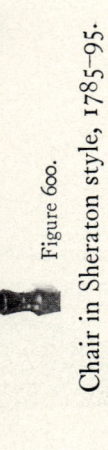

Figure 600. Chair in Sheraton style, 1785-95.

CHAIRS

119

The splat is urn-shaped, with drapery, and above are three feathers. The legs are tapering, with spade feet. This chair is the property of the writer.

Figure 600 shows a Sheraton chair with a round seat. The back is rectangular with rosettes in the corners and a lattice back with rosettes at the crossings. The supports of the arms are spirally twisted and the legs are round and fluted with X underbracing. This chair is the property of the Tiffany Studios.

Figure 601 shows a chair in Sheraton style, the property of Mr. William W. Smith, of Hartford. The cresting is arched at the centre and the entire surface is carved, and at the corners are carved blocks with a rosette in the centre. The stiles have an acanthus-leaf carving at the top resembling capitals, the lower part representing a fluted shaft. Under the arched top and forming a part of the splat is a beautifully carved flower-and-leaf design with pendent flowers, and on either side are columns having the base and top carved in the same leaf design. The legs are in Marlborough form with fluted surfaces.

A form of Sheraton chair quite often found is shown in Figure 602. In the centre of the back is a well-shaped splat below which are carved pendent flowers. The legs are straight and underbraced.

Figure 601.
Chair in Sheraton style, 1785–95.

Figure 603 shows another form of chair in the Sheraton style with a curved seat, in the form known as a conversation chair. The legs are so shaped that a man can sit straddle-legged, resting his arms on the back, and thus keep his coat tails from being creased. Quite a number of designs of these chairs are found in Sheraton's book.

Figure 604 shows a chair in red lacquer and gilt, which is one of a set of side arm chairs and two settees, the property of Professor Barrett Wendell. This set had been painted like the settee of the set shown in Figure 635, but when the paint was removed the design as shown on this chair was disclosed. On the top

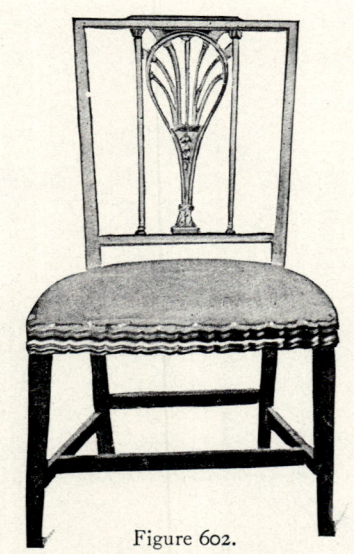

Figure 602.
Chair in Sheraton style, 1785–95.

Figure 603.
Chair in Sheraton style, 1785–95.

Figure 605.
Painted Chair in Sheraton style, about 1800.

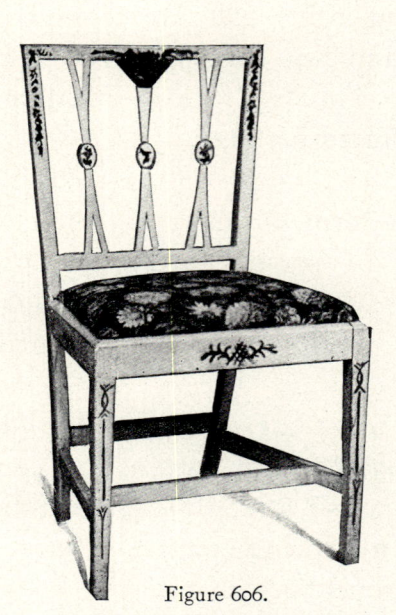

Figure 606.
Painted Chair in Sheraton style, about 1800.

CHAIRS

rail is painted a bow and arrow and a quiver and in the upper section of the splat acanthus leaves in a design found on some of the carved chairs of the Sheraton period. On the flat surface of the front stretcher are painted laurel leaves and a bow knot.

Figures 605 and 606 show two simple forms of Sheraton chairs. The first has three spindles swelling and split at the centre with carved rosettes, and the

Figure 604.
Red Lacquer Chair in Sheraton style, about 1800.

Figure 607.
Upholstered Chair in Sheraton style, 1790–1800.

other has three carved braces with a medallion at the crossings. The decoration on these chairs is painted.

Figure 607 shows an upholstered chair in this style. The frame throughout is finished with a pearl beading and at each corner is a well-carved rosette. The supports to the arm are carved and spirally twisted. The legs are round and fluted with acanthus-leaf carving above. This chair is the property of the Metropolitan Museum of Art.

Another Sheraton upholstered chair is shown in Figure 608. The back is rounded, the arms forming part of the back. The supports for the arms are moulded and there is a slight leaf carving where they join; the legs, which are round, are reeded. This chair is the property of the Tiffany Studios.

Figure 609 shows a tall-backed upholstered chair of the period which resembles the easy-chair, except that it has low wooden arms instead of wings. The supports for the arms are raked in a curve and moulded. The legs are straight and plain. This chair is the property of Mr. Dwight Blaney.

A late form of Sheraton painted chair is shown in Figure 610 and is a design often

Figure 608.
Upholstered Chair in Sheraton style, 1790–1800.

found in this country. The rails of the back are painted, and between them are three groups of spindles consisting of four at the centre and three at either side. The front stretcher on the arm-chair is broadened at the centre and painted in a floral design.

The chair shown in Figure 611 is one of the later

Figure 609.
Upholstered Chair in Sheraton style, 1790–1800.

Sheraton designs in what is called the Empire style. The seat and the back appear to sweep forward in a curve to form the seat rail, and the back is curved backward in the Egyptian style. The legs are an extension of the supports of the arms and are slightly cabriole. This chair is the property of the Tiffany Studios.

CHAIRS

A very ornate chair in the Sheraton Empire style is shown in Figure 612. The back is suggestive of the roundabout style. The supports for the arms are

Figure 610.
Painted Chairs in Sheraton style, about 1800.

Figure 611.
Chair in Sheraton style, 1800–10.

beautifully carved swans standing on cornucopias full of fruit, at which they are pecking, and these stand on a pedestal decorated in the anthemion pattern. The splat, which does not show, is carved to represent Roman arms, banners, and fasces. The front rail is carved in a design which alternates acanthus and anthemion designs, and above the legs is a small panel carved to represent armour and arms. The legs are cabriole, in the Egyptian pattern, ending in griffin's feet, and on the knees are carved the anthemion pattern. Of course, no such ornate chair was probably found in this country, but such designs are found in the third edition of Sheraton's book, and it is thought well, therefore, to show an

Figure 612.
Carved Chair in Sheraton style, 1800–10.

Figure 613.
Chair in Phyfe style, 1810–20.

example. The carving is of the highest order and of the cameo type. This chair is the property of the Metropolitan Museum of Art.

One of the best known of the New York cabinet-makers was Duncan Phyfe, whose shop was at 35 Partition (now Fulton) Street, New York. He made a specialty of the late Empire style, never carried it to excess, and showed a delicacy and refinement of the design which was highly commendable. His workmanship was of the best and his pieces are highly prized.

Figure 613 shows a side chair made by Phyfe. The back, it will be seen, is curved backward in the Empire fashion and the stiles seem to form a part of the seat rails. The surfaces are reeded in the manner he mostly employed. The legs are slightly curved and the lower half of each is carved with a lion's leg and

CHAIRS

claw. The splat is a lyre with acanthus-leaf carving on the scrolls, and there are four strings to the lyre. This chair is the property of Mr. R. T. Haines Halsey, of New York.

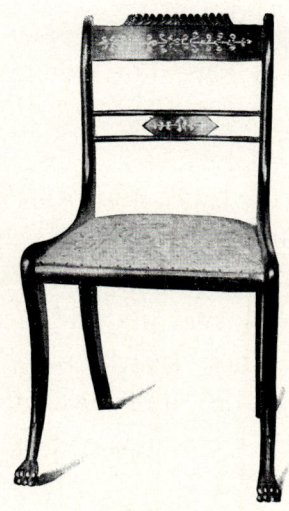

Figure 614.
Chair in late Sheraton style, 1810–20.

Figure 615.
Painted Chair, 1810–25.

Figure 616.
Empire Chair, 1825–30.

Figure 617.
Empire Chairs, about 1840.

Another chair quite suggestive of Phyfe, although much inferior to his work, is shown in Figure 614. The ornamentation is of inlaid brass, and lion's feet finish the legs.

Figure 615 shows a painted variety of the Empire chair such as is quite commonly found in the South. The back and rear legs are raked and are joined to resemble the folding bronze chairs found in Egypt. A brass rosette finishes the imitation hinge. The front legs are heavily fluted. This chair is painted with flowers and gold scrolls and the seat is of cane.

Figure 616 shows the late Empire style as it became modified in this country. The Sheraton influence is seen in the painted lyre on the back. The slat is also painted in fruit designs.

Figure 617 shows two styles of the parlour chairs of our grandmothers' day, which remained in style up to, and indeed later than, 1840. The one to the right has the back and legs made of the same piece, while the other shows a construction where the legs are made separate from the back. The former method of construction makes a stronger and more desirable chair. They clearly have the Empire pieces as their model, and it is amusing to see how the "antique dealers" are to-day advertising such pieces as colonial when they were new within the memory of some of the readers.

VIII
SETTEES, COUCHES, AND SOFAS

THE words settee and sofa have often been used interchangeably, and there seems to have been no uniformity in their use, even among the cabinet-makers of the eighteenth century. For the purpose of this chapter we will call the pieces that do not have upholstered backs, more or less resembling chairs, settees; and those with upholstered backs, not suggestive of chair backs, sofas. It was the fashion throughout the late seventeenth and the entire eighteenth centuries to make settees to resemble two or more chair backs. They are commonly known as double chairs, triple chairs, etc., depending upon the number of chair backs they represent.

The settle seems to have been a direct evolution from the chest. W. H. Pollen, in his book on furniture, says: "As the tops of coffers served for seats, they began in the thirteenth century to be furnished with panelled backs and arms." At any rate, we find beautiful examples of carved settles in England, dating through the fifteenth and sixteenth centuries.

A glance at Figure 618 will clearly show how closely the settle resembles a chest. The lower part of this piece has all the characteristics of a chest, including the lifting top, and the three panels are carved in the same manner and design as are found in chests. The two end stiles are extended to support the arms, and the seat is panelled. The back is divided into three panels, as is the lower part, and the centre panel closely resembles that found below. The top of the back is finished in the fashion of the wainscot chairs, as are also the arms. Many familiar patterns are found in the carving on this settle, most of them of the early periods, as, for instance, the two centre panels and especially the two inside stiles on both top and bottom. The panelled seat suggests that the settle must have been used with a cushion. The piece seems to be made of American oak, and was found at Great Barrington, Massachusetts, where it had been used in a stable to hold salt for cattle. It dates in the latter half of the seventeenth century and is now in the Bulkeley Collection.

Figure 618.
Carved Oak Settle, last half seventeenth century.

Figure 619.
Pine Settle, first half eighteenth century.

SETTEES, COUCHES, AND SOFAS

Settles are mentioned in the inventories of this country from the very first. We find one mentioned in Boston, in 1643, and at Yorktown, in 1647, "1 long wainscot settle"; at Philadelphia, in 1706, "1 settle 17s"; and again, in 1720, "1 long settle 14s"; and at Providence, in 1712, "1 settle 9s."

Such handsome settles as that shown in the last figure were extremely rare in this country, the settle commonly in use being similar to the one shown in

Figure 620.
Cane Settle with three chair backs, about 1675.

Figure 619. It is made of pine, with high back, and the front extends nearly to the floor, thus forming an effective screen against the cold winter winds, for it was the custom to draw these settles up close to the large, open fire, usually in the kitchen, thus making a sort of little inner warm room. This settle is owned by the Misses Andrews, in whose family it has always been. These settles are sometimes furnished with a small shelf fastened in the centre of the back to hold a candle.

Settles of this type were in use in this country for a long period, from the very earliest times down to about 1760, and were, many of them, more carefully made than Figure 619, being of oak and often panelled.

Figure 620 shows a triple chair of the cane period which belongs to the writer. It will be noticed that the two inside stiles of the back are set into the

Figure 621.
Wagon Chair, first half eighteenth century.

Figure 622.
Turned Slat-Back Settle with three chair backs, 1725-50.

SETTEES, COUCHES, AND SOFAS 131

seat rail instead of carrying through to the floor, and that the inside rear legs are not placed under the stiles, the reason apparently being that if the stiles had carried through they would have weakened the seat rail. The trouble, however, with this form of construction is that the entire strain of the back falls upon the end stiles and the arms, which makes the piece rather fragile. The legs are turned, with carved front stretchers, and in the middle the design is double. The piece was intended to be used with a cushion.

Figure 623.
Settee with double chair back in Dutch style, first quarter eighteenth century.

Figure 621 shows a small double chair of the slat-back variety, the property of Mr. Dwight Blaney. Such pieces are called wagon chairs, because they were intended to be placed in the farm wagons to furnish seats when the wagon was to be used as a carriage. Such pieces are fairly common throughout the country places and were probably used through a long period, the earlier ones having large turnings in the usual manner. The outer legs are often notched with a flat outer surface so that they will fit into the sides of the wagon.

Figure 622 is a very unusual example of a triple-back chair of the slat-back variety which belonged to the late Mrs. Frank H. Bosworth. It is the only one of the kind which has come under the writer's observation. The backs and set-back arms are similar to those shown in the rocking-chairs (Figure 425). The seat is of rush and the front stretchers are large and bulbous turned.

Figure 623 shows a double chair in the plain Dutch style, having all the characteristics of a chair of the same period. The lines are all softened into cyma curves, which gives the piece a very graceful appearance, although unrelieved with carving, except on the knees, upon each of which is carved a shell pattern. This double chair is in the Pendleton Collection, owned by the Rhode Island School of Design.

Figure 624 shows another settee, or double chair, of the Dutch period, in which the outline is very similar to that shown in the preceding figure except that

Figure 624.
Settee with double chair back in Dutch style, about 1725.

the surfaces of the splat are ornamented with carving. The centre of the top rail of the back is depressed instead of raised and is carved in a shell pattern with foliated streamers. On the edges of the splat are carved foliated scrolls, and at the centre is an oval piercing which forms the centre of a cartouche, on each side of which is a bird, with beaks coming together at the centre of the top, and above their heads are carved acanthus-leaf scrolls. Below are cords and two tassels. The arms are in the usual form found in this style, making a continuous curve with their supports instead of, as in the last figure, ending in a scroll extending beyond the supports. The front legs are cabriole, terminating in bird's claw and ball feet, and on the knees are carved shells with pendent flowers, and a C scroll

Figure 625.
Settee with three chair backs, Dutch style, 1725–50.

Figure 626.
Settee with two chair backs, Chippendale style, 1750–60.

133

finishes the outer edges of the knees. This piece is the property of the Metropolitan Museum of Art.

Figure 625 shows a settee with three backs, of the same general style, the property of Mr. John J. Gilbert, of Baltimore. At the centre of each back is carved a shell with pendent flowers extending down onto the splats, which are otherwise plain except for piercings. Between each back is a carved flower. The

Figure 627.
Settee with two chair backs, in Chinese taste, 1750–60.

arms are scrolled, terminating in birds' heads, which was a design popular in the period. The legs are cabriole, terminating in animal's claw and ball feet, and on the knees are carved acanthus leaves with a vertical pearl beading through the centre. This piece, as is usual in the period, is made of walnut.

Figure 626 is a very beautiful example of a double chair of the Chippendale period. The backs are separate except for a binding band of wood. The outer ends of the crestings are scrolled and the centre is carved in acanthus-leaf designs. The lower part of the splats are carved with foliated scrolls. The arms terminate in dragons' heads. The legs are cabriole, each terminating in an animal's claw grasping a ball, and on the knees are carved mascarons. This settee belongs to the American Antiquarian Society, of Worcester, Massachusetts.

SETTEES, COUCHES, AND SOFAS 135

Many settees having two or more backs are found in Chippendale style, and yet there is not a single example of one in his book.

Figure 627 shows a settee with two backs, in Chippendale style, showing the Chinese taste, which is at the Ladd house, Portsmouth, and is part of the same set as is the chair shown in Figure 572. The two backs are identical in every way with the back of the arm-chair, but the fretwork under the arms is missing.

Figure 628.
Settee with two chair backs, Chippendale style, third quarter eighteenth century.

Figure 628 shows another example of a Chippendale double chair belonging to Mr. H. W. Erving. A single stile separates the two splats, which are elaborately pierced in a rather late Chippendale design. There are but two front legs, which are cabriole, each terminating in the bird's claw and ball foot. All of the stiles of the back carry through to the floor, forming three legs strengthened by a stretcher.

Figure 629 shows another settee with two chair backs, in the Chippendale style, the property of Mr. Dwight M. Prouty, of Boston. This settee is small and very attractive. An unusual feature of the piece is that there is no stile separating the two splats, it being probably omitted in order to make the piece a little smaller. The splat is cut in a form suggestive of the Gothic. The arms are of the usual type and the legs are cabriole, terminating in Dutch feet. The only carving on the piece is on the knees in a crude acanthus-leaf design. This settee was probably made in this country.

Figure 630 is a particularly interesting example of a four-back settee which was made in the vicinity of Hartford, Connecticut, and belongs to Mr. H. W. Erving. The cabinet-maker had apparently seen a four-back settee, but, not

Figure 629.
Settee with two chair backs, Chippendale style, third quarter eighteenth century.

having the model before him, built this from memory. He apparently forgot that each chair back should have its own cresting, and instead he has made a single, very much elongated, cresting to cover all. The splats are cut in charming designs, but the heavy cresting rather detracts from the symmetry of the piece. There are five straight legs front and back, each underbraced in the manner of the chairs of the period.

Figure 631 shows a double chair, in the Chippendale style, quite different from the foregoing. The backs are filled in with lattice-work, at each crossing of which is carved a piece of wood which appears to bind the sections. Beneath the arms are simple lattices. The front rail is beautifully carved in a fine Gothic design, and a simple fret is carved on the surface of the front legs. There are but four legs underbraced as a chair. The settee belongs to Mr. H. W. Erving.

Figure 630.
Settee with four chair backs, Chippendale style, 1770–80.

Figure 631.
Settee in Chippendale style with two chair backs, 1760–80.

COLONIAL FURNITURE

Figure 632 shows a very interesting triple-back settee in the design of a ladder-back chair. The stiles joining the inside back are pierced, giving the effect of separate stiles for each back. The cresting is complete only on the two ends. The legs are straight, with double ogee and bead mouldings, and there

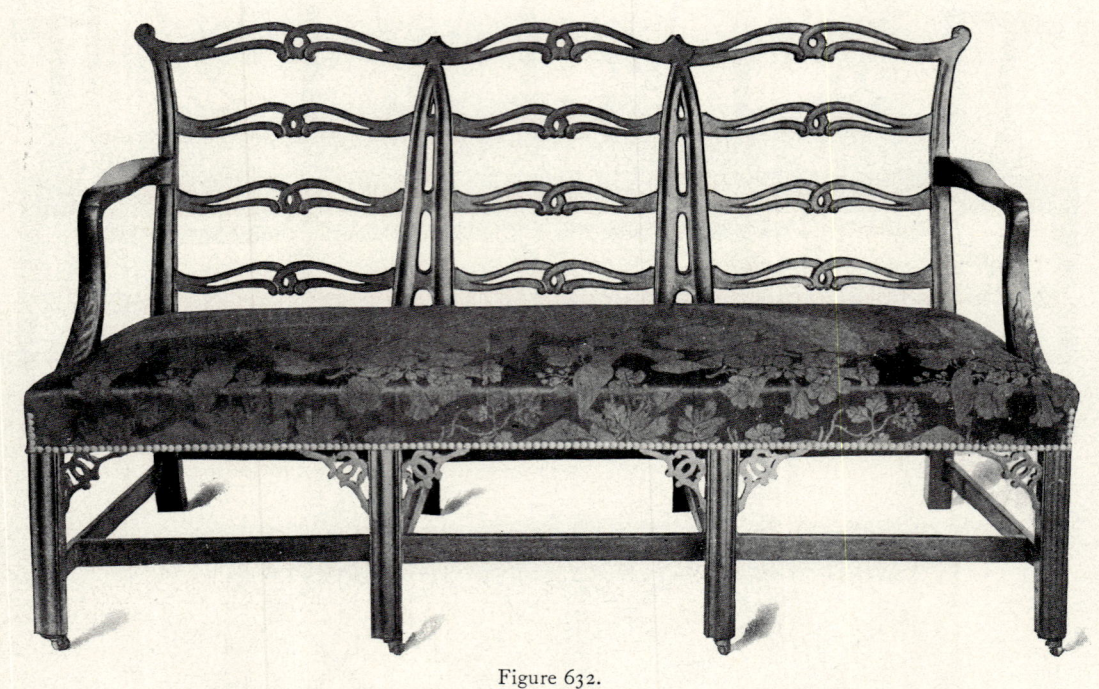

Figure 632.
Settee with three ladder-back chair backs, about 1770.

are pierced brackets where the legs join the seat rail. The arms have a slight acanthus-leaf carving. This settee is the property of Mr. A. C. Hencken, of Greenwich, Connecticut.

Figure 633 shows a settee with two chair backs, in the transition style, between the Chippendale and the Hepplewhite, Shearer, and Sheraton schools. The upper rails of the chair backs are shield-shaped, and at the centre of each is carved an anthemion with pendent flowers extending down on the centre section of the splat, and on either side of this ornament on the top rail are bell flowers. The surfaces of the stiles are moulded. The splat is cut with four piercings which appear to be bound at the centre. The rails of the seat and the legs are plain and the piece is underbraced in the usual manner of this period. This settee is the property of Mr. H. W. Erving.

A settee with three backs, in Hepplewhite style, the property of Mr. William W. Smith, of Hartford, is shown in Figure 634. The backs are shield-shaped, and at the centre of the top of each are carved heads of wheat with pendent flowers.

Figure 633.
Settee with two chair backs, transition style, 1775-85.

Figure 634.
Settee with three chair backs, Hepplewhite style, 1785-95.

140 COLONIAL FURNITURE

The splats are in very much the same shape as shown in the preceding figure, with four piercings bound together at the centre. The front rail is plain and the legs are tapering and fluted.

Figure 635.
Settee with two chair backs, Sheraton style, about 1800.

Figure 636.
Settee with three chair backs, Sheraton style, 1800–20.

Figure 635 shows a double chair in Sheraton style which belongs to the set of which the chair is shown in Figure 604. It was originally decorated like the

SETTEES, COUCHES, AND SOFAS

chair in red lacquer and gilt, but at a subsequent date the piece was painted white and stencilled. It is the property of Professor Barrett Wendell.

Figure 636 shows a triple chair in what is called American Sheraton design. It is plain black, and the stretchers, splats, and frame are enlivened with flowers in gilt, a few of which may be seen in the illustration. The same design of spindles appears under the arms as in the splat, and the front stretchers are cut in the same form.

COUCHES

We now come to a totally different kind of furniture, known in this country as a couch, but in England called a day-bed and by the French a *chaise longue*. The latter name is the best description, for it is truly a long chair.

As the settles and double chairs were pieces on which to sit, so couches were intended to lie upon, and as they are to be found in almost all the designs for chairs, from the turned variety through the Empire style, they very evidently formed parts of sets with their corresponding chairs. To substantiate this the inventories show, at Boston, 1702, "7 cane chairs, 1 couch & squab"; in the same year, "1 Doz. cane chairs with black frames 1 couch ditto"; at Philadelphia, 1686, "1 cane couch & 8 cane chairs."

As might be expected from the character of the settlements and from the fact that the couches were placed at high valuations, they appear first and more frequently in the South; in fact, they were very common throughout the South, as many as twenty-two being mentioned in the inventories at Yorktown between 1645 and 1670. At Yorktown, in 1647, "1 old turned couch" is mentioned, which would indicate that the piece was of considerably earlier date than the entry, and another is mentioned in an inventory of 1645. We do not find couches inventoried among the more sturdy New Englanders earlier than the inventory of John Cotton, of Boston, in 1652.

After that date we find them occasionally mentioned in the North and frequently in the South, but the descriptions give little aid in determining their character. At Yorktown, in 1658, mention is made of "a skin couch"; in 1659, "a wainscoate couch"; in 1667, "1 couch cubbard." At New York, in 1691, we find "3 couches £3"; at Yorktown, in 1692, "1 couch Turkey worked 10s"; at Boston, in 1698, "an old couch," in 1700, "a red couch," and in 1709, "one couch covered"; at Philadelphia, in 1686, "1 cane couch £1," and in 1706, "1 good cane couch £2"; at Providence, in 1732, "an old couch £2."

These early couches were really long chairs; that is, they were without backs on the long side, while on one end there was a back similar to a chair back of the period to which it belongs, with three pairs of front legs making an elongated chair.

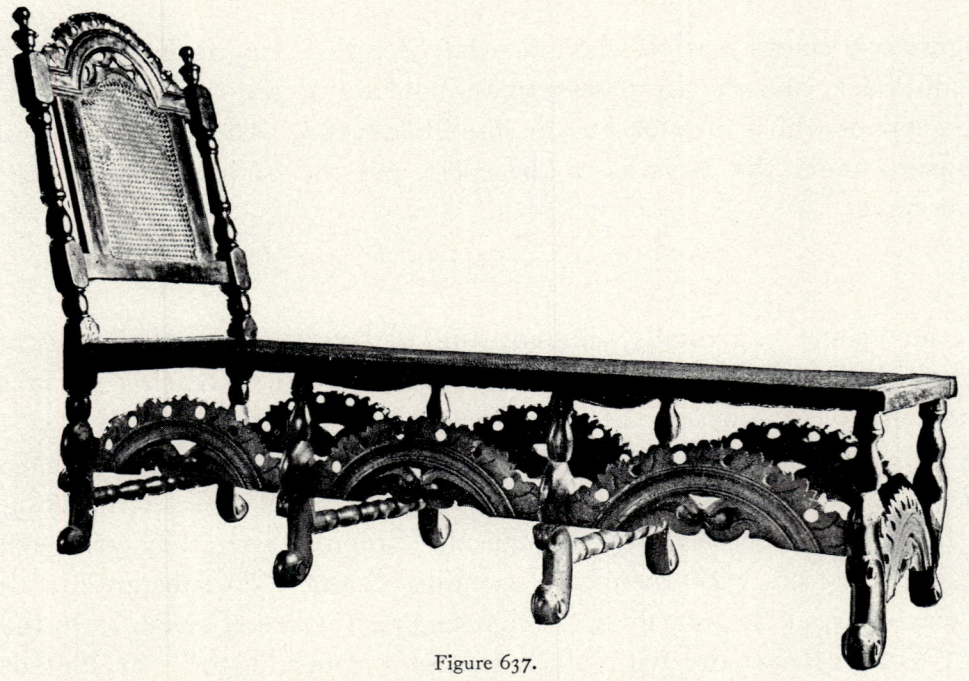

Figure 637.
Cane Couch, Flemish style, 1670–80.

Figure 638.
Cane Couch with Spanish feet, 1680–90.

SETTEES, COUCHES, AND SOFAS 143

Figure 637 shows an example of what was referred to in the inventories as a cane couch. It belongs to the first type of cane chairs. The feet are in the form of the elaborated Flemish scroll. The carved stretchers which follow the design of the cresting extend not only on both sides, but on the end, which is unusual. The splat is hinged at the bottom and lets down on chains to any desired angle. This piece belongs to Mr. F. O. Pierce, of Brooklyn, in whose family it has always been.

Figure 638 is another example of a cane couch; the cresting and stretchers are carved in a mixture of Moorish and European style known as the Mudejar

Figure 639.
Turned Couch, Pennsylvania type, about 1700.

style. The piece really belongs to the second type of cane chairs, although the stiles extend beyond the cresting; but this method of construction was necessary to enable the back to swing out. The legs are turned and terminate in very fine Spanish feet. The stretcher at the end is not carved. This beautiful couch was the property of the late William G. Boardman, of Hartford, Connecticut.

Figures 639 and 640 are two very good examples of turned couches in the form found in Pennsylvania, showing the influence of the Pennsylvania Dutch, the legs resembling those found on the slat-back chairs found in the same vicinity (Figure 429). The turnings are large and the ball feet at each end are slightly different from the centre pair. This is another characteristic of the style. The turned bracings are heavy and are alternately set low and high to avoid weakening the legs. The backs swing as in the preceding type. The turnings of these two couches are identical, except for the stiles, which in Figure 639 are nicely turned. The backs differ slightly. Figure 639 has an arched cresting with three slats, while Figure 640 has a waving cresting with three splats in the well-known Dutch style. Figure 639 is the earlier and is the property of Mrs. Robert W. de Forest. Figure 640 belongs to the writer. It originally had a rush seat.

Figure 641 shows another turned couch in the form found in New England. It will be noted that it is more graceful than the Pennsylvania type, with more

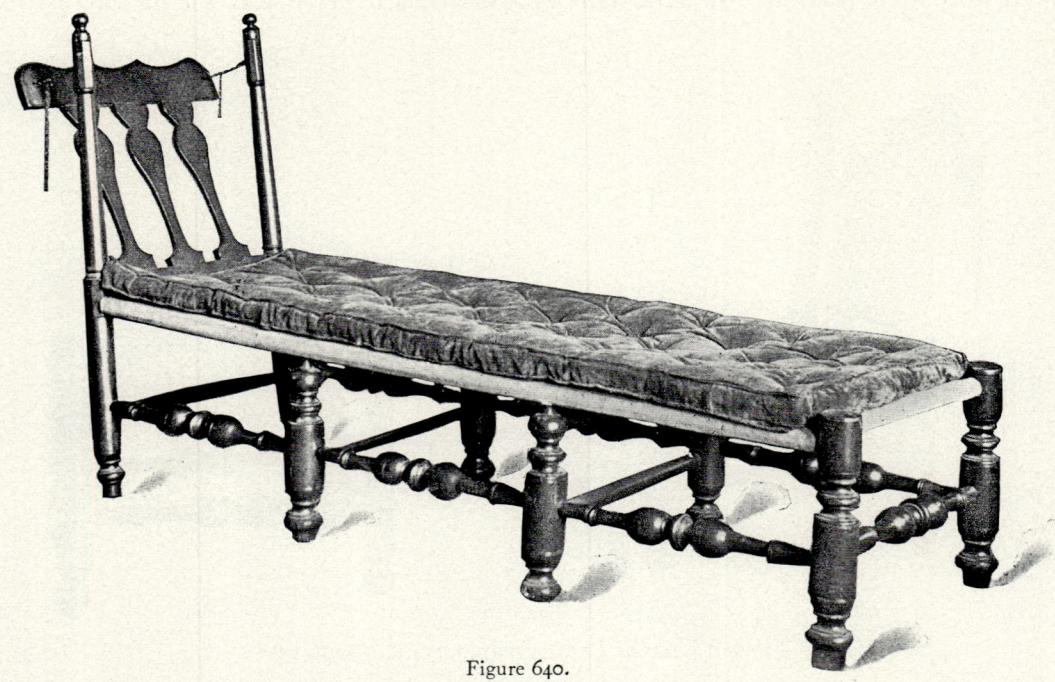

Figure 640.
Turned Couch, Pennsylvania type, about 1700.

delicate turning, and it more clearly resembles the chairs of the period. The cresting is moulded in the same form as the cane couch shown in Figure 638. All of the stretchers, including those inside, are turned in the vase-and-ring pattern. This couch belongs to Mr. Hollis French, of Boston.

Figure 642 shows a very simple couch with a back of the Dutch period. There are but three pairs of legs, and the stretchers, except at the end, are not turned. This couch belongs to Robbins Brothers, of Hartford.

Figure 643 shows a couch in the transition period, closely resembling the chairs shown in Figure 490, and was probably made as a companion piece for such a set. The back is in the Dutch style. The legs are turned, terminating in

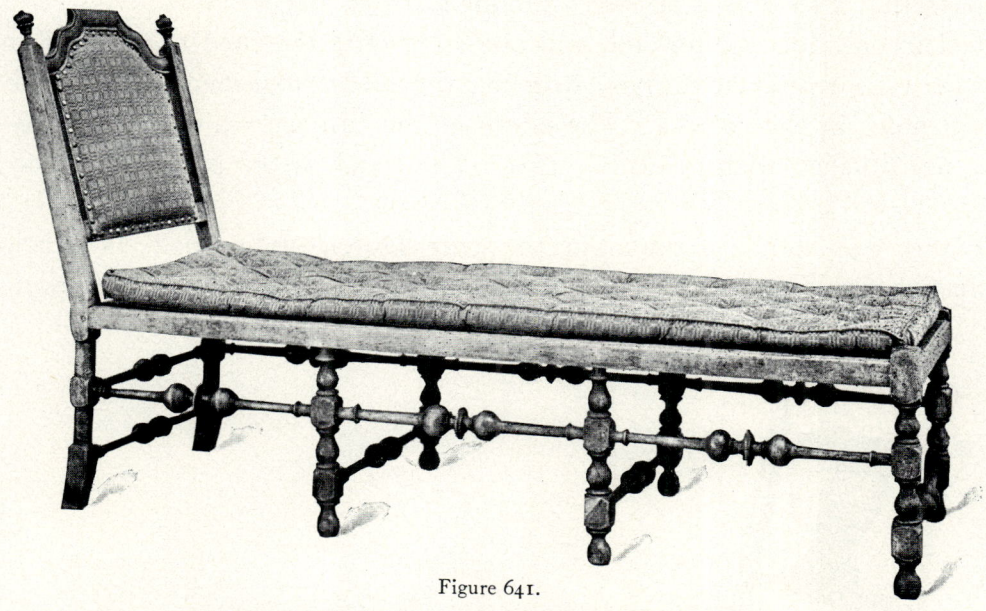

Figure 641.
Turned Couch, New England style, about 1700.

Figure 642.
Turned Couch, Dutch style, 1700–15.

145

Spanish feet, and all of the stretchers and bracings are turned in the vase-and-ring pattern. The seat is of canvas, made in three pieces: two narrow strips, each fastened to one side and an end, and one large strip fastened to one end and side. The canvas is stretched taut by drawing the pieces together with a cord passed through holes in the canvas. The edges of the canvas, which are nailed to the frame, are finished with rawhide strips. The couch is the property of the writer.

Figure 644 shows a couch, in the pure Dutch style, with six cabriole legs terminating in club feet. The back stiles are cut in the characteristic cyma

Figure 643.
Turned Couch, Dutch style, about 1720.

curves. The couch is underbraced with turned stretchers connecting the legs from side to side and connecting the centre of the cross-stretcher. The couch is the property of Mr. Dwight Blaney, of Boston.

Figure 645 shows another couch very similar to the preceding one, except that the back is in the Chippendale instead of Dutch form. The legs are cabriole, terminating in club feet raised on a shoe. The couch is underbraced in the manner described in the preceding figure, and the seat is of canvas fastened in the manner described in Figure 643. The skirt is cut in cyma curves. The stiles rake backward and are very heavy, to withstand the strain of the swinging back. The couch is the property of the writer.

Figure 644.
Cabriole-Legged Couch, Dutch style, 1725-50.

Figure 645.
Cabriole-Legged Couch, Chippendale style, about 1750.

Figure 646.
Ball-and-Claw-Foot Couch, Chippendale style, 1750–60.

Figure 647.
Couch, Chippendale style, 1760–70.

SETTEES, COUCHES, AND SOFAS

Figure 646 shows a form of couch, in the Chippendale style, which belongs to Mr. H. W. Erving. The legs are cabriole, terminating in bird's claw and ball feet, but without any underbracing. The back is stationary and cannot be swung back. The canvas seat is fastened in the manner already described.

Figure 647 shows another couch with a back, in the Chippendale style. The splat is cut in Gothic form, and one of the most popular in the period. About the

Figure 648.
"Duchesse," Chippendale style, about 1760.

lower edge of the skirt is a carved godrooned moulding, and the piece stands on six straight legs, with a stretcher between each pair of legs and two X stretchers. This method of underbracing is uncommon. This settee is in the Bolles Collection, owned by the Metropolitan Museum of Art.

Another form of couch known as a "duchesse" is occasionally found in England. These are composed of two *bergères* and a stool which when placed together form a couch. The writer has never seen an American one.

Figure 648 shows an exceptionally fine specimen of a "duchesse," which is the property of Mr. Marsden J. Perry, of Providence. The upper end is a high-back *bergère* with four beautifully shaped cabriole legs with carved knees and bird's claw and ball feet. The stool is in the same design, and at the lower end is a low-back *bergère*. The pieces lock together with metal clamps.

There do not seem to have been any couches made after the Chippendale

150 COLONIAL FURNITURE

period which followed the design of chairs, probably because the chairs of the Hepplewhite and Sheraton designs were not strong enough to withstand the strain. Upholstered couches, however, came into fashion in England, but very few are found in this country until the Empire period.

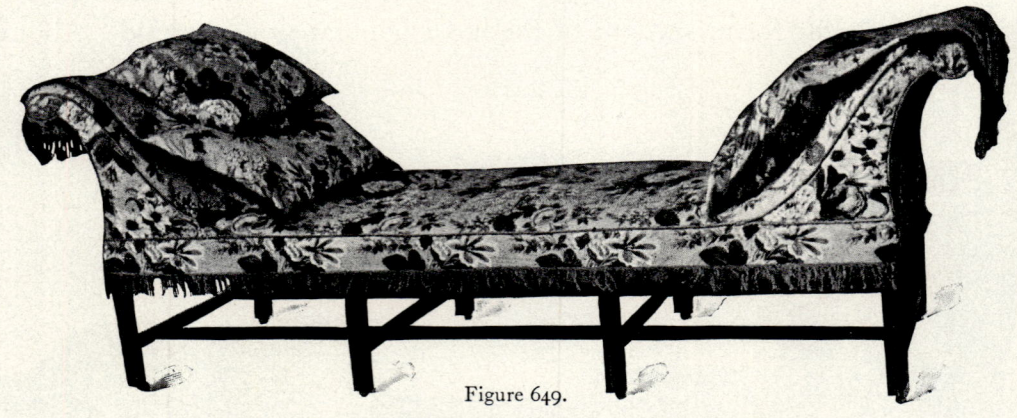

Figure 649.
Couch, Chippendale period, 1770–80.

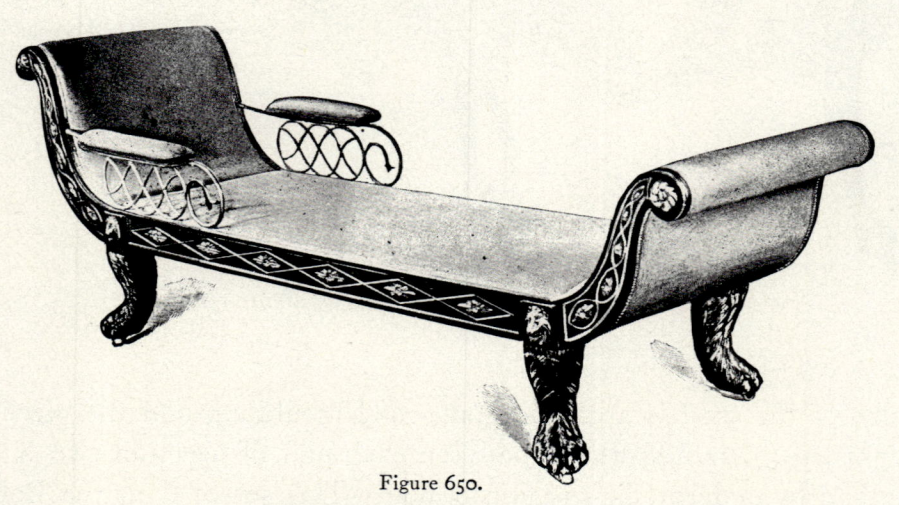

Figure 650.
Chaise-Longue, 1790–1800.

An example of a couch prior to the Empire period is shown in Figure 649 and is the property of Professor Barrett Wendell. The two ends roll and are completely upholstered. The eight legs are straight, with double ogee mouldings on the surfaces, and are strengthened by underbracing across and two underbraces, one on each side, a little recessed, extending the length of the piece.

Figure 650 shows a couch, in the Empire style, which originally belonged to Mr. Joseph Bonaparte and came from his house at Bordentown, New Jersey. It is in the writer's possession. It is made of well-selected mahogany, and the

SETTEES, COUCHES, AND SOFAS

carved bears' or lions' feet are unusually well executed. The arms are of brass and brazed. The sides are enriched with diamond-shaped panels marked off by a raised bead of ebony which is fitted into a channel. At the centre of each panel, graduating in size as the panel becomes smaller at the rolling ends, is a rosette

Figure 651.
Window-Seat, Chippendale style, third quarter eighteenth century.

Figure 652.
Window-Seat, Chippendale style, third quarter eighteenth century.

of ebony. A large rosette of ebony finishes the four ends, and four ebony lions' heads finish where the legs join the frame. The seat is of cane covered with a thin layer of hair.

Throughout the eighteenth century it was common to have small seats to fit into the window recesses, and a number of them have been found in this country, although they are not nearly so common here as they are in England. A very handsome one, in the Chippendale style, is shown in Figure 651, the property of Mr. Marsden J. Perry, of Providence. The ends are scrolled, each scroll being finished with a rosette, and on the front surface are carved acanthus-leaf scrolls. The legs are cabriole, terminating in French scroll feet, and on the knees are carved acanthus leaves. The rear side is straight and the front is serpentine. A lattice design quite similar to that shown in the splat of the chair in Figure 567 finishes the two ends.

Another window-seat, the property of the Tiffany Studios, is shown in Figure 652. The ends are scrolled, terminating in rosettes, and the sides are moulded with a pearl beading through the centre. On the lower edge of the rail is a godrooned moulding and above each leg is carved a rosette. The legs are straight with the surfaces fluted. The seat and two ends are upholstered.

SOFAS

We now come to the discussion of the sofa, which, according to our definition, differs from the settee in that it is upholstered and does not closely follow the design of a chair back. Such pieces are found in every style from the middle of the seventeenth century to and including the Empire style of 1820. In the Dutch period the sofa was often an enlarged arm-chair and was called a love seat, undoubtedly because it would fairly seat but two persons. In Chippendale's first edition of the "Director" he gives but two examples of sofas, and they are in Chinese style, but in his third edition there are found several.

Figure 653 shows an example of a settee, or sofa, of the turned period preceding the Restoration. The legs and stretchers are turned in the knob design. The seat and back are covered with Turkey work. The nature of this upholstery is discussed in Chapter VII. This piece is the property of the Essex Institute, at Salem.

Figure 654 shows a sofa, in the transition style, which belongs to Miss Jessie T. McClellan, of Woodstock, Connecticut. The end legs are straight and the two inside legs are slightly cabriole, terminating in crude Spanish feet. The legs are braced with turned stretchers, connecting the front and back legs, joined at the centre by stretchers running the length of the piece in the manner of the period.

Figure 655 is a sofa preserved at Independence Hall, Philadelphia, and at one time the property of George Washington. It will be interesting to compare this

Figure 653.
Turned Sofa upholstered in Turkey work, about 1660.

piece with the easy-chair shown in Figure 513. It will be seen that the arms and back are in the same design, but the feet of this piece have the animal's claw instead of the bird's claw. The rear legs are slightly cabriole. The knees are carved in an acanthus-leaf design and C scrolls. The sofa is now covered with hair-cloth, which is probably not the original covering. Sofas of similar design but with straight feet are frequently found and are of a little later date.

A very beautiful sofa in the Pendleton Collection, owned by the Rhode Island School of Design, is shown in Figure 656. The entire back is carved in a

Figure 654.
Sofa, about 1700.

series of simple and ogee curves, and at the centre is a shell pattern with flowers and leaves above. At the centre of each side of the top and on the two ends the scrolls are finished with an acanthus-leaf carving. The arms twist outward and are finished in large scrolls with carved surfaces. There are five cabriole legs on the front, terminating in bird's claw and ball feet, and the skirt is so cut that between each two legs on the upper section is a simple serpentine curve and on the lower surface two ogee curves separated by a short serpentine curve. This sofa has many of the characteristics of an early date, but the shell carving at the centre of the top indicates that it belongs to the Chippendale period.

Figure 657 shows a very interesting sofa, in Chippendale style, which was found in a farm-house on Long Island and now belongs to Mr. E. B. Willets, of Brooklyn. The cresting is covered with carving in the design of foliated scrolls and shells. The frame of the back is carved in waving lines, and at either end above the arms are small upholstered wings. The arms are well shaped and orna-

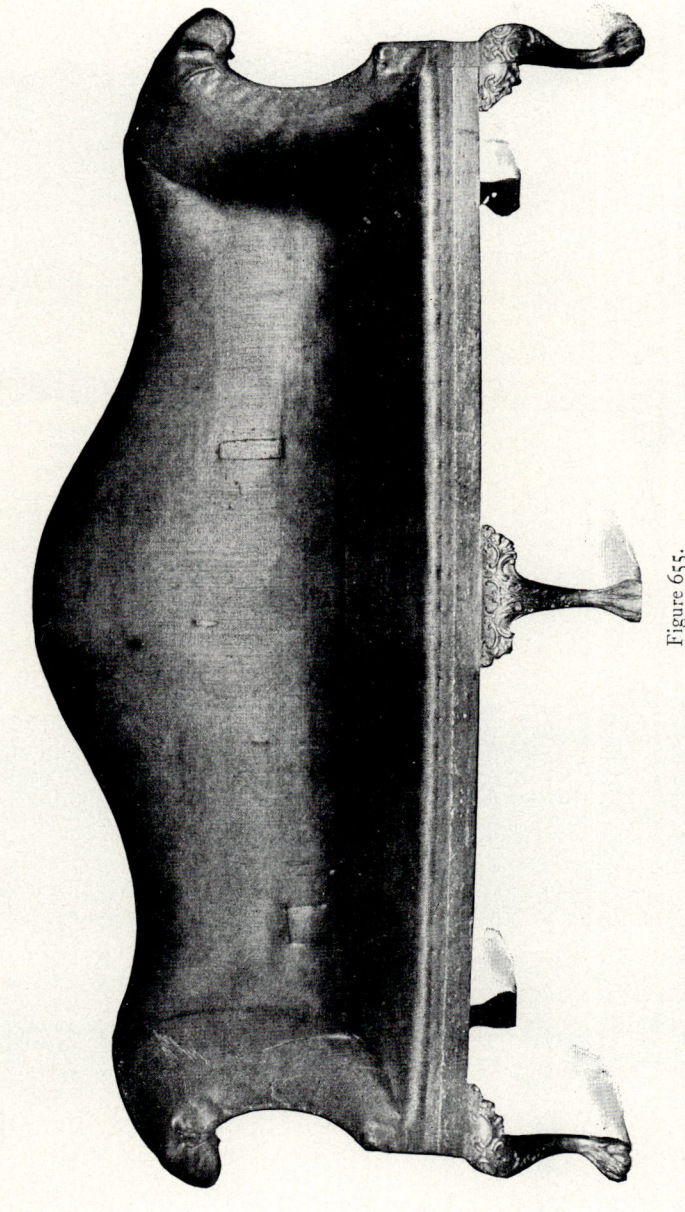

Figure 655.
Sofa, Chippendale style, 1760–80.

mented with acanthus-leaf carving. The four front legs are cabriole, terminating in bird's claw and ball feet, and on the knees are carved conventionalised shells.

Figure 656.
Sofa, Chippendale style, third quarter eighteenth century.

Figure 657.
Sofa, Chippendale style, third quarter eighteenth century.

The skirt is of wood cut in a series of cyma curves with the surfaces carved in a shell design with streamers. The upholstering is shaped to the skirt. It seems quite probable from the nature of the carving and the construction that the piece is of American origin.

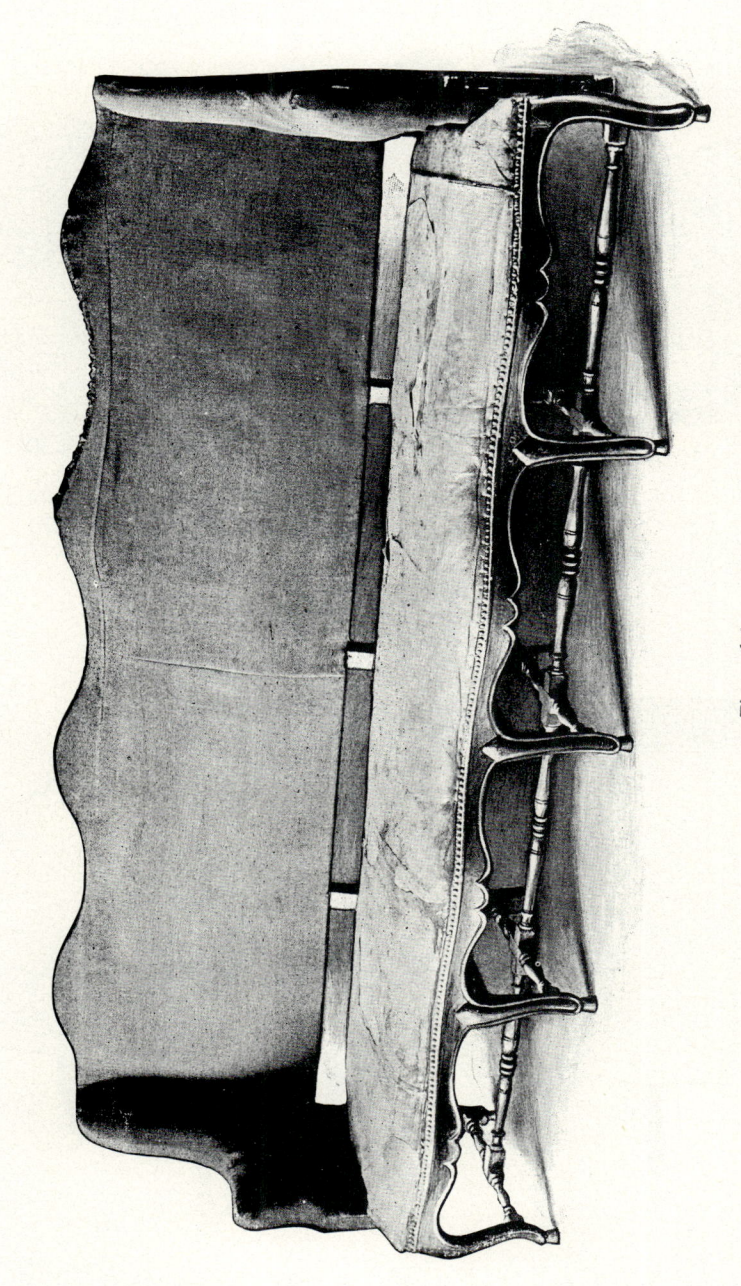

Figure 658.
Upholstered Sofa, 1770–80.

158   COLONIAL FURNITURE

Figure 658 shows an interesting example of an unusually long sofa. The back is shaped to suggest four chair backs but is entirely covered with upholstery. The skirt is cut in cyma curves. The five front legs are in cabriole form,

Figure 659.
Sofa, Sheraton style, about 1785.

Figure 660.
Sofa, Sheraton style, 1790–1800.

each standing on a small ball, and are braced with turned stretchers connecting the front and back legs, joined at the centres by stretchers running the length of the piece. The sofa once belonged to John Hancock, and is now at Pilgrim Hall, Plymouth.

SETTEES, COUCHES, AND SOFAS 159

Figure 659 shows a sofa in Sheraton style, the property of Mr. Marsden J. Perry, of Providence. It is unusual to find a Sheraton piece with cabriole legs, but the form of this piece was apparently influenced by the Louis XVI school. The back is in the form of a serpentine curve, and at the centre is an oval in which is carved a sheaf of wheat with streamers of leaves, and at either end of the back are small rosettes in which are carved anthemions. The entire top rail is beautifully carved, except at the ends, which are upholstered. There are four cabriole

Figure 661.
Sofa, Sheraton style, 1790–1800.

legs in the front terminating in French scroll feet. At the centre is a basket of flowers with wreaths, festoons, ribbons, and medallions, and a similar design is between the two outer legs. Above each leg is carved an anthemion with pendent flowers.

The Sheraton sofa shown in Figure 660 belongs to Mr. R. T. Haines Halsey, of New York. On the surface of the top rail are carved, in cameo carving, festoons of drapery caught up with bow knots. At the centre is an oval panel within which is carved a bunch of arrows. Extending from the oval panel are streamers of bell flowers. The tops of the arms are reeded as are also the bulb-shaped supports. A carved rosette finishes the block above the legs, which are turned and reeded.

A beautiful Sheraton sofa, the property of Mr. H. W. Erving, is shown in Figure 661. The top is carved in an egg-and-dart design, and at the centre is carved a shell with foliated streamers very similar to the design found on the chamber-table (Figure 111). Just below the egg-and-dart pattern is a finely

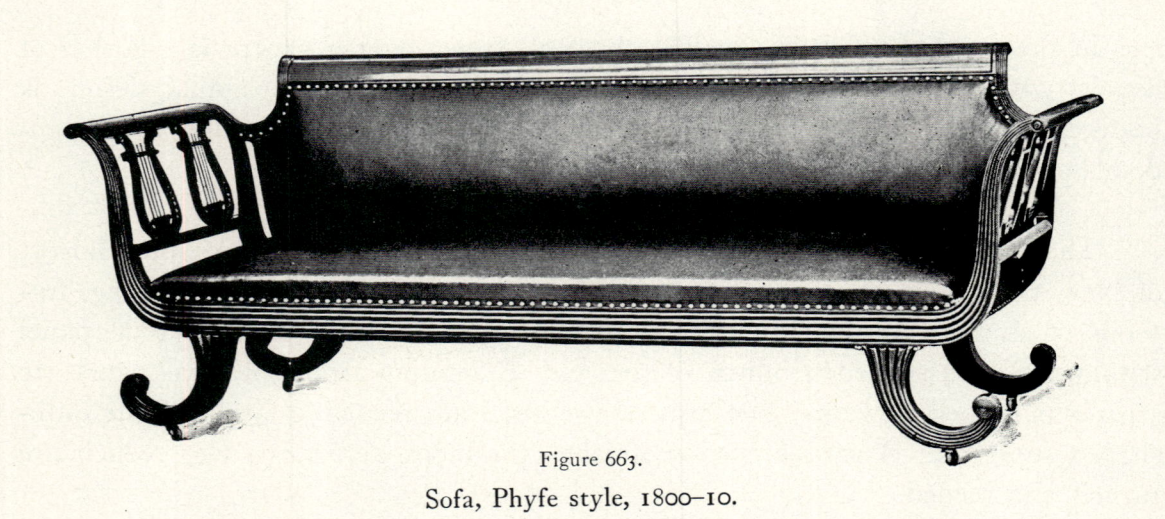

Figure 662.

Sheraton Sofa, about 1800.

Figure 663.

Sofa, Phyfe style, 1800–10.

SETTEES, COUCHES, AND SOFAS

carved narrow border of acanthus leaves. The top and front of the arms are carved in a scale design. The front rail is carved in a beautiful upright acanthus-leaf design with a rosette at the centre. The legs are reeded. The carving on this sofa is of a very fine quality. The shell at the centre of the back is very unusual on a Sheraton piece, but the rosettes and legs place it beyond question in that school.

Figure 664.
Cane Sofa, Phyfe style, 1800–10.

Figure 662 shows a Sheraton sofa which was purchased in 1799 and is now in the possession of the Misses Andrews. The arms with spindle supports and the slender reeded legs are characteristic. Many sofas of this kind, both plain and inlaid, are still to be found in this country.

Following the foregoing type of sofa came the late Sheraton style, with its classic form, of which Figure 663 is a splendid example. This sofa was made by the New York cabinet-maker, Duncan Phyfe, of whom mention is made in the chapter on chairs. The top rail is panelled and is attached to the arms at a single point, giving the piece somewhat the appearance of a French bedstead with a back. The rolling arms are well proportioned and form a continuous line with the front rail. The whole surface is reeded. Each arm consists of two lyres with brass strings. This was a popular theme in the early nineteenth century. The legs are scroll-shaped and reeded. The sofa is the property of Mr. R. T. Haines Halsey, of New York.

Another very fine specimen of a sofa in similar design is shown in Figure 664. The top of the back is divided into three panels; upon the surface of each of the two outer ones is carved, in cameo carving, fasces, and on the centre panel are carved two cornucopias with ends entwined. A smaller pair of cornucopias are carved on each arm. As in the preceding figure, the arms are each composed of two lyres with metal strings. The surface is carved with acanthus leaves. The three cane panels of the back are separated by reeded stiles. The front rail is also reeded. The piece stands on four goats' legs terminating in goats' hoofs. It is the property of Mrs. Ellings, of New York.

Figure 665 shows a small sofa or seat in the Phyfe style. The front is outlined by a long scroll which terminates in the arms on either side. This scroll is

Figure 665.
Cane Sofa, Phyfe style, 1800–10.

finished with rosettes at the ends and at the centre. The legs are curved in an opposite direction and terminate in animal's claw feet. The seat sets within the large scroll and all of the flat surfaces are reeded in the usual manner of the period. The top rail of the back is carved in panels, at the centre is drapery with tassels, and at each side is a bundle of sticks tied at the centre with a bow knot; and the latter pattern is repeated on the sides above the arms. This piece was the property of the late Mrs. Frank H. Bosworth, of New York.

Figure 666 shows another popular design of a sofa of this period. The surfaces are reeded; the legs are scrolled, terminating in brass claw feet. At the turn of the scrolls on the arms are carved rosettes. This style of foot was very pop-

SETTEES, COUCHES, AND SOFAS

ular for tables as well as sofas, and many examples are to be found in this country. One end of the sofa is low, to hold the head reclining. This piece is the property of Mr. Francis H. Bigelow, of Cambridge.

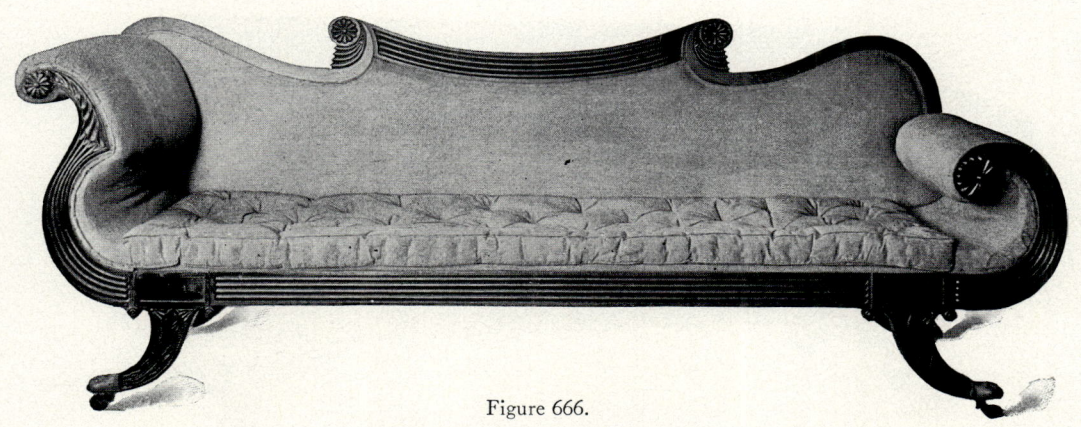

Figure 666.
Sofa in Phyfe style, 1800–10.

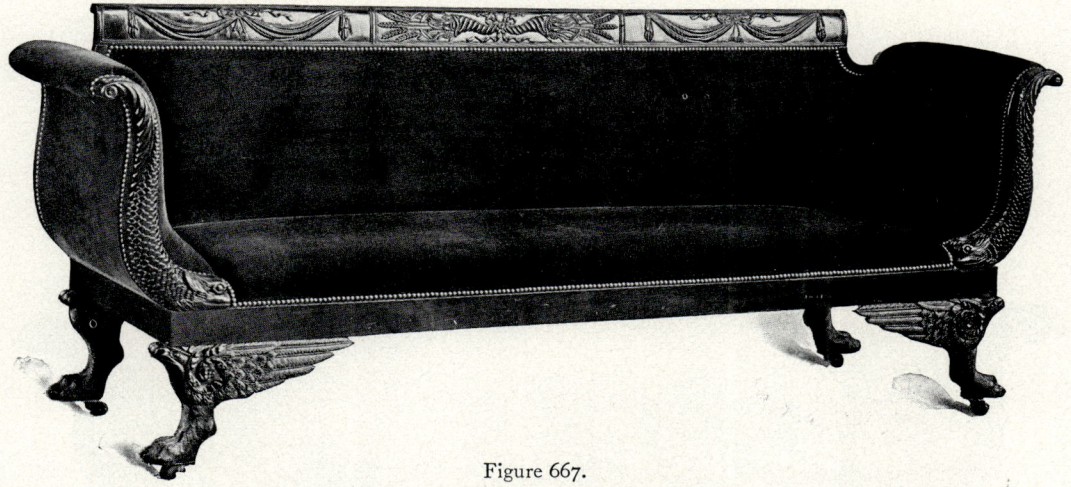

Figure 667.
Sofa in late Sheraton style, 1800–10.

Figure 667 shows a sofa which was the property of the late Judge Arthur F. Eggleston, of Hartford, and which is a good example of the transition between the Sheraton and Empire styles. The top rail is divided into three panels carved in cameo carving, after the manner of the Sheraton school. In the centre one are two cornucopias fastened with a bow knot at the centre out of which project heads of wheat. Drapery caught at the centre with bow knots and tassels decorates the outer panels. The rest of the sofa is in the earlier Empire style. On the front of each arm is carved a dolphin. The feet are well-carved animal's claws, at the head of which are eagle wings extending under the seat rail.

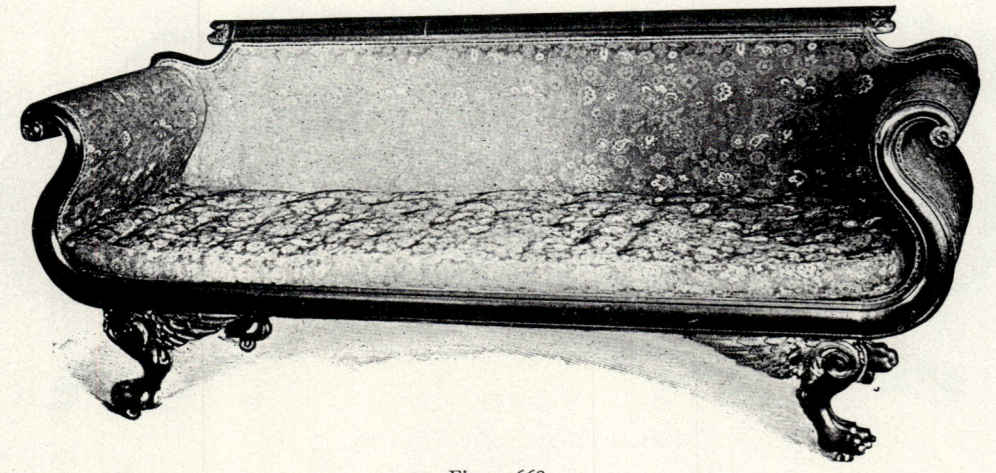

Figure 668.
Empire Sofa, 1810–20.

Figure 669.
Empire Sofa, 1810–20.

SETTEES, COUCHES, AND SOFAS 165

Figure 668 shows another sofa which belongs to the Misses Brown, of Salem, Massachusetts. The arms are in the form known as swan-neck. The legs are made to represent animal's legs with claws, and above are carved wings in imitation of the Egyptian or Assyrian style.

Figure 669 shows a very ornate example of a sofa in the Empire style. The general shape is the same as that shown in the preceding figures. Across the

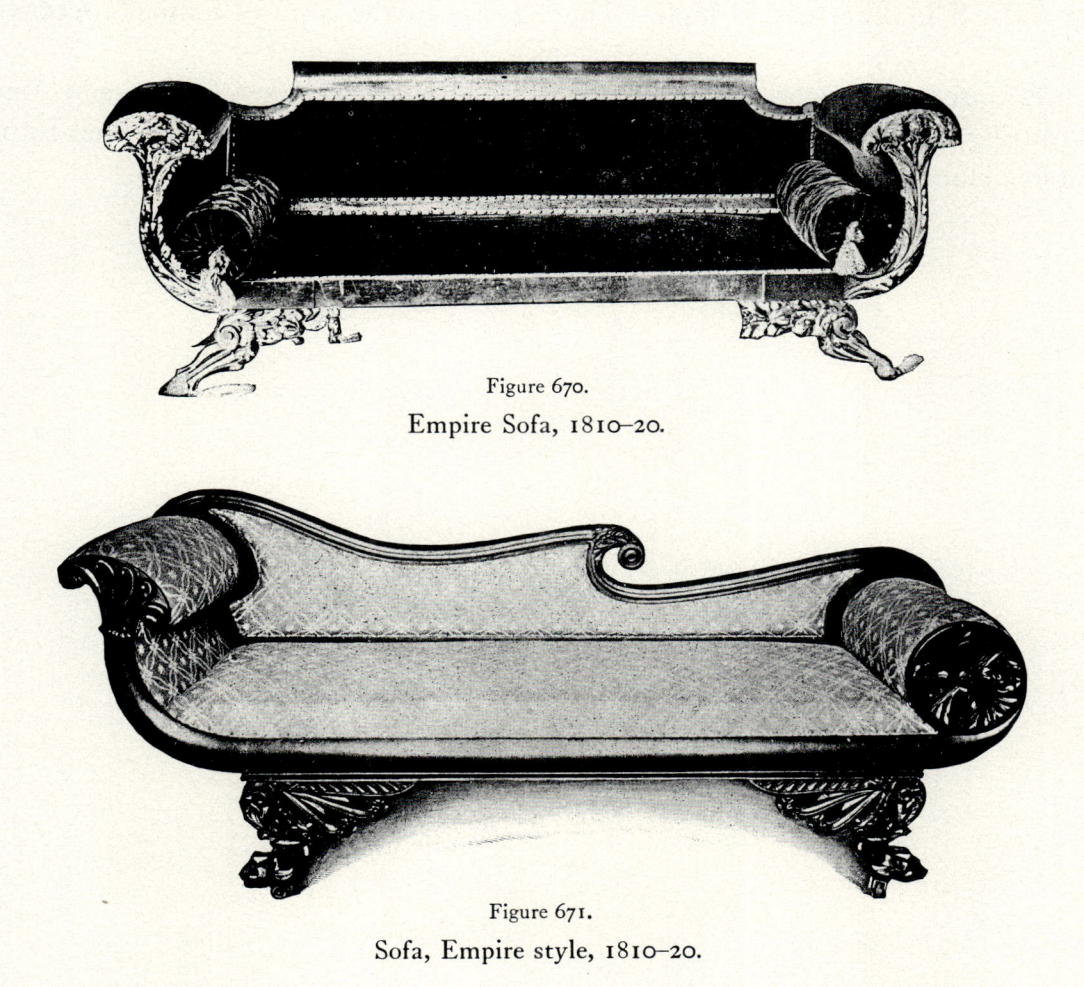

Figure 670.
Empire Sofa, 1810–20.

Figure 671.
Sofa, Empire style, 1810–20.

back is carved an eagle's head with wide, extending wings. The arms are carved to represent dolphins, the tails forming the curves. The legs are also dolphins with heads resting on the floor and the tails twisted and extending to the rails. This sofa is the property of Mr. K. W. Mansfield, of Westport, Connecticut.

Figure 670 is a sofa dating about 1810 to 1820, commonly called the cornucopia sofa, so named from its shape and the carving of the arms. The round pillows shown at the ends of the sofas are known as squabs. The legs of this piece terminate in claw feet and above them is a slab of wood carved in a design of fruits. This sofa is the property of Mrs. L. A. Lockwood.

A common form of Empire sofa had the back finished with a heavy round rail carved at each end.

Another example of an Empire sofa very common in the South is shown in Figure 671. At one end is a squab built in with a large carved rosette finishing the end. The other end is high. The legs are in the form of animal's feet with wings.

Empire sofas such as have been described were extremely popular in America during the early part of the nineteenth century. They were followed by the massive clumsy pieces without carving popular as late as 1850.

IX
TABLES

MANY of the facts already noted regarding chairs are applicable also to tables, as almost every form of chair has its corresponding table.

During Saxon times England did not know or use the word table, but designated what the Normans called tables as "bordes," and that with reason, for their tables were long, narrow "bordes," to be placed on trestles or frames when in use, and it was not until about the year 1600 that standing and dormant tables were freely mentioned.

More early tables have survived than early chairs. The reason is perfectly obvious, as the former were intended to hold dead weight and the chairs were put to the strain of live weight.

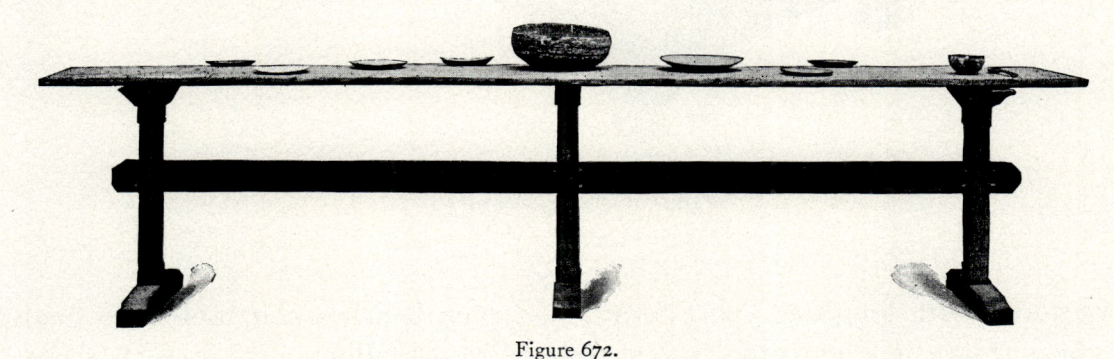

Figure 672.
Table Board and Frame, about 1650.

The oldest American table known and one of the few table boards found in this country is shown in Figure 672 and is from the Bolles Collection. It consists of a loose board 12 feet 2½ inches long and 2 feet wide which rests on three trestles held by a central brace which passes through the trestles and is held firm with wooden pegs. These tables are frequently mentioned in the inventories of the seventeenth century—"1 table board and joyned frame," at Plymouth, in 1638; "1 long table board and frame," at Salem, in 1647; "a great table board and frame," at New York, in 1677; and "a table board," at Philadelphia, in 1687, are some of the items regarding them.

It is not surprising that these table boards did not survive, for they were crude and when no longer used were too bulky to preserve. The only reason that this example has survived is that it had been put in the attic of an old house. The attic had then been partitioned and the table was forgotten until it was discovered a few years ago, when, with great difficulty, it was removed.

Tables referred to as long tables, great tables, and standing tables were probably not made with the frame separate. They are usually accompanied in the

Figure 673.
Wainscot Table, about 1650.

inventories with long and short forms, just such benches and tables, no doubt, as those shown in Figure 158, above referred to. At Plymouth, in 1638, there is mention of "1 table and joyned form," and in 1639, "a framed table"; at New York, in 1669, "1 longe table"; at Salem, in 1673, "a longe table and formes"; at Boston, in 1669, "1 long cedar table"; at Yorktown, in 1647, "1 long framed table"; in 1657, "1 table, 7 feet"; in 1660, "1 long table"—showing that early in the history of the colonies standing tables were also in use.

Figure 673 shows one of these tables in the possession of Mr. H. W. Erving. It is made of American oak. The legs are turned in an early form and the underbracing is very massive and heavy. Each corner of the legs is finished with a bracket, and on the rail is a moulding on which is carved a series of vertical parallel cyma curves above which are carved squares with stars.

TABLES

Figure 674 shows an English frame table belonging to the Metropolitan Museum of Art which is in striking contrast to the simple American frames above shown. The six legs are bulb-turned and at the top of each is carved a crude Ionic capital. The upper part of the bulb is godrooned and below is a grape-and-leaf design. The underbrace is enriched with a dog-toothed inlay and on the rail is carved a flowing pattern of grapes and leaves.

After the table became settled as a distinct piece of furniture, the devices for making it adjustable in size for various occasions came into being. The first of these devices seems to have been the drawing-table, so called because the table was furnished with leaves at the ends which drew out. These leaves were arranged

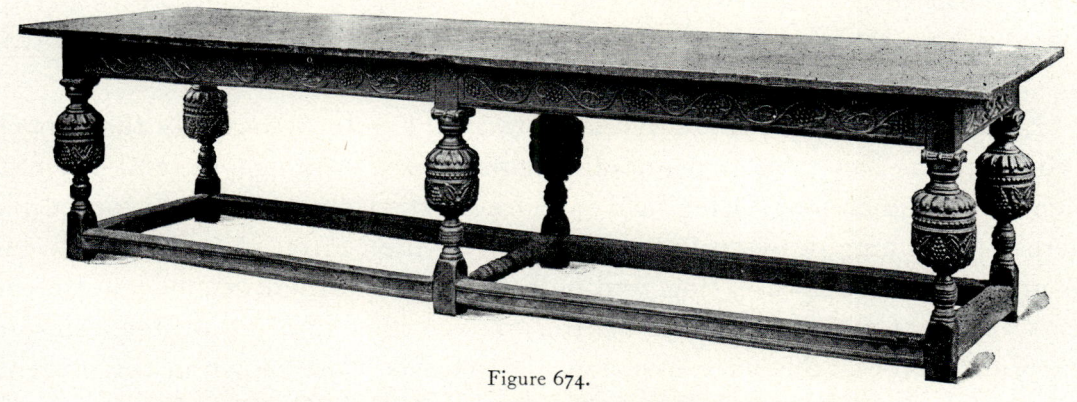

Figure 674.
Carved Oak Dining-Table, first quarter seventeenth century.

to fold back onto or under the main table when not in use, and when drawn out were supported by wooden braces which drew out from the frame and held the ends firmly on a level with the table.

Another method was to have the centre slab of wood held in place by a vertical strip of wood set in a slot which allowed the slab to rise and fall. The two ends were each about half the length of the centre slab and lay under it. They were made to run on a slide tilted toward the centre. The result was that when the slabs were pulled out the centre slab fell into place, making a large table. The frames of drawing-tables were made after the fashion prevailing in the long tables: square and plain, legs slightly turned, or with a large bulb or acorn forming the centre portion.

They are mentioned as follows in the inventories: at Boston, in 1653, "In the parlour, a drawing table £2"; in 1669, "A drawing table and carpett £2 10s"; and at New York, in 1697, "an oak drawing table."

Figure 675 shows a drawing-table preserved at the rooms of the Connecticut Historical Society which is made of American oak, and although the leaves are missing, the place they occupied shows them to have been 2 feet 6½ inches in length, while the top is 6 feet 1 inch in length and 2 feet 11⅜ inches in width. The table, therefore, when opened to its full length, would have been a little over 11 feet long. The rails are ornamented with rectangular bosses with chamfered edges.

Drawing-tables were never common in the colonies if we may judge from the inventories, for they are comparatively seldom mentioned.

Long tables and joined tables continue to be mentioned as late as 1775. They were, it is perhaps needless to say, the dining-tables of their day, and smaller tables made after the same fashion are occasionally found.

Carpets are frequently mentioned with the long tables and were what we should speak of as table-covers or spreads. "A table with a table carpet," in 1690; "a long table and carpett," at Boston, in 1652, are characteristic entries.

Another early American table is shown in Figure 676 and is the property of the writer. The table is made of Virginia walnut throughout, and the top is seven feet one inch long, being held in place on the frame with large turned pins. There are two long drawers and a small one at the centre, all on one side. The legs are turned in the vase, ring, and bulb pattern, and there are heavy stretchers across the ends and through the centre. It is rather difficult to determine just what such tables as this were used for. It suggests those shown in the preceding figures, and the long overhang at the two ends and the underbracing passing through the centre would rather indicate that the table was intended to sit at. It is possible that it was a form of dining-table used contemporaneously with the gate-leg tables. A number of these tables have been found, usually not so large as this one, and occasionally they have underbracing on the sides between the legs. It is possible that this table may have been used for a writing or library table, although it would seem rather large to be used for that purpose. It has also been thought by some that these turned tables were intended to be used as sideboard tables. They are, however, a little low for that purpose, as tables intended for sideboards are usually three or four inches taller than this one.

The form of table most popular in this country during the last half of the seventeenth century was the gate-leg table, so-called because of its construction with one or more gates which swing out from the two sides of the frame to hold the hinged leaves. This style of table is found in many sizes, and when large was the dining-table of the period following the style of dining-table shown in Figure 675. These tables, whether large or small, almost invariably had a drawer at either end. They were commonly made in two ways, one style having six feet touching the floor, and the other having two extra feet below the inner leg of the gate, making eight legs. The frames were made narrow, so that when the leaves were down the table would occupy a comparatively small space. The inner

TABLES

edges of the leaves were usually finished in one of three ways. The more common method was to finish the edges of the top with a quarter-round and the contiguous edges of the leaves with a cove, thus _____ By this method, when the leaves

Figure 675.

Oak Drawing-Table, early seventeenth century.

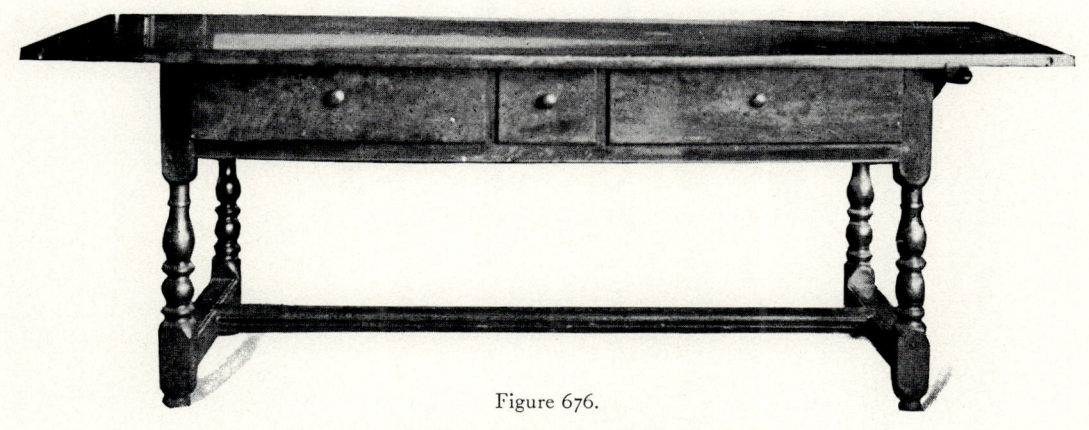

Figure 676.

Walnut Turned Table, about 1700.

are down the hinges are concealed. The second method was to finish the edges of the top with a groove and the contiguous edges of the leaves with a small torus, thus _____ The third method was to finish the edges straight, except for two separate short tenons on each leaf which fitted into two corresponding mortises cut into the edges of the top.

Figure 677 shows a large gate-leg table preserved at Pilgrim Hall, Plymouth, and tradition states that it was used by Governor Edward Winslow in his council chamber. The turnings are of an early pattern and the single gate seems almost too light to hold the large leaf. There are eight feet reaching the floor.

Figure 677.
Gate-Legged Table, first half seventeenth century.

Figure 678.
Gate-Legged Table, about 1650.

A number of medium-sized tables of this sort are found with square tops, and it is probable that they were intended to be used together to form a long dining-table.

Figure 678 shows a gate-leg table with but a single leaf. On the under side of the top were found iron bolts which indicate that it was one of two or three tables intended to be joined to form a long table. It is made of walnut, as were many of the gate tables, and the legs are spiral-turned with plain underbracing. This table is the property of the writer.

TABLES

Figure 679 shows a very good gate-leg table, having the six feet and two gates, which belongs to Mr. Dwight M. Prouty, of Boston. The turnings are all in the knob pattern, which is uncommon on this form of table.

Figure 679.
Gate-Legged Table, third quarter seventeenth century.

Figure 680.
Double Gate-Legged Table, last quarter seventeenth century.

A rare form of gate-leg table is shown in Figure 680 and is from the Bolles Collection. It is very large, and the massive leaves are supported by double gates which swing out from the centre, making twelve legs extending to the floor. It is made of walnut and the turning is in the vase-and-ring pattern. The drawers

Figure 681.

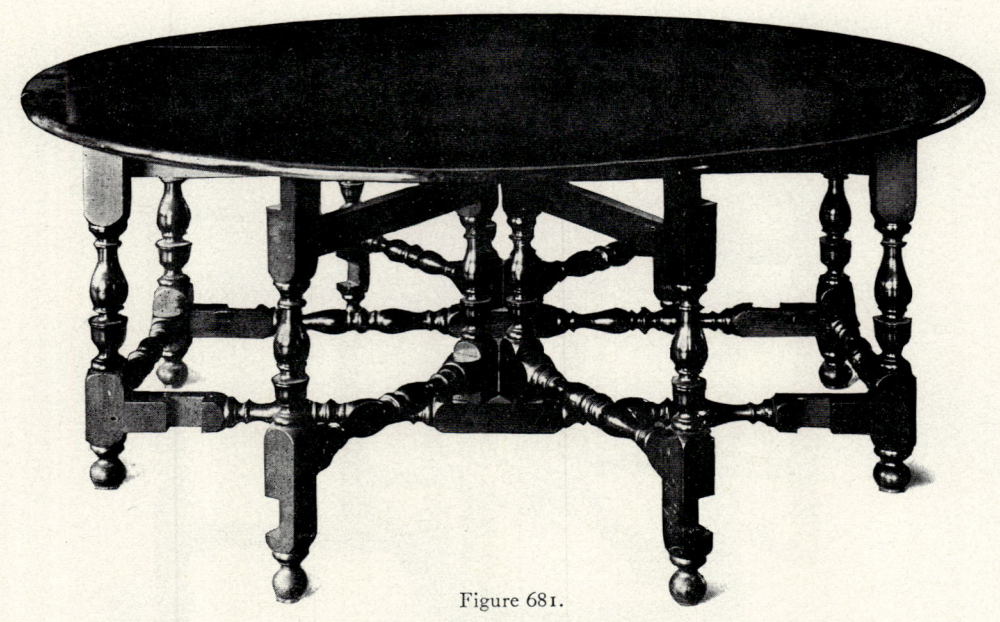

Double Gate-Legged Table, last quarter seventeenth century.

Figure 682.

Gate-Legged Table, last quarter seventeenth century.

TABLES

are missing but were on bottom runners. Very few of these double-gate tables are known. They are generally made of walnut or maple.

Another double-gate table of walnut is shown in Figure 681 and is in the rooms of the Albany Historical Society. It is about the same size as the one last shown, but differs in that the two gates are pivoted at the centre, whereas in the preceding figure they are pivoted at the ends. This form of construction is more

Figure 683.
Gate-Legged Table, late seventeenth century.

graceful as well as more practical, because the legs do not interfere so much with the sitters. The inner legs of the gates do not extend to the floor, consequently the piece stands on but eight feet instead of twelve, as in the preceding figure.

Figure 682 shows a simple gate-leg table of maple, the property of Mr. Dwight Blaney. The legs and stretchers are delicately turned in the vase, ring, and bulb pattern. It is this form of gate-leg table which is most commonly found in this country, although it is unusual to find one with so narrow a frame.

Another gate-leg table in the writer's possession is shown in Figure 683. It is small, measuring but 3 feet 6 inches by 3 feet, and is made of walnut. The turnings are of the type found almost exclusively in the South.

COLONIAL FURNITURE

A rare form of gate-leg table is shown in Figure 684. It has eight Spanish feet and the turnings are in the vase-and-ring pattern. The frame is of cedar and the top is of walnut. At each end is a drawer with a heavy outstanding moulding which acts as a handle. It is the property of the writer.

A small table of the same variety is shown in Figure 685. It likewise has eight Spanish feet, the projection of which beyond the plane of the legs is obtained by applied pieces, while those in the preceding figure are cut from the solid. The turning is in the usual vase, ring, and bulb pattern. It is the property of Mr. G. W. Walker, of New York.

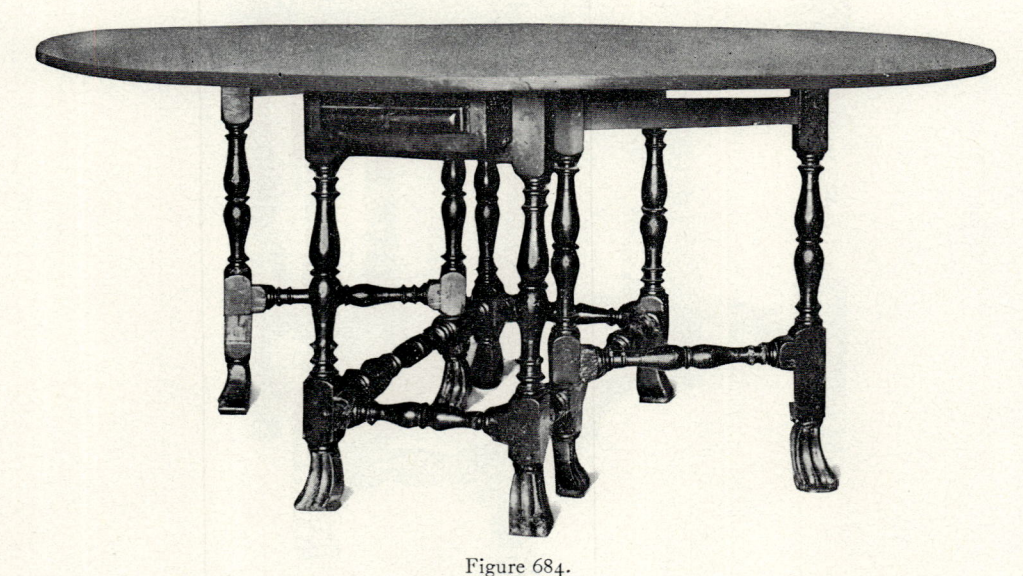

Figure 684.

Gate-Legged Table with Spanish feet, 1690–1700.

Figure 686 shows another gate-leg table with eight legs, made of maple. The turnings are bold and in the usual vase, ring, and bulb pattern, and the corners of the top are rounded.

At Boston, in 1669, "an ovall table £3 10s"; at Philadelphia, in 1688, "a walnut table £2 10s"; at Yorktown, in 1667, "1 ovall table with bolts & catches £3"; at Salem, in 1690, "a round black walnut table £2 5s"; at Boston, in 1699, "a walnut oval table £2"; at Philadelphia, in 1705, "a large oval table £2"; at Providence, 1727, "an ovell table £2 5s," are items which doubtless refer to tables of the gate-leg variety. They are always valued rather high, very seldom under two pounds. These large round and oval tables superseded the long tables and were very generally the dining-tables of their day. Their curved edges must have required the use of chairs rather than the forms used with the long tables. The inventories wherein they appear are those of the well-to-do,

Figure 685.
Gate-Legged Table with Spanish feet, 1690–1700.

Figure 686.
Gate-Legged Table, late seventeenth century.

177

and they may be regarded as the fashionable dining-table of the seventeenth century. The dining-table used by the Van Cortlandt family at the manor-house, Croton-on-Hudson, New York, since early in the seventeenth century, is one very like that shown in Figure 677.

Folding-tables are also often mentioned, and were so constructed that one half of the turned frame folded against the other, and the top fastened by hinges to the frame dropped at the side. The table, when so folded, could not, of course,

Figure 687.
Folding-Table, third quarter seventeenth century.

stand. At Philadelphia, in 1686, a folding-table is valued at six shillings, and, in 1709, "a black walnut folding table" at £1 5s. The "ovall table" at Yorktown, in 1667, "with bolts & catches," above referred to, may have been a folding-table.

Figure 687 shows an early folding-table in the Bolles Collection. It has two turned legs and a gate, all turned, including the upper stretchers, in the sausage pattern. When the gate swings closed the hinged top falls and the piece folds up. It is made of walnut.

Figure 688 shows another folding-table of a little different construction, the property of Mr. H. W. Erving. The pairs of legs are pivoted at the centre, so that when closed the shorter pair fit inside the longer ones and the top falls.

Another form of table, which is practically a folding-table, is shown in Figure 689. It is made on the gate principle with a gate at each side to hold the two

Figure 688.

Folding-Table, late seventeenth century.

Figure 689.

Folding-Table, last quarter seventeenth century.

leaves. The centre portion, however, is narrow and consists of a large turned post with a trestled base. This table, when the leaves are down, is much smaller than the usual gate-leg table. It is the property of Miss C. M. Traver, of New York.

Figure 690 shows another of these tables, from the Blaney Collection, in which the only turning is on the two under posts, the gates and base being of straight strips of wood.

Figure 690.
Folding-Table, last quarter seventeenth century.

Figure 691 shows one of these tables which, when the leaves are down, is but a few inches wide. The table is supported by one leg on each side, as is usual in this type, but it differs from the others in that it has but a single turned stretcher connecting the two legs, and the gates, when closed, are in the plane with them. This type of folding-table was more practicable than those shown in Figures 687 and 688, because when closed it will stand while the others will not. This table is in the Bolles Collection.

A unique table with two leaves is shown in Figure 692, the property of Mr. H. W. Erving. The turned legs are raked after the manner of the so-called "butterfly" table (Figure 693). The legs are braced on the ends and through the

Figure 691.
Folding-Table, last quarter seventeenth century.

Figure 692.
Turned Table with leaves, last quarter seventeenth century.

Figure 693.
"Butterfly" Table, about 1700.

Figure 694.
"Butterfly" Table, about 1700.

TABLES

centre, and from the centre of the middle stretcher is a turning, placed at right angles, to which is fastened the support for the leaves which swing in a similar manner to the gate-leg table. The turnings are in the familiar vase, ring, and bulb pattern.

A style of table of which there are many specimens found in Connecticut is shown in Figure 693. The legs are slightly raked and the leaves are supported by large wings which are pivoted in the stretchers. The form of these supports

Figure 695.
Turned Table, about 1675.

has given the table the name of "butterfly." Of course, were it not for the raked legs, it would be impossible to fasten the supports to the stretchers and have them clear the rail. There is one drawer with raked sides. This piece is the property of Mr. H. W. Erving.

Figure 694 shows another and larger "butterfly" table. The legs have a considerably greater rake than has the one shown in the preceding figure. Tables of this kind usually have straight instead of turned stretchers, and are made of maple or cherry, and rarely of oak.

All through the turned-leg period are found innumerable small tables with round, oval, or rectangular tops, each differing slightly from the other. The earliest were of oak, and the stretchers and the rails were moulded in the manner of the chests.

Figure 695 shows one of these small tables made of oak with a rectangular top. The heavy turnings and underbracings are suggestive of the large oak table shown in Figure 673, and it belongs to the same period. The skirt is cut in ogee curves, and two pendent drops finish the centres of the arches. This table is the property of the Historical Society of Old Newbury.

Figure 696 shows a table a little better than the usual run of small tables. It is made of oak with knob-turned legs and stretchers. The skirt is cut in ogee curves, as in the preceding figure, and three drops finish the lower edge. The drawer is on side runners and has two panels in the manner of the oak chests. On

Figure 696.
Turned Table with panel drawer, last quarter seventeenth century.

the sides and between the panels on the drawers are split spindles, and turtle-head bosses are in the panels. This table is very low and was probably intended to hold a desk-box. It is the property of the writer.

Another small wainscot table made of oak is shown in Figure 697. The turnings are large and the underbracings heavy, which indicates an early date. The skirt is cut from the solid with a flaring serrated edge. This method of ornamentation is quite commonly met with on the tables before 1700. This table is the property of Mr. H. W. Erving.

An interesting table, the property of Mr. Dwight M. Prouty, of Boston, is shown in Figure 698. The legs are turned in the vase, ring, and bulb pattern. Across the front is a drawer on side runners, and another drawer on side runners is shown at the end. The latter is divided into compartments, showing that the piece was intended to be used as a dressing-table.

Figure 697.
Turned Table, last quarter seventeenth century.

Figure 698.
Turned Table, last quarter seventeenth century.

185

An early style of table that was popular both here and in England is shown in Figure 699. The bracing, instead of continuing about the base of the piece as it does in the preceding figures, joins the front and rear legs with a cross-bracing through the centre, and about half-way up the legs are stretchers between the front legs and between the rear legs. The purpose of so arranging the stretchers is apparent, for it would enable a person to sit at the table. It seems almost incredible that so small a table should require so many stretchers, but such was the fashion of the time and it is one of the chief characteristics

Figure 699.
Spiral Turned Table, about 1650.

of the period. The legs and stretchers on this table are spiral-turned, similar to the chair shown in Figure 447, to which period it belongs. It is in the Bolles Collection at the Metropolitan Museum of Art.

Another table in the same collection is shown in Figure 700. The heavy underbracings are seen on the back and two sides, but the front one is turned and placed high, as in the preceding figure. The legs are ball-turned. Two large, elaborately cut frets, separated by a pendant, finish the skirt, and on the stiles on either side of the drawer are rectangular chamfered bosses. A dentil moulding finishes the edge under the top.

Figure 701 shows another table of the same form and construction as that shown in Figure 699. The skirt is cut in a serrated edge and a single-arch moulding is about the lower edge of the rail. The drawer, as is usual in these early pieces, is on side runners. The turning is particularly good, being knob-turned

Figure 700.
Turned Table, second half seventeenth century.

Figure 701.
Turned Table, last quarter seventeenth century.

with a double vase-turning at the centre. This table is the property of Mr. Dwight M. Prouty, of Boston.

Another table of the same sort, but of a little later date, is shown in Figure 702 and is the property of Mr. H. W. Erving, of Hartford. The turning is of the vase, ring, and bulb pattern.

It is probable that such tables as these and the small table shown later are such as were referred to at Salem, in 1684, as "a table with a drawer"; at

Figure 702.
Turned Table, last quarter seventeenth century.

Philadelphia, in 1686, as "1 table with a drawer, 6s"; at Boston, in 1709, as "a square table, 2s." In fact, there was hardly an inventory that did not contain an entry of at least one table of small valuation, called "small," "square," or "short."

It is believed that the small tables above shown were intended to be used to write upon or as dressing-tables.

Figure 703 shows another form of the oval table. The legs are braced at the end and through the centre. The peculiarity about this piece is that the turning of the legs is in the vase-and-ring pattern and the stretchers are in the knob-turning instead of being the same as the legs. There is one drawer on bottom runners. This table is the property of the writer.

Figure 704 shows one of these tables with the legs and stretchers unusually well turned in the vase, ring, and bulb pattern. The top is made in the usual

Figure 703.
Turned Table, about 1700.

Figure 704.
Turned Table, about 1700.

way with a grooved and tongued piece across the ends nailed on. This table is the property of Miss C. M. Traver, of New York.

Figure 705 shows a table with a hexagonal top within which is placed a slate. The inlaid border (Figure 706), it will be seen, is in the same form as that shown on the dressing-table (Figure 63), at which place the reader will find a discussion

Figure 705.
Turned Table, last quarter seventeenth century.

of the slate tables. The legs and stretchers are turned in the usual manner. This table is the property of the American Antiquarian Society of Worcester.

Figure 707 shows a three-legged table with three leaves and a triangular centre. The top turns, thus supporting the leaves by the corners of the frame. The legs are turned in the usual manner and are strengthened with straight stretchers. This table is in the Bolles Collection. Tripod tables with solid tops are not uncommon, but those with leaves are rare.

Figure 708 shows an oval table in the Erving Collection, with raked legs and turned stretchers at the ends and through the centre. The skirt is cut in a double cyma curve so popular in the period. The turnings are a little unusual, with three rings at the centre.

Figure 706.
Top of foregoing table.

Figure 707.

Three-Legged Table, about 1700.

Figure 708.

Turned Table, about 1700.

192

TABLES

Two similar tables from the Bolles Collection are shown in Figure 709. They both have the raked legs and plain straight stretchers. The skirt of the first

Figure 709.
Two Turned Tables, 1700–10

Figure 710.
Candle-Stand, about 1700.

Figure 711.
Tripod Candle-Stand, first quarter eighteenth century.

one is cut in a series of cyma curves and the second in a double cyma curve. The tops of both are oval.

Figure 710 shows an early form of pillar stand with four legs. The legs are turned, heavily raked, and braced at the ends and through the centre with turned stretchers. The top is round. This stand is the property of Mr. H. W. Erving, of Hartford.

Figure 711 shows a tripod candle-stand, the property of Mr. Dwight M. Prouty, of Boston. The round stand is held by a long screw pole which enables one to raise it to any desired height.

An interesting tea-table is shown in Figure 712. The legs are cut and turned similar to the dressing-tables, commonly called low-boys, except that they are

Figure 712.
Tea-Table with tile top, 1690–1700.

in one piece instead of having the ball feet separate, and the X stretcher is mortised into the legs instead of joining the legs and ball feet. The skirt is cut in the early half-round shape, and at the centre of the front is an enormous drop as large as the legs themselves. There is one drawer which has a single-arch moulding about it and early hollow drop handles. A rim extends about the surface of the top and within are set delft tiles. This piece is in the Bolles Collection.

Another table in the same collection is shown in Figure 713. The turnings and cross-bracings show it to be contemporaneous with the six-legged high chest of drawers. The ball feet are separated from the legs in the usual manner by the stretchers instead of being mortised into the legs as in the last figure. The top is octagon, with a slate, and has an inlaid edge, as shown in Figure 706.

Figure 713.
Slate-Top Table, last quarter seventeenth century.

Figure 714.
X-Braced Table, about 1700.

Figure 715.
Card-Table, front view, 1690–1700.

Figure 715.
Card-Table, back view, 1690–1700.

TABLES

Figure 714 shows a simple table in the Erving Collection, and, although the legs are not turned in the cup or trumpet shapes, the cross-stretchers and the separate ball feet stamp it as belonging to the period of the six-legged high chest of drawers. The lower edge of the rail is well moulded and there is one drawer.

Figure 715 shows an interesting card-table both opened and closed. It is built in a half circle with four stationary legs and two which swing out to hold the leaf, a half circle which folds on the half attached to the table frame when not

Figure 716.
Hutch-Table, about 1700.

in use. The legs are turned in the cup shape found in the six-legged high chests of drawers and the stretchers are cut in cyma curves. The feet are scrolls. There are three drawers with double-arch moulding about them, and the skirt is cut in cyma curves with a round arch at the centre in the manner common in the period. The skirt at the back is also finished with the same curves. The top and sides are fine walnut veneer. This is the earliest example of a card-table that has been found in this country. It is the property of Mrs. Bosanko, of Hartford.

Figure 716 shows an interesting tilt-table of walnut in the writer's possession. The top is supported by planks of wood the edges of which are cut in double cyma curves. These sides are mortised into shoes upon which the piece stands. About the base are notched carvings similar to those found on desk-boxes and chests. The top tilts and discloses a small hutch which gives the piece its name, hutch-table.

Figure 717 shows a turned table, quite different from those heretofore shown, which strongly suggests the Dutch influence. The legs are similar to those shown on the scrutoire (Figure 249). The bracings on the ends and through the centre are similar to those found on many chairs. The corners are rounded. This piece belongs to Miss C. M. Traver, of New York.

It may be well to pause here at the end of the seventeenth century, which, as we have seen, marks the end of the oak period, to consider a number of kinds of tables mentioned in the inventories that we are unable to place among any of

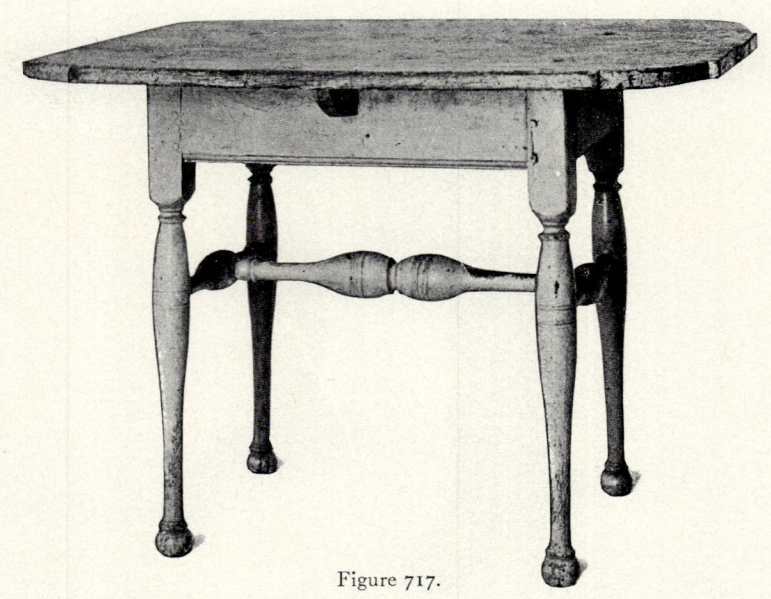

Figure 717.
Turned Table, first quarter eighteenth century.

those already mentioned: at New York, in 1677, "4 Spanish tables 10s"; at Boston, in 1698, "a Jappan table," of what shape and style it is impossible to tell; at New York, in 1686, "2 speck tables"; in 1689, "a dansick table £1," meaning a table from that place, undoubtedly; at Philadelphia, in 1687, "1 inlaid table with a drawer and two stands damnified £1," which may have been a stone table with marquetry border; at New York, in 1702, "1 French table with balls thereunto belonging £3," probably referring to a billiard-table, for they had been invented as early as 1371 by a French artist, and may for that reason have been called French tables; also, in 1702, "a billyard table £3."

With the radical change in style which took place about 1700 came new forms of tables which still followed the fashion of the chairs of the period. The chief characteristics of the tables of this period are the cabriole legs and the use of the cyma curve. Turned tables doubtless continued to be made and used long after the new style came into vogue. The dining-tables of the period had usually two drop leaves which were supported by the swinging out of one or more legs on each side. Tables large enough to seat a family of ten or more are very rare. After the large oak tables were replaced by the gate-leg type, we find, with the exception of perhaps a dozen known examples, that few tables are large enough to accommodate more than eight persons, and the same is true of the period now under discussion. Great quantities of small tables, however, are found. There would seem to be one of two explanations for this: either that several of these tables would be put together, which, of course, would apply only to those having rectangular tops, or that more than one table was used.

Figure 718.
Dining-Table with eight legs, second quarter eighteenth century.

One of the largest dining-tables of this period is shown in Figure 718 and is the property of Mr. H. W. Erving. There are four stationary cabriole legs at each end of the frame, and on each side two cabriole legs swing out to hold the leaf, making eight legs in all. When open, the top is large enough to seat ten or twelve people. The legs all terminate in Dutch feet

Another example of a very large dining-table, owned by Yale University, is shown in Figure 719. It is of unusual construction in that the two legs at each end swing out to hold the leaves and one leg at either side at the centre is stationary. The six legs are cabriole and terminate in well-carved bird's claw and ball feet.

Figure 720 shows an example of the medium-size dining-table of the period, the property of Miss C. M. Traver, of New York. One leg at either end is stationary and the others swing out to hold the leaves. This is the common mode

Figure 719.
Dining-Table with six legs, second quarter eighteenth century.

Figure 720.
Drop-Leaf Table, second quarter eighteenth century.

of construction of the vast majority of these tables. The legs are cabriole and terminate in hoof Dutch feet. The wood is maple.

Figure 721.
Drop-Leaf Table, second quarter eighteenth century.

Figure 722.
Drop-Leaf Table, second quarter eighteenth century.

A large dining-table of the same construction is shown in Figure 721. The legs are cabriole and terminate in the animal's claw and ball feet, and on the legs are carved acanthus leaves. This table is of mahogany and can seat eight to ten people.

Figure 722 shows a rectangular table of the same sort made of walnut. The legs swing in the manner last described and the top is large enough to seat eight

Figure 723.
Twelve-Sided Table, drop leaves, second quarter eighteenth century.

Figure 724.
Drop-Leaf Table, second quarter eighteenth century.

persons. The skirt at the ends is cut in cyma curves and a half circle. The corners of the top are cut in a double ogee curve. The legs are cabriole and terminate in bird's claw and ball feet. This table is in the writer's possession.

Figure 723 shows a twelve-sided table, the property of Mr. B. E. Helme, of Kingston, Rhode Island. Two of the legs swing out in the manner of the tables now under discussion and are straight, terminating in Dutch feet. This form

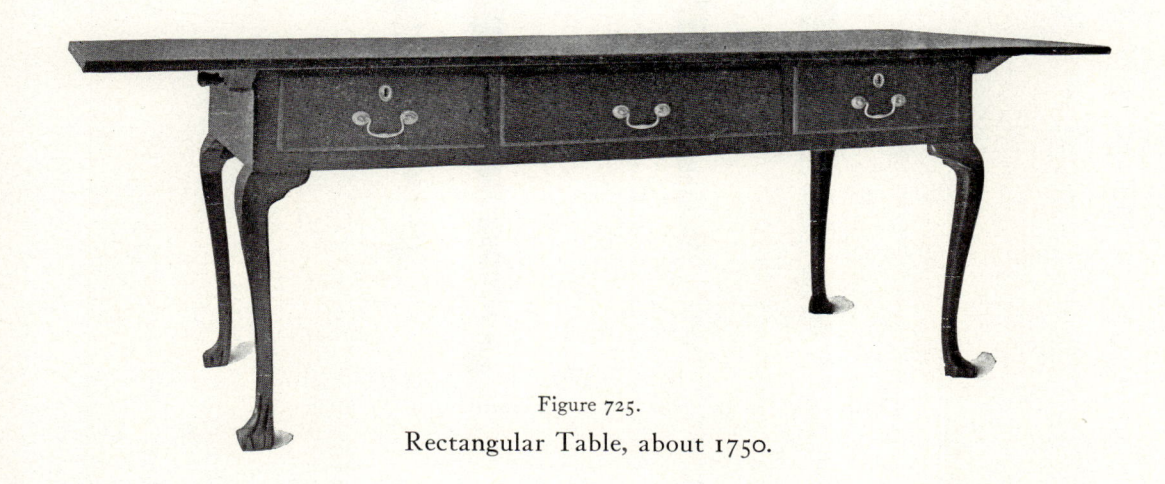

Figure 725.
Rectangular Table, about 1750.

of leg is found almost exclusively in Rhode Island. The writer has seen all sizes and descriptions of tables of this period in that State with the same sort of leg. At either end of the table the skirt is cut in a circular design rarely met with. This table is made of walnut and was probably intended to be used as a dining-table.

An oval table is shown in Figure 724 and is the property of the Tiffany Studios, of New York. The legs are cabriole, with a carved shell on each knee, and terminate in bird's claw and ball feet. The skirt at the ends is cut in cyma curves and a half-round.

Figure 725 shows a rectangular table, the top of which is a large slab of wood fastened to the frame with wooden pegs in a manner similar to that shown in Figure 676. There are three drawers on the side, and the piece stands on cabriole legs terminating in angular Dutch feet. The wood is walnut. As to the use to which this table was put, the reader is referred to the discussion on the subject under Figure 676. This piece is the property of Mr. Dwight M. Prouty, of Boston.

A very small table, the property of the writer, is shown in Figure 726. When the leaves are raised the top is two feet three and one-half inches in

Figure 726.
Drop-Leaf Table, third quarter eighteenth century.

Figure 727.
Three-Legged Drop-Leaf Table, third quarter eighteenth century.

TABLES

diameter. The legs are cabriole, terminating in Dutch feet, and the skirt at either end is cut in a half circle.

Figure 727 shows an interesting three-legged table, the property of the late Mrs. Frank H. Bosworth, of New York. There is one leaf which is held in place by a pull, making a round top. The legs are slightly cabriole and terminate in Dutch feet.

A few tables are found in this country where the cabriole legs are raked in the manner of the turned tables of the earlier period.

Figure 728.
Oak Table Frame with bandy legs, first quarter eighteenth century.

Figure 729.
Tea-Table, about 1725.

Figure 728 shows a frame of one of these tables in the writer's possession. It is made of oak and is perfectly plain, and probably represents an early example of the style. The wooden top is missing.

Tea-tables were popular throughout this period. The earliest record we find in the inventories was at New York in 1705, one at Philadelphia in 1720, and one at Boston in 1732. They were of two varieties, those having four cabriole legs and those on tripod bases.

The first of these varieties was made in two ways, those having a deep skirt and those having a shallow one, and these in turn are subdivided into those having a flaring skirt and those having a straight one.

The first type is shown in Figure 729. The top is rectangular with a raised moulded edge applied. The skirt is cut in sections of a circle. The legs are cabriole, terminating in Dutch feet. This table is in the Bolles Collection at the Metropolitan Museum of Art.

Figure 730 shows another tea-table of this type, the property of the late Miss Esther Bidwell, of Wethersfield. It differs from the preceding one only in the cut of the skirt, which in this example is entirely in cyma curves instead of sections of a circle.

Another example of this type of tea-table in the Bolles Collection is shown in Figure 731. The raised edge of the top is missing. The skirt is cut in a double series of cyma curves and a half circle. The cabriole legs terminate in Dutch feet with a shoe below.

Figure 730.
Tea-Table, about 1725.

The second style of the first type with a flaring skirt is shown in Figure 732, the property of Mr. George S. Palmer, of New London. It has the regular rectangular top with raised edges, and the skirt is flared and moulded, the moulding termi-

Figure 731.
Tea-Table, about 1725.

nating on the legs in a scroll. The legs are cabriole and delicate and are finished with the bird's claw and ball feet. At either end are candle-slides.

A very beautiful little table of mahogany of this same type is shown in Figure 733. The rectangular top does not project over the frame, and the flaring skirt

Figure 732.
Tea-Table, second quarter eighteenth century.

Figure 733.
Tea-Table, third quarter eighteenth century.

is well carved in a leaf pattern. The legs are cabriole, terminating in bird's claw and ball feet, and on the legs is carved an acanthus-leaf design. This table is in the Bulkeley Collection.

The second type of tea-table with a heavy skirt is shown in Figure 734. The top is cut in cyma curves without the raised edge and the skirt is cut in cyma curves and half circles.

Another example of a tea-table of this second type with a flaring skirt, in the

Figure 734.
Tea-Table, second quarter eighteenth century.

writer's possession, is shown in Figure 735. Below the tray top is a wide plain surface and below that a flaring skirt cut in a series of double cyma curves. The piece stands on cabriole legs which terminate in Dutch feet.

Figure 735.
Tea-Table, second quarter eighteenth century.

Another example of this style of tea-table is shown in Figure 736. Under the tray is a drawer and below is a flaring skirt with a small projection at the centre cut in cyma curves and a half circle. The legs are cabriole and terminate in Dutch feet.

Figure 736.
Tea-Table, third quarter eighteenth century.

A little different form of tray-top table, the property of Mrs. E. W. Jenkins, of New Haven, is shown in Figure 737. The tray edge of the top is composed of a fret design with handles at the centre of the sides and ends. The skirt is cut in a series of curves and finished with a carved godrooned edge. At the centre of the skirt is carved a shell with

Figure 737.
Tea-Table, third quarter eighteenth century.

Figure 738.
Tea-Table, domed stretchers, third quarter eighteenth century.

streamers. The legs are cabriole and terminate in bird's claw and ball feet, and the knees are carved in the acanthus-leaf design.

Still a different form of tea-table is shown in Figure 738 and is the property of Professor Barrett Wendell. It is underbraced, with a domed centre composed of C scrolls. The legs are straight, with double ogee moulded surfaces, and at the corners are bracket frets. The top originally had a fret gallery. Very few of this type of tea-table are found in this country.

Figure 739.
Tea-Table, domed stretchers, about 1760.

Figure 739 is shown to illustrate the model from which the preceding table was probably taken. The domed underbracing is the same but with detail carried out to its perfection. The legs are cabriole, terminating in French scroll feet, with surfaces carved in acanthus scrolls. The lower edge of the top is also carved in the same design. The sides and ends are serpentine and a very beautiful fret gallery finishes the top. The table is, of course, English and is the property of Mr. Richard A. Canfield.

Another form of X-braced table is shown in Figure 740 and is the property of Mr. Richard A. Canfield. Small tables with two short leaves became popular in the last half of the eighteenth century and were called "Pembroke" tables. They seem to have been used principally as breakfast-tables. They are found cross-braced and without bracing, and in Chippendale, Shearer, Hepplewhite, and Sheraton styles. This table has cluster-column legs and cross-bracing, and the skirt is cut in Gothic form. The top is serpentine on the sides and ends and the edges are carved in a leaf pattern.

Figure 740.
Pembroke Table, Chippendale style, 1760–70.

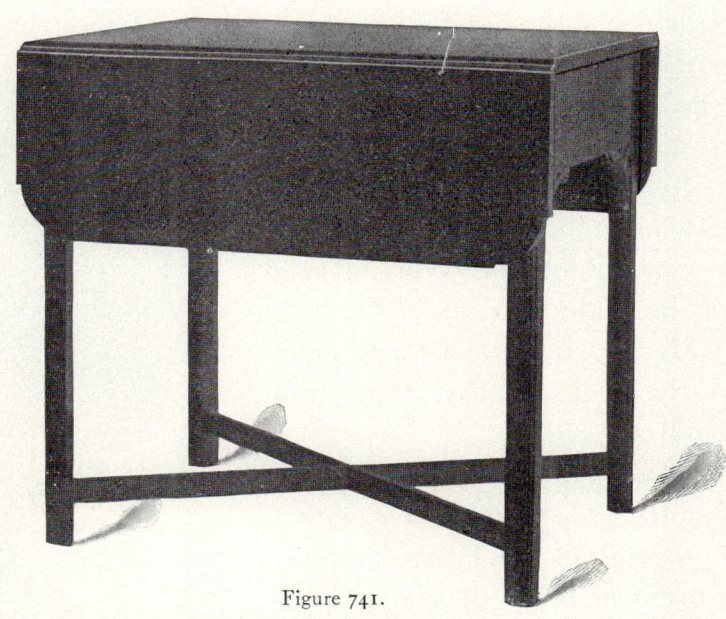

Figure 741.
Pembroke Table, Chippendale style, 1770–80.

A plain form of these tables, of which many examples are found, is shown in Figure 741. The legs and cross-bracing are perfectly plain, but it is apparent that the table is of the same kind as that shown in the preceding figure reduced to its lowest terms. The corners of the leaves are rounded and there are frets at the angles formed by the legs and rails.

Figure 742 shows a bedside-table, the property of the late Mrs. Frank H. Bosworth, of New York. The top has the tray edge. There are three drawers, and the piece stands on small cabriole legs terminating in Dutch feet.

The second variety of tea-table has the tripod base. They are found in great numbers and commonly have either a plain, a dish, a pie-crust, or a scalloped top.

We find an advertisement in the Pennsylvania *Gazette* for July 7, 1737, of tea-table bolts which could have referred to no other type than this.

Figure 742.
Bedside-Table, second quarter eighteenth century.

Tables of this sort were made in many sizes, from the large tea-table to the little candle-stands. The tripod form of construction, though graceful, is faulty, because a strain on the top tends to spread the legs and break them from their sockets. For this reason many of them have iron supports on the under side of the turned centre, strengthening the legs.

The larger tables of this type tilt and many of them both tilt and turn. The tops almost invariably are cut from a single plank of wood, and the edge, if any, is cut from the solid and not applied.

Figure 743 shows a tripod-table with a tray top, the property of the Tiffany Studios. The name is derived from the raised edge cut from the solid. The legs are plain and terminate in bird's claw and ball feet.

The type of tripod-table most sought for is in the form commonly called pie-crust

Figure 743.
Tripod-Table with tray top, second quarter eighteenth century.

TABLES

because of the curving on the raised edge. The almost universal edge is a repetition of a segment of a circle, a recessed half-round, and a serpentine curve. The relative size of these curves vary in different pieces, giving them a different appearance, but upon analysis they will be found to contain the above combination.

Figure 744 shows a plain pie-crust table in the possession of the writer. The top is about twenty-eight inches in diameter and both tilts and turns. The pie-

Figure 744.
Tripod-Table with pie-crust top, 1750–75.

Figure 745.
Tripod-Table with pie-crust top, 1750–75.

crust edge is in the conventional form above described and the turned pedestal and legs are plain.

Figure 745 shows a more ornate pie-crust table in the writer's possession. The top is in the usual form and both tilts and turns. The base has a fluted column and the bulb is carved in an acanthus-leaf design, and on the torus moulding between is a border carved in a design alternating a leaf and a flower. On the knees are carved long acanthus leaves extending nearly to the feet, and on the base between the legs is carved a foliated C scroll. The legs terminate in bird's claw and ball feet.

Another pie-crust table, the property of Mr. George S. Palmer, of New London, is shown in Figure 746. The top is conventional except that the segment curve is a little longer than usual. On the base is a spiral fluting and just above the bulb is a godrooned edge. The lower sections of the bulb are carved in a leaf pattern as is also the small torus moulding below. On the legs are carved acanthus leaves and a cartouche. The legs terminate in bird's claw and ball feet.

Figure 747 shows a pie-crust table where the recessed half circles are accentuated in a manner which quite changes the appearance of the piece, and yet it

Figure 746.
Tripod-Table, pie-crust top, 1750–75.

will be seen to contain a repetition of the three conventional curves above referred to. On the bulb are carved acanthus leaves and on the small torus moulding is carved the egg-and-dart pattern. The knees are carved in the acanthus-leaf design and the legs terminate in animal's claw and ball feet. This table is the property of Mr. Richard A. Canfield.

A variation of a pie-crust edge is shown in Figure 748. The maker, instead of following the series of curves usually employed, has cut the edge in a series of small double ogee curves, within which is a simple raised edge, such as is found on a dish-top table.

The pie-crust tables above shown are the regular type and the simpler modifications. Figure 749 shows one developed to its highest perfection. The edge

Figure 748.
Tripod-Table, ogee edge, 1750–75.

Figure 747.
Tripod-Table, pie-crust top, 1750–75.

216   **COLONIAL FURNITURE**

is composed of a repetition of the double cyma curve and a segment of a circle, but without the concave section which is found in the ordinary type. The edge is carved in a moulding intended to represent lions' teeth, and on the highest point is carved a rope moulding. Inside, next to the plain surface, is a delicately carved

Figure 749.
Tripod-Table, Chippendale style, 1750–60.

acanthus-leaf border. The column of the base is fluted, below which is a lion-tooth border, then a pearl bead edge and an acanthus-leaf moulding similar to that on the edge of the top. The bulb is ornamented with well-carved acanthus leaves. Above the column is a pearl bead edge and an egg-and-dart moulding. On the knees are carved lions' heads and paws. The legs are composed of a series of C scrolls and terminate in scroll feet. The surfaces below the lions are carved in a raised acanthus-leaf pattern and the sides in rococo. This table is the property of Mr. Richard A. Canfield and is, of course, English.

TABLES

Figure 750 shows a pie-crust table with a gallery top in the possession of Mr. John J. Gilbert, of Baltimore. The top is composed of two long serpentine curves on the sides and a large and two small half-round curves on each end. The base is carved with a spiral fluting below which is a godrooned edge, and the

Figure 750.
Tripod-Table with gallery top, 1750–75.

Figure 751.
Tripod-Table with human legs, 1750–75.

lower part of the bulb is also godrooned. The small torus moulding is carved in a leaf design. On the knees are carved acanthus leaves and the legs terminate in bird's claw and ball feet.

Figure 751 shows a very homely form of table, of which quite a number are found, having human legs with low shoes and shoe buckles. The top is round with a carved edge. This table is the property of the Tiffany Studios, of New York.

Figure 752 shows a tripod-table with a scalloped edge, sometimes called a plate or dish top table, because a plate or saucer would about fit in the curves. The base is carved in a spiral turning and on the knees are carved acanthus

218   COLONIAL FURNITURE

leaves. The legs terminate in the rat's claw and ball feet. This table is the property of the writer.

Another form of tripod-table, which is more often found in England than here, is shown in Figure 753 and is known as a dumb-waiter table. There are three tray tops, each carved with a raised pearl edge. Between the trays are vase-

Figure 752.
Tripod-Table with dish top, 1750–75.

turned columns, fluted and reeded, and upon the bulb under the lower tray is carved a leaf design. The knees are ornamented with carving in the form of acanthus leaves, and the legs terminate in rat's claw and ball feet. Each of the trays revolve. This table is the property of the writer.

Figure 754 shows a candle-stand having a raised edge. It closely resembles that shown in Figure 743. The diameter of the top is nineteen inches.

Figure 755 shows still another candle-stand which is in the Erving Collection. The edge of the top is godrooned, otherwise the piece is plain except for the bird's claw and ball feet.

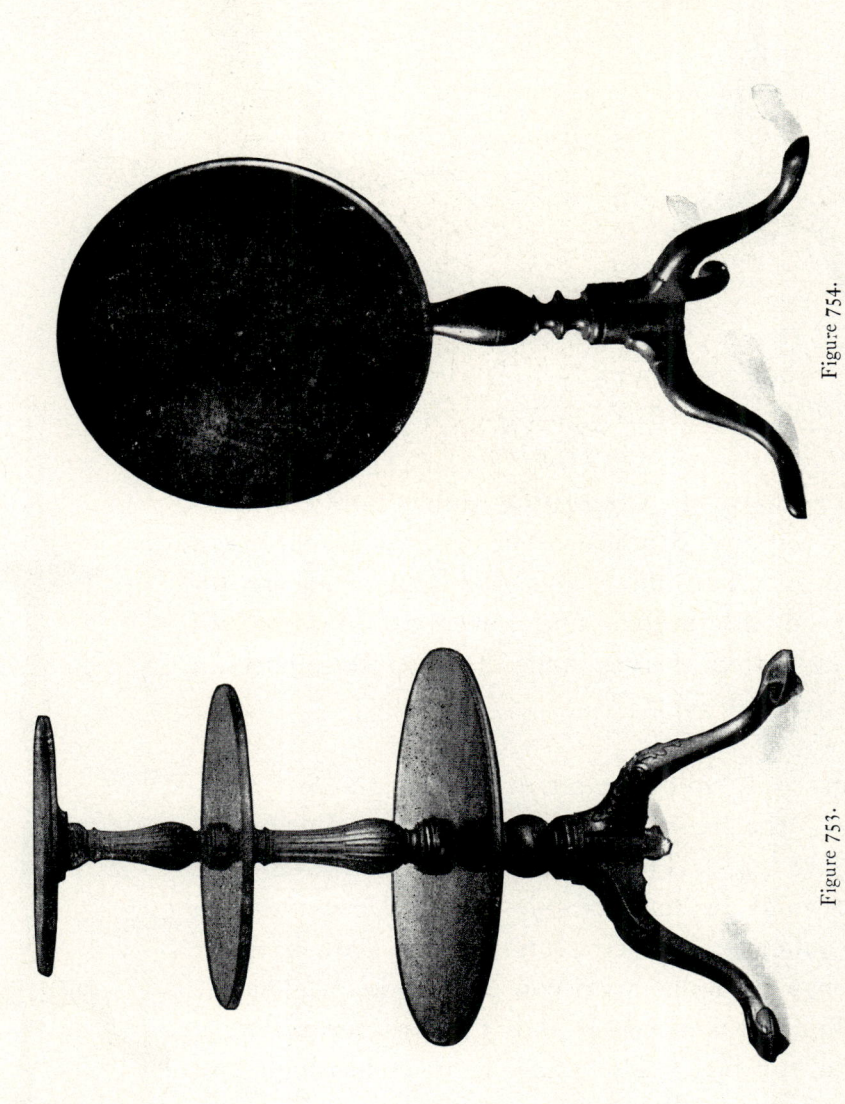

Figure 753.
Dumb-Waiter Table, 1750–75.

Figure 754.
Small Tripod-Table with tray top, second quarter eighteenth century.

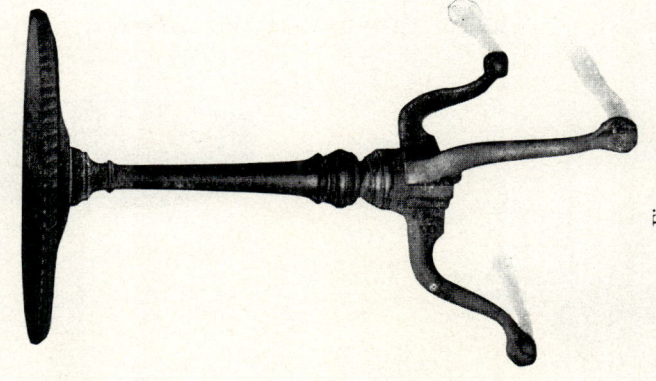

Figure 755.
Small Tripod-Table with godrooned edge, second quarter eighteenth century.

220 COLONIAL FURNITURE

Figure 756 shows a candle-stand in tripod shape, the property of the Misses Andrews. It is exactly like the larger pieces above shown except in size. Tables of this sort were very plentiful throughout the colonies.

Figure 756.
Small Tripod-Table, last half eighteenth century.

Figure 757.
Tripod-Table with octagonal gallery top, 1725–50.

Figure 757 shows an interesting gallery-top table belonging to the Tiffany Studios. The gallery is cut in a fret design and is rather high. The base is plain except for spiral carving on the bulb. The knees are ornamented with carved acanthus leaves and the legs terminate in animal's claw and ball feet.

A very graceful candle-stand in the Pendleton Collection, owned by the Rhode Island School of Design, is shown in Figure 758. The small top has a raised edge cut from the solid in four double cyma curves with a flower at the juncture of each section. The base is made up of two elongated bulbs with concave surfaces. On the knees is a slight leaf carving and the legs terminate in bird's claw and ball feet. This stand is 36 inches high and the top is 9⅜ inches in diameter.

Tall candle-stands are not very common in this country, although a number have been found in the South.

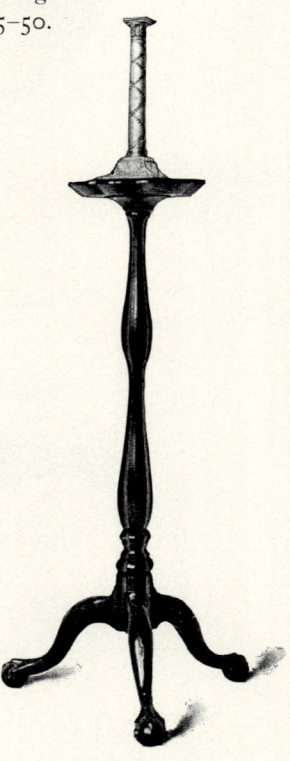

Figure 758.
Candle-Stand, 1725–50.

TABLES

In England they were rather plentiful, and Chippendale shows a number of designs.

Card-tables were plentiful throughout the eighteenth century, and Figure 759 shows a fairly early one made of mahogany. It resembles quite closely the tea-tables of the period. The two top sections are hinged at the back, and when open the leaf is supported by one of the legs which swings out for that purpose. Occasionally these tables are made with both rear legs swinging out to hold the leaf. The corners are blocked, making squares to hold the candle-sticks. The legs are cabriole and terminate in bird's claw and ball feet, and on the knees are carved acanthus leaves.

Figure 759.
Card-Table, 1725–50.

Figure 760 shows another card-table with a plain rectangular top which opens in the manner described above. There is one drawer, and the lower edge of the skirt is godrooned. The legs are cabriole and the feet are of the bird's claw and ball type, and on the knees are carved acanthus leaves.

Figure 760.
Card-Table, 1725–50.

Another card-table which is the property of the Tiffany Studios is shown in Figure 761. It is made in the usual way, the top folding over and being supported by one of the rear legs which swings out. There are circular places at the corners for holding the candle-sticks. On the front is a well-executed design of scrolls in the Chippendale style. The legs are cabriole, terminating in bird's claw and ball feet, and on the knees are carved acanthus leaves and a foliated cartouche from which are pendent a cord and tassel.

Another card-table is shown in Figure 762. The top is shown raised. At the four corners are rounded sections to hold the candles and there are four oval wells to hold chips. The frame is cut with round ends and follows the outline of the top. A godrooned edge with a shell at the centre finishes the skirt. The

Figure 761.
Card-Table, 1750–75.

legs are cabriole and terminate in bird's claw and ball feet, and on each of the front legs is carved a shell and pendent flower which extend up onto the frame. The table is the property of the Tiffany Studios, of New York.

Another form of card-table is shown in Figure 763 and was the property of the late Judge Arthur F. Eggleston, of Hartford. It is in the style known as Chinese, so popular in the time of Chippendale and not uncommon in this country, judging from the advertisements in the newspapers of the day, although very few have been actually found. The top is rectangular, and on the frame is carved a cut fret design in straight lines, while on the legs is carved a fret design in curved lines, and a delicately carved bracket finishes the angles of the table formed by the legs. A carved astragal moulding finishes the lower edges of the frame. Both of the rear legs pull out straight on a hinged frame instead of swinging out in the usual manner; this gives them the name of grasshopper legs.

The later forms of card-tables will be shown with the tables of that period.

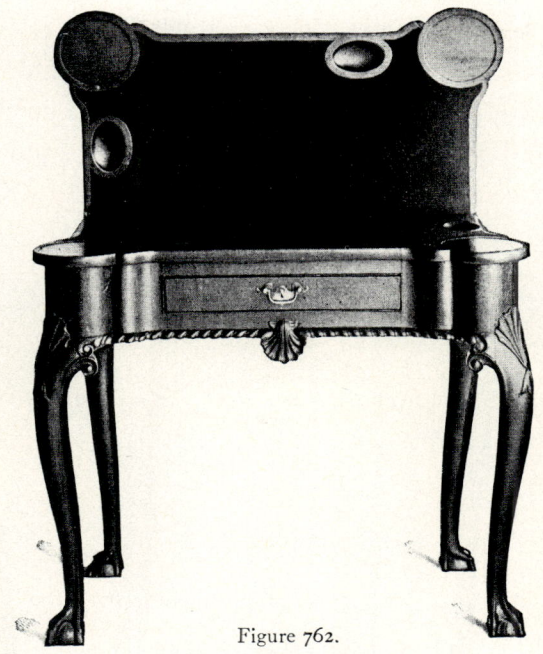

Figure 762.
Card-Table, 1725–50.

Figure 763.
Card-Table, 1750–75.

224 COLONIAL FURNITURE

Another form of table of which a few specimens are found in this country is shown in Figure 764 and are called pier-tables. Such as have been found are more ornate than other kinds of tables, probably because they were only used in the more pretentious houses where the finer furniture would naturally be found. This table is in pure Chippendale style and was found in Philadelphia, and is quite in keeping with the high chest of drawers shown in Figure 107 and the chair in Figure 556, both of which likewise came from that city. On the skirt are cut

Figure 764.
Pier-Table, marble top, 1750–75.

foliated scrolls which originally extended below the lower edge, but most of these have been broken off. At the centre is a carved figure. The legs are cabriole and terminate in French scroll feet with rococo shoes, a favourite design of the Chippendale school. The surfaces of the legs are carved with C scrolls, foliated scrolls, and acanthus leaves. The top is marble and follows the outline of the frame cut in cyma curves. This table is the property of Mr. George S. Palmer, of New London.

A number of pole screens have been found in this country, of which Figure 765, the property of Mr. Dwight Blaney, is a typical example. The base is of the usual tripod type with turned columns similar to that found on the tilt-top tables. Above the base is a pole which terminates in a turned finial. A rectangular screen slides on the pole to any desired height. These screens were usually covered with needle-work, brocade, or other fabric.

Another pole screen a little more elaborate is shown in Figure 766. It is constructed in the same way as that last shown, but the knees are carved with

TABLES

shells and pendent flowers and the legs terminate in rat's claw and ball feet. A piece of needle-work is framed in the rectangular screen which has a carved moulded edge.

Tables of walnut, cherry, and mahogany, with more or less carving, with cabriole legs with and without ball and claw feet, remained in fashion from about

Figure 765.
Pole Screen, third quarter eighteenth century.

Figure 766.
Pole Screen, second quarter eighteenth century.

1720 until 1780, when the Hepplewhite designs became very generally used. The tables just considered, covering the period between 1740 and 1780, correspond in date with the Chippendale period in England, and it may be correctly said that they are in general Chippendale; the wood is commonly mahogany, except in Pennsylvania and Virginia, where walnut continued to be extensively used for the finer pieces throughout this period, and the decoration, carving, and the outlines are those that he elaborated and perfected.

It is somewhat of a problem to determine what were the dining-tables of

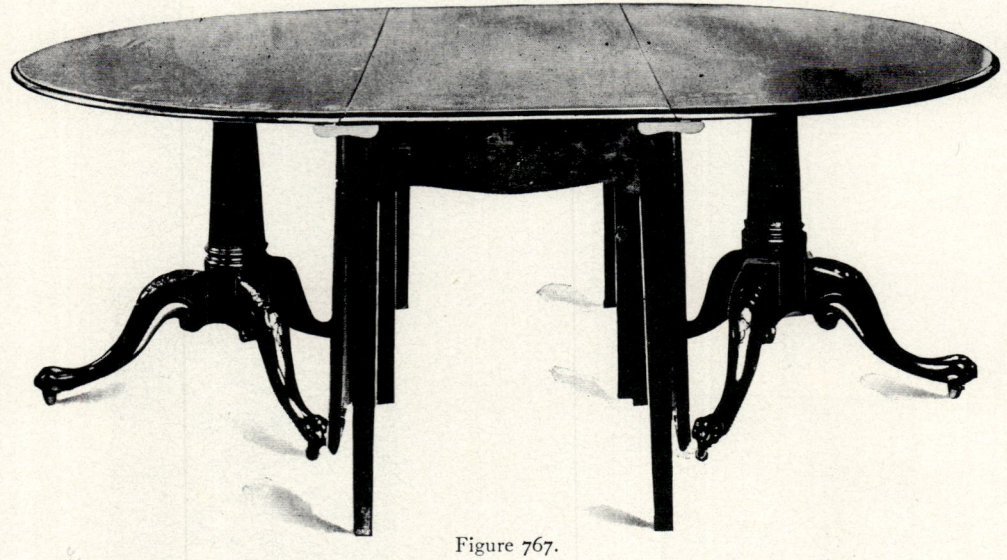

Figure 767.
Dining-Table, about 1775.

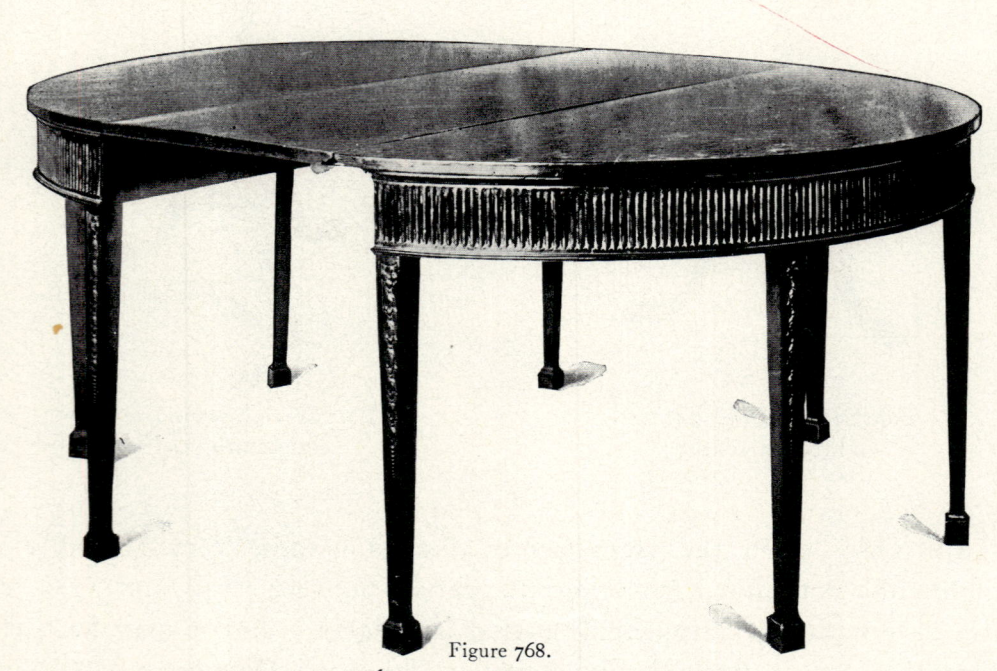

Figure 768.
Dining-Table, last quarter eighteenth century.

TABLES

the Chippendale period. Neither Chippendale nor his contemporaries give any designs for them, and it is probable that the same form of table continued to be used that was popular in the Dutch period. At Boston, in 1760, appears the following entry in an inventory: "2 square mahogany tables 6s," and in 1770, "2 mahogany ends for tables." These were probably the tables made in twos and threes to be placed together.

A late Chippendale dining-table is shown in Figure 767. It is the property of Dr. G. C. F. Williams, of Hartford. It consists of two tripod standards at the ends with bird's claw and ball feet and with carved acanthus leaves on the knees,

Figure 769.
Dining-Table, 1800–10.

and at the centre is a frame with six straight legs and two leaves. These leaves can be raised and joined to the tripod ends, making a long dining-table. The columns are fluted and reeded and the surfaces of the straight legs are finished with a double ogee and bead moulding.

After the adoption of the Hepplewhite and Sheraton styles, between the years 1780 and 1800, the cabriole leg was dropped and the straight square leg or the slender fluted leg took its place on furniture of every kind, and carving was superseded by inlay or marquetry. The wood continued to be principally mahogany.

Figure 768 shows a dining-table composed of two half-round tables, to one of which is attached a leaf which raises and attaches to the other. The frame is fluted and the eight legs are tapering and terminate in spade feet and are ornamented with carved pendent flowers. This table is the property of the Tiffany Studios.

A form of dining-table quite popular in the early nineteenth century is shown in Figure 769. There are three bases, each with four columns carved in the acanthus-leaf design, and four legs the upper surfaces of which are composed of a convex and a concave curve terminating in brass claw feet. On the convex surface of the legs are carved acanthus leaves. The centre standard has no leaves, but each of the ends has one on the inside which, when open, locks into the centre section. This form of table was popular with the cabinet-makers of the period, of whom Duncan Phyfe, of New York, is the best known. This table is the property of the Metropolitan Museum of Art.

Figure 770 shows another dining-table of the same period, closed, which was the property of the late Mrs. Frank H. Bosworth, of New York. There are

Figure 770.
Dining-Table, 1800–20.

Figure 771.
Dining-Table, about 1810.

four lyre-shaped standards. The outer ones have three cyma curved legs and the inner ones have but two legs, and all terminate in brass claw feet. The inner standards are attached to the frame, and when the table is opened they separate, supporting the leaves at proper intervals.

The extension top in this form was invented by Robert Gillow, of London, in 1800 and is the same as that found on the modern tables.

TABLES

Another form of extension dining-table is shown in Figure 771. When closed the legs fold up and it forms a square table. When open the legs spread, as are shown, and four leaves can be inserted. The legs are turned and the only ornaments are rosette bosses at the ends. This table is the property of the Tiffany Studios.

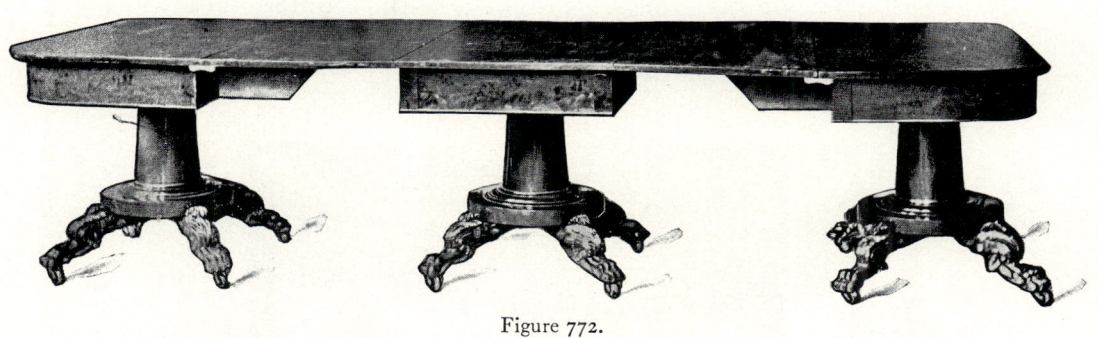

Figure 772.
Dining-Table, about 1820.

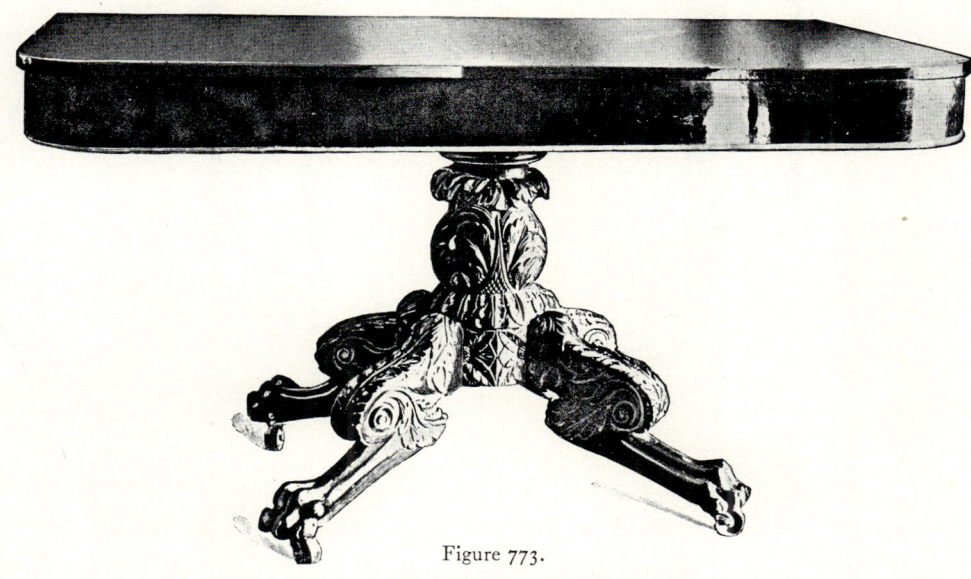

Figure 773.
Part of Dining-Table, about 1820.

A still later form of dining-table is shown in Figure 772. It has three pedestals, circular in form, with four carved claw feet in Empire style. The ends have no leaves but the centre section has two which raise and fasten to the ends. This table is the property of Mr. Charles R. Morson, of Brooklyn.

Figure 773 shows an end of a table similar to that shown in the last figure. The base is well carved in the characteristic coarse Empire carving in acanthus-leaf and pineapple designs. The legs have the usual shoulders and claw feet. This table is the property of Mr. Merle Forman, of Brooklyn.

During the last quarter of the eighteenth century card-tables were very common, and large numbers of them have survived in Hepplewhite and Sheraton styles.

A very beautiful inlaid card-table, in Hepplewhite style, is shown in Figure 774 and is the property of Mr. John J. Gilbert, of Baltimore. The top is a half-round and is divided into five panels. A wide border of inlay finishes the outer

Figure 774.
Card-Table, 1775–1800.

edge of the top and a half circle of inlay is at the back. A satin-wood border forms panels on the frame and at the top of each leg is an inlaid medallion. The legs are tapering and have a pendent flower design inlaid on their surfaces.

Another Hepplewhite card-table, the property of the Misses Andrews, is shown in Figure 775. The corners are cut in the recessed quarter-round design which was very popular during the last ten years of the eighteenth century. The inlay consists of a narrow border of holly on the frame and forming panels on the legs, and at the centre of the skirt and above the leg are lozenge-shaped panels formed with the same wood. When the top is opened it is supported by one of the rear legs which swings out in the usual manner.

Figure 776 shows a card-table in Sheraton style, the property of Miss Manning, of Hartford. The front of the frame is swelled and the sides are formed in

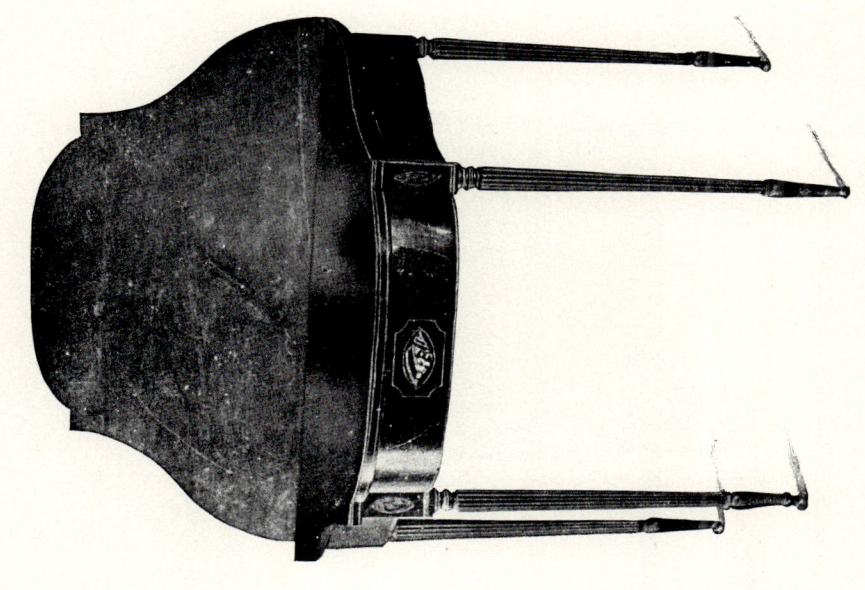

Figure 776.
Card-Table, 1790–1800.

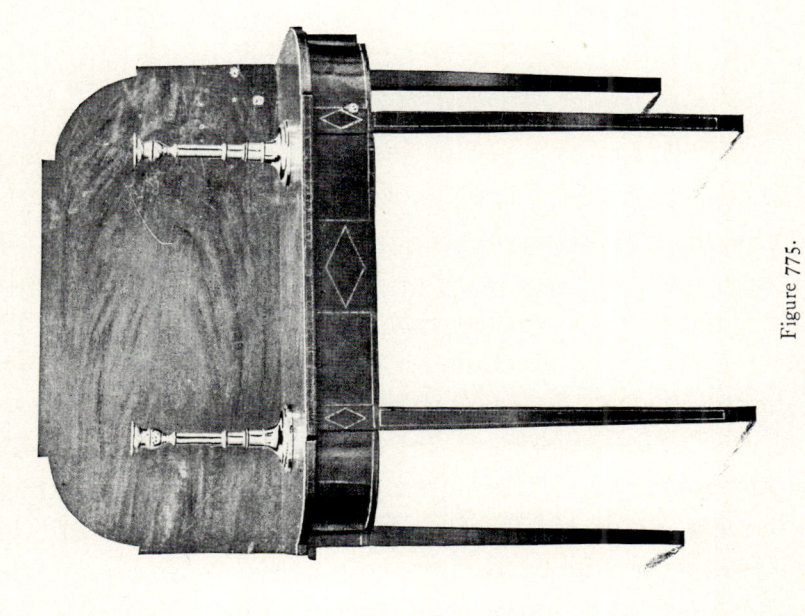

Figure 775.
Card-Table, 1790–1800.

cyma curves. The top follows the outline of the frame. The table, when open, therefore, has a serpentine curve on the long sides. At the centre of the frame and above the legs are inlaid shells. The legs are tapering and reeded.

A form of card-table of the Sheraton period, which is very graceful and of which many examples are found, is shown in Figure 777. The front is slightly

Figure 777.
Card-Table, 1790–1800.

swelled and the top curves out over the round top of the legs. The front and sides have inner panels of satin-wood and a narrow border finishes the edge of the top and skirt. The legs are turned and reeded in the form common on Sheraton pieces. This table is from the Bolles Collection.

With Sheraton's late designs, about the year 1800, the fine outlines that distinguished the cabinet-work of the eighteenth century passed out of style, and in their place came the rather uncouth and heavy designs known as Empire. As almost all the genuine old furniture now to be found for sale in this country follows this fashion, it will be well to consider it somewhat. After the French Revolution there was a reaction against everything that had formerly been in favour in art as well as in social realms, and there was an effort to bring in a completely new fashion in furniture. The design of Empire furniture is largely a

TABLES

revival of the classic, particularly of the Egyptian classic, brought about by the Napoleonic expedition. The use of the sphinx head, with the bear's and lion's foot, the column mounted in brass or gilt, the classic tripod for the frames of tables are all distinguishing features of this style. American Empire followed, to some extent, a fashion of its own, and adopted from the French what best suited the maker. The use of bronze was not extensive here, but brass was used to some extent for the feet of the tables, chairs, etc., and for pillar mountings; the handles were very generally the lion's head with the ring or rosettes. The lyre, one of Sheraton's favourite designs, was much liked for table supports and for decorating the backs of chairs. It may be said with truth that no finer

Figure 778.
Card-Table, Phyfe style, about 1810.

mahogany was ever used than that employed in the Empire sideboards and tables. The carving often is very good, but coarse, and the veneering the very best of its kind.

A card-table made by Duncan Phyfe, the New York cabinet-maker, is shown in Figure 778 and is the property of Mr. R. T. Haines Halsey, of New York. The top is octagonal and turns on the frame to support the top when open. The base is composed of two lyres crossing each other at right angles, and the strings on the lyres are brass. These strings are occasionally made of whalebone. The lyre frames are carved in an acanthus-leaf design, and on the sides and edges is carved a curve in a rope pattern. There are four legs, the edges curved and carved in a rope pattern. The feet are brass lions' claws.

234　　　　　　COLONIAL FURNITURE

The Empire card-table shown in Figure 779 is in the style of Duncan Phyfe. The standard has the double lyres and the legs have a concave curve terminating in brass claw feet, which was his usual design. The top turns on the frame and is supported by bringing the hinges across the frame. It is the property of Mr. Meggat, of Wethersfield.

Figure 780 shows a late form of card-table made at Salem, Massachusetts, by Nathaniel Appleton about the year 1820 and now in the possession of his

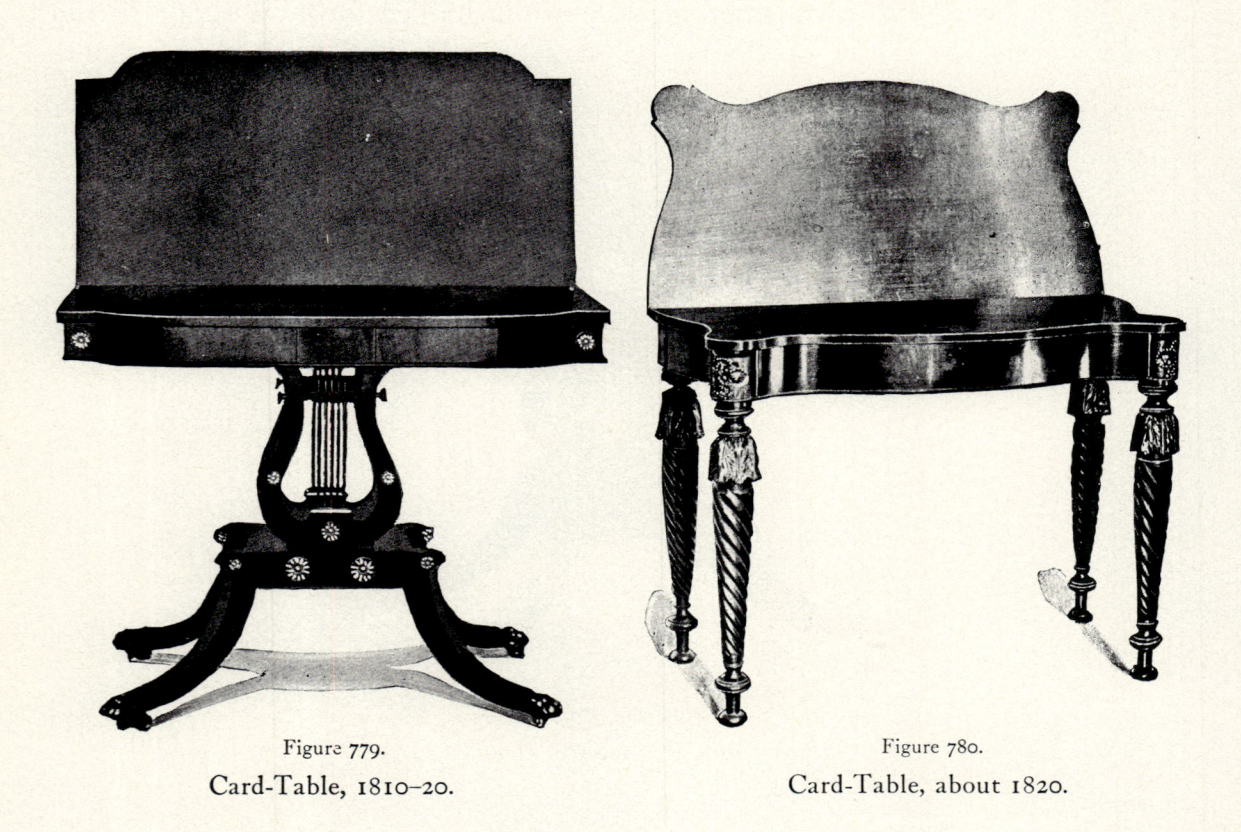

Figure 779.
Card-Table, 1810–20.

Figure 780.
Card-Table, about 1820.

granddaughter, Mrs. Brown. The spiral carving on the legs and the acanthus cup-shaped capitals are familiar designs on the bedsteads and other furniture of the period.

Figure 781 shows a Pembroke table which is the property of Mr. H. W. Erving. The top is cut in serpentine curves. At the top of each leg is a carved rosette and the drawer front is fluted. On the lower edge of the skirt is carved the reel-and-bead pattern. The legs are tapering and the surfaces are slightly concave.

Figure 782 shows an oval table in French walnut which is a Pembroke table in Hepplewhite style. The top is inlaid about an inch from the edge with a narrow

Figure 781.
Pembroke Table, last quarter eighteenth century.

Figure 782.
Pembroke Table, 1780–90.

Figure 783.
Pembroke Table, 1780–90.

Figure 784.
Table, Phyfe style, 1800–10.

TABLES

line of ebony outlined with white holly. On the legs are inlaid pendent flowers bordered with ebony and holly, and above the legs are three inlaid strips of holly.

Figure 783 shows a Pembroke table in Sheraton style. The top is of satin-wood bordered with rosewood. The decoration on the legs consists of strips a quarter of an inch in width at the top, tapering to an eighth of an inch at the

Figure 785.
Table, Phyfe style, 1800–10.

bottom, of rosewood inlaid in satin-wood. The two preceding tables are the property of the writer.

Figure 784 shows another table made by Duncan Phyfe, in the Halsey Collection. There are two drop leaves with triple curves. The frame has one drawer and at each corner are drops. The base has a centre column carved in an acanthus-leaf design, and the four legs are in the characteristic form with acanthus leaf and reeding carved on the surfaces. The legs terminate in brass lions' feet.

Still another form of Duncan Phyfe table, the property of the Metropolitan Museum of Art, is shown in Figure 785. There are two drop leaves with triple curves, and in the frame is one drawer; and drops are at the four corners, as in the preceding figure. The base is composed of four small columns carved in an acanthus-leaf design and the legs are cabriole. The edges are carved in a fern-leaf design, and at the end of each leg are a rosette and a small leaf.

238   COLONIAL FURNITURE

Figure 786 shows a tripod tilt-table with a square top, the property of Mr. H. W. Erving. The edge of the top is raised and the turning indicates a rather late date. The legs terminate in rat's claw and ball feet.

Figure 787 shows a tripod-table in Sheraton style. The top is octagonal with raised edge. The column is reeded and the feet turn under in the manner

Figure 786.
Tripod-Table, about 1780–90.

Figure 787.
Tripod-Table, 1790–1800.

characteristic of the Sheraton school, which is the reverse of the earlier type. This table is the property of Mr. H. W. Erving.

Another tripod table in Sheraton style, the property of the Metropolitan Museum of Art, is shown in Figure 788. The top is octagonal, the base is turned in a vase pattern, and the legs are in the usual Sheraton form, terminating in spade feet.

A handsome dumb-waiter table of this style, the property of the Metropolitan Museum of Art, is shown in Figure 789. There are two trays, the edges of which are finished with the reel-and-bead moulding. The two columns are fluted, and fern leaves are carved on the vase-turnings below. The legs, four in number,

TABLES

are in the usual Sheraton form, ending in spade feet, and on the edges of the legs is carved a simple fret design.

Figure 790 shows a pole screen of the period on a plain tripod base. The screen is oval and filled in with needle-work. It is the property of the Metropolitan Museum of Art.

Figure 788.
Tripod-Table, about 1800.

Figure 789.
Dumb-Waiter Table, 1785–90.

Figure 791 shows another pole screen of the period, the property of Mrs. Eustace L. Allen, of Hartford. The base is in the usual tripod style, perfectly plain. The screen is shield-shaped with an embroidered picture. The finial on the pole is a carved flame.

An interesting dressing-case on legs is shown in Figure 792, the property of the Metropolitan Museum of Art. The top contains a toilet-box, and at either end are lion ring handles. The four legs are in the concave curve of the Phyfe school and terminate in brass lions' claws, and the base is supported by a circular stretcher.

240 COLONIAL FURNITURE

Figure 793 shows a music-rack in the Phyfe style. There are five compartments for music in the upper section. Below that is a long drawer and still lower is an open shelf. The sides are lyre-shaped, the base representing inverted lyres. This is the property of Mr. Dwight M. Prouty, of Boston.

Figure 790.
Pole Screen, about 1790.

Figure 791.
Pole Screen, about 1790.

Delicate little sewing-tables were popular in the late years of the eighteenth century. Sometimes the tops would lift, disclosing a cabinet with compartments designed to fit sewing utensils. Often there was a pocket attached to a frame at the bottom within which to keep the sewing.

Figure 794 shows a Sheraton work-table in the writer's possession. It is made throughout of satin-wood and painted. On the top is an allegorical group and a border of flowers and leaves, and vines and flowers are painted on the

Figure 792.
Toilet-Case, 1800–10.

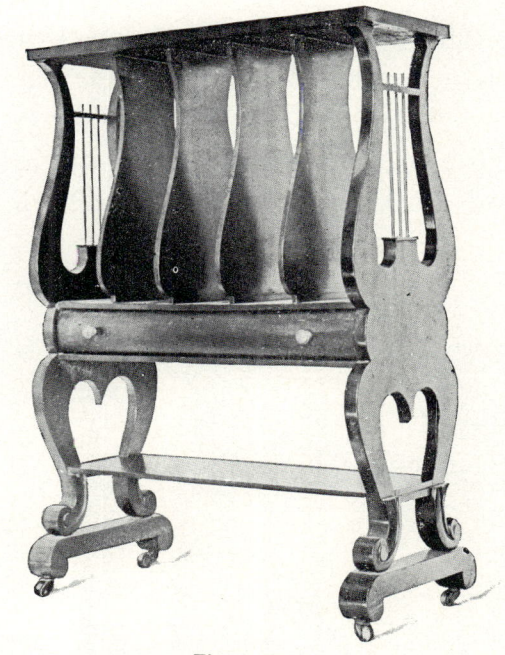

Figure 793.
Music-Rack, 1810–20.

Figure 794.
Sewing-Table, 1800–10.

Figure 795.
Sewing-Table, 1800–10.

drawer, sides, and back, and at the centre of the back is the monogram of the owner. There is one drawer below which is the pocket drawer. The legs are round, with turned rings, and the surface is covered with painted leaves and vines.

Figure 795 shows another form of sewing-table. The cylinder ends are tambour and are intended to hold the sewing. The top lifts, disclosing a place to

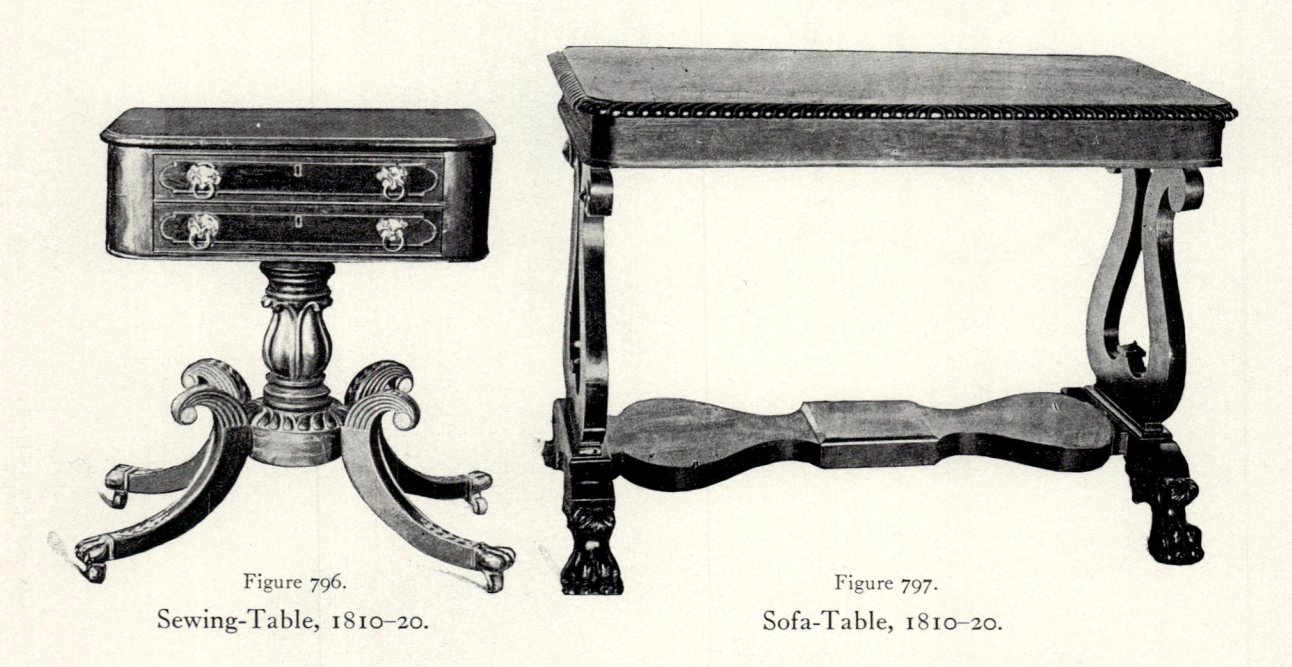

Figure 796.
Sewing-Table, 1810–20.

Figure 797.
Sofa-Table, 1810–20.

write, and small compartments are at the sides. These side compartments contain trays which lift off to give access to the space below. There are two drawers. The piece stands on a pedestal with four concave curved legs, typical of the Phyfe period, and the feet are balls. This table is the property of Mr. H. W. Erving.

Figure 796 shows a work-table with brass lions' feet. It stands on a curved base with four C-shaped legs on which is carved a leaf pattern.

Figure 797 shows a long, narrow table finished alike on all sides, which is known as a sofa-table, because it was intended to be used for books and papers beside such a piece. The edge of the top is godrooned and the standard is lyre-shaped. The feet are the usual animals' claw feet found on Empire pieces.

X
BEDSTEADS

THERE is, perhaps, no branch of the subject of furniture more difficult to approach than that of bedsteads, and this not because they were by any means scarce, but because the bedsteads of the seventeenth century in this country have utterly disappeared, and the inventories give such meagre descriptions that almost the only clues are the valuations there given, and a study of the English bedstead of the same period.

There is, of course, a distinction between a bed and a bedstead, more marked a century ago than to-day—the bedstead being the frame or furniture part, while the bed referred to the mattress.

In England, before the Norman Conquest (1066), and even in the period immediately following, bedsteads were scarce, reserved for the master of the house or ladies, there often being but one to a house, while the other members of the household lay on mattresses of straw laid on the floor or on tables, chests, or benches.

The bedsteads were sometimes built into the walls like bunks, but more often had four massive posts, with top and sometimes sides of wood, and heavy curtains, making a sort of sleeping-chamber in itself, and, it is asserted, were sometimes placed out of doors. However this may be, in some of the old manuscripts and tapestries we find bedsteads represented with tiled roofs, which would indicate that they were exposed to the weather. At any rate, when we consider that the castles and homes of that early day were without glass or other protection for the windows, we can readily understand why that particular style should have originated.

The style, having been brought into existence by necessity, developed along the same line toward a more graceful and delicate design, first losing the sides of wood but retaining the high head-board; then in the early Jacobean period the high head-board gave way to a lower one with curtains at the back and with smaller posts; later the solid wood top was superseded by a frame designed merely to hold a canopy of various kinds of cloth.

The bedsteads in use in England at the time this country was settled were made of oak, often elaborately carved in designs such as are found on the oak furniture here. They were large and cumbersome, and therefore difficult of transportation, and, except in the South, whither English life had been transported bodily, we doubt very much whether in the first fifty years very many found their way to this country. Some, however, must have found their way to New England, for Miss Helen E. Smith, in "Colonial Days and Ways," gives a portion of a letter sent to a correspondent in England, in 1647, by Mrs. Margaret Lake, a sister-in-law of Governor Winthrop, in which she asks to have sent her, among other things, "a bedsteede of carven oake (ye one in which I sleept in my fathers house) with ye valances and curtayns and tapistry coverlid belongyngs."

During the last three-quarters of the seventeenth century the fashion in England was to have plain, slender bed-posts, which were covered with fabric so that no wood showed. The oak bedsteads continued to be used until as late as 1700.

Figure 798 shows the famous Countess of Devon's bedstead which is preserved at the South Kensington Museum. This illustration is given, not because we believe such beautiful bedsteads were in use in this country, but because it is a splendid example of the general type of carved oak bedsteads which must have been here, such as was mentioned by Mrs. Lake, and also because it combines to an unusual degree the patterns of carving found on many of the chests and other carved oak pieces in this country, thus tending to prove the statement heretofore made that practically all of the early carving on oak furniture in this country was taken from English models. Many of the designs shown on this bedstead are to be seen on the chests and cupboards found in this country. The carving is, however, of a much higher order, and the grotesque figures seen on the bedstead we have never found on American pieces. This bedstead, with its heavy oak tester and head-board, also illustrates the development of the bedstead from an enclosed chamber. It dates in the last years of the sixteenth century.

This bedstead represents very well the carved oak bedsteads of the better class in use in England during the early seventeenth century, and there is no reason to doubt that some of the bedsteads inventoried at high figures in the colonial records were much like this one, though far less elaborate. Thus, at Yorktown, Virginia, in the estate of a Dr. McKenzie, who died in 1755, are mentioned "1 oak Marlbrough bedstead £8," and another of the same sort valued at £6, both of which are far above the usual valuation.

In New England records we find, from the first, in nearly every inventory, mention of feather beds, valued at from £2 to £3, a very high valuation, often equal to that of all the rest of the furniture put together. The probable reason is that all the early feather beds were brought here by the settlers, for it could be

BEDSTEADS

hardly possible that such a quantity of feathers as these beds would require could have been taken so early from domestic chickens and geese. At Plymouth, in 1633, is mentioned "1 flock bed and old bolster £1 3s"—flock beds being

Figure 798.
Oak Bedstead, late sixteenth century.

made of chopped rags; at Salem, in 1647, "a straw bed," and in 1673, "a canvas bed filled with cattails" and "a silk grass bed"; in 1654, "a hair bed"; and at New York, in 1676, "a chaff bed"; all of which items are repeatedly met with throughout the inventories both North and South, showing that almost any soft substance was utilised for the beds when feathers were not obtainable. In many instances these beds were probably placed on the floor, for in many inventories they are mentioned without any bedsteads whatever.

Many of the earliest bedsteads of which the records speak were doubtless merely frames on which to place the mattresses or beds; judging from the valuations, such frames may be referred to at Plymouth, in 1633, "1 old bedstead and form 2s"; at Yorktown, in 1667, "2 bedsteads, 2s"; one at 5s., and "one bedstead & buckrum teaster 6s"; at New York, in 1669, "2 bedsteads 16s"; at Philadelphia, in 1682, "1 bed bolster and bedstead £1"; at Providence, in 1670, "two bedsteads £1"; and in the inventory of John Sharp, taken at New York in 1680, the following somewhat minute descriptions of the furnishings of the sleeping-rooms occur: "In the small room, a bedstead with a feather bed, bolster, a couple of blanketts, a rugg and an old pair of curtains and valins £5 3s"; in the middle room, "a bedstead with a feather bed and bolster, a rugg, a blankett, a little square table and a form £5 5s"; in the great room, "a bedstead with a feather bed, a bolster, 2 pillows, a blankett, a rugg, old hangings about the bed and old green hangings about the room and a carpett £6," while "a feather bed, bolster, blankett and coverlid" are inventoried separately as worth £3 10s., thus intimating that rather a small part of the total values can belong to the bedstead. We may also conclude that these simple bedsteads, whatever they were, were furnished with curtains and valances, which are mentioned with them almost without exception. In fact, throughout the inventories, with the exception of those of a few of the wealthier settlers, the values of bedsteads when given by themselves are surprisingly low. Again, we find throughout the Philadelphia records the expression "ordinary bedsteads," and these placed at valuations not exceeding 15s., and more often below 10s.; and, further, the bedsteads, in a large majority of inventories both North and South, are included with the beds and furnishings, usually mentioned last, as of least importance.

On the other hand, we find occasional mention in wills of bedsteads in particular rooms left specifically, as property having special value, and, as in the case of Mrs. Lake before mentioned, some at least of the finer sort must have reached this country.

At Plymouth, in 1639, "a framed bedstead" is spoken of, and at Salem, in 1647, "a joyned bedstead." As "framed" and "joyned" are terms used to describe the wainscot chests and chairs, the bedsteads described in this way were probably something more than simply frames for drapery. Their valuations in these cases, however, 14s. and 16s., respectively, do not allow us to think that they were carved or ornamented in any pretentious way.

In 1643 a bedstead with tester, and in the same year a half-headed bedstead, are among the items. The word tester is derived from the old French word *testiere*, a kind of head-piece, or helmet, and came to mean in English the frame for holding the canopy about a high-post bedstead. A tester, or headed bedstead, would therefore imply a high one, while a half-headed bedstead doubtless was one without the tester, or head-piece, and with low posts.

That some of the bedsteads were built bunk fashion into the walls is implied by the use of the term "standing bedstead," as though to distinguish them from those built in this way.

"Close bedsteads," "cupboard bedsteads," and "presse bedsteads" are also mentioned and must have been arranged so that when not in use they could be folded into a cupboard in the wall and probably hidden by doors. These are valued somewhat higher than the kinds already mentioned, averaging about 30s. A "presse bed" we find defined in Johnson's dictionary as "a bed so constructed that it may be folded and shut up in a case."

In the South the bedsteads during this period are more highly valued, as might be expected, for nearly all the furniture of Virginia and Maryland was imported from England and was doubtless of the carved wainscot variety then prevalent in that country. At Yorktown, in 1647, is a record of "2 old bedsteads," which would indicate that they were imported, and, in 1657, another of "1 bedstead £3."

Although many of the bedsteads of the South were imported, yet we occasionally find in the inventories some which were made here, as, for instance, in 1659, "a Virginia-made bedstead" is mentioned.

After about 1660 the values of the bedsteads and furnishings are much higher, and those in the North and South became more nearly alike. At Boston, in 1660, one is valued at £24; at Richmond, Virginia, in 1678, one is valued at £24 5s.; at Plymouth, in 1682, the "best bedstead and furnishings" was £9; at New York, in 1691, "bed and furniture in the great room £24"; "one in the dinning room £18"; "one in the lodging room £15"; and "four others £36"; at Boston, in 1696, two very handsome bedsteads and furnishings were valued at £70 and £100 respectively; but, of course, it is impossible to tell what was the value of the bedstead and what that of the furnishings, which were often extremely valuable.

Such bedsteads as these might easily have been of the handsome carved oak kind shown in Figure 798, for when we consider the fact that the prevailing style for all other kinds of furniture during this time was the wainscot carved or the panelled style, and that the bedsteads in England during this time were of that same type, there is every reason to believe that the finer bedsteads in this country were of this same variety.

It has never been the writer's good fortune to find an example of a bedstead which, with any certainty, could be assigned to the seventeenth century, and such pieces seem totally to have disappeared. There are probably two reasons for this. First, as we have before suggested, the large portion of bedsteads were simple frames for holding drapery, and not in themselves worth preserving; and, second, in the South, where there must have been some of the handsomely carved oak bedsteads, there seems to be a complete dearth of seventeenth-century pieces, due to the devastation of two wars and the wealth of many of the people enabling them to replace the old-fashioned with the new, thus relegating the heavy oak furniture, which, in the light of the radically different fashion which replaced it, was probably considered very unsightly, to the cabins of the slaves, where it was broken up or otherwise destroyed.

In New England, where practically all the examples of seventeenth-century furniture now known have been found, the less extravagant habits of the people caused them to be more conservative; but, notwithstanding this, most of the fine chests, cupboards, etc., recently unearthed have been found in attics, woodsheds, or barns, partly destroyed and nearly always painted and maltreated in every way. Cupboards, tables, and chairs could for a while serve their useful purposes in kitchen or woodshed, but a bedstead, when discarded, could not be utilised for any useful purpose and was consequently destroyed.

Miss Helen Evertson Smith, author of "Colonial Days and Ways," informs us that she remembers, many years ago, going to the home of the widow of Peter G. Stuyvesant, at the corner of Eleventh Street and Second Avenue, New York City, and seeing there a state bedstead with elegant hangings which was said to have belonged to Governor Stuyvesant, and on the third floor a bedstead which she describes as follows:

"Another bedstead, not so beautiful as this one, but more plentifully (if not so finely) carved, stood dismantled in a rear third-story room, and had, apparently, been intended to fit into an alcove, as all the carving was on one side. A pair of carved and panelled doors opened beneath the high bed-place. The closet thus formed may have been used for bedding. The place for the beds was a sort of box deep enough to have held three or four mattresses or feather-beds, laid, without the intervention of anything to answer the purpose of springs, directly upon the age-darkened boards. At each corner rose a carved post from six to seven inches in diameter, as I now guess. The two front posts were square as far as they formed the ends of the closet beneath the bed, and round as they rose above this till they merged into a carved cornice of over a foot in depth. The two rear posts were halves laid flat against a heavily panelled rear wall."

This would seem to have been a handsome cupboard-bedstead, but the writer has been unable to locate it or to find whether it is still in existence. These cupboard-bedsteads we find frequently mentioned throughout the inventories, which would indicate that they were popular, probably because, being built into an alcove, they took up but little room; and this would also account for the fact that they have so entirely disappeared, for, being built for a particular room, they would have been of little use elsewhere, and when families moved or remodelled their houses these bedsteads would have been destroyed.

BEDSTEADS

Couch-bedsteads are mentioned occasionally in the Northern inventories, and very frequently in the South; in fact, there is hardly a Southern inventory of any size during the first hundred years which does not mention at least one couch-bedstead. These were, as their name indicates, couches which could be utilised for sleeping purposes.

Figure 799.
Oak Cradle, sixteenth century.

As several cradles dating before 1700 have been found in this country, we will briefly describe them here before proceeding further with the discussion of bedsteads.

There were apparently two styles of cradles, one swinging between uprights which stood firm on the floor, the other swinging on short rockers; but, so far as this country is concerned, the former style, though antedating the latter in Europe, does not seem to have appeared here until much later.

Figure 799 is an example of one of the latter style made of oak, the top and side of the hood made with turned spindles, much after the fashion of Elder Brewster's chair, shown in Figure 415. This turned style is extremely old, and we have found such pieces illustrated as early as the fifteenth century. This particular cradle is the finest that has come under our observation in this country, and is probably late sixteenth or early seventeenth century. It is now at Pilgrim Hall, Plymouth.

Another cradle at the same place is shown in Figure 800. This piece, it will be seen, is made of wicker, and tradition says that it came over in the *Mayflower* and was used for Peregrine White. The fact that it is made of wicker can easily

Figure 800.
Wicker Cradle, early seventeenth century.

be explained by the fact that the Pilgrims came from Holland, which at that time was engaged in the India trade, and this piece was undoubtedly of Eastern origin.

After about 1700, in England, the fashion of high ceilings having been introduced, the bedposts were correspondingly lengthened, and some were twenty feet tall. These, as formerly, were heavily draped, the bedsteads being plain or covered with fabric. In this country the ceilings continued to be made low, and simple slender posts were used which were either round, octagonal, or fluted.

We find at Philadelphia, in 1709, "a black walnut bedstead £1"; at Providence, in 1726, "2 bedsteads 10s," and in the same inventory, "1 bedstead and bedding £13"; and in 1734, "14 new bedsteads £14." Occasionally a will throws a little light on the subject, as in the case of the will of Thomas Meriwether, of South Farnham Parish, Essex County, Virginia, February 10, 1708: "I give my dear and loving wife Susanna my best new bed and furniture and the set of chairs belonging to it. The whole sute of Japan." At Providence, in an inventory of 1730, appears, "a feather bed & pannoled bedstead £10," which was probably an oak bedstead of an earlier date.

BEDSTEADS

The bedsteads in this country were probably heavily draped, as they were in England, and an example of this heavy drapery will be seen in Figure 801, which is an enlargement of the second-floor bed-room of the doll house shown in Figure 1.

Figure 802 shows a simple walnut bedstead dating rather early in the eighteenth century. The lower posts are simply fluted and the base is square. The

Figure 801.
Miniature Bed-Room showing draperies, first quarter eighteenth century.

head-posts have chamfered edges and the head-board is plain. Such a bedstead as this was intended to be fully draped either in stuffs or crewel-work. The back would be covered with the fabric, and head-curtains which would slide on rods were on either side. The tester was finished with a valance and the top was often covered. The foot-posts were covered with curtains, which were likewise on rods and could be so drawn as to enclose the entire bedstead. A bedspread would be made of the same material and a valance would finish the bottom under the bed frame.

Another early bedstead is shown in Figure 803. The foot-posts are round and terminate in crude bandy legs. The head-posts are chamfered and the head-board plain, as in the preceding figure.

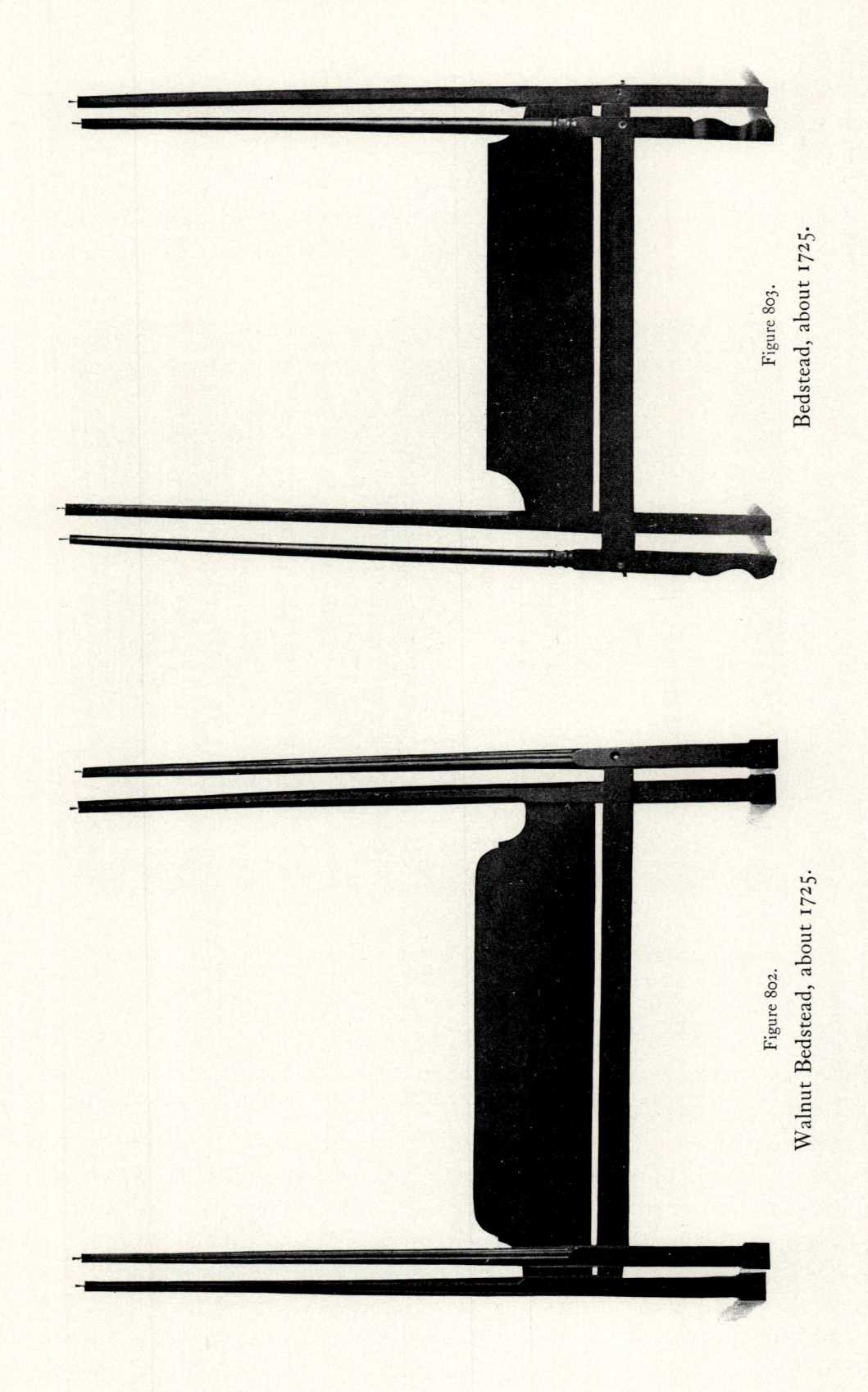

Figure 803.
Bedstead, about 1725.

Figure 802.
Walnut Bedstead, about 1725.

BEDSTEADS

An unusually beautiful set of bed-hangings, made of crewel-work, is shown in Figure 804 and is the property of the museum at the gaol at York, Maine. It was made by Mrs. Mary Bulman, whose husband, Dr. Alexander Bulman, died at the siege of Louisburg in 1745, and in a letter to a friend, dated October, 1745,

Figure 804.
Bedstead draped in crewel-work, 1745.

she mentions beginning the work to occupy her mind. The hangings consist of the head and foot curtains embroidered in a flowing design of flowers and leaves, an upper valance showing trees and verses from hymns, a curtain across the head of the bed embroidered in trees, flowers, baskets of flowers, and birds, and a bedspread to which is fastened the valance embroidered in the same design as the back. Very few of the early bed-hangings have survived, which makes this set doubly interesting.

About 1720, bedsteads became more ornate and the better ones had claw and ball feet.

254   COLONIAL FURNITURE

A very beautiful example of the bedstead of the period is shown in Figure 805. It is the property of Mr. Richard A. Canfield. The foot-posts are carved in a leaf design about one-third the distance up from the bed frame, and above are fluted.

Figure 805.
Mahogany Bedstead, about 1725.

The feet are well-carved animals' claws on balls, but the legs are straight and not cabriole. The head-posts are plain except for a fluting. The bed frame is hidden behind panels of wood on which are carved the meander pattern with a rope edge. The tester-top is unusually well carved in a guilloche design alternating

BEDSTEADS 255

a large and small circle, and in the centre of each large circle is carved a rosette. This design is carried out on the inside as well, and hidden between the two mouldings are the rods upon which the curtains run. Above is a nulled edge, and at each corner is a bold, well-carved acanthus leaf and at the centre of each side

Figure 806.
Cabriole-Legged Bedstead, 1725–50.

and the lower end is carved a cartouche with scrolls and acanthus leaves. No such bedstead has been found in America, but it is shown to emphasise the difference between the elaborate English bedsteads and the simpler ones found here.

A typical example of the simpler bedsteads found in the American colonies is shown in Figure 806 and is in the Pendleton Collection, owned by the Rhode

Island School of Design. The foot-posts are fluted and reeded, the fluting being broken about two-thirds of the way up the post by a ring. There is a rounded capital with a plain shaft above. The legs are cabriole and terminate in bird's claw and ball feet. The head-posts are plain with chamfered edges. This bed-

Figure 807.
Cabriole-Legged Bedstead, 1725–50.

stead had a plain, straight tester-top over which the valance was fastened. Bedsteads of this type are also found with posts a little shorter, with a field top; that is, the tester was cut in a serpentine curve from head to foot.

Figure 807 shows a more elaborate bedstead from the Bolles Collection. The foot-posts are slender and fluted. At the top is a square block above which the posts are plain. The legs are cabriole and terminate in bird's claw and ball feet.

BEDSTEADS

The bolts locking the frames are covered by blocks which accentuate the curves of the legs. These blocks are fastened to the posts by screws which fit into key-hole plates. The surface of the blocks is carved with acanthus leaves and flowers and a scroll at the top standing out beyond the plane of the posts.

Figure 808.
Cabriole-Legged Bedstead, about 1750.

Figure 808 shows another bedstead of the same general type which is the property of the writer. The foot-posts are the same as shown in the preceding figure and blocks of the same style hide the bolts. The blocks in this piece are carved in two-headed pheasants so designed that a head, wing, and tail appear on each side and a rosette finishes the outer edges. The head-posts are plain with chamfered edges. The inner edges of the frame are cut in a recessed square, and knobs of wood are dowelled in, the heads of which come a little below the top surface of the frame. These were intended to hold the cording upon which the mattress was originally placed.

It is probable that this form of bedstead continued to be used in this country until the introduction of the Sheraton style, for we find very few of the Chippendale period.

Figure 809.

Bedstead in Chippendale style, about 1760.

Figure 809 shows an English bedstead of the Chippendale period, the property of Mr. Marsden J. Perry, of Providence. The foot-posts are in cluster form with the surface carved in a pendent-flower design, and above is a capital carved with acanthus leaves above which is an egg-and-dart moulding. The legs are partly chamfered and partly square, and on the surfaces are carved designs of

BEDSTEADS

foliated scrolls and rosettes. The legs swell slightly at the corners of the bottom with carved scrolls, thus forming the feet. The head-posts are perfectly plain.

Figure 810.
Bedstead in Chippendale style, 1750–60.

The tester-top is crested with a bold nulling, and at the corners and centre of the sides and foot are carved acanthus-leaf scrolls.

A very beautiful bedstead of the Chippendale period, with its original draperies, is shown in Figure 810 and is the property of Mr. Marsden J. Perry.

Each foot-post has cluster columns bound by ribbons and a capital carved in an acanthus-leaf design. At the base of each column are carved an acanthus-leaf edge and a bead moulding. Around each post below this is carved a flower pattern, and on the surface of the vase-turning below are well-carved acanthus leaves. The small turnings below are ornamented with a bead and an egg-and-dart moulding. The legs are square, with three mouldings, the upper and lower ones carved in an acanthus-leaf pattern and the centre one in a reel-and-bead pattern. The tester-top is delicately carved in foliated scrolls and acanthus leaves which overhang at the centres and ends. The edges of the valance at the top and bottom are cut in cyma and simple curves, and at the corners of the top are stuffed scrolls of the fabric standing out from the corners of the foot-posts.

Figure 811.
Draped Bedstead, late eighteenth century.

Figure 811 shows one of the bedsteads now preserved at Mount Vernon which illustrates admirably how completely the drapery covered the frame and the bedposts of the simpler sort, thus making any ornamentation of the posts quite unnecessary, the elegant appearance of the bed being made entirely to depend upon the draperies.

One of the features of the style following the Chippendale is that the posts, instead of being plain, fluted, or with a slight vase-shaped turning above the bed frame, are turned in forms which are not architectural, and this turning became more elaborate as time went on.

Figure 812 shows a bedstead in Sheraton style, the property of Mr. Marsden J. Perry, of Providence. The posts are in the form and decoration quite com-

BEDSTEADS

monly found here, but seldom do we find so elaborate a tester. The foot-posts have a carving of drapery and leaves on the bulbs, and above, the post is cut in

Figure 812.
Bedstead, Sheraton style, about 1790.

hexagonal shape, and at the base of this portion, on each surface, is carved a laurel leaf. Below the bulb are narrow medallions, and the square legs terminate in spade feet. The head-posts are plain. The tester-top is domed, and on the edges are gilded rosettes strung on a gilded rod and at the centre is a panel on which is gilded drapery. At the corners and centre of the sides are carved and gilded urns.

Figure 813.
Bedstead in late Sheraton style, about 1800.

A very ornately carved bedstead of this period is shown in Figure 813, the property of Mr. Richard W. Lehne, of Baltimore. The four posts are carved with rosettes just above the rails, and above that is a vase-turning divided into panels within which are carved pendent flowers. Above, the rounded posts are squared. On the two outside surfaces are carved a cornucopia, leaves, flowers, fruits, and acorns extending all the way up the post. The other two sides of the posts are carved in a long, narrow leaf, and above these panels is a slight acanthus-

Figure 814.
Mahogany Bedstead in Sheraton style, 1790–1800.

leaf carved capital. There is a high head-board upon the upper panel of which is a basket filled with fruits, and from either side are streamers of leaves. The legs are square, ornamented with carved leaves and pendent flowers, and terminate in spade feet. The tester-top is simple with a border of oak leaves carved on the surface.

Figure 814 shows a simpler bedstead of the same style, the property of Mr. Merle Forman, of Brooklyn. The four posts are turned in vase shape with a long, swelling shaft above. On the vase part are carved draperies and the rest of the shaft is reeded. The legs originally terminated in spade feet which have at some later date been changed to bird's claw and ball feet.

Figure 815.
Field Bedstead, 1790–1800.

A simple field bedstead is shown in Figure 815. The foot-posts are turned in late form and at the top are urns. The head-posts are plain. The tester is curved in a half-circular form, which makes the top at the centre about the height of the bedsteads, having straight tester-tops.

Figure 816 shows four styles of posts of the Empire period. The ones at the right and left are carved in the usual acanthus-leaf pattern, with pineapple finials, so popular in this period. The second one is a little earlier and plain and the third one is spiral-turned.

BEDSTEADS

Heavily carved mahogany bedsteads, ornamented principally in designs of acanthus leaves and pineapples, with both high and low posts, came into use about 1800–20, when furniture of similar style and design was generally adopted. There have been called to the writer's notice a number of high-post bedsteads of this description which have associated with them traditions of use during the Revolution, either by Washington or Lafayette. This, of course, is impossible,

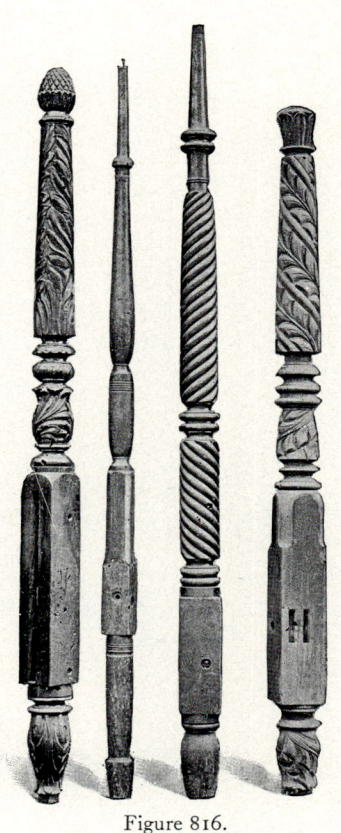

Figure 816.
Empire Bedposts, 1800–20.

and the traditions have been fastened to the wrong bedsteads, for no bedsteads of that type were made prior to 1800.

Figure 817 shows a bedstead of the Empire period. The four posts are carved in the acanthus-leaf and pineapple design and on a portion of the shaft are bold reedings. The bolts are concealed behind panels carved in acanthus-leaf design with a rosette at the centre. The head-board, as is often the case, is carved in the same acanthus-leaf pattern with drapery at the centre. Occasionally a large eagle with outspreading wings is carved at the centre of the bedposts of this period.

Figure 818 shows a low-post bedstead of the Empire period. This style of bedstead was introduced at a time when the tester-top and draped bedsteads were going out of fashion. The posts are carved in acanthus-leaf and pineapple pattern, shown in the preceding figure, and the head-board is bordered with carving.

Figure 817.
Empire Bedstead, about 1810.

Figure 819 shows another low-post bedstead, the property of the writer. The posts are reeded and carved in the acanthus-leaf pattern with pineapple finials. The tops of the head and foot boards are rounded and finished with scrolls carved in acanthus-leaf pattern with large rosettes in the manner commonly found on the sofas of the period.

Figure 818.
Low-Post Bedstead, 1820–30.

Figure 819.
Low-Post Bedstead, 1800–20.

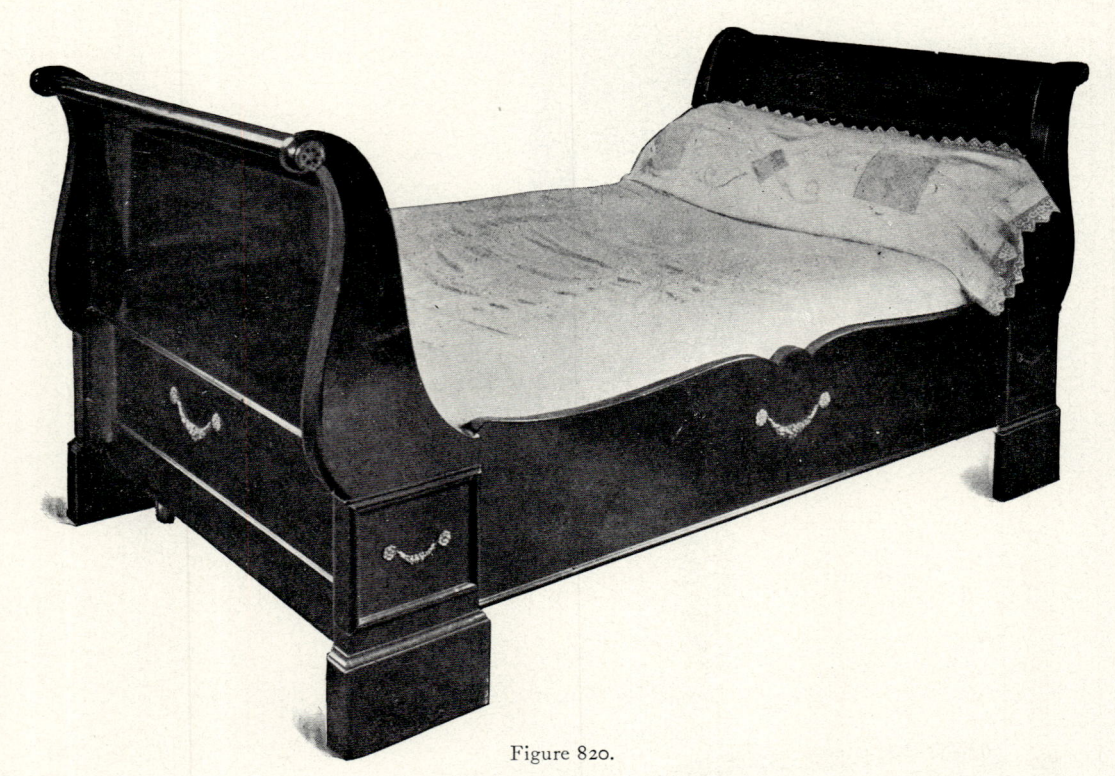

Figure 820.

French Bedstead, about 1830.

Figure 821.

French Bedstead, about 1830.

BEDSTEADS

From 1820–40 great numbers of low-post bedsteads in maple and cherry, with simple turned posts and head-boards, and occasionally with a turned foot-board, were in use throughout New England.

The French Empire bedsteads with rolling head and foot boards were popular here about 1830 and remained in fashion until replaced by the black walnut machine-made bedsteads. The posts of these French bedsteads were ornamented with ormolu or brass mounts and the side rails extended nearly to the floor.

Figure 820 shows a typical example of one of these bedsteads, the property of Miss E. R. Burnell, of Hartford.

A simple bedstead of this style which belongs to Mr. Casper Sommerlad, of Brooklyn, is shown in Figure 821. The side rails are narrower than usual and the feet are turned instead of being a continuation of the sides.

XI
CLOCKS

WE do not consider that clocks technically should be classified as furniture, and still, as there is hardly a collector who does not possess at least one specimen, we think it may be well to give a brief sketch of the subject, having reference more especially to such pieces as have been in the country from colonial times, confining ourselves to clocks in household use, and not speaking of the early clocks in various towers and churches. It is not our intention, in the limited space that can be given to the subject in a general book on colonial furniture, to state more than the leading points which one should know to enable him to buy intelligently, and we would refer the reader for fuller description and information to the excellent books heretofore published exclusively on this subject.

This country was just being settled when the Clockmakers' Company was founded in London, in 1631. This company had for its object the regulation of the clock trade, and, in order to prevent persons from being cheated or deceived by unskilled makers, the members were given the right of search and confiscation of clocks and watches which had "bad and deceitful works." This company seems particularly to have directed its energies against the Dutch, in whose ability as clockmakers, whether justifiably or not, the English had little confidence.

The most important work which this company accomplished was the training of men for the art. There was a carefully arranged apprenticeship, and after serving his turn each apprentice had to make his masterpiece before he was admitted as a workmaster; and therefore the possessor of a clock bearing the name of a member of the guild may rest assured that the piece is at least well made.

At the time our history begins there were two general styles of clocks in use, one which was run with weights, and the other with a spiral spring. The former variety was the older, although, so far as this country is concerned, it was contemporaneous, and of necessity was a stationary clock, while the latter was easily carried about and was often called a portable or table clock.

Clocks are seldom mentioned in any of the records in this country prior to 1700, and were always valued at a fairly high price—the lowest 6s. and the

CLOCKS

highest £20. Descriptions are seldom given, so it is largely a matter of surmise in what style the earliest clocks were.

Thus, at Boston, in 1638, we find "1 clock 18s"; in 1652, "1 brass clock £2," and again "one clock in case £6"; at Salem, in 1660, a clock valued at £2; at New York, in 1689, "one Pendula Clock £6"; and at Boston, in the inventory of Sir William Phips, a very wealthy man, we find, in 1696, a clock valued at £20 and a repeating clock at £10; at New York, in 1691, we find a "diamond watch" mentioned without valuation given, which shows a luxury quite up to date.

Figure 822.
Portable or Table Clock, 1710–20.

The earliest clock mentioned, in 1638, could have been either a lantern clock, described below, or a portable clock; but as the inventories several times refer to brass clocks when describing the lantern variety, the one mentioned in 1638 was probably a portable one, after the fashion of the one shown in Figure 822.

This style of clock came into use about the beginning of the sixteenth century, and this particular clock was made by Jonathan Loundes, a famous clockmaker, of Pall Mall, London, who was admitted to the Clockmakers' Company in 1680. It will be seen that the face has the oval top. This style was introduced by Tompion, who died in 1713, and only appears on his later clocks. The style, however, became very popular in the reign of George I, which began in 1714, and we should place the date of the clock somewhere between 1710 and 1720. The face has not the applied spandrels in the corner, as is usual, but is engraved with an urn at the top and oval figures surrounded with wreaths in the four corners. The case is in the typical style of the portable clock and is japanned. It belongs to the Long Island Historical Society.

Figure 823.
Portable or Table Clock, 1750–60.

Figure 823 shows a portable clock of the Chippendale period, the property of Mr. Richard A. Canfield. The top is domed, and at each corner and on the top is a brass urn with flames. Around the base of the top, on the sides, and in the spandrels above the glass of the doors is elaborate lattice-work. The corners of the case are chamfered and the surfaces are reeded and fluted. The case stands on ogee bracket feet and the skirt is cut in cyma curves. The dial has an oval top in which are two small dials, one regulating the time and the other containing the second-hand. In the spandrels about the main dial are applied brass mounts in Chippendale scrolls. The clock also has a calendar attachment. The works are by James Tregent, of London, a noted clockmaker, who was also watchmaker to the Prince of Wales.

Figure 824 shows another portable clock of a later date made by Isaac Fox, of London, who was admitted to the Clockmakers' Company in 1772. The top is domed in the usual manner, but the round dial indicates that it belongs to a late date.

The clock next found in the inventories is in 1652— "1 brass clock £2." This undoubtedly refers to such a clock as is shown in Figure 825.

Such clocks are known by the following names: "chamber," "lantern," "bird-cage," and "bedpost," all but the last name probably referring to its shape, and the last referring either to its shape or to its being at times fastened to the bedposts; for, as they were often fitted with an alarm attachment, they must have been designed for sleeping-rooms as well as other parts of the house. This style of clock came into existence in England about the year 1600. These clocks were set upon brackets, as shown in this illustration, with weights hanging below, and were wound up by pulling down the opposite end of the cord holding the weights. The face was usually a little larger than the rest, and the centre of the dial was often beautifully etched. The bell at the top was sometimes used for an alarm only, and sometimes to strike the hour as well.

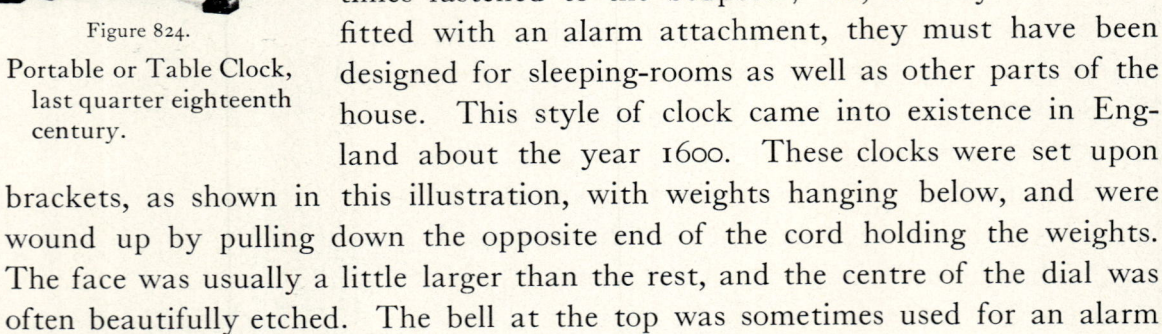

Figure 824.
Portable or Table Clock, last quarter eighteenth century.

The earliest clocks had no pendulum, but a balance controlled the movement, and about the middle of the seventeenth century the pendulum came into use. The original pendulum was short, about the length of the case, and as it swung would fly out at either side of the case, acquiring the name of "bob pendulum." It is sometimes found hung outside the case, and sometimes inside, and when the latter is true little slits are cut in the case to allow the pendulum to swing out on each side. Such clocks run not longer than from twelve to thirty hours. It will be noticed that at the top, on three sides, is a fret, put there partially to conceal the large bell and give finish to the piece, and these frets will often enable one to determine the age of a clock. Many clockmakers had their own

CLOCKS

273

private frets, while others followed the design most popular at that time. The clocks also often have the maker's name engraved on the dial.

The fret on Figure 825 is called the "heraldic fret," and was used from 1600 to 1640, so that this clock is an extremely early one. The next pattern of fret most commonly found is the "dolphin fret" (Figure 827), which appeared about

Figure 825.
Chamber or Lantern Clock, last half seventeenth century.

Figure 826.
Chamber or Lantern Clock, last half seventeenth century.

1650 and remained popular throughout the rest of the time this style of clock was fashionable; consequently it is the pattern most commonly met with. It consisted either of two dolphins with tails crossed, or two dolphins with heads together and tails forming a curve at either side.

Another fret which was used by Charles Fox, clockmaker, and possibly a few others between 1660 and 1680 is shown in Figure 826, and a still later pattern is shown in Figure 828.

To return to Figure 825, it is arranged for an alarm only, and does not strike the hours, the alarm being set by a centre dial. It will be noted that in nearly all of these clocks there is but a single hand, telling the hour, and the space between is divided into fourths instead of fifths. The maker's name does not appear on this clock; it was found at Salem, Massachusetts.

Figure 826 is a more pretentious clock. It both strikes the hour and has the alarm, which is set in the same way as in the preceding clock, and the dial is very

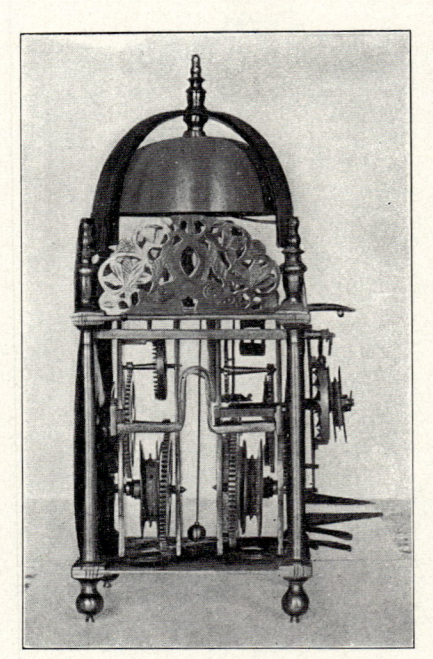

Figure 827.
Chamber or Lantern Clock, last half seventeenth century.

handsomely engraved. The upper side of the inner dial has the following inscription: "Charles Fox at the Fox Lothbury, Londini Fecit." Charles Fox was admitted to the Clockmakers' Company in 1660. This clock was found in New Jersey. It is more compact than Figure 825, but its dimensions are about the same, 15 inches high by 5¾ inches wide, and the dial is 6¼ inches in diameter.

Figures 825 and 826 have the long pendulum substituted for the bob pendulum, probably because they would then keep better time. It was the fashion during the first twenty years of the eighteenth century to have this change made, and many advertisements are to be found of clockmakers who advertised to substitute long pendulums for short ones at reasonable charges.

The long or royal pendulum is supposed to have been invented by Richard Harris, at London, in 1641; but it found little favour at first, and the date when it came into common use is usually placed at 1680. It was also invented on the

CLOCKS

Continent at about the same time, apparently without knowledge of Harris's invention, and it is possible that some of those found their way to this country before 1680.

Figure 827 shows a front and side view of a chamber clock which is particularly interesting because the works are in their original condition; the dial is in the usual form, nicely engraved, and has the centre section to set the alarm. The fret is in the "dolphin" pattern. This clock both strikes and has the alarm. The bob pendulum lies between the go and strike trains, and the release for the strike is bent in a loop to allow for its swing. A single weight runs the clock and strike. On the back plate is an alarm attachment. This has a crescent-shaped strike which rolls on the inner edge of the bell, making a continuous sound. A small separate weight runs the alarm. On the back plate are also two iron spikes meant to hold the clock firmly to the wall or to the bracket. This clock is the property of the writer.

Figure 828 shows another clock of this same style. It is very much smaller than the others shown, being but 9 inches in height and 3¾ inches wide, and the dial is 4¼ inches in diameter. It still has its bob pendulum, which can be seen in the illustration hanging in the middle between the four feet, and it also has the minute-hand. This clock strikes, but has no alarm, and is thought to be of French make.

Figure 829 shows a Dutch bracket clock, the face and ornaments gilded and the face painted. The feet are of wood and in the usual Dutch ball-foot style. It has a bob pendulum and the works are of brass. It differs from the brass clocks above described in that the top of the clock is protected by a wooden hood. A characteristic of the brackets of these clocks is the mermaid cut out of the wood on either side of the back. Such clocks are contemporaneous with the English brass chamber clocks, but are very inferior in workmanship and, we believe, are such as the Clockmakers' Company sought to suppress.

Figure 828. Chamber or Lantern Clock, last quarter seventeenth century.

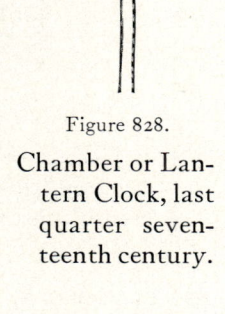

The development from the brass chamber or lantern clock to the tall or "grandfather's" was a natural one. First, a wooden hood was placed over the brass clock for protection, and when the long pendulum came into fashion it had to be enclosed to keep it from injury, the result being a clock with a long case.

The earliest long-case clocks, as well as any seventeenth-century clocks, are extremely scarce.

The inventory at Boston, "1 clock and case £6," in 1652, would be an extremely early entry for a tall clock, although the high price would indicate that it was such; but there can be no doubt about the entry in New York, in 1689, "one Pendulum Clock £6," referring to the tall-case clock.

The earliest clock-cases were very plain, made mostly of oak or walnut, the finer ones being almost entirely of the latter wood; and on the dial-face of the earlier ones the maker's name appears under the dial in Latin; a little later the name appeared on the dial between the figures VII and V within the circle, and about 1715 the name-plate appeared.

At first the dials were square, but they later (about 1710) were made with the straight top broken by a half circle, suggested either by the dome bell on the chamber clock or more probably to cover the top of the bell; and many of the old clock-faces were made over in this way when the fashion changed.

As with the chamber clock the date could be told somewhat by the fret, so in the tall clock an approximation can be made by observing the spandrels or corner ornaments on the face. The earliest faces have a cherub's head, almost perfectly plain, in the four corners (Figure 831), which continued in use as late as 1700. This was followed by cherubs a little more ornate, going out of style about the same time. Then, about the year 1700, came two cupids supporting a crown (Figure 834), which, in its simple or more elaborate form, continued to be used until about 1740; and in George III's reign the pattern became very intricate, sometimes with an Indian or some other head in the centre of a mass of scroll-work, sometimes without the head (Figure 847).

Figure 829.

Dutch Chamber Clock, late seventeenth or early eighteenth century.

It is impossible to tell the age of a clock entirely by its case, as very often the works were brought over here without the case, or, as during the Revolutionary War, the works were taken out and hidden and the case left to be destroyed. Nor can one always judge by the face, as old faces have sometimes been discarded for newer styles. Nor can one always tell from the name-plate, for the writer knows

CLOCKS

of at least one instance where the name-plate had been removed and that of a clockmaker who made repairs substituted. It is really only by taking into consideration all the points heretofore discussed that one can come to an approximation of the age of a clock.

One of the earliest tall clocks in this country is shown in Figure 830, the property of Mr. Richard A. Canfield. The case is of walnut with oyster-shell inlay which consists of cross-sections of the wood set side by side, and narrow lines of light wood divide the surface in geometrical shapes and bull's-eye light is set in the door in front of the pendulum. The top is flat and is supported at the corners by spiral-twisted columns. There is no door in the hood, but on either side of the hood, at the back, is a groove into which the back of the clock fits, and the hood slides up until it clears the back. The dial (Figure 831) is square and in the earliest form, with cupid-head spandrels and narrow numeral dial. It also has a second-hand and a calendar attachment. This clock bears the name "Johannes Fromanteel, Londini," across the base of the dial. This John Fromanteel was a member of an illustrious family of clockmakers who are mentioned as early as 1630. One of them is spoken of by Evelyn as "Our famous Fromantel," and undoubtedly they were at the head of their profession. The regulator, as will be seen in Figure 831, is on the side, and the pendulum is adjusted by moving the hand on the small dial. The winding arbour is in two parts, which is very unusual. Generally the arbour is cast with the barrel, and the main wheel is secured to the barrel by a washer and pin. In this movement, however, the winding end of the arbour and the barrel are in one piece and the main wheel and the other end of the arbour are in another and slide into the winding end, the plates of the movement keeping them together.

Figure 832 shows another early tall clock by the same maker. It is owned by the Philadelphia Library and is said to have belonged to Oliver Cromwell, but

Figure 830.
Tall Clock, last quarter seventeenth century.

278   COLONIAL FURNITURE

this tradition cannot be true. It probably dates about 1690–1700. The name appears below the dial in Latin, "Johannes Fromanteel, Londini fecit." As this John was not admitted to the Clockmakers' Company until 1663, this clock could not have belonged to Oliver Cromwell, who had died before that date, and it is hardly likely that he would have owned a clock made by an apprentice not yet admitted to the guild.

The dial of this clock is silvered and the rest of the face is of brass, without spandrels at the corners, and we can see no signs of there ever having been any.

Figure 831.
Dial and side view of works of foregoing clock.

The clock has a small calendar attachment. The case is made of walnut, and very tall, to make room for the pendulum. These pendulums were sometimes seven feet long. The early single moulding is seen about the doors and the spiral-turned columns are typical of the early clock-cases. It is doubtful whether the interrupted arch pediment is of the same age as the rest of the case. With this exception, the case is very similar to that shown in the preceding figure, including the ball feet.

Figure 833 shows another early clock. The case is made of pine or some other soft wood, and the band of carving at the top is early in design. This clock-case also has the single-arch moulding about the doors, and there is an opening in the lower door to show the swinging of the pendulum. It is at the Van Cortlandt Mansion, Van Cortlandt Park, New York.

Figure 832.
Tall Clock, 1690–1700.

280   COLONIAL FURNITURE

Figure 834 shows a detail of the face of the foregoing clock which is worth noting. It will be seen that the spandrels are of the third order—cupids holding a crown—which came into fashion about 1700. The maker's name, Walter Archer, appears between the numerals VII and V, which shows it to date probably before 1715. We have been unable to find this maker's name among the members of the Clockmakers' Company or elsewhere, and this would seem to indicate that he was probably from one of the smaller towns in England or a colonial maker. The clock is dated 1619, and an examination with the eye failed to detect that the engraved figures were later than the rest of the face; but the photograph shows it to be of a different depth, and it was without doubt added at a rather recent date. The fact that pendulum clocks were not invented until 1641 of itself would disprove the date, apart from the other indications above referred to.

Figure 834.
Dial to foregoing clock.

It will readily be seen that the arched upper part of the dial, which came in a little later, was intended to cover the bell, which in this illustration shows at the top. This clock is wound by pulling up the weights by hand, as is the method in the bird-cage clocks above referred to.

Figure 833.
Tall Clock, 1700–10.

An English marquetry clock is shown in Figure 835, the property of Mr. Richard A. Canfield. The top, instead of being flat, as in the preceding figure, is domed in the manner most frequently found in the early eighteenth century. On either side of the door are twisted columns, and above the door is a carved fret similar to that shown in the preceding figure. The surfaces are covered with exceptionally good marquetry, consisting of flowers, leaves, birds, and butterflies. The dial is square and engraved about the centre and calendar openings, and the spandrels consist of a head and scrolls.

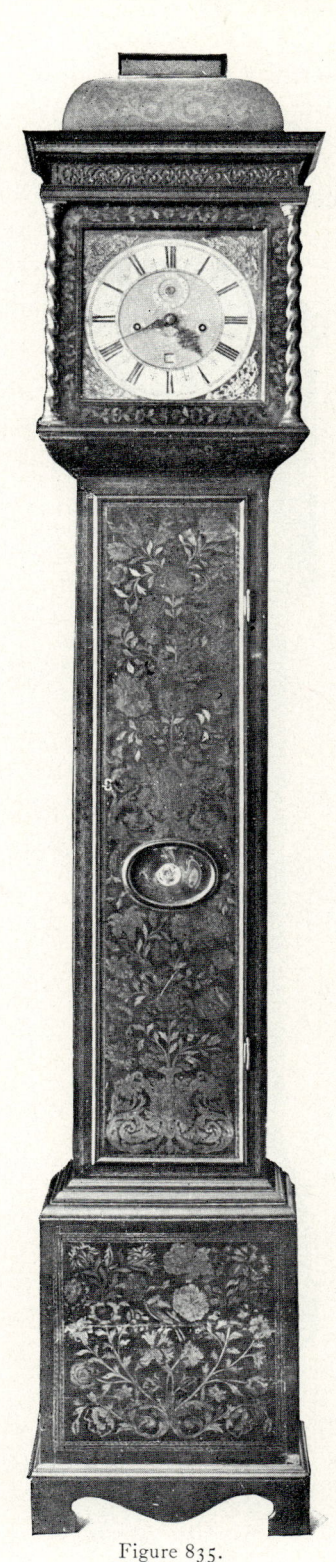

CLOCKS

The maker is "John Barnett, Londini Fecit." This Barnett was admitted to the Clockmakers' Company in 1682. The clock runs for thirty days and has the calendar attachment.

A walnut tall clock of about the same period is shown in Figure 836 and is the property of Rev. George D. Egbert, of Norwalk, Connecticut. The top quite closely resembles the Dutch type of case, but the base has the straight sides in English fashion instead of the Dutch *bombé*. The case stands on ball feet similar to those appearing on chests of drawers. On the top are gilded figures representing at the centre Atlas, at the left Gabriel, and at the right Father Time. The dial has the arched top within which is the dial which controls the strike. The spandrels consist of cupids holding a crown, as in Figure 834. The clock runs for thirty days and strikes the half-hour on a different bell from the one used to indicate the hour. There is the usual calendar attachment. On the face is engraved "Claudini du Chesne, Londini." He was admitted to the Clockmakers' Company in 1693.

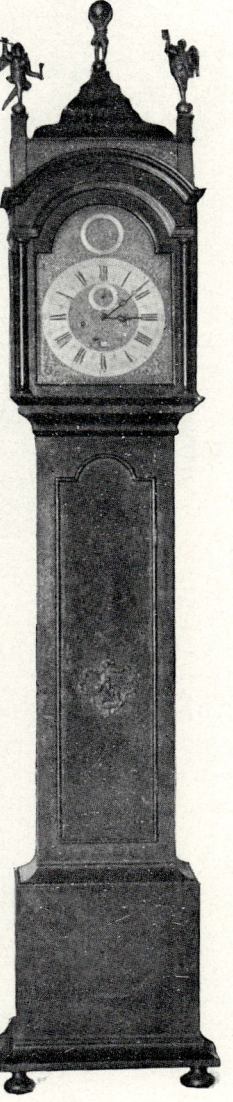

A good dial is shown in Figure 837. The top is arched, and within it is a cartouche containing the name "Peter Stretch, Philadelphia," supported on either side by a cupid and surmounted by a crown. The spandrels are the same as those appearing in the preceding figure, two cupids supporting a crown. The fret top of the case is not original.

Figure 838 shows a tall clock with an English lacquer case, the property of the writer. The hood is arched, following the lines of the dial-plate. This clock has a thirty-day movement and the

Figure 835.
Tall Clock, marquetry case, about 1700.

Figure 836.
Tall Clock, about 1700.

usual calendar attachment. In the arched top is the name "Shedel." On either side of the name-plates are dolphins and scrolls, and the spandrels consist of a head and scrolls.

Nearly all of the early clocks found in this country were made in England and imported. There were, however, a few clockmakers here, and probably one of the best of these was William Claggett. He was born in 1696, was admitted as a freeman at Newport in 1726, and died at Newport in 1749. His dials were especially good and are found in three forms, as shown in the three succeeding figures.

The earliest of his clocks is shown in Figure 839. The dial is square and the case has the square door with single-arch mouldings and a bull's-eye glass. The design of the spandrels is a vase and flowers, with birds and scrolls on either side, similar to that used by the Marot school, and this form was almost invariably used by him (Figure 841). The name-plate is square and is placed just above the calendar. This clock is the property of Mr. G. Winthrop Brown, of Chestnut Hill, Massachusetts.

Figure 837.
Dial of tall clock, showing arched top, 1725-30.

Figure 838.
Tall Clock with japanned case, 1700-25.

Another Claggett clock, which is owned by the Rhode Island Historical Society, is shown in Figure 840. The dial is domed and the spandrels are the same as those shown in the succeeding figure. In the dome is a dial which regulates the strike. The name-plate is square and is placed just above the calendar, as in the preceding figure. The door is domed, and it is interesting to note in passing that the almost universal rule is that if the dial is domed the door is also.

A handsome Claggett dial is shown in Figure 841 and is on a clock, the property of Miss F. F. Hasbrouck, of Providence. The spandrels are in the usual

Figure 839.
Tall Clock made by Claggett,
about 1725.

Figure 840.
Tall Clock made by Claggett,
1725-35.

283

Figure 843.
Dial to following clock.

Figure 841.
Dial to Claggett clock, 1730–40.

CLOCKS

design found on Claggett clocks and the name is in a circular plate arched above the calendar. An eight-pointed star is engraved inside the second-dial. In the dome is a dial which indicates the phases of the moon.

A Claggett clock in a lacquer case, the property of Mr. William Ames, of Providence, is shown in Figure 842. The dial is the most beautiful Claggett one known, and is shown in detail in Figure 843. Above the domed top are engraved the maker's name and the phases of the moon. The semicircular plates on either side are beautifully engraved. The clock has a musical attachment striking on ten bells, and the small dial at the right-hand upper corner regulates the tunes, which are "Britons, Strike Home," and "Happy Swains." The dial at the upper left-hand corner would appear to regulate the time at which the tunes should be played. The small dials at the lower corners are for the calendar attachment, that at the left indicating the days of the month and that at the right indicating the month. Below each month are numerals indicating the number of days that are in that month. The spandrels are composed of scrolls and are, of course, broken at the centre by the small dials. The second-dial is ornamented by a six-pointed star.

An interesting Claggett clock, which is the earliest hanging or mural clock known in this country, is shown in Figure 844. It is owned by the Newport Historical Society, and hangs in the museum, which was the old Seventh Day Baptist Church, in the place for which it was made. The case about the dial is octagonal and the entire case and dial are lacquered. On the edges of the three lower sections of the octagon is painted, "William Claget, Newport." This form of clock became popular in England in the late years of the eighteenth century and is found here in the first quarter of the nineteenth century in the form known as banjo clocks. This clock dates about 1740.

Figure 842.
Tall Clock with japanned case made by Claggett, 1730–40.

Figure 845 shows a clock having a dial very similar to that shown in Figure 841. The case is made of walnut with bands of the early form of inlay. On the square name-plate is engraved, "For John Proud, Newport." The dial, hands,

Figure 845.
Tall Clock, about 1740.

Figure 844.
Wall or Mural Clock, about 1740.

and spandrels are so similar to those made by Claggett that it seems highly probable that this is a Claggett clock and that Proud substituted his own plate, the word "For" indicating that he did not claim to be the maker. This clock is the property of Mr. Thomas G. Hazard, of Narragansett Pier.

From about 1730 down toward the close of the century there was very little change in the general style of the clocks. They were all either the tall "grandfather" or the portable clock.

CLOCKS

Figure 846 shows a musical clock, in a Chippendale case, belonging to Mr. Charles Morson, its chief difference from those heretofore described being that the lower part of the case is kettle shape.

Figure 847.
Dial of clock shown in following figure.

Figure 846.
Musical Clock, Chippendale case, 1760–70.

Figure 847 shows a detail of the face of this clock. It will be seen that the late spandrels are in the two lower corners. This clock was made by Joseph Rose, of London, who, with his son, had a shop at 19 Foster Lane from 1765 to 1768. The clock has both a chime and a musical attachment. The upper dial sets the musical part to play either a polonaise or a march. The dial to the left, as one faces it, regulates the strike, and that on the right the chime. Such clocks as these were not only imported into the colonies, but there were several clockmakers

288 COLONIAL FURNITURE

here who advertised to make them. In the Boston *Gazette* for February 22, 1773, the following advertisement appears: "Benjamin Willard" (first of the famous American clockmakers of that name) "at his shop in Roxbury Street pursues different branches of clock and watch work, has for sale musical clocks playing different tunes, a new tune every day of the week and on Sunday a psalm tune. These tunes perform every hour without any obstruction to the motion or going of the clock and new invention for pricking barrels to perform the music and his clocks are made much cheaper than any ever yet known. All the branches of this business likewise carried on at his shop in Grafton."

Figure 848 shows another tall clock in a lacquer case, the property of Dr. Edward L. Oatman, of Brooklyn. The spandrels are in the form of scrolls, and on the dial in the dome is engraved "White Matlack New York," who worked in New York from 1769 to 1775.

Figure 849 shows a tall clock, the property of Mr. H. W. Erving. The case is inlaid with medallions, fan corners, and scrolls in the manner of the Sheraton school. The base is cut to resemble stone work and stands on ogee bracket feet. The hood has a scroll top. The dial is domed with a luna attachment, and above is the name "Nathaniel Brown, Manchester." The spandrels are in the design of Chippendale scrolls.

Figure 848.
Tall Clock, japanned case, about 1770.

Figure 850.
Burnap Clock, 1799.

Figure 850 illustrates a clock in the possession of the Misses Andrews, made by Daniel Burnap, a well-known American clockmaker, who lived at Andover, Plymouth, and East Windsor, Connecticut, between 1780 and 1800. This clock was bought in 1799. A characteristic of his clocks is the silvered face, usually beautifully engraved, without spandrels. This clock has both the calendar and luna attachments, and the background for the luna attachment is tinted blue. The works are always of brass.

Figure 849.
Tall Clock, inlaid case, last quarter eighteenth century.

Figure 851.
Tall Clock, about 1801.

289

Another tall clock of the period is shown in Figure 851 and is the property of the writer. The case is unusually ornate, the hood is scroll top, the inner ends of the scrolls being finished with rosettes. The surface above the opening is carved in a leaf-and-flower pattern, and about the door is inlaid a vine design in pigment instead of wood. The corners of the case are chamfered and the quarter columns inserted are carved with a leaf-and-flower design. The piece stands on ogee bracket feet. On the door are inlaid in pigment a floral design and "Chr. Fahl 1801." The dial is well enamelled with flowers and at the centre of the top is an American eagle with shield. A calendar attachment is in a semicircular slot. The maker is Benjamin Witman, Reading, and the case is Pennsylvania Dutch in character.

It was the fashion at this time to make miniature tall clocks, and an example, the property of the writer, is shown in Figure 852. The works are of brass and run eight days. In the dome top is a painting of a lake and castle, and the spandrels are United States shields. The clock stands only forty-six inches to the top of the urn.

Another miniature clock is shown in Figure 853 and is the property of Mr. H. W. Erving. The works are of wood and the dial is rather crudely painted. The edges of the case are finished with a reeding.

Figure 852.
Miniature Tall Clock, about 1800.

Figure 853.
Miniature Tall Clock, about 1800.

Toward the close of the eighteenth century there was great demand for cheaper clocks, due to the poverty of the young republic, just recovering from the Revolutionary War, and to an inflated currency. To meet this demand, about 1790 a painted or white enamelled dial came in, taking the place, except in the expensive clocks, of the brass dial. These painted faces were made either of metal or wood, and large numbers were sold to clockmakers throughout the country, who added their names in place of the dials on works often not made by themselves. It was also at this time, and for much the same reason, that the wooden works began to be used. These wooden works usually had either bone or other hard substance for bearings, and there are still many to be found keeping good time.

One of the best-known American clockmakers was Simon Willard. He belonged to an illustrious family of clockmakers whose influence on the clocks

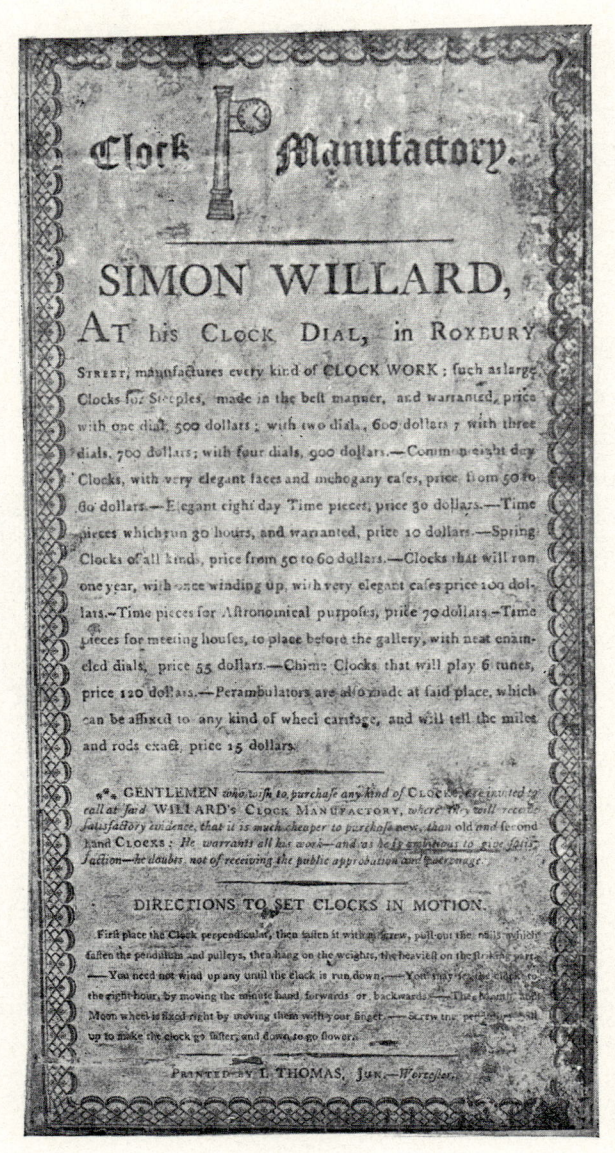

Figure 855.
Advertisement in following clock.

Figure 854.
Tall Clock with painted face, about 1800.

of the late eighteenth and early nineteenth centuries was very great. He had three brothers who were clockmakers, and also a son. The brothers were Benjamin, born in 1743; Ephraim, born in 1755; and Aaron, born in 1757. An interesting history has been written of this famous clockmaker by John Ware Willard, to which the reader is referred for more detailed particulars of the family.

Simon Willard first worked at Grafton, Massachusetts, and later, prior to 1780, moved to Roxbury, where he lived the rest of his life, dying in 1848. His earliest clocks were of the tall variety, of which Figure 854 is a very good example, and is the property of Dr. G. Alder Blumer, of Providence. The dial is domed and is enamelled with flowers. The calendar attachment is in a semicircular slot below which is the name "Simon Willard." The clock is inlaid with fan ornaments in the corners and it stands on ogee bracket feet. Within the door is pasted the advertisement which is given in fac-simile in Figure 855.

Simon Willard also experimented with mantel or bracket clocks and made a number which would run for thirty days. A very good example of one of these thirty-day clocks is shown in Figure 856, which is the property of Mr. G. Winthrop Brown, of Chestnut Hill, Massachusetts. It will be seen that the case merely surrounds the dial and bell. The dial is circular and of metal, and the name appears below the hands. The clock runs and strikes on a single weight.

From 1802 Willard took out a patent for an improved eight-day clock, which at once became a success and was widely imitated by other clockmakers, because never before had it been possible to get an eight-day small clock with weights. Mural or wall clocks had come into general use in England about 1797 and were known as Act-of-Parliament clocks, and it is

Figure 856.
Willard Thirty-Day Clock, about 1800.

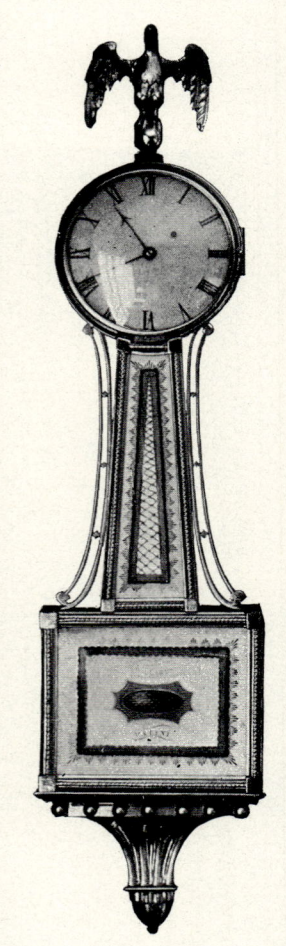

Figure 857.
Willard or Banjo Clock, about 1800.

Figure 858.
Willard Clock, about 1800.

CLOCKS

possible that Willard had heard of these. These clocks had very generally acquired the name of banjo clocks, but the name is modern.

Figure 857 shows a splendid example of this type of clock, the property of Mr. Dwight M. Prouty, of Boston. It is a marriage clock, so-called, is decorated in pink and blue, and is much more elaborate than the usual Willard clocks. On the rectangular base are the words "S. Willard patent." All of the Willard clocks had a rectangular base with straight or curved sides and usually without any ornament below. The painted designs were simple, and there was but little gilding except upon special pieces. The idea was to build an eight-day clock at a reasonable price, and all the maker's energies were directed toward that end.

Figure 858 shows a clock by Willard, Jr., who was Simon, the son of the famous Simon. It differs from most of these clocks in that it has a strike, the bell appearing above the top. The painting on the lower door is Phaeton driving the chariot of the sun.

Of all the clockmakers who adopted Willard's model, probably none made such beautiful clocks as did Lemuel Curtis. Curtis was born in Boston in 1790, moved to Concord, Massachusetts, in 1814, and on January 12, 1816, took out a patent as an improvement on the Willard patent. He lived in Concord until about 1820, when he moved to Burlington, Vermont, where he died in 1857. The form of his clock is much finer than that of the Willards, and they are all quite similar, differing only in minor details.

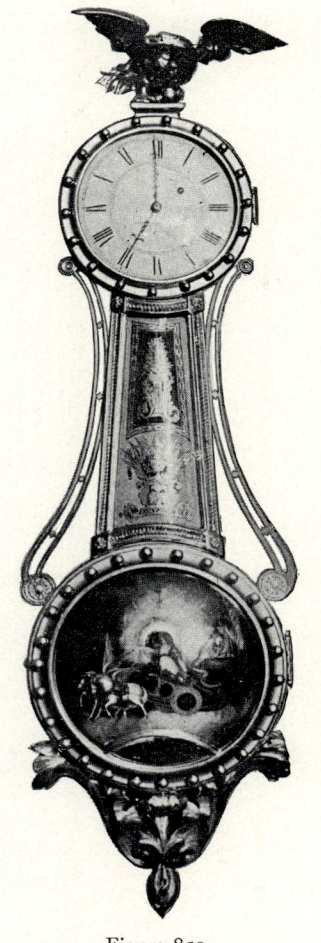

Figure 859.
Curtis Clock, 1800–20.

Figure 859 shows a Curtis clock, the property of Mr. George M. Curtis, of Meriden, Connecticut. Instead of the rectangular base is substituted a circular frame, quite a little larger than the dial, on which is painted on a convex glass Phaeton driving the chariot of the sun. About the dial and base are applied gilded balls. A feature of the Curtis clocks is the hands made of a series of loops. On the dial is printed, "Warranted by L. Curtis." At the foot of the coat of arms "L. Curtis" appears in print, and "Patent" and "L. Curtis" are in script.

Another Curtis clock is shown in Figure 860 and is the property of Mrs. Benjamin Peckham, of Providence. In general form the case is identical with that shown in the preceding figure. In the central section, however, is a thermometer below which is the word "patented." The picture in the lower dial is supposed to represent Paul Revere and Old North Church, Boston. In the background on the dial are the words "Warranted by Curtis & Dunning." An

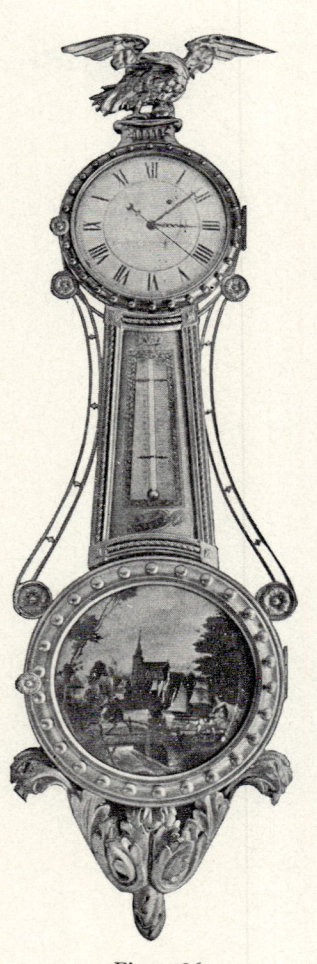

Figure 860.
Curtis Clock, 1800–20.

Figure 861.
Lyre-Shaped Clock, 1815–25.

Figure 862.
Lyre-Shaped Clock, 1815–25.

unusual feature is the sweep second-hand. Curtis clocks are also occasionally found with an eagle with closed instead of spread wings.

Still another form of mural clock is what is known as the lyre clock, a good example of which, the property of Mr. G. Winthrop Brown, of Chestnut Hill, Massachusetts, is shown in Figure 861. The case section is composed of two acanthus-leaf scrolls, and between is painted on glass a female figure with a large lyre. The hands are in the form used by Curtis, and it is possible that he made this clock. An unusual feature of the clock is that it strikes on two wires extend-

CLOCKS

ing diagonally across the clock from the point on the case at the figure IX to the lower right-hand side of the case on two piano stubs over a sounding-board. These wires can be pitched to different tunes. The striking is done with one wheel which lifts a counter-balance to which is attached the hammer which strikes the hour.

Figure 862 shows another lyre clock. The case is composed of two acanthus-leaf scrolls, and on the glass between are painted parallel lines to represent strings.

Figure 864.
Mantel Clock, 1800–20.

Figure 863.
Willard Bracket Clock, 1800–20.

Figure 865.
French Clock, 1800–20.

Figure 863 shows a bracket clock which bears the inscription, "A. Willard, Boston." It is owned by the Misses Brown, of Salem, whose grandfather bought it from Willard. On the lower case is painted a pastoral scene with a floral border. The A. Willard clocks are especially noted for their good painting.

Figure 864 shows another form of mantel clock. The case is mahogany, nicely inlaid, and the dial is painted with a scene and a female figure at the top and fan ornaments in the spandrels. This clock was made by David Wood, of Newburyport, and is in the Bolles Collection, owned by the Metropolitan Museum of Art.

296　COLONIAL FURNITURE

Figure 865 shows a mantel clock such as was popular during the first quarter of the nineteenth century. The frame is composed of alabaster columns and pediment within which are set a dial and a pendulum beautifully embossed. Such clocks as this were intended to be kept under glass.

The earliest mantel clocks without base made in this country were those made by Eli Terry, of Plymouth Hollow, now Thomaston, Connecticut. He was a clockmaker of considerable reputation, and so great was the demand for clocks

Figure 866.
Mantel Clock, 1812.

Figure 867.
Mantel Clock, 1820–30

at the beginning of the nineteenth century that in 1803 he made three thousand clock movements. He then sold out to Calvin Hoadley and Seth Thomas, a well-known American maker, and retired from business. The demand for cheaper clocks than could be made with the tall cases led him to experiment in making small clocks, and about the year 1812 he made six mantel clocks.

Figure 866 shows the first of these clocks. It was a very crude affair and Terry never used it as a model, one of the other five subsequently being adopted for the working model of the later mantel clock, and therefore it has the honour of being the first made and the only one built from this design. It will be seen that it is nothing more nor less than a tall case clock cut down. The works are made of wood and a weight is used for the running power in the same way as in the tall clocks. This clock was bought from Eli Terry by Ozias Goodwin, and is now in the possession of his great-grandson, J. C. Spencer, of Thomaston, Connecticut.

CLOCKS

The model which was adopted for the later mantel clocks was arranged with the pendulum and verge in front of the works behind the face, and was run with a spiral spring.

Figure 867 shows a shelf clock, belonging to the Honourable John R. Buck, which dates between 1820 and 1830 and is a good example of the style. It was quite often the custom to paste in the backs of these clocks a copy of the last census of the principal cities of the United States, and it is thus possible to approximate the year in which they were made.

SUPPLEMENTARY CHAPTER

CHAIRS

A LARGE turned chair of ash is shown in Figure LXXIV, the property of the writer. The back consists of three turnings set horizontal and five well-turned spindles vertical. The finials are not original. It will be seen that this chair differs from the Carver type, Figure 409, in that it has three instead of two horizontal spindles and five instead of three vertical spindles.

Figure LXXV shows a turned slat-back chair with four slats. The finials end in balls, and the turnings are alternating long and short. The arm has a flat surface instead of being turned, and the turnings under the arms and on the front braces are sausage-turned.

Figure LXXVI shows a late turned arm-chair of the Philadelphia type, which is the companion piece to the side-chair shown in Figure 430, except that there are but five instead of six slats. The legs are cabriole, ending in angular Dutch feet with a single turned brace in front, two plain ones on side, and one at back. The skirt on front and sides is cut in cyma curves.

An interesting carved-oak wainscot chair, the property of the Danvers Historical Society, is shown in Figure LXXVII. It is made of American oak throughout. The top overhangs and the surface is carved in a design of gouges and lunettes. A scroll design is carved on the stiles above the arms, and on the upper panel is carved an elaborate lunette design both erect and reversed. On the rail below the panel is an arabesque design, and on the rail below the seat a series of entwined lunettes with acanthus-leaf carving.

Figure LXXVIII shows a cane chair, the property of the Brooklyn Museum. It belongs in classification to the second type of cane chairs; namely, those where the carved cresting extends over the stiles of the back. In this case the stiles curve out and the cresting is considerably wider than the back. The design is a series of scrolls, leaves, and flowers. The stiles are fluted and stopped. The front legs are turned, with cups at top with gadrooning, and terminate in Spanish feet.

Figure LXXVI.
Turned Slat-Back Chair, 1725-50.

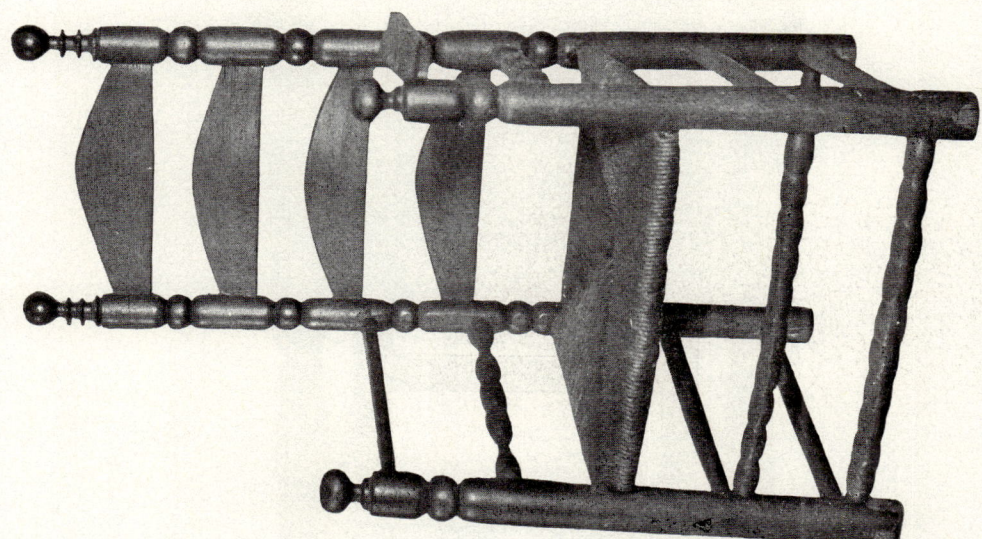

Figure LXXV.
Turned Slat-Back Chair, about 1700.

Figure LXXIV.
Turned Chair, about 1650.

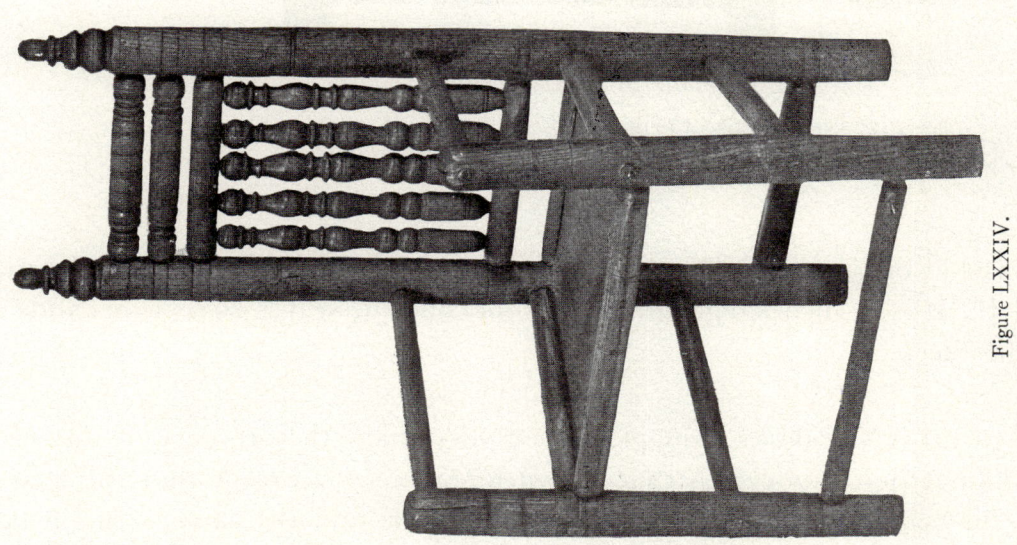

299

At the centre of the brace is a finial. This piece came from Hingham, Massachusetts, where it had been from its probable importation from England about the year 1700.

A very large arm-chair, the property of the writer, is shown in Figure LXXIX. It is in the same design as the side-chair shown in Figure 484. The arms are set

Figure LXXVII.
Carved-Oak Wainscot Chair, about 1650.

back instead of forming an extension of the legs. The Spanish feet are partially restored. It is 47 inches high, 20 inches wide, and the seat is 26¼ inches wide and 20 inches deep.

Figure LXXX shows a maple-turned easy-chair, the property of the writer. This chair is quite similar to that shown in Figure 507 except that the legs terminate in Spanish feet; there is one less stretcher, and the skirt is cut in cyma curves. The arms are in scroll form. The upholstering on the chair is correct, with galloon outlining the scrolls and skirt and a separate cushion.

A well-proportioned maple arm-chair in the Queen Anne style, the property of the writer, is shown in Figure LXXXI. The back is unusually high. The rear legs are in the earliest form, square at bottom and round above. The

Figure LXXVIII.
Cane Chair, about 1700.

Figure LXXIX.
Leather Arm-Chair, Spanish feet, 1700–10.

cabriole legs are slender and stand on club feet. The seat is of needlework of the period.

A Queen Anne side-chair, the property of Mrs. Miles White, is shown in Figure LXXXII. The stiles of the back are rounded, and on the top is a slight carving on either side of a scroll. The splat is plain except for the carved scrolls. The seat is rounded at the front. The legs are cabriole, carved in an acanthus-leaf design, and terminate in ball-and-claw feet. This chair is of Baltimore origin, and although it resembles the Philadelphia pieces in some particulars, its construction is different.

Figure LXXX.
Turned Easy-Chair, 1700–10.

CHAIRS

A Chippendale arm-chair, the property of the Brooklyn Museum, is shown in Figure LXXXIII. It is a companion piece to the side-chair shown in Figure 568. The splat is in Gothic style. Across the top is an acanthus-leaf carving, and the surfaces of the wood connecting the design of the splat are carved in a leaf design.

Figure LXXXI.
Arm-Chair, Dutch style, 1710–30.

The outer edge of the stiles of the back and the front legs are carved in a bead design. These chairs were probably made in New York.

Figure LXXXIV shows a Chippendale arm-chair, the property of Mrs. Miles White. On the surface of the top rail are two ribbon bands, one outlining the top and the other the bottom. On the top at the centre are seven arches with carved pendents. The ribbons join at the top of the stiles. The splat is an intricate design of entwining bands with a cord and tassel at the centre. Fret brackets are under the seat, and the legs are moulded. It is difficult to tell whether this chair was made in the South or was imported when new from England.

A pair of Chippendale chairs from the South, also the property of Mrs. Miles White, are shown in Figure LXXXV. The top of the back is carved in a leaf design, and the splat is composed of a series of entwining scrolls covered with carving in an acanthus-leaf design. The legs are straight, plain, and underbraced.

Another Southern Chippendale chair, the property of Mrs. White, is shown in Figure LXXXVI. The surface of the stiles and back are moulded, and the

Figure LXXXII.
Chair, Dutch style, 1725–50.

splat is in a long scroll design with a slight touch of carving at the top. The legs are plain and underbraced.

The last three figures illustrate the best of the Chippendale chairs found in the South from colonial times, and should be compared with the Philadelphia chairs shown in the chapter on chairs in this volume.

Figure LXXXVII shows a Hepplewhite arm-chair, the property of Mr. G. A. Cluett. The back is shield-shaped, and the splat is carved in drapery and leaf de-

Figure LXXXIV.
Chippendale Arm-Chair, 1760-70.

Figure LXXXIII.
Chippendale Arm-Chair, Gothic taste, 1760-70.

Figure LXXXVI.
Chippendale Side-Chair, 1760-70.

Figure LXXXV.
Pair of Chippendale Side-Chairs, 1760-70.

306

signs with a rosette in a shield. The arms and legs are moulded, and on the turn of the arm is acanthus-leaf carving. The seat is slightly serpentine in front and curved on the sides, and the proportions are perfect.

Figure LXXXVIII shows a Sheraton chair, the property of Mr. Cluett. It is conventional in form, but the surfaces are beautifully inlaid. At the top are fes-

Figure LXXXVII.
Hepplewhite Arm-Chair, 1780–90.

toons of flowers, and an anthemium design is at the head of each splat, below which are pendent flowers. Pendent flowers are also inlaid on the legs.

Figure LXXXIX shows another Sheraton chair, the property of Mr. Cluett. The surfaces of the back are fluted with rosettes at each corner, and the splat is in a fluted lattice design with rosettes at the crossings. The front legs taper and curve out.

308   COLONIAL FURNITURE

Figure XC, the property of Mr. Cluett, shows a variation of the chair shown in Figure 613. It is in Phyfe style. The sides are reeded and the lower part of the legs are carved with a lion's leg and claw. The splat, however, instead of having a lyre, has two sections of an oval back to back.

During the early nineteenth century so-called "fancy" chairs and other ar-

Figure LXXXVIII.
Sheraton Inlaid Chair, 1790–1800.

ticles of painted furniture were made, and it is not uncommon to find advertisements of fancy chairmakers in all the large places. For instance, Thomas Ash, in New York, so advertised. They were called "fancy" because they were painted with designs in bright colors.

Figure XCI shows three fancy chairs owned by Mrs. Miles White. Across the back are three rectangular panels, the outer ones with a border only and the centre one with scrolls of music and musical instruments. The centre splat is

Figure XC.
Sheraton Chair in Phyfe style, 1810–15.

Figure LXXXIX.
Sheraton Chair, 1790–1800.

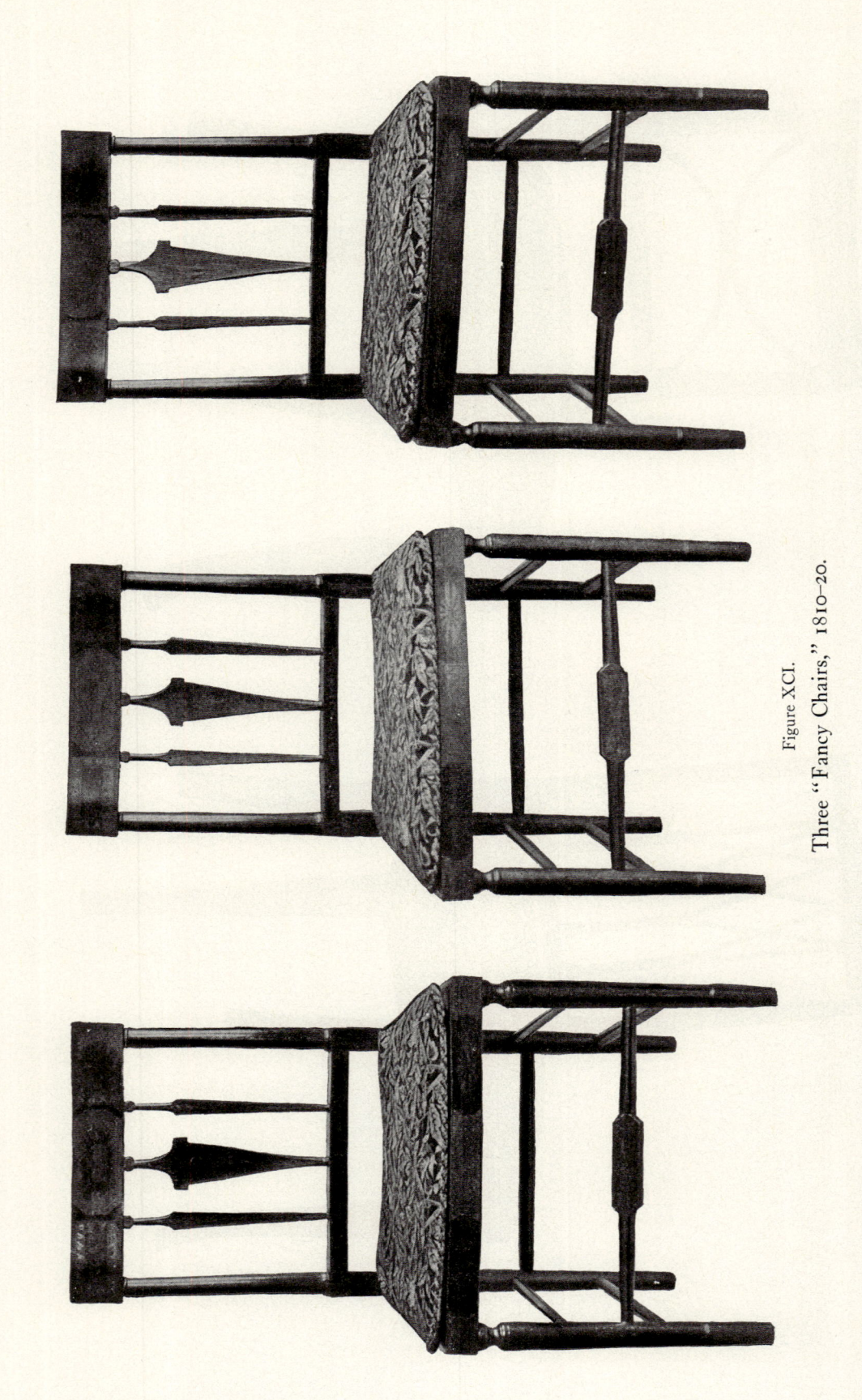

Figure XCI.
Three "Fancy Chairs," 1810–20.

SETTEES, COUCHES, SOFAS

urn-shaped, with painted pendent flowers. There is also a slight design on the outer splats, on the front rail, and the centre of the stretcher.

In addition to these chairs, Mrs. White also owns a settee, Figure XCIV, a window-seat, Figure XCVII, and a card-table, Figure CXIX. These pieces were made by Robert Fisher, of Baltimore. In the Baltimore directory for 1800-1 he appears as a chairmaker at 35 South Gay Street, in 1803 as a fancy chairmaker, 37 South Gay Street. Also in the directories for 1804, 1807, 1810, 1812. In 1814 he appears as a lumber merchant, and in 1822 and subsequently as Gentleman, probably meaning that he had retired from active business.

SETTEES, COUCHES, AND SOFAS

Figure XCII shows a Hepplewhite three-back settee, through the courtesy of Mr. Charles W. Lyon. The backs are shield-shaped, and the splats are three long loops with carved acanthus leaves at the top. The legs are eight in number and tapering.

Figure XCIII shows a Hepplewhite two-back settee, the property of Mr. G. A. Cluett. The backs are shield-shaped. There are inlaid fans at the top of the backs and inlaid urns at the centre, with pendent flowers. The front legs are also inlaid with pendent flowers. The method of lengthening the seat by separating the two backs is an interesting variation.

Figure XCIV shows a painted settee, the property of Mrs. Miles White. It is the companion to the three chairs shown in Figure XCI, and was made by Robert Fisher, of Baltimore. The surfaces are painted in the same manner as the chairs.

Figure XCV shows a pair of charming little window-seats, also the property of Mrs. White. They closely resemble the couch shown in Figure 649. The whole seat is curved. They stand on four plain legs underbraced.

Another window-seat, the property of Mrs. White, is shown in Figure XCVI. The front is serpentine, the ends are scrolled with carved rosettes, and the legs are plain and tapering.

Still another window-seat, the property of Mrs. White, is shown in Figure XCVII. This window-seat is constructed to set into a recess, the front projecting at either side beyond the recess. It is painted, and was made by Robert Fisher, of Baltimore. The legs are in Sheraton form, and the seat is of cane.

A very good Southern sofa is shown in Figure XCVIII, the property of Mrs. Miles White. There are three cabriole legs in front, terminating in ball-and-claw feet, and a shell with pendent flowers is carved on each knee. The rear legs

Figure XCII.
Settee with Three Chair-Backs, Hepplewhite style, 1785–95.

Figure XCIII.
Settee with Two Chair-Backs, Hepplewhite style, 1785–95.

SETTEES, COUCHES, SOFAS 313

terminate in knobs, which is different from the Philadelphia type, where this is omitted.

Figure XCIX shows a handsome Hepplewhite sofa, the property of the Brooklyn Museum. The centre of the back is slightly raised and ornamented with parallel gouges. The arms are composed of two graceful concaves. The front legs are inlaid with pendent flowers with a broad holly band below.

Figure C shows a sofa, the property of Mr. G. A. Cluett. The outline of the top is two long cyma curves, and where joined there is a raised centre upon

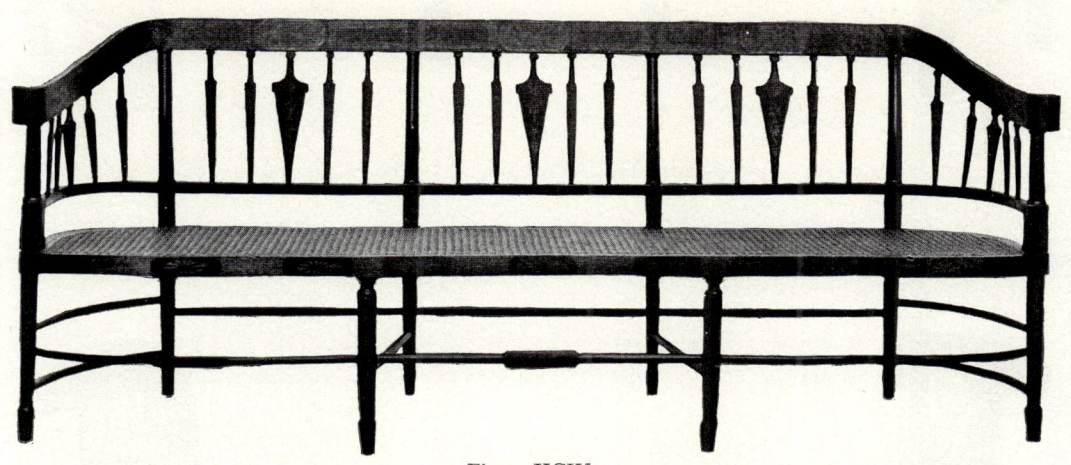

Figure XCIV.
Settee, Painted, Sheraton style, 1810–20.

which is carved a basket of flowers. The arms are scrolled and are finished with carved rosettes and acanthus-leaf carving. Several sofas are known by the same maker, who is supposed to have come from Salem, Massachusetts. (Figures CIII and CVI.) The distinguishing feature is the fine cameo-like carving and the stippled background in the same method found on oak pieces.

Figure CI shows a large Sheraton sofa, the property of Mr. Brooks Reed. On the front of each arm is a reeded bulb with a flat reeded surface behind. The back and seat are upholstered to make three large seats. The front legs are turned.

Figure CII shows a sofa, the property of Mr. G. A. Cluett. It is in the familiar Duncan Phyfe style. The top of the back is divided into three panels. On the outer ones are carved drapery and tassels, and on the centre one cornucopias with heads of wheat, joined at the centre by a bow-knot of ribbon. The top of the arms and the front and side rails are reeded. The fronts of the arms turn in and are

Figure XCV.
Pair Window-Seats, 1775–85.

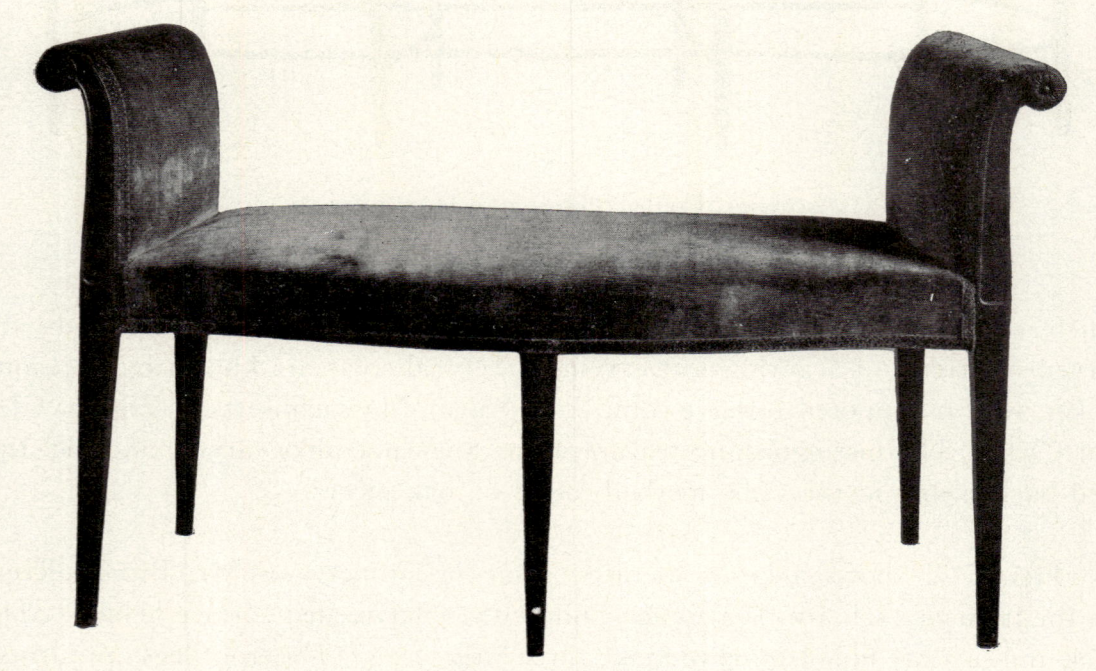

Figure XCVI.
Window-Seat, 1785–95.

314

SETTEES, COUCHES, SOFAS

supported by turned and beautifully carved supports. The side rails are cut in a cyma curve. The feet are reeded.

Figure CIII shows another Salem sofa made by the same cabinet-maker who made Figure C. On the panel at the back is carved a cartouche from which extends drapery, at the centre of which are flowers. The background is stippled in the manner peculiar to this maker. Below the panels is a frieze of four channels separated by rosettes, a design quite commonly used by McIntire. On the arms

Figure XCVII.
Window-Seat, Painted, 1810–20.

are carved rosettes and acanthus leaves, and the supports are also carved in a leaf design with rosettes.

Figure CV shows a sofa in the same general shape as Figure 663 but differently treated. The back is divided into three panels, the outer ones carved in a design of sprays of wheat fastened with a ribbon wound about the stems, and at the centre are two cornucopias full of spears of wheat. On the outside of the arms are again spears of wheat, and on the legs are cornucopias with wheat and terminating in eagles' heads. Across the front rail are curved leaves and rosettes. The arms have splats, each consisting of a curved rectangular design, and below are three sets of three balls. The last two sofas are the property of Mr. G. A. Cluett.

Figure XCVIII.
Sofa, Chippendale style, 1760–80.

Figure XCIX.
Sofa, Hepplewhite style, 1785–95.

Figure C.
Sofa, Hepplewhite style, 1790–1800.

Figure CI.
Sofa, Sheraton style, 1790–1800.

Figure CII.
Sofa, Phyfe style, 1800–10.

Figure CIII.
Sofa, Sheraton style, about 1800.

318

SETTEES, COUCHES, SOFAS 319

Figure CIV shows another sofa in the Duncan Phyfe style, owned by Mr. C. R. Morson. The design carved on the top rail of the back is the same as that shown in Figure 664, fasces in the two outer panels and cornucopias on the centre one. The fronts of the arms are carved in a long acanthus leaf, as are also the legs, which are cabriole terminating in an animal's claw. The front rail of the seat is reeded.

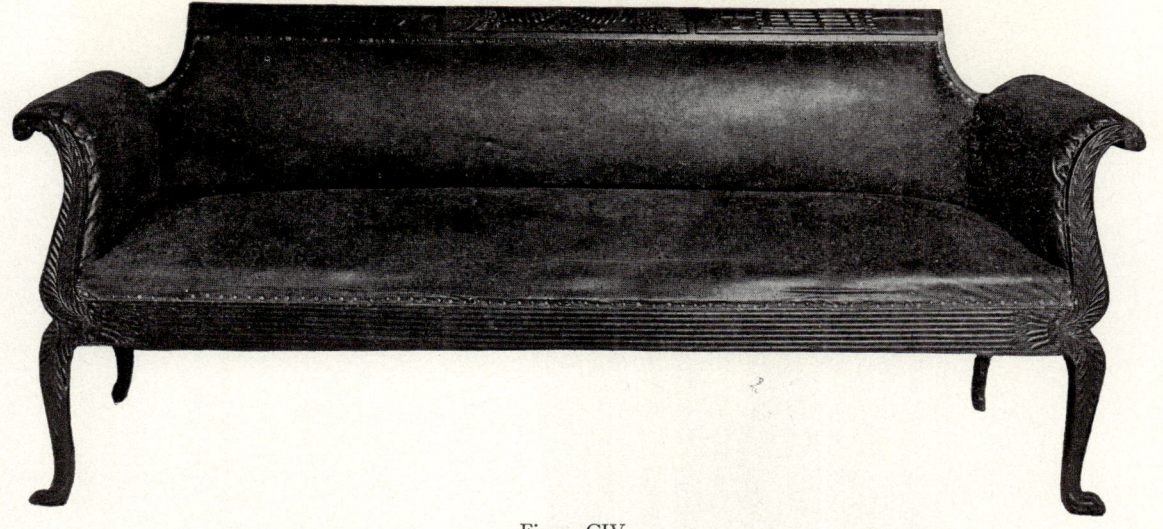

Figure CIV.
Sofa, Phyfe style, 1800–10.

Figure CVI shows a couch by the Salem maker. (See Figures C and CIII.) The top of the back is carved in a design of grapes and leaves. On the arm and roll are carved cornucopias with fruits, flowers, and wheat. The front rail of the seat is carved in a leaf design, the legs are turned and gadrooned. The entire surface back of the cameo carving is stippled, as in the other pieces made by this cabinet-maker.

Figure CVII shows an Empire sofa. The centre of the back is supported by eagle heads. The arms are shaped in Flemish scrolls, the surfaces carved in an acanthus-leaf design, and the legs are eagle heads with wings extending under the seat rail. The last two sofas are the property of Mr. G. A. Cluett.

Figure CV.
Sofa, Phyfe style, 1800–10.

Figure CVI.
Couch, Sheraton style, about 1810.

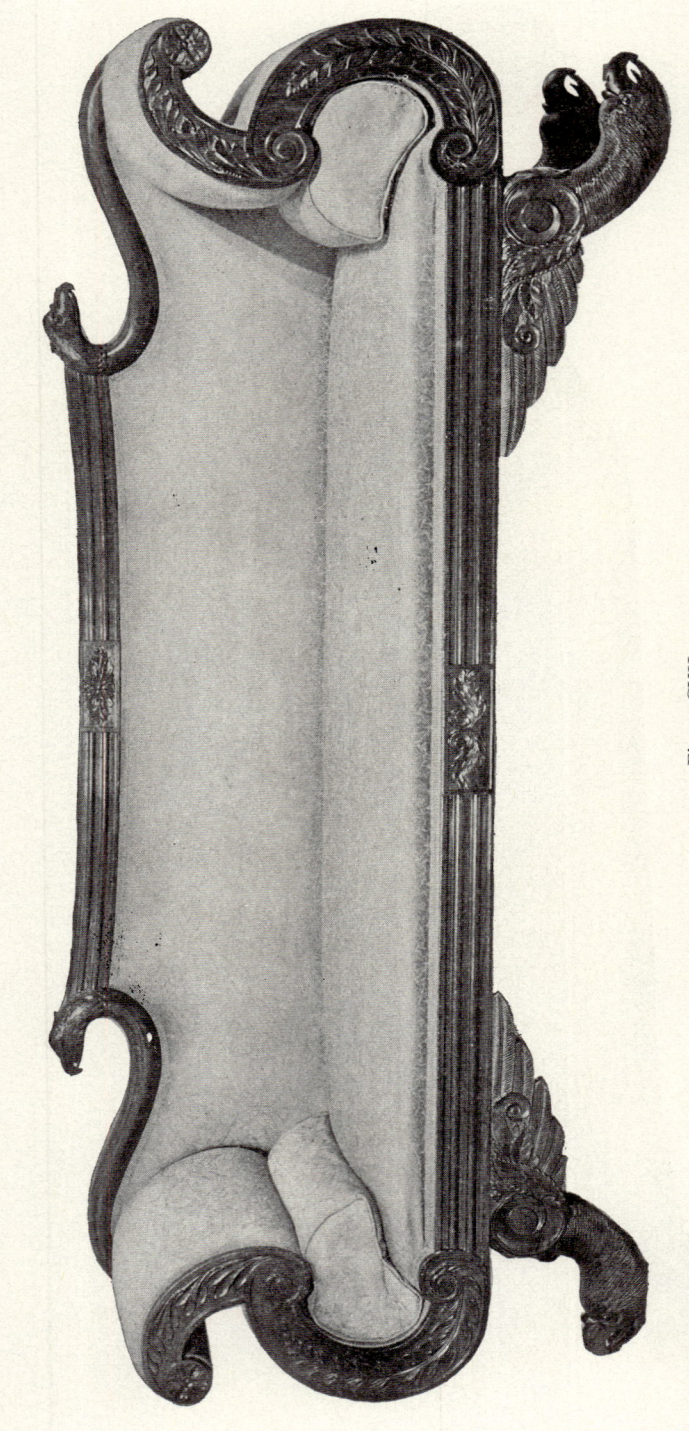

Figure CVII.
Sofa, Empire style, 1810–20.

TABLES

TABLES

Figure CVIII shows a very rare form of wainscot table, the property of Mrs. John I. Blair. It appears to be made of American oak. The shape of the frame is a half octagon, as is also the platform below. The top is oval, folding over similar to a card-table, and the leaf when open is supported by a gate leg similar to that on a gate-leg table. There are four bulbous turned columns supporting the top, similar to those found on court cupboards. The flat surfaces have on them applied bosses and split spindles, and the piece stands on ball feet.

Figure CVIII.
Oak Wainscot Table, 1650–75.

Figure CIX shows a gate-leg table, the property of Mr. Francis P. Garvan. It differs from any which the writer knows in that the legs upholding the leaves do not swing but slide in and out on the track which appears through the centre.

A small folding-table, the property of the writer, is shown in Figure CX. It is 33 inches long, and when closed only 6 inches wide. The turnings are small and the feet are lunette-shaped. There are apparently four types of this table, Figure 689, where the base has a central piece of flat wood instead of turning, the legs swinging from the sides instead of the centre; Figure 690, differing only in that the gates are not turned—they are sometimes plain as those shown or moulded; Figure 691, where the centre section is turned and the gates swing from the centre and when closed are in a plane with the stationary legs, the outer legs supported on flat or moulded wooden slabs; and the fourth kind, that shown in this figure.

Figure CXI shows a turned table the frame of which is entirely of American oak. The top is of pine. The stretchers and legs are sausage-turned and painted black. The drawer is on side runners. The front and back stretchers are set high, showing the table was intended to sit at and to stand away from the wall.

Another oak-turned table is shown in Figure CXII. The frame is also of oak, and on the drawer is a carved lunette design. The front stretcher is set high, but the rear one is low, the same height on the legs as the side stretcher. This would indicate that it was intended to stand against the wall.

An interesting little tea-table, the earliest the writer has seen, is shown in Figure CXIII. The frame is 20½ inches wide and 17¾ inches deep, and the top, which has an edge, has a wide overhang. It is made of pine throughout. There are three little drawers, and the skirt is cut in semicircles. The legs are turned in an unusual pattern. The handles are original.

Figure CXV shows a mahogany dining-table, Chippendale style. The four legs on the frame are stationary, and two legs on each side swing out to hold the leaves. There is a drawer at either end, and the lower edge on each side is carved in a gadroon pattern. On each side of the frame and on the edge above each leg is a small bead carving. The knees are carved in an acanthus-leaf design and terminate in ball-and-claw feet. The last four tables are in the writer's collection.

A mahogany tripod-table is shown in Figure CXIV. The pedestal is well proportioned with fluted columns and a bead. On the top of the legs are acanthus-leaf carving with a pendent flower, a type found south of Philadelphia. The top has a moulded edge cut from the solid.

A pair of card-tables, the property of Mr. Israel Sack, are shown in Figure CXVI. The frame is swelled in front with a long cyma curve on each side. There are three handsome satin-wood panels on the front and one on each side, and over each of the front legs the rectangle is outlined in light and dark inlay. The legs are straight, but taper suddenly below the inlay band near the bottom.

One of another pair of card-tables, the property of Mr. G. A. Cluett, is shown in Figure CXVII. The front of the frame is oval with three oval panels between the legs, separated by an inlaid rosette. On the legs are inlaid pendent flowers, and on the top is inlaid half of an oval rosette.

Figure CIX.
Gate-Leg Table, about 1700.

Figure CX.
Folding-Table, 1675–1700.

Figure CXI.
Turned Table, 1675–1700.

Figure CXII.
Turned Table, 1675–1700.

326

Figure CXIII.
Tea-Table, about 1700.

Figure CXIV.
Tripod-Table, 1760–70.

328 COLONIAL FURNITURE

Figure CXVIII shows a very charming side-table of the Sheraton period, the property of Mr. Cluett. The front is cut in a slight serpentine and the sides in a cyma curve. The panels are mahogany, bordered with satin-wood. The legs are reeded, with acanthus-leaf capitals. There are slender stretchers between the legs, curved inward, with a small platform between the front and rear stretchers.

Figure CXIX shows a card-table, the property of Mrs. Miles White, made by Robert Fisher, of Baltimore. (See note of this cabinet-maker under Figure XCI.) The painting is quite brilliant and well preserved. In the centre is an oc-

Figure CXV.
Dining-Table, Chippendale style, 1760–70.

tagon panel with a tall building painted in the centre. The octagon panels on the side have painted in them musical instruments. The rectangular panels are the same as on the chair, and a similar border is about the edges of the top, which is shaped as the frame, concave in the centre and a large cyma on each side. There are painted lines down the legs to resemble reeding.

A charming small oval table is shown in Figure CXX, the property of Mr. G. A. Cluett. There is one drawer, and a narrow band of holly inlay makes oval panels. There is a satin-wood panel over each leg, and the legs have lines of holly and a band of the same wood near the bottom.

A sofa-table in the style of Phyfe, also the property of Mr. Cluett, is shown in Figure CXXI. At the two ends are lyres, and the feet are carved with acanthus leaves and reeded. A double-reeded and turned stretcher connects the two ends.

A very good example of a Phyfe table is shown in Figure CXXII, the property

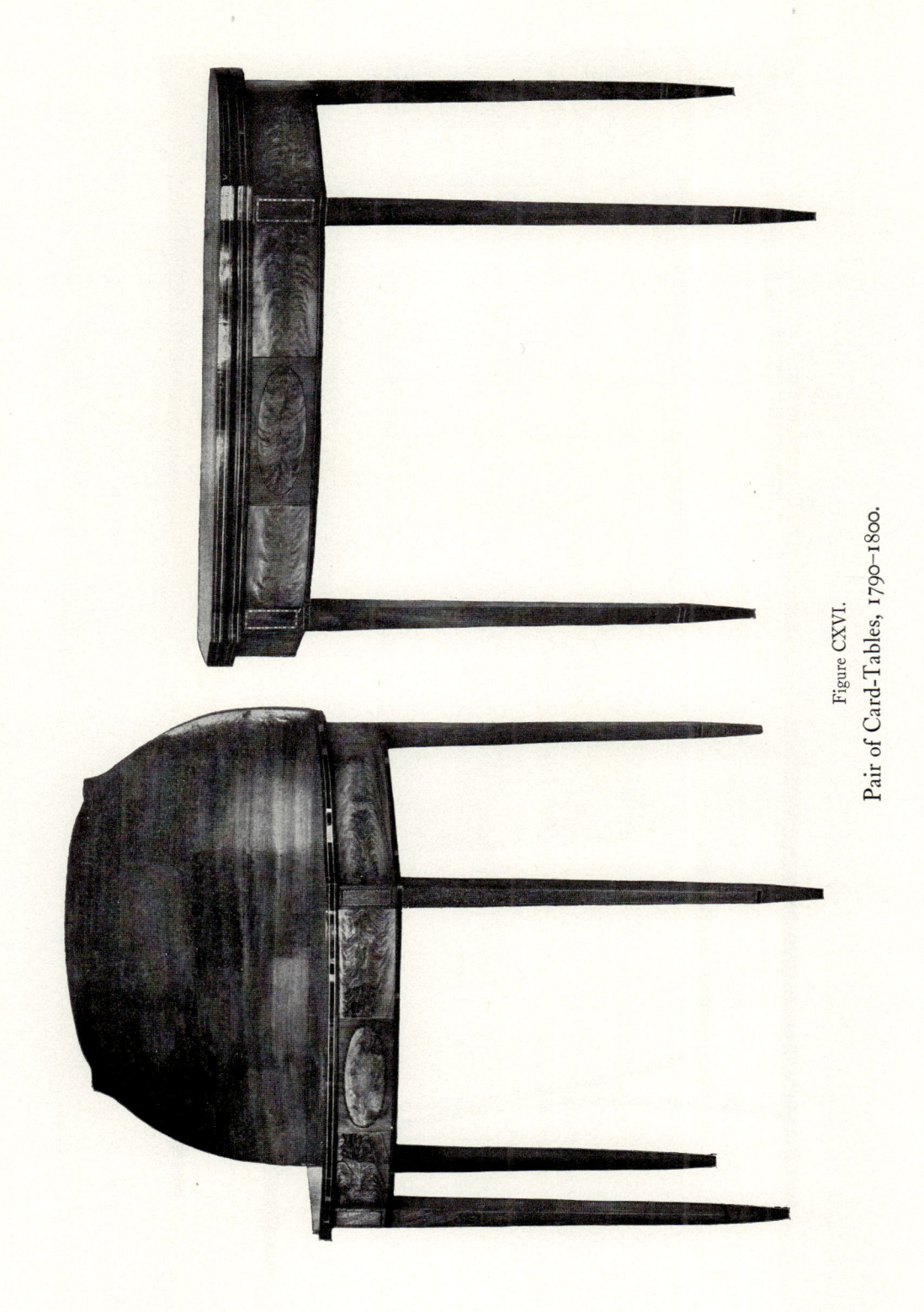

Figure CXVI.
Pair of Card-Tables, 1790–1800.

Figure CXVII.
Card-Table, 1790–1800.

Figure CXVIII.
Side-Table, about 1790.

Figure CXIX.
Painted Card-Table, 1800–10.

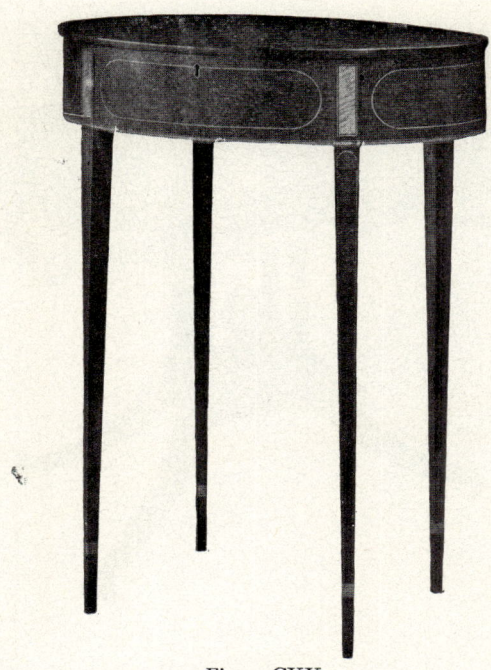

Figure CXX.
Oval Stand, 1790–1800.

332   COLONIAL FURNITURE

of Mr. Charles W. Lyon. There are four small columns in an acanthus-leaf design and a carved pineapple at the centre. The section between the legs is carved

Figure CXXI.
Sofa-Table, Phyfe style, 1800–10.

Figure CXXII.
Phyfe Table, 1800–10.

in a drapery design. The legs are long cyma curves with a fern-leaf design carved on the upper surface, and terminate in lions' feet.

BEDSTEADS

BEDSTEADS

A type of bedstead which the writer has found only in southwestern Connecticut is shown in Figure CXXIII. The four posts are alike, each octagon in

Figure CXXIII.
Bedstead, 1725–50.

shape with fluting on each surface, and the feet are moulded. The hangings, though modern, are a copy of those used prior to 1750.

Figure CXXIV shows a bedstead all four legs of which are cabriole, terminating in Dutch feet. The posts are round. The inner edges of the rails are cut away and the pegs to hold the cording are inserted, making the tops flush with the rails.

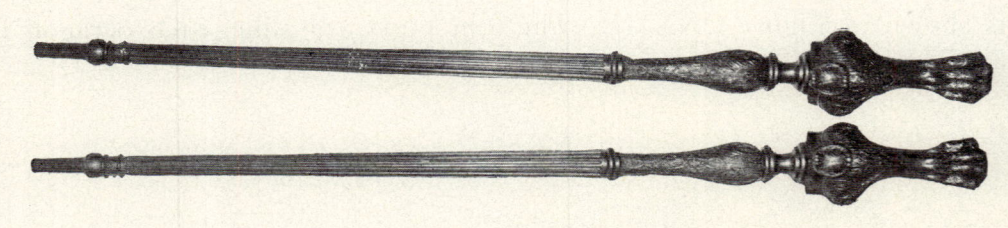

Figure CXXV.
Bedposts, 1760-70.

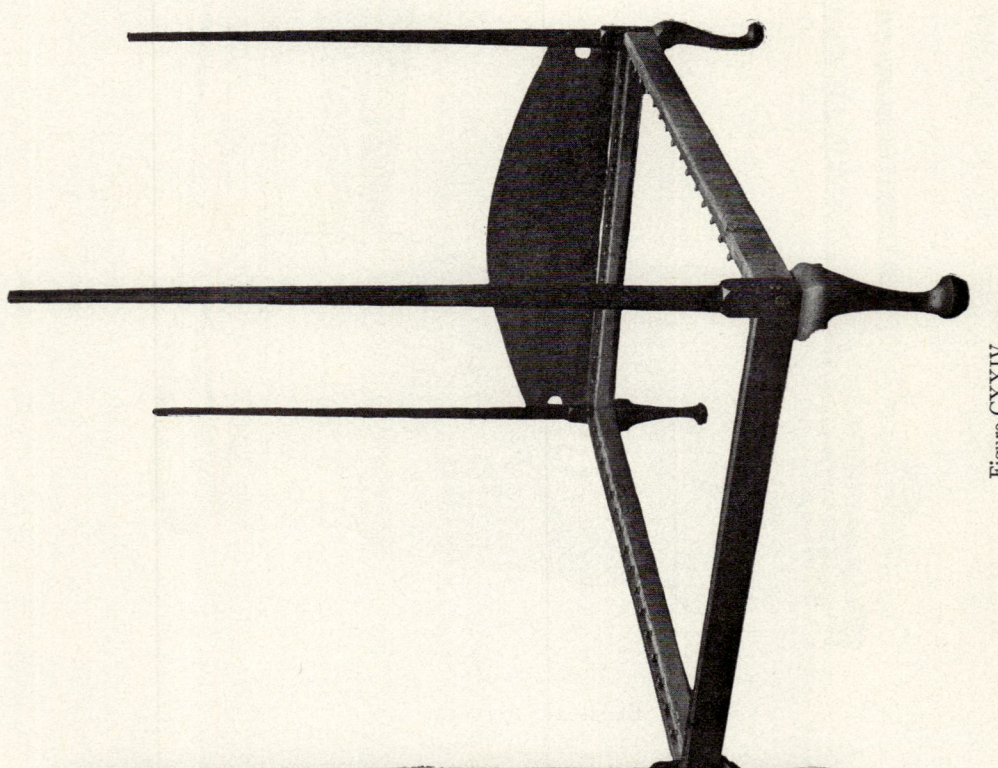

Figure CXXIV.
Bedstead with Cabriole Legs, 1725-50.

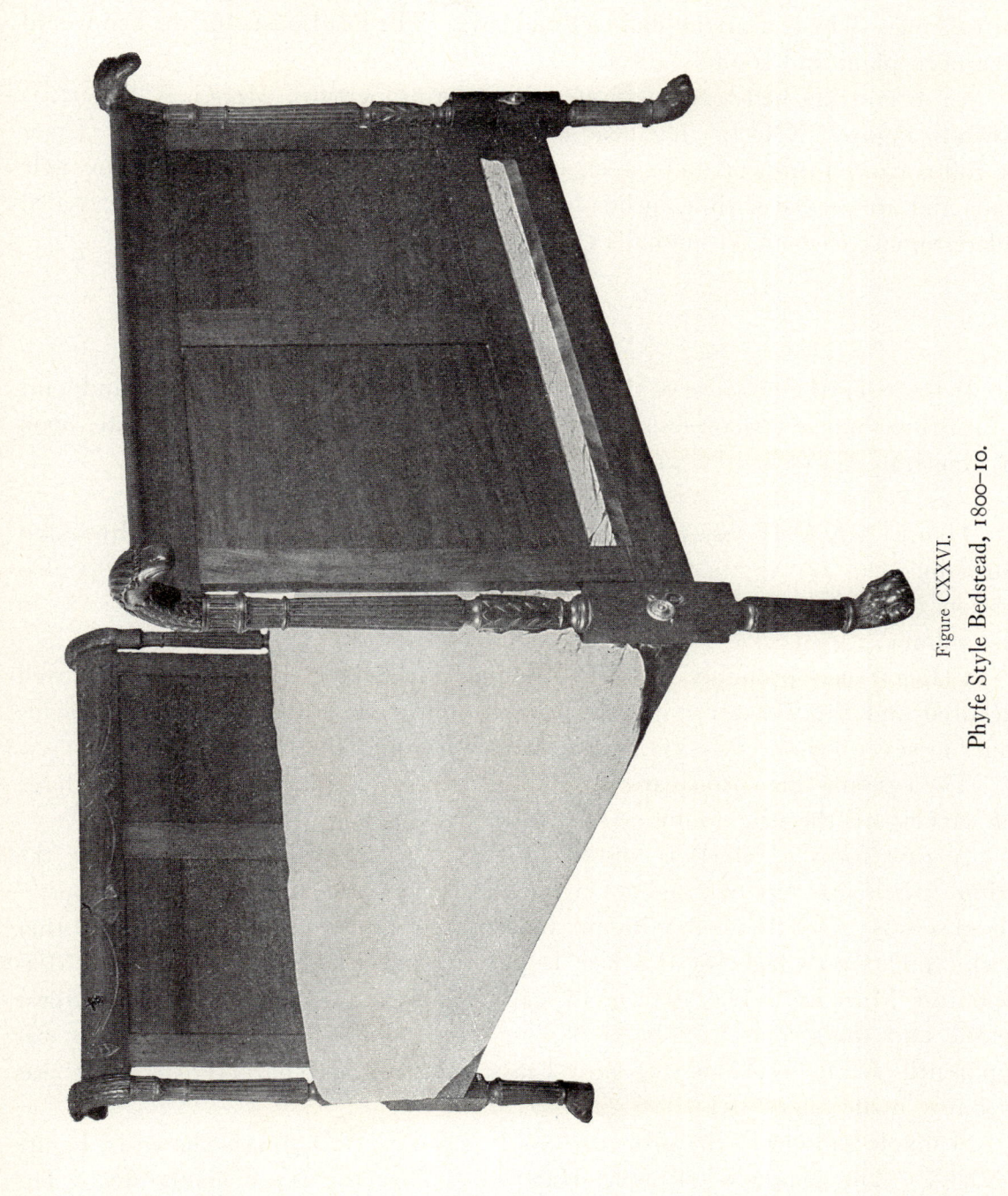

Figure CXXVI.
Phyfe Style Bedstead, 1800–10.

A beautiful pair of foot bedposts are shown in Figure CXXV. The posts are fluted to the bulb turning, which is carved in well-executed acanthus-leaf pattern. The legs are cabriole with a cartouche at the centre of each and acanthus-leaf carving. The feet are animal feet on claws. The head-posts for the bed would have been plain and rounded.

An interesting bedstead in Phyfe style, the property of Mr. G. A. Cluett, is shown in Figure CXXVI. The head and foot boards are high and rounded. Upon the roll is carved drapery and tassels. The columns terminate at the top in eagle heads and are reeded with acanthus-leaf carving at the base. The legs are reeded and terminate each in an animal's claw.

CLOCKS

It has been the purpose of the writer to treat clocks more from the standpoint of furniture than as timepieces. It is to be hoped that some day an adequate book on American clocks will be written.

Figure CXXVII shows a tall clock, the property of the Brooklyn Museum. On the plate is engraved "W. Claggett, Newport." For a discussion of this maker and other examples of his work, see chapter on clocks in this volume.

Claggett was probably the best colonial clockmaker. His dials are all well executed and the works are of the highest order. He seems to have spelled his name in several different ways, sometimes with one g and one t.

The case has the cornice and mouldings used by Goddard, and the finials have the carving on the urns found on his work.

A rare form of clock is shown in Figure CXXVIII, the property of the writer. It is just five feet high. On the dial is engraved "Tho Claget Newport." Thomas was a brother of William and worked at Newport. Only one other clock by Thomas Claget of this size is known, and that is owned by the Metropolitan Museum. The dial is in early form, the spandrels of the earliest period, and there is a little band of engraving edging the dial. The case was apparently made by Goddard, as it bears many of his characteristics. It was probably made about 1745.

A maple tall clock, the property of Mr. Charles W. Lyon, is shown in Figure CXXIX. The maker is Hosmer, Hartford. The case is unusually fine. The cresting is not only on the front but on both sides and is in the form found on mirrors. The finials are tipped with ivory. The slender columns have a twist carving; a rosette and a star are carved on the door of the lower part. The dial has the moon phases. The spandrels are scrolls and differ from any the writer has seen, and the minute dial is especially charming.

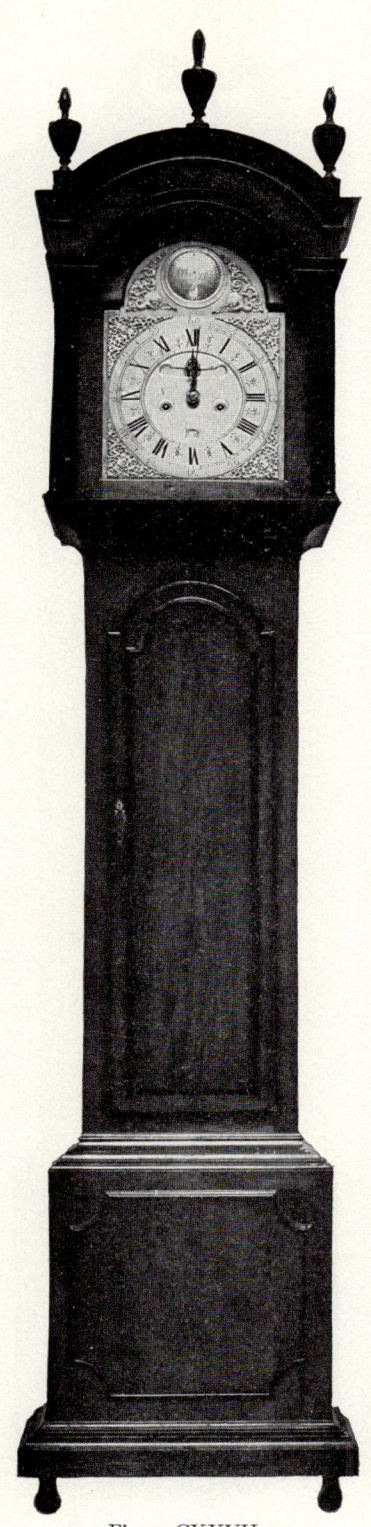

Figure CXXVII.
Tall Clock by Claggett,
about 1745.

Figure CXXVIII.
Miniature Tall Clock by Tho
Claget, about 1745.

Figure CXXIX.
Tall Clock by Hosmer,
about 1790.

Figure CXXX.
Tall Clock by Whiting,
1790–1800.

CLOCKS

Figure CXXX shows a clock with painted dial, the property of Mr. G. A. Cluett. The maker is Whiting, Winchester. On the bonnet are inlaid sprays of flowers, and across the front of the case is inlaid an entwined lunette design.

Figure CXXXI.
Three A. Willard Bracket Clocks, 1800–10.

The quarter-columns are reeded, and below are pendent flowers. At the centre of the door is a large eagle inlaid.

Three Aaron Willard clocks are shown in Figure CXXXI, the property of Mr. Cluett. The outer ones are bracket clocks, without strike. The cases are inlaid and in the centre of the third is an eagle holding a liberty cap on a staff. At the centre is a bracket clock in the banjo form.

Three banjo clocks, also the property of Mr. Cluett, are shown in Figure CXXXII. The first two are by Aaron Willard and the third is by Simon Willard.

340 COLONIAL FURNITURE

It is interesting to compare how closely Aaron followed his father's designs. The second clock has a strike, the bell being on top surmounted by a brass eagle.

Figure CXXXIII shows a modification of the banjo clock, the property of Mr. Philip L. Spalding. The maker is Aaron Willard. The dial is diamond-shaped.

Figure CXXXII.
Three Banjo Clocks, 1800–10.

Above is painted a United States coat of arms, and at the other corners are scrolls. There is a band of reeding on the finial bracket and again below the dial.

Figure CXXXIV shows a Curtis clock, the property of Mr. G. A. Cluett. It is in every respect the same as the Curtis clocks shown in Figures 859 and 860, except the painted picture on the lower dial. On this clock the subject is stated

CLOCKS

341

to be "Venus Resigning Cupid to Calypso." The upper dial is painted in a beautiful shade of blue.

Figure CXXXV shows two clocks, the property of Mr. Philip L. Spalding. They are in a rare form known as Eddystone Lighthouse clocks. They are said

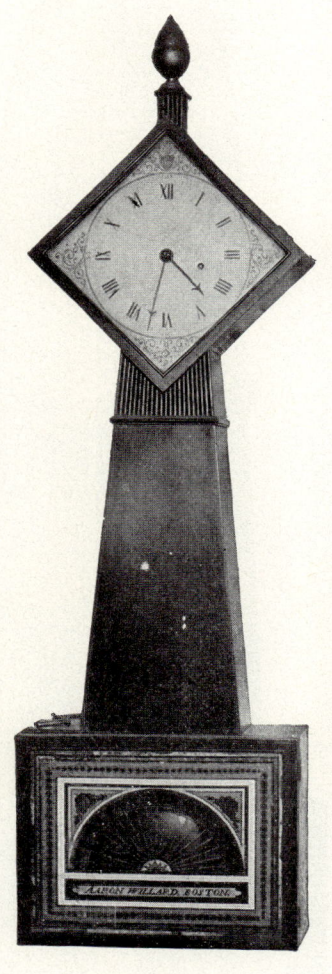

Figure CXXXIII.
Banjo Clock, A. Willard,
1800–10.

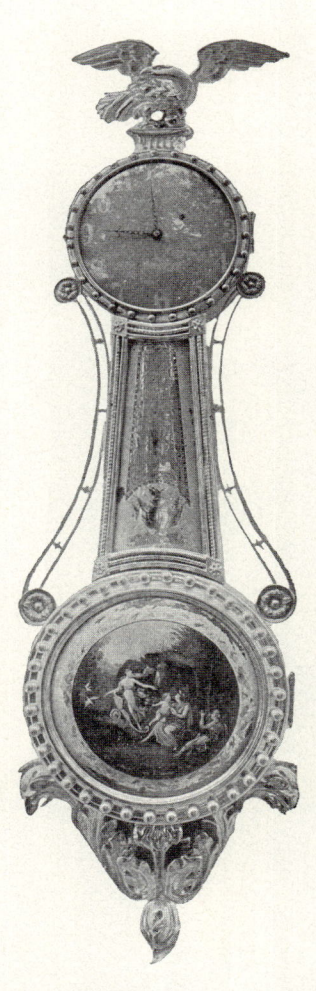

Figure CXXXIV.
Curtis Clock,
1800–20.

not to have been a success, and only a few were made. The clocks run with weights, and because the fall is short the weights were made heavy and more teeth and leaves on the pinions were added, and the strain was so great that the works quickly wore out. They are all made with a glass bell to fit over the works. The two clocks are much alike, differing only in slight details. On the dial of the

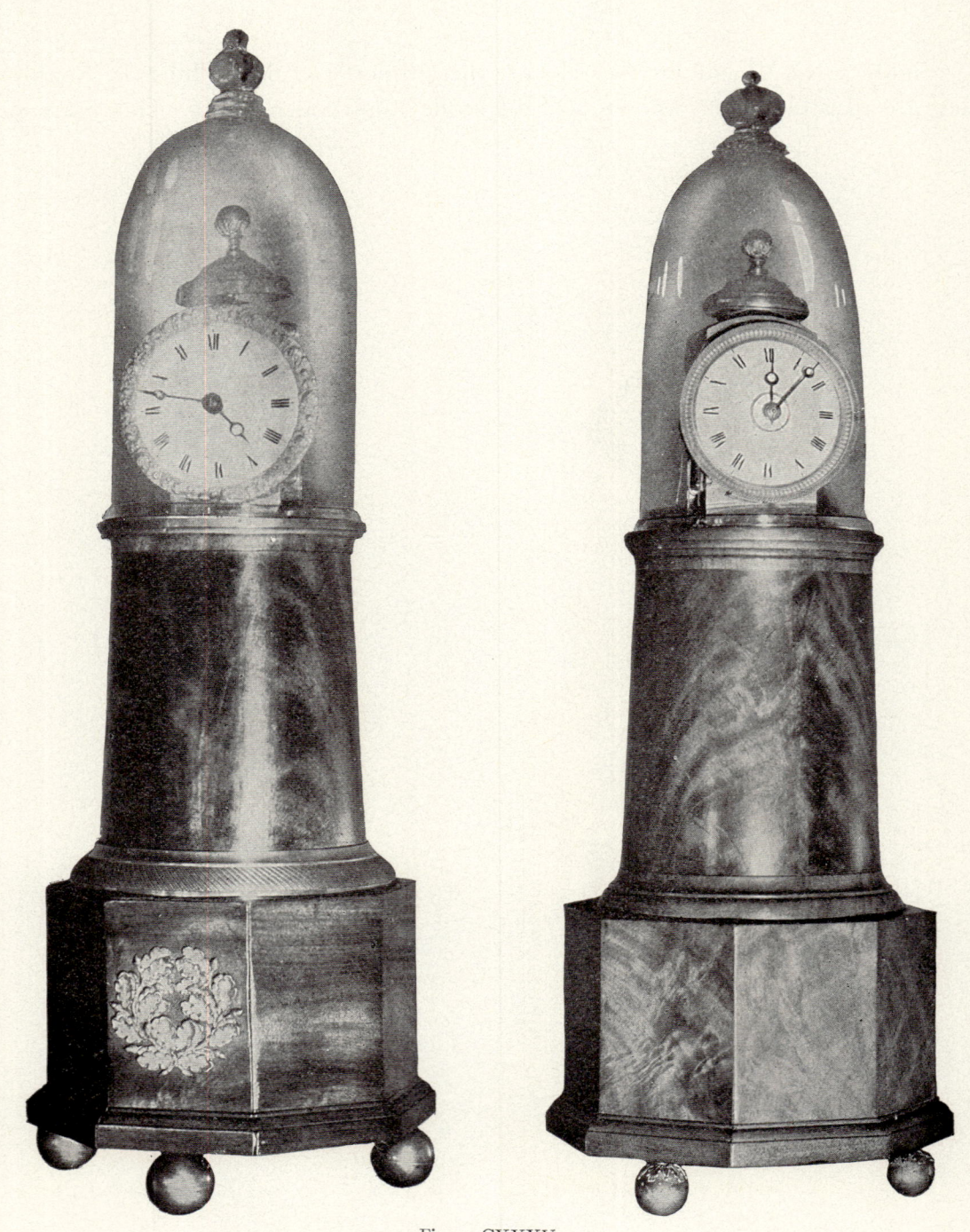

Figure CXXXV.
Two Willard Eddystone Lighthouse Clocks, 1810–20.

Figure CXXXVI.
Two Willard Eddystone Lighthouse Clocks, 1810–20.

first is painted "Simon Willard Patent" and on the other "Simon Willard & Son Patent."

Two other lighthouse clocks are shown in Figure CXXXVI, the property of Mr. G. A. Cluett. The first one has a very short fall and a square base and has painted on the dial "Simon Willard & Son Patent." The other, which is taller, has a square base, and on the case is "Simon Willard Patent."

INDEX

Adam Brothers, I, 11, 17; II, 81, 106, 109
Alarm clocks, II, 272–275
Albany Historical Society, gate-legged table owned by, II, 175
Alden, John, I, 369
Aldersey, Thomas, I, 305
Allen, Mrs. Eustace L., pole screen owned by, II, 239
Allen, Mr. Norman F., looking-glass owned by, I, 314
Allis, Elizabeth, chest made for, I, 341–343
Allis, Ichabod, I, 342
Allis, Captain John, I, 341, 342
Allis, William, I, 342
Allyn, Mary, chest made for, I, 335–337, 341, 342
American Antiquarian Society, furniture owned by: Chippendale settee, II, 134; slate-top table, II, 190
American cabinet-makers, I, 19
American furniture, four periods of, I, 20, 21
Ames, Mr. William, Claggett clock owned by, II, 285
Andrews, Misses, furniture owned by: Burnap clock, II, 288; candle-stand, II, 220; card-table, Hepplewhite, II, 230; chairs: Dutch, II, 56, 59, roundabout, 70; settle, II, 129; sideboard, Hepplewhite, I, 197; sofa, Sheraton, II, 161
Andrews, Rev. Samuel J., D.D., Hepplewhite chair owned by, II, 115
Appleton, Nathaniel, card-table made by, II, 234
Arched carving, I, 24
Ash, Thomas, "fancy" chairs made by, II, 308

Babbitt, Mrs. Anna, furniture owned by: chest on chest, I, 115; sideboard table, 189
Bacon, quoted, I, 210
Banjo clocks, II, 293, 339, 340
Barckley, Duncan & Company, I, 308
Barnett, John, clockmaker, II, 281
Basin-stand, I, 145
"Beaufatts," I, 180, 184
Bed-hangings, II, 251, 253
Bedpost clocks, II, 272–275
Bedposts, II, 250, 336; Empire, 264, 265
Bedside table, II, 212
Bedstead, Countess of Devon's famous, II, 244; Peter Stuyvesant's, 248
Bedsteads, historical sketch of, II, 243, 244; cabriole-legged, 255–257, 333; carved oak, 244; Chippendale, 258–260; kinds of colonial, 247, 248; reasons for disappearance of seventh century, 247, 248; draped, 250–253, 260; Empire, 265–269; English, 244, 258; field, 264; French, 269; low-post, 265, 266; with octagon posts, 333; Phyfe style, 336; prices of, 246, 250; Sheraton, 260–264; of the South, 247
Beekman, Mrs. Henry R., walnut kas owned by, I, 170, 171
Belden & Allis, I, 342

Belden, Samuel, 1, 342
Bible-boxes, I, 210, 211
Bidwell, Miss Esther, furniture owned by: chair, Chippendale, II, 87; chest on chest, I, 125; low-boy, I, 100; tea-table, II, 206. *See also* Bolles Collection
Bigelow, Mr. Francis H., furniture owned by: chair, II, 71; looking-glasses, I, 285, 289; sideboard with china closet, I, 201, 203; sofa, Phyfe, II, 163; scrutoires, I, 235, 243–245, 269; writing-table, I, 272
Bilboa looking-glasses, I, 314, 315, 396
Bird-cage clocks, II, 272–275
Blair, Mrs. John I., furniture owned by: two-drawer chest, I, 338; block-front chest of drawers, I, 358; wainscot table, II, 323
Blaney, Mr. Dwight, furniture owned by: chairs: Carver, II, 11, Chippendale, 84, 89, 108, Dutch, 54, Sheraton, 122, slat-back, 14, wagon, 131; chests: oak, I, 35, Hadley, 42, 43; couch, Dutch, II, 146; dressing-table, I, 91; looking-glass, I, 285; pier-glass, I, 320; pole screen, II, 224; sideboard, Sheraton, I, 199; tables: folding, II, 180, gate-legged, 175; wash-stand, I, 145
Block-front furniture, I, 103, 116, 117; chests on chests, 117–123, 354–357, 359; chests of drawers, 131–133, 355, 358; dressing-tables, 103, 124; scrutoires, 238–255, 380, 385
Blumer, Dr. G. Alder, tall clock owned by, II, 292
Boardman, Mr. William F. J., furniture owned by: chest, I, 47; dressing-table, 73; press cupboard, 172
Boardman, Mr. William G., furniture owned by: cane couch, II, 143; scrutoire, I, 239; wash-stand, I, 145
Bolles Collection, furniture in: bedstead, II, 256; chairs: banister-back, II, 40, 42, Carver, 10, Chippendale, 84, Dutch, 54, 55, knob-turned, 30, 31, leather, 27, 50, slat-back, 13, 17, spindle-turned, 12, 13, three-legged, 7, 8, wainscot, 23–25, Windsor, 77–80; chair-tables, II, 25; chest on chest, I, 117–119; chests: carved oak, I, 25–28, Connecticut, 34, with drawers, 31, 38, Hadley, 40, painted, 47, 48, panelled, 38; chests of drawers: three-drawer, I, 53, inlaid, 59, panelled, 59, scroll-top, 96–99, swell-front, low, 136; cupboards: court, I, 154, 155, with drawers, 165, on frame, 100; clock, mantel, II, 295; couch, Chippendale, II, 149; dressing-tables: earliest, I, 67, bandy-legged, 87, 100, five-legged, 68, japanned, 87, knee-hole, 124, double-arch mouldings, 82, 83, veneered top, 68, 70; desk-boxes, I, 212–214, 216; high-boys: japanned, I, 93, four-legged, 81, five-legged, 70–72, six-legged, 63–65, 68, scroll-top, 96, 98; looking-glasses: "bilboa," I, 315, carved and coloured, 330, carved and gilt, 293, 303, 304, Chinese, 329, Empire, 324, 325, painted, 329, pier, 287; scrutoires: ball-foot, I, 221, 222, block-front, cabinet-top, 242–245, fall front, 218, serpen-

345

INDEX

tine-front, 264, reverse serpentine, 265, on frame, 223; stools, II, 6; table board, II, 167, 168; tables: card, II, 232, folding, 178, 180, gate-legged, 173, slate-top, 194, tea, 194, 205, 206, tripod, 190, turned, 186, 193, writing-table, bookcase-top, I, 272, 274

Bonaparte, Mr. Joseph, Empire couch owned by, II, 150, 151

Bontecou, Mr. Frederic T., furniture owned by: chest of drawers and desk, I, 277; sideboard, Hepplewhite, 197

Bookcases, I, 278–280; Chippendale, 278, 279; Shearer, 279, 280; Sheraton, 276, 280, 389

Books of design, I, 10–14, 17, 21, 193, 198, 297, 298; II, 81

Books of prices, I, 18, 20, 193

Bosanko, Mrs., card-table owned by, II, 197

Bosworth, Mrs. Frank H., furniture owned by: cane chair, II, 52; settle, slat-back, 131; sofa, Phyfe, 162; tables: bedside, 212, dining, 228, tripod, 205

Bracket clock, II, 295, 339

Brasses, early use of, I, 53

Brewster's, Elder, ship chest, I, 23; chair, II, 12

Brinner, John, I, 19

Brooklyn Museum, furniture owned by: bookcase, Sheraton, I, 389; arm-chair, Chippendale, II, 303; cane chair, II, 298; clock, Claggett, II, 336; desk-box, I, 378; sofa, Hepplewhite, II, 313; sideboard table, I, 369

Brown, Misses, furniture owned by: clock, Willard, II, 295; sofa, Empire, 165

Brown, Mrs., furniture owned by: card-table, II, 234; looking-glass, I, 306

Brown, Mr. G. Winthrop, clocks owned by: tall, II, 282, wall, 294, Willard, 292

Brown, Nathaniel, II, 288

Brown & Ives, block-front, cabinet-top scrutoire owned by, I, 246

Buck, Mr. John H., furniture owned by: chest of drawers, I, 135; easy-chair, II, 66

Buck, Hon. John R., furniture owned by: chairs: Chippendale, II, 86, Windsor, 79; looking-glass, I, 326; shelf clock, II, 297

Buek, Mr. G. H., early rocking-chair owned by, II, 16

Buffet chair, II, 7, 8

Bulkeley, Hon. and Mrs. Morgan G., furniture owned by: bookcase, Chippendale, I, 278, 279; carved oak chest, 25

Bulkeley Collection, furniture in: chairs: cane, II, 52, Chippendale, 92, wainscot, 24; chest on chest, I, 120; cupboards: livery, I, 150, press, 156; settle, carved oak, II, 127; sideboard, Hepplewhite corner, I, 197; scrutoire, I, 260; tea-table, II, 208

Bulkley, Miss Mary, Sheraton writing-table owned by, I, 274

Bulman, Mrs. Mary, bed-hangings made by, II, 253

Bureaus, I, 128; origin and meaning of the word, 231–233

Burnap, Daniel, clockmaker, II, 288

Burnell, Miss E. R., furniture owned by: bedstead, French, II, 269; chest of drawers, I, 136

Butterfly table, II, 182, 183

Cabinet-makers, eighteenth century American, I, 19; period of, II, 81–83

Cabriole-legged furniture, I, 4, 18; bedsteads, II, 255–257, 333, 336; chairs: cane, II, 52–55, Chippendale, 84–95, 104, 108, 109, Dutch, 59–62, 301, easy, 65–68, roundabout, 71–73, Sheraton, 124, slat-back, 20, 298, Windsor, 75; chests of drawers, I, 61, 84–90; couches, II, 146, 149; dressing-tables, I, 87–91; scrutoires, I, 224–230, 233; settees, II, 132, 135, 136; sofas, II, 311, 319; tables, II, 198

Candle-stands, II, 193, 194, 218, 220

Cane, use of, I, 4; chairs: characteristics of, II, 32, historical sketch of, 31, 32, three types of, 33, first type, 33–38, second type, 44–47, 298, third type, 47–55; couches, II, 143; settle, II, 129, 131; sofa, II, 161, 162

Canfield, Richard A., furniture owned by: Chippendale collection, I, 16; bedstead, II, 254; chairs: Chippendale, II, 88, 97, 104, 106, Hepplewhite, 114, Manwaring, 98; clocks: marquetry, II, 280, portable, 271, tall, 277; dressing-table, I, 111; high-boy, Philadelphia, I, 104; looking-glass, Chippendale, I, 298; scrutoire, block-front, cabinet-top, I, 246, 253; sideboard table, Chippendale, I, 190, 192; table, pie-crust, II, 214, 216; tea-tables, II, 210; writing-table, knee-hole, I, 238

Card-tables, II, 197, 221–223, 230–234, 324, 328

Carver chairs, I, 8; II, 9–11; side chair, 10; spinning-chair, 11; turned, 9–11

Carving, I, 8, 157; first mention of, 22; arched, 24; on chests, 50, 51, 337; Friesland, 171, 212, 213, 378; scratch, 26, 27, 40

Cellarette in form of dressing-table, I, 113

Chair backs, types of, II, 82

Chairs, banister-back, II, 39–44, 51; Brewster, 12; cane: characteristics of, 32, first type of, 33–38, second type, 44–47, 298, third type, 47–55; Carver, 9–11; Chippendale, 73, 81–83, 92–110, 303, 304; comb-back, 77, 79; to determine date of, 3, 81, 82; how to distinguish Chippendale, Hepplewhite, Sheraton, and Dutch, 82; Dutch: 55–64, 71, 301; characteristics of, 56; early styles of, 6; easy-chairs, 64–69, 300; Empire, 68, 69, 122–126; fan-back, 79; "fancy," 308; French, 92, 108; Hepplewhite, 68, 112–115, 304; imitating bamboo, 104, 105; knob-turned, 30; leather, 27–29, 300; library, 62; Manwaring, 98; Phyfe, 308; rocking, 14–17, 80; roundabout: 69–73, transition style, 70, Dutch style, 71, 72; Sheraton, 115–124, 307, 308; slat-back, turned: 13–20, 298; New England type, 16–19, Pennsylvania type, 19, 20, 298; slipper, 79; spindle-back, turned, 7–13; spiral-turned, 30, 31; three-legged or buffet, 7, 8; transition, 70, 83–91, 111; Turkey-work, 29, 30; upholstered, 38, 39, 50, 62; wagon, 131; wainscot: carved oak, 20–27, 298, construction of, 20, chair-tables, 25–27; wheel, 69, 70; Windsor, 73–80; writing, 79, 80

Chair-tables, II, 25–27

Chaise-longue, II, 141, 150

Chamber clocks, II, 272–275

Chesebrough, Mrs. A. S., furniture owned by: chair, slat-back, II, 17; scrutoire, I, 249

Chesne, Claudini du, clockmaker, II, 281

Chests, I, 4; early English, 22; original colonial, 23; designs and construction of earliest American, 23, 24; carving on, 50, 51, 337; dates of, determined by character of decoration, 50; auger-holes, identification by, 160; to determine whether imported or

INDEX

347

made in America, 51; size of, 51; values of, 50; wood used in, 50; arching and pattern detail, 24, 25; carved oak, 26–28, 335–344; Connecticut, 32, 34, 337–344; Disbrowe, 335–341; with drawers, 30–39, with one drawer, 31, 34, 337, two blind drawers, 48; Dutch, 29, 30; Hadley, 40–44, 341–344; painted, 47, 48; panelled: with two drawers, 35–38, 344, with three drawers, 38, 39, simulating eight drawers, 47, English, 34, mouldings and designs of, 39

Chests of drawers, I, 7; mentioned in early New England records, 52; construction of, 52, 53; brass handles on, early use of, 53; latest development of, foreshadowing six-legged type, 59, 60; block-front, 355, 358; and cupboard, 126, 128; with desk drawer, 277; two-drawer, 53; three-drawer, 53, 54; four-drawer, 54, 55; Dutch, 66, 82; Empire, 141; handles, types of, 83, 84; high-boys, 60–109, 344, 349, 350; inlaid, 59, 350, 363, 367; low-boys, 128–143, 350; miniature, 83; mouldings on, 85; painted, 344; panelled, 54–59, 363, 367; with scroll legs, 349; serpentine-front, 358; Sheraton, 139; six-legged, 344; stencilled, 144; swell-front, 363, 367; woods used in, 85. *See also* high-boys *and* low-boys

Chests on chests, I, 114–116; block-front, 117–123, 354–357, 359; knee-hole, 359; ornate, 363; Philadelphia, 126; reverse serpentine, 125; serpentine-front, 359

Child's chair, II, 23; desk, I, 224

Chinese designs, I, 8, 17; chairs, II, 99–104; dressing-glass, I, 331; looking-glass frames, I, 298, 300, 328; settees, II, 135

Chippendale, Thomas, sketch of, I, 10, 11; his book, 10–14; his carving, 14, 15; versatility of, 15; Adam's influence on, 17

Chippendale furniture, I, 19, 21; bedstead, II, 258–260; bookcase, I, 278, 279; chairs: II, 81–83, 303, how to distinguish genuine, 82, Chinese, 99–104, classic, 106, French, 108, 109, Gothic, 94–99, imitating bamboo, 104, 105, ladder-back, 105, 106, ribbon-back, 93, 94, roundabout, 73, Southern, 304, upholstered, 106–110; chest of drawers, I, 128; chest on chest, I, 126; commodes, I, 15; clock, II, 271, 287; clothes presses, I, 128; couches, II, 146–150; cupboard, corner, I, 184; "duchesse," II, 149; girandole, I, 298; high-boys, I, 104–111; looking-glasses, I, 297–300, 302; low-boys, I, 104–111; scrutoire, I, 260, 261; settees, I, 16, II, 134–137; sideboard table, I, 190, 192; sofas, II, 152–156, 311; tables: II, 225, dining, 227, 324, library, I, 17, 18, pie-crust, II, 216, side, I, 18; torchères, I, 16; window-seats, II, 151, 152

Christ Church College, Oxford, forms in dining-hall of, II, 5

Church, Mrs. N. E., arm and side chairs in transition style, owned by, II, 111

Claget, Thomas, clocks made by, II, 336

Claggett, William, clocks made by, II, 282–286, 336

Clark, Mrs. George Hyde, Empire wardrobe owned by, I, 176

Classic designs, I, 17, 106

Claw and ball foot, II, 60

Claw feet, I, 8

Clay, Daniel, chest of drawers made by, I, 358

Clockmakers' Company, the, II, 270, 275

Clocks, age of, to tell, II, 273, 276, 277; alarm, 272–275; banjo, 293, 339, 340; bracket, 295, 339; Burnap, 288; cases, earliest, 276; Claggett, 282–286, 336; chamber or lantern, 272–275; Chippendale, 287; Curtis, 293, 294, 340; Dutch, 275; earliest mentioned, 271; Eddystone lighthouse, 341–344; French, 296; Hosmer, 336; japanned, 280, 281, 285, 288; lyre-shaped, 294, 295; mantel, 295–297; marquetry, 280; miniature, 290; musical, 287; painted faces, 290; portable or table, 271, 272; prices of, 271; tall, 276–292, 336, 339; thirty-day, 292; wall, 285, 292–294, 339, 340; Whiting, 339; Willard, 292, 293, 295, 339, 340

Clothes press, 1, 172, 369

Cluett, Mr. G. A., furniture owned by: bedstead, Phyfe, II, 336; arm-chair, Hepplewhite, II, 304; side-chairs, Sheraton, II, 307, 308; chests on chests, I, 359; chest of drawers, I, 367; clocks, II, 339, 340, 344; couch, Sheraton, II, 319; desk with bookcase, I, 389; dressing-table, I, 367; mirrors: Bilboa, I, 396, cutwork, 396, oval, 398, pier, 394, 398; scrutoires: block-front, I, 380, serpentine-front, 381, Sheraton, 385; settee, Hepplewhite, II, 311; sideboards: Hepplewhite, I, 372, Sheraton, 377; sofas: Empire, II, 319, Hepplewhite, 313, Phyfe, 313, 315, 319, Sheraton, 315; tables: card, II, 324, mixing, I, 372, oval, II, 328, Sheraton, II, 328, sofa, II, 328; wash-stand, I, 367

Commodes, I, 10, 15, 21, 60; Chippendale, 15

Connecticut furniture, chests, I, 32, 34, 337–344; chest of drawers, 358; cupboards, 160; scrutoires, 229, 233

Connecticut Historical Society, furniture owned by: Bible-box, I, 211; chairs: cane, II, 36, 47, 51, turned, 8, 9; chests: Disbrowe, I, 338, panelled, 34, two-drawer, 33; table, drawing, II, 169

Conversation chair, II, 119

Cooley, Mrs. Charles P., roundabout chair owned by, II, 70, 71

Cooper, George, I, 308

Cooper & Griffith, knee-hole desk owned by, I, 233

Copeland, H., I, 297

Corner cupboards, I, 179–188; Chippendale, 184; inlaid, 186; Sheraton, 187; values of, 179, 180

Corner sideboard, I, 197

Couch-bedsteads, II, 249

Couches, early use of, I, 4; historical sketch of, II, 141; cane, II, 143; Chippendale, 146–150; "duchesse," 149; Dutch, 144–146; Empire, 150, 151; Sheraton, 319; turned, 143, 144; upholstered, 150

Countess of Devon's bedstead, II, 244

Court cupboards, I, 150–155; prices of, 152, 157

Cradles, II, 249, 250

Cromwell, Oliver, clock said to have been owned by, II, 277

Cromwellian chairs, II, 27

Cupboard-bedsteads, II, 247, 248

Cupboards: auger-holes, identification by, I, 160; and chest of drawers, 126, 128; cloths for, 152, 168; Connecticut, 160; construction of, 157, 158; corner, 179–188; court or livery, 7, 150–155; cushions for, 168; Dutch, 169–171; decline in use of, 171, 172; early use of, 4; five-legged, 350; fluted columns, 174, 175; on frame, 100; historical sketch of, 149, 150; miniature, 83; painted, 165–169; panelled, 159, 160, 172; press, 152, 156–158, 160–167, 172, 369; prices of, 152, 157; "Putnam," 163, 164; side, 178–

INDEX

181; with serrated edge, 369; wainscot, 166, 167; wood used in construction of, 153
Cup-shaped legs, use of, I, 4
Curtis, Lemuel, clockmaker, II, 293, 294, 340
Curtis, Mr. George M., furniture owned by: chest of drawers, I, 92; chest on chest, I, 126; clock, II, 293; cupboard, corner, I, 183, 184; looking-glass, I, 313
Cylinder-fall desk, I, 266, 268
Cyma curve, the, I, 8, 21

Danvers Historical Society, oak wainscot chair owned by, II, 298
Davidson, Mr. John, high-boy owned by, I, 344
Davis, Mrs. Joseph E., dressing-table, Sheraton, owned by, I, 143
Deerfield Historical Society, Disbrowe chest owned by, I, 337; Hadley chest owned by, 44
de Forest, Mrs. Robert W., turned couch owned by, II, 143, 144
Derby, Elias Hasket, chest on chest made for, I, 363
Desk, used by Washington, I, 269
Desk-boxes, I, 212–217; Disbrowe design, 378; on frame, 214–217; Hadley pattern, 213; half-octagon, 378; with panels and applied ornaments, 213; scratch carving, 214
Desks, first mention of in America, I, 211; historical sketch of, 210; block-front, 380, 385; with bookcase top, 272, 389; with chest of drawers, 277; cylinder-fall, 266, 268; and dressing-table, 230, 233; on frame, 380; inlaid, 272, 275; knee-hole, 124; Salem, 377; Sheraton, 275, 389; standing, 379; values of, 210; Washington's, 269
Dials, clock, II, 276, 277, 280, 281, 285, 287
Dining-tables, II, 198–203, 227–229, 324
Disbrowe, Nicholas, I, 378; sketch of, 335, 342; chests made by, 335–341
Doll house with early eighteenth-century furniture, I, 8; II, 251
Drake, Mr. Clifford S., sideboard owned by, I, 369
Drawing-tables, II, 169, 170
Dresser, Dutch, I, 176, 177
Dressing-case on legs, II, 239
Dressing-glasses, I, 330–334; Hepplewhite, 331–334; japanned, 331
Dressing-tables, earliest form of, I, 67; bandy-legged, 87–91, 100; block-front, 103, 124; with desk drawer, 230, 233; double-arch mouldings, 81–83; drop-leaf, 73, 74; dummy drawers, 74; Dutch, 82; five-legged, 68; Hepplewhite, 142, 143; inlaid, 350, 367; japanned, 87; knee-hole, 113, 114, 359; knee-hole block-front, 123, 124; Maryland, 350; with mirror, 143, 144; Philadelphia, 110–113; Sheraton, 143, 144; slate-top, 73; veneered, 68, 70, 88. *See also* Lowboys
Duchesse, II, 149
Dumb-waiter table, II, 238
Dutch furniture, introduction of, into England, I, 4, 8; in America, I, 20; chairs: II, 52–64, 71, 72, 301; how to distinguish, 82; chest, I, 29; couches, II, 144, 146; clock, II, 275; cupboards or kasses, I, 7, 152, 168–171; dresser, I, 176, 177; dressing-table, I, 82; scrutoire, I, 226, 229; seat, II, 62; settees, II, 132–134; spoonrack, I, 171; stool, II, 6
Dutch influence in America, I, 5, 6
Dwight, Stephen, I, 282

Eastman, Rev. George P., chest owned by, I, 341
Easy-chairs, II, 64–69; Empire, 68, 69; Hepplewhite, 68; turned, 300
Eddystone lighthouse clocks, II, 341–344
Edwards and Darley designs, I, 10, 298, 300
Egbert, Rev. George D., tall clock owned by, II, 281
Eggleston, Judge Arthur F., furniture owned by: card-table, II, 222; Sheraton sofa, 163
Egyptian classic style, I, 19; II, 233
Ellings, Mrs., Phyfe sofa owned by, II, 162
Empire furniture, I, 19, 21, 139; characteristics of, II, 232, 233; bedposts, II, 264, 265; bedsteads, II, 265–269; card-table, II, 234; chairs: II, 122–126, easy-chair, 68, 69; couches, II, 150, 151; chests of drawers, I, 141, 142; looking-glasses, I, 324–327, 398; sideboards, I, 204–209; sofas, II, 165, 166, 319; scrutoire, I, 277; wardrobe, I, 176; writing-table, I, 277
English furniture: bedsteads, II, 244, 254, 255, 258; chair, II, 37; chest, I, 24, 25; cupboards: court, I, 153, 154, of drawers, 167, 168, press, 162, 167; looking-glass, I, 300; marquetry clock, II, 280; scrutoires, I, 262–264; tables: frame, II, 169, knee-hole, 238, pie-crust, 216, tea, 210
Engs, William, Junior, I, 355
Ernst, Mr. G. G., high chest of drawers owned by, I, 100–103
Erving, Mr. H. W., furniture in collection of: candle-stands, II, 194, 218; chairs: cane, II, 34, 35, 38, Chippendale, 93, easy, 65, 66, Hepplewhite, 112, roundabout, 72, slat-back, turned, 14; chest on chest, block-front, I, 120; chests: carved oak, I, 27, with drawers, 31, 32, Hadley, 40–42, painted, 47, panelled, 37, 38; chests of drawers: block-front, I, 133, contrasting woods, 57, Dutch marquetry, 66, high-boys, 66, 67, 99, panelled, 54, scroll-top, 99; clocks: miniature, II, 290, tall, 288; couch, Chippendale, II, 149; cupboards: corner, I, 187, Connecticut, 160, wainscot, 166, 167; desk-boxes: I, 212–214, on frame, 214, 216; dressing-table, I, 144; form, short, II, 5; looking-glasses: carved and gilt, I, 304, 312, 313, girandole, 298, inlaid, 316, mantel, 319, 320, scroll pediment, 296, 297; scrutoires: block-front, cabinet-top, I, 245, cabriole-legged, cabinet-top, 229, slant-top, 236; settees: Chippendale, II, 135, 136, in transition style, 138; sofa, Sheraton, II, 159; tables: "butterfly," II, 183, dining, 199, folding, 178, 180, oval, 190, Pembroke, 234, sewing, 242, Sheraton, 238, tripod, 238, turned, 188, wainscot, 168, 184, x-braced, 197
Essex Institute, Salem, furniture owned by: carved oak, wainscot chair, II, 21, 22; cupboard, Putnam, I, 163; sofa, Turkey-work, II, 152
Ethridge, Mr., Hepplewhite sideboard owned by, I, 194
Extension tops, table, II, 228

"Fancy" furniture, II, 308
Farr, Mr. W., chest on chest owned by, I, 357
Feather beds, II, 244, 245
Feke, Philadelphia, I, 357
Fellows, John, I, 147
Ferris, Professor H. B., carved chest owned by, I, 26
Field bedstead, II, 264

INDEX

349

Filigree frame looking-glasses, I, 308, 309
Fire-screen scrutoire, I, 269
Fisher, Robert, "fancy" furniture made by, II, 311, 328
Flemish furniture, popularity of, I, 4
Flemish scroll, I, 4, 349; unilateral, II, 44
Foddy, James, I, 282
Folding-tables, II, 178–180, 323
Form of furniture, changes in, I, 8
Forman, Mrs. Alexander, low chest of drawers owned by, I, 136
Forman, Mr. Merle, furniture owned by: bedstead, Sheraton, II, 264; table, dining, II, 229
Forms, II, 3–6
Foster, Mr. George F., cellarette owned by, I, 113
Fowler, Miss Harriet Putnam, I, 163
Fowler, Professor Henry T., Shearer bookcase owned by, I, 279, 280
Fox, Charles, clockmaker, II, 273, 274
Fox, Isaac, clockmaker, II, 272
French, Mr. Hollis, furniture owned by: chests of drawers: panelled, I, 57, scroll-top high-boy, 95, six-legged high-boy, 75, 77; couch, turned, II, 144; cupboard, corner, I, 185; easy-chair, II, 65
French furniture, I, 4, 8, 17; bedsteads, II, 269; chairs, II, 92, 93, 108, 109; clock, II, 295, 296
Fret on clocks, II, 272, 273
Friesland carving, I, 171, 212, 213, 378
Fromanteel, John, clockmaker, II, 277, 278

Garvan, Mr. Francis P., furniture owned by: chest on chest, I, 363; clothes-cupboard, I, 369; gate-legged table, II, 323
Gate-legged tables, II, 170–178, 323
"Gate of Language Unlocked," quoted, II, 3, 28
Gazette and Country Journal, the Providence, I, 354
"Gentlemen's and Cabinet-makers' Director," I, 10–14, 189, 190; II, 82; quoted, II, 94, 100
Gilbert, Mr. John J., furniture owned by: chair, Gothic, II, 98; looking-glasses, I, 288, 289, 316; low-boy, Philadelphia, I, 110, 111; scrutoires: cylinder-fall, I, 266, Sheraton, 269; seat, Dutch, II, 62; settee, Dutch, II, 134; tables: Hepplewhite, II, 230, pie-crust, 217
Gillingham, Mr. Frank C., slat-back, turned chair owned by, II, 19
Gillingham, James, I, 19; II, 95
Gillow, Robert, II, 228
Girandoles, Chippendale, I, 298; circular, 322, 323; Edwards & Darley, 300
Goddard, John, I, 117; sketch of, I, 354, 355; furniture made by: chests on chests, I, 354, 355; clock case, II, 336; high-boy, I, 350; scrutoires, I, 246
Goddard, Thomas, I, 354, 355
Goddard, Townsend, I, 355
Gothic designs, I, 8, 17, 21; chairs, II, 47, 94–99; settees, II, 135, 136
"Grammar of Ornament," by Owen Jones, design from, I, 337
Grandfather's clock, II, 275–292, 336, 339; development of, 275; miniature, 290
Greene, Mr. Maxwell C., press cupboard owned by, I, 162
Gunn, Mr. George M., block-front, cabinet-top scrutoire owned by, I, 253

Hadley chests, I, 40–44, 341–344
Haight, Mr. Frederick E., looking-glass owned by, I, 314
Hallet, William, I, 20
Halsey, Mr. R. T. Haines, furniture owned by: chair, Phyfe Empire, II, 124, 125; sofas: Phyfe, II, 161, Sheraton, 159; tables: card, II, 233, Phyfe, 237
Hammond, Dr. Frank I., furniture owned by: chairs: Chippendale, II, 86, 94, 95; chest of drawers, I, 133
Hancock, John, upholstered sofa owned by, II, 158
Handles, brass, I, 53; different types of, 83, 84; imported, 125
Harris, Richard, II, 274
Harvard College chair, II, 7
Hasbrouck, Miss F. F., Claggett clock owned by, II, 282
Hazard, Mr. Thomas G., furniture owned by: clock, tall, II, 286; dressing-table, knee-hole, I, 124, 125
Hazard, Mr. Thomas G., Jr., Dutch chair owned by, II, 59
Hazard, Mrs. Thomas G., inlaid secretary owned by, I, 271
Helme, Mr. B. E., furniture owned by: scrutoire, I, 249, 250; twelve-sided table, II, 203
Hemstead, Joshua, I, 342
Hencken, Mr. A. C., ladder-back settee owned by, II, 138
Hepplewhite furniture, I, 18, 21; chairs: II, 81, 109, 304; how to distinguish, 82, easy, 65, 68, heart-shaped back, 115, oval back, 114, shield back, 112–114; chests of drawers, I, 60, 135; dressing-glass, I, 331–334; dressing-tables, I, 142, 143; settees, II, 138, 140, 311; sideboards: I, 193–198, 372, period of production of, 198; sofas, II, 313; tables: II, 225, card, 230; wash-stand, corner, I, 145, 146
Herreshoff, Mr. Nathaniel, furniture owned by: chair, roundabout, II, 71; chest on chest, block-front, I, 120
Hickmott, Mr. William J., furniture owned by: chests: Hadley, I, 43, 44, painted, 48; desk-box, 212
High-boys, I, 8; development and construction of, 60–62; block-front, 100–103; bandy-legged, 350; cabriole-legged, 84–91; Dutch marquetry, 66; six-legged, 64–68, 72, 344; early walnut, 88; English six-legged, 63, 64; five-legged, 70–72, 81; flat-top, 90, 92; Goddard, 350; inlaid, 77, 78; japanned, 85, 86, 93; second type of, 75–81; with scroll legs, 349; scroll-top, 92–100, 104–109; Philadelphia, 104–110; veneered, 350
Hillier, Joseph, I, 320
Historical Society of Old Newbury, turned table belonging to, II, 184
Hoadley, Calvin, II, 296
Hogarth chairs, II, 61
Hosmer, Mr. Walter, furniture owned by: chair, Chippendale roundabout, II, 73; cupboard of drawers, I, 167, 168; press cupboard, I, 158; scrutoire, I, 226
Hosmer, clock made by, II, 336
Hutch, I, 48
Hutch-table, II, 197

Ince, I, 17; II, 83
Independence Hall, Philadelphia, Chippendale sofa at, II, 152, 154
Inlaid furniture: chairs, II, 37, 38, 307; chests of

INDEX

drawers, I, 363, 367; clocks, II, 288, 339; cupboards, I, 160, 186; desks, I, 224, 275, 276, 389; dressing-glass, I, 331; dressing-table, I, 350; high-boy, I, 350; looking-glass frames, I, 304, 305, 316; low-boy, I, 350; scrutoire, I, 277, 385; sideboards, I, 192, 193, 372, 377; tables, II, 190, 230, 324, 328; writing-cabinet, I, 274; writing-table, I, 271, 272

Japanned furniture: clocks, II, 281, 282, 285, 288; dressing-glass, I, 331; looking-glass frames, I, 287, 289, 290
Japanning, I, 4, 86, 87
Jekyll, Miss, design from her "Old West Surrey," I, 337
Jenkins, Mrs. E. W., tea-table owned by, II, 208
Johnson, designer, I, 298; pier-glass and table by, 300, 301
Johnson, Edmund, sideboard made by, I, 377
Joined stool, II, 5, 6
Jones, John, I, 147
Jones, Owen, design from his "Grammar of Ornament," I, 337

Kas or Kasse, I, 7, 152, 168–171
Kendal, Mr. George T., Chippendale chair owned by, II, 99
Knee-hole furniture: chest on chest, I, 359; desk, 124, 232; dressing-table, 114, 123–125, 359; writing-table, 271
Knife and spoon box, I, 200, 201
Knife-boxes, I, 200, 206
Knox, General, bookcase owned by, I, 280

Ladd House, Portsmouth, furniture in: chair, Chippendale Chinese, II, 100, 102; settee, Chippendale, 135
Lantern clocks, II, 272–275
Lehne, Mrs. Richard W., Sheraton bedstead owned by, II, 262
Library table, Chippendale, I, 17, 18
Lighthouse clocks, II, 341–344
Livery cupboard, I, 150, 152; prices of, 152
Locke, I, 297
Lockwood, Miss Jane E., scrutoire owned by, I, 224
Lockwood, Mrs. L. A., furniture owned by: banister-back chair, II, 43; Empire sofa, 166
Lockwood, Mr. Luke Burnell, chest of drawers owned by, I, 60
Lockwood, L. V., furniture owned by: bedsteads: cabriole-legged, II, 257, low-post, 266; bookcase, Sheraton, I, 280; chairs: cane, II, 33, 34, 37, 38, 45, 47, 49, 50, Carver, 10, 11, Chippendale, 89–91, 98, 105, 109, Dutch, 55, 61, 62, 64, easy, 65, 66, 68, 300, Hepplewhite, 112, 114, imitating bamboo, 104, 105, leather, 29, 51, 300, Pennsylvania slat-back, 19, 20, Queen Anne, 301, rocking, slat-back, 17, Sheraton, 116, 119, slipper, Windsor, 79, spinning, Carver, 11, turned slat-back, 16, Turkey-work, 29, upholstered, 38, 50, 62, 109, writing, Windsor, 79, 80; chests: two-drawer, I, 32, Connecticut, 338, Disbrowe, 335, Hadley, 44, 47, 343; chest on chest, knee-hole, I, 359; chests of drawers: Chippendale, I, 128, Empire, 141, inlaid, 363; panelled, 55, Sheraton, 139; clocks: chamber, II, 275, Claggett, 336; tall, 281; couches: Chippendale, II, 146, Dutch, 144, 146, Empire, 150, 151, turned, 143, 144; cupboards: corner, I, 182, carved corner, 188, panelled, 172, side, 178; desk on frame, I, 380; dressing-tables: cabriole-legged, I, 88, 91, 111, knee-hole, 359, walnut veneer, 81; high-boys: bandy-legged, I, 88, 90, inlaid, 350, six-legged, 75, 79; looking-glasses: carved and gilt, I, 290, 306, 312, 313, Chinese, 328, Chippendale, 302, Empire, 326, 327, mahogany and gilt, 302, 303, mantel, 389, marquetry, 284, scroll pediment, 295, pier, 286, 287, 390, Sheraton pier, 310; low-boy, inlaid, I, 350; scrutoires: ball-foot, I, 379; ball-foot, cabinet-top, 221, 222, block-front, cabinet-top, 253, 254, cabriole-legged, 226, Dutch turned legs, 226, 229, Sheraton, 265, 266; sideboard, Hepplewhite, I, 193, 194; sideboard table, I, 188; spoon-rack, Dutch, I, 171; tables: Chippendale, II, 324; dining, 203, 324, drop-leaf, 203, folding, 323, gate-legged, 172, 175, 176, oak frame, 205, Pembroke, 234, 237, pie-crust, 213, tea, 208, 324, tilt, 197, tripod, 217, 218, turned, 170, 184, 188, 324
Long Island Historical Society, portable clock owned by, II, 271
Looking-glasses, historical sketch of, I, 281; importation of, 281, 282; values of, 281, two kinds of, 283; remodelling of old, 282, 283; frames of, 282, 283; designers of frames of, 297, 298, 300; bilboa, 314, 315, 396; carved and gilt, 292, 293, 303–306, 311–315; Chinese, 300; Chippendale, 297–302; cutwork, 396; dressing, 330–334; Empire, 324–327; English, 300; filigree, 308, 309; glass frame, 314; gilt frame, 323, 324, 398; girandoles, 298, 322, 323; high cresting, 294; inlaid, 304, 305, 316; marble and gilt, 314, 315; mantel, 298–300, 316–320, 389, 390; olive wood, marquetry, 283, 284; oval, 323, 398; painted glass border, 328, 329; painted scenes, 324, 325; painting at top, 329; pediment top, 294–297, 302–306; pier, 286–291, 310, 320, 321, 390, 394, 398; pier, and table, 300, 301; rectangular with curve at top, 292, 293; Sheraton, 309, 310; shield-shaped, 307, 308; stump-embroidery, 283; walnut, 285
Lord, Richard, cane chair belonging to, II, 35, 36
Louis XV school of designs, I, 298
Louis XVI style, influence of, I, 18
Loundes, Jonathan, clockmaker, II, 271
Low-boys, I, 128; earliest form of, 67; bandy-legged, 87–91, 100; block-front, 103, 131–133; bombé, 131; Chippendale, 128; with desk drawer, 230, 233; double-arch mouldings, 81–83; drop-leaf, 73, 74; dummy drawers, 74; Dutch, 82; five-legged, 68; Hepplewhite, 142, 143; inlaid, 350; japanned, 87; knee-hole, 113, 114, 359; knee-hole block-front, 123, 124; Maryland, 350; Philadelphia, 110–113; serpentine, 135; Sheraton, 143, 144; slate-top, 73; swell-front, 136; veneered, 68, 70, 88; with mirror, 143, 144
Lyon, Dr., work on Colonial Furniture cited, I, 231
Lyon, Mr. Charles Woolsey, furniture owned by: chest, I, 344; Hosmer clock, II, 336; bandy-legged high-boy, I, 350; pier mirror, I, 394; Hepplewhite settee, II, 311; Phyfe table, II, 332
Lyre-shaped clocks, II, 294, 295

McClellan, Miss Jessie T., sofa owned by, II, 152
McIntire, Samuel, I, 372; chest on chest made by, 363

INDEX

Mahogany, introduction of, I, 7, 8, 21; history of, 146, 147; difference between old and new, 147, 148

Manning, Miss Augusta, furniture owned by: chairs: Chippendale, II, 87, 97, Dutch splat, 54; table, Sheraton card, 230

Mansfield, Mr. K. W., Empire sofa owned by, II, 165

Mantel clocks, II, 295–297

Mantel looking-glasses, I, 316–320; Chippendale, 298–300; Georgian, 390; Queen Anne, 389; Sheraton, 317

Manwaring, Robert, chairs made by, II, 83, 98

Marot school designs, I, 286; II, 282

Marquetry, introduction into England, I, 4; little used in America, 5; chest, I, 29; chest of drawers, I, 66; clock, II, 280; looking-glass, I, 283, 284

Matlock, White, clockmaker, II, 288

Matthews, Mrs. John R., looking-glass owned by, I, 294

May, Mrs. James R., dressing-tables owned by: Hepplewhite, I, 142, Sheraton, 144

Mayhew, I, 17; II, 83

Maynard, Mr. R. H., furniture owned by: girandole, I, 323; Sheraton sideboard with china closet, 203

Meggat, Mr. William, furniture owned by: chairs: Chippendale, II, 84, 91, leather, 51; knife and spoon box, I, 200, 201; scrutoire, I, 265; sideboards: Empire, I, 205, 206, Sheraton, 200; card-table, II, 234

Mercury, the Newport, I, 355

Merriam, Mrs. C. S., wainscot chair owned by, II, 23, 24

Metropolitan Museum of Art, furniture owned by: *see* Bolles Collection; chairs: Chippendale, II, 90, 97, 105, Dutch, 61, Sheraton Empire, 123, 124, Sheraton upholstered, 121; chest of drawers, oak, I, 53; Claggett clock, II, 336; cupboards: Chippendale corner, I, 184, court, 153, miniature, 83; dressing-case on legs, II, 239; looking-glass, I, 295; pole screen, II, 239; settee, Dutch, II, 132, 134; tables: dining, II, 227, 228, dumb-waiter, 238, English frame, 169, Phyfe, 237, Sheraton tripod, 238

Millington, Lady Anne, tradition regarding chest belonging to, I, 26

Minshiell, I, 282, 283

Mirrors, *see* Looking-glasses

Mixing-tables, I, 203, 204, 372

Morson, Mr. Charles R., furniture owned by: chair, Empire easy, II, 68, 69; chest on chest, I, 354; clock, musical, II, 287; cupboard, panelled, I, 172; high-boy, I, 350; pier-glass, I, 291; scrutoire, I, 236; sofa, Duncan Phyfe, II, 315; table, dining, II, 229

Mouldings, on high-boys, I, 85

Mount Vernon, draped bedstead at, II, 260

Mudejar design, II, 47, 143

Musical clock, II, 287

Music-rack, II, 240

New Amsterdam, early furniture of, I, 7

New England, early furniture of, I, 7; slat-back chairs, II, 16–19; couches, II, 144

Newport Historical Society, wall clock owned by, II, 285

Nichols House, at Salem, Sheraton furniture in, II, 81; Sheraton chairs, II, 115, 116; mantel looking-glass, I, 316, 317

Nutting, Dr. Wallace, press cupboard owned by, I, 369

Oak, extensive use of, I, 4; English and American, in chests, 51

Oatman, Dr. Edward L., tall clock owned by, II, 288

"Old West Surrey," by Miss Jekyll, I, 337

Painted furniture: chairs, II, 119–122, 126, 308; chest of drawers, I, 344; cupboards, I, 165–169; looking-glasses, I, 324, 325; settee, II, 311; card-table, II, 328; window-seat, II, 311

Palmer, Mr. George S., furniture owned by: cupboard, side, I, 181; high-boys, Philadelphia, I, 107, 108, 110; looking-glass, I, 315; mixing-table, I, 203; scrutoires: block-front, I, 240, bombé-front, cabinet-top, 256, 260, Chippendale, 260, 261; sideboard table, carved, I, 190; tables: pie-crust, II, 213, pier, 224, tea, 206; writing-cabinet, inlaid, I, 274

Peckham, Mrs. Benjamin, Curtis clock owned by, II, 293

Pembroke tables, II, 210–212, 234, 237

Pendleton Collection, furniture in: basin-stand, I, 145; bedstead, II, 255; candle-stand, II, 220; chair, Hepplewhite, II, 114; chest, I, 337; chests of drawers: block-front, I, 131, 132, bombé, 131; dressing-tables: block-front knee-hole, I, 123, 124, carved, 113, with desk drawer, 230; high-boys, Philadelphia, I, 104, 108; looking-glasses: mantel, I, 298–300, 319, pier, 288; scrutoires: block-front, cabinet-top, I, 251–253, 255, bombé-front, cabinet-top, 256, English, 262, 263, Philadelphia, 260; settee, Dutch, II, 132; sofa, Chippendale, II, 154

Pendulums, clock, II, 272, 274, 278

Penn, John, I, 178

Penn, William, scrutoire owned by, I, 222

Pennsylvania Colony, furniture of, I, 6; slat-back chairs, II, 19, 20; couches, II, 143, 144

Pennsylvania Museum, furniture in: chair, Spanish, II, 47; sideboard, Empire, I, 206

Perry, Mr. Marsden J., furniture owned by: bedsteads: Chippendale, II, 258–260, Sheraton, 260, 261; chairs: Chippendale Chinese, II, 102, Chippendale upholstered, 106, 108; desk, Sheraton inlaid, I, 275, 276; "duchesse," Chippendale, II, 149; looking-glasses: carved and gilt, I, 311, Sheraton filigree, 309; pier-glass and table, I, 300, 301; sconces, I, 307; scrutoires: English cabinet-top, I, 263, 264, Rhode Island, 249; sideboard, Sheraton, I, 200; sofa, Sheraton, II, 159; window-seat, Chippendale, II, 152

Philadelphia, early furniture of, I, 7; chairs, II, 92, 93, 298; chests on chests, I, 126; dressing-tables, I, 110–113, 230; high-boys, I, 104–110; scrutoire, I, 260

Philadelphia Library Building, furniture in: cupboard, early Georgian, I, 178, 179; scrutoire, 222

Phillips, J., I, 321

Phyfe, Duncan, I, 19; furniture made by: chairs, Empire, II, 124; clock, tall, II, 277, 278; music-rack, II, 240; sofas, II, 161, 162; tables, II, 228, 233, 237

Phyfe style furniture: bedstead, II, 336; side-chair, 308; sofas, 313, 315; tables, 328, 332

Pie-crust tables, II, 212–217

INDEX

Pierce, Mr. F. O., furniture owned by: chair, Chippendale, II, 86; couch, cane, 143
Pier-glasses, I, 283; carved and gilded, 394; early, gilt frame, 286; Empire, 398; Georgian, 390; japanned, 287, 289, 290; painted panels above, 320, 321; Queen Anne, 390; Sheraton, 310; walnut, 287, 291, 390; walnut and gilt, 288–291; with sconces, 288; and table, 300, 301
Pier-table, II, 224
Pilgrim Hall, Plymouth, furniture at: chairs: Elder Brewster, II, 12, Carver, 9; cradles, 249, 250; sofa, 158; table, 172
Pilgrim Society, panelled chest owned by, I, 36
Pitkin, Mr. Albert H., furniture owned by: chairs: banister-back, II, 43, roundabout, 71, Windsor, 75, 76; cupboard, corner, I, 182; looking-glasses, I, 308, 319; scrutoire, block-front, I, 239
Pole screens, II, 224, 239
Pollen, W. H., quoted, II, 127
Porter, Dr. Ezekiel, furniture owned by: chairs, Dutch, II, 59; cupboard, I, 100; dressing-tables and scroll-top high-boys, I, 92, 95
Pratt, Mr. George D., chest on chest owned by, I, 355
Pray, Mr. Samuel, Sheraton sideboard owned by, I, 199
Press cupboards, I, 152, 156–158; American oak, 172; Connecticut, 160; with drawers, 165–167; English, 162, 167; painted, 165, 166; panelled, 159, 160; "Putnam," 163, 164; serrated-edge, 369; wainscot, 166, 167
Proud, John, clockmaker, II, 286
Prouty, Mr. Dwight M., furniture owned by: candle-stand, II, 194; chairs: banister-back, II, 41, cane, 36, 37, 44, 45, Chippendale roundabout, 73; chests of drawers: block-front low, I, 131, high-boy, 78, panelled, 55; clock, banjo, II, 293; dressing-table, I, 73, 74; looking-glass, I, 297; music-rack, II, 240; scrutoire, block-front, I, 240; settee, Chippendale, II, 135; tables: gate-legged, II, 173, rectangular, 203, turned, 184, 188
"Putnam cupboard," I, 163, 164

Read, Joshua, flat-top high chest of drawers made by, I, 92
Reed, Mr. Brooks, Sheraton sofa owned by, II, 313
Rhode Island furniture, chests of drawers, I, 132, 133; scrutoires, 246–253; sideboard table, 190
Rhode Island Historical Society, tall clock owned by, II, 282
Rhode Island School of Design, *see* Pendleton Collection
Rivington, James, I, 19
Robbins Brothers, Dutch couch owned by, II, 144
Robinson House, side cupboard in, I, 180
Rocking-chairs, earliest, II, 14, 16, 17
Rococo design, I, 8, 21
Room-panelling, first English use of, I, 22
Rose, Joseph, clockmaker, II, 287
Rosenbach Company, looking-glass owned by, I, 283
Rosettes, looking-glass, I, 327, 328
Roundabout chairs, II, 69–73
Russell, Mrs., wardrobe owned by, I, 172

Sack, Mr. Israel, block-front scrutoire owned by, I, 385; card-tables owned by, II, 324

Saint Oswald, Lord, Chippendale chairs owned by, II, 94, 106
Salem furniture: couch, II, 319; desks, I, 377; sofas, II, 313, 315
Savery, William, I, 110
Scallop shell pattern, I, 181
Schutz, Mr. Robert H., inlaid corner cupboard owned by, I, 186
Sconces, I, 288, 298, 306, 307
Scratch carving, I, 26, 27, 40
Scroll design, I, 4, 23, 24, 349
Scrutoires, I, 217; three types of, 218; values of, 218; ball-foot, 218, 221, 222, 379; block-front, 238–255, 380, 385; bombé-front, 255–260; bookcase-top, 269, 276, 277; cabinet-top, 221, 222, 242–264, 380, 381, 385; cabriole-legged, 224–230, 234; Chippendale, 260, 261; cylinder-fall, 266, 268; Dutch turned legs, 226, 229; Empire, 277; English, 262–264; fall front, 218; fire-screen, 269; on frame, 222, 223, 380; inlaid, 271–275; knee-hole, 233, 238; low-boy, 230; Philadelphia, 260; Rhode Island, 246–253; secret drawers, 235, 236; serpentine-front, 264, 381; reverse serpentine-front, 265; Sheraton, 265, 266, 274–276, 385; slant-top, 218, 221, 222, 233–236, 238
Seaman, Mr. Willet, cupboard owned by, I, 350
Seat, Dutch, II, 62
Secretary, inlaid, I, 271
Serrated-edge furniture, I, 369
Settees, Chippendale, I, 16, II, 134–137; Dutch, 132–134; Hepplewhite, 138, 140, 311; ladder-back, 138; painted, 311; Sheraton, 140, 141; transition style, 138
Settles, II, 127–131
Sewall, Judge Samuel, I, 20; chairs owned by, II, 34
Sewing-tables, II, 240, 242
Seymour, Mr. George Dudley, furniture owned by: Carver chair, II, 10; scrutoire, cabinet-top, I, 233; press cupboard, I, 160
Shearer, Thomas, I, 18; furniture designed by: bookcase, I, 279, 280; chairs, II, 109; chests of drawers, II, 60, 135; desk, cylinder-fall, I, 268; fire-screen scrutoire, I, 269; sideboards, I, 18, 193
Sheraton, Thomas, sketch of, I, 18, 19
Sheraton furniture: bedstead, II, 260–264; bookcase, I, 280, 389; cupboard, corner, I, 187; chairs: II, 81, 109, 115–124, 307, 308, how to distinguish, 82, conversation, 119, Empire, 122–124, upholstered, 121, 122; chests of drawers, I, 60, 128, 135, 139; desk, inlaid, I, 275, 276, 389; dressing-tables, I, 143, 144; dumb-waiter table, II, 238; knife-box, I, 200, 201; looking-glasses, I, 309, 310; mantel looking-glasses, I, 316–319; scrutoires: I, 265, 266, 385, bookcase top, 269; secretary, I, 271, 272; settees, II, 140, 141; sideboards: I, 198–203, 377, distinguishing characteristics of, 204, with china closet, 201, 203, 377; sofas, II, 159–161, 313, 315; tables: card, II, 230, 232, side, 328, tripod, 238; wash-stand, corner, I, 146; writing-tables, I, 269, 271, 274
Ship-chest, I, 23
Side cupboards, I, 178–181; early Georgian, 178, 179; scallop-shell pattern, 181
Sideboard tables, carved, I, 190, 192; Chippendale, 190, 192; oak, 188, 189; walnut, with marble top, 189, 190, 369

INDEX

Sideboards, I, 18; historical sketch of, 188, 189; earliest style of, 192, 193; with china closet, 201, 203, 377; corner, 197; Empire, 204–209; Hepplewhite, 193–198, 372; inlaid, 372, 377; Salem desk, 377; Shearer, 193; Sheraton, 198–204, 377; woods employed in, 193
Slate-top tables, I, 73; II, 190, 194
Slipper-chair, Windsor, II, 79
Smith, Miss Helen Evertson, her "Colonial Days and Ways" quoted, II, 244, 248
Smith House, Sharon, Connecticut, pier mirror from, I, 390
Smith, Mr. R. T., furniture owned by: looking-glasses, I, 308, 325; sideboard, Hepplewhite, 197
Smith, Mr. William W., furniture owned by: chairs: Sheraton, II, 119, wheel, 70; chest of drawers, I, 77, 78; high-boy, Philadelphia, I, 107, 108; settee, Hepplewhite, II, 138
Smith & Beck, block-front chest on chest owned by, I, 119, 120
Sofa-table, II, 242, 328
Sofas, cane, II, 161, 162; Chippendale, 154–156, 311; cornucopia, 165; Empire, 165, 166, 319; Hepplewhite, 313; Phyfe, 161, 162, 313, 315; Salem, 313, 315; Sheraton, 159–161, 313, 315; transition style, 152, 163; Turkey-work, 152; upholstered, 158
Sommerlad, Mr. Casper, French bedstead owned by, II, 269
South, the, early furniture of, I, 7; Chippendale chairs from, II, 304; sofa from, II, 311
South Kensington Museum, bedstead at, II, 244
Spalding, Mr. Philip L., clocks owned by, II, 340, 341; standing desk owned by, I, 379
Spanish leather chairs, II, 28, 47
Spencer, Mr. J. C., mantel clock owned by, II, 296
Spinning-chair, II, 11
Spoon-rack, Dutch, I, 171
Stencilled furniture, I, 144
Stools, Dutch, II, 6; joined, 5, 6; turned three-legged, 6
Stretch, Peter, II, 281
Stump embroidery on looking-glass frames, I, 283
Stuyvesant, Peter G., bedsteads in home of, II, 248
Swan, Mrs. Annie B., pier looking-glass owned by, I, 321
Swift, quoted, I, 231

Table board, II, 167, 168
Table carpets, II, 170
Tables, early English, I, 3, 4; early kinds of, mentioned, II, 198; bedside, 212; "butterfly," 183; card, 197, 221–223, 230–234, 324, 328; Chippendale, I, 17, 18, II, 227, 324; dining, II, 198–203, 227–229, 324; drawing, 169, 170; drop-leaf, 199–205; dumb-waiter, 238; folding, 178–180, 323; frame, 169; gallery-top, 217, 220; gate-legged, 170–178, 323; hexagonal top, 190; hutch, 197; inlaid, 324, 328; library, I, 17; oldest American, II, 167–170; painted, 328; "Pembroke," 210–212, 234, 237; Phyfe, 328, 332; pie-crust, 212–217; pier, 224; round and oval, 176; sewing, 240, 242; Sheraton, 328; side, I, 18, II, 328; sofa, II, 242, 328; tea, 194, 205–220, 324; tripod, 190, 205, 212–220, 238, 324; turned, 180–198, 324; twelve-sided, 203; wainscot, 168, 323
Tambour writing-tables, I, 265, 266
Tea-tables, II, 205–210, 324; earliest record of, 205; types of, 205; tile top, 194; tripod, 212–220; with domed stretchers, 210
Terry, Eli, clockmaker, II, 296
Tester, origin of the word, II, 246
Theodore Hook chair, II, 25
Thomas, Seth, clockmaker, II, 296
Tiffany Studios, furniture owned by: chairs: arm, II, 95, cane, 33, Chippendale, 95, 97, 104, Dutch, 59, 60, 62, Hepplewhite, 114, 115, library, 62, Sheraton, 119, Sheraton Empire, 122, Sheraton upholstered, 122; cupboard, I, 174, 175; dressing-glasses, Hepplewhite, I, 331–334; looking-glasses: carved and gilt, I, 292, 304, 311, oval, 323; sideboard table, I, 192; tables: card, II, 221, 222, dining, 227, 229, drop-leaf, 203, tripod, 212, 217, 220; window-seat, Chippendale, II, 152
Tompion, clockmaker, II, 271
Torchères, Chippendale, I, 16
Torr, Mrs. Charles Clarence, girandole owned by, I, 322
Townsend, Edmund, I, 355
Townsend, Hannah, I, 354
Townsend, John, sketch of, I, 357; chest of drawers made by, 358; chests on chests made by, 355–357; cornice used by, 359
Traver, Miss C. M., furniture owned by: chest, panelled, I, 37; chest of drawers, I, 79, 81; dresser, I, 176, 177; scrutoire, with cabinet-top, I, 229; tables: dining, II, 199, folding, 180, turned, 190, 198
"Treatise on Japanning and Varnishing," quoted, I, 87
Tregent, James, clockmaker, II, 272
Trinity College, Connecticut, leather chair owned by, II, 27
Tripod tables, II, 190, 205, 324; Chippendale, 216; dish-top, 217, 218; gallery-top, 217, 220; human legs, 217; pie-crust, 213–217; Sheraton, 238; tray top, 212
Tuileries, the, bookcase from, I, 279, 280
Turkey-work, chairs, I, 7, 20; II, 29, 30; sofas, II, 152

Van Cortlandt Manor, Croton, furniture in: dining-table, II, 178; fire-screen scrutoire, I, 269; looking-glass, I, 290
Van Cortlandt Mansion, Van Cortlandt Park, furniture in: tall clock, II, 278, 280; Dutch cupboard, I, 169
Vitruvian scroll, I, 119, 192
von Falke, Dr., quoted on painted furniture, I, 168

Wadsworth Athenæum, Hartford, I, 369
Wagon chair, II, 131
Wainscot furniture: chairs, II, 20–25, 298; chair-tables, II, 25–27; cupboards, I, 168; tables, II, 168, 323
Waite, Joseph, I, 147
Walker, Mr. G. W., furniture owned by: chair, banister-back, II, 41; cupboard, corner, I, 185; dressing-table, I, 96; high-boys: scroll-top, I, 96, six-legged, 72; pier-glass, I, 291; table, gate-legged, II, 176
Wall clocks, II, 285, 292–294, 339, 340
Walnut, introduction of, I, 4
Wardrobes, Empire, I, 176; scroll-top, 172, 174
Warner House, Portsmouth, early bookcase in, I, 278; ball-foot desk at, 379

INDEX

Wash-stands, I, 145; corner, 145, 146, 367

Washington, George, Chippendale sofa owned by, II, 152, 154; desk used by, I, 269; Sheraton furniture of, II, 81

Watkinson, Mrs. E. B., looking-glass owned by, I, 307

Wellington, Mr. A. W., block-front dressing-table owned by, I, 103

Wendell, Professor Barrett, furniture owned by: chair, Sheraton, II, 119, 121; couch, Chippendale, II, 150; dressing-table with dressing-glass, I, 114; settee, Sheraton, II, 140, 141; tea-table, II, 210

Wheel-chair, II, 69, 70

Whipple House, Ipswich, looking-glass in, I, 284

White, Mrs. Miles, furniture owned by: chairs: Chippendale, II, 303, 304, "fancy," II, 308, Queen Anne, II, 301; low-boys, I, 350; settee, II, 311; sofa, Chippendale, II, 311; card-table, II, 328; window-seats, II, 311

White, Peregrine, II, 250

Whiting, clock made by, II, 339

Whiting, William, I, 335

Willard, Aaron, clockmaker, II, 295; banjo clock by, 340; bracket clocks by, 339

Willard, Benjamin, clockmaker, II, 288

Willard, Simon, clockmaker, II, 290–293; lighthouse clocks made by, 341–344

Willets, Mr. E. B., Chippendale sofa owned by, II, 154

Williams, Dr. G. C. F., Chippendale dining-table owned by, II, 227

Window-seats, II, 151, 152, 311

Windsor chairs, II, 73–80; popularity of, 73–75

Winslow, Governor Edward, chair used by, II, 22, 23; table used by, 172

Witman, Benjamin, clockmaker, II, 290

Wood, David, clockmaker, II, 295

Wright, Mrs. Walter P., Sheraton sideboard owned by, I, 377

Writing-cabinet, inlaid, I, 274

Writing-chair, Windsor, II, 79, 80

Writing-table, used by Washington, I, 269

Writing-tables, Empire, I, 277; inlaid, 272, 274; knee-hole, 238, 271; Sheraton, 274; tambour, 265, 266; with bookcase top, 274

Yale University, dining-table owned by, II, 199

York, Maine, museum, bed-hangings in, II, 253